Sexual Offences

Sexual Offences

Richard Card
Emeritus Professor of Law

Alisdair A Gillespie
Reader in Law

Michael Hirst
Professor of Criminal Justice

all of Leicester De Montfort Law School, De Montfort University

JORDANS

Published by
Jordan Publishing Limited
21 St Thomas Street
Bristol BS1 6JS

British Library Cataloguing-in-Publication Data

A catalogue record for this book is available from the British Library.

ISBN 978 1 84661 122 3

Typeset by Letterpart Ltd, Reigate, Surrey

Printed in Great Britain by CPI Antony Rowe

PREFACE

Sexual offences law is never far from the public eye. This book is intended to provide a thorough exposition of that law as it applies in England and Wales.

The contents are not limited to the Sexual Offences Act 2003. Nevertheless, most of the chapters focus on its provisions. The Sexual Offences Act 2003 has now been in force for over 4 years. Since it was enacted, it has been amended in a number of significant respects and has attracted more than its fair share of appellate decisions. Taken together with developments relating to areas of sexual offences law outside the Act, it is now appropriate to provide an up-to-date exposition of and commentary on it.

The chapters relating to the offences under Part 1 of the Sexual Offences Act 2003 and the management of sex offenders under Part 2 of that Act build on, develop and update *Sexual Offences – The New Law* by the first-named author of this book, published in 2004. This new book, however, has considerably wider scope, dealing additionally with the law relating to prostitution and with child abduction, with relevant aspects of the law of evidence, with the sentencing of dangerous sex offenders and with rules about barring sex offenders from working with children or vulnerable adults.

In writing this book, we have tried to bear in mind the needs not only of the legal profession, but also of the magistracy, of members of police forces, of law students and of others who may read it.

For reasons of simplicity, where a third person pronoun has been employed, we have generally adopted the statutory convention of using the masculine pronoun. However, as in the case of statutory interpretation, 'he' includes 'she', unless the contrary intention appears.

We are grateful to Tony Hawitt and Cheryl Prophett and their colleagues at Jordans for seeing this book through to publication, for producing the Tables of Statutes and Cases and the Index. Above all, we are inordinately grateful to Rachel Card for her invaluable and extensive editorial work on our behalf. For the imperfections which remain, we are solely responsible.

We have summarised and explained the law as it was on 19 August 2008.

Richard Card
Alisdair Gillespie
Michael Hirst
Leicester, August 2008

CONTENTS

TABLE OF CASES

References are to paragraph numbers.

TABLE OF STATUTES

References are to paragraph numbers.

TABLE OF STATUTORY INSTRUMENTS

References are to paragraph numbers.

Sexual Offences

TABLE OF INTERNATIONAL LEGISLATION

References are to paragraph numbers.

TABLE OF INTERNATIONAL LEGISLATION

References are to paragraph numbers

American Law Institute, Model Penal Code ... 8.19
s 2.13.1 ... 7.7

Crimes Act (New Zealand) 1961
s 130 ... 18.07
Criminal Code, RSC 1985 (Canada)
s 182(b) ... 12.67

French Penal Code 1994
Arts 222-33 ... 5.4
arts 227-255 ... 2.28

United Nations Convention against Trans-national Organized Crime ... 11.37

TABLE OF FOREIGN LEGISLATION

References are to paragraph numbers.

Sexual Offences

TABLE OF ABBREVIATIONS

AA	Adoption Act
ABL	Adults' barred list
ACA	Adoption and Children Act
ACPO	Association of Chief Police Officers
AFA	Armed Forces Act
Archbold	Archbold *Criminal Pleading, Evidence and Practice* (Sweet & Maxwell, 2008 edn)
ASBO	Anti-social behaviour order
AWA	Animal Welfare Act
Blackstone's Guide	Stevenson, Davies and Gunn *Blackstone's Guide to the Sexual Offences Act 2003* (OUP, 2004)
CA	Courts Act
CAA	Criminal Attempts Act
CAFCASS	Children and Family Courts Advisory and Support Services
Card, Cross & Jones	Card, Cross and Jones *Criminal Law* (OUP, 18th edn, 2008)
CBL	Children's barred list
CDA	Crime and Disorder Act
CEA	Civil Evidence Act
CEOP	Child Exploitation and Online Protection Centre
CEMA	Customs and Excise Management Act
ChA	Children Act
ChAA	Child Abduction Act
CJA	Criminal Justice Act
CJCSA	Criminal Justice and Court Services Act
CJIA	Criminal Justice and Immigration Act
CJPA	Criminal Justice and Police Act
CJPOA	Criminal Justice and Public Order Act
CJ(S)A	Criminal Justice (Scotland) Act
CLA	Criminal Law Act
CLAA	Criminal Law Amendment Act
CLRC	Criminal Law Revision Committee

Consolidated Criminal Practice Direction	The Consolidated Criminal Practice Direction is a consolidation, with amendments, of existing Practice Directions, Practice Statements and Practice Notes as they affect proceedings in the Court of Appeal (Criminal Division), the Crown Court and the magistrates' courts. It can be found at www.justice.gov.uk/criminal/procrules_fin/contents/practice_direction/pd_consolidated.htm
CPA	Civil Partnership Act
CPS	Crown Prosecution Service
CPS Guidance	CPS Guidance on sexual offences and child abuse (see **1.56**)
CRB	Criminal Records Bureau
Crim PR	Criminal Procedure Rules
C(S)A	Crime (Sentences) Act
CStA	Care Standards Act
CYPA	Children and Young Persons Act
DPA	Data Protection Act
DPP	Director of Public Prosecutions
DTO	Detention and training order
DVCVA	Domestic Violence, Crime and Victims Act
EA	Education Act
ECHR	Convention for the Protection of Human Rights and Fundamental Freedoms 1950 (European Convention on Human Rights)
ECHT	European Convention on Human Trafficking
FA	Firearms Act
FLRA	Family Law Reform Act
FTO	Foreign travel order
Guidance Pt 1	*Guidance on Part 1 of the Sexual Offences Act 2003* (Home Office, 2004) (see **1.56**)
Guidance Pt 2	*Guidance on Part 2 of the Sexual Offences Act 2003* (Home Office, 2004) (see **1.56**)
HRA	Human Rights Act
IBB	Independent Barring Board
IA	Interpretation Act
ICA	Indecency with Children Act
ICT	Information and communication technologies
I(PFD)A	Inheritance (Provision for Family and Dependants) Act
ISO	Individual support order
JPA	Justices of the Peace Act
LA	Licensing Act
LGA	Local Government Act
MA	Marriage Act
MAPPA	Multi-Agency Public Protection Arrangements
MCA	Magistrates' Courts Act
MDA	Misuse of Drugs Act
MHA	Mental Health Act

MPA	Metropolitan Police Act
NO	Notification order
OAPA	Offences Against the Person Act
OPA	Obscene Publications Act
PA	Police Act
PACE	Police and Criminal Evidence Act 1984
PCA	Proceeds of Crime Act
PCC(S)A	Powers of Criminal Courts (Sentencing) Act
PCPSO(S)A	Protection of Children and Prevention of Sexual Offences (Scotland) Act
PHA	Protection from Harassment Act
PJA	Police and Justice Act
PNI	Public nuisance injunction
POA	Public Order Act
PoCA	Protection of Children Act
POCA List	Protection of Children Act List
POVA List	Protection of Vulnerable Adults List
PP	*Protecting the Public: Strengthening Protection Against Sex Offenders and Reforming the Law on Sexual Offences*, Cm 5668 (2002) (see **1.4**)
Review SOffA	*Review of Part 1 of the Sex Offenders Act 1997* (Home Office, 2001)
RO	Restraining order
Rook & Ward	Rook and Ward *Sexual Offences Law & Practice* (Sweet & Maxwell, 3rd edn, 2004)
RSHO	Risk of sexual harm order
RTA	Road Traffic Act
SB	*Setting the Boundaries: Reforming the Law on Sexual Offences* (Home Office, 2000) (see **1.4**)
SCA	Serious Crime Act
SCtA	Supreme Court Act
Scot Law Com No 209	*Report on Rape and Other Sexual Offences* (Scottish Law Commission, 2007)
SGC	Sentencing Guidelines Council
SGC Definitive Guideline	SGC Definitive Guideline Sexual Offences Act 2003 (see Appendix)
Smith & Hogan	Smith and Hogan *Criminal Law* (Ormerod (ed)) (OUP, 12th edn, 2008)
SOA	Sexual Offences Act
SO(A)A	Sexual Offences (Amendment) Act
SOCA	Serious Organised Crime Agency
SO(CI)A	Sexual Offences (Conspiracy and Incitement) Act
SOffA	Sex Offenders Act
SOO	Sex offender order
SOPO	Sexual offences prevention order
StOffA	Street Offences Act

SVGA	Safeguarding Vulnerable Groups Act
TA	Theft Act
TPCA	Town Police Clauses Act
TPO	Safeguarding Vulnerable Groups Act 2006 (Transitional Provisions) Order 2008
UKHTC	UK Human Trafficking Centre
UNCRC	(United Nations) Convention on the Rights of the Child 1989
VA	Vagrancy Act
VCRA	Violent Crime Reduction Act
VISOR	Violent and Sex Offender Register
YJCEA	Youth Justice and Criminal Evidence Act

Chapter 1
INTRODUCTION

1.1   This book concerns the English and Welsh law of sexual offences. It is not restricted to an examination of the Sexual Offences Act (SOA) 2003, although this will, of course, feature heavily within the text since SOA 2003 radically and comprehensively changed the law in this area. However, SOA 2003 is not a code of sexual offences because it does not incorporate certain aspects of the law (perhaps most notably offences relating to street prostitution, indecent photographs of children and the common law offence of outraging public decency) which continue to exist.

1.2   The text also examines some of the key evidential issues relating to sex offences, for example, the special measures that can be used to assist victims and witnesses when testifying in court.

1.3   The text concludes by dealing with various statutory provisions designed to protect the public or members of the public from the risk of harm by a sex offender, namely the dangerous offender sentencing provisions under the Criminal Justice Act (CJA) 2003 and the provisions relating to disqualification from working with, etc children and vulnerable adults, to notification requirements, and to various preventative orders.

MODERNISING THE LAW

1.4   SOA 2003 was the product of two principal reviews into the area of sexual offending. The first was a comprehensive Home Office-led review of sexual offences, whose report is entitled *Setting the Boundaries*.[1] The second was a review of the Sex Offenders Act (SOffA) 1997, which had created the notification system[2] where offenders have to notify the police of their personal details. A protocol for managing these offenders was then developed and the review considered how this could be strengthened. The principal recommendations of both reviews were taken forward to a White Paper, *Protecting the Public*,[3] which set out the key policies on which the Government were to legislate.

1.5   Perhaps the key principle contained within the White Paper was modernising the law. It was widely accepted that the law relating to sex offences was badly in need of reform[4] as it had developed in a piecemeal fashion and was inconsistent. The principal statute before the new Act was SOA 1956. A number of statutes amended it over the

---

[1]   Sex Offences Review *Setting the Boundaries: Reforming the Law on Sexual Offences* (Home Office, 2000) hereafter referred to as *SB*.

[2]   Discussed in Chapter 17.

[3]   *Protecting the Public: Strengthening Protection Against Sex Offenders and Reforming the Law on Sexual Offences*, Cm 5668 (2002) hereafter referred to as *PP*.

[4]   Lacey 'Beset by Boundaries: the Home Office Review of Sex Offences' [2001] Crim LR 3.

years, particularly in relation to offences involving male homosexual activity. In addition, new offences were introduced by the Indecency with Children Act (ICA) 1960 and the Sexual Offences (Amendment) Act (SO(A)A) 2000, whilst SOffA 1997 provided for extraterritorial liability over certain sexual offences against children under 16. SOA 1956, except ss 33–36 (provisions relating to the suppression of brothels and to the prosecution and punishment of those involved), and all of the other Acts just referred to above and various other statutory provisions were repealed by SOA 2003, s 140, Sch 7.

1.6 SOA 1956 was a consolidation statute, and the majority of its offence-creating provisions were drawn from Victorian statutes. Despite amendment after 1956, the law did not reflect changes in morality, society and social attitudes (or in technology) since the Victorian age, particularly in the last 50 years. In particular, many of its offences were gender specific in terms of the sex of the offender and the victim. Where a sex was specified, it was, with one exception, the masculine sex in the case of the offender and, normally, the feminine sex in the case of the other party. SOA 1956 was also discriminatory because it treated male homosexual activity in a different way from other types of sexual activity. Such gender specificity and discrimination was undoubtedly unjustifiable in the twenty-first century, if it had ever been justifiable.

1.7 Another difficulty with the old law was that it did not reflect the increased knowledge of the profound and long-lasting effects of sexual abuse, and neither it nor any other statute provided adequate protection against such abuse. There were unacceptable gaps in the law and many maximum penalties were too low. It also contained a number of terms that were archaic and inappropriate for modern usage.

1.8 The Home Office-led review of sex offences adopted an evidence-based approach to its inquiry. Whilst researchers attached to the team conducted a systematic analysis of the law both within England and Wales and in other jurisdictions, the review also commissioned some of the leading academics in the field to undertake literature reviews and limited empirical work.[5]

1.9 The focus of the review's recommendations was on personal autonomy, on the prevention of sexual abuse or exploitation and on the removal of discrimination in sex offences law. It will be seen throughout this book that SOA 2003 has largely adopted this approach and that the Act is structured on the basis of upholding a person's capacity to choose to engage in sexual conduct and the protection of the vulnerable.

1.10 It would be wrong to suggest that the review, the White Paper and ultimately SOA 2003 have not been controversial. Some commentators argued that the remit of the review was too limited,[6] whilst others have argued that the Act is too wide and that the reach of the criminal law has gone beyond that which is required.[7] Some of these criticisms will be picked up in this book.

1.11 As has been noted, SOA 2003 does not cover all aspects of the law. This is in part because the terms of reference for the review were limited, with perhaps the most notable limitation concerning prostitution. The terms of reference limited the review to the *exploitation* of people through prostitution[8] and accordingly issues that examined the autonomy of sex workers could not be discussed.

5   *SB*, Vol 2 sets out much of this research.
6   Lacey, n 4 above, at p 9 et seq, and see **1.11**.
7   Spencer 'Sexual Offences Act 2003 (2): Child and Family Offences' [2004] Crim LR 347.
8   Lord Falconer of Thoroton, HL Deb, vol 648, col 197.

1.12   Given the emphasis on exploitation it is unfortunate that neither SOA 2003 nor subsequent legislation has taken the long-awaited step of decriminalising loitering or soliciting for prostitution by child prostitutes. They are victims in need of care, not offenders deserving of punishment, and the matter should not simply be left to the law enforcement policies of the various bodies concerned.[9]

1.13   In 2004 the Home Office began a consultation process on prostitution,[10] and some legislative proposals emanating from it were put forward in the early stages of the Criminal Justice and Immigration Bill (2007–2008). However, these were later withdrawn by the Government[11] as it needed the Bill to gain Royal Assent quickly. In consequence, the law of street offences still contains the archaic and offensive term 'common prostitute'.[12]

SEXUAL OFFENCES ACT 2003

1.14   As the principal statute in this area it is prudent to explain the general outline of SOA 2003. The Act is divided into three parts. Part 1 (ss 1–79) sets out a radical framework of sexual offences. Many of the offences focus on the protection of those who are vulnerable to sexual abuse or exploitation, whether because they are young or because they are mentally disordered. Other new offences strengthen the law relating to non-consensual sexual activity and increase the protection of the public against public nuisances or offensive sexually related conduct. Part 2 (ss 80–136) deals with notification requirements and orders designed to prevent sex offending and other sexually harmful behaviour and thereby to protect the public. Part 3 (ss 137–143) contains general provisions, such as those relating to the making of orders and regulations and to commencement.

1.15   Sections 1–4[13] provide for the non-consensual sexual offences of rape (which includes 'oral rape'), assault by non-penile penetration, sexual assault and causing a person to engage in sexual activity without consent. Allied to these offences are corresponding offences in ss 5–8[14], in relation to children under 13, where the absence of consent does not have to be proved on the ground that there is an age below which there should be no question whether a child consented to the sexual activity.

1.16   Sections 9–14[15] deal with sexual activity involving children under 16. Section 15 introduced an offence relating to sexual grooming which is aimed at adults who pursue a course of conduct (by use of the internet or otherwise) with a child leading to a meeting (or intended to lead to a meeting) with intent to sexually abuse the child. This offence is complemented by a civil order, the risk of sexual harm order, referred to below.

---

[9]   In recent years, various children's charities have sought to identify, tackle and publicise the problem of children who engage in prostitution. In addition, the Association of Chief Police Officers has worked in partnership with other agencies to develop new multi-agency ways of treating children who commit offences by engaging in prostitution as victims rather than offenders. In May 2000, the Government published new guidance for the police, social services and other agencies on how to deal with such children. See Home Office Circular 20/2000 and *Safeguarding Children in Prostitution* enclosed therewith. Also see Gillespie 'Diverting Children Involved in Prostitution' [2007] 2 Web JCLI.

[10]   *Paying the Price: A Consultation Paper on Prostitution* (Home Office, 2004).

[11]   'Straw Drops Prostitute Law to Get Ban on Prison Strikes', *The Times*, 28 February 2008.

[12]   See **10.56** et seq.

[13]   Discussed in Chapter 3.

[14]   Discussed in Chapter 3.

[15]   Discussed in Chapter 4.

1.17 Sections 16–44 provide a range of offences to deal with sexual abuse by someone who is in a relationship of trust or care with the victim. Sections 16–24[16] amend and extend the criminal law relating to abuse of a position of trust introduced by SO(A)A 2000. These provisions apply to various types of sexual abuse of children under 18 by people in specified positions of trust. Sections 25–29[17] introduced offences dealing with sexual abuse of children under 18 by people within a range of relationships within the family. Sections 30–44[18] make provisions mirroring those under ss 16–24, to provide greater protection from sexual abuse for mentally disordered people:

- whose choice is impeded;

- who are caused to participate by an inducement, threat or deception; or

- where there is a breach of a relationship of care.

1.18 With the exception of the familial child sex offences, each group of offences in ss 9–44 broadly consists of a similar pattern of offences: engaging in sexual activity with the specified type of vulnerable person; causing or inciting such a person to engage in sexual activity; engaging in sexual activity in the presence of such a person; and causing such a person to watch the sexual activity or to look at pornographic photographs.

1.19 The next group of sections, ss 45–56,[19] amended the law of indecent photographs of children and deals with the abuse of children under 18 through their prostitution or their involvement in pornography, and with the exploitation of prostitution in general. New offences (ss 57–59[20]) were introduced to deal with those who are involved in the growing problem of trafficking of people for sexual exploitation.

1.20 There are three other groups of offences in Pt 1:

- three preparatory offences (ss 61–63);[21]

- offences of sex with an adult relative (ss 64 and 65);[22] and

- a group of miscellaneous offences dealing with exposure; voyeurism; intercourse with an animal; sexual penetration of a corpse; and sexual activity in a public lavatory (ss 66–71[23]).[24]

1.21 Overall, the Act raised the maximum penalty for offences corresponding to those repealed. The main increases were in the areas of sex offences against children and against people with a mental disorder. For example, the maximum sentence for sexual intercourse with a girl under 16 is raised from 2 years' imprisonment to 14 and, in the

---

[16] Discussed in Chapter 5.
[17] Discussed in Chapter 6.
[18] Discussed in Chapter 9.
[19] Discussed in Chapters 8 and 10.
[20] Discussed in Chapter 11.
[21] Discussed in Chapter 12.
[22] Discussed in Chapter 6.
[23] Discussed in Chapter 13.
[24] Offences under SOA 2003, Pt 1 were added to the list of sexual offences in the Police and Criminal Evidence Act 1984 (PACE), s 80(7) for the purpose of the provision in PACE, s 80(3) that a spouse is compellable to give evidence against an accused spouse if the offence is a sexual offence in respect of someone under 16 at the material time: SOA 2003, Sch 6, para 28.

case of a defective woman, from 2 years' to life. Notable reductions are sexual intercourse between adult relatives, reduced from 7 years' imprisonment to 2 years', and intercourse with an animal, reduced from life imprisonment to 2 years'. A significant number of provisions provide a higher maximum where penetrative sexual activity is proved than for non-penetrative activity.

1.22 Minor and consequential amendments were made by s 139 and Sch 6 to various statutes which refer to sexual offences so as to substitute specified offences under Pt 1. For example, CJA 1988, s 32 (evidence through television links) and the Youth Justice and Criminal Evidence Act (YJCEA) 1999, s 35 (prohibition on cross-examination of child-witness by defendant) are amended so as to apply to any offence under Pt 1 of the Act. The anonymity of the complainant provisions of SO(A)A 1992 and the provisions regulating access by defendants and others to certain material disclosed by the prosecution set out by the Sexual Offences (Protected Material) Act 1997[25] were extended to any offence under SOA 2003, Pt 1 besides those of sex with an adult relative, intercourse with an animal and sexual activity in a public lavatory. Despite considerable debate in Parliament, the Act did not extend reciprocal anonymity provisions to suspects or defendants.

1.23 The framework of offences in SOA 2003, Pt 1 goes some way to protect the public and punish sex offenders. Equally important is the management of sex offenders in the community. Part 2 of the Act strengthened the law in five ways in this respect. Sections 80–96[26] deal with the notification requirements automatically imposed on sex offenders who have been convicted or cautioned. Inter alia, they introduced an annual re-notification requirement and tightened the law about the notification of changes. Secondly, ss 97–103[27] introduced a new type of civil order, the notification order (NO), whose effect is to impose notification requirements on people convicted or cautioned for a sexual offence outside the UK. Thirdly, ss 104–113[28] combined two pre-existing types of civil preventative order, the sex offender order and the restraining order which could be imposed on conviction, in a new type of order, the sexual offences prevention order (SOPO). Fourthly, ss 114–122[29] introduced the foreign travel order (FTO) whose effect is to prohibit sex offenders from travelling abroad, to sex-tourism countries in particular, to commit sexual offences. Lastly, ss 123–129[30] introduced the risk of sexual harm order (RSHO), another civil preventative order, which is specifically aimed at preventing harm to children from sexually explicit communication or conduct by an adult where the adult has already engaged in such behaviour towards a child.

SEXUAL OFFENCES AND HUMAN RIGHTS

1.24 Perhaps unsurprisingly, sexual offending has featured heavily in the jurisprudence surrounding human rights. Arguably this dates back as far as the Wolfenden Committee over 50 years ago, which described the purpose of the criminal law in this area as:[31]

---

[25] This Act has not yet been brought into force.

[26] Discussed in Chapter 17.

[27] Discussed in Chapter 18.

[28] Ibid.

[29] Ibid.

[30] Ibid.

[31] *Report of the Committee on Homosexual Offences and Prostitution*, Cmnd 247 (1957), at paras 13 and 14.

'... to preserve public order and decency, to protect the citizen from what is offensive or injurious, and to provide sufficient safeguards against exploitation and corruption of others, particularly of those who are specially vulnerable because they are young, weak in body or mind, inexperienced, or in a state of special physical, official or economic dependence ... It is not, in our view, the function of the law to intervene in the private lives of citizens, or to seek to enforce any particular pattern of behaviour, further than is necessary to carry out the purposes we have outlined.'

1.25   The recognition that the state should not ordinarily intervene in the private lives of citizens recognises the fact that an individual is considered to have sexual autonomy. As will be seen this autonomy exists in two dimensions. In the first, it can be used as an argument that the state should not interfere in consensual activity conducted in private. The second dimension concerns itself with the obligation of the state to protect the sexual autonomy of a person, ie requiring the state to use its resources against those who infringe the autonomy of another.

1.26   The criminal law has been used as a tool to interfere with private activities for many years. There is an inherent tension that exists between allowing individuals to act in an autonomous way whilst at the same time ensuring that society is not harmed by these activities. The criminalisation of obscene and indecent material is sometimes cited as an example of where the law may need to intervene. The traditional basis for doing so is to uphold the moral standards of society. The right of a state to protect the morals of its society has been upheld by the European Court of Human Rights perhaps most famously in *Handyside v UK*.[32] However, the restriction of such material is undoubtedly an interference with, inter alia, the right to freedom of expression[33] and so any restriction must be necessary and proportionate.

1.27   The mere possession of indecent material is ordinarily not a criminal offence since personal use is considered not to be damaging to wider society. Thus criminalising simple possession could be construed as a disproportionate interference with the right to respect for private life[34] or freedom of expression. Where, however, a nexus of harm can be demonstrated, for example, in respect of indecent photographs of children,[35] simple possession can necessarily and proportionately be the subject of the criminal law.

1.28   A more relevant use of the criminal law to interfere with the sexual autonomy of an individual is where it concerns physical activity between individuals. In the past this has included the criminalisation of homosexual activity. The jurisprudence of human rights was an important feature in the relaxation of the prohibitions on that activity and the normalisation of the age of consent.[36] The European Court of Human Rights has accepted that the criminal law does have a role in protecting society, including its vulnerable members,[37] something later confirmed in *Laskey v UK*.[38] In that case the

---

[32]   (1976) 1 EHRR 737.

[33]   European Convention on Human Rights (ECHR), Art 10.

[34]   ECHR, Art 8.

[35]   A child must be abused or, at the very least, exploited for an indecent photograph of a child to be produced. It can be argued that the possession of such photographs fuels the demand for more photographs which, in turn, requires more children to be abused or exploited: see Taylor and Quayle *Child Pornography: An Internet Crime* (Brunner-Routledge, 2003), at p 161.

[36]   See, most notably, *Dudgeon v UK* (1981) 4 EHRR 149 where the higher age of consent for homosexual behaviour was considered to be an unjustified breach of ECHR, Art 8(1).

[37]   Ibid, at [49].

[38]   (1997) 24 EHRR 39. This was a petition by the applicants (including Laskey and Brown) following the dismissal by the House of Lords of their appeal against conviction for non-fatal offences arising from sado-masochistic practices (*Brown* [1994] 1 AC 212).

Court emphasised that states were entitled to interfere with the private rights of individuals so long as that was necessary in a democratic society and proportionate.

1.29 'Necessary in a democratic society' involves determining whether the interference serves a legitimate aim, whether there is a pressing social need for the interference[39] and whether the interference is proportionate to the aim pursued. The test of proportionality was identified as follows by Lord Clyde in *De Freitas v Permanent Secretary of Ministry of Agriculture, Fisheries, Lands and Housing*:[40]

> '... whether: (i) the legislative objective is sufficiently important to justify limiting a fundamental right; (ii) the measures designed to meet the legislative objective are rationally connected to it; and (iii) the means used to impair the right or freedom are no more than is necessary to accomplish the objective.'

Interference with the right may be disproportionate if, for example, it applies to more cases than necessary or if it interferes more than necessary in cases where it properly applies.

1.30 In judging whether there has been an interference with a person's right under Art 8 it is important not just to focus on the legal rule in question since this is, of course, merely one part of the process. It is also relevant to how that rule is applied. The European Court of Human Rights has stated that the effectiveness of the rule of law is an important part of the positive obligation on a state to protect its citizens.[41] In England and Wales the courts have also considered whether the application of the rule of law secures the human rights of individuals. An example of this can be found in Chapter 2, where the issue of the criminalisation of consensual adolescent sexual activity is discussed.[42] In *G*[43] the House of Lords was asked, inter alia, to consider whether the prosecution of an adolescent for consensual behaviour might amount to a disproportionate interference with Art 8.[44] The House decided by a 3-2 majority that no breach of Art 8 occurred in that case,[45] but the House was less clear as to whether prosecutorial policy could ever amount to a breach of Art 8. Lord Hoffmann argued that it could not,[46] but the remaining four members of the Appellate Committee appeared to think otherwise. Lords Hope and Carswell believed that not only was Art 8 engaged but that it had been breached. Baroness Hale stated that she could not agree with Lord Hoffmann's assertion that Art 8 had no role in the prosecutorial process,[47] although she held that it was not breached in this case. Lord Mance appears to have concluded that Art 8(1) was engaged but that the interference with it was justified under Art 8(2). Thus, it would appear that four members of the Appellate Committee accept that Art 8 could be engaged in the prosecutorial process and this will undoubtedly mean that the Crown Prosecution Service (CPS) has to consider carefully the proportionality of not only prosecuting an offender but also the selection of charges.[48]

---

39   *Dudgeon v UK* (1981) 4 EHRR 149.
40   [1999] 1 AC 69 at 80. This statement was applied by Lord Steyn in *A (No 2)* [2002] 1 AC 45, and by the Court of Appeal in *Gough v Chief Constable of Derbyshire* [2002] QB 1213.
41   See **1.31** et seq.
42   See **2.18** et seq. This is also discussed at **4.55** as it can amount to an offence contrary to SOA 2003, s 13.
43   [2008] UKHL 37.
44   Ibid, at [2].
45   For a discussion of the decision in the case see **3.127–3.129**.
46   [2008] UKHL 37, at [10].
47   Ibid, at [34].
48   In *R (S) v DPP* [2006] EWHC 2231 (Admin) the CPS acknowledged that where behaviour is consensual it

1.31　Although it has been said that the object of the ECHR has traditionally been to reduce the area of criminalisation by, for example, rejecting laws that are considered disproportionate or discriminatory,[49] it can be used to require the criminal law to provide adequate safeguards. Perhaps the first case to deal with this issue specifically was *X and Y v Netherlands*[50] where there was a loophole in Dutch sex offences which precluded the guardian of a mentally handicapped girl making a complaint on her behalf, which in essence precluded a criminal investigation. The Dutch Government conceded a loophole existed but suggested that the civil law could provide an effective remedy for a victim in this category, but the European Court of Human Rights rejected this contention and stated:[51]

> 'This is case where fundamental values and essential aspects of private life are at stake. Effective deterrence is indispensable in this area and it can be achieved only by criminal law provisions.'

1.32　This was a major statement by the European Court of Human Rights and confirmed that there is a positive obligation on the state to secure certain aspects of personal autonomy by using the criminal law. This was later followed by the landmark case of *MC v Bulgaria*[52] where the European Court of Human Rights was asked to rule upon the effectiveness of the legal system in relation to a rape complaint. The applicant, aged 14 at the relevant time, had alleged that she had been raped by two different men known to her. Bulgarian law at the time required active resistance or the use of physical force to rape, and since neither could be proved the prosecutor terminated proceedings against both suspects. The applicant claimed that this amounted to a breach of ECHR, Arts 3[53] and 8.[54] The European Court of Human Rights, following its lead in *X and Y v Netherlands*, held that states do have a positive obligation to use the criminal law to provide an effective deterrent from individuals interfering with the sexual autonomy of others.[55]

1.33　It is clear from these decisions that the criminal law must be an effective deterrent and this must include the way in which the law is applied by, for example, the police, prosecutors and the courts. It would not be difficult for someone to take the decision in *MC v Bulgaria* and to argue that a decision not to prosecute infringes these principles; indeed this was part of the argument advanced in *X and Y v Netherlands*. It is quite clear, therefore, that ECHR is capable of being used by both defendants and victims, and that the state has an obligation to ensure that its laws safeguard its citizens. It is likely that SOA 2003 provides an appropriate framework, but the use of it by police and prosecutors may be open to challenge in appropriate cases.

1.34　Outside the substantive criminal law, it is clear that ECHR has had a significant impact on trials relating to sexual offences together with the sentencing and management of those convicted of sex crimes. A good example of this is the tension that was caused by the Government's desire to assist victims of sexual violence and exploitation when it came to giving their testimony. Whilst this is a laudable goal, and

---

　　　is perhaps more appropriate to charge an offence under SOA 2003, s 13 rather than, for example, s 5. The particular facts of that case precluded an argument under Art 8 being advanced (at [14]). See also Lord Hope in *G* [2008] UKHL 37 at [33].

49　See Pitea 'Rape as a Human Rights Violation and a Criminal Offence' [2005] JICJ 447, at p 453.
50　(1985) 8 EHRR 235.
51　Ibid, at [27].
52　(2005) 40 EHRR 20.
53　Prohibition of torture, inhuman or degrading treatment.
54　Right to respect, inter alia, for private life.
55　See (2005) 40 EHRR 20, at [166].

one that is arguably in compliance with certain human rights,[56] it is necessary that these measures do not infringe the defendant's inherent right to a fair trial.[57] The courts have engaged in a careful balancing exercise,[58] something discussed in Chapter 14.

1.35 Challenges have also been brought against sentencing regimes,[59] the ability of courts to disqualify offenders from working with children[60] and the notification requirements. A majority of these challenges has sought to argue that the law cannot act retrospectively.[61] These challenges have failed where the court has held that the provision has a primarily preventative rather than punitive purpose.[62] The management of an offender is obviously capable of interfering with the rights of an individual under Art 8,[63] but it will not breach Art 8 if it is an executive decision relating to offender management which has a legitimate aim, and is necessary and proportionate.[64]

INTERNATIONAL OBLIGATIONS

1.36 The protection of members of society from sexual violence and exploitation has become the subject of action at international level. At United Nations level there have been two principal provisions of relevance. The first is the Optional Protocol to the (United Nations) Convention on the Rights of the Child (UNCRC) on the sale of children, child prostitution and child pornography. This was agreed in 2000 and came into force in January 2002. The UK signed the Convention on 7 September 2000 although it has not yet ratified it. The Optional Protocol requires member states to, inter alia, use the criminal law to safeguard children from prostitution and pornography. It sets out minimum standards for these crimes. The second instrument is the Protocol to the UN Convention against Trans-national Organized Crime, whose purpose is the prevention of the trafficking of humans, especially women and children, and which required contracting states to criminalise trafficking. A weakness of UN Protocols, in particular the UNCRC, is that they are not directly legally enforceable.[65] The UNCRC and its Protocol are simply monitored by the United Nations as member states are required to prepare reports detailing how their legal systems comply. There is no UN court which an individual may petition if he or she believes that the state is breaching its obligations.[66]

1.37 Within the Council of Europe there have been three major instruments of relevance. The earliest of the three is the Convention on Cybercrime which was agreed in November 2001. Article 9 of the Convention requires states to use the criminal law to

---

[56] For example, Arts 3 and 8.

[57] ECHR, Art 6.

[58] Perhaps the most notable example being *A (No 2)* [2002] 1 AC 45.

[59] See, for example, *R (Walker) v Secretary of State for the Home Department* [2008] EWCA Civ 30 which concerned the legality of imprisonment for public protection where a lack of offender management programmes meant the risk of harm could not be ascertained by the Parole Board.

[60] *Field; Young* [2003] 2 Cr App R (S) 175: see **16.6**, n 1 for a discussion of this.

[61] Contrary to ECHR, Art 7.

[62] *Ibbotson v UK* (1998) 27 EHRR CD 332; *Adamson v UK* (1999) 28 EHRR CD 209.

[63] See, for example, *Chief Constable of North Wales ex parte Thorpe* [1999] QB 396.

[64] Ibid, and see *Forbes v Secretary of State for the Home Department* [2007] 1 Cr App R (S) 418.

[65] Although, of course, individual states may decide to legislate in a way compatible with the Convention. The Nationality, Asylum and Immigration Act 2002, s 145 (now repealed and replaced by SOA 2003, ss 57–59) is an example of this as it met the UK's obligation under the UN Protocol on trafficking.

[66] In *R (R) v Durham Constabulary* [2005] 1 WLR 1184 Baroness Hale referred to the obligations under the UNCRC in her opinion; however, she ultimately found that it was not legally enforceable in domestic law (at [44]).

regulate the production and dissemination of child pornography. The Convention is not directly enforceable in the domestic courts, in part because although the UK signed the Treaty on 23 November 2001 it has not yet ratified it.

1.38   The second instrument produced by the Council of Europe is the Convention on Action against Trafficking in Human Beings, which requires states to take measures, including the provision of criminal offences, designed to tackle the trafficking of humans. This Convention was drafted in 2005 but was not signed by the UK until 23 March 2007, after considerable public and political pressure had been applied. The UK has not yet ratified the Convention although it is committed to doing so.

1.39   The final instrument within the Council of Europe is the Convention on the Protection of Children against Sexual Exploitation and Sexual Abuse. This was finalised in October 2007, signed by the UK on 5 May 2008, but not yet ratified. The Convention is a major instrument that covers all aspects of the protection of children from sexual exploitation and abuse. Chapter VI of the Convention details a series of criminal offences that signatory states must ensure are within their domestic criminal law, offering a minimum level of protection to vulnerable members of society. Chapter VII of the Convention prescribes minimum standards for the investigation, prosecution and trial of those who are considered to have breached the law.

1.40   Without domestic legislation, the Conventions and Protocols will not have direct effect in UK law. However, these Conventions, and other international instruments, are referred to by the European Court of Human Rights when determining issues before it and so it is possible that individuals may be able to claim rights in anticipation of ratification through linking the Convention to a claim under the ECHR.[67]

1.41   Action has also been taken at EU level with the production of two EU Council Framework Decisions which require member states to adopt appropriate domestic measures.[68] The first instrument was the EU Framework Decision on combating trafficking in human beings[69] which required member states to create specific criminal offences to criminalise the trafficking of persons for the purposes of labour or sexual exploitation. Unlike the international instruments discussed above, it also prescribed minimum sanctions for these criminal offences. The Decision was made on 19 July 2002 and it required member states to comply by 1 August 2004. The Nationality, Asylum and Immigration Act 2002, s 145 (now repealed and replaced by SOA 2003, ss 57–59) met this obligation, although only in respect of trafficking for sexual exploitation. The second instrument was the EU Framework Decision on combating the sexual exploitation of children and child pornography.[70] The decision was made on 22 December 2003 and it prescribes a number of offences criminalising child prostitution and the production, possession and distribution of child pornography. As with the trafficking Framework Decision, it also set out minimum penalties for the crimes. The Sexual Offences Act 2003 complies with this Decision and the decision to raise the age of 'a child' in respect of offences relating to indecent photographs of children[71] was made to comply with this decision together with, for example, Art 34 of the UNCRC.

---

[67]   For an example of this see *MC v Bulgaria* (2005) 40 EHRR 20, especially at [163].
[68]   Council Framework Decisions being binding on the relevant member states: see EC Treaty, Art 249.
[69]   2002/629/JHA.
[70]   2004/68/JHA.
[71]   See **8.18**.

1.42 Within the EU there has also been discussions by MEPs on the creation of a Europe-wide sex offender register,[72] although that is unlikely to occur since some member states have expressly rejected the suggestion of creating a domestic sex offenders register, and also an EU-wide disqualification system.[73] It is likely that there will continue to be international instruments made in this area, in part as recognition of the fact that sexual exploitation can now take place across geographical boundaries. Whilst the UK has so far been slow to ratify the treaties, pressure will continue to be placed upon it to do so and introduce the necessary legislative change.

MISCELLANEOUS POINTS

1.43 Some offences under SOA 2003 are triable only on indictment. All but one of the rest are triable either way. The maximum punishment on summary conviction is the same in the case of each of these offences: 6 months' imprisonment or a fine not exceeding the statutory maximum,[74] or both. When CJA 2003, s 282(3) is in force, the maximum imprisonment will be raised to 12 months, except in respect of an offence committed before the commencement date. This will also be the case for the other either-way offences discussed in this book, for example, indecent photographs of children,[75] to which s 282(3) applies. Those offences are identified in the following chapters by a cross reference to this paragraph.

1.44 Sexual activity in a public lavatory, contrary to SOA 2003, s 71, is the sole summary-only offence contained in that Act. This is the only offence in SOA 2003 to which the Criminal Attempts Act (CAA) 1981 does not apply.[76]

1.45 The consent of the Attorney-General or Director of Public Prosecutions (DPP) is not required for the institution of proceedings for any of the offences under SOA 2003. The CPS, on behalf of the DPP, does, of course, have the power under the Prosecution of Offences Act 1985 to take over and discontinue a prosecution which may be inappropriate. The consent of the DPP is, however, required for offences relating to indecent photographs of children.[77]

DEFINITIVE SENTENCING GUIDELINE

1.46 The Sentencing Guidelines Council (SGC) has issued a Definitive Guideline on sentencing for sexual offences.[78] It is set out in the Appendix to this book. It deals not only with offences under SOA 2003, Pt 1 (ie all offences under the Act other than those dealing with breach of a notification requirement or preventative order), but also with

---

[72] See, for example, 'MEPs Back Sex Offender List', *The Guardian*, 23 August 2007.
[73] 'Initiative of the Kingdom of Belgium with a view to the adoption by the Council of a Framework Decision on the recognition and enforcement in the EU of prohibitions arising from convictions for sexual offences committed against children.'
[74] The 'statutory maximum' is the prescribed sum within the meaning of the Magistrates' Courts Act (MCA) 1980, s 33 (Interpretation Act 1978, s 5 and Sch 1), which is the maximum fine which can be imposed on a summary conviction for an offence triable either way. At the time of going to press, the statutory maximum was £5,000.
[75] Protection of Children Act (PoCA) 1978, s 6(1) and CJA 1988, s 160(3).
[76] CAA 1981, s 1(4).
[77] PoCA 1978, s 1(3); CJA 1988, s 160(4).
[78] Available at www.sentencing-guidelines.gov.uk/guidelines/council/quick.html.

offences concerning indecent photographs or pseudo-photographs of children, contrary to PoCA 1978, s 1 and CJA 1988, s 160, and with keeping a brothel used for prostitution, contrary to SOA 1956, s 33A. The guideline applies to offenders sentenced on or after 14 May 2007. Where a sexual offence involves domestic violence, it may also be necessary for a court to refer to the *Guideline on Overarching Principles: Domestic Violence*, issued by the SGC in December 2006.

1.47   Courts must have regard to relevant guidelines in sentencing or in exercising any other function relating to the sentencing of offenders,[79] even where the offence was committed before the guideline was issued.[80] Such guidelines are not absolutely binding, but a judge who decides not to follow an applicable guideline must explain why he is not following it.[81]

THE TABLE

1.48   In this text whenever an offence (or group of offences) is presented it will be accompanied by a table which provides information about the application of various statutory provisions to the offence or offences. A specimen of the table is reproduced below.

Class of offence	3	SOA 2003, s 72 applies	✔
Notification requirements	See text	SOPO	✔
CJA 2003, Sch 15 applies	✔	Serious specified offence	✔
Review of lenient sentence	✗	Special provisions of CYPA 1933[82]	✗
Detention of young offender for specified period			✗

1.49   The first box details the class of offence when it is prosecuted on indictment. The class of offence is set out in the *Consolidated Criminal Practice Direction*.[83] Whilst most offences discussed in this book are Class 3, some are Class 2.

1.50   The second box details whether the offence is listed in SOA 2003, Sch 2 as an offence to which SOA 2003, s 72 applies, ie an offence against a child that can be tried in England and Wales although it was committed outside the UK. A detailed discussion of this is given at **2.95–2.103**.

---

79   CJA 2003, s 172.

80   *Bao* [2008] Crim LR 234.

81   *Oosthuizen* [2006] 1 Cr App R (S) 385; *Bowering* [2006] 2 Cr App R (S) 531; *A-G's References (Nos 31, 45, 43, 42, 50 and 51 of 2003)* [2005] 1 Cr App R (S) 377. The explanation may be that there is powerful personal mitigation: see *A-G's Reference (No 8 of 2007)* [2008] 1 Cr App R (S) 1.

82   Children and Young Persons Act 1933.

83   Part III.21. The *Consolidated Criminal Practice Direction* is a consolidation, with amendments, of existing Practice Directions, Practice Statements and Practice Notes as they affect proceedings in the Court of Appeal (Criminal Division), the Crown Court and the magistrates' courts. It can be found at www.justice.gov.uk/criminal/procrules_fin/contents/practice_direction/pd_consolidated.htm.

1.51 The third and fourth boxes detail whether the offence is one which attracts the notification requirements[84] and/or enables a court to make a SOPO.[85] An attempt, conspiracy or incitement[86] to commit any of these substantive offences, and to liability for them as aider, abettor, counsellor or procurer, are also subject to the same provisions.[87] In some cases the box referring to notification requirements will contain the words 'See text', rather than a simple tick or cross. The reason is that in some cases notification requirements only arise if an age or sentence condition[88] is satisfied. In the situations where an age or sentence condition applies, the relevant condition(s) will appear in the text accompanying the table. Age or sentence conditions no longer operate in respect of the offences to which the SOPO provisions apply.[89]

1.52 The fifth and sixth boxes concern the so-called 'dangerous offender' provisions contained within CJA 2003, Pt 12, Ch 5 (ss 224–236). The implications of these provisions are discussed in Chapter 15. The fifth box notes whether the offence is listed within CJA 2003, Sch 15. If it is, the extended sentence provisions of ss 227 and 228 apply to it.[90] The sixth box details whether a specified offence is a serious specified offence. If it is, ss 225 and 226 relating to life sentences and sentences for public protection are also relevant.[91]

1.53 The seventh box details whether the offence is one regarding which the Attorney-General[92] may refer a sentence to the Court of Appeal where he or she believes it to be unduly lenient.[93] Not all sexual offences are so prescribed,[94] but a significant number of the offences relating to abuse and exploitation under SOA 2003 are.[95]

1.54 The eighth box details whether the special provisions of CYPA 1933 apply.[96] These special provisions include a power to proceed with the case in the absence of a child or young person who is a defendant,[97] an extended power to take evidence by way of deposition where attendance at court would involve serious danger to the life or health of the witness[98] and the right for this deposition to be admitted in court as evidence in such circumstances.[99] The offences to which these measures apply are listed in CYPA 1933, Sch 1 and include several offences under SOA 2003.

---

[84]   Ie an offence in SOA 2003, Sch 3. As to notification requirements generally, see Chapter 17.
[85]   Ie an offence in SOA 2003, Sch 3 or Sch 5. As to SOPOs generally, see **18.30–18.134**.
[86]   Serious Crime Act (SCA) 2007, s 63, Sch 6 inserts into SOA 2003, Sch 3 a new paragraph – para 94A (not in force at the time of going to press) – which will state: 'A reference in a preceding paragraph to an offence ("offence A") includes a reference to an offence under [SCA 2007, Pt 2] in relation to which offence A is the offence (or one of the offences) which the person intended or believed would be committed'. This is necessary since Pt 2 of that Act will, when implemented, abolish the common law offence of incitement and replace it with additional offences of encouraging or assisting crime. The same provision adds an identical paragraph (para 173A) to SOA 2003, Sch 5.
[87]   SOA 2003, Sch 3, para 94, Sch 5 para 173.
[88]   See **17.19–17.28**.
[89]   See **18.35**.
[90]   See **15.7–15.10** and **15.51** et seq.
[91]   See **15.11** et seq.
[92]   Or the Solicitor General acting as the Attorney-General's deputy: Law Officers Act 1997, s 1(1).
[93]   Ie under CJA 1988, s 36. The offences are delineated by CJA 1988, s 35(3) and CJA 1988 (Reviews of Sentencing) Order 2006, SI 2006/1116.
[94]   Most notably, offences relating to indecent photographs of children are not prescribed.
[95]   SI 2006/1116, Sch 1, paras 1, 3.
[96]   CYPA 1933, ss 41–43.
[97]   CYPA 1933, s 41.
[98]   CYPA 1933, s 42(1).
[99]   CYPA 1933, s 43.

1.55   The final box indicates whether the offence is one for which a young offender can be detained for a specified period under the Powers of the Criminal Courts (Sentencing) Act (PCC(S)A) 2000, s 91. This provision empowers a court to impose a sentence of detention[100] where it is satisfied that neither a community sentence[101] nor a detention and training order is suitable where an offender aged under 18 is convicted on indictment. Such a sentence can only be passed if the offence carries a maximum term of imprisonment of 14 years or is one of a small number of specified offences (including some under SOA 2003). The term of the sentence is anything up to the maximum prison sentence for the offence. Whilst serving the sentence the offender is held in accordance with the Secretary of State's directions, normally in a young offender institution, although he may be directed to a mental hospital or even allowed to live in a community home.

GUIDANCE

1.56   At appropriate places in this text references are made to:

- Home Office guidance on Parts 1 and 2 of SOA 2003: *Guidance on Part 1 of the Sexual Offences Act 2003* (Circular 021/2004) (*Guidance Pt 1*) (available on the Home Office website) and *Guidance on Part 2 of the Sexual Offences Act 2003* (*Guidance Pt 2*) (available at www.crimereduction.homeoffice.gov.uk/sexual/ sexual027.htm); and

- CPS guidance in relation to most of the offences under SOA 2003: CPS Guidance on Sexual offences and child abuse (*CPS Guidance*) (available at www.cps.gov.uk/ legal/section7/index.html).

---

[100]   Which is considered to be a custodial sentence for the purposes of this Act (PCC(S)A 2000, s 76(1)) and is also subject to CJA 2003, ss 152 (custodial sentence to be imposed only when it is so serious that a non-custodial sentence can be justified) and 153 (custodial sentence to be for the shortest period of time commensurate with the seriousness of the offence).

[101]   As from a date to be appointed, 'community sentence' will be substituted by 'youth rehabilitation order': CJIA 2008, s 6(2), Sch 4, paras 51, 56.

Chapter 2

GENERAL MATTERS RELATING TO SEXUAL OFFENCES

COMMENCEMENT DATES AND APPLICABLE LAW

2.1   As noted in Chapter 1, the law relating to sexual offences in England and Wales is now primarily governed by the Sexual Offences Act (SOA) 2003, which was brought fully into force in England and Wales on 1 May 2004.[1] By SOA 2003, s 141(1)(b), the Secretary of State was empowered to include supplementary, incidental, saving or transitional provisions in any commencement order, but he failed to take advantage of this power. Instead, the vast majority of offences, penalties and procedural provisions hitherto contained within SOA 1956 and other pre-existing sexual offences legislation were abruptly repealed and supplanted as of 1 May 2004 by new offences, penalties and related provisions, none of which were given any retrospective application.

2.2   The repealed provisions of SOA 1956 and related statutes therefore continue to govern offences committed before 1 May 2004. This is entirely normal, but is particularly significant given the number of prosecutions that follow delayed or historic allegations in sex cases. Prosecutions for sexual offences allegedly committed 10, 20 or even 30 years previously are not unknown, particularly where adults complain of offences allegedly committed against them when they were children.

2.3   In other cases, indictments may include counts relating to a series of alleged offences under both old and new law, spanning a period either side of 1 May 2004.[2] It will be many years, therefore, before practising lawyers can safely clear their shelves of works dealing with offences under repealed sexual offences legislation.

2.4   The Home Secretary's failure to include properly drafted supplementary or transitional provisions in the 2004 Commencement Order was quickly proved to be a lamentable oversight. Cases arose in which there was significant doubt or uncertainty as to the dates on which alleged offences had been committed (eg because a child complainant was unfamiliar with the concept of dates). In at least two reported cases,[3] the prosecution found themselves in the frustrating position of being able to prove that

---

[1]   Sexual Offences Act 2003 (Commencement) Order 2004, SI 2004/874. Sections 138 and 141–143 came into force on Royal Assent. Those parts of the Act which apply to Northern Ireland (as specified in s 142) were also brought into force by SI 2004/874; but some of these will cease to apply when the Sexual Offences (Northern Ireland) Order 2008, SI 2008/1769, is brought fully into force. See also Sexual Offences Act 2003 (Commencement) (Scotland) Order 2004, SSI 2004/138.

[2]   See, for example, *Jheeta* [2007] 2 Cr App R 477.

[3]   See *Newbon* [2005] Crim LR 738; *A (Prosecutor's Appeal)* [2006] 1 Cr App R 433. See also *F* [2008] EWCA Crim 994.

D committed either an offence under SOA 1956 or an offence under SOA 2003, without being able to prove which. As the law then stood, trial judges had no option but to direct acquittals.[4]

2.5   The problem was subsequently addressed in the Violent Crime Reduction Act (VCRA) 2006, s 55, which came into force on 12 February 2007 and provides:

'(1) This section applies where, in any proceedings—

    (a)   a person ("the defendant") is charged in respect of the same conduct both with an offence under the Sexual Offences Act 2003 ("the 2003 Act offence") and with an offence specified in subsection (2) ("the pre-commencement offence");[5]

    (b)   the only thing preventing the defendant from being found guilty of the 2003 Act offence is the fact that it has not been proved beyond a reasonable doubt that the time when the conduct took place was after the coming into force of the enactment providing for the offence; and

    (c)   the only thing preventing the defendant from being found guilty of the pre-commencement offence is the fact that it has not been proved beyond a reasonable doubt that that time was before the coming into force of the repeal of the enactment providing for the offence.

    ...

(3) For the purpose of determining the guilt of the defendant it shall be conclusively presumed that the time when the conduct took place was—

    (a)   if the maximum penalty for the pre-commencement offence[6] is less than the maximum penalty for the 2003 Act offence, a time before the coming into force of the repeal of the enactment providing for the pre-commencement offence; and

    (b)   in any other case, a time after the coming into force of the enactment providing for the 2003 Act offence.

    ...

(5) A reference in this section to an offence under the Sexual Offences Act 2003 or to an offence specified in subsection (2) includes a reference to—

    (a)   inciting[7] the commission of that offence;

    (b)   conspiracy to commit that offence; and

    (c)   attempting to commit that offence;

and, in relation to an offence falling within paragraphs (a) to (c), a reference in this section to the enactment providing for the offence so falling has effect as a reference to the enactment providing for the offence under that Act or, as the case may be, for the offence so specified.

---

[4]   Such problems are not unique to sexual offences: see Hirst 'Guilty: But of What?' (2000) 4 E & P 31.

[5]   The offences listed in s 55(2) are those under SOA 1956; the Vagrancy Act 1824, s 4; the Town Police Clauses Act 1847, s 28; the Offences against the Person Act 1861, ss 61–62; the Mental Health Act 1959, s 128; the Indecency with Children Act (ICA) 1960, s 1; SOA 1967, ss 4–5; the Theft Act 1968, s 9; the Criminal Law Act (CLA) 1977, s 54; the Protection of Children Act (PoCA) 1978, s 1; the Sexual Offences (Amendment) Act (SO(A)A) 1976, s 3; and the Nationality, Immigration and Asylum Act 2002, s 145.

[6]   This is a reference to the maximum penalty by way imprisonment or other detention that could be imposed on conviction: s 55(4).

[7]   Given that this provision is in practice concerned with past conduct, it was not considered necessary to amend it so as to refer to the new inchoate offences of assisting or encouraging crime under Serious Crime Act (SCA) 2007, Pt 2.

(6) This section applies to any proceedings, whenever commenced, other than proceedings in which the defendant has been convicted or acquitted of the 2003 Act offence or the pre-commencement offence before the commencement of this section.'

2.6 If an offence under SOA 2003 carries heavier penalties than the equivalent pre-commencement offence, then in cases of doubt as to the date, D may be convicted only of the pre-commencement offence. Where, however, the new penalties are identical or lower, it will be presumed that SOA 2003 applies.

2.7 All three requirements in VCRA 2006, s 55(1) must be satisfied. An indictment must be drafted or amended so as to include counts for offences under both the old and the new law; and these counts must each refer to the same incident, rather than to a series of different incidents. Section 55 is of no assistance where, for example, A is accused of sexually abusing a child, B, on separate occasions before and after 1 May 2004, and the jury concludes that one at least of those allegations must be true (e g because B contracted a sexually transmitted disease from A) but cannot be sure that any particular allegation is true.

2.8 Difficulties may remain if the definition of an offence has changed. It may, for example, be clear that A had no *reasonable* grounds for believing that B consented to sex, but impossible to prove that A did not *unreasonably* believe it. Such a belief is no defence to rape under SOA 2003, but it negated the mens rea required under the old law. In such a case, conviction for rape will remain impossible unless it can be proved to have occurred on or after 1 May 2004.

AGE OF CONSENT

2.9 In English law, as in most other jurisdictions, sexual activity with a child[8] who is below a specified age is unlawful, even if the activity is consented to or initiated by the child in question. The purpose of this age limit (commonly known as the 'age of consent') is to protect children from inappropriate sexual activity at too early a stage when it has the potential to cause them physical, emotional or psychological harm. If A engages in sexual activity with B, when B is below that age, A accordingly commits an offence, and where both parties are under that age each may be guilty of offences against the other.[9]

2.10 The age of consent has been set for most purposes at 16 years of age, which is also the age at which young persons may marry.[10] Many jurisdictions have adopted a similar age of consent, but some have set higher limits and others have set much lower

---

[8] A 'child' includes, in this context, those aged under 16 or in some cases under 18.

[9] In contrast, the *Tyrrell* principle (see *Tyrrell* [1894] QB 719) ensures that children cannot be convicted as secondary parties to offences committed against themselves, or of inchoate offences relating to the commission of such offences against them.

[10] A higher age of consent was previously applicable to male homosexual acts. Under SOA 1967, the age limit for non-criminal consensual acts was originally set at 21. It was later reduced to 18, but this was still perceived as discriminating unfairly against homosexual males and it was lowered again to 16. Some countries still impose a higher age of consent in cases involving homosexual activities; and in others such activities remain criminal at any age.

ones. In the Republic of Ireland and Northern Ireland, for example, the age of consent is 17, but it is 15 in Denmark, France and Sweden, 14 in Iceland and Italy[11] and just 13 in Spain.

2.11   Lower foreign age limits may be significant where a UK resident who is not a UK national engages in consensual sexual activity abroad with a child who is under 16 but old enough to give valid consent according to local law.[12] English law does not purport to undermine local law in such cases, and respects the principle of double criminality. Prior to 14 July 2008 the same was true in respect of British citizens. A British citizen who engaged in consensual sexual activity with his 15-year-old girlfriend (or a local girl or boy of that age) when working or holidaying in France or Spain thus committed no offence. In respect of conduct occurring on or after that date, however, the Criminal Justice and Immigration Act (CJIA) 2008, s 72 (which amends SOA 2003 by substituting a revised version of s 72 of that Act) dispenses with the double criminality requirement as far as British citizens and other UK nationals are concerned.[13] A lawful act in France or Spain may thus be regarded as a criminal one in England.

2.12   Although many countries have adopted lower (and arguably more realistic) ages of consent, it is most unlikely that the age of consent will be lowered in England and Wales. One of the 'basic assumptions' in the Sex Offences Review was that the limit should be no lower than 16. It was argued that despite earlier physical maturity, a child's dependency is now greater than it was a hundred years earlier. Children cannot leave school, enter full-time employment or marry until 16.[14]

2.13   In some circumstances, the age of consent has been raised to 18. This higher limit, first introduced by SO(A)A 2000, s 3, and now found in SOA 2003, ss 16–19, applies to sexual activity between an adult and a young person in relation to whom the adult is an a position of trust, unless the parties are lawfully married or were involved in a lawful sexual relationship before the position of trust arose. It also applies (subject to the same exemptions) in the context of certain family relationships, including fostering relationships and cases in which A was *formerly* a foster parent to B. Finally, the age of consent has also been raised to 18 as far as involvement in prostitution or pornography is concerned.[15]

2.14   Although SOA 2003 has retained 16 as the basic age of consent, it has significantly extended the range of activities that become unlawful when committed with or in respect of children under that age. Under the previous law, the age of consent related only to sexual intercourse and to conduct which was considered indecent or grossly indecent.[16] In contrast, the offences relating to children introduced by the 2003 Act can be committed by any activity which is 'sexual'. 'Sexual activity' is a wider concept than indecent conduct. Kissing, petting or cuddling may sometimes be considered sexual, even when not indecent. Moreover, it is now unlawful to engage for exhibitionist purposes in sexual activity in the presence of a child under 16 (or in some

---

[11]   Sex Offences Review *Setting the Boundaries: Reforming the Law on Sexual Offences* (Home Office, 2000) (*SB*), at para 3.9.9.
[12]   See SOA 2003, s 72(1) (see **2.87** and **2.96**).
[13]   See **2.95**.
[14]   *SB*, at para 3.5.5.
[15]   See SOA 2003, s 45 and ss 47–50.
[16]   ICA 1960, s 1.

cases 18) or to seek sexual gratification by causing such a child to watch a sexual act or show a child images of such an act. This again is a more extensive prohibition than anything that existed before.

2.15 As noted above, the term 'age of consent' is potentially misleading. The fact that a child is under the age of 16 (or 18) does not mean that he is incapable of *actually* consenting for the purposes of offences such as rape, which require an absence of consent on the part of the victim; it means only that a child's consent, if given, is irrelevant for the purposes of those offences, such as sexual activity with a child, where the absence of consent is not an element. There is, however, something more closely resembling a true 'age of consent'. This was first introduced by SOA 2003, and is set at 13.

Conduct involving children under 13

2.16 Under SOA 2003, a child below the age of 13 is effectively deemed incapable of consenting to any sexual activity. Whereas the absence of consent is a specified element in rape, assault by penetration, sexual assault or causing a person to engage in sexual activity without consent, the equivalent offences against children below the age of 13 are defined in such terms that consent or its absence is no longer an issue. If, for example, A penetrates B with his penis, and B is under 13, A is thereby guilty of raping a child. It matters not whether B was willing. In theory her consent or the lack of it is simply irrelevant; but clearly the philosophy behind the creation of this offence (evidenced by use of the term 'rape') is that such a child is deemed incapable of consenting. Moreover, even where a genuine mistake is made, this is likely to constitute only limited mitigation, and the older the offender, the less relevant a mistake as to age, even if reasonably held, is likely to be. Adults having sexual relations with young persons do so at their own risk.[17]

2.17 Hitherto, there had been no minimum age of consent in rape cases. The issue of consent by a child was tested when raised by determining whether the child had any real understanding of what was involved or (in other words) had such a limited knowledge or understanding as not to be in a position to decide whether or not to consent.[18] This could give rise to arguments about a child's capacity to consent and the testing of this by the traumatic practice of cross-examining the child to determine whether it had capacity to consent and, if so, whether it had in fact consented. The introduction of the 13-year-old age threshold should in theory avoid this problem, although it may occasionally be necessary, even on a guilty plea, for a judge to determine by means of a *Newton* hearing[19] whether A forced himself on B or whether B was a willing partner. This would be particularly important where, for example, A and B are children and A's guilty plea is tendered only on the basis that B's consent is no defence to the charge.[20]

---

[17] *A-G's References (Nos 74 and 83 of 2007)* [2007] EWCA Crim 2550. See also *G* [2008] UKHL 37, esp at [3], per Lord Hoffmann, and at [45]–[47], per Baroness Hale.

[18] *Howard* [1966] 1 WLR 13.

[19] After *Newton* (1982) 77 Cr App R 13.

[20] As, for example, in *G* [2008] UKHL 37. Other than the age of criminal responsibility, there is no minimum age for the perpetrator of a sexual offence based on the fact that the other party is under 16 (or 13). In theory, an immature boy aged 10 might become guilty of 'child rape' when seduced by a more experienced girl who is a day short of her thirteenth birthday. It is now settled that the Crime and Disorder Act 1998, s 34 abolished the entire concept of doli incapax (and not merely the former presumption of it) in respect of children over the age of 10: *T* [2008] EWCA Crim 815. A special rule does, however, govern offences under SOA 2003, ss 9-12. A person under the age of 18 who would if aged 18 or more have been guilty of an offence under ss 9-12 will instead be guilty of a less serious offence under s 13 of the Act. See **2.28**.

Appropriateness of the age of consent

2.18   The blanket criminalisation of *all* consensual sexual activity, or related conduct, involving children under 16 is controversial. It is particularly controversial when both participants are under 16, especially when that activity may well involve nothing more than kissing or mild petting. Sexual activity of this kind is widespread amongst youngsters,[21] and has been a part of the adolescent development of most adults. It is far less likely to be exploitative and abusive than when there is a larger age gap between the couple, and (where truly consensual) it is not widely condemned within society. As Lord Millett said in *K*:[22]

> '... the age of consent has long ceased to reflect ordinary life, and in this respect Parliament has signally failed to discharge its responsibility for keeping the criminal law in touch with the needs of society.'

2.19   Is it sensible to make consensual non-exploitative sexual experimentation between two teenagers an offence – especially when the offence is a serious one? The case for saying 'no' is particularly strong where the activity does not involve penetration or significant health risks. Research shows that the criminalisation of underage sexual activity has little effect on behaviour.[23] Indeed, that fact, coupled with the fact that, if the conduct is truly consensual, the Crown Prosecution Service (CPS) is most unlikely to prosecute,[24] may make them think that the law is unreal and can generally be ignored with impunity. On the other hand, the fact that engaging in experimentation in what comes naturally is technically criminal may deter children from seeking advice and assistance about their sexual development or about contraception, pregnancy and sexually transmitted diseases. Where a child is emotionally damaged in the present type of case it is the social welfare and health agencies, rather than the criminal law, which are the appropriate means to deal with the situation, just as they are in counselling before things go 'wrong'. The continued blanket criminalisation of all sexual activity involving children under 16, supported by the Government, sits oddly with a Government-backed scheme to encourage children to experiment with oral sex, as part of a drive to reduce rates of teenage pregnancy. More than 100,000 secondary school children were involved in this scheme in 2002–2003.[25]

2.20   Arguments in favour of criminalisation centre on the need to protect those aged under 16 from the consequences of premature sexual activity which they may not be physically or psychologically equipped to handle.[26] Criminalisation may also help to protect children from coercion, exploitation, abuse or sexual harassment,[27] but (depending on the circumstances) this could equally be dealt with by a prosecution for

---

21   A quarter of women and nearly a third of men in the 16–44 age group first had heterosexual sexual intercourse before reaching the age of 16. The average age for first sexual *activity* was 14 for girls and 13 for boys: *First and Second National Surveys of Sexual Attitudes and Lifestyles* (Penguin, 1994; and (2001) 358 *The Lancet* 1843).

22   [2002] 1 AC 462, at [44].

23   Ford, Halliday and Little 'Changes in the Sexual Lifestyles of Young People in Somerset, 1990–1996' (1999) 25 *British Journal of Family Planning* 55.

24   Prosecutions of boys under 16 for unlawful intercourse with underage girls contrary to SOA 1956, ss 5 or 6 were extremely rare: *SB*, at para 3.9.6 gives the figures.

25   *The Times*, 21 February 2003.

26   See *G* [2008] UKHL 37, at [49], per Baroness Hale: 'The harm which may be done by premature sexual penetration is not necessarily lessened by the age of the person penetrating.'

27   A study conducted on behalf of the NSPCC found that 25–40% of alleged sexual abuse of children involves young perpetrators: Lovell *Children and Young People who Display Sexually Harmful Behaviour* (NSPCC, 2002).

one of the offences referred to in Chapter 3 or for an offence under the general law, such as an offence involving intentional or likely harassment, alarm or distress contrary to the Public Order Act 1986, s 4A or s 5, or an offence contrary to the Protection from Harassment Act 1997. There may also be an argument for dealing with 'consensual' but underage sex by way of a 'welfare response' instead of a criminal law based one. In *G*,[28] Lord Hope refers to the Children's Hearing System established in Scotland by the Children (Scotland) Act 1995 which is considered by its supporters to be preferable to criminal proceedings. Nothing comparable is available under English law.

2.21 Criminalising underage sexual behaviour may perhaps counteract the diffuse pressure to consent to sexual activity, which can come from the media and from the peer group ('Everything I read or hear shows that everyone is having sex. There must be something wrong with me if I don't as well'). It reduces the risk that a young complainant will have to go through the trauma of giving evidence, because her consent or the lack of it will not be an issue and other facts may not be in dispute (and it also avoids trials getting bogged down over such issues or of prosecutions being dropped because of them). The blanket criminalisation of such conduct is nevertheless a heavy price to pay.

2.22 In practice, the proper functioning of the law depends upon the exercise of prosecutorial discretion. The CPS recognises that it is not generally in the public interest to prosecute children of similar ages in respect of consensual sexual activity between them.[29]

2.23 Arguably, it is contrary to the rule of law to enact unworkably draconian laws and then rely upon CPS guidelines to mitigate the more extreme aspects of those laws. This makes CPS policy almost as important as the details of the legislation itself: an unsatisfactory state of affairs, notwithstanding that the application of the policy guidelines by prosecutors is potentially subject to judicial review.[30] Moreover, neither this guidance, nor guidance about the issuing of reprimands and final warnings, can provide a complete answer because, by the time it comes into play, D may already have been arrested and had his private life investigated by the police.

2.24 Even in cases involving truly non-consensual assaults, the prosecution of young or handicapped children may well be inappropriate, unless perhaps the offence in question was very serious. As Hughes LJ observed in *DPP v R*:[31]

> 'Where very young, or very handicapped, children are concerned there may often be better ways of dealing with inappropriate behaviour than the full panoply of a criminal trial. Even where the complaint is of sexual misbehaviour it ought not to be thought that it is invariably in the public interest for it to be investigated by means of a criminal trial, rather than by inter-disciplinary action and co-operation between those who are experienced in dealing with children of this age and handicap.'

2.25 The criminalisation of minor sexual activity involving under-16s may also lead to problems for schoolteachers, youth leaders and parents. By law, they should stop two 15-year-olds who are seen 'snogging' when under their supervision. If they do not, their

---

28 [2008] UKHL 37, at [37]-[38].
29 CPS Guidance on Sexual offences and child abuse (see **1.56**). See also *R (S) v DPP* [2006] EWHC 2231 (Admin).
30 It is by no means a unique state of affairs, however.
31 [2007] EWHC 1842 (Admin).

failure to exercise control over the youngsters' sexual activity could arguably involve liability as a secondary party to the offence.[32]

2.26   During the passage of the Sexual Offences Bill, the Parliamentary Joint Committee on Human Rights questioned whether the proposed criminalisation of all sexual contact between children could be justified under the European Convention on Human Rights (ECHR). The Committee referred specifically to proposals relating to children under 13, but the same points can be made even more forcefully in respect of those just below the age of 16:[33]

> 'Imposing or threatening criminal sanctions on people who kiss consensually is an interference with their right to respect for their private lives under ECHR Article 8.1. It requires justification under Article 8.2, which requires any interference with the right to be in accordance with the law, and necessary in a democratic society for one of the legitimate aims listed in Article 8.2. To be "necessary in a democratic society", an interference must be a proportionate response to a pressing social need. We accept that the interference would be adequately in accordance with the law. The questions are (a) whether the interference serves a legitimate aim, (b) whether there is a pressing social need for the interference, and (c) whether the interference is proportionate to the aim pursued.'

2.27   The Committee concluded that a blanket ban on *all* sexual touching, including kissing, of or by under-13s (which despite criticisms was eventually enacted as SOA 2003, s 7) was considered to be a disproportionate response to any legitimate needs. It was not enough simply to leave it to the discretion of prosecutors to ensure that s 7 did not unjustifiably violate an individual's right to respect for private life under ECHR, Art 8. Consequently, s 7 was over-broad and imposed liability in a way not adequately tailored to the legitimate objective. It interfered with the right to respect for private life more than necessary for that purpose in a democratic society and contained insufficient safeguards against violation of the right.

2.28   SOA 2003 makes (in s 13)[34] one small concession to teenage sexuality by providing that where, in a case involving consensual sexual activity with someone under 16, D is aged under 18, a lesser offence is committed than would have been the case had D been aged 18 or over. With respect, this concession (which does not in any case mitigate liability for the specific offences relating to children under 13)[35] does not go far enough. If the protection of young persons from predatory adults is the real concern, Parliament could have adopted a solution similar to that in the 1994 French Penal Code, Arts 227–225, whereby the offence of consensual sexual behaviour with someone under 15 can be committed only by someone aged 18 or over.

2.29   The terms of the lesser offence are inflexible. If there has to be such an offence, there would have been much to be said for an exemption from liability for underage sexual activity offences where there was a small, defined age difference between D and the complainant (eg 2 years, as in Canada).[36] This approach did not find favour in Parliament,[37] although it has found favour with the draftsmen of the Draft Criminal Code for Scotland, who have proposed limiting liability for consensual sexual behaviour

---

32   Cf *Tuck v Robson* [1970] 1 WLR 741.
33   *Twelfth Report 2002-03 Scrutiny of Bills: Further Progress Report*, HL 119; HC 765 (TSO, 2003–2003).
34   See **4.50**.
35   See *G* [2008] UKHL 37 and **3.127**.
36   Criminal Code, RSC 1985, s 150.1(2).
37   See HC Committee, cols 110–124.

with someone under 16 (other than sexual intercourse between people under that age) to cases where D was at least 2 years older than the complainant, or in a position of responsibility.[38]

2.30 A much stronger case can be made for the prohibition of prostitution involving those under 18. Indeed, one would be hard-pressed to identify any real argument for permitting juvenile prostitution. As for the special rules concerning children under 13, the views of the Parliamentary Joint Committee have already been noted, but it does perhaps make some sense to treat a child's thirteenth birthday as a watershed of some kind. Although the onset of puberty is variable, most children under 13 have not reached puberty, and even pubescent children of 12 may well lack sufficient knowledge or understanding to give a free and informed agreement to sexual activity. An apparent agreement may well be attributable to persuasion, inducement or ignorance; and the younger the child the more likely this will be the case. Beyond 13, the likelihood of this becomes increasingly remote as the birthdays go by. Any age limit is bound to be arbitrary, but 13 may be an appropriate point in those cases where the line should be drawn.

SEXUAL BEHAVIOUR

2.31 Some offences (notably rape) are unequivocally 'sexual'. If it is proved that A penetrated B's mouth, anus or vagina with his penis and that B did not consent, the actus reus of rape is established. No question arises as to A's purpose or as to whether the act can properly be described as sexual. Most offences under SOA 2003 are less straightforward, however. An assault, for example, may or may not be sexual, and will fall within the ambit of the Act only if its sexual character can be established to the satisfaction of the court.

2.32 SOA 2003, s 78, provides guidance as to what amounts to sexual behaviour for the purposes of the Act, but stops short of attempting a full definition:

'For the purposes of [Part 1 of this Act] (except s 71 [sexual activity in a public lavatory]), penetration, touching or any other activity is sexual if a reasonable person would consider that—

(a) whatever its circumstances or any person's purpose in relation to it, it is because of its nature sexual, or

(b) because of its nature it may be sexual and because of its circumstances or the purpose of any person in relation to it (or both) it is sexual.'

2.33 This dichotomy between inherently sexual, potentially sexual and inherently non-sexual conduct is derived from a broadly similar dichotomy adopted by the House of Lords in *Court*,[39] in the context of indecent assaults under SOA 1956.[40] There is, however, a difference between what is 'sexual' and what is 'indecent'. Conduct may be sexual without being indecent or indecent without being sexual. For example, a kiss or a

---

[38] See s 27(2) of the Draft Sexual Offences Bill annexed to *Report on Rape and Other Sexual Offences* (Scottish Law Commission, 2007), hereafter Scot Law Com No 209.

[39] [1989] AC 28.

[40] The provision also has a predecessor in the definition of 'sexual activity' in SO(A)A 2000, s 3(5), for the purposes of the offences of abuse of a position of trust introduced by s 3 of that Act, albeit its precise terms are not identical.

pat on the bottom, which might not nowadays be considered indecent, even when done in public, may be unambiguously sexual. In contrast, an intimate body search might well be considered indecent without being sexual at all.

2.34   Although it does not purport to offer a definition, s 78 may be criticised for its circularity: it tells us that behaviour may be considered sexual if a reasonable person would consider it to be sexual – but what might a reasonable person consider to be sexual? According to the *New Shorter Oxford English Dictionary*, 'sexual' means 'deriving from or relating to desire for sex or for carnal pleasure'. 'Carnal' means, 'pertaining to the body as the seat of passions or appetites; fleshly, sensual; sexual'.

2.35   Ashworth and Temkin[41] acknowledge the limitations of the s 78 tests, but argue that a better test has yet to be found. Moreover:

> 'In ... most cases, it will not be difficult to apply the test in s 78(a). It will be in unusual cases only that s 78(b) will be brought into play. Whilst s 78 might require some fine-tuning, it was wise to have included a provision of this kind. In Canada a decision to exclude any such provision from the legislation has led to a costly proliferation of cases in which courts have been called upon to rule in what circumstances a particular assault may be described as sexual.'

'Sexual': the tests

2.36   SOA 2003, s 78 requires that penetration, touching or other activity must pass one of two tests in order to be labelled as sexual. Given that 'sexual' is an ordinary English word, it must be left to the jury, in the case of a trial on indictment, to decide whether either test is satisfied. Unless the issue is conceded by the defence, it will not be appropriate for a judge to direct the jury that given conduct is or must be sexual, although as with any issue of fact the judge may sometimes be justified in directing an acquittal on the basis that no reasonable jury could find it to be so.[42]

2.37   The first test (in s 78(a)) concentrates on the nature of the conduct. Would a reasonable person consider that because of its *nature* it *is* or must necessarily be sexual? If so, the conduct is sexual for the purposes of SOA 2003. The jury or magistrates must look at the conduct itself, and not at its surrounding circumstances or the purpose with which it is done. This test is not satisfied if objectively the nature of the conduct is merely *capable* of being (ie may or may not be) sexual; it is only satisfied if objectively it is because of its very nature sexual. Examples of conduct which by its very *nature* would always satisfy the present test might include masturbation, genital-oral stimulation and inserting a sex toy into a woman's vagina, although this must ultimately remain a question of fact for a jury to decide. In such cases, because of the nature of the activity, a reasonable person would presumably consider the activity to be sexual, even if the activity was carried out for the purposes of bona fide medical research or in order to provide a sample for forensic or medical analysis.[43] In this context sexual conduct may be committed for purposes other than sexual gratification.

2.38   The second (alternative) test (in s 78(b)) involves two distinct limbs or stages. As Lord Woolf CJ explained in *H*:[44]

---

[41]   'The Sexual Offences Act 2003: Rape, Sexual Assault and Problems of Consent' [2004] Crim LR 328.
[42]   See *Galbraith* [1981] 1 WLR 1039.
[43]   Self-masturbation is the obvious method of providing semen for medical or forensic analysis.
[44]   [2005] 2 Cr App R 149, at [9].

'If there were not two requirements in subs (b), the opening words "because of its nature it may be sexual" would be surplus. If it was not intended by the legislature that effect should be given to those opening words, it would be sufficient to create an offence by looking at the touching and deciding whether because of its circumstances it was sexual. In other words, there is not one comprehensive test. It is necessary for both halves of s 78(b) to be complied with.'

2.39 The first limb of the test involves asking whether a reasonable person would consider that because of its nature the conduct in question *may* be sexual. Examples of such conduct might include inserting a finger into a woman's vagina or someone's anus, removing or pulling at another person's clothes, touching the genital organs (whether one's own, another person's or those of an animal), kissing another person, taking a bath or shower with another, smacking someone's bottom or rubbing suntan lotion onto someone's legs or chest.

2.40 The second limb of the test (which only arises if the answer in respect of the first limb is affirmative) involves asking whether a reasonable person would consider that because of the circumstances of the activity or the purpose of *any* person in relation to it (not just the person who does the act, but – for example – the person to whom it is done or a third person who encourages the act to be done whilst he watches) the activity *is* in this case sexual.

2.41 Thus, for example, where a doctor uses his fingers to examine a patient's vagina or anus, this would not ordinarily be considered sexual; but if he makes inappropriate comments or suggestions whilst doing so, or if there is proof that he knows the examination to be unnecessary, a reasonable person would doubtless conclude that his conduct must indeed be sexual.

2.42 *Court* illustrates how motive and circumstances may be relevant. C, a shop assistant, spanked a 12-year-old girl who had entered his shop. He did this for no immediately apparent reason, but when arrested he admitted that he had a 'buttock fetish'. This was held to be admissible in evidence for the purpose of proving that his conduct was 'indecent' within the meaning of SOA 1956. Such an admission would now be considered equally admissible in order to prove that C's conduct was 'sexual' for the purposes of SOA 2003, s 3 or s 7. Had he purported to be disciplining the child for an offence such a shoplifting, there might have been some possible issue as to whether this was 'sexual' behaviour, but his motives would then have required careful examination. Had he pulled down her pants before spanking her (which he did not) the prosecution's task would have been even easier.

2.43 The first limb of the test in s 78(b) envisages that some conduct may be incapable of being considered sexual, whatever the circumstances or the motives of those involved. If D's conduct is *incapable* of being regarded as sexual, his intention cannot make it so. One can only speculate as to what kind of conduct would be considered incapable of being sexual, given that the 'reasonable person' must presumably be attributed with some knowledge of the enormous range of fetishes and practices that may sexually excite his fellow men and women. Many men and women are sexually stimulated by practices such as bondage, flagellation, uniforms or high heels, and some are similarly excited by horse riding, suffocation, urination, fur or even executions; and these are just a few examples of a much wider phenomenon. So, whereas a judge must remind the jury to consider both limbs of the test, it may be open to a juror to conclude that if some people can derive sexual stimulation from a given type of behaviour, then it must indeed be capable of being sexual. It makes no sense to include obvious fetishes whilst excluding others merely because they are unusual or bizarre.

2.44 In *Court*, the House of Lords appears to have regarded *George*[45] as an example of conduct that could never be indecent. G was charged with indecent assault on the basis that he had removed a shoe from a girl's foot because it gave him sexual gratification; but was acquitted on the basis of the trial judge's ruling that he had done nothing, on this evidence, that could be described as indecent.

2.45 In the context of 'indecency' *George* may perhaps have been correct on its facts,[46] but whether such conduct could properly be described as sexual under SOA 2003 is another matter. In *H*, Lord Woolf CJ said:[47]

> 'We would express reservations as to whether or not it would be possible for the removal of shoes in that way, because of the nature of the act that took place, to be sexual as sexual is defined now in s 78. That in our judgment may well be a question that it would be necessary for a jury to determine.'

2.46 In *H*, the alleged sexual assault consisted of nothing more than grabbing part of the complainant's clothing; but this act was accompanied by the words, 'Do you fancy a shag?', and by an unsuccessful attempt to place a hand across her mouth. In those circumstances, the court had no hesitation in upholding H's conviction for sexual assault. In practice, the perceptions of the reasonable person in the above two tests will be those of the jury or magistrates; it is unlikely that they will have other evidence of what a hypothetical person might think about the conduct, nor will they consider themselves to be anything other than reasonable.

2.47 SOA 2003 does not require the 'reasonable person' in s 78(a) and (b) to be endowed with D's gender, sexual orientation, age, ethnic origin or background. To do so would destroy the essence of s 78, which clearly is intended to lay down an objective test.

2.48 The approach laid down in s 78 might be criticised as liable to lead to arbitrary and inconsistent findings by different juries or benches of magistrates as to what is 'sexual' under the second test. Such criticism is often encountered where there are no clear and watertight definitions for the courts to apply. Nevertheless, the solution to the definition of 'sexual' activity in s 78 is arguably the best one available. The only other realistic solution would have been to provide a list of activities which were or were not to be considered 'sexual'. This would indeed provide greater certainty, but only at the expense of replacing judgment and common sense with a robotic and inflexible approach that would be incapable of responding flexibly to atypical situations. In some cases, whether acts are 'sexual' or not will depend on their circumstances or attendant purpose, which cannot be defined in advance. A list which limits sexual activity to acts per se (ie by their nature) sexual would be far too narrow. On the other hand, a list which refers to acts in more general terms would be incapable of taking sufficient account of the enormous range of circumstances and purposes that may be encountered.

---

[45] [1956] Crim LR 52.

[46] Contrast *Price* [2004] 1 Cr App R 145, in which P's conduct in stroking the complainant's legs through her trousers below the knee whilst begging her to remove her ankle boots was held to be capable of amounting to an indecent assault, contrary to SOA 1956, s 14. It is certainly clear that his motives were sexual and in contrast to *George* this must have been obvious to the complainant.

[47] [2005] 2 Cr App R 149, at [11].

EXCEPTIONS TO LIABILITY FOR AIDING, ABETTING OR COUNSELLING A SEXUAL OFFENCE

2.49 SOA 2003, s 73 makes special provision to protect those who despite acting in good faith might otherwise be in danger (in theory at least) of becoming secondary parties to sexual offences involving children. The Act prohibits sexual activity with or between children below the age of 16, but in practice underage sex does often take place, and the welfare of such children would not be advanced if parents, friends, teachers, medical practitioners and others were prevented from providing frank sex education, counselling or even contraceptives in order to protect them from some of the most serious consequences of such behaviour.

2.50 In order that such advice or assistance can safely be given, those giving it must be sure that they do not risk being charged with assisting or encouraging unlawful sexual behaviour. For this reason, s 73(1) provides:

'(1) A person is not guilty of aiding, abetting or counselling the commission against a child of an offence to which this section applies if he acts for the purpose of—

(a)   protecting the child from sexually transmitted infection,
(b)   protecting the physical safety of the child,
(c)   preventing the child from becoming pregnant, or
(d)   promoting the child's emotional well-being by the giving of advice,

and not for the purpose of obtaining sexual gratification[48] or for the purpose of causing or encouraging the activity constituting the offence or the child's participation in it.

(2) This section applies to—

(a)   an offence under any of sections 5 to 7 (offences against children under 13);
(b)   an offence under section 9 (sexual activity with a child);
(c)   an offence under section 13 which would be an offence under section 9 if the offender were aged 18;
(d)   an offence under any of sections 16, 25, 30, 34 and 38 (sexual activity) against a person under 16.

(3) This section does not affect any other enactment or any rule of law restricting the circumstances in which a person is guilty of aiding, abetting or counselling an offence under this Part.'

2.51 Section 73(1) goes further than the House of Lords' decision in *Gillick v West Norfolk and Wisbech Area Health Authority,*[49] which permitted a doctor to give contraceptives or sexual health advice to patients under 16 in the exercise of his clinical judgment; and s 14(2) and (3) make similar provision to protect against charges of arranging or facilitating the commission of a child sex offence, contrary to s 14(1).

2.52 Section 73 may be invoked by anyone who acts for one of the specified purposes. That person need not be a doctor or parent, or owe a duty of care to the child in question. The friend who provides a condom when asked may equally come within the

---

[48]   Section 78 does not apply to 'sexual gratification'. For the appropriate definition of 'sexual' in the *New Shorter Oxford English Dictionary*, see **2.34**.
[49]   [1986] AC 112.

ambit of the provisions; but protection from liability depends on the purpose for which the assistance or advice is given. If A gives his 15-year-old brother, B, some condoms to prevent him getting his 16-year-old girlfriend, C, pregnant, that would not bring A within the protection of s 73, whereas he would be protected if C was under that age, or if one of his purposes was to safeguard B from sexually transmitted diseases, or from the wrath of C's father, who would be likely to assault anyone who got his daughter pregnant.

2.53 In practice, the real issue is likely to be whether A positively encouraged or assisted underage sexual activity or whether he merely sought to protect the child(ren) concerned from the consequences of such activity. Section 73 provides no exemption to liability for 'procuring' the commission of a child sex offence. This is not surprising since:[50]

> '... a person procures the commission of an offence by setting out to see that it is committed and taking the appropriate steps to produce its commission; more succinctly, "procure" means "to produce by endeavour".'

2.54 D does not bear any persuasive burden of proof in respect of a s 73 defence, although such a defence will have to be raised as an issue by admissible evidence before the prosecution can be required to prove that it does not apply in the case in question. Such evidence need not come from D or his witnesses. It may sometimes be raised by the testimony of the prosecution's own witnesses.

STATUTORY MENS REA OR FAULT ELEMENTS

2.55 The mens rea elements applicable to sexual offences vary, and in most cases different elements are required in respect of different elements of the offence. Rape, for example, requires intention as to the act of penetration, coupled with an absence of any reasonable belief as to the complainant's consent. In other cases, mens rea elements are coupled with some element of strict liability.[51] The following are found in SOA 2003:

- intention to commit an act, cause an event or engage in an activity that is part of the actus reus of the offence, or intention to commit an ulterior offence;

- knowledge, or in some cases a reasonable expectation of knowledge, as to some fact that is an element of the offence (ie it is something that D 'could reasonably be expected to know', even if D does not in fact know it);

- absence of reasonable belief in some fact that would negative the offence;

- belief (or in some cases expectation) as to some future conduct or occurrence; or

- recklessness as to some such fact.

---

[50] *Attorney-General's Reference (No 1 of 1975)* [1975] QB 773, at p 779.
[51] Thus, for an offence under SOA 2003, s 5 (rape of a child) it must be proved that the act of penetration was intentional, but the age of the child is a matter of strict liability, as the House of Lords has confirmed in *G* [2008] UKHL 37. See, in particular, at [3], per Lord Hoffmann, at [46], per Baroness Hale, and at [71], per Lord Mance.

Intention

2.56   Most offences in SOA 2003, Pt 1 (ie in ss 1–71) require some element of intent. D must 'intentionally' do a specified thing or 'intend' a specified consequence of his or her act. Where the act in question is a pure conduct crime (such as exposure of the genitals) or one in which any specified consequence is inseparable in time and space from that conduct (as in the case of an offence involving sexual penetration) what this means in practice is that D must be proved to have acted 'deliberately'.[52] Another way of putting it would be to say that D must have committed the act 'on purpose'.

2.57   Where in contrast the offence in question involves D 'intentionally' causing a consequence that is distinct from his own conduct, as in the s 12 offence of 'causing a child to watch a sexual act', it will no longer suffice that D's conduct was deliberate. He must additionally be proved to have intended the specified consequence, and in this context 'intent' must ordinarily take the form of direct intent (ie aim or purpose),[53] especially where (as in s 12) an ulterior intent or purpose (sexual gratification) is also specified. It can hardly have been D's purpose to derive sexual gratification from a given result unless he aimed to cause that result in the first place.

2.58   Several sexual offences (notably those under SOA 2003, ss 61–63) require proof of an ulterior intent. The same is true, of course, of any attempt to commit a sexual offence.[54] Liability may be incurred in such cases even if the specified intent or purpose remains unfulfilled, but once again it is difficult to see how anything less than direct intent or purpose could suffice in this context. There is little if any room here for 'oblique intent'.[55]

2.59   Indeed, oblique intent probably has little practical application anywhere in the context of sexual offences. The essence of oblique intent is that a court or jury may find D to have 'intended' some obvious and inevitable consequence of his conduct, even though it was merely a side-effect of his actions, rather than part of his aim or purpose in so acting. 'Collateral damage' may in other words be seen as intended, if D knew it would happen, should he succeed in some other aim or purpose.[56] There are, however, a few sexual offences in which oblique intent might potentially be an issue. It is conceivable, for example, that an offence of 'intentionally arranging or facilitating' a child sex offence that it is believed another person will commit, contrary to SOA 2003, s 14(1), might involve something less than direct intent.[57]

2.60   A mistake which prevents D having the intent in question will excuse him, however unreasonable it may be (although the reasonableness of an alleged mistake will be relevant to the credibility of an alleged mistake).[58] The same is true in respect of a requirement of recklessness, knowledge or belief. Whether a mistake has that effect depends on the circumstances and on the definition of the offence in question. Under

---

[52]   *Heard* [2008] QB 43. See **2.81**.
[53]   As to direct intent, see *Mohan* [1976] QB 1 at 11.
[54]   Criminal Attempts Act 1981, s 1.
[55]   As to the meaning of intention in the context of SOA 2003, s 66 (exposure with intent to cause alarm or distress), see **13.18**.
[56]   *Woollin* [1999] AC 82; *Matthews* [2003] 2 Cr App R 461.
[57]   See **4.57**.
[58]   *DPP v Morgan* [1976] AC 182; *Kimber* [1983] 1 WLR 1118; *Williams* [1987] 3 All ER 411, CA; *B v DPP* [2000] 2 AC 428.

the old law, A's honest but mistaken belief that B consented to sexual intercourse negated the mens rea of rape.[59] Under SOA 2003, however, such belief must be based on reasonable grounds.

Knowledge

2.61   A number of offences in SOA 2003 require D to act:

* Knowing of the existence of an element of the actus reus. The preparatory offence of administration of a substance to enable someone to engage in sexual activity with the victim requires D to know that the victim does not consent to the administration of the substance; the offences of voyeurism require D to know that the victim does not consent to being observed, etc for D's sexual gratification.

* Knowing or being reckless about the existence of an element of the actus reus.

* Knowing of an element of the prohibited conduct. For example, in offences against persons with a mental disorder, the mens rea is that D knows (or could reasonably be expected to know[60]) that the victim has such a disorder or disability (and, in some cases, that the victim is likely to be unable to refuse consent) and, in familial sex offences, the mens rea is that D knows or could reasonably be expected to know that he is related to the other person in the prescribed way.

* Knowing or believing something. In the various offences of engaging in sexual activity in the presence of a child or mentally disordered person D must know or believe that the child, etc is aware, or intend that the child, etc should be aware, that D is engaging in it. 'Belief' involves something less than actual knowledge.[61] A person who has no substantial doubt that something is true can be said to 'believe' it; but mere suspicion, however strong, is insufficient.[62]

2.62   Where proof of knowledge is required it means either:

* actual knowledge; or

* where no alternative to knowledge is expressed to be sufficient, wilful blindness. It would, however, be unwise to say that this second meaning invariably applies.[63] Wilful blindness refers to the situation where a person realises the risk that a surrounding circumstance may exist and deliberately refrains from making inquiries, the results of which he may not care to have,[64] or 'what is very much the same thing but put another way, failing to do something or doing something not caring whether contravention takes place or not'.[65] The fact that a person, who did

---

[59]   *DPP v Morgan*, ibid; SO(A)A 1976, s 1. But this was never true of a mistaken belief induced by voluntary intoxication. See **2.74** et seq.

[60]   As to reasonable expectation of knowledge, see **2.64**.

[61]   *Hall* [1973] QB 126.

[62]   Ibid. See also *Grainge* [1974] 1 WLR 619; *Moys* (1984) 79 Cr App Rep 72; *Johnson v Whitehouse* [1984] RTR 38.

[63]   *Westminster City Council v Croyalgrange Ltd* [1986] 1 WLR 674.

[64]   *Roper v Taylor's Central Garages (Exeter) Ltd* (1951) 2 TLR 284, at pp 288–289.

[65]   *Gray's Haulage Co Ltd v Arnold* [1966] 1 All ER 896, at p 898. See also *James & Son Ltd v Smee* [1955] 1 QB 78; *Vehicle Inspectorate v Nuttall* [1999] 3 All ER 833, at p 840, per Lord Steyn.

not know or suspect, ought to have known or suspected and made the inquiries which a reasonable person would have made ('constructive knowledge') is not enough.[66]

2.63 Where knowledge is used in the alternative to some other mens rea, as in the above cases, the effect is to limit the meaning of 'knowledge' in that provision to actual knowledge, because where the alternative word or phrase is 'reckless' or 'could reasonably be expected to know', that phrase embraces what is involved in wilful blindness, or because where the alternative is 'belief' this indicates that awareness of a possible risk is insufficient.

Reasonable expectation of knowledge or absence of reasonable belief

2.64 Most of the major offences under SOA 2003 require proof that D 'did not reasonably believe' some fact that would if true negative the offence.[67] As will be seen:

- in rape and the other non-consensual offences (where the complainant is 13 or over) the mens rea as to the absence of consent is lack of a reasonable belief in the complainant's consent;[68]

- in the child sex offences involving children under 16 years but aged 13 or over, the mens rea as to age is lack of a reasonable belief that the complainant is 16 or over;

- in the offences of abuse of a position of trust or of familial sex in relation to someone under 18, the mens rea as to age where the person is 13 or over is lack of a reasonable belief that the complainant is 18 or over; and

- in the offences of abuse of children under 18 through prostitution or pornography, the mens rea as to age where the complainant is 13 or over is lack of a reasonable belief that the complainant is 18 or over.

2.65 Some offences, however, require proof that D 'knew or could reasonably have been expected to know' that a key component of the actus reus did exist. Thus:

- in offences against persons with a mental disorder, the mens rea as to the complainant's disorder is that D knows or could reasonably be expected to know that the complainant has such a disorder (and, in some cases, that the complainant is likely to be unable to refuse consent);

---

[66] *Roper v Taylor's Central Garages (Exeter) Ltd*, ibid; *Gray's Haulage Co Ltd v Arnold*, ibid.

[67] Whether a jury needs to be directed on this will depend on the evidence. Where there is no evidence whatever to suggest that D was in any way mistaken as to the facts, a direction dealing with reasonable grounds for such belief would not be helpful. Cf *Taran* [2006] EWCA Crim 1498, at [11].

[68] The draftsman unfortunately failed to envisage the kind of mistake that arose in *A-G's Ref (No 79 of 2006); Whitta* [2007] 1 Cr App R (S) 752, where in a darkened room W pushed either his finger or penis into B's vagina, having mistaken her for C. He had reasonable grounds to believe that C wanted sex with him, but had no grounds to believe that of B, who was lying drunk in the bed. W was convicted of sexual assault by penetration, the judge ruling that mistaken identity could not be a defence. Rejecting the Attorney-General's application to increase W's sentence, the court questioned the judge's ruling, suggesting that the offence was committed only if a reasonable (and sober) person would have realised that B was not C.

- in the familial sex offences and in the offences of sex with an adult relative, the mens rea as to the prescribed relationship is that D knows or could reasonably be expected to know that he is related to the other person in the prescribed way; and

- sometimes in the offences of abuse of a position of trust, the mens rea as to the relationship of trust is that D knows or could reasonably be expected to know of the relationship.

2.66 Only a few offences under SOA 2003, notably the preparatory offences and the offences involving matters such as exposure, voyeurism and bestiality, fail to include any requirements as to knowledge, expectation of knowledge, or lack of reasonable belief.

Reasonable belief

2.67 Whether a given belief is reasonable or not is a question of fact. A jury must be directed to both the subjective element involved (what did D in fact believe?) and the objective element (was that a reasonable belief to hold?) Clearly, however, a person does not reasonably believe something if he has given no thought to it, even if grounds for such belief might have been found.

2.68 Absence of reasonable belief postulates an objective test, so that liability is based on negligence, just like 'reasonable cause to believe', 'reason to believe', 'reason to suspect' or 'no reason to suspect'.[69] Whether an alleged belief in consent or age, and so on, was reasonable must be answered by reference to the surrounding circumstances and the antecedent history of the case.

2.69 What then of D's characteristics insofar as they affect his perception of the relevant facts? They can undoubtedly be taken into consideration in assessing whether or not D's claim of a particular belief is credible, but can they also be taken into consideration in assessing the reasonableness of that belief? The only case which says 'yes', where an objective test was posed is *Hudson*,[70] which concerned the defence to a charge of sexual intercourse with a defective woman, contrary to SOA 1956, s 7, that D had 'no reason to suspect her to be a defective'. *Hudson* contains a dictum that not only had there to be an objective reason to suspect but also that account had to be taken of D himself, since there might be cases where he was 'of limited intelligence, or possibly suffering from some handicap which would prevent him from appreciating the state of affairs which an ordinary man might realise'.

2.70 It is, of course, possible for Parliament to provide that an 'absence of reasonable belief' should be assessed by taking into account D's own characteristics. In the context of rape and the other non-consensual offences dealt with in Chapter 3 of this work it is in each case provided that 'whether a belief is reasonable is to be determined having regard to all the circumstances'. This arguably includes any of D's relevant characteristics, but only in respect of those offences where such provision is included.[71]

2.71 The objectivity of the 'lack of reasonable belief' test means that the minimum mens rea required in respect of those offences to which it applies is mere negligence. Some of these offences are amongst the gravest known to English law and are

---

See, for example, *Young* [1984] 1 WLR 654.
[1966] 1 QB 448.
See **3.118** et seq.

punishable with life imprisonment. None of them are minor or trivial offences. It must be questioned whether those who believe, albeit wrongly and unreasonably, that their actions are consented to should be made criminally liable for those actions in the same way as those who know exactly what they are doing or deliberately choose to risk it. To impose criminal liability for a serious offence on the basis of mere negligence runs counter to the modern subjective approach to criminal liability, as affirmed by the House of Lords in *B (A Minor) v DPP*,[72] *K* [73] and *G*.[74]

'Could reasonably be expected to know'

2.72 A requirement that a person 'could reasonably be expected to know' something arguably lays down a different test from that of 'absence of reasonable belief'. Whether a person could reasonably be expected to know something must be judged in the light of all the circumstances, not just the surrounding ones, including D's characteristics and the antecedent history of the case. The objectivity inherent in 'reasonably be expected to know' is, therefore, softened by the subjectivisation of the concept of reasonableness.

Recklessness

2.73 A few offences in SOA 2003 require D to have acted 'knowing or being reckless as to' an element of the actus reus. For example, in the offence of trespass with intent to commit a sexual offence, D must know, or be reckless as to whether, he is a trespasser. Recklessness means the deliberate taking of an unjustified and unreasonable risk that an element of the actus reus may possibly exist or result. A person acts with recklessness as to:

- a circumstance when he is aware of the risk that it exists or will exist;

- a consequence when he is aware of a risk that it will occur,

and it is, in the circumstances known to him, unreasonable to take the risk.[75]

Recklessness may involve indifference as to risk, but a person who deliberately takes an unjustified risk may still be considered reckless even if he fervently hoped that all would be well.[76]

RELEVANCE OF INTOXICATION

2.74 Alcohol, drugs and sex have a close but unfortunate relationship. In the context of alleged sexual offences, intoxication often affects both the alleged offender and the complainant. Various problems can arise from this. Some are evidential, because intoxication can dull or corrupt subsequent recollection of the events, but others have a

---

[72] [2000] 2 AC 428. The House held that in relation to an offence of indecency with a child under 14, contrary to ICA 1960, s 1, it should be implied that D was not liable unless it was proved that he did not believe the child to be aged 14 or over.

[73] [2002] 1 AC 462. The House held that a defendant was entitled to be acquitted of indecent assault on a willing girl under the age of 16 years, if he honestly believed her to be aged 16 years or over.

[74] [2004] 1 AC 1034. This was a case involving arson.

[75] *Stephenson* [1979] QB 695; *G* [2004] 1 AC 1034. Also see *Cunningham* [1957] 2 QB 396.

[76] *Stephenson*, ibid.

bearing on whether any offence is in fact committed. A, for example may be too drunk to notice that B is too drunk to consent to his sexual advances, or too drunk to care whether she consents or not. The consequences, in either case, may be disastrous for them both.

2.75	We are concerned at this point with impact of intoxication on a defendant's criminal liability. It is well established in English law (1) that intoxication, whether voluntary or involuntary, is not in itself a defence to any criminal charge; (2) that evidence of intoxication may sometimes be relied upon in support of a denial of mens rea or a defence such as automatism; and (3) that under the so-called *Majewski* rule, voluntary or self-induced intoxication by alcohol or 'dangerous drugs' can be relied upon in either of those ways only if the offence in question requires proof of 'specific intent' and the intoxication casts doubt on whether D acted with such intent.[77] Where the offence is categorised as one of 'basic intent', evidence of voluntary intoxication cannot be relied upon by D. Instead, a jury may be invited to convict D if satisfied that D would, hypothetically, have known what he was doing and/or appreciated the risks posed by his behaviour, had he been sober at the time.

2.76	There may sometimes be scope for argument as to whether D was or was not 'voluntarily' intoxicated at the time. The principal difficulties, however, are caused by uncertainty over how an offence of 'specific intent' is defined and how it is distinguished from one of basic intent. As a result of this uncertainty, which has been stirred up, rather than settled, by recent case-law, modern sexual offences cannot always be categorised with any degree of confidence.

2.77	The judges have put forward various definitions of an offence of specific intent.[78] The most straightforward, and arguably the only truly workable definition, which can be extracted from the speeches of Lord Elwyn-Jones LC, Lord Edmund-Davies and Lord Russell in *Majewski*,[79] is that where intention or knowledge[80] *and nothing less* is required as to at least one element of the offence, the offence is (in respect of that element) one of specific intent. Where, in contrast, recklessness, maliciousness or negligence suffice, the offence is (in that respect) one of basic intent.

2.78	Even if this relatively straightforward approach is adopted – and it has recently been doubted – some complications remain. In particular, a single offence may have elements of both basic and specific intent. It may in other words require recklessness as to one element but intention as to another. The offence of trespassing with intent to commit a sexual offence[81] provides a good example. A trespasser may have a specific intent to rape a woman on the premises in question and yet not even suspect that he is trespassing. If that is the case, he cannot ordinarily be guilty of an offence under s 63, because the mens rea required under s 63(1)(c) is missing; but under the *Majewski* rule he may be convicted if it transpires that his lack of awareness as to the trespassing results from voluntary intoxication. He acts with the specific or ulterior intent required in respect of the rape, and the missing mens rea as to trespassing is mere recklessness as to circumstances, which is a matter only of basic intent.

77	*DPP v Majewski* [1977] AC 443.
78	See Card, Cross and Jones *Criminal Law* (OUP, 18th edn, 2008), at paras 15.103–15.105.
79	[1977] AC 443.
80	*Durante* [1972] 3 All ER 963.
81	SOA 2003, s 63.

2.79 On this basis, nearly all the offences under SOA 2003 would involve some element of specific intent, because, with one exception,[82] each requires intention (and nothing less) in relation to at least one element of its actus reus. Rape, for example, requires nothing less than intent as to the act of penetration, and sexual assault requires intentional touching of the complainant. If we adopt the straightforward interpretation of the *Majewski* rule suggested above, A would not be guilty of raping (or even of sexual assaulting) B if he penetrated her with his penis whilst in a state of automatism after voluntarily ingesting hallucinogenic drugs.[83] This is of course an extreme and unusual example of intoxication. It is much more common for an alleged rapist to be confused or mistaken as to the complainant's willingness or capacity to consent, which would be no defence unless his intoxication was involuntary, because something less than intent or knowledge suffices in respect of that element of the offence (ie it is a matter of basic intent).

2.80 The idea that offences such as rape and sexual assault could under any circumstances fall to be categorised as crimes of specific intent nevertheless caused some consternation. Under SOA 1956 and SO(A)A 1976, rape had always been described as a crime of basic intent, and this had been reiterated in a number of reported cases.[84] Indecent assault was similarly categorised.[85] Given that the general thrust of SOA 2003 was to tighten the law on such offences, rather than relax it, it seems unlikely that Parliament could have intended to change the law so as to make life easier for intoxicated defendants.

2.81 One possible answer is that rape and indecent assault were always hybrid offences of the kind described above, and that the new offences of rape and sexual assault are essentially similar. An alternative interpretation of the *Majewski* rule was, however, advanced by the Court of Appeal in *Heard*.[86] The prosecution case here was that H, who was drunk, sexually assaulted a police officer by exposing himself and rubbing his penis against the officer's leg. This was a straightforward example of a deliberate sexual assault, and the Court of Appeal upheld his conviction on that basis. He had acted intentionally and when interviewed following his arrest he was even able to explain why he had so acted. A drunken intent, as the Court was quick to point out, remains a form of intent.

2.82 The Court then went on to consider, obiter, whether sexual assault was in any sense a crime of specific intent, and concluded that ordinarily it was not. The Court rejected the idea that if a crime requires intent or knowledge as to one of its elements then it must to that extent be a crime of specific intent. In its place, it adopted a test derived, via Lord Simon's speech in *Majewski*, from Fauteux J's judgment in the Canadian case of *George*,[87] according to which the correct distinction is between crimes requiring 'ordinary' mens rea, and those requiring 'purposive' mens rea:

---

82 Namely, s 65; see **6.77**.
83 Cf *Lipman* [1970] 1 QB 152. A further question might be whether a drunken mistake as to B's identity would negate the specified intent, but the better view is that it would not. Penetration or touching may be intentional, even if there is a mistake as to identity (cf *A-G's Ref (No 79 of 2006); Whitta* [2007] 1 Cr App R (S) 752 (see **2.64**)).
84 *Woods* (1981) 74 Cr App R 312; *Fotheringham* (1988) 88 Cr App R 206.
85 *C* [1992] Crim LR 642; *DPP v H* [1992] COD 266.
86 [2008] QB 43.
87 (1960) 128 Can CC 289. See [1977] AC 443 at 478, per Lord Simon, cited in *Heard* at [31].

'Crimes of specific intent are those where the offence requires proof of purpose or consequence ... amongst which are included those where the purpose goes beyond the actus reus (sometimes referred to as cases of ulterior intent) ...

A distinction is to be made between (i) intention as applied to acts considered in relation to their purposes and (ii) intention as applied to acts apart from their purposes. A general intent attending the commission of an act is, in some cases, the only intent required to constitute the crime while, in others, there must be, in addition to that general intent, a specific intent attending the purpose for the commission of the act.'

2.83 Thus, although both rape and sexual assault require 'intentional' penetration or touching, neither (said the Court) ordinarily requires that conduct to be characterised by any further purpose. On the *Heard* test, both would become crimes of basic intent.[88] In contrast, an offence such as causing criminal damage, being reckless as to endangerment of life[89] would become a crime of specific intent, at least insofar as the recklessness element is concerned. This, said the Court, is because that offence:

'... requires proof of a state of mind addressing something beyond the prohibited act itself, namely its consequences. We regard this as the best explanation of the sometimes elusive distinction between specific and basic intent in the sense used in *Majewski* ...'

This is, with respect, open to argument. As *Smith & Hogan*[90] points out, the 'purpose' test would result in murder being classified as a crime of basic intent, whereas its status as a crime of specific intent has never been doubted.

2.84 Suppose then that D staggers groggily into V and his hands briefly touch her breasts before he falls drunkenly to the floor. Is this to be construed as a sexual assault, as clearly it would be if he had fondled her breasts deliberately? One might suppose that it would be so construed, given that voluntary intoxication is no defence and that such intoxication is the only explanation for his behaviour. But no: just as a drunken intent remains an intent, said the Court,[91] a jury should be reminded that a drunken accident remains an accident:

'Sexual touching must be intentional, that is to say deliberate ... If, whether the defendant is intoxicated or otherwise, the touching is unintentional, this offence is not committed.'

2.85 The 'accident' scenario is however contrasted in *Heard* with the *Lipman* type of scenario in which alcohol or drug abuse induces a confused state of mind in which D believes that 'what he is doing is something different to what he in fact does'. In such a scenario, D would have no defence.

2.86 It is submitted that the classification adopted in *Heard* is unworkable, and ought not to be followed. As long as the *Majeswki* rule remains in place, the only workable interpretation is that any requisite element of intent must be proved, even in cases involving those who are voluntarily intoxicated. In the case of sexual offences such as

---

88   The court in *Heard* did (at [15]) recognise one exception to this, namely where D's purpose is crucial to the question whether his (otherwise equivocal) conduct is 'sexual' in the first place. (see **2.36** et seq). To that extent the court recognised that sexual assault may require proof of specific intent.
89   Criminal Damage Act 1971, s 1(2).
90   Ormerod (ed) *Criminal Law* (OUP, 12th edn, 2008), at p 301.
91   At [33].

rape or sexual assault, this means that voluntary intoxication negating the requisite intent to penetrate, touch, etc would negate liability, but intoxication leading to confusion as to consent would not.

CONDUCT OUTSIDE THE UK

2.87   As a general rule, English criminal law, including that part of the law relating to sexual offences, applies only to things done within England and Wales. It is sometimes said that crimes committed abroad, or in other parts of the UK, fall 'outside the jurisdiction of the English courts', but strictly speaking that is incorrect. Subject to any claims to diplomatic or sovereign immunity, the Crown Court has jurisdiction over any offence that is triable on indictment, wherever it is committed,[92] and as a result of recent reforms magistrates' courts now have a similarly extensive jurisdiction to try both summary offences and offences triable either way.[93] The issue therefore is not one concerning the jurisdiction of the courts (a matter of procedure) but one concerning the ambit of the law itself. To put it another way, acts of rape or sexual assault, etc committed in France or Scotland cannot ordinarily amount to offences under English law. There is no actus reus, because SOA 2003 does not ordinarily apply to such conduct.

2.88   This general rule is, however, subject to a number of statutory exceptions. Some of these are only indirectly concerned with the law relating to sexual offences, and are not examined in any detail here. For example:

- English criminal law now governs behaviour aboard British ships,[94] whether these are at sea or in foreign ports or harbours; and it has also been made applicable (so far as indictable offences are concerned) to acts committed within the territorial waters adjacent to the coasts of England or Wales, even where such acts are committed aboard foreign ships.[95]

- Special provision is also made for offences committed aboard British-controlled aircraft in flight outside the UK, or aboard foreign aircraft that make their next landing in the UK.[96]

- Some individuals, such as members of the Merchant Navy or British armed forces, remain subject to the general corpus of English criminal law when abroad, as well as to the laws of the state they are visiting or residing in at the time. A special rule applies in the case of persons subject to British armed forces discipline. Conduct abroad that would in England and Wales amount to an offence (eg rape) will

---

[92]   Supreme Court Act 1981, s 46(1).

[93]   Magistrates' Courts Act 1980, s 2(1). Jurisdiction over summary offences was previously limited (with some exceptions) to offences committed within a court's commission area, or within 500 yards of the boundary between that and another commission area, but see now the Courts Act 2003, s 44.

[94]   This is true both of registered 'United Kingdom ships', and of small unregistered craft owned by British citizens. Other rules govern conduct on offshore oil and gas platforms. See Hirst *Jurisdiction and the Ambit of the Criminal Law* (OUP, 2003), at Ch 6.

[95]   Territorial Waters Jurisdiction Act 1878, s 2. Territorial waters are not strictly part of England and Wales, but lie adjacent to it.

[96]   Civil Aviation Act 1982, s 92.

instead constitute a corresponding offence (formerly known as a 'civil offence') under the Armed Forces Act 2006, s 42.[97]

Special rules governing sexual offences against children

2.89   SOA 2003, s 72 contains important provisions relating to sexual offences committed abroad by UK nationals or UK residents in respect of children under the age of 16. In its original form,[98] s 72 was largely a re-enactment of the Sex Offenders Act (SOffA) 1997, s 7, which extended the territorial ambit of English sexual offences law so as to apply it for the first time to such conduct. To understand s 72, one must therefore examine the origins of the original provision.

Sexual Offences (Conspiracy and Incitement) Act 1996 and Sex Offenders Act 1997

2.90   During the 1990s, the Government faced increasing demands from MPs and pressure groups,[99] to take action against the sexual abuse of children by British 'sex tourists' in third world countries, such as Thailand, Cambodia and the Philippines.[100] 'Sex-tourism' is a term used to describe a practice whereby individuals (usually men) travel abroad to seek sexual pleasures. In many such cases, they seek encounters with child prostitutes. Third world and poorer Eastern European countries are popular destinations, because child prostitution is often rife in such countries; and the authorities there often lack the resources and/or the resolve to detect, prosecute or punish such conduct effectively.

2.91   The Government initially declined to criminalise extra-territorial child-sex offences, insisting that any legislation purporting to do so would in practice be unworkable because of the difficulties of gathering evidence abroad, and would amount to nothing more than an empty political gesture. The Government did, however, support a private member's Bill which eventually became the Sexual Offences (Conspiracy and Incitement) Act 1996. This made it an offence to conspire or incite,[101] in England and Wales,[102] the commission of specified sexual acts abroad – acts that were not themselves offences under English law, but would have constituted offences if they had been committed within England and Wales.[103] The idea was to hit British-based organisers of sex tourism, who would be more easily prosecuted using evidence obtainable in the UK itself.

---

[97]   This provision (which should be read in conjunction with ss 43-48) will, when brought into force (probably in January 2009), supplant equivalent provisions in the Army Act 1955, s 70, the Air Force Act 1955, s 70 and the Naval Discipline Act 1957, s 42. See *Spear* [2003] 1 AC 734, at [24], per Lord Rodger. Such offences will continue to be triable by court-martial or in some cases by 'service civilian courts' (currently known as 'standing civilian courts').

[98]   A revised version of s 72 was substituted by CJIA 2008, s 72. See **2.95**.

[99]   Notably ECPAT (End Child Prostitution in Asian Tourism), the World Congress against Commercial Sexual Exploitation of Children and the UK Coalition on Child Prostitution & Tourism.

[100] Particular outrage was caused by the fact that most other Western countries appeared willing to exercise jurisdiction over things done by their own nationals abroad. It appeared scandalous that the UK had made no such provision. The UK's willingness to extradite its own nationals (something that many Western countries will not do) was not viewed as a satisfactory alternative.

[101] The conspiracy provisions have since been supplanted by those of CLA 1977, s 1A.

[102] There are corresponding offences under laws of Scotland and Northern Ireland.

[103] The acts in question were originally listed as rape of a child under 16, unlawful intercourse with a girl under 13, unlawful intercourse with a girl under 16, buggery of a child under 16, indecent assault on a boy or girl under 16 and indecent conduct towards a child under 16. On 1 May 2004, these were replaced by offences under SOA 2003, ss 1–2, 14 and 15–26, where the victim is under 16.

2.92 Shortly after the enactment of this legislation, the Government received the Report of an Interdepartmental Committee,[104] which had been established to review wider policy on extra-territorial criminal jurisdiction. The Committee advised that consideration should be given to extending the ambit of specific offences, where policy considerations appear to justify such a measure. It suggested that one at least of the following tests would have to be satisfied:

- the offence must be a serious one;

- by virtue of the nature of the offence, witnesses and evidence must be likely to be available within the UK;

- there must be international consensus as to the reprehensible nature of the crime and the need to take extra-territorial jurisdiction;

- the vulnerability of the victim must make it particularly important that offences are prosecuted;

- it must be in the interests of the standing and reputation of the UK within the international community to criminalise such offences; and

- there must be a danger that such offences would not otherwise be justiciable.

2.93 Offences committed against children by British sex tourists clearly satisfied several of these tests, and as a result the Government quickly reconsidered its position. SOffA 1997, s 7 was then enacted, making it an offence in English law for a British citizen or UK resident to commit abroad any of a wide range of sex offences in respect of a child under the age of 16. This greatly reduced the ambit of the Sexual Offences (Conspiracy and Incitement) Act (SO(CI)A) 1996. The earlier Act remains in force in respect of incitement, although its conspiracy provisions were subsequently supplanted by those in CLA 1977, s 1A,[105] but because it applies only to the incitement of conduct that is *not* itself punishable under English law, any conduct that is criminal under s 7 of the 1997 Act necessarily ceased to be relevant for the purposes of the 1996 Act.

2.94 This remains true of conduct falling under SOA 2003, s 72. If, for example, A in England incites B to sexually abuse children in Bulgaria, the SO(CI)A 1996 applies only where B is a foreign national who is not resident in the UK and who would *not* himself be subject to English criminal law were he to act as A suggests.[106]

---

[104] *Review of Extraterritorial Jurisdiction: Report of the Interdepartmental Steering Committee* (Home Office, unpublished, 1996).

[105] For a rare example of a recent conviction under the 1996 Act, see *Parnell* [2005] 1 WLR 853, in which P in England sent e-mails to what he thought was a 15-year-old boy in Sri Lanka in which he incited the 'boy' to commit buggery with him when he arrived there. The 'boy' was in fact a Sri Lankan police officer. Even so, it seems doubtful whether P was properly convicted under that Act. He did not incite the Sri Lankan officer to commit an offence against a child, but instead he thought he officer *was* the child. Inciting a child (or more accurately attempting to incite a supposed child) to commit a sexual act with oneself does not properly fall within the scope of the Act, although it would amount to an offence under SOA 2003, s 72.

[106] When SCA 2007, Pt 2 comes into force, conduct encouraging or assisting a UK national or UK resident to behave in that way will involve encouraging or assisting the commission of an offence under English law and will be punishable under that Act (ibid, s 63(1) and Sch 6, Pt 1).

Sexual Offences Act 2003, s 72

2.95 In its original form, SOA 2003, s 72 largely re-enacted SOffA 1997, s 7, but a heavily revised version was substituted by CJIA 2008, s 72(1), with effect from 14 July 2008.[107] This differs from the original provision in two main respects. The first is that it is no longer confined to offences against children below the age of 16. In respect of non-consensual offences, such as rape, or offences involving child prostitution or breach of trust, the new age limit is now set at 18. More controversially, the new s 72 deprives UK nationals (as defined in s 72(9)) of any defence based on lack of double criminality. A UK national who engages in consensual sexual activity with a boy or girl of 15 abroad may thus incur criminal liability in England, even if neither lives in the UK and even if the child's consent is fully valid under local law.[108]

2.96 SOA 2003, s 72, as substituted, now provides:

'(1) If—

(a)   a United Kingdom national does an act in a country outside the United Kingdom, and

(b)   the act, if done in England and Wales or Northern Ireland, would constitute a sexual offence to which this section applies,

the United Kingdom national is guilty in that part of the United Kingdom[109] of that sexual offence.

(2) If—

(a)   a United Kingdom resident does an act in a country outside the United Kingdom,

(b)   the act constitutes an offence under the law in force in that country, and

(c)   the act, if done in England and Wales or Northern Ireland, would constitute a sexual offence to which this section applies,

the United Kingdom resident is guilty in that part of the United Kingdom of that sexual offence.

(3) If—

(a)   a person does an act in a country outside the United Kingdom at a time when the person was not a United Kingdom national or a United Kingdom resident,

(b)   the act constituted an offence under the law in force in that country,

---

[107] CJIA 2008, s 72 came into force on that date: Criminal Justice and Immigration Act 2008 (Commencement No 2 and Transitional and Saving Provisions) Order 2008, SI 2008/1586, art 2(1), Sch 1. Section 72 will cease to apply in Northern Ireland when the Sexual Offences (Northern Ireland) Order 2008, SI 2008/1769, art 76, is brought into force: see Sexual Offences (Northern Ireland Consequential Amendments) Order 2008, SI 2008/1779.

[108] This does not apply to persons who become UK nationals only after committing the alleged offence abroad; but such persons may be prosecuted in England if the double criminality test is satisfied: see s 72(3) and (4).

[109] Insofar as the law of Northern Ireland differs from that of England and Wales, each jurisdiction would of course apply its own substantive law. In theory, a person resident in England might be prosecuted under the law of Northern Ireland or vice versa, and this will continue to be the case when the Sexual Offences (Northern Ireland) Order 2008, art 76 is brought into force. As for Scotland, the Criminal Law (Consolidation) (Scotland) Act 1995, s 16B contains provisions analogous to SOA 2003, s 72, but the offences to which it applies are once again different (see s 16B(7)) and in theory an offender resident in England could face prosecution under Scots law for an offence committed in (say) Thailand.

(c)   the act, if done in England and Wales or Northern Ireland, would have constituted a sexual offence to which this section applies, and

(d)   the person meets the residence or nationality condition at the relevant time,

proceedings may be brought against the person in that part of the United Kingdom for that sexual offence as if the person had done the act there.

(4) The person meets the residence or nationality condition at the relevant time if the person is a United Kingdom national or a United Kingdom resident at the time when the proceedings are brought.

(5) An act punishable under the law in force in any country constitutes an offence under that law for the purposes of subsections (2) and (3) however it is described in that law.

(6) The condition in subsection (2)(b) or (3)(b) is to be taken to be met unless, not later than rules of court may provide,[110] the defendant serves on the prosecution a notice—

(a)   stating that, on the facts as alleged with respect to the act in question, the condition is not in the defendant's opinion met,

(b)   showing the grounds for that opinion, and

(c)   requiring the prosecution to prove that it is met.

(7) But the court, if it thinks fit, may permit the defendant to require the prosecution to prove that the condition is met without service of a notice under subsection (6).

(8) In the Crown Court the question whether the condition is met is to be decided by the judge alone.

(9) In this section—

"country" includes territory;

"United Kingdom national" means an individual who is—

(a)   a British citizen, a British overseas territories citizen, a British National (Overseas) or a British Overseas citizen;

(b)   a person who under the British Nationality Act 1981 is a British subject; or

(c)   a British protected person within the meaning of that Act;

"United Kingdom resident" means an individual who is resident in the United Kingdom.'

2.97   SOA 2003, Sch 2 (as amended by CJIA 2008, s 72(2) and (3)) lists the offences to which s 72 applies.[111] As far as English law is concerned, these are:

(a)   an offence under any of ss 5–19, 25 and 26 and 47–50 of the Act;[112]

(b)   an offence under any of ss 1–4, 30–41 and 61 where the victim of the offence was under 18 at the time of the offence;[113]

---

[110]   No rules of court of the type referred to in s 72(6) had been made when this book went to press. Nor were any such rules made during the lifetime of the 1997 Act.

[111]   See n 107 above. Schedule 2, para 1 lists offences under English law. Offences under the law of Northern Ireland are currently listed in para 2, but this is prospectively repealed by the Sexual Offences (Northern Ireland Consequential Amendments) Order 2008, SI 2008/1779.

[112]   In the case of an offence contrary to ss 16-19, 25, 26 or 47-50 committed before 14 July 2008, s 72 applies only where the victim was under 16 at the time of the offence.

[113]   Where the conduct in question occurred before 14 July 2008 the age limit applicable is 16, as originally enacted.

(c)   an offence under s 62 or s 63, where the intended offence was an offence against a person under 18;[114] and

(d)   an offence under PoCA 1978, s 1, or Criminal Justice Act 1988, s 160.[115]

This list is considerably wider than that to which SOffA 1997, s 7 applied.[116] It is also wider than the list which applied prior to amendment by CJIA 2008 (and which still applies in respect of things done between 1 May 2004 and 14 July 2008). One difference is that for many offences the upper age limit for alleged victims is now 18, where before it was 16.

2.98   By para 3, any reference to an offence includes:

(a)   a reference to an attempt, conspiracy or incitement[117] to commit that offence; and

(b)   a reference to aiding and abetting, counselling or procuring the commission of that offence.

2.99   Despite the Government's scepticism as to the effectiveness of such legislation, there have been some prosecutions under SOffA 1997, s 7 and SOA 2003, s 72, but not all have involved the kind of 'sex tourism' that the legislation was intended to address. In *R*,[118] R was initially convicted under the 1997 Act of the rape of his partner's 15-year-old daughter, during a holiday in Barbados. The conviction was quashed because the incident took place before commencement of the Act. In *Holderness*,[119] a youth worker was convicted of assaulting boys during a holiday in Denmark.

2.100   There have been few successful prosecutions for offences committed in third world countries. In one rare example, *Towner*,[120] T pleaded guilty to unlawful intercourse with girls under the age of 13 and to making indecent photographs of children. He was sentenced to 8 years' imprisonment. The offences, committed in Cambodia, came to light when his wife found the photographs on T's computer.[121]

2.101   The effectiveness of this legislation cannot wholly be judged by the number of prosecutions. The real test is whether it has any impact on the British paedophile sex tourism industry. Sex tourism, in the years before its criminalisation, was often a carefully planned activity, involving acts of abuse that were premeditated, rather than impulsive or opportunistic. British paedophiles contemplating trips abroad must now be aware that they will remain liable to prosecution under English law, and some may

---

[114]   Ibid.

[115]   In the case of an offence committed before 14 July 2008, s 72 applies only where the victim was under 16 at the time of the offence. As to pseudo-photographs, see PoCA 1978, s 7(7) and (8) and **8.14** and **8.20**.

[116]   SOffA 1997, s 7, remains applicable to sexual offences allegedly committed against children abroad between 1 September 1997 and 1 May 2004. The only possible exception is that subsequently created by VCRA 2006, s 55 (see **2.5**).

[117]   When the new inchoate offences of encouragement or assistance created by SCA 2007 come into force, the reference to incitement will take effect as a reference to those offences: ibid, s 63 and Sch 6, Pt 1.

[118]   [2001] 1 WLR 1314. See also *Rooney* [2001] EWCA Crim 2844.

[119]   [2004] EWCA Crim 3177.

[120]   (Unreported) 18 June 2001 (Crown Court).

[121]   An unnamed businessman was similarly convicted of raping children in India after incriminating video evidence was discovered by officers searching his London home in connection with a suspected fraud. Eight life sentences were imposed ((unreported) 2007 (Crown Court)).

perhaps be discouraged or dissuaded by this. If only a few are dissuaded in this way, the legislation will have achieved something, to say nothing of the relevance of such legislation to the international image of the UK, which might otherwise have been seen as condoning such behaviour.[122]

2.102 Courts may impose travel restriction orders on offenders.[123] These may be particularly appropriate to persons convicted by virtue of s 72.

Cases to which SOA 2003, s 72 does not apply

2.103 SOA 2003, s 72(1) only applies to acts done in a country or territory outside the UK. It has no obvious application to misconduct by UK nationals or UK residents aboard foreign ships on the high seas.[124] Nor does it apply English law to conduct in Scotland or Northern Ireland. Conduct in Scotland can very rarely amount to an offence under English law. There is, however, one significant exception, which concerns offences involving abuse of trust under SOA 2003, ss 16–19.[125]

Abuse of trust offences committed in Scotland

2.104 SOA 2003, s 21, contains extensive provisions dealing with sexual relationships that are considered to involve a position of trust. These are in some respects more extensive than the corresponding provisions of SO(A)A 2000, which no longer apply in England and Wales but remain applicable in Scotland, where SOA 2003, Pt 1 does not apply.[126] It follows that in this respect Scots law is less draconian than English law. It was feared that someone living in England who is in a position of trust in relation to a child (aged under 18) under s 21 (but not under the 2000 Act) might engage in sexual activity with the child whilst they were in Scotland. This was seen as a potential loophole, and to close this loophole SOA 2003, s 20 provides (in respect of English or Northern Irish law):[127]

> 'Anything which, if done in England and Wales or Northern Ireland, would constitute an offence under any of sections 16 to 19 also constitutes that offence if done in Scotland.'

2.105 This is a remarkable provision. The general rule is that conduct in Scotland cannot be an offence under English law, even if it is criminal in Scotland and punishable in England when committed outside the UK. But in this case, conduct in Scotland that is *not* criminal in Scotland may in theory be prosecuted in England, even if everyone involved is domiciled in Scotland. No principle of double jeopardy applies: indeed, s 20

---

[122] A greater deterrent is provided by increased levels of policing in some of the countries concerned. Cambodia and Vietnam (where Gary Glitter's conviction for child sex offences was well publicised in the UK) are now considered to be 'dangerous' countries for Western paedophiles to visit, although child prostitution remains a major problem in those countries.

[123] See SOA 2003, ss 114–122 (see **18.135-18.170**).

[124] The Merchant Shipping Act 1995, s 281, may apply if D does not belong to that ship: *Kelly* [1982] AC 665 (decided under the Merchant Shipping Act 1894, s 686). See Hirst, n 94 above, at pp 291–295.

[125] See **5.4** et seq.

[126] The Scottish Law Commission has recommended the re-formulation of the abuse of trust offences but the offence recommended would still leave Scots law considerably more restricted than English law in terms of the behaviour covered and the types of position of trust covered: see Scot Law Com No 209, paras 4.126-4.134.

[127] Section 20 will cease to apply in Northern Ireland when the Sexual Offences (Northern Ireland) Order 2008, SI 2008/1769, art 27, is brought into force: see the Sexual Offences (Northern Ireland) Consequential Amendments) Order 2008, SI 2008/1779, art 5; but in England and Wales s 20 will then apply to things done in Northern Ireland as well as to things done in Scotland.

was enacted for the purpose of violating that principle. Where conduct consists of an offence under both English law and under Scots law, it can be dealt with in either jurisdiction, but that is not the purpose of this provision.

Chapter 3

NON-CONSENSUAL SEXUAL OFFENCES

3.1   Many of the most serious sexual offences involve things done to another person without consent. The absence of consent may turn an otherwise lawful activity into one of the gravest of crimes, but consent can be hard to define and its absence can be even harder to prove.

3.2   The problem in terms of definition is that a clear line cannot always be drawn between consensual acts and those in which consent is lacking. In particular, the distinction between reluctant consent, on the one hand, and non-consensual submission, on the other, can be very difficult to draw, and there may often be room for disagreement as to where and how it should be drawn. Factors such as ignorance, misunderstanding, coercion, sleep and intoxication can each complicate the position.

3.3   For reasons of public policy, there are legal constraints on the ability of an individual to give valid consent to certain activities, notably sado-masochistic acts in which injury is knowingly or recklessly inflicted. One may for that reason encounter a 'non-consensual' sexual offence that was instigated by the complainant,[1] and in respect of which the complainant herself makes no complaint at all.

3.4   This chapter includes consideration of certain offences involving child complainants under the age of 13, where, strictly speaking, the presence or absence of consent is not a relevant consideration. These offences are included because they are each based on the implicit doctrine that a child under that age cannot be considered capable of giving legally valid consent. In practice, such offences are treated as 'non-consensual' and are worded in non-consensual terms, such as 'rape of a child under 13', even though evidence as to consent or its absence will be relevant (if at all) only to sentencing.

NON-CONSENSUAL OFFENCES UNDER THE SEXUAL OFFENCES ACT 1956

3.5   The SOA 1956 contained a number of essentially non-consensual sexual offences, namely rape (s 1), indecent assault on a woman (s 14); indecent assault on a man (s 15) and assault with intent to commit buggery (s 16).[2] It also contained two related but rarely prosecuted offences, namely procuring a woman to have sexual intercourse anywhere in the world by threats or intimidation (s 2) or by false pretences or

---

[1]   A complainant is not the person who actually complains of the offence, but the person against or in respect of whom the offence charged was allegedly committed. See **14.1**, n 1. Sexual Offences Act (SOA) 2003 uses the term only in ss 75–77, referring elsewhere to the defendant or offender as 'A' and the complainant or victim as 'B'.

[2]   As to the s 16 offence and the old common law offence of assault with intent to rape, see **12.33**.

representations (s 3). These were not strictly speaking non-consensual offences, because they dealt with cases in which the threat or false pretence may have been insufficient to vitiate consent and support a charge of rape.[3] There were no specifically non-consensual child-sex offences, but ss 14 and 15 each provided that a person under the age of 16 was incapable of giving valid consent to acts that would otherwise be indecent assaults. D might thus be acquitted of rape on the basis of a 15-year-old complainant's actual consent, but convicted of indecently assaulting her in the course of the same incident on the basis that her consent was, for the purposes of that particular offence, invalid.

NON-CONSENSUAL OFFENCES UNDER THE SEXUAL OFFENCES ACT 2003

3.6   SOA 2003 repealed the provisions noted at **3.5** and replaced them with a more coherent structure of offences, coupled with a corresponding set of offences in relation to children under the age of 13 in which the possibility of consent is effectively discounted. The current offences are:

- rape, contrary to s 1;

- rape of a child under 13, contrary to s 5;

- assault by penetration, contrary to s 2;

- assault of a child under 13 by penetration, contrary to s 6;

- sexual assault, contrary to s 3;

- sexual assault of a child under 13, contrary to s 7;

- causing a person to engage in sexual activity without consent, contrary to s 4; and

- causing or inciting a child under 13 to engage in sexual activity, contrary to s 8.[4]

3.7   SOA 2003 does not, however, provide any direct replacement for the offences of procuring a woman to have sexual intercourse anywhere in the world by threats or intimidation or by false pretences or representations.[5] One might perhaps have expected these offences to be supplanted by a new offence of obtaining sexual penetration or sexual activity in any part of the world by threats or deception,[6] especially given that SOA 2003, s 35 creates an analogous offence of causing a mentally disordered person to engage in sexual activity by threats or deception.[7] The absence of such an offence leaves

---

3   See *Jheeta* [2007] 2 Cr App R 477; see **3.8**.

4   To the above list of non-consensual offences may be added those relating to persons with a mental disorder impeding choice, which are examined in Chapter 9; the offence of voyeurism (s 67) which is examined at **13.26** et seq; and that of administering a substance with intent to stupefy, etc (s 61) which is examined at **12.3** et seq.

5   The 'trafficking' provisions in ss 57–59 (see Chapter 11) cover some of the ground previously covered by SOA 1956, ss 2 and 3, but do not assist in cases such as *Jheeta* [2007] 2 Cr App R 477 (see **3.8**).

6   *Setting the Boundaries: Reforming the Law on Sexual Offences* (Home Office, 2000) (*SB*), Recommendation 14.

7   See **9.74**.

a surprising gap in the overall scheme of the Act. As Ashworth and Temkin point out,[8] it means that 'in the unusual case where this issue occurs, the vague terms of s 74, which partially defines consent, now assume a heightened importance'.

3.8   This is illustrated by *Jheeta*,[9] in which J weaved a bizarre pattern of deceit and intimidation in order to persuade his credulous girlfriend to have more frequent sexual intercourse with him than she would otherwise have done. In respect of incidents occurring before 1 May 2004, J was charged with procuring sexual intercourse by false pretences, contrary to SOA 1956, s 3; but in respect of incidents occurring after that date the only possible charge was rape, and doubts concerning the application of that offence to such circumstances gave rise to the appeal in that case. Although it was eventually concluded that the deceit practised by J was sufficient to vitiate consent, other cases may arise in which it might not.[10] It seems unlikely that Parliament intended to decriminalise any such behaviour, but SOA 2003 appears to have done so.

CONSENT

Consent at common law and under SOA 1956

3.9   SOA 2003 is the first legislation in English law to attempt a statutory definition of 'consent' in the context of sexual offences. SOA 1956 made no attempt to define it. In prosecutions for offences under that Act, the courts treated consent as an ordinary word, and thus as ultimately a matter for the jury. In *Olugboja*,[11] the Court of Appeal rejected submissions that consent in cases of rape could be vitiated only by incapacity, physical force, threats of violence or fraud as to the essential nature of the act in question. The Court held instead that where an issue of consent arose, the question for the jury was whether the complainant consented in the 'ordinary meaning' of the word, which covered 'a wide range of states of mind ... ranging from actual desire on the one hand to reluctant acquiescence on the other'. A question of consent should not be left to the jury without some explanation to help it: the jury should be told that 'real consent' was a different state of mind from 'mere submission', and that it should draw the line between these two states by 'applying their combined good sense, experience, and knowledge of human nature and modern behaviour'.

3.10   Although the Court in *Olugboja* took a modern and enlightened approach to the concept of consent, rejecting any suggestion that physical resistance or insensibility was required in order to negate it, the ruling was widely considered to be problematic. The distinction between 'reluctant acquiescence', which amounted to consent, and 'mere submission', which did not, inevitably gave rise to uncertainty. One could all too easily posit scenarios that some might regard as examples of 'reluctant acquiescence' but others would regard as cases of mere submission. For example, A persuades his employee, B, to have sex with him by threatening to sack her if she does not. This looks at first like a case of submission by B under duress; but what if A already had ample grounds for sacking B? What if the possibility of sex in place of dismissal was B's idea, rather than A's? And what if B submitted reluctantly to sex in order to secure promotion, rather than from fear of dismissal?

---

8   'The Sexual Offences Act 2003: (1) Rape, Sexual Assaults and the Problems of Consent' [2004] Crim LR 328, at p 346.
9   [2007] 2 Cr App R 477.
10   Some kinds of deceit would not be capable of vitiating consent. See **3.52** et seq.
11   [1982] QB 320.

3.11 As these examples demonstrate, the distinction between involuntary submission and reluctant acquiescence may in practice be difficult to draw. One jury could easily draw the line differently from another. According to Glanville Williams,[12] *Olugboja* represented 'one more manifestation of the deplorable tendency of the criminal courts to leave important questions of legal policy to the jury'. Subsequent cases did little to remedy the problem; and it was a significant problem because the issue of consent is often crucial to the outcome of a trial, especially in cases of 'date rape' or 'acquaintance rape'.[13]

3.12 In its Policy Paper for the Sex Offences Review, the Law Commission recommended that there should be a statutory definition of consent for the purposes of any non-consensual sexual offence.[14] The Sex Offences Review agreed. A definition of consent was accordingly included in SOA 2003; but how far it succeeds in resolving such uncertainties is very much open to question.

Consent under SOA 2003

3.13 SOA 2003, s 74, defines consent in these terms:

> 'A person consents if he agrees by choice, and has the freedom and capacity to make that choice.'

It is implicit in this definition that consent can be given only by the person in question, and not (for example) by a partner or parent or someone in authority over that person.

3.14 This basic definition, which is supplemented in certain circumstances by 'evidential' and 'conclusive' presumptions contained in ss 75 and 76, may initially appear straightforward, but it is not. As Ashworth and Temkin rightly point out:[15]

> '"Freedom" and "choice" are ideas which raise philosophical issues of such complexity as to be ill-suited to the needs of criminal justice – clearly those words do not refer to total freedom or choice, so all the questions about how much liberty of action satisfies the "definition" remain at large.'

3.15 Tadros[16] makes a similar point, and is troubled by what he considers to be a paradox within s 74:

> 'On the one hand, the definition supposes that it is possible for a person to agree by choice whilst lacking capacity or freedom. Otherwise the second part of the definition would appear to be redundant. It would only be necessary to define consent as an agreement made by choice *with* capacity and freedom if there was the possibility that an agreement might be made by choice *without* the capacity and freedom. But, on the other hand, the definition suggests that if one lacks capacity and freedom one cannot agree by choice at all. For the definition suggests that one must have the capacity and freedom *to make that choice*. Hence,

---

[12] *Textbook of Criminal Law* (Stevens, 2nd edn, 1983), at para 25.3. *Olugboja* does, however, have its defenders: see, for example, Gardner 'Appreciating *Olugboja*' (1996) 16 LS 275.

[13] The relationship between women complainants and defendants in cases of alleged rape is: current partners 45%; acquaintances 16%; ex-partners 11%; dates 11%; other intimates 10%; strangers 8%: Myhill and Allen *Rape and Sexual Assault of Women: The Extent and Nature of the Problem*: Home Office Research Study 237 (Home Office, 2002).

[14] *Consent in Sex Offences* set out in *SB*, Vol 2, App C, at para 2.12.

[15] Note 8 above, at p 336.

[16] 'Rape without Consent' (2006) 26 OJLS 449.

the definition implies that the complainant might have agreed by choice and yet lacked the capacity and freedom to make that choice, which is paradoxical. Are the jury to determine whether the complainant agreed by choice first, and then determine whether she had the relevant capacity and freedom? Or are they to address the question of capacity and freedom first and, if either capacity or freedom are lacking, conclude that she did not agree by choice?'

3.16 With respect, this paradox is more apparent than real. The Sex Offences Review[17] recommended that consent should be defined as 'free agreement'. SOA 2003, s 74 comes close to this. It assumes there can be no valid 'agreement by choice' in the absence of freedom and capacity to make that choice. If, for example, the agreement is made under duress it amounts to submission rather than consent. A few extra words in s 74 might have made this clearer: for example, 'A person consents if he agrees by choice, *and in order to do this he must have* the freedom and capacity to make that choice'. But this does not resolve the problem of interpreting terms such as 'freedom', 'choice' and 'agreement'. These are complex and ambiguous concepts, which defy precise definition.

Rejected proposals as to consent

3.17 The Sex Offences Review recommended that there should be set out in legislation a non-exhaustive list of circumstances where consent is not present,[18] an approach adopted by some Australian states[19] and by the American Law Institute's Model Penal Code.[20] The proposed circumstances were that the complainant:

- submits or is unable to resist because of force or fear of force;

- submits because of threats or fear of serious harm or serious detriment of any type to himself or another person;

- is asleep, unconscious or too affected by alcohol or drugs to give free agreement;

- does not understand the purpose of the act, whether because of lack of capacity to understand or deception as to the purpose of the act;

- is mistaken or deceived as to the identity of the person or the nature of the act;

- submits or is unable to resist because abducted or unlawfully detained; or

- has agreement given for him or her by a third party.

3.18 There would have been a 'conclusive presumption' (in effect, a rule of law) that consent was absent in those circumstances. The aim was to clarify the existing case-law and to give a clear indication to the courts and to society at large about circumstances where sexual activity was unacceptable and deemed to be non-consensual; but with the exception of two circumstances set out in SOA 2003, s 76(2) for the purposes of SOA 2003, ss 1–4, the 2003 Act eschews this approach. The Government was not satisfied that the other circumstances in the Review's proposed list were ones where it could safely be assumed conclusively that consent was absent. It did, however, recognise that some of

---

17   *SB*, at para 2.10; Recommendation 4.
18   *SB*, at para 2.10.6; Recommendation 5.
19   Crimes Act 1900 (NSW), s 61R; Crimes Act 1958 (Vict), s 36.
20   Section 213.1.

the other circumstances in the proposed list would give rise to serious doubts about the complainant's ability to exercise a free choice, and in those circumstances s 75 lays down for the purposes of ss 1–4 an evidential presumption as to the absence of consent. For the most part, the meaning of consent depends on judicial interpretation of 'freedom', 'choice' and 'agreement'.

Agreement

3.19 Agreement can be expressed or implied, and may be evidenced by words or conduct, past or present. The same is true of a refusal to consent. As the Court of Appeal pointed out in _Malone_,[21] and later confirmed in _Hysa_:[22]

'There is no requirement that the absence of consent has to be demonstrated or that it has to be communicated to the defendant for the actus reus of rape to exist.'

3.20 SOA 2003, s 74 clearly recognises that 'yes' does not necessarily amount to valid consent. Anti-rape campaigners frequently insist that 'no' must always be construed as an effective refusal of consent; but there has never been any rule of law to that effect and in real life a verbal refusal may in some cases be undermined (at the time or shortly afterwards) by conduct that is clearly indicative of consent.

3.21 There must be a subsisting agreement at the time of the sexual activity in question. If what is relied on is a prior agreement to the act being done at a later time, there will be no effective consent if the agreement has lapsed or been withdrawn (eg following a quarrel) before the act was done. Consent may even be withdrawn during the course of sexual activity. B may, for example, consent to sexual penetration but withdraw that consent when she begins to feel pain or when A says or does something that offends her. The sexual activity in question will become non-consensual from that moment unless A at once desists.[23]

3.22 As was the case at common law, a person who is asleep or unconscious at the time of the relevant act cannot ordinarily consent, because although he may not object either at the time or when he wakes, he cannot whilst asleep or unconscious agree to what is being done. It is, however, possible that a person may expressly encourage his partner to initiate sexual activity even when he is asleep. This possibility is implicitly recognised in SOA 2003, s 75 and is considered at **3.61** et seq.

3.23 Issues of consent may arise even in the context of marriage or other long-term relationships. If it was ever good law that a wife was deemed to consent to sex with her husband merely by virtue of being his wife, that has long ceased to be the case. Nevertheless, the courts still recognise that the dynamics of consent within such a relationship may differ from those between a couple on an occasional date. A direction given to the jury by Pill J in _Zafar_[24] is still commended by the Judicial Studies Board

---

21 [1998] 2 Cr App R 447.
22 [2007] EWCA Crim 2056, at [16].
23 _Kaitamaki v R_ [1985] AC 147; _Hysa_ [2007] EWCA Crim 2056.
24 (Unreported) 1992, 92/2762/W2.

(JSB)[25] although in places it requires updating so as to more accurately reflect the new statutory definition of consent. This passage appears to remain equally valid under the new law:[26]

> 'In considering whether it is proved that the complainant ... did not consent, bear in mind when considering the evidence the relationship between them. When people enter into long-term relationships either within or outside marriage they usually contemplate regular sexual relations. In most partnerships, even not entirely happy ones, there is often give and take between the partners on sexual as on other matters. A female partner may not particularly want sexual intercourse on a particular occasion but because it is her husband or her partner who is asking for it she will consent to sexual intercourse. The fact that such consent is given reluctantly or out of a sense of duty to her partner, is still a consent [sic].'

3.24 Arguably, the dynamics of a settled relationship have an even greater bearing on cases involving sexual intimacies falling short of intercourse. A wife may reject an ill-timed hug, pat or caress from her husband (or vice versa), but this does not mean that the rejected advance amounted to a sexual assault. The dynamics of the relationship may well be such that consent to sexual contact is presumed until and unless a contrary indication is issued. Whether that is so must be a question of fact in every case, but if the principle were not recognised it would mean that the vast majority of married or cohabiting partners must at some time have committed (and/or been the victims of) sexual assaults.

Capacity to choose

3.25 A person's agreement to sexual activity will be invalid if he lacks the mental capacity to consent because of extreme youth, mental impairment or serious intoxication. Neither SOA 2003, s 74 nor any other section in SOA 2003 lays down a specific test of capacity. In a public law decision, *X City Council v MB*,[27] however, Munby J regarded the common law test of capacity to consent as being preserved by s 74. A person will thus lack capacity to consent if he has no real understanding of what is involved, or has such limited knowledge, awareness or understanding as to be in no position to decide whether to agree.[28] In *Morgan* the Supreme Court of Victoria held that for a woman to be found to lack capacity to consent to intercourse:[29]

> '... it must be proved that she has not sufficient knowledge or understanding to comprehend (a) that what is proposed to be done is the physical fact of penetration of her body by the male organ or, if that is not proved, (b) that the act of penetration proposed is one of sexual connection as distinct from an act of a totally different character.'

The Court went on to say:[30]

> 'That knowledge or understanding need not, of course, be a complete or sophisticated one. It is enough that she has sufficient "rudimentary knowledge" of what the act comprises and of its character to enable her to decide whether to give or withhold consent.'

---

25   Specimen Directions (rev 2007), Direction No 53.
26   There is clearly some error in this last sentence, but the essential point is clear: reluctant consent may still be valid consent.
27   [2007] 3 FCR 371, at [82]. Munby J held that the test of incapacity to consent to sexual activity should be the same under criminal and civil law. This was approved by the Court of Appeal in *C* [2008] EWCA Crim 1155.
28   *Howard* [1966] 1 WLR 13.
29   [1970] VR 337 at 341.
30   Ibid, at 342.

In *X City Council v MB* Munby J held that *Morgan* was 'an essentially correct summary and statement of the common law rule'. He continued:[31]

> 'The ... question is whether she (or he) lacks the capacity to understand the sexual nature of the act. Her knowledge and understanding need not be complete or sophisticated. It is enough that she has sufficient rudimentary knowledge of what the act comprises and of its sexual character to enable her to decide whether to give or withhold consent.'

Munby J also pointed out that not only is capacity 'issue specific' in relation to different types of transaction (so that someone may have capacity for one purpose but not for another), but it is also in relation to different transactions of the same type (so that a vulnerable adult may have the capacity to consent to one type of sexual activity whilst lacking the capacity to consent to some other (and to them unfamiliar) type of sexual activity). Munby J enlarged on this point in the following terms, pointing out that, although capacity to consent to sexual relations is issue specific, it is not person specific:[32]

> 'The question is issue specific, both in the general sense and, as I have already pointed out, in the sense that capacity has to be assessed in relation to the particular kind of sexual activity in question. But capacity to consent to sexual relations is, in my judgment, a question directed to the nature of the activity rather than to the identity of the sexual partner.
>
> A woman either has capacity, for example, to consent to "normal" penetrative vaginal intercourse or she does not. It is difficult to see how it can sensibly be said that she has capacity to consent to a particular sexual act with Y whilst at the same time lacking capacity to consent to precisely the same sexual act with Z ... Put shortly capacity to consent to sexual relations is issue specific; it is not person (partner) specific.'

In *C*[33] the Court of Appeal agreed with this conclusion. It added that capacity to choose to agree to sexual activity is not 'situation specific' either. Elliott[34] criticises this on the ground that:

> '[I]n relation to adults, English law adopts a "functional" approach to capacity: "the assessor asks whether an individual is able, at the time when a particular decision has to be made, to understand its nature and effects" (Law Commission No 231 *Mental Incapacity* (1995), at 3.3. See e g *In the Estate of Park* [1954] P 112). Although generally capacity to consent to sexual relations will not be "person specific", there may be rare cases in which this will not be the case: e g if a mentally disordered person suffers from a severe phobia in relation to a specific person or type of person and, faced with such a person, "seizes up" and is unable to make any rational choice. Furthermore, the suggestion that capacity to agree to sexual activity is not "situation specific" must be incorrect. The situation in which the activity took place may be highly relevant to the assessment of capacity, particularly in the case of sexual activity other than penile penetration, since touching etc may take place in all manner of situations.'

The Court of Appeal in *C* also stated that an irrational fear that prevents the exercise of choice cannot be equated with lack of capacity to choose. Elliott[35] also criticises this on the ground that irrational fear that prevents the exercise of choice must mean that the person lacks capacity to choose, being unable to choose.

---

31   [2007] 3 FCR 371, at [74]. See Elliott 'Capacity, Sex and the Mentally Disordered' [2008] 2 *Archbold News* 6.
32   [2007] 3 FCR 371, at [86], [87].
33   [2008] EWCA Crim 1155. See also **9.17**.
34   [2008] 6 *Archbold News* 5.
35   Ibid.

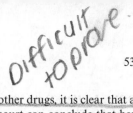

3.26   In a case involving intoxication caused by alcohol or other drugs, it is clear that a complainant must have been seriously intoxicated before a court can conclude that her ability to consent was undermined. In *Bree*,[36] it was held that 'on a proper construction' of s 74:

> 'If, through drink (or for any other reason) the complainant has temporarily lost her capacity to choose whether to have intercourse on the relevant occasion, she is not consenting, and subject to questions about the defendant's state of mind, if intercourse takes place, this would be rape. However, where the complainant has voluntarily consumed even substantial quantities of alcohol, but nevertheless remains capable of choosing whether or not to have intercourse, and in drink agrees to do so, this would not be rape ... As a matter of practical reality, capacity to consent may evaporate well before a complainant becomes unconscious. Whether this is so or not ... depends on the actual state of mind of the individuals involved.'[37]

where is the line drawn?

3.27   It may perhaps be possible to take account of consent that has been given previously and not withdrawn. Suppose, for example, that A and B agree to get drunk and then have sex. B drinks herself into a state of confused intoxication. By the time that they go to bed, she is so drunk that she would not ordinarily have been adjudged capable of giving consent, but A has sexual contact with her without any protest or resistance on her part. It is at least arguable that B's earlier agreement remains valid, and this argument becomes stronger if drunken sex of this kind has been a regular feature of their relationship, and one to which B has never objected.[38]

3.28   If, however, B is asleep or unconsciousness, or A has caused her to take a stupefying drug without her knowledge, certain evidential presumptions as to her lack of consent may arise under SOA 2003, s 75.[39]

3.29   Where B's incapacity is due to mental disorder, it will often be more appropriate to charge A with an offence under SOA 2003, s 30 (sexual activity with a person with a mental disorder impeding choice).[40] Where B is aged under 13, the obvious charge will be one under SOA 2003, ss 5–8. Such charges may also be easier to prove.

Evidence of capacity

people not reporting – problem

3.30   Where B was clearly intoxicated at the time of the alleged offence, evidential difficulties may arise as to whether any reliance can be placed on B's account of events. If, owing to that intoxication, B cannot remember whether she consented or not, and there is no independent evidence to prove that she did not (or could not) consent, there may be no case to answer.[41] But even if B's memory is incomplete, she may recall enough to give rise to a case to answer, and if there is some independent evidence as to the circumstances or as to B's condition, the case may still be a strong one.

believed? made to feel like her own fault

---

[36]   [2008] QB 131. See also *Malone* [1998] 2 Cr App R 447; *Hysa* [2007] EWCA Crim 2056.

[37]   The court acknowledged the assistance derived from its earlier judgment in *Lang* (1975) 62 Cr App R 50.

[38]   See the view of the Law Commission, n 14 above, at para 4.54. Some critics appear uncomfortable with this reasoning. Temkin argues in *Rape and the Legal Process* (OUP, 2nd edn, 2002), at pp 98–99 that it undermines the principle of sexual autonomy; but (with respect) why should B *not* say in advance what she wants A to do in such circumstances?

[39]   These apply only where A is charged with an offence under SOA 2003, ss 1–4. See **3.39**, n 46.

[40]   See **9.34**.

[41]   This explains the judge's ruling in *Dougal* (unreported) 2005, Crown Court, where the complainant admitted under cross-examination that she could not be sure she had not consented because she was too drunk to remember. The ruling was not opposed by the prosecution, but became the target of much ill-informed criticism.

3.31 In *Hysa*,[42] the complainant, aged 16, had been drinking heavily and smoking cannabis. She got into a car with H and two other men. She did not know them. One of them fingered her vagina and another then had intercourse with her. He was identified by DNA evidence as H, although he initially denied it. The complainant testified that she did not want to have sex with H, that she did not think that she did so willingly and she did not think that she would have consented. But she could not remember what she had said because she was drunk.

3.32 The trial judge ruled that there was no case to answer, because the evidence as to consent was not clear, but the Court of Appeal allowed a prosecution appeal against that ruling. It would, said the Court, be open to a jury to regard the circumstances of the case, together with H's lies, as providing support for the prosecution case:[43]

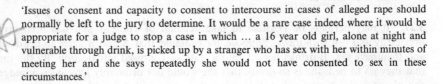

> 'Issues of consent and capacity to consent to intercourse in cases of alleged rape should normally be left to the jury to determine. It would be a rare case indeed where it would be appropriate for a judge to stop a case in which ... a 16 year old girl, alone at night and vulnerable through drink, is picked up by a stranger who has sex with her within minutes of meeting her and she says repeatedly she would not have consented to sex in these circumstances.'

Freedom to choose

3.33 Under SOA 2003, s 74, as under the *Olugboja* test it replaces, consent can range from enthusiastic agreement to reluctant acquiescence. The difficulty arises, as before, when we attempt to distinguish consensual acquiescence from non-consensual submission. Section 74 offers little improvement over *Olugboja* in that context. Where the offence in issue is rape, assault by penetration, sexual assault or causing a person to engage in sexual activity without consent, proof of the absence of consent in some of the situations described above may be aided by an evidential presumption of lack of consent provided by s 75,[44] but such presumptions largely deal with circumstances in which the answer is already likely to be obvious. They offer little real assistance where the more difficult borderline scenarios are concerned.[45]

3.34 Freedom of choice is a relative concept. Few choices in life are wholly free or wholly involuntary. One woman may feel that she has 'no choice' but to acquiesce to sex with her employer, because she fears that her career will not otherwise progress as she wishes, whereas another may choose to fight the armed men who are trying to rape her, even though she fully expects that this will cause them to kill her. We all have some 'freedom of choice', even in life and death situations. That indeed is why the law makes no concession to those who commit murder under duress.

3.35 When a court or jury determines that a complainant who reluctantly submitted to sex was or was not 'free to choose' it passes a judgment on her choice. Regardless of s 75, no reasonable jury would decide that a complainant who submitted at knifepoint 'consented', but many juries would doubtless react differently to a complainant who submitted in order to advance her career or reputation. A jury might also distinguish between one who agrees to sex in order to avoid well-deserved dismissal and one who agrees to it only when wrongfully threatened with dismissal based on false evidence.

---

42 [2007] EWCA Crim 2056.
43 When the trial resumed, H did not testify and the jury took just 40 minutes to convict him of rape.
44 See **3.61** et seq.
45 See, for example, *Jheeta* [2007] 2 Cr App R 477.

3.36 A jury may also take account of the nature of any threat, along with other circumstances (including the complainant's age and mental capacity, whether there was any realistic possibility that it would be carried out and whether the complainant could have taken steps to neutralise it) and whether in the light of these factors the complainant was in its view free to give or withhold consent. *unclear*

3.37 It would seem that consent can be stifled only by duress or coercion. The hope or promise of profit or advantage cannot suffice. Coercion may deprive the complainant of her freedom to consent, but bribery, however 'irresistible', surely cannot. On the other hand, there is no reason why fear induced by an implied threat should not suffice, nor is there any reason why the threat or other conduct should not come from a third party.

Deception and mistake

3.38 A mistake may sometimes vitiate any apparent agreement, especially if it is induced by deception. Two kinds of deception are specifically addressed in SOA 2003, s 76, by means of 'conclusive presumptions', but only in the context of alleged offences under SOA 2003, ss 1–4. Other forms of deception or mistake are not specifically addressed, and some may prove problematic in practice.

Conclusive presumptions about consent

3.39 SOA 2003, s 76(1) provides:

> 'If in proceedings for an offence to which this section applies[46] it is proved that the defendant did the relevant act and that any of the circumstances specified in subsection (2) existed, it is to be conclusively presumed—
>
> (a) that the complainant did not consent to the relevant act, and
> (b) that the defendant did not believe that the complainant consented to the relevant act.'

3.40 The two circumstances specified in s 76(2) are that:

> '(a) the defendant intentionally deceived the complainant as to the nature or purpose of the relevant act,
> (b) the defendant intentionally induced the complainant to consent to the relevant act by impersonating a person known personally to the complainant.'

3.41 A 'conclusive presumption' of this kind is not really a presumption at all, but a rule of substantive law. It would be more logical to provide that 'where the defendant intentionally deceives the complainant as to the nature or purpose of the relevant act, etc, the act in question is non-consensual',[47] but the effect is the same.

---

[46] These are confined to the four offences listed in s 77 (see **3.42**). See ss 1(3), 2(3), 3(3) and 4(3). Inchoate offences are not included, which may greatly complicate the task of directing a jury where D faces counts both for a substantive offence and for an attempt to commit that or a related offence. See Rodwell 'Problems with the Sexual Offences Act 2003' [2005] Crim LR 290.

[47] Cf SOA 1956, s 1(2), which provided: 'A man who induces a married woman to have sexual intercourse with him by impersonating her husband commits rape.'

The relevant act

3.42   By SOA 2003, s 77, in relation to an offence to which ss 75 and 76 apply, references to the relevant act and to the complainant are to be read as follows.

Offence	Relevant act
An offence under s 1 (rape)	The defendant intentionally penetrating, with his penis, the vagina, anus or mouth of another person ('the complainant').
An offence under s 2 (assault by penetration)	The defendant intentionally penetrating, with a part of his body or anything else, the vagina or anus of another person ('the complainant'), where the penetration is sexual.
An offence under s 3 (sexual assault)	The defendant intentionally touching another person ('the complainant'), where the touching is sexual.
An offence under s 4 (causing a person to engage in sexual activity without consent)	The defendant intentionally causing another person ('the complainant') to engage in an activity, where the activity is sexual.

Deception as to the nature or purpose of the relevant act

3.43   SOA 2003, s 76(2)(a) gives statutory effect to the common law principle adopted in the notorious case of *Williams*,[48] in which an otherwise normal girl of 16 had been kept so ignorant of sexual matters that she was tricked into submitting to sexual intercourse on the pretext that it was some kind of operation to improve her breathing when singing. The Court of Criminal Appeal held that:[49]

> 'Where [the complainant] is persuaded that what is being done to her is not the ordinary act of sexual intercourse, but is some medical or surgical operation in order to give her relief from some disability from which she is suffering, then that is rape although the actual thing that was done was done with her consent, because she never consented to the act of sexual intercourse.'

3.44   A more likely scenario today is that A, a medical professional (whether genuine or false), tricks B into 'consenting' to an intimate breast or genital examination on the pretext that he is checking for cancer or some other ailment, whereas he is in fact merely acting for the purposes of his own sexual gratification. One might perhaps argue here as to whether the 'nature' of the act is different to the one B consents to, but there is no doubt that A's purpose is different, and that must suffice to trigger the conclusive presumption in s 76(2)(a).[50]

3.45   Deceptions as to other matters may not suffice. If, as in the Australian case of *Papadimitropolous*,[51] A merely deceives B into thinking that they are validly married (or that he intends to marry her) it cannot be said that this concerns the nature or purpose of the act. This would not be covered by s 76(2) and arguably would not be rape at all.

---

48   [1923] 1 KB 340.
49   Ibid, at p 347. See also *Flattery* (1877) 2 QBD 410.
50   Cf *Green* [2002] EWCA Crim 1501; *Piper* [2007] EWCA Crim 2151.
51   (1958) 98 CLR 247, HCA.

3.46 In *Linekar*,[52] A deceived B, a prostitute, into thinking that he would pay her for her services. He had no intention of paying her. His conviction for rape was quashed on appeal, on the basis that his deception did not relate to nature of the act, but only to the payment. Section 76 does additionally refer to the *purpose* of the act, but clearly A's purpose was sexual gratification and B's purpose was to provide it. The fact that she expected payment did not alter that, unless purpose is to be equated with motive. Section 76 does not apply to cases such as this.[53]

3.47 A more difficult scenario would be provided by a case such as *Gill*,[54] where G, a therapist, enticed one of his clients into having a 'threesome' with him and another woman on the basis that it would 'release her inhibitions' and facilitate her recovery from depression, etc. G's real purpose was his own sexual gratification. This scenario differs from *Williams* in that the client understood exactly what sexual intercourse involved. But could it be distinguished from *Linekar*, and is it analogous to the scenario involving the fake medical examination?

3.48 It is submitted that the answer must in each case be 'no'. G's client was deceived only as to G's 'wider purpose', and knew that the mutual enjoyment of sex was the immediate purpose. Any anticipated therapeutic benefits were akin to the complainant's expectation of payment in *Linekar*.[55] In contrast, the complainant in the false medical examination is fundamentally deceived as to what the defendant is doing to her. She does not realise that he is not conducting a medical examination at all.

3.49 In the context of alleged offences under SOA 2003, ss 1–3, any reference to 'nature or purpose' means D's purpose in doing the 'relevant act' or the nature of that act. In relation to offences under s 4, it might initially be supposed that 'the relevant act' must be the sexual activity that the complainant engages in, but s 77 provides that the 'relevant act' is D's act in causing him to so engage. The complainant need not be deceived as to the nature of his own act. In *Devonald*,[56] D sought to exact revenge on his daughter's former boyfriend, V, by contacting him online and pretending to be a young woman who wanted to see him expose himself on a webcam and masturbate for her. His real purpose was to humiliate V. V fell for the deception. D was convicted of an offence under s 4. Upholding this conviction, the Court of Appeal said:[57]

> 'It is difficult to see how the jury could have concluded otherwise than that the complainant was deceived into believing that he was indulging in sexual acts with, and for the sexual gratification of, a 20-year-old girl with whom he was having an on line relationship. That is why he agreed to masturbate over the sex cam. In fact, he was doing so for the father of his ex girlfriend who was anxious to teach him a lesson, doubtless by later embarrassing him or exposing what he had done.'

Impersonating a person known personally to the complainant

3.50 For the purposes of SOA 2003, s 76(2)(b) it is not enough merely to impersonate someone else, or to assume a fictitious identity (as where A seduces B by pretending to be the Crown Prince of Ruritania or a famous sportsman or entertainer to whom he

---

52 [1995] 2 Cr App R 49.
53 See *Jheeta* [2007] 2 Cr App R 477, at [27].
54 (Unreported) September 1989, Crown Court.
55 The issue did not in the end fall to be resolved in *Gill*, where A agreed to plead guilty to indecent assault in return for charges of rape being dropped.
56 [2008] EWCA Crim 527.
57 Ibid, at [7].

bears a striking resemblance). The person impersonated must be personally known to the complainant and the complainant must intentionally have been induced to consent by the impersonation. The classic scenario is one in which A impersonates his twin brother so as to trick B (his brother's wife or partner) into having sex with him, but in respect of offences other than rape the offence could equally be committed by a woman impersonating her sister, or some other woman personally known to the complainant.

3.51 The conclusive presumptions under s 76 might at first glance be thought to raise questions about their compatibility with the presumption of innocence under the European Convention on Human Rights (ECHR), Art 6(2); but they do not. They merely help to define the concept of consent, and are no more open to challenge than was SOA 1956, s 1(2), which stated that: 'A man who induces a married woman to have sexual intercourse with him by impersonating her husband commits rape.'

Deception or mistake not covered by s 76

3.52 The circumstances referred to in SOA 2003, s 76 do not purport to be exhaustive of those in which consent may be considered to be absent. One might perhaps infer that true consent will also be lacking where B mistakes A for her husband or lover, even if A did not intentionally impersonate him or induce that mistake. For example, B is drunk, and gets into A's bed thinking A is her husband. A foolishly assumes B is simply 'hitting on him' because her husband is away, and has sexual intercourse with her. The jury concludes that a reasonable man would have spotted B's mistake. That may be enough to make A guilty of rape, but a judge would be well advised to leave that decision to the jury, rather than direct it as he would do in a s 76 case.

3.53 Section 76 is not applicable to a deception relating to the quality of the act, rather than its nature or purpose. In *Tabassum*,[58] several women allowed T to examine their breasts on the basis of his false representation that he was medically qualified and conducting a survey into breast cancer. He had no medical qualification, and his claim to have been conducting research was at best suspect. One might reasonably infer, on those facts, that T's real purpose must have been sexual gratification (in which case s 76 would indeed apply) but the Court of Appeal declined to draw any such inference, and concentrated instead on the fact that T had deceived his victims as to his medical qualifications. Upholding his conviction for indecent assault under SOA 1956, s 14, Rose LJ said: 'There was consent to the nature of the act, but not its quality.'

3.54 *Tabassum* is a suspect authority,[59] being difficult to reconcile with *Richardson*,[60] in which it was held that no Offences against the Person Act (OAPA) offence was committed by a dentist who filled patients' teeth without disclosing that she had been struck off the dental register. It can thus be argued that on facts such as those in

---

[58] [2000] 2 Cr App R 328. See also *Piper* [2007] EWCA Crim 2151, in which P invited young women who were 'willing to flaunt it' to attend interviews for non-existent modelling work and strut around in front of him in their underwear. He then insisted on measuring them for bikinis and 'was more careless with his hands than one might have expected him to be if he were doing it with any sense of appropriateness'. He pleaded guilty to sexual assault. Dismissing his appeal against sentence, the Court of Appeal noted that by his plea he had 'acknowledged that the women would not have consented to allow themselves to be measured ... if they had appreciated that it was a charade'.

[59] See the analysis of *Tabassum* by Smith at [2000] Crim LR 687.

[60] [1998] 2 Cr App R 200.

[margin note: However, lawyers can be reluctant to use]

*[margin note: * wrongly decided]*

Tabassum, no offence can be established under SOA 2003, unless the court or jury first concludes that A has deceived B as to A's purpose.[61]

3.55 Writing shortly after SOA 2003 came into force, Herring[62] proposed a more radical approach to the question of consent. He argued that: 'If we are to regard the right to sexual autonomy or integrity seriously then we need to be strict about what is meant by consent.' Where A and B engage in sexual behaviour, B's consent should, on that view, be regarded as invalid if, at the relevant time, B is mistaken as to any fact (including some fact concerning A's state of mind); and would not have consented if aware of the truth.

Tabarrum

3.56 This interpretation, which in Herring's view was open to the courts when SOA 2003 first came into force, would have made A guilty of raping B if he failed to warn her before having unprotected intercourse that he had recently tested positive for a sexually transmitted disease. Many would support that particular outcome; but Herring's test would also require convictions on facts such as those in *Linekar* or *Papadimitropolous*;[63] and it would not stop there. Take a case in which A has been unfaithful to his wife, B. He realises that B would almost certainly walk out on him if she found out; but for the sake of the children, etc he decides never to tell her. A and B continue to enjoy a full and mutually satisfying sex life for several more years. Adopting Herring's argument, A's undisclosed infidelity invalidates B's consent; but can it seriously be argued that A has repeatedly raped B over several years? With respect, that is simply not a realistic view.[64]

3.57 The strict approach advocated by Herring has not been adopted. In *B*, the Court of Appeal held that, even where the complainant is unaware that her partner has been confirmed as being infected with HIV, her consent to unprotected sexual intercourse would not thereby be invalidated as far as a charge of rape is concerned:[65]

> 'As a matter of law, the fact that the defendant may not have disclosed his HIV status is not a matter which could in any way be relevant to the issue of consent under section 74 of the 2003 Act in relation to the sexual activity in this case.'[66]

3.58 On a charge of maliciously inflicting grievous bodily harm,[67] however, a lack of 'informed consent' may be crucial. If B does not know of A's infection she does not give informed consent to the risk of being infected (and thus injured) by him and her consent to sexual intercourse does not prevent A from being convicted of the OAPA offence.

3.59 Assuming that *B* is correctly decided, the following examples would equally appear to involve valid consent to sexual activity:

- B allows A to have unprotected intercourse with her, because he has told her (falsely) that he has had a vasectomy; and

---

[61] If A's real purpose was (say) medical research, another argument would be that his acts were not made 'sexual' by the mere lack of formal medical qualifications. See **2.36** et seq.

[62] 'Mistaken Sex' [2005] Crim LR 511.

[63] See **3.45**.

[64] See Bohlander 'Mistaken Consent to Sex, Political Correctness and Correct Policy' (2007) 71 Jo Crim L 412. As Herring has since acknowledged (*Criminal Law, Text, Cases and Materials* (OUP, 2nd edn, 2006), at p 485) this argument is one 'which very few commentators have been willing to adopt'.

[65] [2006] 1 WLR 1567, at [21].

[66] See also *Dica* [2004] QB 1257; *Konzani* [2005] 2 Cr App R 198.

[67] OAPA 1861, s 20.

- B allows A to have intercourse with her, because he has falsely promised to marry her.

It would not necessarily make any difference if B expressly made her consent conditional on the fact in question.

3.60 A more difficult scenario would be one in which B, a lesbian, encourages A to have intercourse with her in order to become pregnant by him. A deceives her into thinking he is fertile, when in fact he knows himself to be sterile. The complication here is that B might claim to have been deceived as to the *purpose* of the act (impregnation), which would bring the case within s 76.

Evidential presumptions as to lack of consent and the mens rea relating to it: s 75

3.61 SOA 2003, s 75, like s 76, applies only to the offences of rape, assault by penetration, sexual assault and causing a person to engage in sexual activity without consent. It does not apply to inchoate offences or to any other offence under the Act where consent is relevant.[68] But in contrast to s 76, s 75 defines the limits of consent only to the extent that the circumstances with which it deals must at least be capable of negativing consent. Its principal function is evidential.

3.62 Section 75(1) provides: *D can argue against.*

'If in proceedings for an offence to which this section applies it is proved—

  (a)   that the defendant did the relevant act,[69]
  (b)   that any of the circumstances specified in subsection (2) existed, and
  (c)   that the defendant knew[70] that those circumstances existed,

the complainant is to be taken not to have consented to the relevant act unless sufficient evidence is adduced to raise an issue as to whether he consented, and the defendant is to be taken not to have reasonably believed that the complainant consented unless sufficient evidence is adduced to raise an issue as to whether he reasonably believed it.'

3.63 Prior to the enactment of the Human Rights Act 1998, presumptions imposed on defendants in criminal cases were almost invariably of the kind that reversed the legal or persuasive burden of proof. Such presumptions must be rebutted by evidence that proves the contrary on (at least) a balance of probabilities. Whether evidence called by the defence for that purpose suffices to rebut the presumption is ultimately a question of fact for the jury, and the jury must be directed accordingly.

3.64 Many such presumptions still exist, but some are open to challenge on the basis that they unjustifiably undermine the presumption of innocence that is protected by ECHR, Art 6(2), according to which a defendant is entitled to be presumed innocent until proved guilty according to law.[71] Section 75 avoids any such difficulty by imposing a more limited and less controversial form of presumption. The presumption of

---

[68]   See **3.39**, n 46.
[69]   As defined in s 77; see **3.42**.
[70]   See **2.61**.
[71]   See *Salabiaku v France* (1988) 13 EHRR 379; *Lambert* [2002] 2 AC 545; *Sheldrake v DPP*; *A-G's Reference (No 4 of 2002)* [2005] 1 AC 264.

non-consent will be rebutted if sufficient evidence is adduced to raise an issue as to whether the complainant did indeed consent; and the presumption that D knew the complainant did not consent will similarly be rebutted by any credible evidence that D did not know this. Such evidential presumptions are not incompatible with the presumption of innocence under ECHR, Art 6(2).[72] It is for the judge to decide whether sufficient evidence has been adduced to rebut either or both presumptions.[73]

3.65   There will be sufficient evidence if the evidence is sufficient to raise a prima facie case,[74] and D's own testimony to that effect will ordinarily suffice, unless it is inherently incredible. The evidence relied on will normally be adduced by D in evidence given by him or one of his witnesses in the course of the case for the defence, but it could be adduced in the course of the prosecution case from evidence given by the complainant during cross-examination. Indeed, it could come from a prosecution witness in evidence-in-chief,[75] in which case D will have no evidential burden to discharge.

3.66   Where the judge is satisfied that an issue has been raised on the evidence, he must leave it to the jury (whether D has mentioned it or not)[76] and in the normal way it will be for the prosecution to prove the absence of consent. The jury will have to be directed to this effect.

3.67   On the other hand, if the judge does not consider that any evidence adduced is sufficient to raise the issue (e g because it is vague, speculative or incredible) or if no such evidence is adduced, he must direct the jury to convict if it is sure that D intentionally did the relevant act, that one or more of the six circumstances in s 75(2) is proved, and that D knew of that circumstance.[77]

3.68   Sufficient evidence to raise an issue may be adduced in relation to either or both of the two evidential presumptions. If, for example, sufficient evidence is adduced to rebut the presumption that A did not *reasonably believe* B to have consented, that will not necessarily affect the presumption that B did not *in fact* consent. Evidence that B *did* in fact consent is likely to undermine any presumption relating to A's belief concerning it, but there is no rule of law to that effect. It depends on the circumstances of the case.

3.69   The circumstances specified in s 75(2) are that:

(a)   any person was, at the time of the relevant act or immediately[78] before it began, using violence against the complainant or causing the complainant to fear that immediate violence would be used against him;

---

72   *Lambert* [2002] 2 AC 545; *A-G's Reference (No 1 of 2004)* [2004] 1 WLR 2111; *Sheldrake v DPP* [2005] 1 AC 264.
73   *Hendry* (1989) 88 Cr App R 187.
74   See *Bonnick* (1978) 66 Cr App R 266.
75   Prosecution witnesses may testify as to facts that suggest consent when D's case is that the incident never happened. If credible, this will rebut any presumption of non-consent under s 75.
76   *Palmer v R* [1971] AC 814.
77   As to intention and knowledge, see **2.56** and **2.61**.
78   The reference to the time immediately before the relevant act began is, in the case of an act which is one of a continuous series of sexual activities, a reference to the time immediately before the first sexual activity began: s 75(3). It is likely that 'immediately' will be given a generous interpretation, as has 'immediate' in other contexts in the criminal law: see *Horseferry Road Magistrates' Court ex parte Siadatan* [1991] 1 QB 260; *Ireland; Burstow* [1998] AC 147; *Constanza* (1997) 2 Cr App R 492.

(b) any person was, at the time of the relevant act or immediately[79] before it began, causing the complainant to fear that violence was being used, or that immediate violence would be used, against another person;

(c) the complainant was, and the defendant was not, unlawfully detained at the time of the relevant act;

(d) the complainant was asleep or otherwise unconscious at the time of the relevant act;

(e) because of the complainant's physical disability, the complainant would not have been able at the time of the relevant act to communicate to the defendant whether the complainant consented;

(f) any person had administered to or caused to be taken[80] by the complainant, without the complainant's consent, a substance which, having regard to when it was administered or taken, was capable of causing or enabling the complainant to be stupefied or overpowered at the time of the relevant act.'

3.70 The imposition of an evidential presumption in these circumstances is not unreasonable.[81] In each case, consent is unlikely to be present and D is unlikely to have any reasonable grounds for believing otherwise. But clearly there may be exceptions, and for that reason the imposition of irrebuttable presumptions (as used in s 76) could easily lead to injustice in any of the circumstances covered by s 75.

3.71 Not everyone agrees. Ashworth and Temkin[82] note that:

'Obtaining compliance by using violence or threats of immediate violence seems no less heinous than doing so by deception, and yet the Act creates a conclusive presumption in the latter case and only a rebuttable presumption in the former.'

3.72 With respect, SOA 2003 does not 'create a rebuttable presumption' in cases where A secures B's compliance or submission *by* using violence or threats of violence. Such cases must inevitably be non-consensual and juries surely do not need statutory presumptions to tell them so. What the Act does do (in s 75(2)(a)) is to create a rebuttable presumption of non-consent in cases where violence is being or has been used or threatened against B. Such violence may not necessarily have emanated from A and may not necessarily have occurred against B's will. Violence is *likely* to negate consent, but the Act recognises that it will not always do so. If, for example, A and B, who are sado-masochists or spanking fetishists, happily engage in sexual activity immediately after one has soundly spanked or whipped the other (or has been spanked, etc by a third party), it would be absurd to insist that this sexual activity must by law be considered non-consensual.[83]

3.73 Ashworth and Temkin then ask:

---

[79] Ibid.

[80] For the meaning of these terms, see **12.8–12.11**.

[81] In its *Fifth Report for Session 2002–03: Sexual Offences Bill*, HC 639, at para 31 the Home Affairs Select Committee of the House of Commons shared this view. For other examples of statutory provision of evidential burdens, see Homicide Act 1957, s 3; Regulation of Investigatory Powers Act 2000, s 53; Terrorism Act 2000, s 118.

[82] 'The Sexual Offences Act 2003 (1) Rape, Sexual Assaults and the Problems of Consent' [2004] Crim LR 328.

[83] Any whipping that intentionally causes actual bodily harm may itself be unlawful under the principles established by the House of Lords in *Brown* [1994] 1 AC 212, but this need not have any bearing on the legality of subsequent sexual activity between the parties.

'Is there any good reason why it should be the case that, if D deceives C by means of impersonation or as to the nature of the act, non-consent is conclusively proved under s 76, but if D has sex with C when C is asleep or unconscious this supports only a rebuttable presumption?'

3.74 The short answer is 'yes'. The distinction is necessary in order to accommodate the possibility that the parties have an agreement or understanding by which 'sleepy sex' is consented to or indeed welcomed. If B asks A to wake him on his birthday by performing a sexual act on him, and A gives him the very present he asked for, can we seriously even consider describing B as the victim of a sexual assault?[84] A rule requiring this would drag the law into disrepute. As the Court of Appeal noted in *Jheeta*:[85]

'It would seem pretty surprising to couples sharing a bed to be told that the law prohibited either of them from intimately touching the other while asleep, and that they would be potentially liable to prosecution and punishment, for a sexual touch of the sleeping partner as a preliminary to possible sexual activity which the sleeping partner, on awakening, might welcome.'

3.75 It is even possible that a complainant who has been abducted and unlawfully detained might consent to sexual activity with her abductor; it is not unknown for such persons to develop a sexual attraction for each other. For this and other reasons, it is right that the evidential presumptions imposed by s 75 are open to rebuttal.

3.76 Section 75(2)(e) differs from the other paragraphs in s 75(2) because it is not limited to circumstances in which there is some doubt as to whether the complainant was able to exercise free choice. Instead, it addresses the problem of a physically disabled complainant who (although capable of giving valid consent) would not have been able to communicate such consent at the relevant time. If, for example, B is partially paralysed and can communicate only by means of a sign language which A cannot understand, and A was discovered stroking B's breasts, this will ordinarily give rise to an evidential presumption that he thereby committed a sexual assault on her; but this presumption would be nullified by any credible evidence that B did in fact consent, or that A had reasonable grounds to believe she consented. Such evidence might include something that B told a third person with whom she could communicate (e g she told X, 'I like it when A comes to pleasure me: tell him I wish he would do it more often'). If such evidence is adduced, the prosecution must then prove B's lack of consent (and A's mens rea) in the usual way.

3.77 Section 75(2) does not create such an evidential presumption where B (the complainant) is unable to communicate whether or not she consents because of a mental disorder. Such a case is dealt with instead by the offence of penetrative sexual activity with a person with a mental disorder who is unable to refuse.[86]

3.78 Section 75(2)(f) deals with the situation where someone, not necessarily the defendant, has, without the consent of the complainant, B, administered to B or caused to be taken by[87] B something which, having regard to when it was administered, etc, was capable of stupefying or overpowering B at the time of the relevant act, or was capable

---

84   Ashworth and Temkin's answer to such criticism is that their critics are merely 'uncomfortable with the full implications of sexual autonomy', but the authors eventually concede that mere touching in sleep ought perhaps to be kept outside the scope of any irrebuttable presumption of non-consent.
85   [2007] 2 Cr App R 477, at [22].
86   See **9.31** et seq.
87   For the meaning of these terms, see **12.8–12.11**.

of enabling B to be so overpowered or stupefied. Cases where B was actually rendered unconscious fall within s 75(2)(d). Section 75(2)(f) complements the offence in s 61 of administering, etc a substance with intent to stupefy or overpower the other person, so as to enable sexual activity to occur. Section 75(2)(f) deals with the well-known problem of drug-assisted sexual activity. The drugs used commonly, Rohypnol[88] or GHB[89], are typically put in the complainant's drink surreptitiously.

3.79   The effect of Rohypnol or GHB has been described as follows:[90]

'The drugs have common effects in that they lower anxiety, alertness and inhibition whilst inducing passivity, euphoria and a sense of relaxation and well-being; effects that are more profound when taken in conjunction with alcohol … Therefore, the drugs may reduce the victim's ability to resist sexual advances, render her unable to communicate her wishes regarding intercourse, or engender an uncharacteristic inclination to participate in sexual activity … rather than … reducing her to a state of unconsciousness. That is not to say that victims are misrepresenting their experience when they report that intercourse has occurred whilst they were unconscious as these drugs induce anterograde amnesia causing the victim to experience a memory void that the brain rationalises as a period of unconsciousness. The amnesiac effects prevent victims from recollecting events after the initial onset of drowsiness until awakening several hours later to a realisation that intercourse has occurred.'

3.80   Section 75(2)(f) refers to any substance, whether a drug or alcohol or any other substance, which is capable of having the requisite effect. It does not cover cases in which the complainant consents to the administration of such a drug,[91] or voluntarily drinks too much (not even if someone encourages this in the hope that it will lower her sexual inhibitions). It might, however, cover cases in which B's usual alcopop drinks are repeatedly spiked by A with extra shots of vodka until B becomes helplessly drunk. The fact that B knows she is consuming some alcohol should not prevent the presumption from arising if it is proved that she has been tricked into doubling or tripling her usual or intended consumption.

Rebutting an evidential presumption under s 75

3.81   Where evidence is adduced which the court or judge regards as sufficient to rebut the evidential presumptions imposed by SOA 2003, s 75 it will then be for the prosecution to prove that there was no consent and/or no reasonable belief in consent, as the case may be. A will be entitled to the benefit of any reasonable doubt. Once it is clear that the presumption has been rebutted by credible evidence, no direction as to that presumption will be required, and indeed the provision of such a direction would only mislead or confuse the jury.

3.82   Directing the jury in other cases may well require great care. It would be all too easy for a judge to confuse a jury as to the nature of the presumption, by making it appear persuasive or even irrebuttable.[92] Furthermore, A may allege that B consented and may adduce credible evidence of such consent, whilst at the same time wholly denying the facts on which the presumption is founded.

---

[88]   Also known as flunitrazepam.
[89]   Gamma hydroxy butyrate acid.
[90]   Finch and Munro 'Intoxicated Consent and the Boundaries of Drug-assisted Rape' [2003] Crim LR 773, at p 775. For a discussion of s 75(2)(f) see Finch and Munro 'The Sexual Offences Act 2003: Intoxicated Consent and Drug Assisted Rape Revisited' [2004] Crim LR 789.
[91]   See, for example, *Meachen* [2006] EWCA Crim 2414.
[92]   See, for example, *Zhang* [2007] EWCA Crim 2018.

3.83   Assume, for example, that the prosecution's case is that B was unconscious at the time. A's defence is that B was awake and willingly consented. There is no evidence from any quarter that might suggest B consented despite being unconscious. The jury here must be directed (in relation to the actus reus element):

- that it is for the prosecution to prove B did not consent;

- that if they are in any doubt as to whether B was conscious, no presumption applies (A is entitled to the benefit of any reasonable doubt as to her consent); but

- if they are sure that B was unconscious, they must (in the absence of any evidence to suggest the contrary) conclude that she did not consent.

3.84   If the prosecution case is that B was asleep or unconscious, whereas A's defence is that B was awake and consenting, a finding that B was indeed asleep is clearly fatal to that defence, and may leave A's entire case in ruins.

Other circumstances

3.85   The circumstances which give rise to evidential or conclusive presumptions under SOA 2003, s 75 or s 76 are not, of course, the only ones where an apparent consent may not be a true consent. The question of consent can be in issue for various reasons because communication between those involved in sexual activity may be unclear as to its meaning or precise meaning or because of factors other than those referred to in ss 75 and 76 (eg a threat of dismissal or economic harm, threats of non-immediate violence, abuse of a relationship of power and a self-induced mistake as to the nature or purpose of an act or the complainant's voluntary intoxication). In the case of other circumstances, it will be for the prosecution from the start to prove the absence of consent (as defined above) and of any reasonable belief in consent.

Consent to physical harm

3.86   The validity of apparent consent may sometimes be impugned on public policy grounds, notably where conduct that is otherwise consented to involves the deliberate or reckless infliction of actual bodily harm or worse. Much of the case-law in this area focuses on offences under OAPA 1861, but it is clear that the principles applicable to offences under the 1861 Act apply equally to charges of sexual assault, or sexual assault by penetration.

3.87   One must distinguish here between two main types of case. In the first, bodily harm is both intended and caused. In the context of sexual offences, we are primarily concerned here with sado-masochism and flagellation. If, as in *Donovan*,[93] A administers a severe or moderately severe (and sexually motivated) beating to B, which leaves B seriously marked and bruised, then B's consent will be invalid and A may face charges either of assault occasioning actual bodily harm or of sexual assault. In cases involving more serious forms of sado-masochism, charges under the OAPA 1861, s 20 may also be available. The thinking behind this approach to the issue of consent was expressed with some force by Lord Templeman in *Brown*:[94]

---

[93]   [1934] 2 KB 498.
[94]   [1994] 1 AC 212.

'The question whether the defence of consent should be extended to the consequences of sado-masochistic encounters can only be decided by consideration of policy and public interest ...

The violence of sado-masochistic encounters involves the indulgence of cruelty by sadists and the degradation of victims. Such violence is injurious to the participants and unpredictably dangerous. I am not prepared to invent a defence of consent for sado-masochistic encounters which breed and glorify cruelty ...'

3.88 A playful spanking, in contrast, remains perfectly lawful, as long as no real harm is done and as long as it is consented to.[95] Arguably the law interferes too closely with the sexual autonomy of sado-masochists,[96] but the law here is firmly established, and has survived direct challenge in Strasbourg.[97]

3.89 A second and more difficult type of case is one in which outré, but consensual, sexual activity leads to unintended injury. Activities such as 'fisting' and anal intercourse are known to carry a significant risk of injury unless great care is taken. Games involving suffocation or asphyxiation may involve a risk of serious or even fatal harm, should things go wrong. If some such injury is caused, is consent thereby invalidated? *Donovan* appears to suggest an affirmative answer to that question, at least where acts of violence (eg sexual beating) are involved; but a more measured response was adopted by the Court of Appeal in *Boyea*,[98] in which it was implicitly accepted that some risks may lawfully be taken in the context of sexual activity.

3.90 One may thus give valid consent to the risk of a given injury, even where one could not validly consent to the deliberate infliction of that injury. In *Dica*[99] the Court of Appeal explained why this is so:

'The problems of criminalising the consensual taking of risks include the sheer impracticability of enforcement and the haphazard nature of its impact. The process would undermine the general understanding of the community that sexual relationships are pre-eminently private and essentially personal to the individuals involved in them. And if adults were to be liable to prosecution for the consequences of taking known risks with their health, it would seem odd that this should be confined to risks taken in the context of sexual intercourse, while they are nevertheless permitted to take the risks inherent in so many other aspects of everyday life ...'

3.91 *Dica* concerned the question of consent to the risk of sexually transmitted infection, but must on principle be applicable to any hazardous sexual activity. This must, however, be qualified. In some cases, the conduct in question may be so dangerous or foolhardy that consent to the risks may still be deemed invalid. This was noted (obiter) in *Boyea*, where, during what was otherwise consensual sexual activity, the appellant inserted his hand into the complainant's vagina and twisted it around inside

---

[95] In the event of a genuine misunderstanding, where A wrongly believed B to be consenting, A has a defence to a charge of common assault, even if his mistake was a foolish one; but if charged with sexual assault, his mistake would be a defence only if found to be reasonable having regard to all the circumstances. See SOA 2003, s 3(2).

[96] See Giles '*R v Brown*: Consensual Harm and the Public Interest' (1994) 57 MLR 101.

[97] *Laskey v UK* (1997) 24 EHRR 39.

[98] (1992) 156 JP 505.

[99] [2004] QB 1257.

her, causing significant injuries to her labia and vagina. He was charged with indecent assault and convicted. His conviction was upheld on appeal, where it was said that:[100]

'... the extent of the violence inflicted on the complainant went far beyond the risk of minor injury to which, if she did consent, her consent would have been a defence.'

3.92 In another 'fisting' case, *Slingsby*,[101] the complainant suffered cuts caused by a signet ring worn by S as he penetrated her vagina and rectum with his hand; septicaemia developed and she died. He was charged with manslaughter. The prosecution submitted that although there was nothing unlawful in the act of fingering or fisting per se, it would become criminal if some foreseeable injury was in fact caused. In a ruling at trial, Judge J rejected this submission:[102]

'[T]he sexual activity to which both the deceased and the defendant agreed did not involve deliberate infliction of injury or harm and but for the coincidental fact that the defendant happened to be wearing a signet ring, no injury at all would have been caused or could have been contemplated. The question of consent to injury did not, in fact, arise because neither anticipated or considered it. At the time, all they were considering was this vigorous sexual activity. Therefore, the reality was that the deceased sustained her unfortunate injuries, not when she or the defendant were consenting to injury, but as an accidental consequence of the sexual activity which was taking place with her consent. It would be contrary to principle to treat as criminal activity which would not otherwise amount to assault merely because in the course of the activity an injury occurred.'

3.93 The injury caused in *Slingsby* may thus have been an accident that neither party had foreseen; but *Boyea* suggests that subjectively reckless behaviour involving a grave and known risk of serious injury cannot be met by a defence of consent if such an injury is in fact occasioned. This interpretation is more explicitly supported by *Emmett*,[103] in which E and the complainant engaged consensually in what was described as 'outré' sexual activity. In one incident, E partially asphyxiated the complainant by placing a plastic bag over her head; she lost consciousness and suffered sub-conjunctival haemorrhages. In a second incident, he poured lighter fuel over her breasts and ignited it; she suffered burns when they failed to extinguish the fire in time. He was convicted of offences under OAPA 1861, s 47, following this ruling by the judge, with which the Court of Appeal 'entirely agreed':[104]

'In this case, the degree of actual and potential harm was such and also the degree of unpredictability as to injury was such as to make it a proper cause for the criminal law to intervene. This was not tattooing,[105] it was not something which absented pain or dangerousness and the agreed medical evidence is in each case, certainly on the first occasion, there was a very considerable degree of danger to life, on the second there was a degree of injury to the body.'

---

[100] (1992) 156 JP 505, at p 507. On close analysis, however, this case was decided on the basis that the victim did not in fact consent: see *Dica*, at [44].

[101] [1995] Crim LR 570.

[102] Transcript of ruling cited in *Meachen* [2006] EWCA Crim 2414, at [39]. In *Meachen* M was charged with causing serious injuries to the complainant's anus during vigorous sexual activity. The Court of Appeal accepted that, if his version of the incident were believed, and the complainant's injuries were caused by him penetrating her anus with three of his fingers whilst she 'rode' him, then her consent to that activity would have been a valid defence to the charges, including a charge of indecent assault.

[103] [1999] All ER (D) 641; Case No: 9901191 Z2.

[104] From transcript.

[105] Contrast *Wilson* [1997] QB 47.

RAPE

3.94 Rape is one of the oldest and most serious sexual offences in English law, but it has been radically redefined in recent years. Originally a common law offence in which the victim was necessarily female, and penetration necessarily vaginal, it became a statutory offence under SOA 1956, s 1, and was redefined, first by the Sexual Offences (Amendment) Act (SO(A)A) 1976, s 1, and then again by the Criminal Justice and Public Order Act (CJPOA) 1994, s 142, which for the first time classified non-consensual anal sex as capable of constituting rape, thus enabling males to be recognised as potential rape victims. SOA 2003 enlarged the scope of the offence still further by including within it the concept of 'oral rape', and it has also made significant changes to the mens rea component of the offence.[106] Some, but not all, of these latest changes were recommended in the Sex Offences Review, whose proposals were only partly put into effect.[107]

3.95 SOA 2003, s 1(1) provides:

'A person (A) commits an offence if—

(a) he intentionally penetrates the vagina, anus or mouth of another person (B) with his penis,

(b) B does not consent to the penetration, and

(c) A does not reasonably believe that B consents.'

3.96 Rape remains triable only on indictment. The maximum punishment in the case of an adult offender is life imprisonment.[108] See the Sentencing Guidelines Council (SGC) Definitive Guideline in the Appendix.[109] Rape is a specified offence to which CJPOA 1994, s 25 applies, whereby a person who has been charged with or convicted of a specified offence, and who has a previous conviction[110] in the UK for any such offence,[111] may be granted bail only if the court or, as the case may be, the constable considering the grant of bail is satisfied that there are exceptional circumstances that justify it.[112]

Class of offence	2	SOA 2003, s 72 applies	✔[113]
Notification requirements	✔	SOPO[114]	✔
CJA 2003,[115] Sch 15 applies	✔	Serious specified offence	✔

---

[106] The new offence came into force on 1 May 2004. As to the position in respect of rapes allegedly committed before that date see **2.1** et seq.

[107] See Rumney 'Review of Sex Offenders and Rape Law Reform: Another False Dawn?' (2001) 64 MLR 890.

[108] SOA 2003, s 1(4).

[109] At pp 5–26.

[110] 'Conviction' in this context includes a finding of insanity or unfitness to plead, or a conviction for which D was discharged absolutely or conditionally: s 25(5).

[111] This includes convictions for rape under SOA 1956 or under the law of Scotland or Northern Ireland: s 25(2).

[112] Section 25(1) and (3).

[113] But only where the complainant is within the age limit to which s 72 applies: see **2.97**.

[114] Sexual offences prevention order.

[115] Criminal Justice Act (CJA) 2003.

Review of lenient sentence	✔	Special provisions of CYPA 1933[116]	✔
Detention of young offender for specified period			✔

See **1.48** et seq.

3.97 SOA 2003 does not give effect to arguments that reckless or negligent rape should be classified differently from deliberate rape,[117] or that 'acquaintance rape' (including 'date rape') should become a less serious offence than 'stranger rape'.[118] According to evidence considered by the Sex Offences Review,[119] it can be just as traumatic – if not more so – to be raped by a friend or trusted acquaintance as by a stranger. Nor is there any real evidence that juries are less inclined to convict in cases of acquaintance rape. One modern study actually suggests that stranger rape charges have a higher acquittal rate than cases where D was an acquaintance or an intimate,[120] although cases involving disputes as to consent often prove more problematic than cases in which consent is not an issue. Under the SGC Definitive Guideline[121], acquaintance rape and marital rape are prima facie treated as no less serious than rape by a stranger. Male rape, anal rape and oral rape are likewise to be treated as no less serious than vaginal rape; but the rape of a child or young person will ordinarily attract a significantly heavier sentence than a comparable adult rape.[122]

Marital rape

3.98 There is no longer any special rule concerning rape within marriage, although questions of consent between married or cohabiting couples may need to be considered in the light of the observations in *Zafar*.[123] Sir Matthew Hale's notorious statement that a man could never be guilty of raping his own wife ceased to have any validity in English law long before the enactment of SOA 2003, being wholly rejected by the House of Lords in *R*.[124] As a result of *R*, successful prosecutions have subsequently been brought even in respect of incidents predating that case by several years.[125] Such prosecutions are of course for rape under SOA 1956.

Penetration

3.99 The requirements of the actus reus set out in SOA 2003, s 1(1)(a) and (b) are essentially the same as those required for rape under SOA 1956 (as amended), except that the current offence extends to non-consensual penile penetration of a victim's

---

[116] Children and Young Persons Act (CYPA) 1933.
[117] See Power 'Towards a Redefinition of the Mens Rea of Rape' (2003) 23 OJLS 379.
[118] The relationship between women and their rape attackers is: current partners 45%; acquaintances 16%; ex-partners 11%; dates 11%; other intimates 10%; and strangers 8%: Myhill and Allen *Rape and Sexual Assault of Women: The Extent and Nature of the Problem*: Home Office Research Study 237 (Home Office, 2002). See also Harris and Grace *A Question of Evidence? Investigating and Prosecuting Rape in the 1990s*: Home Office Research Study 196 (Home Office, 1999).
[119] *SB*, at para 2.8.6; Recommendation 2.
[120] See Harris and Grace, n 118 above, at p 31.
[121] See also the Court of Appeal's guidance in *Millberry* [2003] 1 Cr App R 396, from which many of the Guideline's principles are derived.
[122] See the Definitive Guideline set out in the Appendix, at p 23, para 2A.3.
[123] (Unreported) 1992, 92/2762/W2; see **3.23**.
[124] [1992] 1 AC 599.
[125] See, for example, *Crooks* [2005] Crim LR 238.

mouth (oral rape) – an act that could previously be charged only as an indecent assault. There is only one offence of rape, albeit that it can be committed in different ways.[126] The Sex Offences Review[127] concluded that: 'forced oral sex is as horrible, as demeaning and as traumatising as other forms of forced penile penetration', and recommended that it should fall within the definition of rape. The inclusion of non-consensual oral penile penetration as a species of rape survived attacks in Parliament based on arguments that the inclusion of oral penetration within the definition of rape would diminish the gravity of the offence and make juries less willing to convict offenders.[128]

3.100 'Penetration' is a continuing act from entry to withdrawal.[129] It follows that, if B consents to initial penetration by A, but withdraws this consent (eg) as a result of experiencing pain, A may be guilty of rape if he fails promptly to desist when B asks him to do so. It also follows that if A begins to have sexual intercourse (or fellatio, etc) with B, and only realises that B is not consenting after he has penetrated her, he will become guilty of rape if he fails to desist after realising his mistake.[130]

3.101 It is clear that rape need not involve the ejaculation of semen. Ejaculation was expressly stated to be unnecessary in respect of offences involving intercourse under SOA 1956, s 44 which stated that penetration alone would suffice, and the concept of penetration is again used in SOA 2003. It will doubtless continue to be the case that the slightest degree of penetration suffices.[131] In the case of vaginal penetration, the hymen need not be broken.[132] 'Vagina' is defined by s 79(9) as including the vulva (the external female genitals[133]). It follows that if A's penis pushes only between only the outer lips of B's vagina, and no further, a complete act of penetration may still have been committed, even though from A's viewpoint this would doubtless be considered a failed attempt at intercourse.

3.102 References in the Act to 'penis', 'vagina' and other parts of the body include references to a part surgically constructed (in particular through gender reassignment surgery).[134] It follows that vaginal rape can be committed by a female-to-male transsexual or in respect of a male-to-female transsexual.

CPS Guidance

3.103 Crown Prosecution Service (CPS) guidance to prosecutors advises that an indictment for rape should specify whether the vagina, anus or mouth was penetrated. If more than one type of penetration is alleged, separate counts should be preferred for each. If it is not clear whether the complainant's anus or vagina was penetrated by a penis or by some other means, prosecutors are advised that 'an alternative of assault by

---

[126] As to charging practice and the form of indictments, see **3.103**.

[127] *SB*, at para 2.8.5; Recommendation 1.

[128] See, in particular HL Committee, vol 646, cols 1048–1059 and HL Report, vol 648, cols 1077–1079. There is no evidence that such fears were justified or that juries are reluctant to label non-consensual oral penetration as rape.

[129] SOA 2003, s 79(2). As was the case under the old law: *Kaitamaki v R* [1984] 3 WLR 137; *Schaub* [1994] Crim LR 531.

[130] *Kaitamaki v R* [1984] 3 WLR 137.

[131] *Hughes* (1841) 9 C & P 752; *Lines* (1844) 1 Car & Kir 393.

[132] Ibid.

[133] These include the labia majora, labia minora and vestibule of the vagina. Contrast the definition given by the High Court of Australia. Dealing with a statute requiring 'penetration of the vagina', it held that this meant the vagina in its strict anatomical sense. See *Holland v R* (1993) 117 ALR 193, HCA.

[134] SOA 2003, s 79(3).

penetration would be appropriate',[135] but alternative counts should otherwise be used sparingly and only where there are doubts concerning the issues.

3.104 Under the Code for Crown Prosecutors, a prosecution must usually take place unless there are public interest factors tending against prosecution which clearly outweigh those tending in favour. Rape is so serious that a prosecution is almost certainly required in the public interest; but evidential weakness may sometimes indicate that charges should be dropped or reduced. CPS policy on charging and dropping charges requires that:

> 'All rape cases should be allocated to specialist lawyers, who should be responsible for the case from advice or charging decision stage to conclusion of any proceedings ... All decisions to drop or substantially reduce the prosecution case should be discussed with a second specialist lawyer before a final decision is taken. If a Duty Prosecutor is not a specialist, he should contact a specialist to decide whether or not to charge a suspect.'

Women as rapists?

3.105 The offences of rape and of rape of a child under 13[136] arguably provide exceptions to the otherwise strictly gender-neutral approach of SOA 2003,[137] because a woman cannot ordinarily commit either offence. The Sex Offences Review[138] concluded that rape should be limited to active penile penetration, and not extended to cover other forms of sexual penetration. It considered that rape was clearly understood by the public as an offence that was committed by men, and also took the view that penile penetration was of a particularly personal nature, which carried risks of pregnancy and disease transmission.

3.106 The statement that rape offences are an exception to the principle of gender neutrality admits of at least one exception. As previously noted, if A is a female-to-male transsexual who penetrates B with a surgically constructed penis, without B's consent, A can be convicted of rape; even though in law A remains a woman.[139]

3.107 Women can of course be secondary parties to offences committed by men,[140] and there is some authority for the argument that a woman may also be convicted of rape as a principal offender, if she uses a man or boy as her innocent agent in committing the offence.[141] Alternatively, she might be convicted of procuring the offence despite the lack of any true principal offender. The latter of these two solutions is arguably the less problematic and has been adopted in other contexts,[142] but the former remains arguable.

---

[135] Assault by penetration includes penetration by a penis. See **3.139** and **3.141**.

[136] SOA 2003, s 5; see **3.124**.

[137] The only other apparent exception is the offence of active penetrative intercourse with an animal under SOA 2003, s 69(1); and this offence is mirrored by one of passive penetrative intercourse under s 69(2).

[138] *SB*, at para 2.8.4; Recommendation 1.

[139] See **3.102**. In law, the sex of a person is fixed at birth, and is determined biologically by reference to chromosomal and genital features at that time: *Bellinger v Bellinger* [2003] 2 All ER 593. A person born a 'woman', for example, remains a woman, despite undergoing a 'sex-change' operation which gives her a male appearance. The fact that she may be philosophically, psychologically or socially male is irrelevant: ibid.

[140] This was also possible at common law: *Ram* (1893) 17 Cox CC 609. They can also be guilty of inchoate offences of assisting or encouraging rape under the Serious Crime Act (SCA) 2007, Pt 2 when the relevant provisions are in force.

[141] *Cogan* [1976] QB 217.

[142] *Bourne* (1952) 36 Cr App R 125; *Millward* (1994) 158 JP 1091.

3.108 What then of a woman who causes a man to penetrate her without his consent? A penis need not be erect to be fellated; and an erection or partial erection (sufficient for vaginal penetration) can sometimes be induced even in a reluctant (perhaps bound or incapacitated) male. Alternatively, men can be tricked or coerced into compliance that falls short of true consent.

3.109 In some jurisdictions, an adult woman who encourages an underage boy to have sex with her risks charges of child or statutory rape, on the basis that his consent must be deemed legally irrelevant. Rightly or wrongly, however, this is not the position under English law. In defence of that law, it must be noted that the same rules apply equally to a man who causes another man (or child) to penetrate him without consent. The distinction is not specifically a gender-based one, but is based on the premise that only active penetration with a penis can properly be called rape.

Absence of consent

3.110 Penetration must occur without the consent of the complainant, and in many case the presence or absence of consent is the critical issue at trial. The question is not whether or not there was consent to sexual activity or even penetration in any general sense, but whether or not there was ongoing consent to the specific type of penetration: for example, consent to vaginal penetration is not consent to anal penetration; and consent to 'safe sex' penetration (using a condom) might not cover penetration without a condom. The often difficult concept of consent is examined at **3.13–3.93**.

Mens rea

3.111 A's penetration of B must be committed intentionally.[143] Arguably, this makes rape an offence of specific intent insofar as that particular element is concerned, although in all other respects (notably in respect of B's lack of consent) it is clearly a crime of basic intent to which evidence of A's self-induced intoxication would be irrelevant.[144]

3.112 Even if A was sober at the time, any mistaken belief on his part that B consented must be judged reasonable before it can afford him a defence.[145] We saw in **2.68** that absence of reasonable belief is an objective test; negligence thus suffices as to B's lack of consent, whereas under the previous law nothing less than recklessness sufficed.

3.113 The adoption of an objective test was controversial and met resistance when the Bill was before the House of Lords. Under the old law, as established in *DPP v Morgan*[146] and restated in the SO(A)A 1976, a defendant who made no real attempt to ascertain whether the complainant consented could not in practice expect to be acquitted, because although a genuine mistake as to consent would in theory negate mens rea, the reasonableness of the alleged mistake was always relevant to the credibility of an allegation of such a mistake.[147] A jury was unlikely to accept an alleged mistake as

---

[143] See **2.56–2.60**.
[144] But see *Heard* [2008] QB 43; **2.81** et seq.
[145] As to the difficulties that may arise where A mistakes B for C, whom he has reasonable grounds for believing would consent, see *A-G's Reference (No 79 of 2006)* [2006] EWCA Crim 2626.
[146] [1976] AC 182.
[147] SO(A)A 1976, s 1(2). In its Policy Paper, *Consent in Sex Offences*, set out in *SB*, Vol 2, Appendix C, the Law Commission advised the Sex Offences Review that a properly directed jury would 'be well able to root out the true from the bogus defence of belief in consent'.

genuine unless there were reasonable grounds for believing it, or unless the circumstances were highly unusual.[148] Even a genuine mistake or misunderstanding was doomed to fail if it arose from voluntary intoxication, because rape was and remains (in that respect at least) a crime of basic intent.

3.114 The Government's case for requiring any mistaken belief to be reasonable was that by so doing it would increase the conviction rate for rape, which was considered unacceptably low;[149] but if this was the Government's purpose, it failed. Conviction rates have not improved.[150] The choice between a subjective and an objective test in such cases ought in any case to be one of principle, rather than expediency, and to its credit the Government did also add an appeal to principle:[151]

> 'The unsatisfactory elements of the current position are, first, that it implicitly authorises the assumption of consent regardless of the views of the victim. Secondly, it is easy for the defendant to seek consent – the cost to him is very slight and the cost to the victim of forced sexual activity is very high indeed ... It is not unfair to ask any person to take care to ensure that their partner is consenting and for them to be at risk of a prosecution if they do not ... So we take a strong view that there should be an objective element in the matter.'

3.115 SOA 2003, s 1(2) provides:

> 'Whether a belief [in consent] is reasonable is to be determined having regard to all the circumstances, including any steps A has taken to ascertain whether B consents.'

3.116 The words '*all* the circumstances' must refer to any which might be relevant to the issue. The jury can take into account, for example, the actions of those involved, including any third parties,[152] the circumstances in which A and B have placed themselves, the nature of their relationship (if any) and, specifically, 'any steps A has taken to ascertain whether B consents'. Section 1(2) does not, however, require any specific steps to be taken.[153] Such a requirement would often be unrealistic and unfair, particularly where A and B were in a well-established sexual relationship. But where reasonable steps have been taken (and have not revealed any absence of consent) they may provide strong evidence of reasonable belief.

3.117 Evidence of B's sexual history or experience is not ordinarily admissible, unless it suits the prosecution to raise it,[154] but there are certain circumstances in which the defence may adduce evidence of that history, and where such history is before the jury it may become relevant to an issue of reasonable belief.

3.118 It is not clear whether 'circumstances' can include any personal characteristics that might affect A's ability to perceive whether B is consenting. Examples might include

---

[148] For that reason, the Law Commission (n 147 above) added that that '*Morgan* is not, in practice, a problem'.

[149] Lord Falconer of Thoroton, HL Deb, vol 646, col 1088; *Protecting the Public: Strengthening Protection Against Sex Offenders and Reforming the Law on Sexual Offences*, Cm 5668 (2002) (*PP*), at para 32. The conviction rate for those charged with rape and brought to court in 2001 was cited by Lord Falconer as 41.2% compared with a corresponding figure of 73.4% for all offences tried by jury. The real problem lies in the fact that, compared with other crimes, fewer reports of rape (14% of reported cases) get to court: ibid.

[150] As to the conviction rate in rape cases, see **14.2**.

[151] Lord Falconer of Thoroton, HL Deb, vol 646, col 1060.

[152] In *Cogan* [1976] QB 217, C was told by L that L's wife wanted to have sex with C. This was a lie, but it seems that C may genuinely have believed it. The jury was specifically asked to determine whether C's belief was reasonably held and determined that in the circumstances it was not.

[153] Contrast the conclusion of the Sex Offences Review: *SB*, at paras 2.13.8–2.13.14.

[154] Youth Justice and Criminal Evidence Act 1999, s 41. See **14.45** et seq.

learning disabilities, mental illness, deafness, blindness, youth and sexual inexperience. In New Zealand, where the corresponding provision requires belief in consent to be based on 'reasonable grounds',[155] the courts have held that mental illness must be disregarded;[156] but the New Zealand statute does not refer (as does SOA 2003) to 'all the circumstances' being taken into consideration, and this may be a crucial distinction.

3.119 The strongest argument in favour of requiring juries to take A's personal characteristics into account is that it would accord with the Government's own statements during the passage of the Bill through Parliament,[157] but there must be some limits on the extent to which such considerations could make a difference. The psychotic delusions of a mentally ill defendant, however understandable in medical terms, cannot be described as 'reasonable' without doing extreme violence to the English language.[158] On the other hand, a mistake might perhaps be excused as reasonable in light of A's youth or inexperience, when it would not be so perceived coming from an experienced man of the world.

3.120 One characteristic which clearly cannot be taken into account is A's voluntary intoxication through alcohol or 'dangerous drugs'. On general principles, this can never be used to support a defence, other than a denial of specific intent, where such intent is required.[159] To exclude such a circumstance when s 1(2) says that regard may be had to all the circumstances may seem to do violence to the wording of the provision, but there is a precedent for so doing,[160] and in any event a mistaken belief that can only be explained on the basis of intoxication is most unlikely to be considered 'reasonable'.

3.121 Subject to the exclusion of any particular circumstances, on which the judge would have to direct the jury, it should be left to the jury to determine whether any of A's characteristics are relevant, before taking any relevant ones into consideration.

3.122 In order to avoid any unnecessary complication of the jury's task, a direction concerning absence of reasonable belief falls to be given only when there is material on which a jury might come to the conclusion (1) that B did not consent, but (2) A might have thought she was consenting.[161] If there is some such evidence, the direction may have to be given, even if neither the Crown nor the defence specifically alleges that such a mistake was made.[162]

Legal and evidential presumptions

3.123 The prosecution may in some cases be assisted in relation to the issues of absence of consent and of a reasonable belief in consent by the evidential and conclusive

---

[155] NZ Crimes Act 1961, s 128(2) and (3).

[156] *P (T129/92)* (1993) 10 CRNZ 250.

[157] Baroness Scotland of Asthal, HL Deb, vol 649, col 678.

[158] This issue did not arise in *Sultan* [2008] EWCA Crim 6, because the incident giving rise to prosecution in that case occurred shortly before SOA 2003 came into force. S's Asperger's syndrome, which apparently made it 'difficult for him to understand others' beliefs, desires or intentions or to consider alternative views to his own' could thus be put forward as evidence that he did not knowingly or recklessly rape the complainant; but it is submitted that this would not so easily have afforded him a defence under SOA 2003.

[159] See **2.74–2.87**.

[160] Voluntary intoxication could not be taken into account in relation to a claimed belief in consent under the 'old' law, even though SO(A)A 1976, s 1(2), required a jury to take into account 'any ... relevant matters': *Woods* (1981) 74 Cr App R 312.

[161] *Taran* [2006] EWCA Crim 1498, at [11].

[162] Ibid, at [12].

presumptions in SOA 2003, ss 75 and 76,[163] which by s 1(3) apply to the present offence. These refer to the defendant having done the 'relevant act'. For the purposes of rape, the 'relevant act' is that he intentionally penetrates the complainant's vagina, anus or mouth with his penis.[164]

RAPE OF A CHILD UNDER 13

3.124 As noted at **2.16**, SOA 2003 effectively introduced a rule under which a child under 13 becomes legally incapable of giving any legally significant consent to sexual activity. It will thus no longer be possible for a defendant to claim successfully that such a child consented to sexual intercourse. By SOA 2003, s 5, penetrative intercourse with such a child is declared to be 'rape of a child'.

3.125 SOA 2003, s 5(1) provides:

'A person commits an offence if—

(a)   he intentionally penetrates the vagina, anus or mouth of another person with his penis, and
(b)   the other person is under 13.'

The elements specified in s 5(1)(a) are identical to those of rape under s 1(1)(a) The difference lies in s 5(1)(b), by which the complainant's age supplants lack of consent as the remaining element of the actus reus.

3.126 An offence under s 5 is triable only on indictment. By s 5(2) the maximum penalty is life imprisonment. See the SGC Definitive Guideline in the Appendix.[165] It is an offence to which CJPOA 1994, s 25 (restrictions on granting of bail) applies.[166] A defence to a charge of aiding, abetting or procuring the commission of an offence under s 5 may in appropriate cases by provided by SOA 2003, s 73.[167]

Class of offence	2	SOA 2003, s 72 applies	✔
Notification requirements	✔	SOPO	✔
CJA 2003, Sch 15 applies	✔	Serious specified offence	✔
Review of lenient sentence	✔	Special provisions of CYPA 1933	✔
Detention of young offender for specified period			✔

See **1.48** et seq.

---

[163] See **3.38** et seq.
[164] See s 77; see **3.42**.
[165] At pp 5–26.
[166] See **3.96**.
[167] See **2.49** et seq.

3.127 Other offences in the Act dealing with sexual activity in respect of children under 16 or children under 18 include detailed provisions as to mens rea in respect of the complainant's age. The absence of any such provision in SOA 2003, ss 5–8 clearly implies that no such mens rea is required there, and that the offences in question are of strict liability in that respect. A mistaken belief that the complainant was aged 13 or over cannot, in other words, be a defence, even if it was a reasonable mistake in the circumstances. The House of Lords has confirmed this in *G*,[168] where a boy of 15 pleaded guilty to the rape of a girl of 12, but only on the basis that she had been willing and that on the basis of what she herself had told him he had reasonably believed her to be 15. The Appellate Committee upheld this conviction, rejecting arguments that the imposition of strict liability in such a case is incompatible with ECHR, Art 6 or that the prosecution of a child in such circumstances is an unjustified interference with his rights under Art 8(1).[169] Moreover, even where a genuine mistake is made, this is likely to constitute only very limited mitigation in the case of an adult offender. Adults having sexual relations with young persons do so at their own risk.[170]

3.128 The minimum age at which this offence can be committed is the age of criminal responsibility, which is the tenth birthday. If A and B, aged between 10 and 13, consensually experiment together and A intentionally penetrates B with his penis, it follows that he is guilty or raping a child, even if he is younger and less experienced or knowledgeable than B, and acts in accordance with B's instructions.[171] B, who in reality is the instigator, becomes in law the victim.[172] B cannot even be prosecuted for aiding and abetting the 'rape'.[173] B may, however, be guilty of committing other offences against A, notably under SOA 2003, s 7 or s 13.[174]

3.129 Many of the more absurd consequences of the modern law can, however, be avoided by the proper exercise of prosecutorial discretion. It is recognised that the prosecution of a young offender may not always be appropriate, and an inappropriate decision to prosecute may be open to judicial review.[175] Even if some form of prosecution is appropriate, a charge under s 5 may be considered unduly heavy-handed if it is clear that the complainant fully understood and consented to what took place.[176]

---

[168] [2008] UKHL 37.

[169] Their Lordships were unanimous on the former issue. On the latter, Lords Hope and Carswell dissented on the basis that, in the absence of any proof of an actual lack of consent (either at trial or in the course of a *Newton* hearing following G's qualified guilty plea), the continued use of a s 5 charge was disproportionate and incompatible with G's rights under Art 8. Of the Law Lords on the majority, Lord Hoffmann held that Art 8 had no possible application in such cases, but none of the other Lords went that far: see **1.30**. Baroness Hale's view was that G's Art 8 rights were not engaged on the facts, and that the strict nature of the law was in any event justified on the basis that it protected the physical and moral integrity of children such as the complainant.

[170] *G* [2008] UKHL 37, esp at [46], per Baroness Hale. See also *A-G's References (Nos 74 and 83 of 2007)* [2007] EWCA Crim 2550. CPS guidance indicates that, where D is an adult, prosecution of a s 5 offence will usually be required in the public interest unless there are factors tending against it which clearly outweigh those tending in favour.

[171] If, however, A passively allows B to fellate him, without fully understanding what B is doing, it may be possible to argue that he does not 'intentionally penetrate' B at all.

[172] It may be considered paradoxical that a child under 13 cannot understand the implications of sexual activity sufficiently to give a valid consent to it; but may nevertheless be regarded as criminally culpable for any such actions of his own. Such, however, is the law.

[173] *Tyrrell* [1894] 1 QB 710. See Bohlander 'The Sexual Offences Act 2003 and the *Tyrrell* Principle – Criminalising the Victims?' [2005] Crim LR 701. Nor when Serious Crime Act (SCA) 2007, Pt 2 is in force could B be prosecuted for encouraging or assisting A contrary to Pt 2: SCA 2007, s 51.

[174] See **4.50**.

[175] See *R (S) v DPP* [2006] EWHC 2231 (Admin), at [14] et seq.

[176] Conviction of a child under s 5 labels him a rapist and subjects him to notification requirements as a sex

The Court of Appeal acknowledged this in *G*[177] and the H
appear to have dissented from that. But the initial complair
forcible rape, which would fully have justified the initial charg
pleaded guilty on the basis of de facto consent and his mista
was appropriate for this to be reflected merely in the sentenc
the substitution of a lesser charge. Baroness Hale concluded:

> 'The word "rape" does indeed connote a lack of consent. But the law has disabled children
> under 13 from giving their consent. So there was no consent. In view of all the dangers
> resulting from under age sexual activity, it cannot be wrong for the law to apply that label
> even if it cannot be proved that the child was in fact unwilling. The fact that the appellant
> was under 16 is obviously relevant to his relative blameworthiness and has been reflected in
> the second most lenient disposal available to a criminal court. But it does not alter the fact of
> what he did or the fact that he should not have done it. In my view the prosecution,
> conviction and sentence were both rational and proportionate in the pursuit of the legitimate
> aims of the protection of health and morals and of the rights and freedoms of others.'

3.130 CPS guidance to prosecutors confirms that they must indeed consider
alternatives to prosecution where D is a child. The overriding public concern must be to
protect children, not to criminalise them.[179]

Proof of age

3.131 A person reaches a particular age at the commencement of the relevant
anniversary of his birth (ie his birthday).[180]

3.132 CYPA 1933, s 99(2) may assist in the proof of age. It provides that:

> 'Where in any charge or indictment for [rape of a child under 13 or any other offence]
> mentioned in the First Schedule[181] to this Act, it is alleged that the person by or in respect of
> whom the offence was committed was a child or young person or was under or had attained
> any specified age, and he appears to the court to have been at the date of the commission of
> the alleged offence a child or young person, or to have been under or to have attained the
> specified age, as the case may be, he shall for the purposes of this Act be presumed at that
> date to have been a child or young person or to have been under or to have attained that age,
> as the case may be, unless the contrary is proved.'

---

offender. Conviction under s 13 merely labels a child one who has had sexual activity with another child, and
does not subject him to notification requirements unless sentenced to at least 12 months' imprisonment.

[177] [2006] 2 Cr App R 270.

[178] [2008] UKHL 37, at [55].

[179] Guidelines issued by the DPP state that only Crown Prosecutors should decide whether a person under 18 be
charged with an offence under SOA 2003. Furthermore, youth offender specialists should review all such
files and take all major decisions in relation to those cases, in particular, whether or not a prosecution should
take place. The guidance stresses that before any decision is made on whether or not to prosecute,
prosecutors must have as much information as possible from sources, such as the police, youth offending
teams and any professionals assisting those agencies about D's home circumstances and the circumstances
surrounding the alleged offence, as well as any information known about the complainant. It may also be
important to obtain the views of the complainant and where appropriate those of the complainant's family.

[180] Family Law Reform Act 1969, s 9.

[181] CYPA 1933, Sch 1 mentions the following offences dealt with in this book: any offence against a child or
young person under any of SOA 2003, ss 1–41, 47–53, 57–61, 66 and 67, or any attempt to commit such an
offence; any offence under SOA 2003, s 62 or s 63 where the intended offence was an offence against a child
or young person, or any attempt to commit such an offence; any offence under CYPA 1933, s 3; and any
other offence involving bodily harm to a child or young person.

her method of proving B's age at the time of the alleged offence is to produce a tified copy of an entry in the register of births purporting to be sealed or stamped with the seal of the General Register Office (since this may be used to prove an entry in that register, and is admissible evidence of the date of birth[182]) and to adduce evidence to identify B as the person named in the certified copy.[183] The same applies where it is sought to prove B's age by production of a birth certificate.[184] The date of birth of an adopted child may be proved by a certified copy of an entry in the Adopted Children Register,[185] similarly sealed or stamped, coupled with identification of the child named in the certificate with the person in question. Age may also be proved, where this is permissible,[186] by the production of a certified copy of the entry in a foreign register of births or adoption, coupled with identification of the child named in the certificate with the person in question.[187] Age may also be proved by any other admissible means (e g the testimony of someone present at the time of birth, by inference from appearance or by hearsay evidence as to pedigree).[188]

OFFENCES INVOLVING ASSAULT

3.133 SOA 2003, ss 2, 3, 6 and 7 (which replaced the old offences of indecent assault on a woman and indecent assault on a man, contrary to SOA 1956, ss 14 and 15) create offences of:

- assault by penetration;

- assault of a child under 13 by penetration;

- sexual assault; and

- sexual assault of a child under 13.

3.134 Whereas an assault can usually be committed by causing another merely to apprehend the infliction of unlawful force, an assault under SOA 2003 must involve actual touching (or battery). An indecent assault under SOA 1956 could be committed in either way,[189] so this change narrows the scope of the offence. It seems that the Sex Offences Review deliberately adopted the term 'assault' to describe the offence of sexual assault which it proposed, because it wanted to retain 'not only the touching element but

---

[182] Births and Deaths Registration Act 1953, s 34.

[183] *Bellis* (1911) 6 Cr App R 283.

[184] *Rogers* (1914) 10 Cr App R 276. Under Government proposals, not yet enacted, there may eventually be an electronic system of registration of births, deaths and marriages. If and when this system is ever enacted and brought into force, birth, etc certificates would no longer be issued. Documents containing registered details obtainable by the public would have no evidential force, but certified copies would still be available for production in court. See *Civil Registration: Delivering Vital Change*, Cm 5355 (2002); *Modernising Civil Registration: Consultation Document* (General Register Office, 2003).

[185] Adoption Act 1976, s 50(2).

[186] Where an Order in Council has been made under the Oaths and Evidence (Overseas Authorities and Countries) Act 1963, s 5(1).

[187] Evidence (Foreign, Dominion and Colonial Documents) Act 1933, s 1.

[188] *Cox* [1898] 1 QB 179. Common law principles governing the admission of hearsay in this context are preserved under CJA 2003, s 118(1). As to establishing age from photographs or video, see *Land* [1999] QB 65, at p 71.

[189] *Rolfe* (1952) 36 Cr App R 4; *Rogers* [1953] 1 WLR 1017; *Kimber* [1983] 3 All ER 316.

also behaviour which puts the victim in fear of force of some kind (ie where no touching occurs)'.[190] Parliament retained the terminology, but rejected the wider meaning that is ordinarily embraced by that terminology.

3.135 Although a person who merely causes another to fear an immediate sexual touching does not thereby commit an assault under SOA 2003, they may in some cases be guilty of attempting to commit such an offence or of an offence under SOA 2003, s 62 (committing an offence with intent to commit a sexual offence).[191]

3.136 Under SOA 1956, a person who was a 'defective'[192] or aged under 16 could not give a valid consent to the indecent conduct in question,[193] so as to render it lawful and therefore prevent an assault being committed. Even if that person had in fact consented, this consent was deemed invalid. Thus any person (male or female) who indulged in sexual petting with a willing girl of 15 indecently assaulted her.[194]

3.137 The modern offences of assault by penetration and sexual assault do not 'deem' consent to be invalid on such grounds. Consent, even by a child, negates the commission of any such offence. Where, however, A has engaged in sexual acts with B, a mentally disordered or 'underage' complainant, there may be no need to establish whether B consented, because SOA 2003 provides specific offences of sexual activity with a child under 16[195] and sexual activity with a person with a mental disorder impeding consent[196] under which consent would be irrelevant to anything other than sentencing. Sections 6 and 7 meanwhile create specific offences of assault by penetration of a child under 13 and of touching a child under 13, where once again consent is not an issue.

ASSAULT BY PENETRATION

3.138 The Sex Offences Review[197] concluded that the 10-year maximum imprisonment for indecent assault was inadequate for the worst cases of sexual penetration otherwise than by a penis, which could be as serious in their impact on the victim as rape; they could leave the victim physically and psychologically damaged for years. Accordingly, it recommended a new offence of sexual assault by penetration of a non-penile type. SOA 2003, s 2, implements this recommendation.

3.139 SOA 2003, s 2(1) provides:

'A person (A) commits an offence if—

    (a)   he intentionally penetrates the vagina or anus of another person (B) with a part of his body or anything else,

    (b)   the penetration is sexual,

    (c)   B does not consent to the penetration, and

---

[190]   *SB*, at para 2.14.2.
[191]   See **12.20**.
[192]   See **9.3**.
[193]   SOA 1956, ss 14(4) and 15(3) (defective) and ss 14(2) and 15(2) (children under 16).
[194]   Moreover, the 'young man's defence', which might have enabled a defendant aged under 24 to escape conviction for unlawful sexual intercourse if he had honestly and reasonably mistaken her age, was inapplicable on a charge of indecent assault.
[195]   In s 9. See **4.9**.
[196]   In ss 30–41. See generally Chapter 9.
[197]   *SB*, at paras 2.8.2 and 2.9.1; Recommendation 3.

(d)   A does not reasonably believe that B consents.'

3.140   The offence is triable only on indictment and by s 2(4) the maximum punishment is life imprisonment. See the SGC Definitive Guideline in the Appendix.[198] It is an offence to which CJPOA 1994, s 25 (restrictions on granting of bail) applies.[199] Under CPS guidance prosecutors should regard the offence as essentially similar to rape which means that a prosecution is almost certainly required in the public interest.

Class of offence	2	SOA 2003, s 72 applies	✔[200]
Notification requirements	✔	SOPO	✔
CJA 2003, Sch 15 applies	✔	Serious specified offence	✔
Review of lenient sentence	✔	Special provisions of CYPA 1933	✔
Detention of young offender for specified period			✔

See **1.48** et seq.

Actus reus

3.141   The penetration[201] of B's vagina[202] or anus without B's consent[203] may be by A using any part of his body (eg his hand or tongue). Penetration by A's penis is not excluded. If penile penetration can be proved, a charge of rape may be more appropriate, but cases may arise in which a drunk or incapacitated complainant can testify only that she felt *something* push into her,[204] and in that case an offence under SOA 2003, s 2 will usually be much easier to establish.[205] Alternatively, A may commit the offence by using an object (such as a sex toy, vegetable or bottle); the hand of an unwilling third party; or even an animal. Because the nature of the penetration is at large, the offence may be capable of proof even where it is impossible to establish what exactly was used.[206]

3.142   In contrast to rape or child rape (which can be committed only by someone with a penis) an offence of assault by penetration can be committed by anyone. There is no need for a hostile intent to be proved, but the penetration must be done without the victim's consent. Penetration of the mouth is not an offence under s 2, but 'French kissing' or any other penetration of the mouth (if sexual) without the victim's consent may involve an offence of sexual assault under SOA 2003, s 3.

---

[198]   At pp 5–21 and 28–30.
[199]   See **3.96**.
[200]   But only where the complainant is within the age limit to which s 72 applies: see **2.97**.
[201]   As to what amounts to penetration, see **3.100–3.101**.
[202]   See **3.102**.
[203]   See **3.13** et seq.
[204]   See, for example, *A-G's Reference (No 79 of 2006)* [2006] EWCA Crim 2626.
[205]   CPS guidance recommends charging under s 2 in such cases.
[206]   If physical injury is caused by acts of unlawful penetration, charges under OAPA 1861, ss 47, 20 or s 18 may be appropriate: see *Meachen* [2006] EWCA Crim 1414.

3.143 Because the penetration must be sexual,[207] a doctor who, for genuine clinical reasons, inserts a speculum in the vagina or anus of a patient who has refused consent would not commit the present offence. (The doctor would, however, be guilty of common assault if the patient was an adult capable of judging his own best interests, whose refusal of consent posed no threat to anyone else.[208]) Nor would a doctor commit a s 2 offence by penetrating an unconscious patient for clinical reasons, even if his actions are adjudged to be unlawful in other ways.

Mens rea

3.144 The mens rea required for assault by penetration is similar to that required for rape. The prosecution must prove that A's act was intentional[209] and that A did not reasonably believe[210] B consented to it. As in the case of rape contrary to s 1, whether a belief is reasonable is to be determined having regard to all the circumstances, including any steps A took in order to ascertain whether B consented.[211] Mistaken belief as to consent arising from voluntary intoxication must be disregarded, because the offence is deemed to be one of basic intent.[212]

Legal and evidential presumptions

3.145 If it is proved that A intentionally penetrated B's anus or vagina, that the penetration was sexual, and that to A's knowledge one of the circumstances in SOA 2003, s 75(2) existed, the evidential presumptions about the absence of consent and of a reasonable belief in consent in s 75 apply.[213] If instead it is proved that A intentionally deceived B as to the nature or purpose of the act, or that A intentionally induced B to consent to that act by impersonating someone known to B, it must be conclusively presumed[214] that B did not consent to that act and that A did not believe that the complainant consented to the relevant act.[215]

ASSAULT OF A CHILD UNDER 13 BY PENETRATION

3.146 SOA 2003, s 6(1) provides:

'A person commits an offence if—

    (a)   he intentionally penetrates the vagina or anus of another person with a part of his body or anything else,

    (b)   the penetration is sexual, and

    (c)   the other person is under 13.'

---

[207] See **2.36** et seq.

[208] See Card, Cross and Jones *Criminal Law* (OUP, 18th edn, 2008), at para 19.44, based on *St George's Healthcare NHS Trust v SD* [1998] 3 WLR 936.

[209] See **2.56–2.60**.

[210] See **2.67**.

[211] SOA 2003, s 2(2).

[212] See **2.74** et seq.

[213] See ss 2(3) and 77. See **3.61** et seq.

[214] Such a presumption is in effect a legal rule.

[215] See **3.38** et seq.

3.147 This offence is closely based on that of assault by penetration, contrary to s 2, in the same way that child rape is based on that of rape. In each case, what must be proved are the elements of the basic offence, other than lack of consent, in place of which it must be proved that the complainant was under the age of 13.[216] The underlying (but unstated) rationale is that children below this age are incapable of giving valid consent.

3.148 The elements of s 6(1)(a) and (b) are identical to those of s 2(1)(a) and (b), discussed in **3.141–3.143**.[217] The offence, like that under s 5 (rape of a child under 13), is one of strict liability as to age.[218] As with ss 5 and 7, a defence to a charge of aiding, abetting or procuring the commission of an offence under s 6 may in appropriate cases be provided by SOA 2003, s 73.[219]

3.149 An offence under s 6 is triable only on indictment (s 6(2)). The maximum penalty is life imprisonment (s 6(2)). See Part 2A of the SGC Definitive Guideline in the Appendix.[220] It is an offence to which CJPOA 1994, s 25 (restrictions on granting of bail) applies.[221] As to CPS policy in respect of prosecutions, the relevant considerations are much the same in this case as they are for rape of a child under s 5.[222]

Class of offence	2	SOA 2003, s 72 applies	✔
Notification requirements	✔	SOPO	✔
CJA 2003, Sch 15 applies	✔	Serious specified offence	✔
Review of lenient sentence	✔	Special provisions of CYPA 1933	✔
Detention of young offender for specified period			✔

See **1.48** et seq.

SEXUAL ASSAULT

3.150 The Sex Offences Review[223] concluded that its proposals relating to non-consensual oral sex and penetrative assault had removed some of the most serious types of non-consensual conduct from what was covered by the offences of indecent assault under SOA 1956. It considered, however, that these proposals still left:[224]

'... a range of unacceptable behaviour, including "frottage" (rubbing up against someone else in a sexual manner) on the Tube, fondling and groping to quite serious assaults. All of these

---

[216] See **3.131** and **3.132**.
[217] For exceptions from liability for aiding, abetting or counselling this offence, see **2.49** et seq.
[218] See **3.127**.
[219] See **2.50**.
[220] At pp 5–21 and 28–30. See also *Corran* [2005] 2 Cr App R (S) 453; *A-G's References (Nos 74 and 83 of 2007)* [2007] EWCA Crim 2550.
[221] See **3.96**.
[222] See **3.127–3.130**, together with accompanying notes.
[223] *SB*, at para 2.14.1.
[224] *SB*, at para 2.14.1.

are distressing to the victim because there is a clear sexual intention, and they are often directed at the more sensitive and private parts of the body or carried out by the use of the private parts of the perpetrator.'

Consequently, it recommended that there should be a new offence of sexual assault to cover sexual touching without consent.[225]

3.151 SOA 2003, s 3(1) provides:

'A person (A) commits an offence if—

(a)   he intentionally touches another person (B),
(b)   the touching is sexual,
(c)   B does not consent to the touching, and
(d)   A does not reasonably believe that B consents.'

3.152 A s 3 offence is triable either way and by s 3(4) is punishable on indictment by up to 10 years' imprisonment.[226] This reflects the fact that even non-penetrative sexual assaults can involve high levels of fear, degradation and trauma.[227] See the SGC Definitive Guideline in the Appendix.[228]

Class of offence	3	SOA 2003, s 72 applies	✔[229]
Notification requirements	See **3.153**	SOPO	✔
CJA 2003, Sch 15 applies	✔	Serious specified offence	✔
Review of lenient sentence	✔	Special provisions of CYPA 1933	✔
Detention of young offender for specified period			✔

See **1.48** et seq.

3.153 The notification requirements apply if:[230]

'(a)   where the offender was under 18, he is or has been sentenced, in respect of the offence, to imprisonment for a term of at least 12 months;
(b)   in any other case—
  (i)   the victim was under 18, or
  (ii)   the offender, in respect of the offence or finding, is or has been—
    (a)   sentenced to a term of imprisonment,
    (b)   detained in a hospital, or
    (c)   made the subject of a community sentence of at least 12 months.'

---

[225]   *SB*, at Recommendation 10.
[226]   Maximum on summary conviction: see **1.43**.
[227]   *PP*, at para 45.
[228]   At pp 5–21 and 31–34.
[229]   But only where the complainant is within the age limit to which SOA 2003, s 72 applies: see **2.97**.
[230]   SOA 2003, s 80 and Sch 3, para 18.

Touching

3.154 The use of 'touch' in SOA 2003, s 3(1)(a) means that the most minimal contact with B suffices under s 3. By SOA 2003, s 79(8), 'touching' includes:

'... touching—

(a) with any part of the body,
(b) with anything else,
(c) through anything,

and in particular includes touching amounting to penetration.'

3.155 The reference in s 79(8)(a) is to touching with any part of *the* body, and not necessarily with A's own body. If A seizes X's hand and, before X can resist, places it on B's breast, A will thereby have touched B.[231] An example of a touching by something other than a part of the body would be where A pushes a sex toy against B's breasts or genitals. Since touching can be done through anything, it would be irrelevant that B was fully dressed at the time. Patting a woman's bottom through her clothing may constitute the offence, but CPS guidance on charging practice suggests that prosecutors must have regard to whether the public interest warrants a prosecution in respect of conduct 'at the lower end of the scale'.[232]

3.156 In *H*,[233] it was argued that under s 79(8)(c) there can be no touching of another unless pressure in some form is brought against the body of the person concerned. Thus, although a sexual assault may involve A stroking or fondling B's body through her clothing, it cannot merely take the form of touching or tugging at B's clothing. The Court of Appeal rejected that argument, which would have had the unfortunate consequence that if A attempts to tear off B's clothes, that might not involve any touching for the purpose of sexual assault. The Court said:[234]

'Subsection (8) is not a definition section ... It was not Parliament's intention by the use of that language to make it impossible to regard as a sexual assault touching which took place by touching what the victim was wearing at the time.'

Sexual touching

3.157 The requirement that the 'touching' be sexual[235] marks an important demarcation line between a sexual assault and a mere battery. Sexual assault nevertheless covers a wider range of touching than did indecent assault under the old law, because as previously explained[236] a touching can be sexual without being indecent.

3.158 The fact that 'touching' can include penetration means that it would be no defence to a charge under SOA 2003, s 3 for a defendant to allege that, in fact, A

---

[231] X would not be liable because his involvement is involuntary and the touching unintentional on his part.
[232] There may, however, be features that make such an offence more serious. Examples listed in CPS guidance include abuse of position, use of drugs, etc, use of violence or coercion and repeated offending.
[233] [2005] 1 WLR 2005; see **2.46**.
[234] Ibid, at [26].
[235] See **2.31** et seq.
[236] See **2.33**.

committed rape or assault by penetration. This is significant, because in some cases it will be clear that A has sexually assaulted B, but not clear what conduct that assault involved.

Absence of consent

3.159 The touching in question must be without B's consent.[237] Although consent to physical contact may be implied in appropriate circumstances under the law relating to the offence of battery,[238] and may in principle be implied in a case of sexual touching, it is almost inconceivable that B would impliedly consent to being sexually touched by A unless they were already in some form of sexual relationship. Where there is such a relationship, however, there must ordinarily be some element of sexual give and take within it, and although A's mistimed sexual touch might be rejected by B, B would not ordinarily be considered (or consider herself to be) the victim of a sexual assault. It might of course be different if sexual relations between them have broken down or if A persists in touching B despite clear indications that she does not consent at that time or indeed to that kind of touching.[239]

Mens rea

3.160 A must not reasonably believe[240] that B consents to his touch. He must intentionally[241] touch B but he need not intend it to be sexual.[242] In some cases his purpose may help to determine whether it is sexual or not.[243] As in the case of rape, whether a belief is reasonable must be determined with regard to all the circumstances, including any steps A has taken to ascertain whether B consents.[244] A mistaken belief as to consent arising from voluntary intoxication must be disregarded, because this is treated as a matter of basic intent.[245]

Legal and evidential presumptions as to consent etc

3.161 The prosecution may in some cases be assisted by the evidential and conclusive presumptions in SOA 2003, ss 75 and 76 as to the absence of consent and of a reasonable belief in consent,[246] which by SOA 2003, s 3(3) apply to the present offence. Both s 75 and s 76 refer to the defendant having done the 'relevant act'. For the purposes of the present offence, the 'relevant act' is that he intentionally touched the complainant, where the touching was sexual.[247]

---

[237] Consent is discussed at **3.9** et seq.
[238] See *Collins v Wilcock* [1984] 3 All ER 374, at p 378.
[239] See Pill J's observations in *Zafar* (unreported) 1992, 92/2762/W2; see **3.23**.
[240] See **3.112** et seq.
[241] See **2.56–2.60**.
[242] *Heard* [2008] QB 43.
[243] See **2.36** et seq.
[244] SOA 2003, s 3(2).
[245] See **2.74–2.86**.
[246] See **3.38** et seq.
[247] SOA 2003, s 77; see **3.42**.

SEXUAL ASSAULT OF A CHILD UNDER 13

3.162 This offence follows the same pattern as child rape and assault of a child by penetration. What must be proved are the elements of the basic offence (sexual assault, contrary to SOA 2003, s 3), but omitting lack of consent. In place of this, the prosecution must prove (if required) that the complainant was under the age of 13 at the time of the alleged offence.[248] The underlying (but unstated) rationale is that children below this age must be deemed incapable of giving legally valid consent.

3.163 SOA 2003, s 7(1) provides:

'A person commits an offence if—

    (a)   he intentionally touches another person,
    (b)   the touching is sexual, and
    (c)   the other person is under 13.'

3.164 The offence is triable either way and by s 7(2) is punishable on indictment with a maximum of 14 years' imprisonment.[249] The higher maximum punishment under s 7 compared with that under s 3 reflects the view that sexual assault can cause even greater harm where the victim is a child. As to sentencing, see the SGC Definitive Guideline in the Appendix.[250]

Class of offence	3	SOA 2003, s 72 applies	✔
Notification requirements	See **3.165**	SOPO	✔
CJA 2003, Sch 15 applies	✔	Serious specified offence	✔
Review of lenient sentence	✔	Special provisions of CYPA 1933	✔
Detention of young offender for specified period			✔

See **1.48** et seq.

3.165 The notification requirements apply if the offender:[251]

(a)   was aged 18 or over; or

(b)   is or has been sentenced, in respect of the offence, to imprisonment for a term of at least 12 months.

3.166 The elements of s 7(1)(a) and (b) are identical to those of s 3(1)(a) and (b).[252] As with an offence under s 5 or s 6 (rape of a child under 13 or assault by penetration of

---

[248]   See **3.131** and **3.132**.
[249]   Maximum on summary conviction: see **1.43**.
[250]   At pp 5–21 and 31–34.
[251]   SOA 2003, s 80 and Sch 3, para 20.
[252]   See **3.151** and **3.154–3.158**.

such a child), an offence under s 7 is one of strict liability as to age.[253] As with s 5 or s 6, a defence to a charge of aiding, abetting or procuring the commission of an offence under s 7 may in appropriate cases be provided by SOA 2003, s 73.[254] As in the case of the offences under ss 5 and 6, however, there is no exemption for the case of consensual sexual touching, including kissing or fondling over clothes, or where the toucher is also a youngster, perhaps under 13 as well, and no exploitation or abuse is involved. Prosecutors may however be expected to use some discretion in such cases, in accordance with CPS guidance governing such offences.[255]

CAUSING A PERSON TO ENGAGE IN SEXUAL ACTIVITY WITHOUT CONSENT

3.167 Compelling or otherwise causing someone to engage in sexual activity without consent is potentially a very serious infringement of that person's sexual autonomy, and clearly deserves the label of 'criminal'. Where compulsion is used, this can be very frightening, and in any event the sexual behaviour involved can be distressing and leave the victim feeling guilty or ashamed.[256] Where A causes B to engage in non-consensual activity with A himself, there is obviously some overlap with offences under SOA 2003, ss 1, 2 or s 3 and one of these may well provide the more appropriate charge in such a case.

3.168 SOA 2003, s 4(1) provides:

'A person (A) commits an offence if—

    (a)   he intentionally causes another person (B) to engage in an activity,
    (b)   the activity is sexual,
    (c)   B does not consent to engaging in the activity, and
    (d)   A does not reasonably believe that B consents.'

3.169 By s 4(4)), where the activity caused by A involved:

(a)   penetration of B's anus or vagina (whether by a penis, other part of the body or anything else);

(b)   penetration of B's mouth with a person's penis;

(c)   penetration of a person's anus or vagina with a part of B's body or by B with anything else; or

(d)   penetration of a person's mouth with B's penis,

the offence is triable only on indictment and is punishable with a maximum of life imprisonment. It is also (but in those circumstances only) an offence to which CJPOA 1994, s 25 (restriction on grant of bail) applies.[257] In any other case (eg where A causes

---

[253] See **3.127**. As to proof of age, see **3.131** and **3.132**.
[254] See **2.50**.
[255] See **3.127–3.130**, together with accompanying notes.
[256] *PP*, at para 46.
[257] See **3.96**.

B to have sexual contact with an animal, but without penetration of B's vagina or anus), an offence under s 4(1) is triable either way and punishable on indictment with a maximum of 10 years' imprisonment.[258] See the SGC Definitive Guideline in the Appendix.[259]

Class of offence	2 or 3[260]	SOA 2003, s 72 applies	✔[261]
Notification requirements	✔	SOPO	✔
CJA 2003, Sch 15 applies	✔	Serious specified offence	✔
Review of lenient sentence	✔	Special provisions of CYPA 1933	✔
Detention of young offender for specified period			✔[262]

See **1.48** et seq.

3.170 It is clear that two separate offences are created by s 4, each carrying different penalties: causing B to engage in penetrative sexual activity; and causing B to engage in 'non-penetrative' sexual activity. As the House of Lords ruled in *Courtie*,[263] if a different maximum punishment can be imposed if a particular factual ingredient can be established than if it is not, two or more distinct offences presumptively exist. There is nothing to rebut the presumption. It follows from the fact that there are two separate offences that it is essential for any indictment to specify whether the alleged sexual activity was penetrative or non-penetrative.

3.171 SOA 2003, s 4 covers cases where A forces or otherwise causes B to perform some sexual activity without consent. This may be self-penetration with fingers or objects, self-masturbation or some other 'sexual' activity (such as erotic dancing or striptease). In addition, it covers a case where A causes B to engage without her consent in sexual activity with a third party or an animal (eg to masturbate X or be penetrated by an animal). There was previously no specific offence dealing with such conduct.

3.172 As previously noted, a woman cannot ordinarily commit an offence of rape, although she can be a secondary party to such an offence. One of the purposes of the s 4 offence (according to CPS guidance to prosecutors) 'is to create a female equivalent of the offence of rape, which carries the same level of punishment for what amounts to the same type of offending behaviour'. A more accurate analysis is that s 4(4) enables A to be convicted of such an offence where A forces or tricks B into penetrative sexual acts to which B does not genuinely consent; and it does not matter for this purpose if A is 'merely' the passive or receptive partner in the sexual act.

---

[258] SOA 2003, s 4(5). As to the maximum penalty on summary conviction, see **1.43**.
[259] At pp 5–21 and 35–41.
[260] Class 2 where s 4(4) applies; otherwise Class 3.
[261] But only where the complainant is within the age limit to which s 72 applies: see **2.97**.
[262] But only if the conviction is for an offence under s 4(4).
[263] [1984] AC 463. Where it is uncertain whether a particular factual ingredient of the offence existed, charges which include allegations of factual ingredients which attract different maximum penalties should be put into separate counts on the indictment to simplify the task of the judge when summing up to the jury and that of the jury in understanding what alternatives are open to it when it retires to deliberate on its verdict: ibid.

3.173 Where A has caused B to engage in sexual activity with a third party (X) in which X penetrated B, it may be more appropriate to charge A with rape (or assault by penetration) if A can be said to have aided, abetted, counselled or procured X's act. If X lacked the mens rea for such an offence, A might still be charged with that offence as a perpetrator on the basis of X's innocent agency, but a charge under s 4(4) may perhaps be more straightforward on such facts.

Causing non-consensual sexual behaviour

3.174 A causes B to engage in sexual activity if B engages in the activity in consequence of A exerting a capacity which he possesses to control or influence B's acts.[264] It is not enough simply to prove that some antecedent event or condition produced by A contributed to the determination of the will of B to engage in the sexual activity, or that in producing that antecedent event or condition A was actuated by desire that B should engage in it.[265] The prosecution must prove that B did not consent to the sexual activity in which A caused him to engage.

3.175 As previously explained, trickery or deception may negate consent just as effectively as force or coercion.[266] In *Devonald*,[267] D deceived V into thinking that D was a young woman who was excited at the thought of watching V masturbate in front of his internet webcam. D was in fact the father of a girl V had recently jilted, and sought to humiliate V by this trick. V did as D asked. The deception practised by D was held to invalidate V's consent.

3.176 Causing requires proof of an act.[268] It cannot suffice that A failed to stop a third party (X) engaging in sexual activity with B without B's consent, even if A owed a legal duty of care in respect of B or had a right of control over X[269] (although in these cases A could be convicted as a secondary party to the offence committed by X if he failed to take reasonable steps to prevent that offence being committed).[270]

Mens rea

3.177 A must intentionally[271] cause B to engage in the relevant sexual activity, and must not reasonably believe[272] that B consents to so doing.[273] As in a case of rape, whether a belief is reasonable must be determined with regard to all the circumstances,

---

[264] Cf *O'Sullivan* v *Truth and Sportsman Ltd* (1957) 96 CLR 220, HCA; approved in *A-G of Hong Kong v Tse Hung-lit* [1986] AC 876.

[265] Ibid.

[266] See **3.52–3.60**.

[267] [2008] EWCA Crim 527; see **3.49**.

[268] *Price v Cromack* [1975] 1 WLR 988. Cf *Chainey* [1914] 1 KB 137 and *Ralphs* (1913) 9 Cr App R 86, where it was held that offences of causing or encouraging sexual intercourse with a girl under 16 for whom D was responsible could be committed by deliberately failing to prevent it. The court in *Chainey* based this view on a provision which deemed D to have caused or encouraged the intercourse if he knowingly allowed the girl to consort with someone of known immoral character; but the court in *Ralphs* based its view on the word 'encouragement' rather than 'cause', as did the court in *Drury* (1974) 60 Cr App R 195, in relation to a charge under SOA 1956, s 28.

[269] *Price v Cromack*, ibid.

[270] Ibid.

[271] See **2.56–2.60**.

[272] See **2.64** et seq.

[273] SOA 2003, s 4(1)(d).

including any steps A has taken to ascertain whether B consents.[274] What was said about absence of reasonable belief in the context of rape[275] is equally relevant here.[276]

Legal and evidential presumptions as to consent, etc

3.178 The prosecution may be assisted by the evidential and conclusive presumptions in SOA 2003, ss 75 and 76 as to the absence of consent or of a reasonable belief in consent. For the purposes of the present offence, the 'relevant act' (as defined in s 77) is that A intentionally caused B to engage in an activity, where the activity was sexual. In other words, the 'relevant act' must be A's act, not B's.[277]

CAUSING OR INCITING A CHILD UNDER 13 TO ENGAGE IN SEXUAL ACTIVITY

3.179 As with the offences of rape, assault by penetration and sexual assault, separate offences of causing engagement in sexual activity are provided by SOA 2003, s 8 in respect of victims under 13, in which (for the same reasons) absence of consent is not an element. Section 8, however, covers a wider range of conduct than SOA 2003, s 4 because it also makes it an offence to incite a child aged under 13 to engage in sexual activity.

3.180 SOA 2003, s 8(1) provides:

'A person commits an offence if—

    (a)   he intentionally causes or incites another person (B) to engage in an activity,
    (b)   the activity is sexual, and
    (c)   B is under 13.'

3.181 By s 8(2), an offence under s 8(1) is triable only on indictment (and carries a maximum penalty of life imprisonment) if the activity caused or incited involved 'penetration' (which has the same definition as in s 4).[278] In other cases, offences under s 8(1) are triable either way and by s 8(3) are punishable with a maximum of 14 years' imprisonment.[279] Offences involving penetration within s 8(2) are also offences to which CJPOA 1994, s 25 (restriction on grant of bail) applies.[280] As to sentencing, see the SGC Definitive Guideline in the Appendix.[281]

Class of offence	2 or 3[282]	SOA 2003, s 72 applies	✔
Notification requirements	✔	SOPO	✔

---

[274] SOA 2003, s 4(2).
[275] At **3.111** et seq.
[276] See also **2.67**.
[277] See *Devonald* (para **3.49**).
[278] See **3.169**.
[279] As to the maximum penalty on summary conviction, see **1.43**.
[280] See **3.96**.
[281] At pp 5–21 and 35–41.
[282] Class 2 where s 8(2) applies; otherwise Class 3.

CJA 2003, Sch 15 applies	✔	Serious specified offence	✔
Review of lenient sentence	✔	Special provisions of CYPA 1933	✔
Detention of young offender for specified period			✔

See **1.48** et seq.

3.182 In the light of the *Courtie* principle[283] and of the fact that 'causing' and 'inciting' would seem to involve separate offences,[284] there are at least two, and arguably four, potential offences under s 8, namely:

- causing a child under 13 to engage in penetrative sexual activity (in one of the ways defined in s 8(2));

- inciting a child under 13 to engage in such activity;

- causing a child under 13 to engage in 'non-penetrative' sexual activity; and

- inciting a child to engage in such activity.

3.183 In drafting charges and indictments, prosecutors must at least specify whether the alleged sexual activity involved penetration or not.[285] Support for this view that causing and inciting involve different offences can be found in *Walker*,[286] in which the trial judge and Court of Appeal each criticised an indictment in which one count alleged a single offence of 'causing or inciting' a child to engage in sexual activity; but in *Walker* it was at least clear from the particulars of offence that the true basis of the count was incitement, and the conviction was upheld.[287]

3.184 With the exception of the element of incitement, the elements of s 8(1)(a) and (b) are similar to those already examined in the context of the s 4 offence.[288] In contrast to the offences under ss 5–7, however, the defence to charges of aiding, abetting or procuring provided by SOA 2003, s 73 is not available in respect of s 8. This means that if A discovers that B, aged 12, has been having sexual intercourse with her boyfriend, C,

---

[283] See **3.170**.

[284] A provision may create two (or more) offences or it may create one offence with alternative ways of committing it. An examination of the case-law (which is not always easy to reconcile) and the structure of the present provision (and other offences of causing or inciting in SOA 2003) seems to indicate that there are separate offences of causing and of inciting because the section refers to two separate types of conduct as constituting an offence (see *Surrey Justices ex parte Witherick* [1932] 1 KB 450; *Naismith* [1961] 1 WLR 952; *Mallon v Allon* [1964] 1 QB 385; *Bolton Justices ex parte Khan* [1999] Crim LR 912) as opposed to referring to various ways of committing one specified piece of conduct (*Bale v Rosier* [1977] 2 All ER 160; *Nicklin* [1977] 1 WLR 403).

[285] This follows from *Courtie* and is acknowledged in CPS guidance to prosecutors.

[286] [2006] EWCA Crim 1907, at [23].

[287] The safer course is to include separate counts for causing the relevant activity and for inciting it if it is wished to allege both (e g because there is doubt as to which can be proved). An indictment bad for duplicity can be amended by the court in accordance with the Indictments Act 1915, s 5. Likewise, the safer course in summary proceedings is to lay separate informations for causing and for inciting. After a summary trial has commenced for one of the either-way offences of 'causing or inciting' under SOA 2003, the information can be amended by the court in accordance with Criminal Procedure Rules, SI 2005/384, r 7.3; and see also Magistrates' Courts Act 1980, s 123.

[288] See **3.167** et seq.

and advises her to engage in oral or non-penetrative sex with C instead, it is no defence that A was seeking only to safeguard B's health by diverting her from a potentially more dangerous form of sexual activity. A is still guilty of inciting B to engage in oral or non-penetrative sex with C.

Incitement: actus reus

3.185 Incitement requires an element of persuasion or encouragement,[289] which may involve a bribe,[290] dare, threat or other form of pressure[291] and may be implied or expressed.[292] The mere expression of a desire that someone should do the act in question may not in itself suffice. The sexual activity incited may be with A himself (as where A incites B to masturbate him) or with a third party (as where A incites B to have sexual intercourse with C) or A may simply incite B to masturbate or expose himself in a sexual way.

3.186 In cases of incitement or solicitation at common law, or under OAPA 1861, s 4, there can be no complete offence unless the incitement or solicitation came to the notice of the person or persons to whom it was addressed, although it need not have been effective in persuading the recipient to act.[293] The same rule has been held to apply to the SOA 2003, s 8 offence. In *Jones*, the Court of Appeal held that:[294]

> 'The offence ... can be committed by a person who, with the requisite intention, makes a statement which in specific terms directly incites a child or children under the age of 13 to engage in sexual activity. It matters not that it is not possible to identify any specific or identifiable person to whom the statement is addressed.'

3.187 It is, however, necessary for the incitement to be communicated to at least one such child. If this cannot be proved (as in *Jones*, where J sent text messages to a police officer who had purported to be such a child), an appropriate charge may be one of attempting to commit such an offence.[295]

Incitement: mens rea

3.188 Like the other offences involving children under the age of 13, an offence under SOA 2003, s 8 is one of strict liability as to age,[296] but intention is expressly required as to the act of incitement. One might perhaps have supposed from this that A must act with the intention of persuading B to do whatever it was that A suggests. A mere joke or put-down could not on that basis constitute an offence of incitement. In *Walker*, however, it was held that no such intent is required:[297]

> 'That encouragement to engage in sexual activity by the defendant must be intentional, that is to say deliberate, or done on purpose; and the defendant must know what he is saying or doing ... [but] it is not a necessary ingredient of the offence of intentional incitement to

---

[289] *Hendricksen* [1977] Crim LR 356; *Marlow* [1997] Crim LR 897.
[290] *Wade v Broughton* (1814) 3 V & B 172.
[291] *Race Relations Board v Applin* [1973] QB 815; *Invicta Plastics Ltd v Clare* [1976] RTR 251.
[292] *Invicta Plastics Ltd v Clare*, ibid.
[293] *Krause* (1902) 18 TLR 238, at p 243.
[294] [2007] EWCA Crim 1118, at [18].
[295] See also *Walker* [2006] EWCA Crim 1907, at [37]. Cf *Ransford* (1874) 13 Cox CC 9.
[296] *G* [2006] 2 Cr App R 270; *A-G's References (Nos 74 and 83 of 2007)* [2007] EWCA Crim 2550; see **3.127**. As to proof of age, see **3.131** and **3.132**.
[297] [2006] EWCA Crim 1907, at [30] and [31].

engage in sexual activity, and the prosecution does not have to prove, that the defendant intended that the particular sexual activity should take place. That is because the essence of the offence is the incitement of the person under 13 to engage in sexual activity.'

3.189 In *Walker* itself, W was guilty of inciting a girl to 'show him her fanny' regardless of whether he ever had the slightest intention of actually persuading her to show it to him. It was enough that he intended her to hear (and presumably understand) what he said. This, with respect, is a surprising interpretation of the concept of incitement. Is it even necessary for A to intend that B should take his suggestion seriously, rather than treat it as an insult or joke? This is not made clear in *Walker*. On the other hand, if something is quite obviously only a sexually explicit insult (eg 'go fuck yourselves') it surely cannot properly be described as incitement to anything.

3.190 As in the case of the offences under SOA 2003, ss 5–7, s 8 creates no exceptions or defences to cover cases where A and B are of similar ages, but (particularly where no exploitation or abuse is involved) prosecutors are expected to use some discretion in such cases, in accordance with CPS guidance.[298] Where in contrast A is an adult, there will ordinarily be a strong public interest in prosecuting.

---

[298] See **3.127** and **3.130**, together with accompanying notes.

Chapter 4

CHILD SEX OFFENCES

4.1   Before the Sexual Offences Act (SOA) 2003, the major sexual offences relating specifically to children under the age of legal consent were, with one exception, provided by SOA 1956:

- s 5 (sexual intercourse by a man (or boy) with a girl under 13);

- s 6 (sexual intercourse by a man (or boy) with a girl under 16);

- s 12 (buggery with a boy or girl under 16);

- s 13 (gross indecency by a man (or boy) with a boy under 16);

- ss 14 and 15 (indecent assault by a person of either sex on a girl or boy respectively; a girl or boy under 16 could not in law give a valid consent which would prevent an act being an assault); and

- s 28 (causing or encouraging unlawful sexual intercourse with, or an indecent assault on, a girl under 16 by a person with parental responsibility for, or in care of, her).

In addition, the Indecency with Children Act (ICA) 1960 made it an offence to commit an act of gross indecency with or towards a child under 16, or to incite a child to such an act.

4.2   The offences above had evolved over time in a piecemeal fashion, largely to protect girls and boys from older men. Although the coverage given by these offences was comprehensive, the law was made more complicated and incoherent than necessary by having offences which distinguished between boy and girl victims and between men and women as perpetrators, and between types of sexual activity. This complication was enhanced by the facts that the necessary mens rea differed as between the various offences, and that in the case of the offences under SOA 1956, s 6 or s 13 there was a one-year time-limit on prosecutions.[1] In addition, the level of penalties lacked consistency. For example, an offence of unlawful intercourse with a girl under 16 carried a maximum penalty (2 years' imprisonment) which was one-fifth of that available in respect of a consensual indecent assault (eg 'petting') on that girl and insignificant compared with the life sentence available in respect of buggery of her.

4.3   The Sex Offences Review considered that a reformed law should not only address the above unnecessary complications but should also distinguish between the case where an adult sexually abuses a child and the case where a child engages in sexual activity

---

[1]   SOA 1956, s 37 and Sch 2; SOA 1967, s 7.

with another child. The Review considered activity between an adult and a child to be a serious violation of the law, requiring a strong message to the public that such behaviour was wrong, whereas it believed that sexual conduct between children was less serious.[2]

4.4   The above proposals were largely put into effect by SOA 2003, ss 9–15, which provide the offences of:

- sexual activity with a child (s 9);

- causing or inciting a child to engage in sexual activity (s 10);

- engaging in sexual activity in the presence of a child (s 11);

- causing a child to watch a sexual act (s 12);

- child sex offences committed by children or young persons (s 13);

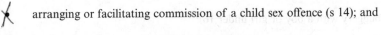 arranging or facilitating commission of a child sex offence (s 14); and

meeting a child following sexual grooming, etc (s 15).

4.5   There is a significant overlap between a number of these offences and the non-consensual offences in SOA 2003, ss 1–4.[3] The latter should ordinarily be prosecuted where there is a lack of consent.[4] Where, however, it is difficult to prove a lack of consent then it may be more appropriate to charge s 9 or use s 9 as an alternative count to a non-consensual offence in the indictment.

4.6   Where B (the complainant) is under 13 and A (the defendant) is 18 or over a significant overlap also exists between the offences under ss 9 and 10 and those under ss 5–8;[5] if A is under 18 there is an overlap in such cases between s 13 and ss 5–8. The effect of this overlap is discussed elsewhere in the book[6] and it will be necessary for prosecutors to consider carefully the circumstances of the case before deciding which charge is most appropriate.

4.7   There may also be overlap between the offences under ss 9 and 10 and the familial sex offences (SOA 2003, ss 25–26). Where there is sufficient evidence in such circumstances to prove the family relationship, the familial offence should be charged rather than the equivalent child sex offence.[7]

---

2   *Setting the Boundaries: Reforming the Law on Sexual Offences* (Home Office, 2000) (*SB*), at para 3.6.4; Recommendation 19.
3   This overlap has been criticised as legislative overkill and one that potentially creates confusion as to the mens rea requirements: Spencer 'Sexual Offences Act 2003 (2): Child and Family Offences' [2004] Crim LR 347, at p 352.
4   CPS Guidance on Sexual offences and child abuse (*CPS Guidance*) (see **1.56**).
5   See **3.124** et seq.
6   See **3.129**.
7   *CPS Guidance.*

4.8 In respect of the first two offences many of the definitions are shared with the offences relating to non-consensual offences, particularly ss 6–8.[8] The offences under SOA 1956 referred to above and under ICA 1960 were repealed by SOA 2003.[9]

SEXUAL ACTIVITY WITH A CHILD

4.9 SOA 2003, s 9(1) provides:

'A person aged 18 or over (A) commits an offence if—

(a)   he intentionally touches another person (B),

(b)   the touching is sexual, and

(c)   either—

(i)   B is under 16 and A does not reasonably believe that B is 16 or over, or

(ii)   B is under 13.'

Class of offence	3	SOA 2003, s 72 applies	✔
Notification requirements	✔	SOPO[10]	✔
CJA 2003,[11] Sch 15 applies	✔	Serious specified offence	✔
Review of lenient sentence	✔	Special provisions of CYPA 1933[12]	✔
Detention of young offender for specified period			✔

See **1.48** et seq. The exceptions in SOA 2003, s 73 from liability for aiding, abetting or counselling where the defendant acts for 'for the child's protection'[13] apply to this offence. As to proof of age, see **3.131, 3.132**.

4.10 The mode of trial depends on the actions of the defendant. Where the touching involves:

(a)   penetration of B's anus or vagina with a part of A's body or anything else;

(b)   penetration of B's mouth with A's penis;

(c)   penetration of A's anus or vagina with a part of B's body; or

(d)   penetration of A's mouth with B's penis,

---

8   See **3.146** et seq.
9   See **1.5**.
10   Sexual offences prevention order.
11   Criminal Justice Act (CJA) 2003.
12   Children and Young Persons Act (CYPA) 1933.
13   See **2.49** et seq.

then the offence is triable only on indictment and punishable by a maximum sentence of 14 years' imprisonment.[14] In all other cases the offence is triable either way but still punishable, on indictment, to a maximum sentence of 14 years' imprisonment.[15] See the Sentencing Guidelines Council (SGC) Definitive Guideline in the Appendix.[16]

4.11   Because there are two different modes of trial dependent on the alleged facts of the matter, there are two separate offences under the rule in *Courtie*.[17] The first offence is engaging in penetrative sexual activity with a child, and the second is engaging in non-penetrative sexual activity with the child.

4.12   Where it can be proven that B is under 13 at the material time, it may be more appropriate for A to be charged with rape of a child under 13, or assault by penetration of such a child, or sexual assault of such a child, as appropriate, contrary to SOA 2003, ss 5, 6 or s 7 respectively,[18] the first two of which carry a maximum of life imprisonment. However, the fact that the present offence is not limited to cases where B is 13 or over means that if A was prosecuted under s 9 (eg because it was then thought that B was 13 at the material time, and it only transpired at the trial that B was 12), there would be no need to apply to the judge to amend the indictment. Nevertheless, if penetration was involved, the maximum of a life sentence for an offence under s 5 or s 6 might make it desirable to do so.

Actus reus

4.13   A must touch another person, B, aged under 16, and the touching must be sexual.[19] The ambit of s 9 is not as wide as the heading to the section ('Sexual activity with a child') suggests since it is limited to sexual touching and does not include other forms of sexual activity (eg inviting a touching) which are dealt with by SOA 2003, ss 10–12. There is the potential for a particular type of sexual activity to fall 'between the gaps'. As mentioned in **3.154**, 'touching' is defined in SOA 2003, s 79(8): it covers all forms of physical contact, including penetration, and can be committed by touching a person's clothing. Because of the requirement of 'touching' if an under-16-year-old B takes the only active part in sexual activity (so that he or she is not touched by A), as, for example, where B masturbates a supine, but acquiescent, A, A does not commit the present offence, although he would commit the equally serious offence under s 10 if he caused or incited B to engage in the activity. As has been pointed out,[20] if A masturbates over B and emits semen which hits B there could only be a 'touching' by a rather strained interpretation of that term. However, the less serious offence under s 11 would be committed in any event. There is, of course, no requirement that B does not consent. A, aged 18, who has sexual intercourse with his 15-year-old girlfriend, or otherwise sexually touches her, with her consent commits an offence under s 9.

---

[14]   SOA 2003, s 9(2).
[15]   SOA 2003, s 9(3).
[16]   At pp 5–18 and 48–54.
[17]   See **3.170**.
[18]   See *CPS Guidance* and *Guidance on Part 1 of the Sexual Offences Act 2003* (Home Office, 2004) (hereafter *Guidance Pt 1*), at para 49: **1.56**. As to these offences see **3.125**, **3.146** and **3.163**.
[19]   See **2.31–2.48**.
[20]   Stevenson, Davies and Gunn *Blackstone's Guide to the Sexual Offences Act 2003* (OUP, 2004) (hereafter *Blackstone's Guide*), at para 4.3.2.1.

Mens rea

4.14   The requirement for the touching to be intentional[21] means that accidental touching will not be caught by this provision, but it is not necessary for A to have intended to touch sexually. So long as there is an intention to touch the offence will be satisfied if the touching *is* sexual.[22] Where B is under 13 then any belief as to age is irrelevant. Where B is aged 13 or over, or it is not possible for whatever reason to prove B's age, then the prosecution must prove that A did not reasonably believe that B was over 16.[23]

4.15   As to the requirement that A must not reasonably believe that B is 16 or over, see **2.67–2.71**. A does not have an evidential burden in respect of the absence of a reasonable belief[24] that B is under 16. The burden of proof in this respect is on the prosecution ab initio.

4.16   Where B is under 13 at the time of the touching the offence is one of strict liability as to age, like the offences under SOA 2003, ss 5–8, so that not even a reasonable belief that B is aged 16 or over will excuse. The structure of s 9(1)(c) would seem to make it much clearer than the corresponding provision in s 5 (child rape), which has been held to impose strict liability, that the presumption that mens rea (as to age) is required is rebutted in this type of case.

4.17   SOA 2003 does not abolish the common law principle in *Tyrrell*[25] that a girl under 16 is not responsible for aiding or abetting a sexual offence against her, however willing her participation, on the basis that the purpose of the sexual offence is to protect her against exploitation.

No marriage exception

4.18   The repealed offences of unlawful sexual intercourse with a girl under 16 or with a girl under 13 were subject to the defence that the parties were married to each other. The defence ensured that the criminal law did not interfere with the consensual intercourse within marriage. Whilst the original Sexual Offences Bill had proposed to continue this exemption so as to ensure that international obligations were respected as regards valid marriages in other jurisdictions where the age of consent was lower than 16, it was decided at the Report Stage in the House of Commons that this was contrary to one of the principal themes of the Act, the protection of children. Accordingly the exemption was removed and consequently, for example, an 18-year-old husband who gives his 15-year-old wife lawfully married abroad a sexual kiss commits an offence under s 9.

CAUSING OR INCITING A CHILD TO ENGAGE IN SEXUAL ACTIVITY

4.19   SOA 2003, s 10(1) provides:

---

21   See **2.56–2.60**.
22   See **2.31 et seq**.
23   SOA 2003, s 9(1)(c).
24   See **2.67–2.71**.
25   [1894] 1 QB 710.

'A person aged 18 or over (A) commits an offence if—

(a) he intentionally causes or incites another person (B) to engage in an activity,
(b) the activity is sexual, and
(c) either—
    (i)   B is under 16 and A does not reasonably believe that B is 16 or over, or
    (ii) B is under 13.'

Class of offence	3[26]	SOA 2003, s 72 applies	✔
Notification requirements	✔	SOPO	✔
CJA 2003, Sch 15 applies	✔	Serious specified offence	✔
Review of lenient sentence	✔	Special provisions of CYPA 1933	✔
Detention of young offender for specified period			✔

See **1.48** et seq.

4.20 Like an offence under SOA 2003, s 9, an offence under s 10 is, by s 10(2), triable only on indictment if the activity caused or incited involves:

(a) penetration of B's anus or vagina (with a part of the body or anything else);

(b) penetration of B's mouth with a person's penis;

(c) penetration of a person's anus or vagina with a part of B's body or by B with anything else; or

(d) penetration of a person's mouth with B's penis.

4.21 Where s 10(2) applies, the maximum sentence is 14 years' imprisonment. In all other cases, s 10 is triable either way[27] and the maximum punishment on conviction of indictment is also 14 years' imprisonment.[28] See the SGC Definitive Guideline in the Appendix.[29]

4.22 Where a child under 13 has been caused or incited to engage in sexual activity, it is expected that A would be charged with causing or inciting a child under 13 to engage in sexual activity, contrary to SOA 2003, s 8. However, if the offence under s 10 was charged there would be no need to apply to the judge to amend the indictment.

---

[26] According to Archbold *Criminal Pleading, Evidence and Practice* (Sweet & Maxwell, 2008 edn), at para 20.66, it would seem that if ever a case involving a child under 13 and falling within s 10(2) were to be prosecuted (as to which see **4.22**), then it would properly be regarded as a Class 2 offence. Class 2 includes 'causing or inciting a child under 13 to engage in sexual activity, where penetration is involved'.

[27] SOA 2003, s 10(3).

[28] Maximum on summary conviction: see **1.43**.

[29] At pp 5–18 and 48–54.

4.23 In the light of the *Courtie* principle[30] and of the fact that 'causing' and 'inciting' would seem to involve separate offences, there are at least two, and arguably four, offences created by s 10:

• causing a child under 16 to engage in penetrative sexual activity;

• causing a child under 16 to engage in non-penetrative sexual activity;

• inciting a child under 16 to engage in penetrative sexual activity; and

• inciting a child under 16 to engage in non-penetrative sexual activity.[31]

Actus reus

Cause or incite

4.24 SOA 2003, s 10 simply requires A to cause or incite B, aged under 16,[32] to engage in an activity which is sexual. The meaning of these terms have been discussed earlier in this book[33] and that discussion applies equally here. There is no requirement that A and B are spatially close, so the offence would be established, for example, where A and B are talking on an internet chatroom and A asks B to masturbate herself. There is no requirement that A takes an active part in the activity. Whilst the activity could occur with him (e g A could incite B to perform fellatio on him) it could equally involve a third party (e g A could cause or incite B to have sexual intercourse with C, another person under the age of 16) or even involving B performing activity with an animal or corpse. Where a third party is involved the age of that third party is immaterial.

Sexual activity

4.25 'Sexual activity' is a wider phrase than the comparable offence found in ICA 1960, s 1, which required an act of gross indecency. The offence under SOA 2003, s 9 simply requires an activity that is sexual, the latter being defined widely in SOA 2003, s 78.[34] An example of a difference between the two statutes would be causing or inciting a child to strip or expose itself. It is extremely unlikely that this would have amounted to an act of gross indecency under the 1960 Act but is certainly an 'activity' for the purposes of SOA 2003. Where the strip or exposure is sexual (e g A and B are talking on the internet and A asks B to lift her top up and bare her breasts to the webcam) this could amount to an offence under s 10.[35]

Mens rea

4.26 The defendant must intentionally[36] cause or incite the sexual activity. The limited meaning attached to 'intentionally incite' was explained in **3.188–3.189**.

---

[30] See **3.170**.
[31] See also **3.183**.
[32] As to proof of age, see **3.131, 3.132**.
[33] See **2.31–2.48, 3.174, 3.176** and **3.185–3.187**.
[34] See **2.31–2.48**.
[35] It may also lead to an offence contrary to the Protection of Children Act (PoCA) 1978 (indecent photographs of children). These offences are discussed in Chapter 8.
[36] See **2.56–2.60**.

Sexual Offences

4.27 What has been said earlier about mens rea as to the fact that the child is aged 16 or over[37] applies equally to this offence.

ENGAGING IN SEXUAL ACTIVITY IN THE PRESENCE OF A CHILD

4.28 SOA 2003, s 11(1) provides:

'A person aged 18 or over (A) commits an offence if—

(a) he intentionally engages in an activity,

(b) the activity is sexual,

(c) for the purposes of sexual gratification, he engages in it—
  (i) when another person (B) is present or in a place from which A can be observed, and
  (ii) knowing or believing that B is aware, or intending that B should be aware, that is engaging in it, and

(d) either—
  (i) B is under 16 and A does not reasonably believe that B is 16 or over, or
  (ii) B is under 13.'

Class of offence	3	SOA 2003, s 72 applies	✔
Notification requirements	✔	SOPO	✔
CJA 2003, Sch 15 applies	✔	Serious specified offence	✔
Review of lenient sentence	✔	Special provisions of CYPA 1933	✔
Detention of young offender for specified period			✘

See **1.48** et seq.

4.29 The offence under s 11 is triable either way and the maximum punishment on conviction of indictment is 10 years' imprisonment.[38] See the SGC Definitive Guideline in the Appendix.[39]

4.30 Unlike the offences under SOA 2003, ss 9 and 10, the present offence does not have a counterpart in the special provisions in SOA 2003, ss 5–8 relating to under-13-year-olds.

Actus reus

Engaging in sexual activity

4.31 Together with the incitement provisions under s 10, SOA 2003, s 11 covers conduct which would previously have fallen within ICA 1960 as well as conduct which

---

[37] See **4.15** and **4.16**.
[38] SOA 2003, s 11(2). Maximum on summary conviction: see **1.43**.
[39] At pp 5–18 and 43–45.

would not. Although A will normally engage in a sexual activity by *doing* something, it is submitted that A can also do so by acquiescing in sexual[40] activity performed by another, as where A, aged 18, acquiesces in masturbation performed on him by X, aged 15, in the presence of B, also aged 15. In such a case, X would also commit an offence of engaging in sexual activity in the presence of a child but, as B is under 18, it would be the less serious offence under s 13. If acquiescence can constitute 'engaging', could an offence under s 11 be committed if the only child present was the child whose sexual activity is acquiesced in? Such a situation would fall within the literal interpretation of the words of s 11(1). To the extent that the above situations do not fall within s 11, there would be a gap in the law where A has not incited or caused B to act as B did.

4.32   It is important to recognise that 'activity' is not restricted to touching and accordingly it would be perfectly possible, for example, for stripping to be included. So far most of the reported cases involving s 11 have involved a person masturbating in front of a child.[41] Prior to SOA 2003 this activity could be charged under ICA 1960, s 1 but only where it could be proved that the masturbation constituted an act *towards* a child (as where it was done to derive sexual gratification from being watched by the child). Where this could not be shown, for example, where it was simply in the presence of a child, it was necessary, in appropriate circumstances, to rely on the common law offence of outraging public decency,[42] which was not a sexual offence for the purpose of either the notification requirements[43] or for a sex offender order.[44] Outraging public decency also does not differentiate between adult and child victims, something that s 11 obviously does. The Government was keen to recognise that a person masturbating in front of anyone (but particularly a child) can cause significant harm and should not be dismissed as a trivial offence or the equivalent of exposure.[45]

Engaging in presence of B or in place where A can be observed

4.33   Whilst masturbating in front of children has occurred for many years, technology has permitted new ways for this behaviour to occur. The growth in the use of webcams to facilitate online communication is significant, but such growth also brings new dangers. A person may now masturbate in front of a webcam, 'broadcasting' this behaviour to the viewer who is logged on. It would appear that this behaviour can be covered by SOA 2003, s 11 since the requirement is for A to be '*in a place from which A can be observed*'[46] and 'observed' is defined in the statute as including looking at an image.[47] 'Image' is defined as including a moving image and thus a live 'webcast' must be included within the section, meaning that s 11 applies where A performs an act in front of a webcam knowing, believing or intending that B will see the image. There is undoubtedly an overlap between these circumstances and the offence of causing a child to watch a sexual act,[48] but they are distinct and the overlap will be expanded upon below.[49]

---

40   See **2.31–2.48**.
41   For example, *Brown* [2006] EWCA Crim 1560; *Jones* [2006] EWCA Crim 3109; and *WH* [2005] EWCA Crim 1917.
42   See, for example, *Pedley* (unreported) 2000.
43   Ie those under the Sex Offenders Act 1997; see **17.2**.
44   See **18.30, 18.31** and **18.33**. But see **13.87**, n 101.
45   *SB*, at para 8.2.3.
46   SOA 2003, s 11(1)(c)(i).
47   SOA 2003, s 79(7).
48   SOA 2003, s 12 and see **4.38** et seq.
49   See **4.42**.

4.34 It will be noted that s 11 does not require a person who is in a place from which A can be observed actually to observe A engaging in the sexual activity. It is submitted that B must be in the place from which A can be observed at the time that A engaged in the sexual activity. Provided that B is 'present' the offence would also be committed where, for example, B is somewhere where he cannot observe what A is doing but is aware from what he hears that A is having sexual intercourse with C (or because A describes to B, whom he has locked in a cupboard, what he is doing as he masturbates himself). This type of case does raise questions about the meaning of 'present'. It is submitted that B need not be in the same room as A or close to A, but he must be in earshot. If he can only hear A's activity (or about it) because of the use of sound amplification used by A, B could not be said to be 'present'. It remains to be decided whether B would be present if he could have heard (without some amplification) but did not actually do so.

Mens rea

4.35 A must intentionally[50] engage in the sexual activity. A must believe or intend B to observe activity, or know that B is observing him. This means that where A does not have this belief (eg because A mistakenly believes that B is asleep) then the offence will not be satisfied irrespective of the fact that B did in fact observe the activity.

4.36 A's purpose in engaging in the sexual activity in B's presence must be the purpose of obtaining sexual gratification[51] from doing so in B's presence or in a place from which A can be observed. If A, aged 21, has sexual intercourse with his 18-year-old partner in the presence of B, his one-year-old daughter, who is lying awake in her cot alongside them, he may know that the child is aware that he is engaging in the activity (presumably B is not required to understand that the activity is sexual, otherwise the offence could not be committed where B is young) but he would be most unlikely to be engaging in intercourse in B's presence for the purpose of obtaining sexual gratification from being watched. Likewise, if a couple of adults kiss each other in a sexual way in the presence of a 15-year-old whilst they are standing in a bus queue, knowing that the child is aware of what they are doing, it would be unlikely that they would be engaging in the kiss to get sexual gratification from being watched. SOA 2003, s 11 does not require that A's purpose of engaging in the sexual activity should be solely that of deriving sexual gratification from doing so in B's presence, etc. Thus, it would not excuse A that he *also* engaged in the sexual activity for the purpose of deriving sexual gratification from the activity itself. The present requirement may make the offence difficult to prove in some cases.[52]

4.37 As in the case of offences under SOA 2003, ss 9 and 10, it is clear that the offence is one of strict liability as to B's age if B was under 13 at the material time; otherwise (ie when B is aged 13–15), it is up to the prosecution to prove that A does not reasonably believe[53] that B is under 16.

---

[50] See **2.56–2.60**.
[51] SOA 2003, s 78 (see **2.32**) does not apply to 'sexual gratification' (as that section refers to activities and not motivation). For the appropriate definition of 'sexual' in the *New Shorter Oxford English Dictionary* see **2.34**.
[52] Wherever 'for the purpose of sexual gratification' appears in SOA 2003, proof of that purpose may involve evidence of circumstances, written material, emails and text messages.
[53] See **2.67–2.71**. As to proof of age, see **3.131, 3.132**.

CAUSING A CHILD TO WATCH A SEXUAL ACT

4.38   SOA 2003, s 12(1) provides:

'A person aged 18 or over (A) commits an offence if—

(a)   for the purpose of obtaining sexual gratification, he intentionally causes another person (B) to watch a third person engaging in an activity, or to look at an image of any person engaging in an activity,
(b)   the activity is sexual, and
(c)   either—
   (i)   B is under 16 and A does not reasonably believe that B is 16 or over, or
   (ii)   B is under 13.'

Class of offence	3	SOA 2003, s 72 applies	✔
Notification requirements	✔	SOPO	✔
CJA 2003, Sch 15 applies	✔	Serious specified offence	✔
Review of lenient sentence	✔	Special provisions of CYPA 1933	✔
Detention of young offender for specified period			✘

See **1.48** et seq.

4.39   The offence under s 12 is triable either way and the maximum punishment on conviction of indictment is 10 years' imprisonment.[54] See the SGC Definitive Guideline in the Appendix.[55]

4.40   Unlike the offences under SOA 2003, ss 9 and 10, the present offence does not have a counterpart in the special provisions in SOA 2003, ss 5–8 relating to under-13-year-olds.

4.41   There is a recognition that sexual imagery and acts, including adult pornography, can be used as part of a grooming process in order to help normalise sexual activity.[56] Where child pornography is shown to a child this was already an offence,[57] but no comparable offence existed in respect of adult pornography. Where the pornography was obscene it was possible that the Obscene Publications Acts could have been used, but these have had a somewhat chequered history in contemporary times and also would not address the behaviour of the offender. The sentence under those Acts is relatively minor and they are not qualifying offences for the purposes of the provisions relating to the management of sex offenders and the sentencing of dangerous sex offenders.[58]

4.42   As a result of the shared genesis, there is an obvious overlap between this offence and that contained in SOA 2003, s 11. The principal distinction is that where the activity

---

54   SOA 2003, s 12(2). Maximum on summary conviction: see **1.43**.
55   At pp 5–18, 43 and 46–47.
56   Lord Falconer of Thoroton, HL Deb, vol 646, col 1205.
57   PoCA 1978, s 1: see **8.41**.
58   Now to be found in SOA 2003, Pt 2 and CJA 2003, Pt 12.

is being watched then it must involve a third party and not A.[59] The rationale for this is obvious since where A is involved the offence under s 11 is likely to be committed. The requirement is for A to cause the child to watch the sexual activity and this could occur, for example, through A bringing B to a room where C and D are having sexual intercourse, or where C is masturbating.

Actus reus

Watching or looking

4.43   The first part of SOA 2003, s 12(1)(a) is limited to causing B, aged under 16,[60] to *watch* a third person engaging in sexual[61] activity: causing a child under 16 simply to *hear* a third party engaging in such activity will not do. If it is A who engages in the sexual activity the relevant offence is that under s 11. The third party who engages in such activity, seen or heard, by the child in real time can, of course, be convicted of an offence under s 11 if he has the necessary mens rea.

4.44   Where A is causing B to look at an image, however, then there is no restriction as to who is portrayed within the image. 'Image' is defined under the Act[62] as:

> '... a moving or still image and includes an image produced by any means and, where the context permits, a three-dimensional image.'

This is a very wide definition and is not restricted to photographs or films, but would include computer-generated images, drawings and cartoons. This can be particularly useful since there is some evidence to suggest that offenders will use drawings or cartoons to influence children to act in a sexual manner.[63]

4.45   The fact that anybody may be portrayed in the image must mean that this includes A.[64] Accordingly if A caused B to watch a video showing A masturbating this could come within s 12. It would not be contrary to s 11 because the syntax of that provision appears to require the child to be present at the time the activity occurred. Accordingly whilst A may be guilty under s 11 if he broadcasts his sexual activity over a webcam, it would not apply where he recorded his activity and then emailed it to B.

4.46   The second difference between ss 11 and 12 is that the child must actually see the activity. It was noted that s 11 implies that a child must simply be *aware* of the sexual activity and it need not necessarily occur in the sight of the child.[65] Quite clearly s 12 requires the child to actually see the sexual activity and accordingly if the child merely hears the activity (eg the child is sent an audio file which portrays sexual activity) then the offence would not apply.

---

59   SOA 2003, s 12(1)(a).
60   As to proof of age, see **3.131, 3.132**.
61   See **2.31–2.48**.
62   SOA 2003, s 79(4).
63   Taylor and Quayle *Child Pornography: An Internet Crime* (Routledge, 2003), at p 195.
64   Unlike the position where the activity is merely being watched: see **4.42**.
65   See **4.34**.

Causing

4.47   The offender must *cause* the child to watch the sexual act or image. 'Cause' is discussed elsewhere[66] but it will be remembered that it means that the offender must do something which causes the child to watch the act. During the passage of the Bill through Parliament there was an attempt to broaden the offence to include situations where A 'allows' B to watch a sexual act.[67] An example of this situation would be where A brings B back to his house and there are numerous pornographic videos on display. B plays the video and A lets him do so. The Government argued that this would capture possible innocent behaviour, for example, where a parent shows an '18'-rated video to a 15-year-old but Rook and Ward point out that this misses the point that s 12 only applies where it is for the purposes of sexual gratification.[68] However, the absence of this term means that someone who allows (ie fails to stop) a child watching a pornographic video or other sexual activity does not commit the present offence, even if that failure to act is for the purpose of deriving sexual gratification.

Mens rea

4.48   A must intentionally[69] cause B to watch the activity or image. In addition, A must intentionally cause the watching or inciting for the purpose of obtaining sexual gratification. SOA 2003 does not require sexual gratification to be the defendant's sole purpose in acting as he has. A person who acts only for a purpose other than sexual gratification (eg for the purpose of gain), does not commit an offence under s 12. Thus, if A, a shopkeeper, sells B a pornographic video and B then watches it, A could not be convicted under s 12, even if it could be proved that he intentionally caused B to watch it. A fortiori, a schoolteacher who showed a video of a couple having sexual intercourse to a sex education class would not commit the offence if he showed it solely for educational purposes. On the other hand, if the schoolteacher also acted for the purpose of obtaining sexual gratification he would commit the offence. In *Abdullahi*[70] the Court of Appeal confirmed that sexual gratification did not have be derived at the time of the showing; it would be sufficient for the offence if he shows the video as part of a longer-term 'grooming' process or to 'put the child in the mood' for sexual activity. The Court accepted that this interpretation means there is overlap between ss 12 and 14, something expanded on below.

4.49   As in the case of offences under SOA 2003, ss 9–11, it is clear that the offence is one of strict liability as to B's age if B was under 13 at the material time; otherwise (ie when B is aged 13–15), it is up to the prosecution to prove that A does not reasonably believe[71] that B is under 16.

CHILD SEXUAL OFFENCES COMMITTED BY CHILDREN OR YOUNG PERSONS

4.50   Perhaps one of the most controversial offences contained in SOA 2003 is that set out in s 13(1):

---

[66]   See **3.174** and **3.176**.
[67]   HL Deb, vol 646, col 1208.
[68]   *Sexual Offences Law and Practice* (Sweet & Maxwell, 3rd edn, 2004), at para 4.73.
[69]   See **2.57** et seq.
[70]   [2007] 1 Cr App R 206.
[71]   See **2.67–2.71**.

'A person under 18 commits an offence if he does anything which would be an offence under any of sections 9 to 12 if he were aged 18.'

Class of offence	3	SOA 2003, s 72 applies	✔
Notification requirements	See text	SOPO	✔
CJA 2003, Sch 15 applies	✔	Serious specified offence	✘[72]
Review of lenient sentence	✘	Special provisions of CYPA 1933	✔
Detention of young offender for specified period			✘

See **1.48** et seq.

4.51 The exceptions under SOA 2003, s 73 from liability for aiding, abetting or counselling where the defendant acts 'for the child's protection' apply to an offence under s 13 if what is done would be an offence under s 9 if the offender was 18 or over. The notification requirements in SOA 2003, Pt 2 apply to an offender in respect of the above offence only if a sentence of imprisonment for at least 12 months is or has been imposed.[73]

4.52 The offence under s 13 is triable either way and the maximum punishment on conviction of indictment is 5 years' imprisonment.[74] See the SGC Definitive Guideline in the Appendix.[75]

4.53 As we noted in **2.28**, s 13 recognises the need to treat youngsters differently where they are involved together in sex cases, but as we explained in Chapter 2 it does not go far enough where that involvement is consensual because the blanket prohibition on sexual activity between youngsters criminalises it.[76] Section 13 not only criminalises sexual experimentation but it is also capable of criminalising other aspects of teenage development. For example, the offence of inciting sexual activity is technically capable of criminalising much schoolyard banter.[77]

Relevant offence

4.54 The offence under s 13 is committed where any offence under SOA 2003, ss 9–12 inclusive is committed by an offender under the age of 18. Section 13 realistically alters two principal aspects of these offences. The first is that the defendant (A) is now 10 or

---

[72] In *Blythe* (2008) *The Times*, April 18 the Court of Appeal confirmed that an offence under s 13 is not a serious specified offence even though the offence under s 9, 10, 11 or 12 is.

[73] SOA 2003, s 80 and Sch 3, para 22.

[74] SOA 2003, s 13(2). Maximum on summary conviction: see **1.43**.

[75] At pp 5–18 and 133–138.

[76] Something the subject of considerable criticism, not least because research has shown a significant proportion of adolescents engage in sexual contact before the age of 16: see, for example, Spencer 'The Sexual Offences Act 2003 (2): Child and Family Offences' [2004] Crim LR 347, at p 354.

[77] Smith and Hogan *Criminal Law* (Ormerod (ed)) (OUP, 12th edn, 2008) (*Smith & Hogan*), at p 713.

over[78] but under 18, and the second is the maximum sentence. All other definitional aspects of the offences, including the actus reus and mens rea, are to be found within the appropriate sections.

Victim under 13

4.55 The point was made in **4.6** that there is overlap between the offences under SOA 2003, ss 9 and 10 (sexual activity with a child under 16 and causing or inciting such a child to engage in sexual activity) and SOA 2003, ss 5–8 (corresponding conduct in respect of a child under 13). Thus, for example, an offence under s 5 (rape of a child under 13) is also an offence under s 9. This means that if A, aged 14, has sexual intercourse with B, his 12-year-old girlfriend, he would be liable to a maximum of a life sentence if charged and convicted under s 5, but only to a maximum of 5 years' imprisonment if charged and convicted under s 13 with the commission of what would be the offence of sexual activity with a child contrary to s 9 if he were 18 or over.

4.56 The matter has inevitably been raised in the courts and the overlap between s 13 and s 5 has been fully discussed in Chapter 3.[79]

ARRANGING OR FACILITATING THE COMMISSION OF A CHILD SEX OFFENCE

4.57 SOA 2003, s 14(1) provides:

'A person commits an offence if—

(a) he intentionally arranges or facilitates something that he intends to do, intends another person to do, or believes that another person will do, in any part of the world, and

(b) doing it will involve the commission of an offence under any of sections 9 to 13.'

Class of offence	3	SOA 2003, s 72 applies	✔
Notification requirements	See text	SOPO	✔
CJA 2003, Sch 15 applies	✔	Serious specified offence	✔
Review of lenient sentence	✔	Special provisions of CYPA 1933	✔
Detention of young offender for specified period			✔

See **1.48** et seq.

4.58 The notification requirements in SOA 2003, Pt 2 apply to an offender in respect of the above offence but, where the offender is under 18 at the time of sentencing, only

---

[78] The age of criminal responsibility in England and Wales.
[79] See **3.127–3.130**.

if a sentence of imprisonment for at least 12 months is or has been imposed.[80] An offence contrary to s 14 is a 'lifestyle offence' within the Proceeds of Crime Act (PCA) 2002, Sch 2, in respect of which a confiscation order may be made under PCA 2002 or a financial reporting order under the Serious Organised Crime and Police Act 2005, s 76. An offence under s 14 is also a serious offence for the purposes of making a serious crime prevention order under the Serious Crime Act (SCA) 2007, Pt 1.[81]

4.59 An offence under s 14 is triable either way and the maximum punishment on conviction of indictment is 14 years' imprisonment.[82] See the SGC Definitive Guideline in the Appendix.[83] Although the maximum sentence is the same as for the offences under ss 9 and 10, it is more than the maximum for an offence under ss 11, 12 or s 13. Thus, if A, aged 17, arranges to meet his girlfriend B, aged 15, for sexual activity, he is liable to a maximum sentence of 14 years' imprisonment, but if the sexual activity then takes place he is only liable to a maximum sentence of 5 years' in respect of it.

4.60 Section 14 owes its origins to two principal issues of concern. The first was that the law prior to SOA 2003 was not sufficiently rigorous to deter those who sought to procure children for sexual activity, especially where it was on a non-commercial basis. The second issue was that of grooming. There was concern that the then existing law was not sufficient to tackle those who sought to befriend children and undertake preparatory behaviour designed to condition children to allow them to be abused.[84] As discussed already, the issue of grooming is a complicated one and SOA 2003 creates a number of offences that can be used to tackle this behaviour. The previous response to both grooming and procurement required the law to tackle issues that would otherwise be left to inchoate liability or the rules of complicity.

4.61 Procuring children for sexual activity, whilst relatively uncommon, attracted significant public attention in the early 2000s. One of the most notable cases was that of Kenneth Lockley, who approached an internet-based procurement agency that was, in fact, operated covertly by the FBI. His details were passed to the Metropolitan Police, who set up a 'UK' version of the procurement site. A meeting was arranged where Lockley asked for a young pre-pubescent girl to be brought to the meeting so that he could have sex with her. Lockley was arrested but there was confusion as to what he could be charged with. Eventually he was charged with the offence of attempting to incite an undercover police officer to commit the offence under SOA 1956, s 23 (repealed by SOA 2003) of procuring a girl under the age of 21 for sexual intercourse. The substantive element of this offence was the procurement, but it was necessary to use inchoate liability in terms of attempt[85] and incitement.[86] The maximum sentence for this offence was 2 years' imprisonment and the trial judge deprecated the lenient sentence that he was required to pass.

4.62 Like most of that Act, SOA 1956, s 23 applied only to female victims. Eventually the inevitable occurred and the police came into contact with another would-be procurer, only this time he was interested in boys. Victor van de Walle was a Belgian

---

80 SOA 2003, s 80 and Sch 3, para 7.
81 SCA 2007, s 2(2)(a), Sch 1, Pt 1, para 4(2)(a).
82 SOA 2003, s 14(4). Maximum on summary conviction: see **1.43**.
83 At pp 5–18, 48–51 and 66–67.
84 See, for example, Gillespie 'Children, Chatrooms and the Law' [2001] Crim LR 435.
85 Since the operation was impossible: there was never a girl to be procured.
86 Since the offender did not wish to procure the child himself but asked the undercover officer to procure the girl for him.

national who wanted the covert 'agency' to find him a young boy. A similar operation was launched as against Lockley but there was confusion as to what van de Walle could be charged with. Eventually the offence of inciting an undercover police officer to procure a boy under 16 for an act of indecency was used. Here the substantive element was that of an act of indecency, contrary to ICA 1960, s 1, but it was still necessary to use the inchoate offences of incitement and attempt together with the offence of procurement.[87] van de Walle pleaded guilty to the offence, which was somewhat fortunate. There was an argument that this offence was not known to law – the conduct prescribed would appear to be inciting someone to become a secondary party to an offence, something which appears not to be possible.[88] In any event it was decided that the sentence would need to be comparable to that under SOA 1956, s 23 and again controversy existed over the leniency of this penalty.

Actus reus

Arrange or facilitate

4.63   SOA 2003, s 14 appears to create two separate offences: one of arranging and one of facilitating. A person arranges something if he plans it or settles beforehand its details.[89] An 'arrangement' may well involve an agreement with somebody else (who may be an innocent third party) but it will not necessarily do so. It is submitted that an 'arrangement' requires an element of finality. Merely deciding to commit a child sex offence or expressing a willingness to commit it is insufficient. On the other hand, it would seem that there can be an arrangement even though not all the details have been settled. It will be a matter of degree depending on the details to be settled. If, for example, all the details have been settled except the place where the sexual offence is to be committed (e g the defendant may be undecided about whether it should take place inside his car or in the woods to which he intends to drive it) the defendant could be said to have arranged to commit that sexual offence.

4.64   In *R*[90] the Court of Appeal held that s 14 was designed to tackle preparatory conduct, and noted the section did not further define or limit those steps other than by requiring their object to involve the commission of a relevant child sex offence. It stated that:[91]

> 'An arrangement may be made without the agreement or acquiescence of anyone else. A defendant may take steps by way of a plan with the criminal objective identified in the section without involving anyone else and the mere fact that no-one else is involved would not necessarily mean that no arrangement was made.'

The Court of Appeal also held that, although the offence under s 14 covers preparatory conduct, it remains a substantive offence and there is nothing in the Criminal Attempts Act (CAA) 1981 that precluded the application to s 14 of the offence of attempt. In *R*, A was alleged to have asked a prostitute to find a girl of 12 or 13 for sex. On the evidence the prostitute did not say that she would do so, nor did she give A any reason to believe that she would do so. Allowing the prosecution's appeal against a terminating ruling given by the trial judge, the Court of Appeal held that a mere request was capable

---

87   Accessories and Abettors Act 1861, s 8.
88   See *Bodin* [1979] Crim LR 176; and see *Smith & Hogan*, at p 444; but c f Simester and Sullivan *Criminal Law: Theory and Doctrine* (Hart Publishing, 3rd edn, 2007), at p 274.
89   *New Shorter Oxford English Dictionary*.
90   [2007] EWCA Crim 1880.
91   Ibid, at [8].

of amounting to an attempt to commit an offence under s 14, although whether there had actually been a more than merely preparatory act to the commission of such an offence would have to be left to the jury. It did not need to decide whether the act constituted the substantive offence under s 14, but it stated that nothing it had said was meant to indicate that was alleged might not constitute the substantive offence of arranging contrary to s 14.

4.65 The term 'arrangement' may also cover issues relating to grooming, as is illustrated by *Connolly*, a sentencing appeal.[92] Here A met, and communicated with, a 13-year-old daughter of his wife's friend who lived in the same street. He obtained the girl's telephone number and sent increasingly suggestive text messages to her. One was a message which stated that he had obtained a 'blue movie and some alcohol and cigs' and instructed her to switch on and off her bedroom lights if she received the text. A later message was then sent warning her not to come to the house because A's wife was present and had seen the text message. A's conviction of an offence under s 14 was on the basis that he arranged the commission of a child sex offence. Whilst the actual offence whose commission was arranged is not mentioned in the transcript, it would appear, at the very least, to be an arrangement to commission the child to watch a sexual act (the pornographic video).

4.66 A person 'facilitates' something if he makes it easy or easier, promotes it or moves it forward.[93] An example of facilitation would be where A lends C the key to his (A's) flat so that C can have sexual intercourse with an underage boy. In this case, s 14 is not strictly necessary if the sexual offence is actually committed because A would be a secondary party under ordinary principles to the offence committed by C. However, it does demonstrate the extension of criminal liability in respect of this conduct since if the act did not actually take place it is unlikely that a crime would have been committed by A.

Commission of a child sex offence

4.67 It is immaterial for this offence whether it is the defendant who wishes to undertake the sexual act or whether it is a third person who is to commit the child sex offence (ie an offence under SOA 2003, ss 9–13[94]). The inclusion of s 13 is interesting since it leaves open the possibility that the commission involves a juvenile undertaking sexual activity with another minor. An example of a situation which may involve a child commissioning the offence could be that X, aged 16, arranges for Y, a 14-year-old girl, to come to his house where she will have sexual intercourse with Z, her 15-year-old boyfriend, whilst he records the activity unbeknown to Y and Z. If they acted as arranged Y and Z would each commit an offence under s 13. By making the arrangements for the sexual activity to occur, X would be liable for an offence under s 14.

4.68 This offence also deals with the case where the anticipated offence will be committed by A, the arranger or facilitator, himself (as eg where A sends an underage boy the money for the fare to his flat where he intends to have sexual intercourse with him). It should be noted that nothing in SOA 2003, s 14 requires the substantive crime actually to take place: arranging the commission of the offence will suffice. Accordingly,

---

92   [2007] EWCA Crim 1880.
93   *New Shorter Oxford English Dictionary*.
94   SOA 2003, s 14(1)(b).

this could cover situations where, for example, the subsequent crime does not take place because the police, acting on a 'tip-off', arrest A before the boy arrives or the boy fails to arrive. In the latter case, the facts may well not involve a statutory conspiracy or *common law incitement*. Where the intended sexual offence is to be committed by the defendant, offences under s 14 are preparatory offences; the defendant need not have got as far as attempting the sexual offence in order to be convicted under s 14. Thus, where the police set up a 'sting' operation and an offender contacts them believing they are offenders who can procure him a child for sexual abuse, but no real child is actually involved, an attempt at the s 14 offence may be charged.[95]

In any part of the world

4.69 Quite apart from the fact that the offence is subject to the provisions of SOA 2003, s 72,[96] the offence can occur where the offender intends either they or the other person to commission the offence in any part of the world. An example of this could be as follows. A, an adult living in England, has been talking to B, a 15-year-old girl from Belgium, for some time over the internet. A reserves a hotel room in Belgium over the internet. He intends to have sexual intercourse with B in the hotel and tells B where the hotel is and at what time to meet. Clearly A has arranged the commission of a sex offence[97] that he intends to carry out. The arrangements were made in this country (where A was accessing the internet) even though the actual sex offence will take place in Belgium. This will still amount to an offence under SOA 2003, s 14.

Mens rea

4.70 It is necessary that A intentionally[98] arranges, or intentionally facilitates, doing something which will involve an offence under SOA 2003, ss 9–13, and that A either intends to do, intends another person to do, or believes[99] another person will do, that thing anywhere in the world.

Exceptions

4.71 During the passage of the Bill concern was raised over whether the remit of SOA 2003, s 14 may lead to some legitimate facilitation being criminalised. Whilst it may at first sight be difficult to conceive of how facilitating underage sexual activity could be legitimate, the argument is premised on the basis that we know underage sexual activity does occur and the meaning of 'facilitate' is so wide as to potentially include, for example, sex education or the provision of contraceptives.

4.72 Under pressure from the House of Lords the government introduced an exception to SOA 2003, s 14, and it is contained within s 14(2):

'A person does not commit an offence under this section if—

(a) he arranges or facilitates something he believes another person will do, but that he does not intend to do or intend another person to do, and

---

95 *Guidance Pt 1*, at para 80.
96 See **2.89** et seq.
97 Sexual activity with a child: SOA 2003, s 9.
98 See **2.56–2.60**.
99 See **2.61**.

(b)   any offence within subsection (1)(b) would be an offence against a child for whose
       protection he acts.'

In this context, s 14(3) provides:

'... a person acts for the protection of a child if he acts for the purpose of—

(a)   protecting the child from sexually transmitted infection,
(b)   protecting the physical safety of the child,
(c)   preventing the child from becoming pregnant, or
(d)   promoting the child's emotional well-being by the giving of advice,

and not for the purpose of obtaining sexual gratification or for the purpose of causing or
encouraging the activity constituting the offence within subsection (1)(b) or the child's
participation in it.'

4.73   Examples of conduct falling within s 14(3) would be giving an underage boy a
condom (if done for the purpose of protecting the boy against a sexually-transmitted
infection, but not if done to protect the boy against the risk of his 16-year-old girlfriend
becoming pregnant[100]); giving advice (eg by an 'agony aunt', teacher or counsellor) to
an underage child or children about protected sex (if done for the purpose of protection
against sexually-transmitted infection, or, where the advice is given to a girl, pregnancy,
or to promote the child's emotional well-being). These are all examples of 'facilitation'.
Given the mischief of the exceptions, it is perhaps surprising that they extend to those
who 'arrange' for the commission of an offence.

4.74   The list in s 14(3) is exhaustive. The exceptions do not cover arrangers or
facilitators who act for some other reason in the child's best interests: for example, they
do not cover police officers using a child as a decoy to catch a sex offender.

4.75   The reference in s 14(3)(b) to protecting the physical safety of the child is
somewhat obscure. Baroness Scotland of Asthal said at the Third Reading in the House
of Lords[101] that s 14(3)(b) covered physical well-being, but she based this on the
argument that physical well-being includes physical safety (undoubtedly correct);
however, the point is whether the reverse is true (debatable). A case where s 14(3)(b)
would be applicable would be where a sex counsellor, advising a 15-year-old boy who is
in a homosexual relationship with another boy in which he is being anally penetrated,
gives the boy a lubricant to reduce the risk of serious harm to the boy. On the other
hand, if the lubricant was given simply to reduce the pain felt by the boy, this would fall
outside s 14(3)(b).

4.76   The defence was not universally supported, and indeed Baroness Blatch
considered the defence to be 'unnecessary and dangerous'.[102] It could be considered
unnecessary since the criminal law already recognises the doctrine of double effect,
perhaps most famously encapsulated by the House of Lords in *Gillick v West Norfolk
and Wisbech Area Health Authority*.[103] It is difficult to see how the factors contained

---

[100]   Although the prevention of pregnancy is within the exceptions, the 16-year-old girlfriend is not a 'child' for
        these purposes and so the supplier cannot be acting for the protection of a child.
[101]   HL Deb, vol 649, col 703.
[102]   HL Deb, vol 649, col 692.
[103]   [1986] AC 112.

within s 14(3) would not have come within the *Gillick* ruling, but for whatever reason Parliament decided to make the exceptions explicit.

Sexual gratification

4.77   The exceptions do not apply where the purpose of the arranger or facilitator is to obtain sexual gratification.[104] Applying the logic of *Abdullahi*,[105] it is likely that the courts will hold that there need not be a temporal connection between the sexual gratification and the facilitation. Accordingly, where the offender is using the arranging or facilitation as a method of 'normalising' sexual conduct in order that he may later have sexual relations with the child, this may be sufficient to ensure that the exception does not apply. Proving this may be difficult, although the bad character provisions of CJA 2003 may assist.

MEETING A CHILD FOLLOWING SEXUAL GROOMING, ETC

4.78   SOA 2003, s 15(1), as amended by CJIA 2008,[106] provides:

'A person aged 18 or over (A) commits an offence if—

(a)   A has met or communicated with another person (B) on at least two occasions and subsequently—
  (i)   A intentionally meets B,
  (ii)   A travels with the intention of meeting B in any part of the world or arranges to meet B in any part of the world, or
  (iii)   B travels with the intention of meeting A in any part of the world,
(b)   A intends to do anything to or in respect of B, during or after the meeting mentioned in paragraph (a)(i) to (iii) and in any part of the world, which if done will involve the commission by A of a relevant offence,
(c)   B is under 16, and
(d)   A does not reasonably believe that B is 16 or over.'

Class of offence	3	SOA 2003, s 72 applies	✔
Notification requirements	✔	SOPO	✔
CJA 2003, Sch 15 applies	✔	Serious specified offence	✔
Review of lenient sentence	✔	Special provisions of CYPA 1933	✔
Detention of young offender for specified period			✘

See **1.48** et seq.

---

[104]   SOA 2003, s 14(3).
[105]   [2007] 1 Cr App R 206.
[106]   Section 73, Sch 15.

4.79 The offence under s 15 is triable either way and the maximum punishment on conviction of indictment is 10 years' imprisonment.[107] See the SGC Definitive Guideline in the Appendix.[108]

4.80 At the beginning of the millennium there was increasing concern over the use that sex offenders were beginning to make of information and communication technologies in order to facilitate the abuse of children. Much of this attention was directed towards the issue of 'grooming', which can be loosely described as being the position whereby a person seeks to befriend a child and seek control over the child so as to obtain what the offender perceives as 'consent' (but in reality is acquiescence) to sexual relations. Whilst some of the attention was undoubtedly sensationalised, there was legitimate concern as to whether the law was able to adequately tackle such behaviour.[109] However, the offence under s 15 has been slightly misunderstood in that it does *not* seek to criminalise grooming per se, but rather it is designed to tackle the aftermath of grooming.

Elements of the offence

Having met or communicated with a child

4.81 It must be proved that A has either met or communicated with B on at least two prior occasions. The communication can take place by whatever means including, for example, telephone, text messages or within a chatroom. It is perfectly possible for there to be a mixture, ie one communication and one meeting, and it is not necessary that they amount to a 'course of conduct'[110] or that they take place within a timeframe.

4.82 There is no requirement for the communication or meetings to involve a sexual element. Whilst in many cases they will, this need not be the case, particularly where the behaviour occurs offline. For example, A works in a corner shop. B, a 10-year-old girl, frequently comes into the shop on her way home from school. After a few visits A starts to talk to B about who she is, what school she goes to, etc. When she buys some sweets he always puts in a few more as 'a treat'. After a few weeks, A invites B to meet him in the park for a 'kiss and a cuddle'. Assuming the relevant intention can be satisfied[111] then A could still be culpable in this example, something that would not have been possible had there been a requirement for sexualised meetings or communications.

4.83 It should be noted that the initial meeting(s) can take place in any part of the world and that the initial communication(s) can take place to or from or in any part of the world.[112] Accordingly the following examples are within the scope of SOA 2003, s 15:

- A is in England and is talking to B who lives in Amsterdam;

- A is in Switzerland and is talking to B who lives in Manchester; and

---

[107] SOA 2003, s 15(4). Maximum on summary conviction: see **1.43**. Note when the provision was originally introduced the maximum sentence on indictment was 5 years' imprisonment but it was raised to 10 during the passage of the Act as there was concern that it did not adequately reflect the seriousness of the offence.
[108] At pp 5–18 and 82–83.
[109] See Gillespie 'Children, Chatrooms and the Law' [2001] Crim LR 435.
[110] Cf Protection from Harassment Act 1997.
[111] See **4.84–4.90**.
[112] SOA 2003, s 15(2)(a).

- A is in France and is talking to B who lives in Germany.

Meeting, arranging a meeting or travelling to meet

4.84 After the two communications or meetings with B, one of three things must happen:

- A intentionally[113] meets B;

- A travels with the intention of meeting B in any part of the world or arranges to meet B in any part of the world; or

- B travels with the intention of meeting A in any part of the world.

In this context 'intentionally' must mean 'deliberately' meet and accordingly where A and B meet by chance in a shop or cafe then this would not satisfy the criteria. However, where A spots B entering a shop and follows B in then this would, it is submitted, suffice. 'Intention of meeting' would seem to require direct intent.

4.85 Where A is travelling, it is not necessary that any meeting actually takes place so long as A travels with the intention of meeting a child and that some of that travelling is done in England and Wales. Accordingly, it does not matter that B does not eventually attend the meeting. It should also be noted that the travel must be with the intention of meeting B in any part of the world, so if B is in, for example, Germany, A would satisfy this requirement by travelling to Gatwick airport en route to Germany.

4.86 The amendments which came into force on 14 July 2008[114] extend the range of conduct which has to occur after the initial meetings or communications on two occasions. First, it is now enough in the alternative to A travelling to meet B that A 'arranges to meet' B; thus A can now satisfy SOA 2003, s 15(1)(a)(ii) merely by making arrangements to meet B in any part of the world. The meaning of 'arrangement' has been discussed elsewhere,[115] but in this context could presumably include, for example, reserving a hotel room in Paris at a time A knows B is in Paris on a school trip. When A communicates the name of that hotel to B and says 'meet me there at 3pm' it is likely that this would amount to an arrangement.[116] Secondly, the original wording of s 15 did not expressly cover situations where B travels to meet A.[117] Section 15(1)(a)(iii), inserted by CJIA 2008, means that s 15 now also applies to situations where B travels to A. As with the position discussed at **4.85**, it does not matter that A and B do not eventually meet so long as B was travelling with the intention of meeting A.

4.87 B is defined as a person under the age of 16.[118] B must be under 16 not only at the time of the two initial meetings/communications but also at the time of the intentional meeting or travelling with the intention of meeting or arranging to meet. If, for example, B was under 16 when A began talking to her on the internet but became 16

---

[113] See **2.56–2.60**.
[114] CJIA 2008, s 73, Sch 15; Criminal Justice and Immigration Act 2008 (Commencement No 2 and Transitional and Saving Provisions) Order 2008, SI 2008/1586, art 2(1), Sch 1.
[115] See **4.63** et seq.
[116] See the discussion of *R* [2008] EWCA Crim 619 at **4.64**.
[117] Cf the position in Scotland: Protection of Children and Prevention of Sexual Offences (Scotland) Act 2005, s 1(1)(a)(iii).
[118] As to proof of age, see **3.131, 3.132**.

before the subsequent meeting or when A travelled with the intention of meeting B, no offence would be committed. If A still believed B to be aged under 16 then presumably A could be convicted of attempting to commit an offence contrary to s 15.[119] At the time of the intentional meeting or the travelling with intent to meet, A must be 18 or over, but need not have been at the time of the initial meetings or communications.

Intends to commit a relevant offence

4.88   At the time of any of the activity set out in **4.84**, A must intend to do 'anything to, or in respect of B, during or after the meeting and in any part of the world' which will involve the commission of a relevant offence. The definition of 'relevant offence' for England and Wales is:

(a)   an offence within SOA 2003, Pt 1;

(b)   a corresponding offence under Northern Irish law;[120] or

(c)   anything done outside England and Wales or Northern Ireland which is not an offence included in (a) or (b) but would be an offence under SOA 2003, Pt 1 if done in England and Wales.[121]

The requisite intention would seem to be a direct one. Given that the conduct required to be proved, which if it were committed in England and Wales comes within Pt 1 of SOA 2003, does not require proof of anything ostensibly improper, this element of mens rea is of great importance as a limitation on the offence.

4.89   The fact that it suffices that the relevant offence is intended to take place in any part of the world means that A cannot avoid liability by intending to commit a sex crime outside the jurisdiction. An example would be that A and B have been communicating in a chatroom for several weeks. B tells A that she is going to a school camp in France in a fortnight's time. A arranges to meet B at the campsite so that they can have sex. At this stage an offence under SOA 2003, s 15 is committed.

4.90   Obtaining evidence to prove the intent will be crucial. The source of such evidence is likely to be the items that are brought to the meeting (eg condoms, lubrication gel, etc) or the communications between A and B.[122]

Reasonable belief

4.91   A does not commit an offence if he reasonably believes that B was over 16 even where B was under 13.[123] The concept of 'reasonable belief' has been discussed elsewhere[124] and it is for the prosecution to prove that A does not so believe.

---

[119]   CAA 1981, s 1(2) and (3).

[120]   Currently listed in SOA 2003, Sch 3, paras 61–92. This reference to a corresponding offence so listed (ie (b)) will be omitted from s 15 when the Sexual Offences (Northern Ireland Consequential Amendments) Order 2008, SI 2008/1779, art 4, is brought into force.

[121]   SOA 2003, s 15(2)(b). When the Sexual Offences (Northern Ireland Consequential Amendments) Order 2008, SI 20808/1779, art 4, is brought into force, the reference to Northern Ireland will be omitted from (c), as will the reference in (c) to (b).

[122]   See, for example, *Mohammed* [2007] 1 Cr App R (S) 79.

[123]   SOA 2003, s 15(1)(d).

[124]   See **2.67–2.71**.

Chapter 5

ABUSE OF POSITION OF TRUST

5.1   Sexual activity with a child is inappropriate within relationships of trust, even if the child is 16 or 17 (and therefore over the age of consent to sexual activity). This is not simply because the power differentials make the child vulnerable to abusive or sexually predatory sexual behaviour by someone in a position of trust in respect of the child, but also because sexual activity within such a relationship is incompatible with the ethical and moral responsibilities of those in a position of trust.

5.2   As a result of publicity given in the 1990s to sexual abuse of children by those entrusted with their care, various developments occurred to prevent inappropriate people working with children.[1] In addition, it was made an offence by the Sexual Offences (Amendment) Act (SO(A)A) 2000, s 3 for someone of 18 or over to have sexual intercourse with a person under 18, or to engage in any other sexual activity with, or directed towards, such a person if he or she was in a position of trust in relation to that person. Section 3 was passed following the recommendations of an inter-departmental working group which had been asked, inter alia, to propose measures to protect young people vulnerable to abuse by those in positions of trust.[2] *Protecting the Public* proposed the re-enactment of s 3 of the 2000 Act but with an expanded list of those in a position of trust.[3] Section 3 and an ancillary section, s 4, were repealed by the Sexual Offences Act (SOA 2003),[4] ss 16–19 of which go further than proposed in *Protecting the Public* by providing five offences to deal with abuse of a position of trust involving sexual activity with a child, and by extending even further the list of positions of trust. These provisions are another example of the Act's theme of preventing exploitation.

5.3   Like SO(A)A 2000, s 3, SOA 2003, ss 16–19 are principally designed to protect 16- and 17-year-olds who are vulnerable to sexual abuse and exploitation by particular classes of people in a position of trust in relation to them. Younger children are protected by the offences referred to in Chapter 3 (under-13-year-olds) and Chapter 4 (under-16-year-olds), which carry significantly higher penalties to reflect the fact that the child is below the age of consent.

THE OFFENCES

5.4   The offences of abuse of position of trust under SOA 2003, ss 16–19 are:

*   sexual activity with a child;

---

[1]   See Chapter 16.
[2]   See *Report of the Interdepartmental Working Group on Preventing Unsuitable People from Working with Children and Abuse of Trust* (Home Office, 1998).
[3]   *Protecting the Public: Strengthening Protection Against Sex Offenders and Reforming the Law on Sexual Offences*, Cm 5668 (2002) (*PP*), at para 60.
[4]   See **1.5**. The repeal does not extend to Scotland.

- causing a child to engage in sexual activity;

- inciting a child to engage in sexual activity;

- sexual activity in the presence of a child; and

- causing a child to watch a sexual act.

The prohibited behaviour in each of these somewhat prolix and repetitive sections is identical to that prohibited by the child sex offences in SOA 2003, ss 9–12,[5] except that the defendant must be in a position of trust, and the child may be 16 or 17. As to the identical elements, see Chapter 4. It is not necessary to prove that the defendant abused or exploited the position of trust. It is therefore irrelevant to liability that the defendant was seduced by a sexually experienced 17-year-old who took advantage of the defendant's sexual immaturity.[6] In comparison, the French Penal Code, Arts 222–33 deals with the type of behaviour in issue by an offence of sexual harassment, which includes abusive pressure brought to bear by a teacher or hierarchical superior.[7] Any age limit is open to the objection that it is arbitrary, but any limit lower than 18 would be incompatible with the requirements of the EU Council Framework Decision of 22 December 2003[8] on combating the sexual exploitation of children and child pornography, which requires member states to provide for the punishment of various forms of intentional sexual exploitation of children under 18, including that where abuse is made of a recognised position of trust or authority or influence over a child. The offences under ss 16–19 are triable either way and punishable with a maximum of 5 years' imprisonment on conviction on indictment.[9] No distinction is drawn in any of the offences between penetrative and non-penetrative activity. See the Sentencing Guidelines Council (SGC) Definitive Guideline,[10] in the Appendix.

Class of offence	3	SOA 2003, s 72 applies	✔[11]
Notification requirements	See text	SOPO[12]	✔
CJA 2003,[13] Sch 15 applies	✔	Serious specified offence	✘
Review of lenient sentence	✘	Special provisions of CYPA 1933[14]	✔
Detention of young offender for specified period			✘

See **1.48** et seq.

---

5   Chapter 4.
6   It would, however, be relevant to sentence as a mitigating factor: see the SGC Definitive Guideline in the Appendix.
7   Spencer 'Child and Family Offences' [2004] Crim LR 347, at p 356.
8   2004/68/JHA, Art 2 (22 December 2003).
9   SOA 2003, ss 16(5), 17(5), 18(5) and 19(5); maximum on summary conviction: see **1.43**.
10   At pp 5–18, 49–51 and 60–65.
11   See **2.97**.
12   Sexual offences prevention order.
13   Criminal Justice Act (CJA) 2003.
14   Children and Young Persons Act (CYPA) 1933.

5.5 The notification requirements under SOA 2003, Pt 2 apply to these offences if the offender is or has been sentenced to imprisonment, detained in a hospital or made the subject of a community sentence of at least 12 months.[15]

5.6 Where lack of consent can be proved, an offence under SOA 2003, ss 1–4 should be charged where the child is 16 or 17. Notwithstanding that ss 16–19 apply to under-16s where the child (B) is under 16, prosecutors should charge an offence(s) under the child sex offences (ss 9–12), or the under-13s offences (ss 5–8), if appropriate. It may be appropriate to charge an abuse of trust offence where B is under 16 when it is likely that the person in a position of trust reasonably believed that the child was 16 or over, but it is less probable that he reasonably believed the child to be 18 or over (and therefore lacked the requisite mens rea).[16]

5.7 The offences share a number of common elements relating to mens rea and exemptions. These will be dealt with[17] after the discrete requirements of each offence have been set out.

Abuse of position of trust: sexual activity with a child

5.8 This offence is provided by SOA 2003, s 16. Its discrete elements are set out by s 16(1) as follows:

'A person aged 18 or over (A) commits an offence if—

> (a) he intentionally touches another person (B),
> (b) the touching is sexual,
> (c) A is in a position of trust in relation to B, ... and
> (e) ... B is under 18 ...'

B's consent is, of course, irrelevant, as it is in the case of the offences under ss 17–19. For exceptions from liability for aiding, abetting or counselling this offence where the defendant acts 'for the child's protection', see s 73 (dealt with in **2.49** et seq).

Abuse of position of trust: causing or inciting a child to engage in sexual activity

5.9 SOA 2003, s 17 deals with a person in a position of trust who causes or incites a child under 18 to engage in sexual activity with him- or herself (ie the child), such as masturbation, or with a third party (who need not be in a position of trust with the child), or with the person in a position of trust. If, in the last case, the child actually engages in a sexual activity, a charge under s 16 would be more appropriate.

5.10 The discrete elements are set out by s 17(1) as follows:

'A person aged 18 or over (A) commits an offence if—

> (a) he intentionally causes or incites another person (B) to engage in an activity,
> (b) the activity is sexual,

---

[15]   SOA 2003, s 80 and Sch 3, para 25.
[16]   CPS Guidance on Sexual offences and child abuse (see **1.56**).
[17]   See **5.23** et seq.

> (c)   A is in a position of trust in relation to B, ... and
> (e)   ... B is under 18.'

As in the case of other offences under the Act of causing or inciting under-age sexual activity, there appear to be two offences, one of causing and one of inciting, under s 17.[18]

Abuse of position of trust: sexual activity in the presence of a child

5.11   SOA 2003, s 18 deals with this. The typical example would be the person who masturbates in front of a child in respect of whom he is in a position of trust. Section 18(1) provides:

> 'A person aged 18 or over (A) commits an offence if—
>
> (a)   he intentionally engages in an activity,
> (b)   the activity is sexual,
> (c)   for the purpose of obtaining sexual gratification, he engages in it—
>   (i)   when another person (B) is present or is in a place from which A can be observed, and
>   (ii)   knowing or believing that B is aware, or intending that B should be aware, that he is engaging in it,
> (d)   A is in a position of trust in relation to B, ... and
> (f)   ... B is under 18 ...'

Abuse of position of trust: causing a child to watch a sexual act

5.12   This offence catches the person (A) who causes the child to watch a sexual activity which is being engaged in by a third party and not by A, or to look at an image (eg a photograph) of anyone (including A) engaging in a sexual activity. The discrete elements which must be proved by the prosecution are provided by SOA 2003, s 19, which provides:

> 'A person aged 18 or over (A) commits an offence if—
>
> (a)   for the purpose of obtaining sexual gratification, he intentionally causes another person (B) to watch a third person engaging in an activity, or to look at an image of any person engaging in an activity,
> (b)   the activity is sexual,
> (c)   A is in a position of trust in relation to B, ... and
> (e)   ... B is under 18 ...'

POSITION OF TRUST

5.13   SOA 2003, s 21(1) provides that, for the purposes of the above offences, a person (A) is in a position of trust in relation to another person (B) if:

• any of s 21(2)–(13) of s 21 applies; or

---

[18]   See Chapter 3, n 284.

• any condition specified in an order[19] made by the Secretary of State is met. No order has yet been made.

The specification of the positions of trust under s 21(2)–(13) was guided by three criteria:[20]

'... first, the individual who is particularly vulnerable, for example on probation or in residential care; secondly, the location and/or lack of access to other adults and absence of countervailing influence makes the individual particularly vulnerable; and thirdly, the special influence of the adult: the relationship is in loco parentis.'

These criteria will guide the specification of any further positions of trust.[21]

5.14 For A to be in a position of trust, there is no need to prove that B actually placed trust in A or was even influenced by A (although this would be relevant to an offence under SOA 2003, s 17 or s 19). Once A ceases to be in a position of trust, the offences do not apply to subsequent conduct, even though A may still retain considerable influence over B. Those who are in a position of trust via a familial relationship are not thereby in a position of trust for the purposes of the offences under ss 16–19. They are dealt with by the two familial child sex offences under ss 25 and 26, dealt with in Chapter 6, which cover a narrower range of conduct.

5.15 SOA 2003, s 21(2)–(13) provides a list of positions of trust. Subsections (2)–(5) appeared in essence in SO(A)A 2000, s 3 (save that there has been a widening of the types of institution in s 21(4) and an amendment in respect of s 21(5)). Subsections (6)–(13) are entirely new.

5.16 Section 21(2)–(13) provides that A is in a position of trust in respect of B if:

'(2) ... A looks after persons under 18[22] who are detained in an institution [eg a Young Offender Institution] by virtue of a court order or under an enactment, and B is so detained in that institution.

(3) ... A looks after persons under 18 who are resident in a home or other place in which—

(a) accommodation and maintenance are provided by an authority[23] under section 23(2) of the Children Act (ChA) 1989 or Article 27(2) of the Children (Northern Ireland) Order 1995 (SI 1995/755) (NI 2), or

(b) accommodation is provided by a voluntary organisation under section 59(1) of that Act [or the equivalent Northern Irish provision],

and B is resident, and is so provided with accommodation and maintenance or accommodation, in that place. [Examples are residential care (local authority, private or voluntary (such as Barnado's and National Children's Homes), including secure accommodation) and semi-independent accommodation.]

---

[19] The order must be made by statutory instrument and is subject to the affirmative procedure: SOA 2003, s 138(1) and (2) respectively.

[20] Lord Falconer of Thoroton, HL Deb, vol 646, col 1294.

[21] Ibid.

[22] As to proof of age, see **3.131**, **3.132**.

[23] 'Authority': (a) in relation to England and Wales, means a local authority; (b) in relation to Northern Ireland, has the meaning given by the Children (Northern Ireland) Order 1995, SI 1995/755 (NI 2), art 2(2): SOA 2003, s 22(5).

(4) ... A looks after persons under 18 who are accommodated and cared for in one of the following institutions—

(a)   a hospital,[24]
(b)   an independent clinic,[25]
(c)   a care home,[26] residential care home[27] or private hospital,[28]
(d)   a community home,[29]voluntary home[30] or children's home,[31]
(e)   a home provided under section 82(5) of the ChA 1989,[32] or
(f)   a residential family centre,[33]

and B is accommodated and cared for in that institution. [This covers places where a child with a physical or mental illness, or physical or learning disabilities, or behavioural problems might be accommodated. It includes NHS, private and voluntary accommodation.[34]]

(5) ... if A looks after persons under 18 who are receiving education[35] [whether full- or part-time] at an educational institution and B is receiving, and A is not receiving, education at that institution. [This provision applies whether the educational institution is public or private, and whether it is a school, sixth form or further education college, or even a university (although university students under 18 are uncommon). The requirement that A must not be receiving *education* at the institution means that if A, aged 18 or over, is a pupil

---

[24] 'Hospital': (a) in relation to England and Wales, means a hospital within the meaning given by NHS Act 2006, ss 275(1) or s 206(1), or any other establishment which is a hospital within the meaning given by the Care Standards Act (CStA) 2000, s 2(3); (b) in relation to Northern Ireland, means a hospital within the meaning given by the Health and Personal Social Services (Northern Ireland) Order 1972, SI 1972/1265 (NI 14), art 2(2), or any other establishment which is a hospital within the meaning given by the Health and Personal Social Services (Quality, Improvement and Regulation) (Northern Ireland) Order 2003, SI 2003/431 (NI 9), art 2(2): SOA 2003, s 22(5) (as amended by the NHS (Consequential Provisions) Act 2006, s 2, Sch 1, paras 237, 238).

[25] 'Independent clinic' has: (a) in relation to England and Wales, the meaning given by CStA 2000, s 2(2); and (b) in relation to Northern Ireland, the meaning given by the Health and Personal Social Services (Quality, Improvement and Regulation) (Northern Ireland) Order 2003, SI 2003/431 (NI 9), art 2(2): SOA 2003, s 22(5).

[26] 'Care home' means an establishment which is a care home for the purposes of CStA 2000: SOA 2003, s 22(5).

[27] 'Residential care home' means an establishment which is a residential care home for the purposes of the Health and Personal Social Services (Quality, Improvement and Regulation) (Northern Ireland) Order 2003, SI 2003/431 (NI 9): SOA 2003, s 22(5).

[28] 'Private hospital' has the meaning given by the Mental Health (Northern Ireland) Order 1986, SI 1986/595 (NI 4), art 90(2): SOA 2003, s 22(5).

[29] 'Community home' has the meaning given by the ChA 1989, s 53: SOA 2003, s 22(5).

[30] 'Voluntary home has: (a) in relation to England and Wales, the meaning given by ChA 1989, s 60(3); (b) in relation to Northern Ireland, the meaning given by the Children (Northern Ireland) Order 1995, SI 1995/755 (NI 2), art 74(1): SOA 2003, s 22(5).

[31] 'Children's home' has: (a) in relation to England and Wales, the meaning given by CStA 2000, s 1; and (b) in relation to Northern Ireland, the meaning that would be given by the Health and Personal Social Services (Quality, Improvement and Regulation) (Northern Ireland) Order 2003, SI 2003/431 (NI 9), art 9 if in art 9(4) subparas (d), (f) and (g) were omitted: SOA 2003, s 22(5).

[32] Ie a home arranged by the Secretary of State for children in need of particular facilities unlikely to be readily available in a community home.

[33] 'Residential family centre' has the meaning given by the Health and Personal Social Services Act (Northern Ireland) 2001, s 22: SOA 2003, s 22(5).

[34] Explanatory notes to SOA 2003.

[35] A person receives education at an educational institution if he is registered or otherwise enrolled as a pupil or student at the institution: SOA 2003, s 22(4). Note, however, that where the child (B) is registered or otherwise enrolled at institution X but receives education at a different institution Y under an arrangement which X has with Y, A, at institution Y, will be in a position of trust in relation to B: ibid. Thus, if A, a lecturer at Y institution, engages in consensual sexual activity with B, a 16-year-old girl pupil enrolled at X institution, who attends Y once a week as part of her studies, A could be convicted of an offence under s 16. The same would be true if B is an exchange student enrolled at foreign institution X but attending English institution Y under an exchange agreement between X and Y.

there and looks after under-18-year-old pupils in his capacity as a prefect, A is not in a position of trust in relation to them. On the other hand, a young trainee teacher on teaching practice would be, since he or she is receiving *training* and not *education*. It would make no difference that he or she was an ex-pupil of the school and had known B as a fellow pupil.]

(6) ... A is appointed to be the guardian of B under Article 159 or 160 of the Children (Northern Ireland) Order 1995 (SI 1995/755 (NI 2)) [this covers a guardian appointed by the court or testamentary guardian].

(7) ... A is engaged in the provision of services under, or pursuant to anything done under—

(a)   sections 8 to 10 of the Employment and Training Act 1973 [provision of careers service for school and college students and others], or
(b)   section 114 of the Learning and Skills Act 2000 [provision of services to encourage, enable or assist effective participation by young persons in education or training],

and, in that capacity, looks after B on an individual basis. [If A is a Connexions Personal Adviser, whose normal means of communication with the child is telephone or e-mail, for example, A falls within this provision.]

(8) ... A regularly has unsupervised contact with B (whether face to face or by any other means [eg by telephone or e-mail])—

(a)   in the exercise of functions of a local authority under section 20 or 21 of the Children Act 1989 [provision of accommodation for children in need thereof (because no one has parental responsibility for them, because they are lost or abandoned, or because the person caring for them is unable to provide suitable accommodation) or in police protection or detention or on remand], or
(b)   in the exercise of functions of an authority under Article 21 or 23 of the Children (Northern Ireland) Order 1995. [This refers to people such as social workers and family centre staff employed by the relevant authority who arrange accommodation for such children and visit the accommodation to check the child's welfare.]

(9) ... A, as a person who is to report to the court under section 7 of the Children Act 1989 or Article 4 of the Children (Northern Ireland) Order 1995 on matters relating to the welfare of B, regularly has unsupervised contact with B (whether face to face or by any other means). [This refers to people like probation officers (offender management officers), local authority officers and independent Children and Family Reporters appointed by CAFCASS (the Children and Family Court Advisory and Support Service).]

(10) ... A is a personal adviser appointed for B under—

(a)   section 23B(2) of, or paragraph 19C of Schedule 2 to, the Children Act 1989 [appointment by the local authority], or
(b)   Article 34A(10) or 34C(2) of the Children (Northern Ireland) Order 1995,

and, in that capacity, looks after B on an individual basis. [Such advisers generally help and support 16- and 17-year-olds who have been in local authority care.]

(11) ...

(a) B is subject to a care order,[36] a supervision order[37] or an education supervision order,[38] and

(b) in the exercise of functions conferred by virtue of the order on an authorised person or the authority[39] designated by the order, A looks after B on an individual basis. [This refers to adults supervising children pursuant to a care order, supervision order or education supervision order.]

(12) ... A—

(a) is an officer of the service appointed for B under section 41(1) of the Children Act 1989 [CAFCASS] or Welsh family proceedings officer (within the meaning given by section 35 of the Children Act 2004)[40] [eg in respect of an application for a care order or supervision order (or for the discharge thereof or an appeal in relation to such an application), or where the court is considering making a residence order or a contact order in respect of a child subject to a care order],

(b) is appointed a children's guardian of B under rule 6 or rule 18 of the Adoption Rules 1984 (SI 1984/265), or

(c) is appointed to be the guardian ad litem of B under rule 9.5 of the Family Proceedings Rules 1991 (SI 1991/1247) [guardians ad litem appointed by the court in family proceedings (ie proceedings which in the High Court are assigned solely to the Family Division, namely private law proceedings under ChA 1989 and wardship proceedings)] or under Article 60(1) of the Children (Northern Ireland) Order 1995,

and, in that capacity, regularly has unsupervised contact with B (whether face to face or by any other means).

(13) ...

(a) B is subject to requirements imposed by or under an enactment on his release from detention for a criminal offence, or is subject to requirements imposed by a court order made in criminal proceedings, and

(b) A looks after B on an individual basis in pursuance of the requirements.

[This includes adults who supervise children under bail supervision, children under a community sentence and children under conditions following release (eg on licence from a young offender institution). It also includes adults who provide a treatment programme as part of a sentence. Consequently, a member of a youth offending team could be in a position of trust if he had sufficient contact with the child. So could someone providing counselling or drug rehabilitation services to the child under a court order.]'

When the Sexual Offences (Northern Ireland Consequential Amendments) Order 2008, SI 2008/1779, art 6, is in force the whole of s 21(4)(f), (6), (8)(b) and (10)(b), the references to Northern Irish legislation in s 21(3), (9) and (12)(c), and the references to 'residential care home or private hospital' in s 21(4)(c) will be omitted.

---

[36] 'Care order' has: (a) in relation to England and Wales, the same meaning as in ChA 1989; and (b) in relation to Northern Ireland, the same meaning as in the Children (Northern Ireland) Order 1995, SI 1995/755 (NI 2): SOA 2003, s 22(5).

[37] 'Supervision order' has: (a) in relation to England and Wales, the same meaning as in ChA 1989, s 31(11); and (b) in relation to Northern Ireland, the meaning given by the Children (Northern Ireland) Order 1995, SI 1995/755 (NI 2), Art 49(1): SOA 2003, s 22(5).

[38] 'Education supervision order' has: (a) in relation to England and Wales, the meaning given by ChA 1989, s 36; and (b) in relation to Northern Ireland, the meaning given by the Children (Northern Ireland) Order 1995, SI 1995/755 (NI 2), Art 49(1): SOA 2003, s 22(5).

[39] See n 23 above.

[40] As amended.

'Looking after'

5.17 For the purposes of SOA 2003, s 21(2), (3), (4) and (5), a person looks after persons under 18 at an institution, etc if that person is *regularly* involved in *caring for, training, supervising or being in sole charge of such persons* at that institution, etc,[41] not necessarily the child abused. The scope of this definition is wider than may have been intended. Hospitals and educational institutions, for example, may have thousands of patients or pupils, who may be spread across different departments and, even, sites. According to the definition, nurse A who works on the accident and emergency department would have a relationship of trust with B, aged 17, who is an in-patient in a ward after routine surgery, even though A never had the care, etc of B. So would A, a lecturer in building at a further education college who is employed solely at the Bruddersfield campus of the college, in relation to B, a 16-year-old hairdressing student, who only attends the Wethersfield campus of the college 6 miles away, even though A never had care or supervision of B or been in sole charge of her.[42] The definition raises questions (as does the next definition) about when someone becomes regularly involved.[43] It would seem to exclude a 'supply teacher' who only works in that capacity in the particular school on an intermittent basis. The same point can be made about the use of temporary staff in children's homes and other institutions where attendance is irregular.

5.18 SOA 2003, s 21(7), (10), (11) and (13) refers to a person looking after another *on an individual basis*. A person (A) looks after another (B) on such a basis if:

(a) A is *regularly* involved in caring for, training or supervising B; *and*

(b) in the course of their involvement, A *regularly has unsupervised contact* with B (whether face to face or by any other means, e g by telephone or e-mail).[44]

The unsupervised contact need not be with the child alone. It will be for the jury or magistrates to decide, on the facts, whether there has been unsupervised contact. The presence, for example, of a younger sibling at a meeting would not in itself prevent unsupervised contact. The points made above about the effect of the 'regularly' requirement are equally applicable here.

---

[41] SOA, s 22(2).

[42] Because it considers it far too wide, the Scottish Law Commission has recommended that the corresponding identically worded definition which applies to the same range of cases in SO(A)A 2000, s 4 (which still applies in Scotland) should be replaced by a provision that one person looks after another where he or she regularly cares for, trains, supervises or is in sole charge of that other person: *Justice, Clarity and Consent: New Sex Laws for Scotland*, Scot Law Com No 209 (2007), at para 4.132.

[43] 'Regularly' is not defined by the Act. In the House of Lords, Lord Falconer of Thoroton opined that teaching for one day 'would not be regular enough, but doing so for a whole term probably could be. It is a question of fact in every case': HL Deb, vol 644, col 879. The latter part of the first sentence seems unduly cautious. His Lordship was rather more precise at the Committee stage: 'What constitutes "regular" will depend on the particular factor or individual situation, but is obviously expected to cover not only the full-time class teacher or matron in a children's home but, for example, the peripatetic teacher who takes a child for music lessons once a week; the supply teacher who provides cover during the maternity leave of the regular teacher; or the physiotherapist who treats a child daily during a short period of convalescence in hospital': HL Deb, vol 646, col 1301.

[44] SOA 2003, s 22(3).

5.19   The requirements of regularity under these definitions are questionable; the position of trust of a schoolteacher, for example, derives from his or her position vis-à-vis pupils, and not from the regularity with which he or she performs his or her functions.

5.20   Neither definition of 'looking after' seems to catch an ancillary worker, such as a caretaker, school secretary or dinner lady, who may well have the opportunity to gain the trust of a child but cannot be said to satisfy the terms of the definitions.

5.21   A number of other people who have (or may have) a relationship of trust with a youngster also fall outside the categories in s 21. Examples are doctors; health-care employees outside residential units; clergymen; sports coaches; youth and community workers; voluntary group leaders; choir masters; and scout masters *in their positions as such*.[45] The Government resisted the inclusion of such persons in s 21 on the ground that they did not meet the three criteria referred to in **5.13**.[46] Other examples are child-minders and babysitters, but they would be unlikely to gain a position of trust vis-à-vis a child of 16 or 17, on whom the abuse of trust offences focus. Nannies and au pairs also fall outside the categories in s 21 but they can fall within the range of familial relationships for the purposes of familial child sex offences.[47]

MENS REA

5.22   In addition to requiring the defendant intentionally to do the thing specified by each individual section, SOA 2003, ss 16–19 contain somewhat involved provisions as to the mens rea in respect of the child's age and the existence of a position of trust.

As to age

5.23   In terms of the mens rea as to the age of the child (B), ss 16(1)(e), 17(1)(e), 18(1)(f) and 19(1)(e) provide:

'either—

---

[45]   Such persons may, of course, fall within one of the specified categories in s 21 depending on the circumstances.

[46]   Lord Falconer of Thoroton, HL Deb, vol 646, cols 1151 and 1294.

[47]   It has been argued that the sports coach-trainee relationship can involve the parties 'living in the same household' and consequently give rise to a familial relationship within the meaning of that term for the purposes of the familial child sex offences described in **6.1–6.69**: Brackenridge and Williams 'Incest in the "Family" of Sport' (2004) 154 NLJ 179. For a discussion of this argument, see **6.59** et seq.
       During the passage of the Sexual Offences Bill, the Government acknowledged that there could be occasions where a sports coach acts in loco parentis, for example, during intensive training, but it considered that the UK Coaching Certificate which has now been developed was a more appropriate means of dealing with the risk of abuse of trust by sports coaches. It acknowledged that if this proves inadequate, sports coaches could be added to the list of those in a position of trust by an order made under SOA 2003, s 21(1): Lord Falconer of Thoroton, HL Deb, vol 648, col 1153; Baroness Scotland of Asthal, HL Deb, vol 649, col 719. In 2005, the Government undertook a consultation exercise *Consultation on the Scope and Implementation of the Sexual Offences Act 2003 in Relation to Sports Coaches* about whether sports coaches should be brought within the list of positions of trust under SOA 2003. The consultation closed on 21 March 2005 but nothing has been forthcoming as a result. The UK Coaching Certificate is not primarily a code of conduct but does seek to address concerns about abuse of trust; a coach with a certificate who uses his or her position to manipulate a trainee into a sexual relationship may lose his or her qualification: see Williams 'Playing it Safe' (2005) 155 NLJ 234. The Certificate scheme currently does not apply to all sports and, even where it applies, is not mandatory.

(i)   B is under 18 and A does not reasonably believe that B is 18 or over, or

(ii)   B is under 13.'

5.24   Note that (i) above does not apply if B is under 13 at the material time; in such a case the offences are undoubtedly ones of strict liability as to age, like their counterparts under ss 9–12 (and like the offences under ss 5–8).[48] Although the prosecution ultimately has the persuasive burden of proof of the mens rea as to the age of B where B is aged 13–17, the prosecution is assisted by the following for which there are no counterparts in ss 9–12:[49]

> 'Where in proceedings for an offence under this section it is proved that the other person was under 18, the defendant is to be taken not to have reasonably believed that that person was 18 or over unless sufficient evidence is adduced to raise an issue as to whether he reasonably believed it.'

In other words, if it is proved by the prosecution that B was under 18 at the material time, this mens rea will be presumed proved unless evidence supporting a prima facie case to the contrary is adduced, in which case the prosecution will have to prove that element. Imposing an evidential burden is sensible overall; adults in most of the positions of trust can normally be assumed not to have reasonably believed that a child within the relationship of trust was 18 or over unless there is evidence to the contrary. Adults in those positions will find it particularly difficult to discharge the evidential burden.

As to position of trust

5.25   Sections 16(1)(d), 17(1)(d), 18(1)(e) and 19(1)(d) deal with the mens rea in relation to the existence of a position of trust in cases to which subs (2) of each section applies. Sections 16(2), 17(2), 18(2) and 19(2) apply where A is in a position of trust in relation to B by virtue of circumstances within:

- s 21(2) (B detained in an institution by virtue of a court order or under an enactment);

- s 21(3) (B in residential care, etc);

- s 21(4) (B accommodated and cared for in a hospital, care home, children's or residential family centre, etc); or

- s 21(5) (B receiving education at an educational institution),

and, in each case, A is not also in a position of trust by virtue of other circumstances.

These four circumstances are ones where A looks after persons under 18 at an institution and B is at that institution (but not necessarily looked after by A).

5.26   Sections 16(1)(d), 17(1)(d), 18(1)(e) and 19(1)(d) provide that in these cases, it must be proved that A knew or could reasonably be expected to know of the circumstances by virtue of which he or she is in a position of trust in relation to B. Proof

---

48   See **4.16**.

49   Sections 16(3), 17(3), 18(3) and 19(3).

of this mens rea is aided by ss 16(4), 17(4), 18(4) and 19(4), which provide that, where it is proved that A was in a position of trust in relation to the other person by virtue of circumstances within s 21(2), (3), (4) or (5), and it is not proved that he or she was in such a position of trust by virtue of other circumstances, it is to be presumed that A knew or could reasonably have been expected to know of the circumstances by virtue of which he or she was in such a position of trust unless sufficient evidence is adduced to raise an issue[50] as to whether he or she knew or could reasonably have been expected to know of those circumstances. If such evidence is adduced the prosecution will have to prove the mens rea as to a position of trust.

5.27　These provisions are designed to cover cases where, for example, the institution is very large or has a number of sites, so that the defendant may not know that the child is at the institution.[51] An example of where a person might not reasonably be expected to know that he is in a position of trust in relation to a particular child would be where a teacher meets in a bar, and subsequently has sex with, a sixth-form student who he is not aware attends the school at which he teaches.[52]

5.28　Where a position of trust arises wholly or partly by virtue of the other categories of circumstance referred to in s 21, it does so on the basis of an individual's personal relationship of trust between A and B. Not surprisingly, SOA 2003 does not require proof of any mens rea as to the position of trust where such a position of trust is involved. There can be no doubt, in view of the special provision made as to the mens rea in respect of the other types of positions of trust, that the presumption that any mens rea is required in these types of case is rebutted. The offence is therefore one of strict liability in this respect in these cases.

EXCEPTIONS: SPOUSES AND CIVIL PARTNERS, AND PRE-EXISTING SEXUAL RELATIONSHIPS

5.29　SOA 2003, ss 23 and 24 set out exceptions from liability for the above offences under ss 15–19.

The exception for spouses and civil partners

5.30　SOA 2003, s 23 (as amended by the Civil Partnership Act (CPA) 2004, s 261(1) and Sch 27, para 173) provides:

> '(1) Conduct by a person (A) which would otherwise be an offence under any of sections 16 to 19 against another person (B) is not an offence under that section if at the time—
>
> (a)　B is 16 or over, and
> (b)　A and B are lawfully married or civil partners of each other.
>
> (2) In proceedings for such an offence it is for the defendant to prove that A and B were at the time lawfully married or civil partners[53] of each other.'

51　Explanatory notes to SOA 2003.
52　*Guidance on Part 1 of the Sexual Offences Act 2003* (Home Office, 2003), at para 102.
53　A civil partnership is a relationship between two people of the same sex ('civil partners'): (a) which is formed

5.31 This exception applies even if the marriage or civil partnership registration only took place after the position of trust arose. As a matter of good practice, of course, one would not expect a married couple or civil partners to remain in a relationship of trust within s 21. Where the marriage or civil partnership registration occurs after A has come into a position of trust with respect to B, the exception implicitly recognises the acceptability of parents condoning or promoting a sexual relationship between A and B by giving their consent to the marriage or registration, and apparently ignores the risk that A may have pressurised B into the marriage.[54]

5.32 It will be noted that the defendant does not have the legal or persuasive burden of proof that B was 16[55] or over at the time of the alleged offence, although doubtless the defendant has an evidential burden in this respect (so that unless that burden is satisfied a judge must not leave the defence to the jury, and that, if it is, the burden is on the prosecution to prove that B was under 16). The burden imposed on the defendant to prove the element in s 23(1)(b), ie that the other party (A) is lawfully married (ie the marriage was recognised in English law) to B or the civil partner of B, is discussed in **5.41–5.43**. It is not necessary that B should have been 16 or over at the time of the marriage or civil partnership registration. There could be a valid marriage or registration even though B was under 16 when married, etc if A and B were married, etc abroad and under the law of the country (or countries) of domicile they had capacity to the other at the time of the marriage, etc.[56] It will be noted, however, that this defence does not cover the case where B was validly married, etc to A at the time of the alleged offence but was under 16 at that time, having been married, etc under the law of a country permitting marriage, etc at an earlier age. It must also be remembered that if a spouse, etc is under 16 an adult in a position of trust who engaged in sexual activity with that person can be convicted of the relevant child-sex offence under ss 5–12, because there is no similar exception to those offences for a spouse, etc. Provided that a marriage is recognised in English law, it would be irrelevant that it was actually or potentially polygamous. A void marriage is, of course, not recognised in law.

5.33 If the exception is raised, there will have to be proof of the celebration of the marriage (or registration of the civil partnership) between A and B; proof of acknowledgement, repute or cohabitation is insufficient.[57] The simplest way of proving celebration of a marriage is the production of the marriage certificate[58] (or, where this is permissible,[59] production of a certified copy of the entry in the foreign register of marriages[60]) and evidence from someone who was present at the marriage that A and B were the parties to the marriage. Where the celebration of a marriage cannot be proved by a certificate or certified entry, it may be proved by the evidence of someone who was present at it, but it will be necessary to call expert evidence as to its validity.[61] Similar comments apply to proof of a civil partnership.

---

by registration in accordance with Ch 1 of CPA 2004, Pts 2, 3, 4 or 5, or (b) which they are treated under CPA 2004, Pt 5, Ch 2, as having formed by virtue of having registered a relationship in a specified country or territory outside the UK: CPA 2004, s 1(1).

54 See Stevenson, Davies and Gunn *Blackstone's Guide to the Sexual Offences Act 2003* (OUP, 2004), at p 85.

55 As to proof of age, see **3.131, 3.132**.

56 For a simple account of the law relating to the recognition of foreign marriages, monogamous or polygamous, see *Halsbury's Laws of England* (4th edn) *Conflict of Laws*, vol 8(3) (reissue), at paras 208–240.

57 *Morris v Miller* (1767) 4 Burr 2057, at p 2058 in relation to the question of marriage. Doubtless the same is true in respect of civil partnership.

58 Marriage Act 1949, s 65(3).

59 Where an Order in Council has been made under the Oaths and Evidence (Overseas Authorities and Countries) Act 1963, s 5(1).

60 Evidence (Foreign, Dominion and Colonial Documents) Act 1933, s 1.

61 Lord Falconer of Thoroton, HL Deb, vol 646, col 1255.

5.34 The defendant's mistaken belief that the marriage was lawful (or that a civil partnership was validly registered) appears to be no defence, however reasonable it may be.

5.35 The marriage exception (and the subsequent civil partnership exception) are in SOA 2003 because of the right of everyone to respect for their private and family life. However, this rationale is only partially put into effect. As Rook and Ward have put it:[62]

> 'The Government seems to have considered it a bridge too far to extend the exception to cases where one spouse is under 16. However, if the parties are validly married, it is not clear on what basis their Convention right to enjoy married life together, including sexual relations, can be denied them. There is also potential for the marriage exception in s 23 to be attacked via the Convention on grounds that it discriminates against long-term cohabitees.'

Existing sexual relationship

5.36 SOA 2003, s 24 provides:

> '(1) Conduct by a person (A) which would otherwise be an offence under any of sections 16 to 19 against another person (B) is not an offence under that section if, immediately before the position of trust arose, a sexual relationship existed between A and B.
>
> (2) Subsection (1) does not apply if at that time sexual intercourse between A and B would have been unlawful.
>
> (3) In proceedings for an offence under any of sections 16 to 19 it is for the defendant to prove that such a relationship existed at that time.'

Thus the defendant (A) will have a defence if he or she proves[63] that immediately before[64] the position of trust arose a sexual relationship existed between him- or herself and B, as where A and B were in a sexual relationship immediately before B became a hospital patient or pupil of A (but this exception does not apply if at *that* time sexual intercourse between A and B would have been unlawful,[65] eg because B was under 16).

5.37 There was no exception corresponding to SOA 2003, s 24(1) under SO(A)A 2000. The exception avoids interference with a pre-existing lawful sexual relationship, whether heterosexual or homosexual, which has not been obtained by manipulation of a position of trust. It follows from the exception that, although a nurse (or teacher) who starts an affair with a 17-year-old patient (or pupil) a day after he or she starts a job at a hospital (or school) can be convicted, some such person who had begun the sexual relationship before cannot. Although misguided, the continuation of the former relationship would not be an offence. The exception will also cover someone who has a pre-existing sexual relationship with a 16-year-old schoolgirl if he then gets a job involving a position of trust in relation to her in order to have better access to her. The relationship need not have commenced before the defendant was aware (or should have been aware) that he would be in a position of trust with the child. If A, in April, obtains a teaching post at a school, to commence in September, and he commences a sexual relationship with a 16-year-old pupil at the school in May, the defence is available.

---

62 *Sexual Offences Law & Practice* (Sweet & Maxwell, 3rd edn, 2004), at p 169.
63 SOA 2003, s 24(3); see **5.41–5.43**.
64 Ie with no intervening break: *New Shorter Oxford English Dictionary.* Thus the sexual relationship must be ongoing (and not suspended or broken-off) when the position of trust begins.
65 This would seem to mean 'criminal', as it did under SOA 1956: *Chapman* [1959] 1 QB 100.

5.38 On the other hand, unlike the provisions under SO(A)A 2000, it is no defence that *immediately before the offence-creating section came into force*, a sexual relationship had developed between A and B, in relation to whom A was in a position of trust. This exception under the 2000 Act was a transitional provision and could be regarded as having 'served its day'.

5.39 SOA 2003 does not define a 'sexual relationship'. According to Lord Falconer of Thoroton,[66] a 'one-night stand' immediately before the position of trust arose would not be a sexual relationship. This would seem to be correct. The couple will have had 'sexual relations' but they cannot be said to have developed the emotional association required for a sexual relationship. Determining whether a sexual relationship had arisen is a matter of fact and degree.

5.40 The wisdom of the exception is open to doubt. A sexual relationship will be intrinsically unequal within a relationship of trust, whether it began before or after the start of that relationship of trust. Would it not have been better if a person who has a sexual relationship with someone with whom a position of trust arises was forced by the criminal law to choose between continuing the relationship or the position of trust? Is it enough to leave the matter to be dealt with by professional codes of conduct and the internal procedures of the institution or employer? The exception is open to abuse; it is not inconceivable that it will be spuriously, but successfully, claimed by a defendant supported by the youngster whose trust has been abused.

Proof

5.41 Putting the burden of proving an issue on the defendant is open to the objection that a court or jury may have to convict the defendant although it thinks it quite possible that he or she is not guilty of it. Provisions which expressly or impliedly place a persuasive (as opposed to an evidential)[67] burden on the defendant may for that reason be incompatible with the European Convention on Human Rights (ECHR), Art 6(2), which provides: 'Everyone charged with a criminal offence shall be presumed innocent until proved guilty according to law.' Article 6(2) does not, however, create an absolute rule.[68] There can be circumstances where the imposition of a burden of proof on the defendant is permissible under ECHR.[69] The question of compatibility of an express or implied reverse onus provision has to be decided by the courts and if a court finds that such a provision is incompatible with Art 6(2) it is required by the Human Rights Act 1998, s 3 wherever possible to 'read down' that provision so as to impose only an evidential burden, even where Parliament appears clearly to have intended to impose a persuasive burden on the defendant.[70]

5.42 In deciding whether the imposition of a reverse persuasive burden is or is not compatible with the ECHR, the task of the court is not to decide whether a reverse burden should be imposed on a defendant; instead its task is to assess whether a burden

66   HL Deb, vol 647, col 353.
67   Placing an evidential burden on the defendant does not ordinarily contravene ECHR, Art 6(2): *Lingens v Austria* 26 DR 171 (1981); *Lambert* [2002] 2 AC 545; *A-G's Reference (No 1 of 2004); Edwards* [2004] 2 Cr App R 424.
68   *Salabiaku v France* (1988) 13 EHRR 379; *Brown v Stott* [2003] 1 AC 681.
69   *DPP, ex p Kebiline* [2000] 2 AC 326; *Lambert*, n 67 above; *Johnstone* [2003] 2 Cr App R 493; *A-G's Reference (No 1 of 2004)*, n 67 above; *Sheldrake v DPP; A-G's Reference (No 4 of 2002)* [2005] 1 AC 264.
70   *DPP, ex p Kebiline*, n 69 above; *Lambert*, n 67 above; *Johnstone*, n 69 above; *A-G's Reference (No 1 of 2004)*, n 67 above; *Sheldrake v DPP*, n 69 above.

enacted by Parliament unjustifiably infringes the presumption of innocence.[71] Where the imposition of such a burden goes no further than is reasonably necessary to achieve its objective (ie where it is proportionate) and is reasonably necessary in all the circumstances, it will ordinarily be justified.[72] The factors which the court may need to take into account were listed by the Court of Appeal in *A-G's Reference (No 1 of 2004); Edwards*[73] as follows:

- When ascertaining whether the reverse burden was justified, the court must construe the provision to ascertain what would be the realistic effects of the reverse burden.

- In doing that the courts should be more concerned with substance than form. If the proper interpretation is that the statutory provision created an offence plus an exception that will in itself be a strong indication that there was no contravention of ECHR, Art 6(2).

- The easier it is for the defendant to discharge the burden the more likely it is that the reverse burden was justified. That would be the case where the facts were within the defendant's own knowledge. How difficult it would be for the prosecution to establish the facts is also indicative of whether a reverse legal burden was justified.

- The ultimate question is: would the exception prevent a fair trial? If it would, it must either be read down if that is possible; otherwise it should be declared incompatible.

- Caution must be exercised when considering the seriousness of the offence and the power of punishment. The need for a reverse burden is not necessarily reflected by the gravity of the offence:[74]

    'The overriding concern is that a trial should be fair, and the presumption of innocence is a fundamental right directed to that end. The Convention does not outlaw presumptions of fact or law but requires that these should be kept within reasonable limits and should not be arbitrary. It is open to states to define the constituent elements of a criminal offence, excluding the requirement of mens rea. But the substance and effect of any presumption adverse to a defendant must be examined, and must be reasonable. Relevant to any judgment on reasonableness or proportionality will be the opportunity given to the defendant to rebut the presumption, maintenance of the rights of the defence, flexibility in application of the presumption, retention by the court of a power to assess the evidence, the importance of what is at stake and the difficulty which a prosecutor may face in the absence of a presumption ... The justifiability of any infringement of the presumption of innocence cannot be resolved by any rule of thumb, but on examination of all the facts and circumstances of the particular provision as applied in the particular case.'

The application of these factors can often be a matter of considerable difficulty and uncertainty, so that one cannot be confident in advance of a judicial decision on a particular reverse onus provision whether or not it will be held compatible with Art 6(2).

[71] *Sheldrake v DPP*, n 69 above, per Lord Bingham.
[72] *Salabiaku v France*, n 68 above; *A-G's Reference (No 1 of 2004)* , n 67 above; *Sheldrake v DPP*, n 69 above.
[73] [2004] 2 Cr App R 424, at [52].
[74] *Sheldrake v DPP*, n 69 above, at [21], per Lord Bingham.

So far, however, of those reverse onus provisions which have been considered by the courts more have been held compatible with Art 6(2)[75] than those which have not.[76]

5.43 On that basis, it is submitted that placing a persuasive burden (rather than simply an evidential one) on the defendant in respect of the specified matters in ss 23 and 24 is, on balance, a justifiable and proportionate response to the legitimate aim identified above, despite the nature of the offences and the maximum punishment available for them. If this view is rejected, it would be easy to read down the provisions so as to impose only an evidential burden.

ACTS DONE IN SCOTLAND

5.44 See **2.104** and **2.105**.

---

[75] See *Davies* [2003] 1 ICR 586; *R (Grundy & Co Excavations Ltd) v Halton Division Magistrates' Court* (2003) 167 JP 387; *SL (a juvenile) v DPP* [2003] QB 137; *Matthews* [2004] QB 690; *Drummond* [2002] 2 Cr App Rep 371; *S* [2003] 1 Cr App R 602; *Johnstone*, n 69 above; *A-G's Reference (No 1 of 2004)*; *Edwards*, n 67 above; *Sheldrake v DPP*, n 69 above; *DPP v Baker* (2004) 168 JP 617.

[76] See *Lambert*, n 67 above; *A-G's Reference (No 4 of 2002)*, n 69 above.

Chapter 6

FAMILIAL SEX OFFENCES

INTRODUCTION

6.1   Under the pre-existing law, familial sexual relations were only specifically dealt with by the offences of incest under the Sexual Offences Act (SOA) 1956, ss 10 and 11, which were gender specific and confined to vaginal sexual intercourse. By s 10, it was an offence for a man to have intercourse with his granddaughter, daughter, sister (including half-sister) or mother. By s 11, it was an offence for a woman aged 16 or over to permit her grandfather, father, brother (including half-brother) or son to have intercourse with her. Limited to people closely related by a whole or half blood tie, these offences did not reflect modern looser family structures. Familial sexual activity falling outside the offences of incest was left to be dealt with by the various general offences relating to sexual conduct which – if the conduct was consensual – only applied to 'victims' under 16.[1]

6.2   SOA 2003 repealed the offences under SOA 1956, ss 10 and 11 and replaced them with gender-neutral offences concerned with:

- sexual activity with a child member of the 'family', as broadly defined; and

- penetrative sexual activity with an adult relative.

FAMILIAL CHILD SEX OFFENCES

6.3   Sexual relations with a child in a familial relationship with the other party almost inevitably involve serious abuse and exploitation because of the balance of power in the family unit and the close and trusting relationships within it.[2] Fathers may exploit their power to induce a daughter into sexual activity from an early age and exert pressure on her not to reveal it; this can have serious repercussions on the child's development. Abuse and exploitation can occur even though both parties are children.

6.4   The Sex Offences Review (see **1.4**) concluded that the offences of adult sexual abuse of a child and sexual activity between children did not remove the need for a separate offence specifically dealing with sex with a child by someone in a family relationship with the child. It proposed an offence of familial sexual abuse of a child which extended to any form of sexual penetration of a child under 18 by a wide range of

---

[1]   See **4.1**.

[2]   Home Office *Protecting the Public: Strengthening Protection Against Sex Offenders and Reforming the Law on Sexual Offences,* Cm 5668 (2002) (*PP*), at para 58.

people in a familial relationship not limited to a blood tie.[3] The rationale was protection against sexual abuse and exploitation, and not – in the case of incestuous intercourse – the prevention of inbreeding.[4] The Review favoured an upper age of 18 because:[5]

> '... children up to the age of 18 deserve protection from abuse and exploitation in situations where they might not be able to make an informed and mature choice of sexual partner because of their dependence on members of the family. Children in a family are particularly vulnerable ... Until [18] they are still legally children and dependent in many ways on adult parents or guardians.'

A defect with the proposal was that it was limited to penetrative sex, whereas father-daughter abuse often commences with other types of sexual behaviour, such as masturbation.[6] The Review's proposal was adopted in an extended form in SOA 2003, s 25.

6.5   SOA 2003, ss 25 and 26 provide two groups of offences respectively dealing with:

- sexual activity with a child family member (B) aged under 18 (s 25); and

- inciting a child family member aged under 18 to engage in sexual activity (s 26).

The age of 18 can be justified on the grounds referred to by the Sex Offences Review, mentioned above. In addition, the law would be incompatible with the European Framework Decision referred to in **5.4** if it failed to penalise those who intentionally engaged in sexual activities with an under-18-year-old where abuse is made of a recognised position of trust, authority or influence over that person. As to proof of age, see **3.131**, **3.132**. The consent of B to the sexual activity (or being incited) is irrelevant.

6.6   Both groups of offences have a number of elements common to offences under SOA 2003, ss 9 and 10 (child sex offences) and ss 16 and 17 (abuse of a position of trust). There are, however, no offences of familial child sex offences corresponding to those of causing a child to engage in sexual activity (although many who cause such activity involving familial child sex no doubt commit the offence of incitement under s 26), engaging in sexual activity in the child's presence and causing a child to watch a sexual act. The offences under SOA 2003, ss 25 and 26 are of particular importance where B is aged 16 or 17. If B is under 16 the conduct is also an offence, triable and punishable in the same way as an offence under s 25 or s 26, by virtue of s 9, 10 or 13, as the case may be.

6.7   Where a child is under 13, prosecutors should charge the relevant under-13 offence under SOA 2003, ss 5–8, if appropriate, notwithstanding that ss 25 and 26 apply to such a child. If there is difficulty in proving that the child was under 13 at the material time, then an offence under s 25 or s 26 should be charged, so long as the other elements of the offence can be proved.[7]

---

[3]   *Setting the Boundaries: Reforming the Law on Sexual Offences* (Home Office, 2000) (*SB*), at paras 5.1.5–5.1.9.

[4]   Ibid, Recommendations 35–42.

[5]   Ibid, at para 5.5.7.

[6]   Butler *Conspiracy of Silence – The Trauma of Incest* (Volcano Press, 1978), at pp 31–32, cited by Temkin *Rape and the Legal Process* (Oxford University Press, 2nd edn, 2002), at p 59.

[7]   CPS Guidance on Sexual offences and child abuse (*CPS Guidance*) (see **1.56**).

6.8 Where an offence falls within s 25 or s 26 and also within an equivalent offence where there is no familial relationship, such as s 9 or s 10, prosecutors should charge an offence under s 25 or s 26, as the case may be, if there is sufficient evidence to prove the family relationship, rather than the equivalent offence.[8]

6.9 The offences under ss 25 and 26 depend upon proof of a 'family relationship' described in **6.32-6.62** whose definition covers a much wider range of relationships than those to which the old offences of incest applied. The offences are subject to two exceptions described in **6.63-6.69**. They do not require proof that there actually was exploitation.

Sexual activity with a child family member

6.10 SOA 2003, s 25(1) provides:

'A person (A) commits an offence if—

(a) he intentionally touches another person (B),
(b) the touching is sexual,
(c) the relation of A to B is within section 27,
(d) A knows or could reasonably be expected to know that his relation to B is of a description falling within that section, and
(e) either—
  (i) B is under 18 and A does not reasonably believe that B is 18 or over, or
  (ii) B is under 13[9].'

Class of offence	3	SOA 2003, s 72 applies	✔[10]
Notification requirements	See text	SOPO[11]	✔
CJA 2003,[12] Sch 15 applies	✔	Serious specified offence	✔[13]
Review of lenient sentence	✔	Special provisions of CYPA 1933[14]	✔
Detention of young offender for specified period			✔

See **1.48** et seq.

6.11 The exceptions from liability for aiding, abetting or counselling an offence, provided by SOA 2003, s 73,[15] apply to an offence under s 25 if B is under 16. The notification requirements in SOA 2003, Pt 2 apply in respect of such offences where the

---

[8]   Ibid.
[9]   As to proof of age, see **3.131, 3.132**.
[10] See **2.97**.
[11] Sexual offences prevention order.
[12] Criminal Justice Act (CJA) 2003.
[13] Unless offender under 18 at time of offence.
[14] Children and Young Persons Act (CYPA) 1933.
[15] See **2.49-2.54**.

offender was 18 or over at the time of the offence, or is or has been sentenced, in respect of the offence, to at least 12 months' imprisonment.[16]

6.12   Where A is 18 or over at the time of the offence and the touching involved:

(a)   penetration of B's anus or vagina with a part of A's body or anything else;

(b)   penetration of B's mouth with A's penis;

(c)   penetration of A's anus or vagina with part of B's body (but not with anything else); or

(d)   penetration of A's mouth by B's penis,

an offence under s 25 is triable only on indictment and punishable with a maximum of 14 years' imprisonment.[17] In any other case where A was 18 or over at the material time, the offence is triable either way. The maximum punishment on conviction on indictment is, however, the same as in a case of penetration.[18]

6.13   Where A was not 18 or over at the material time, an offence under s 25 is triable either way and punishable with a maximum of 5 years' imprisonment on conviction on indictment.[19]

6.14   See the Sentencing Guidelines Council (SGC) Definitive Guideline[20] in the Appendix.

6.15   It may be noted in comparison that the maximum for the either-way offences of penetrative sex with an adult relative contrary to ss 64 and 65 is only 2 years' imprisonment on conviction on indictment, despite the fact that such conduct may well be exploitative or abusive.

6.16   Because there are different maximum punishments depending on the facts established, the application of the principle in *Courtie*[21] means that there are two separate offences under s 25:

•   sexual touching of someone under 18 in a familial relationship by someone aged 18 or over;[22] and

•   sexual touching of someone under 18 in a familial relationship by someone not proved to be 18 or over.

---

16   SOA 2003, s 80 and Sch 3, para 26.
17   SOA 2003, s 25(4) and (6).
18   SOA 2003, s 25(4); maximum on summary conviction: **1.43**.
19   SOA 2003, s 25(5); maximum on summary conviction: **1.43**.
20   At pp 5–18, 49–51, 56–58, 133, 134 and 139.
21   [1984] AC 463; **3.170**. There is nothing to rebut the presumption to this effect.
22   Presumably, the principle in *Tyrrell* [1894] 1 QB 710 (**4.17**) applies to prevent the child being liable as an accomplice to the offence perpetrated by the adult.

Where penetration (as specified in s 25(6)) is alleged a charge for the former offence should particularise that circumstance so as to ensure that the case is tried on indictment, and good practice would be to set out such particulars in the indictment.[23]

6.17 As indicated above,[24] these offences can overlap with other offences against children. Reference should be made to the prosecution guidance given there.

Actus reus

6.18 The elements specified in s 25(1)(a) and (b) are identical to those in the corresponding offences under ss 9 and 16. As to the relevant provisions of ss 9 and 16, see **4.13** and **5.8**.

6.19 The present offences extend to any form of sexual touching (as defined in ss 78 and 79); they do not distinguish between heterosexual and homosexual activity. It does not take much imagination to think of non-penetrative sexual activity within a familial relationship which could be highly exploitative and abusive. On the other hand, one can think of cases where it would not be: for example, experimental French kissing between two 16-year-olds who are first cousins is an offence under s 25.

6.20 As in the case of the offences of engaging in sexual activity with a child under s 9 and s 16, whether or not a child consented is irrelevant. If both A and B are under 18 and engage in sexual activity during which each touches the other, both can be convicted of the either-way offence. In the repealed offence of incest by a woman under SOA 1956, s 11, the woman had to be 16 or over. Under the present offences, there is no minimum age for the defendant, A, except the age of criminal responsibility. No doubt the younger an offender the more likely it will be that the discretion to prosecute will be exercised against a prosecution.

6.21 It would not excuse a defendant that he or she did not consent to commit the actus reus but was compelled to do so, unless he or she was compelled to do so by a reasonable belief in a threat of death or serious injury (and the requirements of the defence of duress were satisfied). In such a case, however, it would be unlikely that the CPS would institute a prosecution if satisfied that there had been coercion.

Mens rea

6.22 In addition to proving that A intentionally[25] touched B, the prosecution has to prove that A knew or could reasonably be expected to know that his relation to B was of a description falling within s 27.[26] Where, however, it is proved that the relation of A to B was of such a description, it is to be taken that A knew or could reasonably have been expected to know that his relation to B was of that description unless sufficient evidence is adduced to raise an issue[27] as to whether A knew or could reasonably have been expected to know that it was.[28] Suppose that A, adopted soon after birth, meets B, his natural younger sister, aged 17, when he is 22 and has sexual intercourse with her without realising that she is his natural sister. A will not be guilty under s 25 if he did

---

[23]   *Archbold* 20.115.
[24]   See **6.7** and **6.8**.
[25]   See **2.56**.
[26]   SOA 2003, s 25(1)(d).
[27]   See **3.63–3.68**.
[28]   SOA 2003, s 25(3). See **2.62**, **2.63** and **2.72**.

not know and could not reasonably be expected to know that his relation to B was that of brother-sister or any other prescribed relationship, but he will be taken to have had the requisite mens rea unless sufficient evidence is adduced to raise an issue as to whether he knew or could reasonably have been expected to know that his relation to B was of a description within s 27. The wording of s 25(1)(d) indicates that this would be the case even if A wrongly believed that B fell within another description (e g he thought that B was his stepsister).

6.23   The prosecution must also prove that either:

(a)   B is under 18 and A did not reasonably believe that B was 18 or over; or

(b)   B is under 13.[29]

There can be no doubt from this formulation and the case-law relating to it under s 5[30] that where B is proved to have been under 13 the offence is one of strict liability as to age. Otherwise, where it is proved that B was under 18, A is to be taken not to have reasonably believed that B was 18 or over unless sufficient evidence is adduced to raise an issue as to whether he or she reasonably believed it.[31]

6.24   These provisions are similar to those under ss 16–19, described in **5.23–5.28**.

Inciting a child family member to engage in sexual activity

6.25   SOA 2003, s 26(1) provides:

'A person (A) commits an offence if—

(a)   he intentionally incites another person (B) to touch, or allow himself to be touched by, A,
(b)   the touching is sexual,
(c)   the relation of A to B is within section 27,
(d)   A knows or could reasonably be expected to know that his relation to B is of a description falling within that section, and
(e)   either—
        (i)   B is under 18 and A does not reasonably believe that B is 18 or over, or
        (ii)   B is under 13[32].'

Class of offence	3	SOA 2003, s 72 applies	✔[33]
Notification requirements	See text	SOPO	✔
CJA 2003, Sch 15 applies	✔	Serious specified offence	✔[34]

---

[29]   SOA 2003, s 25(1)(e). As to 'not reasonably believe', see **2.67–2.71**.
[30]   See **3.124** et seq.
[31]   SOA 2003, s 25(2).
[32]   As to proof of age, see **3.131**, **3.132**.
[33]   See **2.97**.
[34]   Unless offender under 18 at the time of offence.

Review of lenient sentence	✗	Special provisions of CYPA 1933	✔
Detention of young offender for specified period			✔

See **1.48** et seq.

6.26 The notification requirements in SOA 2003, Pt 2 apply in respect of such offences where the offender was 18 or over at the time of the offence, or is or has been sentenced, in respect of the offence, to at least 12 months' imprisonment.[35]

6.27 An offence under s 26 is triable and punishable in the same way as an offence under s 25.[36] For the same reasons as in s 25, because the maximum punishment differs there are two offences under s 26:

- one committed by someone aged 18 or over inciting a sexual touching (as defined in **6.12**); and

- the other committed by someone under 18 who incites any form of sexual touching.

6.28 The requirement in s 26(1)(a) and (b) is differently worded from that in the corresponding offences under ss 10 and 17. Not only is there not the alternative of 'causing', but those offences speak of 'inciting sexual activity' with someone (who need not be the inciter), whereas here the sexual touching incited by A must relate to a touching of A or a touching by A. A would incite B to touch A if he incited B to touch his penis. A would incite B to allow herself to be touched by A if he incited her to let him touch her breasts or to have sexual intercourse with him. The incitement need not succeed. If B actually allows touching to occur, the appropriate offence would be that under s 25. As to the terminology of s 26(1)(a) and (b), see **2.31–2.48**, **3.154–3.158** and **3.183–3.189**.

6.29 The mens rea in respect of the fact that the relation of A to B is within s 27 is the same as that in s 25. Thus, where it is proved that the relation of A to B was of a description falling within s 27, it is to be taken that A knew or could reasonably have been expected to know that his relation to B was of that description unless sufficient evidence is adduced to raise an issue as to whether he knew or could reasonably have been expected to know that it was.[37]

6.30 Likewise, in respect of the mens rea in s 26(1)(e)(i) (reasonable belief (where B is not under 13) that B is 18 or over), where it is proved that B was under 18, A is to be taken not to have reasonably believed that B was 18 or over unless sufficient evidence is adduced to raise an issue as to whether he reasonably believed it.[38]

6.31 As in the case of an offence under s 25, an offence under s 26 is one of strict liability as to age if B is under 13.

---

[35] SOA 2003, s 80 and Sch 3, para 25.
[36] SOA 2003, s 26(4), (5) and (6): **6.12–6.14**.
[37] SOA 2003, s 26(3).
[38] SOA 2003, s 26(2).

Family relationships

6.32   Under SOA 2003, ss 25 and 26 the relation of the defendant and the 'victim' must be within s 27. Section 27 reflects the looser structure of modern families by extending the family relationship to include relatively distant relatives and other types of people likely to be in a position of trust or control in relation to the child. If a relationship within s 27 is proved it is unnecessary also to prove that A abused it. Where what has occurred is not abusive, or is insufficiently harmful to warrant criminal liability, this is a matter to be dealt with by the discretion to prosecute and by the discretion which exists in sentencing if a successful prosecution is brought.

6.33   The relationships within s 27 are defined widely in an attempt to cover anyone of any age who has a familial relationship with a child by virtue not only of blood ties, but also by virtue of adoption, fostering or marriage or quasi-marital relationship, or by virtue of living in the same household as the child and having a position of trust/authority in relation to it. This is sensible; the balance of power and the trusting relationships which exist within a family unit are not limited to those related by blood. The definition of 'family relationships' is considerably wider than the prohibited degrees of marriage under the Marriage Act (MA) 1949, Sch 1, under which someone aged 16 or over is legally capable of marrying not only a cousin, but also most of the other people within s 27. Thus, A who could legally marry B may be liable for engaging in extra-marital sexual activity with B if he or she falls within that definition. The appropriateness of this has been questioned.[39] It marks a reversal from the situation in respect of the old offences of incest where the range of prohibited relationships was narrower than the list of prohibited degrees of marriage.

6.34   By SOA 2003, s 27(1), as amended by CJIA 2008:[40]

> 'The relation of any person (A) to another person (B) is within this section if—
>
> (a)   it is within any of subsections (2) to (4), or
> (b)   it would be within one of those sections but for section 39 of the Adoption Act 1976 or section 67 of the Adoption and Children Act 2002 (status conferred by adoption).'

6.35   The terms of s 27(1)(a) can be satisfied by an adoptive relationship, as well as by a biological one.[41] This is because the Adoption Act (AA) 1976, s 39 (which applies to adoptions made before 30 December 2005) and the Adoption and Children Act (ACA) 2002, s 67 (which applies to adoptions made on or after 30 December 2005) provide that an adopted child is to be treated in law as the child of the adoptive parent or parents and not of the biological parents. Adoptive relationships were not recognised for the purposes of the offences of incest under SOA 1956. The Sex Offences Review[42] recommended, however, that they should be because of the trust and responsibility undertaken by adoptive parents to their adopted children and because adoptive siblings are intrinsically part of the family.

6.36   The effect of s 27(1)(b) is that the categories of relationship set out in s 27(2)-(4) continue to apply to an adopted child's biological family relationships. As enacted, s 27(1)(b) only referred to ACA 2002, s 67, with the result that s 27(1)(b) only had the

---

[39]   By Spencer 'Child and Family Offences' [2004] Crim LR 347, at p 357.
[40]   Section 73, Sch 15, paras 2, 3.
[41]   As to the biological relationship, see **6.36**.
[42]   *SB*, at paras 5.6.1–5.6.2; Recommendations 38 and 39.

above effect in relation to cases where the child was adopted on or after 30 December 2005. The amendments made by CJIA 2008, which came into force on 8 July 2008,[43] added AA 1976, s 39 in the alternative to ACA 2002, s 67 so as to make s 27(2)–(4) applicable to adoptions made before 30 December 2005, as had been the initial intention. Thus, contrary to the normal legal rule that an adopted child is the child of the adoptive parent(s), and not the biological parents,[44] an adopted child will be treated as the child of both sets of parents and as the sibling of both biological and adoptive siblings, irrespective of the date of the adoption.

6.37   The categories in s 27(2)–(4) deal respectively with:

- certain core family relationships;

- some other relationships (less close ones) where those involved live or have lived in the same household or one is or has been regularly involved in the care, etc of the other; and

- some more remote relationships where those involved live in the same household *and* one is regularly involved in caring, etc for the other.

6.38   These relationships apply whether the two people are of the same sex or are of different sexes. As will be seen, the relationships are widely drawn. The result is, for example, that 'sexual' kissing between two 16-year-old first cousins related through a half-bloodline is an offence under s 25 if they have ever lived in the same household.

Core family relationships

6.39   SOA 2003, s 27(2) provides:

'The relation of A and B is within this subsection if—

(a)   one of them is the other's parent, grandparent,[45] brother, sister, half-brother, half-sister, aunt or uncle, or

(b)   A is or has been B's foster parent.'

6.40   A relationship referred to in (a) does not need to be traced through lawful wedlock. 'Aunt' means the sister or half-sister, and uncle the brother or half-brother, of a person's parent.[46] Section 27(2) does not include a stepsibling (ie the child of a person's step-parent by someone other than that person's parent), nor a 'foster sibling' (ie the child of a foster parent). This is not surprising, since such persons may never live in the same household and may rarely, if ever, come into contact with each other. Where they do live, or have lived, in the same household, the relationships of stepsibling and of foster sibling fall within s 27(3)(c) and (d) respectively.

6.41   Incest under SOA 1956 did not include the uncle-niece and aunt-nephew relationships. This was a significant omission. In one study, for example, it was found, in one of two samples, that sexual contact between a child and an adult uncle was the most

---

43   CJIA 2008, s 153(2)(e).

44   See **6.35**.

45   The absence of a great-grandparent from this list may be noted. Such a person can, nevertheless, be within a family relationship if the terms of s 27(4) are satisfied.

46   SOA 2003, s 27(5)(a).

prevalent form of sexual contact between relatives.[47] It is unfortunate that uncles by marriage (ie those married to a child's blood aunt) or putative uncles (the partners of a child's blood aunt) do not fall with s 27(2), and are only caught if they satisfy the stricter requirements of s 27(4).

6.42   The extension of the proscribed relationship to a foster parent was recommended by the Sex Offences Review[48] on the ground that any sexual relationship with a foster child is a particular abuse of trust. A person is a foster parent for the purposes of the present offences if:[49]

• he is a person with whom the child has been placed under the Children Act (ChA) 1989, s 23(2)(a) or s 59(1)(a) (fostering for local authority or voluntary organisation); or

• he fosters the child privately, within the meaning given by s 66(1)(b) of that Act.

It will be noted that even a temporary foster parent falls within s 27(2). If a relationship based on foster parentage ceases before the child is 18, an offence can still be committed under s 25 or s 26 as long as the victim is under 18.

6.43   Because there is no minimum age which A must have obtained for this or any other of the relationships, A, aged 16, the aunt of B, aged 17, would commit an offence under s 26 by engaging in sexual activity with B, and so would B by engaging in that activity with A.

Less close relationships

6.44   SOA 2003, s 27(3) provides:

'The relation of A to B is within this subsection if A and B live or have lived in the same household, or A is or has been regularly involved in caring for, training, supervising or being in sole charge of B, and—

(a)   one of them is or has been the other's step-parent,
(b)   A and B are cousins,
(c)   one of them is or has been the other's stepbrother or stepsister, or
(d)   the parent or present or former foster parent of one of them is or has been the other's foster parent.'

6.45   The inclusion of the relationship referred to in (a) is important because of the influence which step-parents can exercise over their stepchildren; reference to press reports shows that stepdaughters, at least, are particularly vulnerable to sexual abuse from their stepfathers.

6.46   A 'step-parent' includes a parent's partner.[50] This is not as wide as may at first seem because a person is another's partner (whether they are of different sexes or the

---

[47]   West *Sexual Victimisation* (Gower, 1985), at p 56. See also Temkin 'Do We Need the Crime of Incest?' (1991) 44 CLP 185, at pp 202–203.
[48]   *SB*, at para 5.6.6; Recommendation 41.
[49]   SOA 2003, s 27(5)(c).
[50]   SOA 2003, s 27(5)(e).

same sex) only if they live together as partners in an enduring family relationship.[51] Nevertheless, tricky questions are liable to arise about what constitutes an 'enduring family relationship' (undefined by SOA 2003), how long a relationship must last to be 'enduring' and whether an 'enduring family relationship' has commenced. It remains to be seen whether the answer depends on the duration of the relationship or on whether the parties intended it to be permanent, or a combination of these. There must be questions about whether this requirement can be defined with the degree of precision required for the criminal law. There are potential problems in respect of the European Convention on Human Rights (ECHR), Art 7 and other Articles. The step-parent of a person (X) also includes a person who is the civil partner of X's parent (but is not X's parent).[52]

6.47 In (b), 'cousin' means the child of an 'aunt' or 'uncle', as defined by s 27(5)(a).[53] It follows that a second (or more remote) cousin does not fall within (b).

6.48 In (c), 'stepbrother' and 'stepsister' are not limited to the case where one child's parent is married to the parent of the other child; the terms include the child of a parent's 'partner', as defined above.[54] A person's (X's) stepbrother or stepsister also includes a person who is the son or daughter, as the case may be, of the civil partner of X's parent (but is not the son or daughter, as the case may be, of either of X's parents).[55]

6.49 Paragraph (d) refers to foster siblings. Like stepsiblings, they are particularly vulnerable to peer sexual abuse when they live, or have lived, in the same household.[56]

6.50 The wide definition in s 27(3) reflects the fact that sometimes familial relationships are transitory in nature. It may be noted that none of the relationships referred to fall within the prohibited degrees of marriage. As with the other relationships referred to in s 27, there is no exemption where both parties are under 18.

6.51 For a case to fall within s 27(3), something more is required than the simple relationship referred to in s 27(3)(a)–(d); A and B must live or have lived in the same household, or A must be or have been regularly involved in caring for, training or supervising or being in sole charge of B. It is not enough, for example, simply for A to be the partner of B's parent or a cousin of B.

6.52 It is submitted that, for A and B to live (or have lived) 'in the same household', there must be (or have been) a sharing (however minimal) of a common life on a permanent or temporary basis, rather than on a casual basis. What was said by the Court of Appeal in *Santos v Santos*[57] about 'living with each other in the same household' may provide guidance in respect of 'living in the same household' in s 27(3), although the context is very different since that was a case about when the separation of spouses commenced.[58] Sachs LJ, delivering the judgment of the Court, said that the

---

[51] SOA 2003, s 27(5)(d).

[52] Civil Partnership Act (CPA) 2004, ss 246(1), 247(1)(a), Sch 21, para 61.

[53] SOA 2003, s 27(5)(b): **6.40**.

[54] SOA 2003, s 27(5)(e).

[55] CPA 2004, ss 246(1), 247(1)(a), Sch 21, para 61.

[56] Epps 'Causal Explanation: Filling the Theoretical Reservoir' in Calder (ed) *Working with Young People who Sexually Abuse* (Russell House, 1999), at p 7.

[57] [1972] Fam 247.

[58] In *Santos* the question was the meaning of a provision in the Divorce Reform Act 1969, s 2(5) (repealed) that 'a husband and wife shall be treated as living apart unless they are living with each other in the same household'.

phraseology did 'not use the word "house", which relates to something physical, but "household", which has an abstract meaning', and said that 'household' was 'a word which essentially refers to people held together by a particular kind of tie, even if temporarily separated'.[59] A similar view was taken by the Court of Appeal in *Gully v Dix*[60] where *Santos v Santos* was applied. Assuming that *Santos v Santos* does provide guidance in the present context, it does not decide that people held together by a particular kind of tie can be said to live (or have lived) in the same household if they have never resided under the same roof. Sachs LJ's reference to 'even if temporarily separated' (in the context of spouses) implies that there must have been a time when the parties lived under the same roof. This implication is supported by the natural meaning of 'live in' which, in the present context, is 'reside among'.

6.53 There is no minimum time during which A and B must have lived in the same household.

6.54 The alternative, 'regular involvement in care', etc provides protection in looser familial relationships.

6.55 Once the relationship is established under s 27(3), it continues as long as B is under 18 even if, de facto, A and B ceased to live in the same household or A ceased to care, etc for B, however long before the alleged offence.

More remote relationships

6.56 SOA 2003, s 27(4) provides:

'The relation of A and B is within section 27(4) if—

(a) A and B live in the same household, *and*
(b) A is regularly involved in caring for, training, supervising or being in sole charge of B.'
(Emphasis added.)

The definition in (a) can be satisfied by someone who would not normally be regarded as being in a family relationship with other members of the household (e g a nanny or au pair).

6.57 It must be emphasised that proof of the s 27(4) category of relationship requires proof of both requirements. Thus, for example, if A is the husband or partner of B's aunt (ie an uncle by marriage or a putative uncle) and he is regularly involved in caring for the child, he does not fall within s 27(4) unless he also lives in the same household as B.

6.58 This category of relationship is different from the other two since the relationship ends when A and B cease to live in the same household or when the involvement in caring, etc for B by A ceases. If B is looked after by a nanny (A) and she leaves the household on finding employment elsewhere or B goes to boarding school and A is regularly involved in caring for X, a younger sibling of B, A and B are no longer in a relationship within s 27(4).

---

[59] [1972] Fam 247, at p 262.
[60] [2004] 1 WLR 1399.

6.59   It has been argued[61] that the relationship between a sports coach and his or her trainee can in itself satisfy s 27(4). The writers have stated that it would be consistent with SOA 2003's theme of preventing sexual exploitation if it could because:

> 'At the highest level, athletes may devolve all their living decisions (food choices, travel arrangements and so on) to a coach, and this will be with the full consent of the athlete's natural family. It is a question of fact, then, that a coach can have considerable confidence and status accorded to him by his athlete's family – they trust him to take care of their child.'

6.60   The relationship of sports coach and trainee clearly satisfies the criterion in s 27(4)(b) but whether it can satisfy s 27(4)(a) is doubtful. It has been argued[62] that the relationship of sports coach and trainee can be so close that in itself it satisfies s 27(4)(a). This argument, partly based on *Santos v Santos* (**6.52**) and *G v F*,[63] seems, however, to ignore the fact that the phraseology requires the parties to be '*living* in the same household', which (as stated in **6.52**) seems to require 'residing' in the same household.

6.61   *G v F* is a case concerned with whether the parties were 'associated' for the purposes of the Family Law Act 1996, s 62(3), which provides that a person is associated with another for the purpose of making a non-molestation order if, inter alia, 'they are cohabitants or former cohabitants or have lived in the same household'. Wall J said that the non-molestation provisions in the Act were:[64]

> '... designed to provide swift and accessible protective remedies to persons of both sexes who are the victims of domestic violence, provided they fall within the criteria laid down by s 62. It would, I think, be most unfortunate if s 62(3) was narrowly construed so as to exclude borderline cases where swift and effective protection for the victims of domestic violence is required ... In the light of my finding that these parties are former cohabitants, it is unnecessary for me to ... discuss the difference between cohabitants and those who have lived together in the same household.'

6.62   *G v F* does not provide any guidance as to the meaning of 'living in the same household'. All it does is to decide that s 62(3) should be given a wide, purposive construction. Section 62 is concerned with the making of a civil order. A wide construction of 'living in the same household' in SOA 2003, s 27(4)(a) in favour of the prosecution might well contravene the strict interpretation rule which applies to criminal statutes.[65]

Exceptions: spouses and civil partners, and pre-existing sexual relationships

6.63   Conduct by a person (A) which would otherwise be an offence under SOA 2003, s 25 or s 26 against another person (B) is not an offence if one of the two exemptions provided by s 28 or s 29 respectively applies. The exceptions correspond (the second broadly) to those which apply to offences of abuse of trust. The points made in **5.30–5.43** about those exceptions are equally applicable to ss 28 and 29.

---

[61]   Brackenridge and Williams 'Incest in the "Family" of Sport' (2004) 154 NLJ 179. See also Brackenridge *Spoilsports: Understanding and Preventing Sexual Exploitation in Sport* (Routledge, 2001), at pp 94–95.
[62]   Brackenridge and Williams, ibid.
[63]   [2000] Fam 186.
[64]   [2000] Fam 186, at pp 196–197.
[65]   See *Sweet v Parsley* [1970] AC 132, at p 149, per Lord Reid; *DPP v Ottewell* [1970] AC 642, at p 649, per Lord Reid; *A-G's Reference (No 1 of 1988)* [1989] AC 971.

6.64   SOA 2003, s 28, as amended by CPA 2004,[66] provides:

'(1) Conduct by a person (A) which would otherwise be an offence under section 25 or 26 against another person (B) is not an offence under that section if at the time—

(a)   B is 16 or over, and

(b)   A and B are lawfully married or civil partners of each other.

(2) In proceedings for such an offence it is for the defendant to prove that A and B were at the time lawfully married or civil partners of each other.'

6.65   Adoptive siblings, for example, can marry each other provided that they have both reached the age of 16, and so can people in many of the other relationships referred to in s 27. It will be noted that this defence does not cover the case where B was validly married to A at the time of the alleged offence but was under 16, having been married under the law of a country permitting marriage at an earlier age. A's mistaken belief that he or she is lawfully married to B is apparently no defence, however reasonable the mistake.

6.66   SOA 2003, s 29, as amended by CJIA 2008,[67] provides:

'(1) Conduct by a person (A) which would otherwise be an offence under section 25 or 26 against another person (B) is not an offence under that section if—

(a)   the relation of A to B is not within subsection (2) of s 27,

(b)   it would not be within that subsection if section 39 of the Adoption Act 1976 or section 67 of the Adoption and Children Act 2002[68] did not apply, and

(c)   immediately before the relation of A to B first became such as to fall within section 27, a sexual relationship existed between A and B.

(2) Subsection (1) does not apply if at the time referred to in subsection (1)(c) sexual intercourse between A and B would have been unlawful.

(3) In proceedings for an offence under s 25 or 26 it is for the defendant to prove the matters mentioned in subsection (1)(a) to (c).'

Put more simply, this means that the exception under s 29 applies where the defendant proves that:

(a)   the relation of A to B is not within s 27(2) (the core family relationships: see **6.39–6.41**);

(b)   where A or B (or both) is adopted, the relationship would not be within s 27(2) if there had not been the adoption; and

(c)   immediately before the relation of A to B first became such as to fall within s 27, a sexual relationship existed between A and B.[69]

---

[66]   Section 261(1), Sch 27, para 174.
[67]   Section 73, Sch 15, paras 2, 4.
[68]   See **6.35**.
[69]   SOA 2003, s 29(1).

As enacted, s 29(1)(b) only referred to ACA 2002, s 67, with the result that it only applied where the adoption was made on or after 30 December 2005. The amendment made by CJIA 2008, which came into force on 8 July 2008,[70] added AA 1976, s 39 (which makes the like provision to ACA 2002, s 67 in respect of an adoption made before 30 December 2005) to SOA 2003, s 29(1)(b) in the alternative to ACA 2002, s 67, so that the defence for sexual relationships predating family relationships does not apply where A or B (or both) is adopted unless the defendant proves that the relation of A and B does not fall within s 29(1)(a) (whether by blood or adoption). Section 29(1)(c) means that the exception under s 29 does not apply if A and B, who had been in a sexual relationship, had broken it by the time the family relationship first came into existence but later resumed it.

6.67 Section 29(1) does not apply if immediately[71] before the relation of A to B first became such as to fall within s 27 sexual intercourse between A and B would have been unlawful,[72] as where B was under 16.

6.68 An example of the result of this exception is this. Suppose that A's father marries (or becomes a partner of) B's mother, having met because A and B, both aged 16, have a sexual relationship and all four thereafter live in the same household. A and B are exempt from the offences under ss 25 and 26 if they continue their sexual relationship as stepsiblings, even though that relationship, previously limited to petting, develops into sexual intercourse when they are living under the same roof. Another example would be where A, aged 20, who has a sexual relationship with cousin B, aged 17, continues that relationship after moving into B's household.

6.69 There is no transitional exception for the situation where, immediately before the commencement of s 25 or s 26, as the case may be, a sexual relationship existed between A and B.

SEX WITH AN ADULT RELATIVE

6.70 Rejecting the recommendation of the Criminal Law Revision Committee (CLRC) in 1984 that incest between parties of 21 or over should cease to be an offence,[73] the Sex Offences Review concluded that sexual intercourse between consenting adult relatives should continue to be criminal.[74] Its rationale was not the prevention of inbreeding and genetic abnormalities but protection against abuse.[75]

6.71 Not all forms of inter-relative penetrative sexual activity are abusive. Suppose, for example, that siblings or half-siblings meet as adults. Initially, at least, they may be unaware of their relationship. They are attracted and have sexual relations. The case for criminality here is not strong, especially when weighed against the couple's right to

---

[70] CJIA 2008, s 153(2)(e).
[71] Ie with no intervening break: *New Shorter Oxford English Dictionary*. Thus the sexual relationship must be ongoing (and not suspended or broken off) when the position of trust begins.
[72] SOA 2003, s 29(2).
[73] *Fifteenth Report, Sexual Offences*, Cmnd 9213 (1984), at para 8.22.
[74] For criticism of this conclusion, see Spencer 'Child and Family Offences' [2004] Crim LR 347, at p 358. For a review of the arguments relating to whether or not such conduct should be criminalised, see Temkin 'Do We Need the Crime of Incest?' (1991) 44 *Current Legal Problems* 185.
[75] *SB*, at para 5.8; Recommendation 43.

private life under ECHR, Art 8. According to the Sex Offences Review, such cases of incest rarely came to the attention of the police or were prosecuted.[76]

6.72 The more common type of relationship, however, begins when one of the partners is a child, and involves long-term abuse. There is evidence that many adult incestuous relationships are based on long-term grooming and pressure from childhood, and are not genuinely consensual.[77] The particular nature of close family relationships and the importance of protecting the family as an institution, as well as members of a family, were regarded by the Sex Offences Review as justifying a limitation through the criminal law on an adult's right to exercise sexual autonomy in their private life.[78]

6.73 Despite recognising that not all cases of sex between adult relatives involve abuse, the Sex Offences Review did not recommend any exemption from criminal liability. Nor did *Protecting the Public*, which stated (without citing any evidence) that:[79]

> 'Despite involving consensual adults it is generally believed that all such behaviour [ie sexual activity between adult blood relatives] is wrong and should be covered by the criminal law.'

This statement is surprising in the light of its apparent rejection of the 'Wolfenden principle'.[80]

6.74 Sections 64 and 65 provide gender-neutral offences to deal with those who engage in consensual penetrative sex with an adult blood relative. The offences differ significantly from those relating to children.

6.75 The offences under ss 64 and 65 are described somewhat prosaically by the heading to s 64 as 'Sex with an adult relative: penetration' and by s 65 as 'Sex with an adult relative: consenting to penetration'. 'Incest' would have been an inappropriate description because it is not generally understood as including oral or anal penetration, or as including homosexual intercourse between relatives. Life might have been easier for those trying to explain these two offences if one could talk in terms of 'man' and 'woman', but the gender-neutral philosophy (and wording) of the sections does not permit this nor does the fact that the Act recognises that transsexuals can have a penis or a vagina.[81]

6.76 Assuming that prosecutions are likely to be brought only where there has been an element of abuse by one party of the other, the offence to be charged will depend on whether the 'abuser' party was the *penetrator* (as is the more likely) or was the *penetrated*. The fact that the other party may have committed an offence by being penetrated or by penetrating, as the case may be, may discourage her or him from coming forward to make a complaint.

---

[76] Ibid.
[77] Ibid. This factor is an aggravating factor meriting imprisonment under the SGC Definitive Guideline at p 93: see the Appendix. In other cases, even if there is grooming by an adult of another, the starting point in sentencing is a community order.
[78] *SB*, at para 5.8; Recommendation 43.
[79] *PP*, at para 59.
[80] See **1.24**.
[81] See **3.102**.

6.77 The definitions of the two offences are set out in ss 64(1) and 65(1) respectively, as amended by CJIA 2008.[82] By s 64(1):

'A person aged 16 or over (A) (subject to subsection (3A))[83] commits an offence if—

(a) he intentionally penetrates another person's vagina or anus with a part of his body or anything else, or penetrates another person's mouth with his penis,

(b) the penetration is sexual,

(c) the other person (B) is aged 18 or over,

(d) A is related to B in a way mentioned in subsection (2), and

(e) A knows or could reasonably be expected to know that he is related to B in that way.'

Section 65(1) provides:

'A person aged 16 or over (A) (subject to subsection (3A)) commits an offence if—

(a) another person (B) penetrates A's vagina or anus with a part of B's body or anything else, or penetrates A's mouth with B's penis,

(b) A consents to the penetration,

(c) the penetration is sexual,

(d) B is aged 18 or over,

(e) A is related to B in a way mentioned in subsection (2), and

(f) A knows or could reasonably be expected to know that he is related to B in that way.'

Class of offence	3	SOA 2003, s 72 applies	✗
Notification requirements	See text	SOPO	✔
CJA 2003, Sch 15 applies	✔	Serious specified offence	✗
Review of lenient sentence	✗	Special provisions of CYPA 1933	✗
Detention of young offender for specified period			✗

See **1.48** et seq.

6.78 Both offences are triable either way and punishable with a maximum of 2 years' imprisonment on conviction on indictment.[84] See the SGC Definitive Guideline,[85] in the Appendix. The notification requirements under SOA 2003, Pt 2 apply to these offences in specified circumstances. These are:

• where the offender was under 18, he is or has been sentenced in respect of the offence to at least 12 months' imprisonment;

• in any other case, the offender, in respect of the offence or finding, is or has been:

---

[82] Section 73, Sch 15, paras 2, 5(1), (2), 6(1), (2).

[83] The amendment, the insertion of '(subject to subsection (3A))' in each of s 64(1) and 65(1), came into force on 8 July 2008: CJIA 2008, s 153(2)(e).

[84] SOA 2003, ss 64(4), 65(5). Maximum on summary conviction: **1.43**.

[85] At pp 5–18 and 92–93.

–   sentenced to a term of imprisonment, or
–   detained in a hospital.[86]

Actus reus

6.79   It will be noted that essentially these two offences deal with the two sides of the same coin. They both require penetration in one of the ways described in subs (1)(a) of each section (although s 65 does not require the penetration to be intentional, a point of no great substance). The penetration must be sexual and it must be of a relative. It will be noted that both offences are gender neutral, although the ways in which a female could perpetrate the s 64 offence are limited.[87] A must be aged 16 or over and B 18 or over. The Home Office guidance on the Act states:[88]

> 'In cases where sexual activity was initiated when one of the parties was an adult and the other was a child under 18, there will normally be a presumption that the criminal responsibility for the offence should rest only with the person who was adult at onset and that no criminal responsibility should attach to the younger party. This will always be the case where the younger party was aged under 16 at the time of the alleged offence. However, these offences have specifically been drafted to apply to defendants aged 16 or over to cover the situation where, for example, a dominant brother aged 17 incites his submissive sister aged 18 into a sexual relationship, having groomed her for this purpose and with the expectation that she will be held responsible because she is an adult. Applying the offences to 16 and 17 year olds means that where a child of 17 is having sex with a family member aged 18, the 18 year old could be prosecuted for a familial child sex offence and the 17 year old could be prosecuted for one of the "sex with an adult relative" offences, with the decision about which party should be charged being based on the facts of the individual case.'

6.80   Sections 64(2) and 65(2) define the ways that A may be related to B: as a parent, grandparent, child, grandchild, brother, sister, half-brother, half-sister, uncle, aunt, nephew or niece. Penetrative sexual activity between relatives not included in this list is not unlawful, nor is non-penetrative sexual activity between adult relatives, however closely related.

6.81   For the purposes of ss 64(2) and 65(2), 'uncle' means the brother of a person's parent, and 'aunt' has a corresponding meaning.[89] In contrast, these terms include the half-brother and half-sister of a person's parent for the purposes of the familial child sex offences under ss 25 and 26. Consequent on the present definition of 'uncle' and 'aunt', 'nephew' and 'niece' mean the child of a person's brother or sister.[90] The uncle/aunt-niece/nephew relationships were not covered by the old offences of incest, despite the fact that they are within the prohibited degrees of marriage.[91]

6.82   Subject to what is said in **6.83**, where a person is adopted adoptive relationships are excluded from the application of s 64 or 65 but biological ones are not. Thus, an offence is not committed where, for example, A and B are adoptive brother and sister, adoptive grandparent and grandchild or adoptive uncle and niece. Until 8 July 2008, this was the case only where the adoption was made on or after 30 December 2005. If the

---

86   SOA 2003, s 80, Sch 3, para 32.
87   A woman could be convicted as a secondary party to the commission of a s 64 offence in any of the ways described by s 64: *Ram and Ram* (1893) 17 Cox CC 609.
88   *Guidance on Part 1 of the Sexual Offences Act 2003* (Home Office, 2003) (*Guidance Pt 1*), at para 290.
89   SOA 2003, ss 64(3)(a) and 65(3)(a).
90   SOA 2003, ss 64(3)(b) and 65(3)(b).
91   MA 1949, Sch 1.

adoption was made before that date, adoptive relationships were included in the application of s 64 or 65 and the biological relationships of an adopted person were not. This was because, by oversight, only one of the two statutory provisions relating to the effect of adoption on the legal relationship of the parties was originally disapplied.[92] CJIA 2008[93] has rectified the situation by amending the relevant legislation so as to disapply the other provision in this respect. This amendment came into force on 8 July 2008.[94]

6.83 The statements at the beginning of **6.82** are subject to an exception in respect of penetration involving an adoptive parent and his or her adopted child. This is because CJIA 2008 has amended ss 64 and 65 so as to provide in each section that 'parent' includes an adoptive parent and that 'child' includes an adopted person.[95] However, s 64(3A) and s 65(3A) (both inserted by CJIA 2008[96]) provide that, where s 64(1) or s 65(1) apply in a case where A is related to B as B's child by virtue of being B's adopted child, A does not commit an offence under s 64(1) or 65(1), as the case may be, unless A is 18 or over. These amendments came into force on 8 July 2008.[97]

6.84 It will be noted that, unlike the list of relationships for the purposes of an offence under ss 25 and 26, the list does not include step-relationships or the other wider familial relations which apply to the familial child sex offences under ss 25 and 26. The context where adults are concerned is rather different and, with the possible exception of step-parents (and their stepchildren), the line seems to have been drawn in the right place. The gender neutralisation of the present offences and the fact that they are not limited to penile/vaginal penetration means that they cannot be justified as a whole on the basis of avoiding the risk of genetic abnormalities. Their justification lies in the potential for continued abuse, and that potential depends on context rather than a blood tie. Consequently, the limitation of the offences to sexual penetration is puzzling. If the offences are necessary to deal with abuse, why should they not apply to non-penetrative sexual activity, such as masturbation of B by A?

6.85 The requirement that a penetration be sexual is clearly going to be satisfied with ease where the penetration is by a penis. In the case of other penetration, it will depend

---

[92] Although an adopted person is treated in law as if born as the child of the adopters or adopter, and not as the child of its biological parents (ACA 2002, s 67), this does not apply for the purposes of an offence under SOA 2003, s 64 or 65. This is because ACA 2002, s 67 is disapplied by s 74(1)(b) (as amended) of that Act. Section 74(1)(b), however, only applies to adoptions made on or after 30 December 2005. AA 1976, s 39 (which has the like effect to ACA 2002, s 67 in relation to adoptions made before 30 December 2005), was not disapplied at the same time as ACA 2002, s 67.

[93] CJIA 2008, s 73, Sch 15, paras 2, 7 amends AA 1976, s 47(1) so as to disapply AA 1976, s 39 for the purposes of SOA 2003, s 64 or 65.

[94] CJIA 2008, s 153(2)(e).

[95] SOA 2003, ss 64(3)(za), (zb), 65(3)(za), (zb) (inserted by CJIA 2008, Sch 15, paras 2, 5(1), (3), 6(1), (3). Nothing in AA 1976, s 47 or ACA 2002, s 74 is to be read as preventing the application of AA 1976, s 39 or ACA 2002, s 67 for the purposes of SOA 2003, s 64(3)(za) and (zb) or s 65(3)(za) and (zb): SOA 2003, ss 64(6), 65(6) (inserted by CJIA 2008, Sch 15, paras 2, 5(1), (5), 6(1), (5)). The reference to an 'adopted person' is to an adopted person within the meaning of ACA 2002, Pt 1, Ch 4, ie a person adopted under an adoption order made in the UK, the Channel Islands, the Isle of Man and countries outside the British Isles which have implemented the Hague Convention on Adoption (1999), overseas adoptions (as defined by ACA 2002, s 87) and adoptions recognised by the law of England and Wales and effected under the law of any other country: ACA 2002, s 66(1).

[96] CJIA 2008, Sch 15, paras 2, 5(1), (4), 6(1), (4).

[97] CJIA 2008, s 153(2)(e).

on the circumstances. An example of a case where the requirement would serve to exclude conduct from the offence would be where one sibling helps another to insert a pessary for medical reasons.[98]

6.86   In the offence under s 65, the prosecution must prove that A consented to the penetrative sexual activity.

Mens rea

6.87   The offences of incest under SOA 1956 required the prosecution to prove that the defendant knew that he or she and the other party were related. The offences under ss 64 and 65 make life easier for prosecutors. They are required by ss 64(1)(e) and 65(1)(f) respectively to prove that the defendant (A) knew or *could reasonably be expected to know* that he or she is related to B in a way mentioned in s 64(2) or s 65(2), as the case may be. According to the Home Office guidance, '[e]xcept in the most unusual circumstances, a person can reasonably be expected to be aware of such close familial ties'.[99] The type of requirement in ss 64(1)(e) and 65(1)(f) has already been discussed in another context in **6.22**. So has the evidential presumption laid down by s 64(4) and s 65(4) in respect of the proof of it, namely that:

> 'Where ... it is proved that the defendant was related to the other person in any of [the specified] ways, it is to be taken that the defendant knew or could reasonably have been expected to know that he was related in that way unless sufficient evidence is adduced to raise an issue as to whether he knew or could reasonably have been expected to know that he was.'

Other points

6.88   The statement above that the two offences essentially deal with the two sides of the same coin is not completely true. If brother X penetrates sister Y with Y's consent, X and Y will normally each commit the relevant offence if both are 18 or older. On the other hand, if X is only aged 16 and Y is 18 or older, X will commit an offence on Y under s 64(1) but Y will not commit an offence against X under s 65(1) because X is under the age limit of 18 for a 'victim' under s 65(1). The relevant offence by Y would be the more serious offence under s 25. If X and Y had both been under 18, no offence would have been committed under s 64 or s 65, even though one or both was aged 16 or 17; the relevant offence would be under s 25, as it would be if one (or both) of them was (were) under 16. It may seem odd that a person under 16 cannot be convicted of an offence under s 64 or s 65 with an adult relative but can be convicted under s 25 in relation to a much wider range of sexual activity with a much wider range of people under 18 in a familial relationship. The explanation, however, is that the offences under ss 64 and 65 are aimed at protection from abuse of B by A and B must be 18 or over. It is unlikely that A would be able to exploit and abuse B if significantly younger.

6.89   Although the essence of the offence in s 65 is that the perpetrator consents to the penetration (in essence 'permits' it), and no reference to consent is made by s 64, the s 64 offence is designed to deal with consensual penetration.[100] Nevertheless, this does not mean that the offences cannot be committed where A, aged 16 or over, induces relative B, aged 18 or over, to engage in a penetrative sexual activity by a threat which is

---

98   Explanatory notes to SOA 2003.
99   *Guidance Pt 1*, at para 291.
100   'Consent' in the present context means 'consent' as defined by SOA 2003, s 74 (see **3.13** et seq).

insufficient to vitiate B's consent. Indeed, as the law stands both parties would commit an offence under ss 64 and 65 respectively, since the defence of duress by threats would not be available to B in such a case.[101]

6.90 The offence under s 64 can technically be committed by non-consensual penetration. However, if consent is alleged to be lacking, the appropriate course of action would be to charge the penetrator with rape or assault by penetration as the more serious offence; on conviction for such an offence, the sentence will then reflect the absence of consent.[102] As in the case of the old offence of buggery (where no reference was made in its definition to absence of consent), a sentence on conviction for a s 64 offence cannot be imposed which reflects the conclusion that the victim was not consenting.[103]

6.91 The absence of the marriage exception which applies to the offences under ss 25 and 26, and to various other offences under SOA 2003, is open to criticism in the light of the fact that marriages between uncles and nieces and nephews and aunts are potentially legal in some countries.[104]

6.92 The fact that relatives who engage in sexual activity on a fully consensual basis (or that a person who engages in sexual activity with a relative after being groomed or induced to do so by a threat) are (or is) criminally liable under s 25 or s 26 is open to particular objection. It is a good example of the dangers of drafting offences widely and leaving it to the discretion of the prosecution or the sentencer to mitigate the rigour of the law.

---

[101] See *Card, Cross & Jones*, para 16.31 et seq.
[102] *Davies* [1998] 1 Cr App R (S) 380.
[103] Ibid.
[104] A point made by Spencer 'Child and Family Offences' [2004] Crim LR 347, at p 357.

Chapter 7

CHILD ABDUCTION

7.1 This chapter considers the offence of child abduction by a person other than a person connected with the child in a prescribed way, contrary to the Child Abduction Act (ChAA) 1984, s 2, under which (unlike the offences of kidnapping and false imprisonment) the consent of the child taken or detained is immaterial. Child abduction by a person connected with the child, contrary to ChAA 1984, s 1, is outside the scope of this book. The offence under s 2 is included in this book because the abductor is often sexually motivated.

7.2 Criminal liability for abduction goes back to the thirteenth century.[1] Thereafter, the law was developed by further legislation, principally in the nineteenth century, aimed at protecting young girls and unmarried women against sexual or financial depredation. This line of legislation culminated in the Sexual Offences Act (SOA) 1956, ss 17–21, which provided the following offences:

- taking or detaining a woman of any age against her will with intent that she should marry or have unlawful sexual intercourse with the defendant or another, if she was so taken or detained by force or for the sake of her property or expectation of property (s 17);

- taking or detaining a girl under 21 out of the possession of her parent or guardian against his will, if she had property or expectation of property and was so taken or detained by fraud and with intent that she should marry or have extra-marital intercourse with the defendant or another (s 18);

- taking an unmarried girl under 18 out of the possession of her parent or guardian against his will with intent that she should have extra-marital intercourse with men or a particular man (s 19);

- taking, without lawful authority or excuse, an unmarried girl under 16 out of the possession of her parent or guardian against his will (s 20); and

- taking a mentally defective woman out of the possession of her parent or guardian against his will with intent that she should have extra-marital intercourse with men or a particular man (s 21).

The offence under s 18 was repealed by the Family Law Reform Act (FLRA) 1969, s 11(c), but the other offences survived until they were repealed by SOA 2003.[2] They have not been replaced.

---

[1]   Statute of Westminster 1275, c 13.
[2]   See **1.5**.

CHILD ABDUCTION ACT 1984, S 2

7.3   ChAA 1984, s 2 stems from the recommendations of the Criminal Law Revision Committee (CLRC) in 1980,[3] although it differs from them in a number of significant respects. The offence recommended by the Committee was intended to replace SOA 1956, s 20.[4] In recommending that offence the CLRC was influenced by the fact that the requirement in s 20 of a taking out of the possession of a parent or guardian against his will had been given a restricted interpretation in *Jones*,[5] so as to mean that there must be some conduct of the defendant amounting to a substantial interference with the possessory relationship of parent, etc and child. Thus, whilst permanent deprivation was not required, merely taking a girl for a short walk without her parent's permission did not constitute a taking out of parental possession for the purposes of the offence. The CLRC considered that a substantial interference with possession should not be required and that the degree of interference which should be covered was interference with the responsibilities of persons having the lawful control of the child, whether permanently or for the time being, for the well-being of the child.[6]

7.4   Like the offence recommended by the CLRC, and unlike the offences under SOA 1956, ss 17-21, the offence under ChAA 1984, s 2 protects boys as well as girls.

7.5   ChAA 1984, s 2(1)[7] provides:

'Subject to subsection (3) below, a person, other than one mentioned in subsection (2) below commits an offence if, without lawful authority or reasonable excuse, he takes or detains a child under the age of sixteen—

(a)   so as to remove him from the lawful control of any person having lawful control of the child; or

(b)   so as to keep him out of the lawful control of any person entitled to lawful control of the child.'

An offence under s 2(1) is triable either way and punishable on conviction on indictment with a maximum of 7 years' imprisonment.[8]

Class of offence	3	SOA 2003, s 72 applies	✗

---

3   *Fourteenth Report: Offences against the Person*, Cmnd 7844 (1980), at paras 239–246, 251(c).
4   Ibid, at para 240.
5   [1973] Crim LR 621.
6   *Fourteenth Report: Offences against the Person*, Cmnd 7844 (1980), at para 242.
7   As amended by ChA 1989, s 108(4), Sch 12, para 38.
8   ChAA 1984, s 4(1)(b). On summary conviction an offender is liable to imprisonment for a term not exceeding 6 (to be increased to 12, see **1.43**) months or to a fine not exceeding the statutory maximum, or to both: s 4(1)(a) (as amended).
     There is no definitive sentencing guideline, nor a guideline case in relation to ChAA 1984, s 2. For sentencing cases see: *Dean* [2000] 2 Cr App R (S) 253; *Parsons* [1996] 1 Cr App R (S) 36; *Mohammed Raza* [2007] 1 Cr App R (S) 79; *Prime* [2005] 1 Cr App R (S) 203; *Whitlock* (1993) 15 Cr App R (S) 146; *Kidd* [2004] EWCA Crim 17; *Nelmes* (2001) *The Times*, February 6; *Cooper* (1994) 15 Cr App R (S) 470; *M (Martin Graham)* [2008] EWCA Crim 313; *JA, DA, ET* [2002] 1 Cr App R (S) 473.

Notification requirements	✗	SOPO[9]	✓[10]
CJA 2003,[11] Sch 15 applies	✗	Serious specified offence	✗
Review of lenient sentence	✗	Special provisions of CYPA 1933[12]	✗
Detention of young offender for specified period			✗

See **1.48** et seq.

7.6   Section 2(1) creates two separate forms of the same offence.[13] These forms are:

- taking or detaining a child under 16 so as to remove him or her from the lawful control of a person having lawful control of the child; and

- taking or detaining a child under 16 so as to keep him or her out of the lawful control of any person entitled to lawful control of the child.

Actus reus

7.7   It must be proved that the defendant, D, not being connected with the child, took or detained a child under 16 (C) either so as to remove C from the lawful control of any person having lawful control of C or so as to keep C out of the lawful control of any person entitled to have lawful control of him or her. The reference in s 2(1) to 'without lawful authority or reasonable excuse' would seem to be to a defence to be raised by the defendant's or other evidence but then to be disproved by the prosecution. Unless it provides a lawful authority or reasonable excuse, the reason why D committed the actus reus is irrelevant; an improper or immoral motive is not required. C's consent is irrelevant.

Who can commit the offence?

7.8   The offence under s 2 can be committed by anyone, male or female, other than a person mentioned in s 2(2). The persons so mentioned are the following persons connected with C:

'(a)   where the father and mother of the child in question were married to each other at the time of his birth, the child's father and mother;[14]

(b)   where the father and mother of the child in question were not married to each other at the time of his birth, the child's mother; and

(c)   any other person mentioned in section 1(2)(c) to (e) above.'

---

9   Sexual offences prevention order.
10   SOA 2003, s 104, Sch 5, para 43B (inserted by SOA 2003 (Amendment of Schedules 3 and 5) Order 2007, SI 2007/296).
11   Criminal Justice Act 2003.
12   Children and Young Persons Act 1933.
13   *Foster v DPP* [2005] 1 WLR 1400, at p 1402.
14   References to a child's parents and to a child whose parents were (or were not) married to each other at the time of its birth are to be construed in accordance with the FLRA 1987, s 1 (which extends their meaning): ChAA 1984, s 3(d).

The persons mentioned in s 1(2)(c) to (e) are:

• a guardian of C;

• a special guardian of C;

• a person in whose favour a residence order is in force with respect to C; and

• a person who has custody of C.[15]

7.9   Where a certificate issued by the Secretary of State under ChA 1989, s 51 (refuges for children at risk) is in force, ChAA 1984, s 2 does not apply to a person providing a refuge for any child at risk of harm in a voluntary home or private children's home nor to the provision by a local authority foster parent or a foster parent with whom children are placed by a local authority.[16]

7.10   It will be noted from the above that the above exceptions do not apply to the father of C if he was not married to the mother at the time of C's birth. However, the father has a defence under s 2(3)(a)(i)[17] if he proves that he is C's father.

Child under 16

7.11   An offence under ChAA 1984, s 2 can be committed against any child under 16[18] other than one connected with the defendant in one of the ways described in s 2(2).[19]

Take or detain

7.12   D must be proved to have taken *or* detained a child under 16 (C) either so as to remove C from the lawful control of any person having lawful control of C or so as to keep C out of the lawful control of any person entitled to have lawful control of him or her.

7.13   For the purposes of s 2, D is regarded by s 3(a) as taking C if he causes or induces C to accompany him or any other person or causes C to be taken. This would seem to be an exclusive definition of 'taking' for the purposes of s 2, although the Court of Appeal has declined to express a view on the point.[20] D's acts need not be the sole cause of C accompanying him; it is immaterial that there are also other causes, such as

---

[15]   For the meaning of 'guardian of a child', see Children Act (ChA) 1989, s 105(1); for the meaning of 'special guardian', see ChA 1989, s 14A, and for the meaning of 'residence order', see ChA 1989, s 8(1). The definitions in ChA 1989 referred to are applied to ChAA 1984, s 1(7)(a) (as substituted). A person is treated as having custody of a child if there is in force an order of a court in the UK awarding them (whether solely or jointly with another person) custody, legal custody or care and control of the child: ChAA 1984, s 1(7)(b) (as substituted). The provisions whereby a court can award custody, legal custody or care and control of a child were all replaced by ChA 1989 as from 14 October 1991 (ChA 1989, Sch 15; Children Act 1989 (Commencement and Transitional Provisions) Order 1991, SI 1991/828, art 3(2)); consequently the reference to a person who has custody of a child is for practical purposes obsolescent.

[16]   ChA 1989, s 51(5), (6).

[17]   See **7.27**, **7.28**.

[18]   As to proof of age, see **3.131**, **3.132**.

[19]   Presumably, the principle in *Tyrrell* [1894] 1 QB 710 (para **4.17**) applies to prevent a child being liable as accomplice to an offence perpetrated under ChAA 1984, s 2.

[20]   *A (Child Abduction)* [2000] 1 Cr App R 418.

C's state of mind (eg a wish to go with him).[21] Thus, and by analogy with the offences under SOA 1956 (and its predecessors), not only is no force required,[22] but the fact that C consents or proposes the taking does not prevent 'taking' if D's acts are an effective cause of C accompanying him, as where he has made a bargain with C to take him away (even if at C's instigation)[23] or if he has otherwise persuaded or induced C to accompany him.[24] On the other hand, unlike the offences under the old legislation,[25] the use of the word 'accompany' indicates that if D is not present when C leaves home by prior agreement or at his persuasion or inducement, D does not 'take' C. A fortiori, D would not take C if C came entirely of his volition without any persuasion or inducement by D and D simply fails to restore C to the lawful control of the person with such control.

7.14 By ChAA 1984, s 3(c), for the purposes of s 2, a person is to be regarded as detaining a child if he causes C to be detained or induces C to remain with him or any other person. This leaves open the meaning of 'detain' in this context. There is nothing in ChAA 1984 to warrant limiting the term to compelling a child to remain in a place.[26] On this basis, a person who deceives or persuades a child into staying detains the child. By analogy with 'taking' and consistent with the purpose of ChAA 1984 the child's consent is immaterial.

7.15 It is clear from what has been said about 'taking' and 'detaining' that they refer to conduct which is almost inevitably continuous, the period of continuous time depending on the facts. This may be of practical importance in relation to the defences under ChAA 1984, s 2(3)[27] and the defences of lawful authority or reasonable excuse.[28] Thus, for example, detaining with lawful authority will become a detaining without lawful authority if during the period of its continuity that authority ceases to exist. Is the contrary true? Can a person who initially satisfies requirements for liability under s 2 and who does not have one of the above defences cease to be so liable simply because by the time that the taking or detention ends he has a defence? In principle, the answer is 'no'. Against this may be cited *Packer*,[29] a case concerned with the offence of abduction of a girl under 18, contrary to the Offences against the Person Act (OAPA) 1861, s 54, to which there was a defence of reasonable belief that the girl was 18 or over. It was held that a 'taking' under s 54 (re-enacted as SOA 1956, s 19) could be continuous over a period of time, and that if the defendant (who initially did not have that reasonable belief) formed it before the taking was 'complete' he could rely on the defence. The fallacy with this is that it ignores the fact that as soon as the taking commenced the defendant became guilty of the offence and if he had been charged with a taking at the precise place and time when it commenced would have had no excuse. How could the subsequent availability of a defence at a later point of time undo that initial liability?

---

[21] Ibid.
[22] *Mankletow* (1853) 6 Cox CC 143.
[23] *Robins* (1844) 1 C & K 456.
[24] *Mankletow* (1853) 6 Cox CC 143.
[25] *Handley* (1859) 1 F & F 648; *Robb* (1864) 5 F & F 59.
[26] Contrast *Moore and Grazier* (1971) 1 CCC (2d) 521, at p 537, cited by Rook and Ward *Sexual Offences Law & Practice* (Sweet & Maxwell, 3rd edn, 2004) (*Rook & Ward*), at para 9.18 (a decision on a Canadian offence similar to that under SOA 1956, s 17, described in **7.1**, which spoke in terms of 'some form of compulsion' whereby a person's liberty was restrained).
[27] See **7.27**.
[28] See **7.30** et seq.
[29] (1886) 16 Cox CC 57.

So as to remove from or keep out of

7.16   D must take or detain C so as to remove C from the lawful control[30] of any person having lawful control of C, or so as to keep C out of the lawful control of any person entitled to lawful control of C. 'So as to' remove or keep means to have the objective consequence (ie have the effect) of so removing or keeping.[31] The question whether any taking or detaining of C has had the consequence of removing C from (or keeping him or her out of) the lawful control of the person having (or entitled to) lawful control of C is a question of fact, and the jury must have regard to the meaning of 'lawful control'.[32]

7.17   No removal from the geographical area of control of the person with lawful control is required by the words 'so as to remove him from the lawful control of any person having lawful control of the child'. This was held by the Court of Appeal in *Leather*,[33] where A was charged, inter alia, with five counts of taking children so as to remove them from the lawful control of their parents. In each case, D had induced the children to accompany him in search for an allegedly stolen bicycle. D did not try to stop any of the children leaving. It appeared that the children had been to the places to which they went with D on previous occasions with the consent of their parents. At the end of the prosecution's case, defence counsel had submitted that there was no case to answer because there was no evidence that the children had been removed from the control of their parents or other lawful custodian because the prosecution had to prove not only (a) that C was in the lawful control of his parent and (b) that he moved or was moved physically, but also (c) that at the end of the movement C was outside the geographical area of control. The judge rejected that submission, ruling that 'control' did not involve a geographical element.

7.18   The Court of Appeal held that the judge was correct in rejecting the submission of no case to answer. It held that 'control' in s 2(1) does not have a necessary spatial element. It continued:[34]

> 'Who has control of a child is a question of fact. If, for example, "physical control", by which is meant a taking hold of the child and continuing to hold the child, is taken by a stranger at a time when the child has been, up to that time, in the control of its parents, then that would inevitably amount to a removal of the child from the control of its parents. Of course, it may be that in such circumstances there would also be a detaining of a child so as to move him from the lawful control of his parent or other person ...

> We are satisfied that the words with which we are concerned do not require the removal of the child but the removal of the control of the child from the parent or other person having lawful control to the accused. There is no need for any complicated definition of the word "control". It is a perfectly ordinary English word in everyday use.

---

[30]   ChAA 1984 does not define 'lawful control'. In *Mousir* [1987] Crim LR 561, the Court of Appeal held that it was not necessary or desirable to try to define the phrase. It stated that the concept of control may vary according to the person having control at the relevant time, whether it be a parent or a schoolmaster or a nanny. In *Re Owens* [2000] 1 Cr App R 195, 'it did not seem [to Simon Brown LJ (as he then was) with whose words Newman J entirely agreed] that, for the purposes of s 2(1), lawful control can be equated with legal custody. That, indeed is plain from the language of the provision itself: paragraph (a) speaks of someone "having lawful control", paragraph (b) of someone "entitled to lawful control"' (at p 200).

[31]   See **7.24**.

[32]   *Mousir* [1987] Crim LR 561.

[33]   (1993) 98 Cr App R 179.

[34]   (1993) 98 Cr App R 179, at pp 183–184.

[A] question which would have been relevant in each case was: Was the child concerned, without any lawful authority or reasonable excuse, deflected by some action of the accused from that which with the consent of his parents, or other person at the time having lawful control, he would otherwise have been doing into some activity induced by the accused? If, as must have been the case, the answer to that question was "yes", then it was open to the jury to say that the offence was made out. Clearly, they would have to consider the individual circumstances of each individual allegation. No doubt here they would wish to take into account that each child, bar one for whom there was an acquittal, was led away from that which he or she had been doing by a suggestion made by the appellant.'

7.19   Further explanation was provided by the Divisional Court in *Foster v DPP*,[35] where it was held that 'remove' means 'a substitution of the authority by an accused for that of the person lawfully having it and not physical removal'.

7.20   The distinction between removal from a person *having* lawful control (s 2(1)(a)), and keeping from a person *entitled* to lawful control (s 2(1)(b)), is intended to reflect materially different states of affairs. The first (s 2(1)(a)) requires C there and then to be in the lawful control of someone when taken or detained. The second (s 2(1)(b)) requires only that C is kept out of lawful control of someone entitled to it when taken or detained, and would cover a situation (such as that in *Foster v DPP*) where C had run away from lawful control and was, whilst out of lawful control, detained unlawfully by D or a situation where a childminder kept C beyond the time permitted by its parent. The importance of this distinction is shown by *Foster v DPP*. A 15-year-old child, C, was in the lawful control of her foster parents. Believing that C was over the age of 16, D1 took her to his address. C's foster father reported C missing when she did not return home. The police telephoned D1 and told him that they were looking for C and that she was under age. That information was also made known to D2. Soon after, the police arrived at D1's home. D1 and D2 falsely told them that C had been there but had left. When the police revisited 5 hours later they found C in the living room. D1 and D2 were charged with detaining C so as to remove her from the lawful control of a person having lawful control of her, contrary to ChAA 1984, s 2(1)(a). They were convicted but the Divisional Court allowed their appeals. It held that, on the facts, by the time that D1 and D2 knew that their inducements to C were unlawful, ie when they learnt that C was under age, C was no longer in the lawful control of her foster parents, and the fact that this was so because of their conduct was immaterial.

7.21   Clearly, in *Foster v DPP*, there could not have been liability under s 2(1)(a) since:

* when C accompanied D1 home (ie when there was a *taking* so as to remove C from the foster parents' lawful control), D1 believed that she was over the age of 16 (and therefore D1 was not liable at that stage: see **7.27**); and

* when D1 and D2 detained C after learning that she was under age, she was no longer in the lawful control of the foster parents or anyone else.

The appropriate charge would have been under s 2(1)(b), of detaining C so as to keep her out of the lawful control of a person (the foster parents) entitled to lawful control.

---

35   [2005] 1 WLR 1400.

Mens rea

7.22   The mens rea for an offence under ChAA 1984, s 2 required to be proved by the prosecution, at least in the first instance, is limited, as explained below.

7.23   ChAA 1984, s 2(1)(a) and (b) requires that D takes or detains C under 16 *so as* (a) *to* remove C from the lawful control of any person having lawful control of C or (b) *to* keep C out of the lawful control of any person entitled to lawful control of C. 'So as to' has been the cause of a difference of opinion in the courts. In *Mousir*[36] it was conceded, and the Court of Appeal agreed, that 'so as to' was concerned with the objective consequence (effect) of the taking or detaining (ie the removal of C from the lawful control of any person having lawful control of him or the keeping of C out of the lawful control of any person entitled to such lawful control, respectively), and was not concerned with the D's purpose (intention) to achieve that consequence. In *Leather* the Court of Appeal saw no defect in a direction which was solely in objective terms.[37] On the other hand, in *Re Owens*,[38] an extradition case, where *Mousir* was not cited, the Divisional Court held that 'so as to' meant 'with the intention of' keeping C out of the control of someone known to be entitled to such control, rather than merely 'with the effect of' the taking or detaining.

7.24   The matter was resolved by the Divisional Court in *Foster v DPP*,[39] where the Court held that it was bound by *Mousir* and *Leather* and that the emphasis on mens rea in *Re Owens* was unnecessary to reach the result in that case. The Divisional Court stated that the mens rea under s 2 is:[40]

> '... an intentional or reckless taking of a child under the age of 16, the effect or objective consequence of which is to remove or to keep that child within the meaning of s 2(1)(a) or (b).'

7.25   Examination of this reveals that this requirement does not add up to much because, quite apart from the fact that it does not require D to have mens rea as to the objective consequence:

- mens rea as to C's age is not something which the prosecution must prove, at least in the first instance, because lack of mens rea as to C's age is made the subject of a defence under s 2(3)(b), below. It would have been better if the Court of Appeal had put 'under the age of 16' in square brackets or not used the phrase at all; and

- mens rea as to the fact that another person had lawful control of, or was entitled to such control of, C does not have to be proved.

The defence under s 2(3)

7.26   A person who, with the above mens rea, has committed the actus reus without lawful authority or reasonable excuse will be guilty of an offence under ChAA 1984, s 2 unless he proves that he has a defence under s 2(3).

---

36   [1987] Crim LR 561.
37   (1993) 98 Cr App R 179.
38   [2000] 1 Cr App R 195.
39   [2005] 1 WLR 1400.
40   [2005] 1 WLR 1400 at [27].

7.27 ChAA 1984, s 2(3) provides:

'In proceedings against any person for an offence under this section, it shall be a defence for that person to prove—

(a) where the father and mother of the child in question were not married to each other at the time of his birth—

    (i) that he is the child's father; or

    (ii) that, at the time of the alleged offence, he believed, on reasonable grounds, that he was the child's father; or

(b) that, at the time of the alleged offence, he believed that the child had attained the age of sixteen.'

As to whether 'a defence for that person to prove' imposes a legal (or persuasive) burden or an evidential one, and, if the former, its compatibility with the presumption of innocence under the European Convention on Human Rights, Art 6(2), see the approach to this issue set out in **5.41, 5.42**. Analogy with the defence of 'without lawful authority or reasonable excuse' (below) suggests that D does not bear the legal burden in respect of s 2(3).

7.28 The defences under s 2(3)(a) apply only to the father of the 'child in question', ie the child taken or detained. This was affirmed by the Court of Appeal in *Berry*,[41] which went on to hold that consequently s 2(3)(a) had no application to a case where D had made a mistake of identity and took child C thinking that the child was E whose father he was; in such a case, it held, the defence on the facts raised by D fell to be considered by reference to the phrase 'without lawful authority or reasonable excuse'[42] in s 2(1).

7.29 The defence under s 2(3)(a)(ii) clearly postulates (a) a subjective test (did the defendant believe[43] that he was the father of the child in question?), and (b) an objective test (did he have reasonable grounds for believing that?) under which no account is taken of D's characteristics as they affect his perception of the relevant facts. In contrast the defence of belief under s 2(3)(b), which is available to any defendant, is purely subjective in nature, so that even an unreasonable belief that C is 16 or over will excuse the defendant.[44]

Without lawful authority or reasonable excuse

7.30 The taking or detention of C must be without lawful authority or reasonable excuse. In *Berry*[45] it was common ground, which the Court of Appeal apparently accepted, that the prosecution has the burden of proving this.[46] It is, however, submitted that an evidential burden in respect of lawful authority or reasonable excuse must be satisfied before the prosecution has the task of disproving such a defence. Proving a negative is not easy and it would be unfortunate if the prosecution had to prove the absence of lawful authority or reasonable excuse beyond reasonable doubt when the

---

[41] [1996] 2 Cr App R 226. For criticism of this decision see Smith's commentary at [1996] Crim LR 574.

[42] See **7.30** et seq.

[43] For the meaning of 'believe' see **2.61**.

[44] *Kimber* [1983] 3 All ER 316; *Gladstone Williams* (1984) 78 Cr App R 276; *Beckford v R* [1988] AC 130; *B v DPP* [2000] 2 AC 428; *K* [2002] 1 AC 462.

[45] [1996] 2 Cr App R 226, at pp 229, 230.

[46] Contrast the defence under ChAA 1984, s 2(3).

issue was not raised on the evidence. It is for this reason that it is submitted that 'without lawful authority or reasonable excuse' is a matter of defence.

Lawful authority

7.31 'Lawful authority' presumably means that the taking or detaining was authorised by law, as where a statute authorises the removal into care of children, or where a child is deprived of liberty following the sentence of a court or the exercise of a right of arrest, or where a parent or guardian with lawful control of a child consents.

7.32 For the purposes of the old offence of abduction contrary to what became SOA 1956, s 20, which spoke of taking 'against the will of a parent etc', it was held that there was such a taking if, though the parent etc consented, his or her consent was induced by the fraudulent representation of D.[47] It would appear that this was so even though the mistake induced did not relate to D's identity or the nature of the act or its quality.[48] There is no reason to doubt that the law is the same in respect of 'without lawful authority' in ChAA 1984, s 2. Presumably, consent given under a self-induced mistake would be equated with one induced by misrepresentation, as it can in other contexts.[49]

Reasonable excuse

7.33 'Reasonable excuse' is presumably meant to add something to 'lawful authority', but what that is is not clear. 'Reasonable excuse' clearly refers to an excuse, other than lawful authority, which is reasonable.

7.34 The Court of Appeal in *Berry*[50] concluded that, although D who mistakenly believed that the child in question was his would have mens rea, it would be open to a jury to conclude that he had a reasonable excuse; consequently, the judge had been wrong to direct the jury to forget about 'reasonable excuse'. The Court stated:[51]

> 'It is ... common ground that on general principles if the facts as the appellant believed[52] them to be would have afforded him lawful authority or reasonable excuse, then the prosecution would have failed to prove the offence. Thus if the appellant may honestly but mistakenly have believed the child ... was his daughter it would be open to the jury to conclude that that constituted reasonable excuse.'

The flaw with this is that it is not apparent how the facts as D believed them to be would have afforded him a lawful authority or reasonable excuse. If they had been as he believed they would not have given him lawful authority to take C and it seems very odd to base a reasonable excuse on a belief in facts which, had they been true, would have amounted for some unexplained reason to a reasonable excuse.

---

47   *Hopkins* (1842) Car & M 254 (D falsely represented to child's mother that he was taking the child into service in another town and thereby persuaded mother to consent; taking against mother's will. D convicted of abduction. Trial judge stated that he would reserve the point for the consideration of the court for Crown Cases Reserved but afterwards did not do so because D was convicted of attempted sexual intercourse with the child and sentenced only for that.)

48   The mother's consent in *Hopkins* ibid did not relate to any of these matters.

49   See *Richardson* [1999] QB 444, at p 450.

50   [1996] 2 Cr App R 226.

51   Ibid, at pp 229–230.

52   Whether or not the belief was reasonable, it would seem.

7.35 Reasonable excuse can be contrasted with 'lawful excuse' which appeared in the offence of abduction of a girl under 16, contrary to SOA 1956, s 20, and 'unlawfully' which appeared in the predecessors to that offence. Case-law under that legislation which stated that D acted without lawful excuse or unlawfully should be viewed with caution because 'reasonable' does not imply 'lawful' and seems to embrace a wider range of excuses. On the other hand, a decision that there could be a lawful excuse or lawful taking under the old legislation would necessarily seem equally applicable to the issue of reasonable excuse under ChAA 1984, s 2.

7.36 In *Prince*[53] Denman J thought, obiter, that D would not have acted 'unlawfully' for the purposes of the abduction offence under OAPA 1861, s 55, if he proved that he had the authority of a competent court or some legal warrant (ie lawful authority) or that he acted to prevent some illegal violence requiring forcible intervention by way of protection because that would provide a lawful excuse. In *Tinkler*,[54] a case under the predecessor to OAPA 1861, s 55, D took his orphaned niece away from her guardian, having promised her father that he would take care of her. He was acquitted of abducting the girl after the judge had directed the jury:

> '... inasmuch as no improper motive was suggested on the part of the prosecution, it might very well be concluded, that the prisoner wished the child to live with him, and that he meant to discharge the promise which he alleged he had made to her father, and that he did not suppose he was breaking the law when he took the child away ... [I]f the jury should take that view of the case, and be of opinion that the prisoner honestly believed that he had a right to the custody of the child [ie a claim of right], then ... he would be entitled to an acquittal.'

7.37 On the other hand, it was clear that the mere fact that D acted with a good motive could not render his taking lawful for the purposes of OAPA 1861, s 55, or give him a lawful excuse for the purposes of SOA 1956, s 20. In respect of the former provision there are two cases, *Booth*[55] and *Prince*,[56] to which reference may be made. In *Booth* it was held that motive afforded no defence. D induced his 15-year-old girl servant, C, to leave home, without the knowledge or consent of her parents, and to accompany him by train to a town some 30 miles away, where he left her at a respectable house. D's defence at his trial for abduction was, inter alia, that, actuated by religious and philanthropic motives, he had taken C in order to save her from seclusion in a convent. The jury was directed that, even if C's father did propose to place her in a convent, D's motives were immaterial. Thus the accused in *Booth* acted unlawfully despite his philanthropic motives. In *Prince*, it is clear that Bramwell B, with whom five other judges agreed, did not consider that a good motive could render a taking lawful. He stated, in an obiter dictum:[57]

> 'I have not lost sight of this, that though the statute probably principally aims at seduction for carnal purposes, the taking may be by a female, with a good motive.'

7.38 In respect of lawful excuse in SOA 1956, s 20, there is *Tegerdine*,[58] where D took a 5-year-old child, C, of whom he was the putative father, from her mother. He claimed that he was not guilty of the offence under s 20, claiming that he had taken C because it

---

53 (1875) LR 2 CCR 154, at p 178.
54 (1859) 1 F & F 513.
55 (1872) 12 Cox CC 231.
56 (1875) LR 2 CCR 154.
57 Ibid, at p 174.
58 (1982) 75 Cr App R 298.

was in her interests to be with him because she was not being well cared for. The judge withdrew this defence from the jury on the basis that, whatever D's motives, they could not constitute a defence to the offence charged. The Court of Appeal agreed that in the circumstances D did not have a lawful excuse to take the child. A good motive provided no excuse. The Court of Appeal considered that *Tinkler* was wrongly decided because of this. However, as has been pointed out, *Tinkler* was distinguishable as a case where there was evidence that the defendant had a claim of right, as opposed to a mere philanthropic motive.[59]

---

[59] Smith [1983] Crim LR 164. Also see *Rook & Ward*, at para 9.14.

Chapter 8

INDECENT PHOTOGRAPHS OF A CHILD

8.1   The regulation of indecent images of children is a relatively recent concept, with the legislation originating in the Protection of Children Act (PoCA) 1978. Prior to this, it was necessary to rely on the Obscene Publications Act (OPA) 1959 to regulate such material. However, there were concerns that the obscenity legislation was focusing on the wrong issue and it is clear that the then Government believed it was necessary to introduce new legislation to protect children who were at risk of being abused and exploited to produce indecent photographs. The title of the Act was not accidental; the emphasis was on the protection of children[1] rather than the proliferation of the material.

8.2   Ten years later, concern changed from the production and dissemination of material to the need to regulate simple possession of photographs, resulting in the offence in the Criminal Justice Act (CJA) 1988, s 160, which deals with this. In the absence of any definitive link between the possession of indecent images and contact offending[2] it could be argued that the possession of an image does not contribute to the protection of a child. The counter-argument to this, and one that the courts have repeatedly argued,[3] is that by its very nature it is necessary to abuse or exploit a child in order to produce an indecent image of a child and that accordingly the possession of images encourages the market for such images, requiring further children to be exploited.

8.3   Since 1988 there have been significant alterations to the law relating to indecent photographs of children. The Criminal Justice and Public Order Act 1994, s 84(2) introduced the concept of 'pseudo-photographs'[4] and also introduced a new offence of 'making' an indecent photograph or pseudo-photograph of a child. The Criminal Justice and Court Services Act 2000, s 41 substantially increased the maximum penalty that could be imposed for conviction under either PoCA 1978 or CJA 1988. The Sexual Offences Act (SOA) 2003, s 45 raised the age of 'a child' to 18[5] and ss 48–50 introduced three new offences that complement PoCA 1978.[6] The Violent Crime Reduction Act 2006, s 39 introduced new forfeiture arrangements and, finally, the Criminal Justice and Immigration Act (CJIA) 2008, s 69 widened the scope of these offences to include

---

[1]   See McCarthy and Moodie 'Parliament and Pornography: The 1978 Child Protection Act' (1981) 34 *Parliamentary Affairs* 47, at pp 47–62 for a comprehensive analysis of the origins of the Act.

[2]   There is, as yet, no definitive answer to whether such a link exists. Whilst research has been conducted, it tends to be limited and the results are equivocal (Taylor and Quayle *Child Pornography: An Internet Crime* (Brunner-Routledge, 2003), at pp 74–78).

[3]   See, for example, *Harrison* [2007] EWCA Crim 2976, at [4].

[4]   See **8.14**.

[5]   See **8.18**.

[6]   Discussed in Chapter 10.

tracings or other images derived from photographs.[7] The amount of amendment which the law in this area has received raises concern that it is moving away from its original purpose.[8]

MAKING, TAKING OR DISSEMINATING INDECENT IMAGES

8.4   PoCA 1978, s 1[9] provides:

'(1) ... it is an offence for a person—

(a)   to take, or permit to be taken or to make, any indecent photograph or pseudo-photograph of a child; or
(b)   to distribute or show such indecent photographs or pseudo-photographs; or
(c)   to have in his possession such indecent photographs or pseudo-photographs, with a view to their being distributed or shown by himself or others; or
(d)   to publish or cause to be published any advertisement likely to be understood to be conveying that the advertiser distributes or shows such indecent photographs or pseudo-photographs, or intends to do so.'

An offence under s 1(1) can be committed in respect of one or more photographs or pseudo-photographs, since words in the singular include the plural and vice versa.[10]

Class of offence	3	SOA 2003, s 72 applies	✔[11]
Notification requirements	See text	SOPO[12]	✔
CJA 2003,[13] Sch 15 applies	✔	Serious specified offence	✔
Review of lenient sentence	✘	Special provisions of CYPA 1933[14]	✘
Detention of young offender for specified period			✘

See **1.48** et seq.

8.5   An offence under PoCA 1978, s 1 is triable either way and punishable by a maximum sentence on indictment of 10 years' imprisonment.[15] See the Sentencing Guidelines Council (SGC) Definitive Guideline in the Appendix.[16] The notification requirements apply to this offence where the indecent photographs or pseudo-photographs showed persons under 16:

---

[7]   See **8.17**.
[8]   See, for example, Gillespie 'Tinkering with Child Pornography' [2004] Crim LR 361.
[9]   As amended.
[10]   Interpretation Act 1978, s 6(c).
[11]   See **2.97**.
[12]   Sexual offences prevention order.
[13]   Criminal Justice Act (CJA) 2003.
[14]   Children and Young Persons Act (CYPA) 1933.
[15]   PoCA 1978, s 6(2). Maximum on summary conviction: see **1.43**.
        At pp 5–18, 109–114.

- if the conviction, finding or caution was before 1 May 2004; or

- if the offender was 18 or over; or

- if the offender was under 18, he or she is sentenced in respect of the offence to imprisonment for a term of at least 12 months.[17]

8.6 An offence under PoCA 1978, s 1 requires the consent of the Director of Public Prosecutions (DPP) before it can be prosecuted.[18] A Crown prosecutor can give consent to the prosecution on behalf of the DPP.[19] However, the mere fact that a Crown prosecutor is involved in the case does not mean consent has been given: it must be a conscious decision taken by the Crown prosecutor after examining all the circumstances of the case. However, the consent need not be written so long as the Crown prosecutor had the need for consent in his or her mind when preparing the draft indictment.[20]

8.7 There appear to be seven offences under PoCA 1978, s 11 relating to an indecent photograph or pseudo-photograph of a child:

- taking it;

- permitting it to be taken;

- making it;

- distributing it;

- showing it;

- possessing with a view to its being distributed or shown; and

- publishing an advertisement likely to be understood to be conveying that the advertiser distributes or shows it, or intends to do so.

Arguably the total number of ways of breaching the offences could be 14 since each type of conduct could be divided into an offence relating to a photograph and one relating to a pseudo-photograph. Section 1 is a wide-ranging provision but there are a number of common elements to all of these offences, the most important of which are 'indecent', 'photograph' and 'child'.

Indecent

8.8 Arguably the first and most important aspect of the definition is 'indecent'. The statute is silent as to the meaning of indecent but it is a word that is found in different areas of the law. In *Stamford*[21] it was held that 'indecent' and 'obscene' were at opposite ends of the same spectrum, with obscenity being the graver of the two.[22] In

---

17   SOA 2003, s 80 and Sch 3, para 13.
18   PoCA 1978, s 1(3).
19   Prosecution of Offences Act 1985, s 1(7).
20   *Jackson* [1997] Crim LR 293.
21   [1972] 2 QB 391.
22   Ibid, at p 398, per Ashworth J.

Graham-Kerr[23] the Court of Appeal held that 'indecent' meant offending against the recognised standards of propriety, and that whether a photograph, etc was indecent was an objective question and one wholly within the province of the jury.

8.9   The effect of the objective test is that it focuses on the image and not on the circumstances or the intentions of the person who took the photograph. It does not matter *why* an image has been taken; it is sufficient that it is indecent. This has caused several controversies over the years when art installations have been investigated by the police when investigating whether a particular image is an indecent photograph of a child.[24] However, the test was recently confirmed in *Smethurst*[25] where the Court of Appeal held that the objective test was not incompatible with the European Convention on Human Rights.

8.10   The Court of Appeal decision in *Murray*[26] clarified what has to be indecent. In this case a person made a 'video-clip' of a child from legitimate sources. The appellant had recorded a documentary film that included a gynaecological examination of a child. The appellant deleted the soundtrack (an explanation of the examination) and spliced the tape so that it showed only the genital areas. He argued that the resulting image could have been produced by using the 'pause' feature on his video-recorder and that since it originated from a legitimate source it could not be indecent. The Court of Appeal rejected this argument saying that the resultant product was a new image and the jury was right to consider only that image and not the circumstances surrounding where it was made.

8.11   Notwithstanding the objective test it has been held that age is relevant when deciding whether an image is indecent.[27] This has been criticised for altering the definition of indecency,[28] especially where the age of a child is not always known.[29] However, the ruling is making clear that the mischief of the act is protecting children from being abused or exploited through the production of indecent photographs of children. Accordingly the issue of age is important in qualifying whether an *indecent photograph of a child* has been created. This permits a jury to decide that a photograph which would not be indecent if the subject of a photograph was an adult would be indecent because it is of a child.

Photograph or pseudo-photograph

8.12   The second common element within s 1 is that of 'photograph'. This is defined in PoCA 1978, s 7(2) as:

> 'References to an indecent photograph include an indecent film,[30] a copy of an indecent photograph or film, and an indecent photograph comprised in a film.'

---

23   (1988) 88 Cr App R 302.
24   In 2001 the 'I am Camera' exhibition at the Saatchi Gallery in London was visited by the police and the gallery told to remove at least one image from this exhibition which was considered to be indecent. In 2007 an exhibition at the Baltic Gallery in Gateshead was investigated by Northumbria Police following a complaint that one of the photographs in the exhibition (depicting two children, one of which was naked from the waist down) was indecent. No action was taken in respect of this picture.
25   [2002] 1 Cr App R 50.
26   [2004] EWCA Crim 2211.
27   *Owen* (1986) 86 Cr App R 291.
28   Smith's commentary on *Owen* [1988] Crim LR 120.
29   See **8.19**.
30   Including any form of video-recording: s 7(5).

Section 7(4)[31] adds to this definition by stating that:

'References to an indecent photograph include—

(a)   the negative as well as the positive version; and
(b)   data stored on a computer disc or by other electronic means which is capable of conversion into a photograph.'

Accordingly 'photograph' bears a relatively wide definition, albeit one that is linked by the notion of photography. In *Fellows; Arnold*[32] the Court of Appeal held that scanning a copy of an image into a computer created a 'copy of a photograph' and so was within the remit of PoCA 1978, s 1. Section 7(4)(b) covers digital photography where no film negative is produced and instead the photograph is recorded onto memory cards as data that is capable of being converted into a photograph.

8.13   PoCA 1978, s 7(3) provides:

'Photographs (including those comprised in a film) shall, if they show children and are indecent, be treated for all purposes of this Act as indecent photographs of children and so as respects pseudo-photographs.'

In *Owen* the Court of Appeal stated that s 7(3):[33]

'... would be apt to prohibit a photograph of ... a highly indecent act being carried out by adults in which children appeared, albeit the children themselves were not photographed in any indecent manner.'

8.14   Technological developments led to a more significant change in the wording of s 1. The police were concerned that they were finding images that appeared to be of children but which had been electronically altered by a computer program. It was not immediately clear to the police whether these were indecent images of children or not. Parliament responded by the introduction of 'pseudo-photograph', something defined in s 7(7) as:

'"Pseudo-photograph" means an image, whether made by computer-graphics or otherwise howsoever, which appears to be a photograph.'

8.15   This definition is expanded in s 7(9) which states that the term 'pseudo-photograph' includes:

'(a)   a copy of an indecent photograph; and
(b)   data stored on a computer disc or by other electronic means which is capable of conversion into [an indecent][34] pseudo-photograph.'

8.16   There has been limited authority on the meaning of pseudo-photograph but in *Goodland*[35] the Divisional Court held that it must look like a photograph, and accordingly where something is obviously not a photograph then it will not come within

---

[31]   As amended.
[32]   [1997] 1 Cr App R 244.
[33]   (1988) 86 Cr App R 291, at p 295.
[34]   Words in square brackets inserted by CJIA 2008, s 69(1), (4) (in force from 8 July 2008: see CJIA 2008, s 153(2)).
[35]   [2001] 1 WLR 1427.

this definition. It was held that an image made by an exhibit which obviously consisted of parts of two different photographs taped together could not be said to 'appear to be a photograph' and was therefore not a 'pseudo-photograph', although if it was itself photocopied it could.

8.17　Technological advancement has made some computer-generated images almost of photographic quality and there is an argument that these may, therefore, be within s 7(7) irrespective of the fact that no child has ever existed.[36] However, most images are still not of that quality and so would probably fall within the *Goodland* ruling that they are obviously not a photograph. CJIA 2008[37] amended PoCA 1978 by the insertion of a new provision, s 7(4A), to the following effect:

> '(4A) References to a photograph also include—
>
> (a)　a tracing or other image, whether made by electronic or other means (of whatever nature)—
>> (i)　which is not itself a photograph or pseudo-photograph, but
>> (ii)　which is derived from the whole or part of a photograph or pseudo-photograph (or a combination of either or both); and
> (b)　data stored on a computer disc or by other electronic means which is capable of conversion into an image within paragraph (a);
>
> and subsection (8) [below] applies in relation to such an image as it applies in relation to a pseudo-photograph.'

Child

8.18　Subject to PoCA 1978, s 7(8) (below), 'child' means a person under the age of 18.[38] The age limit had been 16 but it was increased by SOA 2003, s 45. The formal reason for this change was that it was necessary to comply with an impending EU Framework Decision,[39] but it has been criticised on the basis that it does appear incompatible with the usual age of sexual consent.[40] The counter-argument is that it recognises the permanency of the conduct. If a sexual image is posted on the internet then it becomes virtually impossible for it to be removed,[41] and so it has been argued that the decision to expose oneself to this permanency should only be made by an adult. However, it is difficult to reconcile this with personal and sexual autonomy where, for example, a 16-year-old could willingly decide to have unprotected sexual intercourse with someone who is HIV positive[42] but cannot be the subject of a photograph. It is also notable that although the offence is now committed whenever the victim is under 18, an offender is only subject to the notification requirements where the victim is under 16.[43]

8.19　Where the identity of the child is known its age can be proved in the ways explained in **3.132**, but in many cases the identity of the child, and therefore its age, will not be known. Consequently, PoCA 1978, s 2(3) states:

---

[36]　Which would be irrelevant since they 'appear' to be of a child: s 2(3).
[37]　CJIA 2008, s 69(1), (3); see ibid, s 153(2). The amendment relates to things done as mentioned in PoCA 1978, s 1 on or after 8 July 2008: CJIA 2008, s 148(2), Sch 27, para 24.
[38]　PoCA 1978, s 7(6).
[39]　Council Framework Decision 2004/68/JHA.
[40]　Gillespie 'Tinkering with Child Pornography' [2004] Crim LR 361, at pp 361–362.
[41]　Taylor and Quayle, n 2 above, at p 24.
[42]　Implicit within the decision in *Dica* [2004] QB 1257.
[43]　See **8.5**.

'In proceedings ... relating to indecent photographs of children a person is to be taken as having been a child at any material time if it appears from the evidence as a whole that he was then under the age of 18.'

This is a matter of fact for the jury to decide. In *Land*[44] the Court of Appeal held that age was an issue that the jury could decide without the assistance of expert evidence.

8.20 A similar provision exists in respect of pseudo-photographs. Section 7(8) states:

'If the impression conveyed by a pseudo-photograph is that the person shown is a child, the pseudo-photograph shall be treated for all purposes of this Act as showing a child and so shall a pseudo-photograph where the predominant impression conveyed is that the person shown is a child notwithstanding that some of the physical characteristics shown are those of an adult.'

Again this must mean that the matter is one for the jury and, following *Land*, expert evidence would be inadmissible on the point. This provision is required because some pseudo-photographs will be doctored images of adults (eg where a photograph of a naked young adult is taken and then a graphics manipulation package is used to airbrush out the pubic hair and reduce the size of the hips and breasts, making the resulting image look like a naked child), and also because some pseudo-photographs may include features that are obviously of an adult.[45]

Making or taking an indecent photograph or pseudo-photograph

Actus reus

8.21 PoCA 1978, s 1(1)(a) makes it an offence to make, take or permit to be taken an indecent photograph or pseudo-photograph of a child. 'Take' is a word in ordinary usage and clearly refers to the person who actually takes a photograph of a child using photographic equipment. 'Make' is another word of ordinary meaning and the dictionary definition of 'to cause to exist; to produce by action, to bring about' has been approved.[46] This can include, but is not restricted to, the creation of pseudo-photographs. Making by creation could be found, for example, in the example of splicing two photographs together to create a single pseudo-photograph. Other examples of making a photograph or pseudo-photograph are duplicating an image by photocopying a photograph, or scanning a photograph into a computer,[47] or duplicating an existing electronic file.

8.22 Particular attention has been paid to the accessing of indecent photographs on the internet. In *Bowden*[48] the Court of Appeal was called upon to consider the provisions in connection with someone who had downloaded a photograph from the internet. It rejected the appellant's assertion that 'make' should not include the duplication of an existing image and expressly held that downloading a photograph from the internet constitutes making.[49] The logic of this definition is understandable in

44 [1998] 1 Cr App R 301.
45 In *Goodland* the item was two photographs 'hinged' together. The top was that of a child's head. The Divisional Court argued that a photocopied version of the 'hinged' photograph may have amounted to a pseudo-photograph, presumably relying on s 7(8) since the body would be obviously that of an adult.
46 *Bowden* [2000] 1 QB 88.
47 See **8.12**.
48 [2000] 1 QB 88.
49 Ibid, at p 95.

a literal context. When a person downloads the photograph a file has been created. This file never existed before and has undoubtedly been 'made'.

8.23   It is, however, difficult to justify the above interpretation. Interpreting 'make' to mean 'create' (as the appellant had suggested) would give it a meaning comparable to the term 'take', ie the creation of a *new* image. Such a construction would not have meant that downloading images would be beyond the reach of the criminal law since, at the very least, a person who has downloaded something to his or her PC has possession of it.[50] It is notable that for the purposes of sentencing this position has now been adopted,[51] with the SGC Definitive Guideline stating that the sentence for downloading should ordinarily be comparable to that for possession.[52]

8.24   The logic of *Bowden* was taken further in the case of *Smith; Jayson*[53] where it was held that viewing an image online or opening up an e-mail attachment could, subject to the mens rea being satisfied, amount to an infringement of s 1. The logic of this decision is again technically correct. When a person views an image online the computer creates an automatic copy of the image and stores it in its temporary internet cache,[54] and the same principle exists in respect of opening an e-mail: a copy will be created irrespective of whether the user wishes this or not.

Mens rea

8.25   Section 1(1)(a) is silent as to any mens rea requirement but the courts have made it clear that the offence of 'making' is not one of strict liability, and doubtless the same is true (and the same mens rea is required) for the offence of 'taking'. The leading case is *Smith; Jayson*[55] where the Court of Appeal was called upon to consider the requisite mens rea in respect of two situations where making was in issue. In the case of *Smith* the appellant had been sent an e-mail which had, as an attachment, an indecent photograph of a child. Smith contended that unless he *knew* the attachment contained an indecent photograph of a child he could not be said to have the necessary mens rea. In the case of *Jayson* the appellant had accessed indecent photographs of a child on the internet and, although he had called them to the screen, he had not downloaded them. When a user browses the internet the images which appear on the screen are automatically downloaded and placed in the computer's temporary internet cache. The user does not have any control over this downloading although many people are now aware that this occurs, and certainly in this case Jayson was aware of this. The Court of Appeal held that the mens rea for 'making' is that the act of 'making' should be a 'deliberate and intentional act with knowledge that the image made was, or was likely to be, an indecent photograph or pseudo-photograph of a child'.[56] By parity of reasoning the Court held that a person calling an image onto his screen would be guilty of the offence of making if he knew it was, or was likely to be, an indecent photograph or pseudo-photograph of a child.[57] The Court expressly stated that it was not necessary for a person to intend that

---

50   See **8.68**.
51   Although an offence under PoCA 1978, s 1(1)(a) is still charged in preference to one under CJA 1988, s 160 on the basis that it avoids a discussion on deleted images (**8.68**).
52   See SGC Definitive Guideline, at p 109, in the Appendix.
53   [2003] 1 Cr App R 212.
54   A succinct analysis of the technical process involved in the creation of an image within the cache is provided by ibid, at [25]–[30].
55   Ibid.
56   Ibid, at [19].
57   Ibid, at [33].

the image would be stored for later retrieval,[58] but that in order to show the deliberate and intentional act of making the user would have to know that images are automatically stored in the cache.

8.26 As is apparent from the above, an unintended copying or storing of an image does not result in criminal liability for 'making' it.[59] Consequently, someone who opens a doubtful e-mail attachment (which turns out to be indecent photographs) or whose computer automatically saves it on its cache is not guilty of making those photographs.[60] Nor will he be in possession of them whilst they are stored on the cache if he is are unaware of the existence and effect of the cache, although he will be in possession of them in respect of their transient downloading onto the computer's screen.[61]

8.27 The mens rea was extended, in a problematic way, in *Harrison*.[62] The judgment in this case focused on the issue of automatic 'pop ups'. The Court of Appeal stated:[63]

> '[the jury] has to be sure not only that ... the appellant knew about automatic "pop up" activity when he accessed adult pornographic sites, but that he knew that in accessing certain sites there was a likelihood that these "pop ups" would be illegal images.'

In other words, the Court of Appeal stated that even where a person is accessing lawful websites containing (adult) pornographic pictures, a person can be guilty of 'making' if he foresees that it is *likely* that an automatic 'pop up' may include an illegal image. 'Pop ups' have been problematic for many years, with the adult industry seeing them as an important part of its advertising.[64]

8.28 This would appear an extension too far. A user has no control over whether a 'pop up' appears (unlike, e g an e-mail attachment where a user has to make a deliberate choice as to whether to open the e-mail). Reducing the mens rea to a knowledge that it is *likely* a 'pop up' could include an indecent photograph of a child could criminalise those who are seeking lawful pornographic images. For example, if a person is seeking photographs of girls aged 18 or 19 (which are perfectly lawful) then it is quite possible that a 'pop up' may include younger girls, especially where the website is based in a country where the age of 'a child' differs from that in the UK.[65]

8.29 *Harrison* may, in fact, be purely obiter since the appellant was convicted of the offence of possession and yet the judgment of the Court of Appeal related wholly to 'making'. If so, it is to be hoped that the decision will not be followed. The use of 'likelihood' in *Smith; Jayson* can be justified by the fact that a person makes a conscious decision to open an e-mail attachment. There may be circumstantial evidence which will guide the choice of an offender in doing so (e g who the e-mail is from, whether he has previously sought indecent photographs of children, etc). Those same factors are not necessarily present for 'pop ups' where a person could be seeking perfectly lawful images

---

[58] Ibid.
[59] *Atkins v DPP* [2000] 2 Cr App R 248.
[60] Ibid.
[61] Ibid.
[62] [2008] 1 Cr App R 387.
[63] Ibid, at [19].
[64] See Lane *Obscene Profits: The Entrepreneurs of Pornography* (Routledge, 2001).
[65] Some countries continue to adopt the age of 16 as England and Wales did prior to the changes made by SOA 2003.

yet realising that an illegal photograph may well pop up. Such an interpretation would seem to restrict the activities of a person browsing the internet, beyond the scope of the law.

Defences

8.30   Until SOA 2003 there was no statutory defence to an offence under s 1(1)(a). However SOA 2003, ss 45 and 46 inserted two defences. The first relates to a defence of marriage or other relationship and the second is a defence of making, etc for the purposes of criminal proceedings, investigations and security functions.

Marital or other relationship

8.31   PoCA 1978, s 1A states:

> '(1) This section applies where, in proceedings for an offence under section 1(1)(a) of taking or making an indecent photograph of a child ... the defendant proves that the photograph was of the child aged 16 or over, and that at the time of the offence charged the child and he—

> (a)   were married or civil partners of each other, or
> (b)   lived together as partners in an enduring family relationship.

> ...

> (3) This section applies whether the photograph showed the child alone or with the defendant, but not if it showed any other person.

> (4) In the case of an offence under section 1(1)(a), if sufficient evidence is adduced to raise an issue as to whether the child consented to the photograph being taken or made, or as to whether the defendant reasonably believed that the child so consented, the defendant is not guilty of the offence unless it is proved that the child did not so consent and that the defendant did not reasonably believe that the child so consented.'

8.32   This is a bizarre defence. As noted already, SOA 2003 raised the age of a child from 16 to 18.[66] The purpose of the defence (and the similar defences in respect of the other offences under PoCA 1978, s 1) is to prevent criminal liability where the offences would interfere with certain lawful consensual relationships. It is clear from the section that it imposes a legal or persuasive burden on the defence[67] in one respect and an evidential burden in another respect.[68] Quite how a jury is supposed to understand these differences is perhaps open to question.

8.33   The requirement that the defendant and the child be married or in a civil partnership is legally unproblematic and can be easily proved. However, the term 'enduring family relationship' is not defined but it is clear that it only applies where they are living together. This could create some perverse results. Let us assume that A is a 17-year-old soldier and B is his sweetheart. They have been boyfriend and girlfriend since the age of 13 and are currently engaged to be married, but A lives in barracks and B with her parents. When A deploys, B lets him take an indecent photograph so 'he can

---

[66]   See **8.18**.
[67]   Section 1A(1) – 'the defendant proves' – which must mean a legal burden.
[68]   Section 1A(4) – 'if sufficient evidence is adduced to raise an issue'.

remember her'. As they do not live together, the defence does not apply. Whereas if A and B have been together for only 3 months but now they live together as lovers then, subject to whatever an 'enduring family relationship' means, the defence could apply to them.[69]

8.34 The issue of consent only applies where evidence is adduced as to make it an issue. If it does become an issue then the burden is imposed on the prosecution to prove an absence of consent or that B did not reasonably believe that B consented. Discharging such a burden could be quite challenging, particularly given the private nature of these offences.

8.35 The defence also only applies where the photograph shows either the child alone or the defendant and child, but not if it shows anyone else. It does not matter how old the other person is.

Defence for criminal proceedings and investigations

8.36 PoCA 1978, s 1B which, unlike s 1A, applies in the case of pseudo-photographs as well as photographs, states:

'(1) In proceedings for an offence under section 1(1)(a) of making an indecent photograph or pseudo-photograph of a child, the defendant is not guilty of the offence if he proves that—

(a) it was necessary for him to make the photograph or pseudo-photograph for the purposes of the prevention, detection or investigation of crime, or for the purposes of criminal proceedings, in any part of the world,

(b) at the time of the offence charged he was a member of the Security Service[or Secret Intelligence Service],[70] and it was necessary for him to make the photograph or pseudo-photograph for the exercise of any of the functions of [that] Service, or

(c) at the time of the offence he was a member of GCHQ,[71] and it was necessary for him to make the photograph or pseudo-photograph for the exercise of any of the functions of GCHQ.'

8.37 Section 1B(1)(a) is not restricted to police officers or those employed by the police and will cover, for example, the Criminal Prosecution Service (CPS), which may need to duplicate images in order to provide sufficient bundles of evidence for the jury and counsel. It would also cover those who report matters to the police, including companies, internet service providers and even those who operate 'hotlines'. Placing the burden of proof on the defendant to show that it is 'necessary' for the prevention, detection or investigation of crime should ensure that only bona fide people will come within the defence, which will presumably be a matter of fact for the jury to decide.

8.38 Section 1B(1)(b) and (c) may seem surprising at first sight but this is a reflection of the fact that indecent photographs of children have become a global issue and one that can involve international gangs and rings being created to deal in this commodity. Increasingly in recent years the intelligence services[72] have been used to tackle this behaviour and s 1B simply ensures there is a defence where they need to make indecent photographs for this purpose.

---

[69] The comment in **6.46** applies equally here.
[70] Words in square brackets inserted by CJIA 2008, s 69(1), (2) (in force from 8 July 2008: see CJIA 2008, s 153(2)).
[71] 'GCHQ' having the same meaning as in the Intelligence Services Act 1994: PoCA 1978, s 1B(2).
[72] Including the SIS.

Distributes or shows an indecent photograph or pseudo-photograph

Actus reus

8.39   PoCA 1978, s 1(1)(b) makes it an offence to distribute or show an indecent photograph or pseudo-photograph of a child. In terms of distribution, s 1(2) provides:

> 'For the purposes of this Act, a person is to be regarded as distributing an indecent photograph or pseudo-photograph if he parts with possession of it to, or exposes or offers it for acquisition by, another person.'

8.40   This demonstrates that it is not necessary actually to distribute an image, offering it will suffice. This undoubtedly means that there is an overlap between this offence and that under s 1(1)(c), possession with intention to distribute or show. Distribution or showing is considered to be serious offending behaviour[73] because it is actively increasing the number of people that are able to access the indecent photograph thus increasing the exploitation. Sending indecent photographs from a website abroad to a computer in this country constitutes an offence of 'distribution' in this country contrary to s 1(1)(b).[74]

8.41   'Show' is, to an extent, self-explanatory but a person will not be guilty where the showing is to himself.[75] Accordingly the offence is not committed where A calls up a previously saved image to his or her computer screen. However, where this creates a duplicate image (because, e g the saved image was in a compressed file or was encrypted) then it is likely that this would be a 'making' contrary to s 1(1)(a).

Mens rea

8.42   The mens rea requirement for s 1(1)(b) was discussed in *Price*.[76] The Court of Appeal confirmed that it was not necessary for the prosecution to prove that a person knowingly distributed indecent images of children. It was sufficient for the prosecution to prove that the defendant knowingly distributed an item and that item contained indecent photographs of a child. This creates a strict liability offence, although this is subject to the statutory defences.

Defences

8.43   Section 1(4) creates two statutory defences:

> 'Where a person is charged with an offence under subsection (1)(b) or (c), it shall be a defence for him to prove—
>
> (a)   that he had a legitimate reason for distributing or showing the photographs or pseudo-photographs or (as the case may be) having them in his possession; or
> (b)   that he had not himself seen the photographs or pseudo-photographs and did not know, nor had any cause to suspect, them to be indecent.'

---

73   SGC Definitive Guideline, at p 110: see the Appendix.
74   *Tompkins* [2007] Crim LR 234.
75   *ET* [1999] Crim LR 749.
76   [2006] EWCA Crim 3363.

8.44 'Legitimate reason' in (a) is not defined in the statute and this will be explored elsewhere in this text when the comparable defence under CJA 1988, s 160(2) is examined.[77] However, in this context examples could include education or training where, for example, images of the sexual organs of a child need to be displayed, or where a police officer shows an indecent photograph to a CPS prosecutor during an investigation.

8.45 As the Court of Appeal stated in *Price* the defendant bears the legal or persuasive burden of proof in relation to this defence. The principal reason that the Court of Appeal in *Price* held that there was no mens rea requirement in s 1(1)(b) as to the fact that the item was an indecent image of a child was that, if the prosecution had to prove this, the defence within s 1(4)(b) would never be triggered.

Marital or other relationship

8.46 In the context of an offence under s 1(1)(b), s 1A provides:

'(1) This section applies where, in proceedings for an offence under ... section 1(1)(b) ... relating to an indecent photograph of a child, the defendant ... proves that the photograph was of the child aged 16 or over, and that at the time of the offence charged the child and he—

(a)   were married or civil partners of each other, or
(b)   lived together as partners in an enduring family relationship.

(2) [Subsection (5) ... also applies] where, in proceedings for an offence under section 1(1)(b) relating to an indecent photograph of a child, the defendant ... proves that the photograph was of the child aged 16 or over, and that at the time when he obtained it the child and he—

(a)   were married or civil partners of each other, or
(b)   lived together as partners in an enduring family relationship.

(3) This section applies whether the photograph showed the child alone or with the defendant, but not if it showed any other person.

. . .

(5) In the case of an offence under section 1(1)(b), the defendant is not guilty of the offence unless it is proved that the showing or distributing was to a person other than the child.'

8.47 Much of this defence has been discussed earlier[78] but the addition here is s 1A(5) where the prosecution must prove that, so long as the defendant and child were married, in a civil partnership or living together in an 'enduring family relationship', the showing or distribution was to a person other than the child.

---

[77]   See **8.74**.
[78]   At **8.32**.

Inciting the distribution of an indecent photograph or pseudo-photograph of a child

8.48 Linked to the offence of distribution under PoCA 1978, s 1(1)(b) is that of inciting the distribution of an indecent photograph. This relies on the common law offence of incitement, to be replaced, at a date not yet announced, by the provisions under the Serious Crime Act 2007, Pt 2.

8.49 The first principal circumstance when common law incitement has been used is where a person has replied to an advertisement offering the supply of indecent photographs of children. *Goldman*[79] is an example of this situation. The appellant sought to argue that because he was responding to an advert it could not be said that he was inciting someone to distribute the images, because the company was itself committing an offence. The Court of Appeal rejected the argument and suggested that, irrespective of whether the company was committing an offence, it could still be said that the appellant had incited the company to perform an illegal act, namely the distribution of indecent photographs of children.

8.50 The second contemporary use of incitement arose from 'Operation Ore',[80] the national law enforcement action arising out of the arrest in the US of Thomas and Janice Reedy, who operated Landslide Productions. Operation Ore was a long-running inquiry and by the time some named individuals were investigated by the police there was no forensic evidence to show the existence of indecent photographs on their computer, although there was evidence from credit-card billings that they had accessed the Landslide Productions website.

8.51 In *R (O'Shea) v City of Coventry Magistrates' Court*[81] the appellant had been convicted of the offence of inciting the distribution of indecent photographs of children on the basis of his subscription to Landslide. He appealed by way of case stated on the basis that Landslide was a fully automated system and that incitement required a human to be involved so that he can be persuaded to commit the relevant crime. The Divisional Court rejected this argument by stating that a human was behind the computers and thus whilst it may have been an automated computer system, it still required human involvement (at the very least the creation of the software and the compilation of the images that would be accessed) and this was sufficient for an incitement.[82] It is also worth noting that it is immaterial where the person to be incited is based because the incitement takes place within this country even though the distribution may occur outside of the jurisdiction.[83]

---

[79]   [2001] EWCA Crim 1684.
[80]   See, e g 'Cracking Down on Net Predators', *Sunday Times*, 15 February 2004.
[81]   [2004] EWHC 905 (Admin).
[82]   It should be noted the decision is somewhat controversial and Ormerod has noted that the fact that the owners continually added to the material may be the reason why this ruling was acceptable on the facts: [2004] Crim LR 948, at pp 950–951.
[83]   Ibid. See also *C* [2006] EWCA Crim 2132.

Possessing an indecent photograph or pseudo-photograph of a child with a view to its being distributed or shown

Actus reus

8.52   This offence under PoCA 1978, s 1(1)(c) overlaps slightly with the offences under s 1(1)(b) as a result of the definition given to 'distribution' by s 1(2). However, it does not require an actual offer to be made but rather that the photographs or pseudo-photographs are possessed with a view to them being distributed. In other words, if it can be proved that the defendant wishes to show or distribute the photographs or pseudo-photographs in his or her possession then this will suffice. The meaning of 'possession' is discussed below.[84]

8.53   It is clear that the possessor does not need to be the owner of the material. In *Matrix*[85] the appellant (M) was employed as an assistant in a sex shop. The police executed a warrant to search the premises and found a number of video cassettes containing indecent photographs of children. M was charged with, and convicted of, an offence under s 1(1)(c) and appealed arguing that he was not in possession of the images since it should mean more than mere physical control. The Court of Appeal rejected this, stating that M was clearly in possession of the video as it was under his control as part of the stock of the shop and the possession was clearly for the purpose of distribution.

8.54   In *Fellows; Arnold*[86] the first appellant produced a website which included indecent photographs of children. He supplied people (including the second appellant) with a password that allowed them to access these images. His conviction for an offence contrary to s 1(1)(c) was upheld on the basis that supplying the passwords demonstrated that he was in possession of the images with a view to them being shown to by others (ie those with the password). It is now possible to have a 'virtual hard drive', ie space on the internet where data can be stored and displayed. If this virtual hard drive is outside the UK (eg it is housed on an Eastern European server) then it is unlikely that a person can be truly said to be in possession of these images and so s 1(1)(c) may not be satisfied.

Mens rea

8.55   The mens rea element for this offence is the 'view to' the indecent photograph, etc being distributed or shown. In *Dooley*[87] this provision was examined. Here, the appellant used a peer-to-peer network. Such networks allow people freely to access files in a folder known as 'my shared folder'. Anything within that folder will be accessible whereas material on other parts of the computer will not. The appellant in this case had downloaded a significant amount of material using the peer-to-peer network. When the appellant was arrested some images were still in this folder and he was convicted of the offence under s 1(1)(c) on the basis that the files were possessed with a view to them being distributed (via the peer-to-peer network). The Court of Appeal quashed his conviction and held that whilst it need not be the person's intention to distribute or show images, it must be one of his purposes for possessing the material. In this case the

---

84   At **8.68**.
85   [1997] Crim LR 901.
86   [1997] 1 Cr App R 244.
87   [2006] 1 Cr App R 349.

appellant claimed that he had simply not moved the images from the 'my download folder' to another folder and therefore there was no proof that one of his purposes was distribution.

Defences

8.56   A defence exists under s 1(4) where the defendant proves:

'(a)   that he had a legitimate reason for distributing or showing the photographs or pseudo-photographs or (as the case may be) having them in his possession; or

(b)   that he had not himself seen the photographs or pseudo-photographs and did not know, nor had any cause to suspect, them to be indecent.'

These defences were discussed above.[88]

Marital or other relationship

8.57   The defence under PoCA 1978, s 1A applies as follows:

'(1) This section applies where in proceedings for an offence ... under section 1(1) ... (c) relating to an indecent photograph of a child, the defendant proves that the photograph was of the child aged 16 or over, and that at the time of the offence charged the child and he—

(a)   were married or civil partners of each other, or

(b)   lived together as partners in an enduring family relationship.

(2) [Subsection (6) also applies] where, in proceedings for an offence under section 1(1)(c) relating to an indecent photograph of a child, the defendant proves that the photograph was of the child aged 16 or over, and that at the time when he obtained it the child and he—

(a)   were married or civil partners of each other, or

(b)   lived together as partners in an enduring family relationship.

...

(6) In the case of an offence under section 1(1)(c), if sufficient evidence is adduced to raise an issue both—

(a)   as to whether the child consented to the photograph being in the defendant's possession, or as to whether the defendant reasonably believed that the child so consented, and

(b)   as to whether the defendant had the photograph in his possession with a view to its being distributed or shown to anyone other than the child,

the defendant is not guilty of the offence unless it is proved either that the child did not so consent and that the defendant did not reasonably believe that the child so consented, or that the defendant had the photograph in his possession with a view to its being distributed or shown to a person other than the child.'

---

[88]   At **8.43** et seq.

This defence was discussed above[89] but the addition here is s 1A(6). Here, the defendant would bear only an evidential burden which, when discharged, will result in the prosecution having to prove the relevant factors.

Publish or cause to be published any advertisement

Actus reus

8.58 PoCA 1978, s 1(1)(d) creates the offence of publishing or causing a photograph to be published likely to be understood as conveying that the advertiser distributes or shows indecent photographs or pseudo-photographs of a child or intends to do so.

8.59 The Act does not define the term 'publish' but it is likely the term will be construed in a similar way to the definition of that term in OPA 1959, s 1, which includes distribution, circulation, selling, letting, giving or lending of an article. Whilst there is no comparable statutory definition within PoCA 1978, the OPA 1959 definition is compatible with the dictionary definition, which refers to issuing, announcing and communicating. In *Taylor*,[90] a case under OPA 1959, s 1, the Court of Appeal held that the act of developing and printing obscene photographs which were then sold or passed back to the owners was capable of amounting to 'publication'.

8.60 'Advertisement' is not defined but it is a word of everyday usage and would be a matter of fact for the jury. A contemporary example could be where a defendant posts an indecent photograph onto a newsgroup and says, 'if you want more, go to [website]'. Under these circumstances the defendant would be guilty under s 1(1)(b) but also, it is submitted, under s 1(1)(d).

8.61 It has been held that circulating material between a circle of friends or subscribers for a private purpose is not 'publishing'.[91] Rook and Ward have suggested that this should not be followed for s 1(1)(d)[92] and there are good public policy reasons for not doing so. It is known that many offenders operate in closed groups operating in private chatrooms or distribution lists.[93] It would be inappropriate if a person who advertised a series of pictures[94] within a list for sale or distribution escaped liability under s 1(1)(d).

Mens rea

8.62 No mens rea is to be found on the face of s 1(1)(d) but in common with the other subsections it is likely that the defendant must intentionally publish or cause to be published the advertisement. Following the ruling in *Collier*,[95] which will be discussed below,[96] it is likely that the prosecution must prove that the defendant knew he was publishing an advert in relation to an indecent photograph or pseudo-photograph *of a child* and not just an indecent photograph or pseudo-photograph.

---

[89] At **8.31**.
[90] [1995] 1 Cr App R 131.
[91] *Exchange Telegraph Company v Central News* [1897] 2 Ch 48.
[92] Rook and Ward *Sexual Offences Law & Practice* (Sweet & Maxwell, 3rd edn, 2004), at para 8.41.
[93] Taylor and Quayle, n 2 above, at pp 130–143.
[94] A series of images is often produced in respect of a single child, particularly as the child grows up. Child pornographers frequently spend considerable effort tracking down every image within a series or collection: ibid, at p 161.
[95] [2005] 1 Cr App R 129.
[96] At **8.74**.

Defences

8.63   No defence to an offence under s 1(1)(d) is provided by POCA 1978.

POSSESSION OF INDECENT PHOTOGRAPHS

8.64   As noted already there is an offence of simple possession of an indecent photograph of children which is set out in CJA 1988, s 160(1).

> '[Subject to section 160A][97], it is an offence for a person to have any indecent photograph or pseudo-photograph of a child in his possession.'

Class of offence	3	SOA 2003, s 72 applies	✓[98]
Notification requirements	See text	SOPO	✓
CJA 2003, Sch 15 applies	✓	Serious specified offence	✗
Review of lenient sentence	✗	Special provisions of CYPA 1933	✗
Detention of young offender for specified period			✗

See **1.48** et seq.

8.65   An offence under s 160 is triable either way and punishable by a maximum sentence on indictment of 5 years' imprisonment.[99] See the SGC Definitive Guideline in the Appendix.[100] The notification requirements apply to this offence where the indecent photographs or pseudo-photographs showed persons under 16:

- if the conviction, finding or caution was before 1 May 2004; or

- if the offender was 18 or over; or

- if the offender was under 18, he is sentenced in respect of the offence to imprisonment for a term of at least 12 months.[101]

8.66   An offence under CJA 1988, s 160 requires the consent of the DPP before it can be prosecuted.[102]

---

[97]   Words in square brackets substituted by CJIA 2008, s 148(1), Sch 26, para 24, in force 8 July 2008: ibid s 153(2).
[98]   See **2.97**.
[99]   CJA 1988, s 160(2A). Maximum on summary conviction: **1.43**.
[100]   At pp 5–18, 109–114.
[101]   SOA 2003, s 80 and Sch 3, para 15.
[102]   PoCA 1978, s 1(3) applied by CJA 1988, s 160(4). See **8.6**.

8.67   The definitions of 'photograph', 'pseudo-photograph' and 'child' bear the same definition as with PoCA 1978, s 1.[103] There can be no doubt that the definition of 'indecent'[104] will be the same. Following the decision in *Bowden*[105] there is a considerable overlap between this offence and the offence of 'making' under PoCA 1978, s 1 because where a person downloads from the internet a photograph or pseudo-photograph to a storage device it must now also be in his possession. When an indictment is drafted it is not unusual to use s 160 as a 'catch-all' offence on the indictment. Most collections on the internet now involve several thousand images and clearly it would not be desirous to have separate counts on the indictment for each offence. However, following the decision in *Canavan*[106] a person can only be sentenced for what he or she either pleads guilty to or is convicted of.[107] In order to indicate the full seriousness of the offending to the attention of the court it is not unusual for the residuary images to be placed within one or more counts of possession. In *Thompson*[108] the Court of Appeal stated that where this practice was used then the indictment should be phrased in such a way that it demonstrated the number of images in each of the levels within the typology.

Actus reus

8.68   The meaning of possession was explored in *Porter*.[109] Here the appellant had downloaded a number of indecent images but had deleted them. They were, however, forensically retrievable although the prosecution conceded that an ordinary member of the public would not usually be able to gain access to the images once deleted. The appellant was convicted of possessing the images forensically recovered but the Court of Appeal quashed his conviction on the basis that possession involved having an element of custody or control[110] and that since they were deleted they were no longer under his control. This is a pragmatic approach but also one of limited practical application since the 'solution' to the issue in such a case is to charge the offence of 'making' under PoCA 1978, s 1.[111] Assuming it is possible to show that it was the defendant who downloaded the images, the fact that they have been deleted would be irrelevant since the fact that the image is present on the machine (albeit deleted) shows that it has been *made*. Under this construction the deletion would be relevant only to mitigation not liability.

8.69   Possession must be a continuing act. This has implications for the change of age of 'a child' introduced by SOA 2003. Where, prior to 1 May 2004,[112] A was in possession of several hundred indecent photographs of 16- and 17-year-olds his possession of them was not an offence under CJA 1988, s 160 but his continued possession of them thereafter is an offence.

---

[103]   CJA 1988, s 160(4). That is, by PoCA 1978, ss 7(2)–(5), 7(7)–(9), and 2(3) and 7(6) respectively; see **8.12–8.20**. The amendment to the meaning of 'photograph' in PoCA 1978, s 1 made by CJIA 2008, s 69(3) applies equally in relation to things done as mentioned in CJA 1988, s 160(1): CJIA 2008, s 148(2), Sch 27, para 24; see n 37 above.

[104]   See **8.8**.

[105]   [2000] 1 QB 88.

[106]   [1998] 1 Cr App R (S) 243.

[107]   In *Pardue* [2004] 1 Cr App R (S) 105 this point was expressly made by the Court of Appeal in connection with indecent photographs. The appellant had been found with in excess of 1,000 images on his computer but the indictment did not specifically identify this. The judge sentenced on the basis of his admission (during police interview) that he had downloaded such images but the Court of Appeal reduced the sentence because the indictment did not reflect the actual quantity.

[108]   [2004] 2 Cr App R 262.

[109]   [2006] 2 Cr App R 359.

[110]   Ibid, at [18]–[22].

[111]   See **8.21** et seq.

[112]   The date of commencement for SOA 2003.

Mens rea

8.70 In *Atkins v DPP*[113] it was held that an offence of possession was not committed under s 160 unless the defendant knew that he had, or once had, the photographs or pseudo-photographs within his possession, something confirmed in the case of *Porter*.[114] In *Land*,[115] a case that dealt with an offence under PoCA 1978, s 1(1)(c) which has a similar mens rea requirement,[116] the Court of Appeal stated that it was not necessary for the prosecution to prove that the defendant knew that the items in his possession were indecent photographs or pseudo-photographs of children, merely that he knew he was in possession of indecent photographs or pseudo-photographs. It will also be remembered that it is immaterial whether the defendant himself considers the items to be indecent; it is a purely objective test.[117]

Defences

8.71 Four defences exist in respect of an offence under s 160. Three are contained within s 160(2), which states that a defence exists where the defendant proves:

'(a) that he had a legitimate reason for having the photograph or pseudo-photograph in his possession; or

(b) that he had not himself seen the photograph or pseudo-photograph and did not know, nor had any cause to suspect, it to be indecent; or

(c) that the photograph or pseudo-photograph was sent to him without any prior request made by him or on his behalf and he did not keep it for an unreasonable time.'

Legitimate reason

8.72 'Legitimate reason' is not defined in CJA 1988 and in *Atkins v DPP*[118] the Divisional Court held that what would amount to a legitimate reason will be a question of fact in each case. The appellant in *Atkins* tried to argue that academic research could qualify as a defence. The Divisional Court did not rule out academic research as being a legitimate reason but did say:[119]

'... the central question will be whether the defendant is essentially a person of unhealthy interests in possession of indecent photographs in the pretence of undertaking research or by contrast a genuine researcher with no alternative but to have this sort of unpleasant material in his possession'.

8.73 The Court continued by stating that courts should show a degree of scepticism when the defence was pleaded and it is submitted that this is correct. Accordingly a court will be required to assess whether it was truly necessary for a defendant to have access to indecent photographs for the research. It is also important to note that this defence does not, in any event, apply to POCA 1978, s 1(1)(a) and thus where an image is made (including through downloading from the internet) the legitimacy of the research is theoretically irrelevant, although it would invariably form part of the public interest prosecution test.

---

113 [2000] 2 Cr App R 248.
114 [2006] 2 Cr App R 359.
115 [1998] 1 Cr App R 301.
116 At **8.52** et seq.
117 See **8.8**.
118 [2000] 2 Cr App R 248.
119 Ibid, at p 257.

Had not seen the photograph

8.74 The second defence contained within s 160(2) is that the defendant had not seen the photograph or pseudo-photograph and had no reason to suspect that it was indecent. It is notable that s 160(2) does not refer to 'of a child' which would, on a literal interpretation, mean that the defendant would only have the defence if he could prove that he did not know, or have any reason to suspect, that the images were indecent per se. In *Collier*[120] the Court of Appeal confirmed that this approach was wrong and that Parliament must have intended the lack of knowledge, etc to relate to indecent photographs of children. The facts of *Collier* demonstrate the potential use of this defence. The appellant ordered CDs that he thought contained adult homosexual pornographic images. Unbeknown to him there were four indecent images of children on the discs. The appellant contended that he had not seen those images and he had bought them legitimately. There was no doubt that some of the images on the discs could be considered indecent per se but the Court of Appeal, quashing his conviction, held that if the defendant could prove that he did not know the indecent photographs were *of children* then he should be acquitted.

Unsolicited photographs

8.75 The third defence is that the defendant was sent the photograph or pseudo-photograph unsolicited and that he did not keep it for an unreasonable length of time. There has been no guidance on what amounts to a reasonable period of time and it is almost certainly a matter of fact in each case.

Marital or other relationship

8.76 CJA 1988, s 160 has a comparable defence to the marital or other relationship defences under PoCA 1978. It is set out in s 160A:

'(1) This section applies where, in proceedings for an offence under section 160 relating to an indecent photograph of a child, the defendant proves that the photograph was of the child aged 16 or over, and that at the time of the offence charged the child and he—

(a)   were married or civil partners of each other, or
(b)   lived together as partners in an enduring family relationship.

(2) This section also applies where, in proceedings for an offence under section 160 relating to an indecent photograph of a child, the defendant proves that the photograph was of the child aged 16 or over, and that at the time when he obtained it the child and he—

(a)   were married or civil partners of each other, or
(b)   lived together as partners in an enduring family relationship.

(3) This section applies whether the photograph showed the child alone or with the defendant, but not if it showed any other person.

(4) If sufficient evidence is adduced to raise an issue as to whether the child consented to the photograph being in the defendant's possession, or as to whether the defendant reasonably

---

[120]   [2005] 1 Cr App R 129.

believed that the child so consented, the defendant is not guilty of the offence unless it is proved that the child did not so consent and that the defendant did not reasonably believe that the child so consented.'

8.77 The constituent elements of this defence are equivalent to those in PoCA 1978, s 1A[121] and what was said in respect of that provision[122] applies equally here. It is notable that this defence applies if the defendant and the child were married, civil partners or living as partners in an enduring family relationship at one of two times: either when the defendant obtained the photograph or pseudo-photograph (and accordingly it would not seem to matter if he continues to possess the photograph even after the marriage or civil partnership has been dissolved or after the 'enduring family relationship' has broken down) or at the time of the offence charged.

INDECENT PHOTOGRAPHS: ANCILLARY MATTERS

8.78 The preceding sections of this chapter have examined the key features of the offences under PoCA 1978, s 1 and CJA 1988, s 160 but there are some other matters that need to be discussed, namely:

- offences committed by corporations;

- entry, search and seizure; and

- forfeiture of the indecent photographs.

Offences committed by corporations

8.79 PoCA 1978, s 3 states:

'(1) Where a body corporate is guilty of an offence under this Act and it is proved that the offence occurred with the consent or connivance of, or was attributable to any neglect on the part of, any director, manager, secretary or other officer of the body, or any person who was purporting to act in any such capacity he, as well as the body corporate, shall be deemed to be guilty of that offence and shall be liable to be proceeded against and punished accordingly.

(2) Where the affairs of a body corporate are managed by its members, subsection (1) shall apply in relation to the acts and defaults of a member in connection with his functions of management as if he were a director of the body corporate.'

Section 3 is applied to an offence under CJA 1988, s 160 by CJA 1988, s 1(4).

8.80 Comparable provisions apply elsewhere in the criminal law.[123] In *Boal*[124] it was held that it applies to those who are in positions of real authority and who have the power to decide policy and not just those who are designated as having an internal (junior) management role but without any real authority.

---

[121] See **8.31**, **8.46** and **8.57**.
[122] See **8.31**.
[123] For a discussion of the elements of this provision, see *Card, Cross & Jones*, at paras 18.43–18.45.
[124] [1992] QB 591.

Entry, search and seizure

8.81 PoCA 1978, s 4 governs the entry, search and seizure by police officers:

'(1) The following applies where a justice of the peace is satisfied by information on oath, laid by or on behalf of the Director of Public Prosecutions or by a constable, that there is reasonable ground for suspecting that, in any premises, there is an indecent photograph or pseudo-photograph of a child.

(2) The justice may issue a warrant under his hand authorising any constable to enter (if need be by force) and search the premises and to seize and remove any articles which he believes (with reasonable cause) to be or include indecent photographs or pseudo-photographs of children.

(3) [Repealed: see below]

(4) In this section "premises" has the same meaning as in the Police and Criminal Evidence Act 1984[125].'

8.82 Section 4(3) was repealed by the Police and Justice Act (PJA) 2006, s 39 to take account of the fact that there are new forfeiture provisions introduced by that Act.

Forfeiture

8.83 PoCA 1978, s 5 deals with forfeiture. The PJA 2006, s 39 replaced PoCA 1978, s 5 and inserted a Schedule into the Act. The revised s 5 simply states that the Schedule deals with the forfeiture of the indecent photographs. The Schedule has effect regardless of whether the property was seized before or after it came into force.[126] The Schedule is important where indecent photographs, etc have been seized but the case has been dealt with by a caution or the CPS decides not to prosecute. The Schedule provides an administrative procedure to deal with the forfeiture of property save where it is contested by the offender (which in most situations it will not). Where the matter proceeds to conviction, the court may order forfeiture under its general powers[127] to make forfeiture orders.

8.84 The Schedule applies where:

(a) property is in the custody of a constable through lawful seizure;

(b) ignoring the Schedule, there is no legitimate reason for the constable to retain custody of the property;

---

[125] PACE, s 23 states 'premises includes any place and, in particular, includes—
  (a) any vehicle, vessel, aircraft or hovercraft;
  (b) any offshore installation;
  (ba) any renewable energy installation;
  (c) any tent or moveable structure.'
[126] PJA 2006, s 39(6) except where the items had been brought before the court under the provisions of PoCA 1978, s 4(3) before the Schedule came into force (1 April 2008: Police and Justice Act 2006 (Commencement No 8) Order 2008, SI 2008/790, art 2).
[127] Powers of Criminal Courts (Sentencing) Act 2000, s 143.

(c)   where the constable is satisfied that there are reasonable grounds for believing that the property is or is likely to be forfeitable property;[128] and

(d)   where, ignoring the Schedule, the constable is not aware of any person who has a legitimate reason for possessing the property or any readily separable[129] part of it.[130]

8.85   The property must be retained in the custody of a constable until it is returned or otherwise disposed of in pursuance of the Schedule.[131] The constable for the time being with custody of the property must then serve a notice on:

(a)   every person whom he believes to have been the owner of the property, or one of its owners, at the time of the seizure of the property;

(b)   where the property was seized from premises, every person whom the relevant officer believes to have been an occupier of the premises at that time; and

(c)   where the property was seized as a result of a search of any person, that person.[132]

8.86   This notice describes the property and explains how a person can make a claim to have the property back.[133] Where a person claims that he or she has a legitimate reason for possessing the property or a part of it he or she may, within one month of the notice above being served,[134] provide written notice of this at a police station in the police area where the property was seized.[135] The police must then decide whether to apply to the magistrates' court to condemn the property as forfeited[136] or to return the property.[137] Where no claim is made, the property is automatically forfeited.[138]

8.87   Where forfeiture proceedings are instituted, the court must order the forfeiture of the property if it is satisfied that it is forfeitable property and that no one has a legitimate reason for possessing the property.[139] Where the court is satisfied that it is reasonably practicable to separate the property, it can order the forfeiture only of that part which contains forfeitable property.[140]

---

[128]   Ie any indecent photograph or pseudo-photograph of a child and any property which it is not reasonably practicable to separate from an indecent photograph or pseudo-photograph of a child: PoCA 1978, Sch, para 1(2).
[129]   A part of the property is 'readily separable' if, in all the circumstances (including time and costs) it is reasonably practicable for it to be separated from the remainder of that property without prejudicing the remainder of the property or another part of it: PoCA 1978, Sch, para 1(3), (4).
[130]   PoCA 1978, Sch, para 1(1).
[131]   PoCA 1978, Sch, para 2. The Police (Property) Act 1897 does not apply to this Schedule.
[132]   PoCA 1978, Sch, para 4(1).
[133]   PoCA 1978, Sch, para 4(2).
[134]   PoCA 1978, Sch, para 6(1).
[135]   PoCA 1978, Sch, paras 5, 6(1)(a). If no notice of intended forfeiture has been given, notice of claim must be given within one month of the date when the property began to be retained in the custody of a constable: para 6(1)(b).
[136]   PoCA 1978, Sch, para 8.
[137]   PoCA 1978, Sch, para 9.
[138]   PoCA 1978, Sch, para 7.
[139]   PoCA 1978, Sch, para 10(2).
[140]   PoCA 1978, Sch, para 10(5).

Chapter 9

OFFENCES AGAINST PEOPLE WITH A MENTAL DISORDER

INTRODUCTION

Protection of the mentally disordered

9.1   Considerable attention has been given in modern times to the risks to children from sexual abuse. Much less attention has been paid to the risk of sexual exploitation and abuse to which people with a mental disorder are particularly vulnerable. In some situations mental disorder may be so severe as to prevent meaningful understanding of, and consent to, sexual activity. Even if it does not have this effect, mentally disordered people may be suggestible and unable to resist inappropriate sexual behaviour. In addition, they may be targeted by others for their own sexual gratification. Research has estimated that the incidence of sexual exploitation and abuse amongst people with disabilities may be as much as four times higher than that for the non-disabled population,[1] and that a high proportion of those abused are women and girls (most of whom know the abuser).[2] The risks of this have been enhanced by the fact that mentally disordered adults are now far more likely to be living in the community (in sheltered or supported houses or with families), rather than in an institution. Sexual exploitation and abuse of those with a mental disorder by those with the responsibility to care for them is a matter of particular concern. It has been suggested that abusers may deliberately seek employment as care workers in order to facilitate abuse of the mentally vulnerable.[3]

9.2   The issue of sexual relations and the mentally disordered confronts the law with a balancing act between the need to protect the vulnerable against exploitation and abuse and the need to respect their rights to a private life, including the expression of their sexuality and the enjoyment of tender (potentially beneficial) relationships.

The law before the Sexual Offences Act 2003

9.3   Apart from cases where the victim was too mentally impaired to consent, the criminal law used to offer limited protection to mentally disordered adults against sexual abuse and exploitation. The offences under the previous legislation,[4] all of which were

---

[1]   *Setting the Boundaries: Reforming the Law on Sexual Offences* (Home Office, 2000) (*SB*), at para 4.2.5 (citing Muccigrosso (1991)).

[2]   Ibid (citing Sobsey and Doe (1991) who suggest that 81% of victims were female and 99% knew the abuser).

[3]   *Behind Closed Doors: Preventing Sexual Abuse against Adults with a Learning Disability* (Voice, Respond, Mencap, 2001), at p 11.

[4]   These were the offences of: unlawful sexual intercourse by a man with a 'defective' woman (SOA 1956, s 7); procuring a 'defective' woman to have unlawful sexual intercourse anywhere in the world (SOA 1956, s 9); abduction of a 'defective' woman from her parent or guardian (SOA 1956, s 21); permitting a 'defective' woman to use premises for intercourse (SOA 1956, s 27); causing or encouraging the prostitution of a female 'defective' (SOA 1956, s 29); and sexual intercourse by a male employee or manager of a hospital or care home with a woman patient being treated for mental disorder, or by a man with a mentally disordered

repealed by the Sexual Offences Act (SOA) 2003,[5] were gender specific and, with one exception,[6] were limited to 'defectives', ie persons suffering from a state of arrested or incomplete development of mind which included *severe* impairment of intelligence and social functioning.[7] The term therefore did not cover those with an arrested or incomplete development of mind whose impairment, though significant, was not severe, nor those whose minds had developed normally but who then suffered dementia or whose brains had been damaged in an accident, for example. Nor did it cover people with other types of mental disorder.

Sexual Offences Act 2003

9.4   SOA 2003, ss 30–41 provide a range of non-gender-specific offences specifically aimed at protecting people with any mental disorder, as defined by the Mental Health Act (MHA) 1983, s 1, whether permanent or temporary, of whatever degree at the material time. The age of the victim is irrelevant.

Three groups of offences

9.5   The offences are grouped as follows under three headings:

- Offences against persons with a mental disorder impeding choice (ss 30–33).
  Offences in this group are designed to protect a mentally disordered person who because of, or for a reason related to, their mental disorder is unable to refuse to participate in the activity concerned.

- Inducements, etc to persons with a mental disorder (ss 34–37).
  Offences in this group are designed to protect a mentally disordered person who is capable of giving consent to sexual activity, but who has a mental disorder making him vulnerable to low levels of inducement, threat or deception.

- Offences by care workers against persons with a mental disorder (ss 38–41).
  Offences in this group are designed to protect a mentally disordered person who has the capacity to consent but may be vulnerable to exploitative behaviour by someone on whose care he relies and may agree to sexual activity because of this.

9.6   Each of the three groups of offences covers the same range of sexually related conduct as the child sex offences and abuse of trust offences described in Chapters 4 and 5 (ie sexual touching of a mentally disordered person (B), causing or inciting sexual activity by B, engaging in sexual activity in B's presence and causing B to watch sexual activity). This is a much wider range of conduct than that penalised by the 'mental disorder provisions' repealed by SOA 2003.[8] To the extent that the new offences

---

female patient under his guardianship or care (MHA 1959, s 128). By SOA 1967, s 1(4), this section had effect as if 'unlawful sexual intercourse with a woman' included buggery or an act of gross indecency with another man.
In addition, a 'defective' woman or man could not give a valid consent under the law relating to indecent assault (SOA 1956, ss 14(4) and 15(3)), and nor could a 'defective' man validly consent to homosexual gross indecency (SOA 1967, s 1(3)).
Mentally disordered men were given no protection against heterosexual sexual exploitation.

5   See **1.5**.
6   MHA 1959, s 128.
7   SOA 1956, s 45; SOA 1967, s 1(3A).
8   See **9.3**, n 4.

correspond with those which they replaced, their maximum term of imprisonment is greater, thereby responding to criticisms that sentencing powers under the previous legislation were too limited.

9.7 The three groups of offences have the potential for overlap between themselves and with others. As pointed out in *Smith & Hogan*:[9]

> 'If the activity is seemingly non-consensual (or at least B is unable to refuse), and involves a child complainant and a carer who is in a family relationship with B, the possible range of offences committed is vast.'

9.8 Outside the bounds of the three groups of offences, those with mental disorders have the same rights to engage in consensual sexual activity as anyone else, and so do those with whom they so engage. Overall, the offences under ss 30–41 achieve the appropriate balance between the need to protect the mentally disordered from sexual abuse and the need to give maximum recognition to their right to a sexual life. Perhaps surprisingly, there is no equivalent of the offence under SOA 2003, s 15 to deal with 'grooming' people who are mentally disordered, and who may be as vulnerable to it as are children.

Evidential matters

9.9 Witnesses suffering from mental disorder clearly raise issues in terms of their competence and vulnerability. These matters are dealt with in Chapter 14.

MENTAL DISORDER

9.10 For the purposes of the offences under SOA 2003, ss 30–41, 'mental disorder' has the meaning given by MHA 1983, s 1,[10] namely 'mental illness,[11] arrested or incomplete development of mind, psychopathic disorder[12] and any other disorder or disability of mind'.[13] When an amendment made by MHA 2007, s 1(1) and (2) comes into force on 3 November 2008, 'mental disorder' will be redefined as 'any disorder or disability of the mind'.[14] Both definitions cover a much wider range of mental states than 'defective', the term whose definition was referred to in **9.3**. Examples of clinically recognised mental disorders include mental illnesses such as schizophrenia, bipolar disorder, anxiety and depression, as well as personality disorders. Disorders or disabilities of the brain are not mental disorders unless (and only to the extent that) they give rise to a disability or

---

9   Smith and Hogan *Criminal Law* (Ormerod (ed)) (OUP, 12th edn, 2008), at p 721.
10   SOA 2003, s 79(6).
11   There is no statutory definition of 'mental illness'. For the general meaning of the term see *W v L* [1974] QB 711.
12   'Psychopathic disorder' in this definition 'means a persistent disorder or disability of mind (whether or not including significant impairment of intelligence) which results in abnormally aggressive or seriously irresponsible conduct on the part of the person concerned': MHA 1983, s 1(2). This definition will be omitted from MHA 1983, s 1(2) as from 3 November 2008 when MHA 2007, s 1 comes into force.
13   MHA 1983, s 1(2).
14   MHA 2007 (Commencement No 7 and Transitional Provisions) Order 2008, SI 2008/1900, art 2(a). As from 3 November 2008, MHA 1983, s 1(3) will provide: 'Dependence on alcohol or drugs is not considered to be a disorder or disability of the mind for the purposes of subsection (2) above.'
     Like the exclusion under the original s 1(3) (for which it has been substituted), this will not prevent a person being categorised as suffering a mental disorder if, as well as alcohol or drug dependence, he is suffering from an unrelated mental disorder, or a mental disorder arising from alcohol or drug dependence or from the withdrawal of alcohol or drugs, or brain damage resulting from long-term alcohol or drug use.

disorder of the mind as well, such as certain types of psychological dysfunction arising from brain injury or damage in adulthood.[15] Although mental health professionals broadly agree about what constitutes mental disorder, there is potential for disagreement in some situations.[16] It is for the prosecution to prove that the complainant was mentally disordered at the relevant time. Medical evidence will be required to prove that the complainant had a mental disorder at such a time.

9.11 Both the existing and the substituted definitions of mental disorder include a 'learning disability'. According to the White Paper, *Valuing People: A New Strategy for the 21st Century*:[17]

'Learning disability includes the presence of:

–   a significantly reduced ability to understand new or complex information, to learn new skills (impaired intelligence); with
–   a reduced ability to cope independently (impaired social functioning);
–   which started before adulthood, with a lasting effect on development.'[18]

MENCAP estimates that there are over 200,000 people with severe or profound learning disability in England and Wales.[19] There would be many more with medium to mild learning disabilities.

9.12 To lump people with a learning disability together with those who have other forms of mental disorder has the potential to inhibit sexual behaviour involving persons with a learning disability which are socially acceptable and it may be regarded as demeaning. Although it is unfortunate that the Act does not make this distinction, it has to be admitted that to have done so would have produced even greater proliferation of offences and more distinctions between them.[20]

OFFENCES AGAINST PERSONS WITH A MENTAL DISORDER IMPEDING CHOICE

9.13 The offences in SOA 2003, ss 30–33 deal with cases where A:

*   engages in sexual activity with B, a person with a mental disorder (s 30);

*   causes or incites B, a person with a mental disorder, to engage in sexual activity (s 31);

*   engages in sexual activity in the presence of B, a person with a mental disorder (s 32); or

15   Explanatory notes to MHA 2007.
16   Bartlett and Sandland *Mental Health Law: Policy and Practice* (Oxford University Press, 2nd edn, 2003) cited in Rook and Ward *Sexual Offences Law & Practice* (Sweet & Maxwell, 3rd edn, 2004), at p 217.
17   Cm 5086 (2001).
18   In some cases, learning disability directly results from organic damage, e g the malfunction of the nervous system during or soon after birth. In others it is due to chromosomal abnormality, such as Down's syndrome. More commonly, people with learning disability have no organic defects: VOICE *Competent to Tell the Truth* (Voice UK, 1998).
19   *SB*, at para 4.1.5.
20   As observed in *Smith & Hogan Criminal Law* (Ormerod (ed)) (OUP, 11th edn, 2005), at p 640.

- causes B, a person with a person with a mental disorder, to watch a sexual act (s 33),

and, because B has a mental disorder or for a reason related to it, B is unable to refuse.

9.14 Where a person is unable to refuse *because of* a mental disorder, there is a direct causal link between the disorder and the inability to refuse. The alternative, that a person is unable to refuse consent *for a reason related to* a mental disorder, widens the test to cover other people who are equally vulnerable. This is because the alternative covers people who are unable to refuse partly for a reason other than the fact of their mental disorder as such but related to their mental disorder. One example would be where someone taking medication for a mental disorder was rendered unable to refuse. Others would be where someone is unable to refuse because he has spent all his life in an institutional environment, and has become very compliant with requests that staff make of him, or has had no opportunity to become aware of what sexual activity entails, or does not know that there is a choice to be made when it comes to engaging in sexual activity.[21]

9.15 Proof of inability to refuse may depend on the degree and extent of the mental disorder. Expert evidence is admissible in this regard, as it is in respect of the existence of the mental disorder, but is not always necessary since the complainant's mental state may be established from other evidence and from the jury's observation of the complainant's behaviour and reactions.[22] Thus, expert evidence giving an opinion as to the extent of a mental impairment can properly be rejected by a jury if it considers that it is contradicted by other evidence or by the jury's own observations of the complainant.[23]

Inability to refuse

9.16 The question in relation to the offences under ss 30–33 is not whether there was an absence of consent but whether there was an inability to refuse.[24] Subsection (2) of each of ss 30–33 provides a comprehensive definition of what is meant by the requirement of inability to refuse in the context of the particular section in terms of:

(a) the absence of the capacity to choose whether to agree to the material conduct (whether because he or she lacks sufficient understanding of the nature – or, in ss 30(2) and 31(2), reasonably foreseeable consequences – of that conduct, or for any other reason); or

(b) inability to communicate such a choice to the defendant.

Thus, the concept of inability to refuse covers cases where the complainant lacks the mental capacity to choose and cases where, whether or not the complainant lacks the capacity to choose whether to agree to the material conduct, the complainant is unable to communicate his or her choice to the defendant. People with severe brain damage, severe learning disabilities or severe dementia are clear examples of people who would be unable to refuse under the above rules.

---

[21] Paul Goggins MP, HC Deb, vol 412, col 600.
[22] *Hall* (1987) 86 Cr App R 159; *Robbins* [1988] Crim LR 744.
[23] *Hall*, ibid.
[24] Lord Falconer, HL Deb, vol 647, col 398.

Absence of mental capacity to choose[25]

9.17   The test in (a) above not merely involves the complainant (B) being unable to choose to refuse to submit to the material conduct (or to engage in the material conduct, as the case may be); it involves B being unable to *choose to agree* to the material conduct (or to engage in it).[26] Reference to the test of capacity to consent to sexual relations set out in **3.25** indicates that, for the purposes of (a), a person 'lacks sufficient understanding of the nature' of the material conduct if he or she does not understand the sexual nature of the material conduct. Thus, the mere fact that a mentally disordered person gave way to 'animal instincts' in response to conduct is not enough.[27] Sufficient understanding of the sexual nature of the conduct might include knowing that sexual activity is different from personal care.[28] The 'understanding of sexual nature' test can be satisfied by a relatively low level of knowledge and understanding. In respect of the offences under ss 30 and 31 which require the mentally disordered person to be touched sexually or to be caused or incited to engage in sexual activity, ss 30(2) and 31(2) indicate that a person may also not have the capacity to choose (for the purposes of those sections) because he or she lacks sufficient understanding of the reasonably foreseeable consequences of the touching or activity. Sufficient understanding of the reasonably foreseeable consequences of that conduct would seem to refer to understanding that some sexual activities can lead to pregnancy or the transmission of disease. In inserting this alternative test of understanding in ss 30(2) and 31(2), Parliament presumably thought that a person could understand the nature of sexual touching or activity without understanding its reasonably foreseeable consequences. On the other hand, given that the test of understanding of the nature of conduct in ss 30 and 31 relates to its sexual nature it is arguable that one cannot understand that nature without being aware of its reasonably foreseeable consequences, in which case the alternative test of understanding adds nothing to the common law test of capacity to consent referred to in **3.25**. In *C*[29] the Court of Appeal agreed with Munby J's view in *X City Council v MB*[30] that there was little, if anything, between the test of capacity to choose in s 30(2) and the common law test of capacity to consent.

9.18   The phrase 'or for any other reason' in the test in (a) was considered by the Court of Appeal in *C*. The case concerned an appeal by A against conviction for sexual activity with a person with a mental disorder impeding choice, contrary to s 30(1). The complainant, B, had a long history of mental disorder. She met A, who was 'doing crack', and took drugs with him and engaged in sexual activity with him. There was evidence that at the time in question B was suffering a relapse of her mental illness, that she had gone to a flat with A because he had offered to help her in her distressed state and that because she was frightened of A she had consented to the sexual activity. Dealing with what might constitute a lack of capacity to choose to agree to sexual activity, the judge chose as an example 'an irrational fear arising from her mental disorder such that she felt that she was unable to refuse any request the defendant . . . made for sex'. This was wrong, said the Court of Appeal, because it could have led the jury to conclude that if B agreed to A's proposals out of an irrational fear arising from

---

25   See Elliott 'Capacity, Sex and the Mentally Disordered' [2008] 2 *Archbold News* 6.
26   *C* [2008] EWCA Crim 1155 at [48].
27   A person who had given way to animal instincts had been held in pre-SOA 2003 cases to have consented: *Fletcher* [1866] LR 1 CCR 39 (disapproved by Palles CB in *Dee* (1884) 15 Cox CC 579 at 594 and by Munby J in *X City Council v MB* [2007] 3 FCR 371, at [73]). See also *Jenkins* (2000) an unreported Crown Court case where the judge ruled that a severely impaired woman could give consent through her 'animal instincts'.
28   *Guidance on Part 1 of the Sexual Offences Act 2003* (Home Office, 2003) (*Guidance Pt 1*), at para 134.
29   [2008] EWCA Crim 1155 at [49].
30   [2007] 3 FCR 371 at [82].

her mental disorder, this would, of itself, amount to incapacity to choose whether to agree to the sexual activity, and this did not follow for the reasons given below.

9.19 In *C* the Court of Appeal stated that the words 'or for any other reason' set a similarly high hurdle for the prosecution to those that had gone before them in s 30(2). The effect of a mental disorder necessarily had to be severe before it would have the effect that a person was unable to choose whether to submit to sexual activity. It would not, said the Court of Appeal, be very helpful to attempt to exemplify the type of mental condition that might have that effect, notwithstanding that the person suffering from it was able to understand the nature of sexual activity. It was, however, possible to conceive of an acute episode of a mental disorder resulting in an inability to take a rational decision about sexual activity, or indeed other activities, notwithstanding that the person suffering from it had an understanding of the nature of sexual activity. Such a mental condition could fall within the words 'or for any other reason'. On the other hand, if B had consented to sexual activity against her inclination because she was frightened of A, even if her fear was irrational and caused by her mental disorder, it did not follow that she lacked the capacity to choose whether to agree to sexual activity. It did not follow from that irrational fear that B would not have been capable of choosing whether or not to agree to sexual activity in circumstances which did not give rise to that fear. Irrational fear that prevented the exercise of choice could not be equated with lack of capacity to choose. A lack of capacity to choose to agree to sexual activity could not be 'person specific' or 'situation specific'. For criticism of the latter part of this statement see **3.25**.

9.20 *C* was a case where it was alleged that B lacked the capacity to choose *because* of her mental disorder. An example of a case where a person might lack the capacity to choose 'for any other reason' *for a reason related* to his mental disorder might be that he had no choice because of the effect of institutionalisation.[31]

Inability to communicate choice

9.21 The second type of inability to refuse covers people who may be able to make a choice but are unable because of mental disorder, or a reason related to it, to communicate that choice. According to the decision of the Divisional Court in *Hulme v DPP*[32] a person who is physically able to speak but who is unable effectively to do so in the way that someone of his age, not suffering from his disabilities, would have done in similar circumstances, is unable to communicate his choice. In that case, B, a woman aged 27, suffered from cerebral palsy and had a mental age well below 27. A touched B on her private parts and caused her to touch his penis. A was convicted of sexual activity with a person with a mental disorder impeding choice, contrary to s 30. On appeal the Divisional Court held that there was evidence on which the magistrates could conclude that B was unable to refuse to be touched sexually. Although the magistrates' findings indicated that B did not want A to act in the way that he did (ie she was capable of choosing whether to agree to his conduct), their findings also indicated that B was unable effectively to communicate her choice to A. There was evidence to support that finding because:

---

[31] *Guidance Pt 1*, para 134.
[32] (2006) 170 JP 598.

- in her evidence, B had said that on A touching her private parts and pressing hard, she did not know what to do or say, and that could only sensibly be because of her mental condition; and

- in her evidence, B had said that when she touched A's penis she did so because A made her and because he wanted her to, although she did not want to, and that was explicable on the basis that B was unable effectively to communicate her wishes in the way that a woman of 27, not suffering from her disabilities, would have done.

A's conviction was therefore upheld. In such cases it may be difficult to prove lack of consent on a charge under ss 1–4 but there would be an inability to choose for the purposes of an offence under s 30 or 31 if the inability is due to (or by a reason related to) mental disorder. The liberal interpretation in *Hulme v DPP* can be supported by reference to the mischief behind the present group of offences.

9.22   In *C*, referred to above, the trial judge had also left the case to the jury that B would have been unable to refuse if through her mental disorder she was unable to communicate her choice to A because of her irrational fear. The Court of Appeal held that this was wrong; the second type of inability to refuse was designed to address those whose mental disorders impair their ability to communicate, and there was no evidence that B was unable to communicate any choice that she had made. This part of the decision may be inconsistent with *Hulme v DPP*, to which the Court of Appeal referred without comment.[33]

9.23   Where B is *physically* incapable of communicating a choice, he or she is presumed not to have consented for the purposes of an offence under SOA 2003, ss 1–4 (rape, sexual assault, etc) unless there is evidence to the contrary.[34] An example would be someone paralysed by a stroke.

9.24   There is an obvious degree of overlap between the offences under SOA 2003, ss 30 and 31 and those under ss 1–4 but the definition of inability to refuse is such that the overlap is not complete. Given that the offences under ss 30 and 31 have the same maximum punishment as (or in some instances a higher maximum than) offences under ss 1–4 and that 'inability to refuse' may be easier to prove than 'without consent', a charge under s 30 or s 31 would seem more appropriate where there is overlap.

General

9.25   Proof of the requisite relationship between the mental disorder and the inability to refuse does not necessarily require the complainant to be called as a witness. Such proof may be satisfied by means of expert medical evidence. Alternatively, use may be made of the Criminal Justice Act (CJA) 2003, s 116.[35]

9.26   Where a person with a mental disorder is unable to refuse consent because he is not free to do so, and not because of the disorder or a reason related to it, as where he

---

33   See Elliott [2008] 6 *Archbold News* 6.
34   SOA 2003, s 75. See **3.61** et seq.
35   Inter alia, s 116 permits an out-of-court statement by the complainant to be admitted where that person is unfit to be a witness because of his mental condition.

is subject to violence or a threat of violence, the relevant offence will be one under SOA 2003, ss 1–4, as appropriate depending on the type of sexual activity.

9.27 Where it cannot be proved that a person with a mental disorder was thereby (or for a reason related to it) unable to refuse, a prosecution for one of the offences under SOA 2003, ss 34–37[36] may succeed, depending on the facts. On the other hand, an alternative verdict for one of these offences under the Criminal Law Act 1967, s 6(3) would not be possible on a trial for an offence under SOA 2003, ss 30–33 because an allegation in the indictment for one of these offences will not expressly amount to, expressly include, impliedly amount to or impliedly include an allegation[37] of any of the offences under ss 34–37.

Some other common points

9.28 Because each of the offences in ss 30–33 is concerned with conduct that replicates conduct dealt with by the child sex offences (ss 9–12) and abuse of trust offences (ss 16–19), many of their elements can be explained by cross-reference.

Knows or could reasonably be expected to know

9.29 Each offence requires that A knows or could reasonably be expected to know that B has a mental disorder *and* knows or could reasonably be expected to know that because of it, or a reason related to it, B is likely to be 'unable to refuse'. If it is proved that B has a mental disorder and that it was to *such a degree* as to render B 'unable to refuse', it will be a rare case where the first limb of the present requirement could not be proved. It is the second limb which will normally be the important one if a case is contested in respect of the present requirement; the more severe B's mental impairment is, the more apparent its severity will be and the easier it should be to prove that requirement.

9.30 As stated in **2.72**, 'could reasonably be *expected* to know' suggests that the test is not wholly objective, but that the objective test should be applied on the basis of A's mental ability and understanding.

9.31 Apart from the degree of mental impairment, other factors which may be relevant to proof of the requirement include the extent to which the mental disorder was manifested, the relationship between the parties, the age, intelligence and maturity of A and A's familiarity with mental disorder. Assuming that A was fit to plead, it would be unlikely that the requirement could be proved against A if he or she had a mental disorder making him or her unable to make or communicate choices.

No exception for spouses, civil partners or pre-existing sexual relationships

9.32 Unlike corresponding offences elsewhere in the Act (e g under ss 38–41),[38] it is no defence under ss 30–33 for A to prove that he or she was lawfully married to, or the civil partner of, or had a pre-existing sexual relationship with, B at the material time. A mental disorder could supervene a valid marriage between A and B.

---

[36]   See **9.60–9.85**.
[37]   *Wilson* [1984] AC 242.
[38]   See **9.125–9.130**.

CPS guidance for prosecutors

9.33 A prosecution under ss 30–33 will usually take place unless public interest factors tending against prosecution clearly outweigh those tending in favour. Given the seriousness of such an offence a prosecution will almost certainly be required.[39]

Sexual activity with a person with a mental disorder impeding choice

9.34 SOA 2003, s 30(1) provides:

'A person (A) commits an offence if—

(a) he intentionally touches another person (B),

(b) the touching is sexual,

(c) B is unable to refuse because of or for a reason related to a mental disorder, and

(d) A knows or could reasonably be expected to know that B has a mental disorder and that because of it or for a reason related to it B is likely to be unable to refuse.'

Trial, punishment and miscellaneous points

9.35 An offence under s 30 is triable only on indictment and the maximum punishment is life imprisonment if the touching involved:

(a) penetration of B's anus or vagina[40] with a part of A's body or anything else;

(b) penetration of B's mouth with A's penis;[41]

(c) penetration of A's anus or vagina with a part of B's body (but not with anything else); or

(d) penetration of A's mouth with B's penis.[42]

Otherwise, the offence is triable either way and punishable on conviction on indictment with a maximum of 14 years' imprisonment.[43] See the Sentencing Guidelines Council (SGC) Definitive Guideline,[44] in the Appendix.

9.36 By virtue of the principle in *Courtie*,[45] there are two separate offences under s 30: one requires penetration in a specified way; the other 'non-penetrative' sexual touching.

Class of offence	See text	SOA 2003, s 72 applies	✔[46]
Notification requirements	✔	SOPO[47]	✔

---

39 CPS Guidance on Sexual offences and child abuse (*CPS Guidance*): see **1.56**.
40 See **3.100–3.102**.
41 See **3.100** and **3.102**.
42 SOA 2003, s 30(3).
43 SOA 2003, s 30(4); maximum on summary conviction: **1.43**.
44 At pp 5–18, 68–72.
45 [1984] AC 463; **3.170**. There is nothing to rebut the presumption to this effect.
46 But only where the complainant is within the age limit to which s 72 applies: see **2.97**.

CJA 2003, Sch 15 applies	✔	Serious specified offence	✔
Review of lenient sentence	See text	Special provisions of CYPA 1933[48]	✔
Detention of young offender for specified period			✔

See **1.48** et seq.

9.37   The provisions of CJA 1988, ss 35 and 36 relating to Attorney-General's references for a review of a sentence as unduly lenient apply to the penetrative offence but not the non-penetrative one. This is probably an oversight.[49] The former is a Class 2 offence, the latter Class 3.[50]

9.38   The restriction on bail under the Criminal Justice and Public Order Act (CJPOA) 1994, s 25 referred to in **3.96** applies to the penetrative offence under SOA 2003, s 30(1) and (3) or an attempt to commit it.[51] The exceptions under SOA 2003, s 73[52] from liability for aiding, abetting or counselling the commission of an offence against a child under 16 apply to an offence under s 30.[53]

Intentional touching: sexual touching

9.39   These terms in s 30(1)(a) and (b) are identical to s 9(1)(a) and (b) referred to in **4.9**, **4.13** and **4.14**.

Inability to refuse etc

9.40   Section 30(2) provides that B is unable to refuse if:

'(a)   he lacks the capacity to choose whether to agree to the touching (whether because he lacks sufficient understanding of the nature or reasonably foreseeable consequences of what is being done, or for any other reason), or

(b)   he is unable to communicate such a choice to A.'

See further **9.10–9.24**. The reference to 'reasonably foreseeable consequences' in (a) clearly refers to the complainant's understanding that the touching in question may result in injury to his or her health or, where sexual intercourse is involved, and at least when the complainant is a woman, pregnancy.

Knows or could reasonably be expected to know, etc

9.41   See **9.29–9.31**.

---

[47]   Sexual offences prevention order.
[48]   Children and Young Persons Act 1933.
[49]   There would seem to be a similar oversight in respect of offences under SOA 2003, ss 31, 34, 35, 38 and 39.
[50]   *Consolidated Criminal Practice Direction*(see **1.49**), at para III.21.1.
[51]   CJPOA 1994, s 25(2)(i), (n).
[52]   See **2.49–2.54**.
[53]   SOA 2003, s 73(2)(d).

Human rights

9.42 The effect of s 30 is that it is unlawful sexually to touch people who are unable to make or communicate choices about sexual activity. It also means that, if such people have the necessary mens rea, they are guilty of an offence if they touch someone else with such a disorder or disability. Clearly, this engages the right to respect for private life under the European Convention on Human Rights (ECHR), Art 8.[54] In the light of the decision of the European Court of Human Rights in *X and Y v The Netherlands*,[55] the Joint Committee on Human Rights[56] considered that s 30 was generally compatible with ECHR rights. This is no doubt generally correct where only one of the two parties is unable to refuse because of or for a reason related to mental disorder. In such a case that party's sexual autonomy needs generally to be protected against exploitation by the other. The Committee concluded that s 30 was unlikely to result in the imposition of criminal liability on mentally disordered people who engage in sexual activity with similarly affected people. The mens rea would be unlikely to be established and the discretion to prosecute would probably be exercised against any such prosecution. Moreover, there are ways of diverting such people from the mainstream penal system towards medical care following a finding of unfitness to plead or after a conviction.

Causing or inciting a person with a mental disorder impeding choice to engage in sexual activity

9.43 SOA 2003, s 31(1) provides:

'A person (A) commits an offence if—

(a)   he intentionally causes or incites another person (B) to engage in an activity,

(b)   the activity is sexual,

(c)   B is unable to refuse because of or for a reason related to a mental disorder, and

(d)   A knows or could reasonably be expected to know that B has a mental disorder and that because of it or for a reason related to it B is likely to be unable to refuse.'

9.44 An offence under s 31 is triable and punishable in the same way as one under s 30[57] depending on whether the activity caused or incited is penetrative,[58] in the sense that it is proved to have involved:

(a)   penetration of B's anus or vagina (by part of the body or anything else);

(b)   penetration of B's mouth with a person's penis;

(c)   penetration of a person's anus or vagina with a part of B's body or by B with anything else; or

(d)   penetration of a person's mouth with B's penis.

---

54   As to the ECHR generally, see **1.24** et seq.

55   (1985) 8 EHRR 235: see **1.31**.

56   *Twelfth Report 2002–03 Scrutiny of Bills: Further Progress Report* (HL 119; HC 765), at paras 2.21–2.25. The Committee emphasised that s 30 was far more carefully targeted on its objective than s 7 (sexual assault of child under 13) (see **3.163**), and that the systems for diverting offenders are much better regulated by statute in relation to mental health than in relation to child offenders, where agencies have great discretion.

57   See **9.35** and the SGC Definitive Guideline, at pp 5–18, 35–41, in the Appendix.

58   Section 31(3) and (4); see **9.35**.

Because of this and because 'causing' and 'inciting' appear to be separate offences,[59] the effect is to create at least two, and arguably four, offences under s 31:

- causing a person with a mental disorder who is thereby unable to refuse to engage in penetrative sexual activity as defined above;

- causing such a person to engage in 'non-penetrative' sexual activity;

- inciting such a person to engage in 'penetrative' sexual activity; and

- inciting such a person to engage in 'non-penetrative' sexual activity.

Class of offence	3	SOA 2003, s 72 applies	✔[60]
Notification requirements	✔	SOPO	✔
CJA 2003, Sch 15 applies	✔	Serious specified offence	✔
Review of lenient sentence	See text	Special provisions of CYPA 1933	✔
Detention of young offender for specified period			✔

See **1.48** et seq.

9.45   The restriction on bail under CJPOA 1994, s 25 referred to in **3.96** applies to the penetrative offence under SOA 2003, s 31 or an attempt to commit it.[61] The provisions of CJA 1988, ss 35 and 36 relating to Attorney-General references for a review of a sentence as unduly lenient apply to s 31 offences relating to penetrative activity but not the others.[62]

9.46   An example of an offence under s 31 would be where A causes B, whom he or she knows is unable to refuse because of a mental disorder, to have sexual intercourse with A's friend. Another would be where A incites B, whom he or she should know is unable to refuse because of a mental disorder, to undress for A's sexual gratification. A third example would be where A causes B, whom he or she knows is unable to refuse because of a mental disorder, to have sexual intercourse with him or her. However, a prosecution under s 30[63] would be more appropriate in such a case.

Intentionally causing or inciting activity; activity sexual

9.47   Section 31(1)(a) and (b) are identical to SOA 2003, s 10(1)(a) and (b); see **4.19** and **4.24–4.26**.

Inability to refuse, etc

9.48   Section 31(2) provides that B is unable to refuse if:

---

[59]   See **3.182**.
[60]   But only where the complainant is within the age limit to which s 72 applies: see **2.97**.
[61]   CJPOA 1994, s 25(2)(m), (n).
[62]   As for s 30, this is probably an oversight.
[63]   See **9.34**.

'(a) he lacks the capacity to choose whether to agree to engaging in the activity caused or incited (whether because he lacks sufficient understanding of the nature or reasonably foreseeable consequences of the activity, or for any other reason), or

(b) he is unable to communicate such a choice to A.'

See further **9.10–9.24**.

Knows or could reasonably be expected to know

9.49   See **9.29–9.31**.

Engaging in sexual activity in the presence of a person with a mental disorder impeding choice

9.50   SOA 2003, s 32(1) provides:

'A person (A) commits an offence if—

(a) he intentionally engages in an activity,
(b) the activity is sexual,
(c) for the purpose of obtaining sexual gratification, he engages in it—
    (i)   when another person (B) is present or is in a place from which A can be observed, and
    (ii) knowing or believing that B is aware, or intending that B should be aware, that he is engaging in it,
(d) B is unable to refuse because of or for a reason related to a mental disorder, and
(e) A knows or could reasonably be expected to know that B has a mental disorder and that because of it or for a reason related to it B is likely to be unable to refuse.'

9.51   An offence under s 32 is triable either way and punishable with a maximum of 10 years' imprisonment on conviction on indictment.[64] See the SGC Definitive Guideline[65] in the Appendix.

Class of offence	3	SOA 2003, s 72 applies	✔[66]
Notification requirements	✔	SOPO	✔
CJA 2003, Sch 15 applies	✔	Serious specified offence	✔
Review of lenient sentence	✘	Special Provisions of CYPA 1933	✔
Detention of young offender for specified period			✘

See **1.48** et seq.

---

[64] SOA 2003, s 32(3); maximum on summary conviction: see **1.43**.
[65] At pp 5–18, 43–45.
[66] But only where the complainant is within the age limit to which s 72 applies: see **2.97**.

Intentionally engaging in sexual activity, etc for the purpose of obtaining sexual gratification

9.52 Section 32(1)(a), (b) and (c) are identical to s 11(1)(a), (b) and (c): see **4.28** and **4.31–4.36**.

Inability to refuse, etc

9.53 Section 32(2) provides that B is unable to refuse if:

'(a) he lacks the capacity to choose whether to agree to being present [sic] (whether because he lacks sufficient understanding of the nature of the activity, or for any other reason), or

(b) he is unable to communicate such a choice to A.'

See further **9.10–9.24**. Presumably, 'present' in s 32(2)(a) will be interpreted as including 'in a place from which A can be observed'. The non-inclusion of these words, which were added to s 32(1)(c)(i) in Parliament, would seem to be a drafting error.

Knows or could reasonably be expected to know

9.54 See **9.29–9.31**.

Causing a person with a mental disorder impeding choice to watch a sexual act

9.55 SOA 2003, s 33(1) provides:

'A person (A) commits an offence if—

(a) for the purpose of obtaining sexual gratification, he intentionally causes another person (B) to watch a third person engaging in an activity, or to look at an image of any person engaging in an activity,

(b) the activity is sexual,

(c) B is unable to refuse because of or for a reason related to a mental disorder, and

(d) A knows or could reasonably be expected to know that B has a mental disorder and that because of it or for a reason related to it B is likely to be unable to refuse.'

9.56 An offence under s 33 is triable and punishable in the same way as one under s 32 and as its corresponding offence under s 12.[67] See the SGC Definitive Guideline[68] in the Appendix.

Class of offence	3	SOA 2003, s 72 applies	✔[69]
Notification requirements	✔	SOPO	✔
CJA 2003, Sch 15 applies	✔	Serious specified offence	✔

---

[67] SOA 2003, s 33(3).

[68] At pp 5–18, 43, 44, 46 and 47.

[69] But only where the complainant is within the age limit to which s 72 applies: see **2.97**.

Review of lenient sentence	✗	Special provisions of CYPA 1933	✔
Detention of young offender for specified period			✗

See **1.48** et seq.

For purpose of sexual gratification, intentionally causing another to watch, etc

9.57 Section 33(1)(a) and (b) are identical to s 12(1)(a) and (b); see **4.38** and **4.43–4.48**.

Inability to refuse, etc

9.58 Section 33(2) provides that B is unable to refuse if:

'(a)   he lacks the capacity to choose whether to agree to watching or looking (whether because he lacks sufficient understanding of the nature of the activity, or for any other reason), or

(b)   he is unable to communicate such a choice to A.'

See further **9.10-9.24**.

Knows or could reasonably be expected to know

9.59 See **9.29–9.31**.

INDUCEMENT, THREAT OR DECEPTION TO A PERSON WITH A MENTAL DISORDER

9.60 SOA 2003, ss 34–37 create the following offences:

- inducement, threat or deception to procure sexual activity with a person with a mental disorder (s 34);

- causing a person with a mental disorder to engage in or agree to engage in sexual activity by inducement, threat or deception (s 35);

- engaging in sexual activity in the presence, procured by inducement, threat or deception, of a person with a mental disorder (s 36);

- causing a person with a mental disorder to watch a sexual act by inducement, threat or deception (s 37).

9.61 The difference between these offences and those in ss 30–33 is that it is not necessary to prove that the complainant was unable to refuse. Indeed these offences are concerned with ostensibly consensual conduct, since it is an element of each offence that the complainant agrees,[70] and it is irrelevant that he or she has consented. If he or she

---

[70]   Or engages or agrees to in the case of an offence under s 35.

has not, or was unable to refuse, the appropriate charge would be under ss 1 to 4, if the conduct falls within those provisions, or ss 30 to 33 respectively. It is necessary to prove that the complainant's agreement was procured by inducement, threat or deception on the part of the defendant. It is this element of improper persuasion which puts the 'sting' in what has occurred in respect of a person whose mental disorder may not be of the same depth as required for an offence under ss 30–33. Because of this element the interference with the right to private life under ECHR, Art 8 would seem to be compatible with that right on the ground that it is necessary in order to protect the right of the mentally vulnerable to sexual autonomy.[71]

9.62 It would seem that the references to inducement, threat or deception are simply references to various ways of committing the specified conduct which lies at the heart of each offence.[72]

9.63 The present offences recognise that, although a mentally disordered person may well be capable of understanding the nature and reasonably foreseeable consequences of the activity in question, and consequently be able to refuse to be involved in it, such a person's capacity to consent may be more compromised than that of someone who is not mentally disordered: he or she may be vulnerable to relatively low levels of inducement, threat and deception which would seem implausible to most people. In *PP*[73] it was said:

> 'For example, case studies show that it is possible for a person with a learning disability to be induced into sexual activity by offers of gifts. They can be seriously distressed by threats of withholding treats and favours or telling tales to their friends and family, and they can also be deceived by claims that sexual activity is all part of routine health care or a game that everyone plays.'

Inducement, threat or deception

9.64 Each of SOA 2003, ss 34–37 speaks of 'an inducement offered or given, a threat made or a deception practised by A [the perpetrator of the offence]'. The dictionary meaning of 'inducement' is 'a thing which induces [ie causes] someone to do something'.[74] It adds something to the other two terms since it covers persuasion or other forms of inducing (eg by a gift). Because the inducement need only be 'offered', a promise which induces the relevant conduct can suffice. If something is offered or given, and B's agreement is obtained thereby, there is no reason why the offer to give (or giving) should relate to a giving to B, as opposed to a third party. The inducement, threat or deception is not required to occur immediately before the specified result. It may occur at any time before then, although the greater the temporal gap the more difficult it may be to prove that it was a cause of that result. Because the inducement, threat or deception must be given, made or practised by A, it would seem that one of these things done by a third party at A's instigation would not suffice; if so, this is an unfortunate and unnecessary restriction on the offence.

9.65 There seems no reason why a threat should not be made by implication. The nature of the threat is left at large. It need not be such as would vitiate consent for the

---

[71] See **1.29**.
[72] As opposed to referring to three separate types of conduct: see the comments in **3.182**, n 284.
[73] *Protecting the Public: Strengthening Protection Against Sex Offenders and Reforming the Law on Sexual Offences*, Cm 5668 (2002), at para 63.
[74] *New Shorter Oxford English Dictionary*.

purposes of a non-consensual sexual offence.[75] It is submitted that, as with 'menaces' in blackmail, a 'threat' must relate to 'action detrimental to or unpleasant to the person addressed'.[76] There is no reason why it should not relate to action by someone other than A. Thus, the statement that B will be in trouble if he or she does not agree to engage in one of the two specified activities will suffice. The 'harm' threatened need not be immediate harm. The threat may relate to action against someone other than B (eg a threat that X will get B's brother into trouble if B does not agree).

9.66　As Buckley J famously said: 'To deceive is … to induce a man to believe that a thing is true which is false.'[77] The falsity may be conveyed expressly or by implication from conduct. There is no reason why it should be limited to a matter of fact; a false representation of law or as to A's intentions should suffice.

9.67　In each offence, the inducement must be offered or given, or the threat made or deception practised, for the purpose of causing B to agree to, or (in s 35) to engage in, the relevant conduct, and it must be effective in this respect. If an inducement, etc offered, etc for another purpose accidentally has a relevant effect an offence under ss 34–37 will not be committed. Likewise, if an inducement, etc offered, etc for a specified purpose has no effect, none of these offences is committed. In determining whether it caused B to agree to, or engage in, the relevant conduct, account should be taken of B's mental disorder. For example, in the case of a threat it might be important to consider B's ability or inability to assess the gravity or imminence of the threat.

Other common points

Other elements

9.68　Apart from the element of inducement, threat or deception just discussed, the other elements of the offences in ss 34–37 are common to other offences already described. Consequently, the description of the offences in ss 34–37 is largely done by cross-referencing.

No exception for spouses or civil partners, or pre-existing sexual relationships

9.69　As with the offences under ss 30–33, it is no defence under ss 34–37 for A to prove that he or she was lawfully married (etc) to B at the material time.

CPS guidance for prosecutors

9.70　A prosecution for an offence under ss 34–37 will usually take place unless there are public interest factors tending against prosecution which clearly outweigh those tending in favour. Given the seriousness of such an offence a prosecution will almost certainly be required.[78]

---

[75]　See **3.33** et seq.

[76]　*Thorne v Motor Trade Association* [1937] AC 797, at p 817, per Lord Wright.

[77]　*Re London and Globe Finance Corporation Ltd* [1903] 1 Ch 728, at p 732. See also *DPP v Ray* [1974] AC 370.

[78]　*CPS Guidance.*

Inducement, threat or deception to procure sexual activity with a person with a mental disorder

9.71 SOA 2003, s 34(1) provides:

'A person (A) commits an offence if—

(a) with the agreement of another person (B) he intentionally touches[79] that person,

(b) the touching is sexual,[80]

(c) A obtains B's agreement by means of an inducement offered or given, a threat made or a deception practised by A for that purpose,[81]

(d) B has a mental disorder,[82] and

(e) A knows or could reasonably be expected to know[83] that B has a mental disorder.'

9.72 An offence under s 34 is triable only on indictment and the maximum punishment is life imprisonment if the touching involved penetration in one of the ways set out in **9.35**.[84] Otherwise, an offence is triable either way, the maximum punishment on conviction on indictment being 14 years' imprisonment.[85]. The effect is that there are two offences under s 34: one requiring penetration in one of the above ways; and the other 'non-penetrative' sexual touching.[86] As to sentencing, see the SGC Definitive Guideline[87] in the Appendix.

Class of offence	See text	SOA 2003, s 72 applies	✔[88]
Notification requirements	✔	SOPO	✔
CJA 2003, Sch 15 applies	✔	Serious specified offence	✔
Review of lenient sentence	See text	Special provisions of CYPA 1933	✔
Detention of young offender for specified period			✔

See **1.48** et seq.

9.73 The provisions of CJA 1988, ss 35 and 36 relating to Attorney-General references for a review of a sentence as unduly lenient apply to the penetrative offence but not the other.[89] The former is a Class 2 offence, the latter Class 3.[90] The exceptions under SOA 2003, s 73[91] from liability for aiding, abetting or counselling the commission of an offence against a child under 16 apply to an offence under s 34.[92]

---

[79] See **2.56, 3.154–3.156**.

[80] See **2.31–2.48**.

[81] See **9.64–9.67**.

[82] See **9.10–9.12**.

[83] See **9.29–9.31**.

[84] Section 34(2).

[85] Section 34(3); maximum on summary conviction: **1.43**.

[86] See *Courtie* [1984] AC 463: **3.170**. There is nothing to rebut the presumption to this effect.

[87] At pp 5–18, 68–72.

[88] But only where the complainant is within the age limit to which s 72 applies: see **2.97**.

[89] As for s 30, this is probably an oversight.

[90] *Consolidated Criminal Practice Direction*, at para III.21.1.

[91] See **2.49–2.54**.

[92] Section 73(2)(d).

Causing a person with a mental disorder to engage in or agree to engage in sexual activity by inducement, threat or deception

9.74   SOA 2003, s 35(1) provides:

'A person (A) commits an offence if—

(a)   by means of an inducement offered or given, a threat made or a deception practised by him for this purpose,[93] he intentionally[94] causes another person (B) to engage in, or to agree to engage in, an activity,

(b)   the activity is sexual,[95]

(c)   B has a mental disorder,[96] and

(d)   A knows or could reasonably be expected to know[97] that B has a mental disorder.'

9.75   An offence under s 35 is triable and punishable in the same way[98] as an offence under s 34 depending on whether or not the activity caused or agreed on is penetrative in the sense set out in **9.44**; this is the effect of s 35(2) and (3). As in the case of s 34, this means that there are at least two separate offences under s 35. Indeed, until the matter is judicially resolved the safe course would be to interpret s 35 as also involving separate offences relating to causing another to engage, and causing another to agree to engage, in sexual activity by various acts. On this basis there are four offences under s 35.

Class of offence	3	SOA 2003, s 72 applies	✔[99]
Notification requirements	✔	SOPO	✔
CJA 2003, Sch 15 applies	✔	Serious specified offence	✔
Review of lenient sentence	See text	Special provisions of CYPA 1933	✔
Detention of young offender for specified period			✔

See **1.48** et seq.

9.76   The provisions of CJA 1988, ss 35 and 36 relating to Attorney-General references for a review of a sentence as unduly lenient apply to the offences relating to penetration but not the others.[100]

9.77   Section 35 covers where, by inducement, etc, A causes B, a person with a mental disorder, to engage in a sexual activity with A (eg masturbating A), with him- or herself (eg B masturbating himself) or with a third party. Of course, if a person is caused to engage in a sexual activity with the inducer, an offence would be committed under s 34.[101] There is nothing in the Act, however, to prevent a prosecution for an offence under s 35 in such a case.

---

[93]   See **9.64–9.67**.

[94]   See **2.57** et seq.

[95]   See **2.32–2.48**.

[96]   See **9.10–9.12**.

[97]   See **9.29–9.31**.

[98]   See the SGC Definitive Guideline, at pp 5–18, 68–72, in the Appendix.

[99]   But only where the complainant is within the age limit to which s 72 applies: see **2.97**.

[100]   As for s 34, this is probably an oversight.

[101]   See **9.71**.

9.78 Because it is sufficient under s 35 that B is induced to agree to engage in sexual activity, it is not necessary to prove that the sexual activity took place, provided that it is alleged and proved that B was induced to agree that it should. There will be few cases where B is caused to engage in sexual activity which B had not previously agreed to (albeit reluctantly or confusedly in many cases).

9.79 The counterparts of s 35 in the other similar groupings of offences in the Act, those relating to child sex offences, to abuse of a position of trust, and to persons with a mental disorder impeding choice, are offences of causing or *inciting* sexual activity. An *incitement* need not result in agreement by the person incited to undertake the activity incited.[102] For an offence under s 35, however, B, the person to whom the inducement is offered or given, or to whom the threat is made or deception practised, must either be caused to engage or be caused to agree to engage in a sexual activity. If the inducement, threat or deception is unsuccessful, there could be a conviction for an attempt to commit an offence under s 35, contrary to the Criminal Attempts Act 1981.

Engaging in sexual activity in the presence, procured by inducement, threat or deception, of a person with a mental disorder

9.80 SOA 2003, s 36(1) provides:

'A person (A) commits an offence if—

(a) he intentionally engages in an activity,
(b) the activity is sexual,
(c) for the purpose of obtaining sexual gratification, he engages in it—
(i) when another person (B) is present or is in a place from which A can be observed, and
(ii) knowing or believing that B is aware, or intending that B should be aware, that he is engaging in it,
(d) B agrees to be present or in the place referred to in paragraph (c)(i) because of an inducement offered or given, a threat made or a deception practised by A for the purpose of obtaining that agreement,[103]
(e) B has a mental disorder,[104] and
(f) A knows or could reasonably be expected to know[105] that B has a mental disorder.'

This offence is triable either way and punishable with a maximum of 10 years' imprisonment on conviction on indictment,[106] the same as for its counterpart under s 32. See the SGC Definitive Guideline[107] in the Appendix.

Class of offence	3	SOA 2003, s 72 applies	✔[108]
Notification requirements	✔	SOPO	✔
CJA 2003, Sch 15 applies	✔	Serious specified offence	✔

---

[102] *Krause* (1902) 18 TLR 238 at 243.
[103] See **9.64–9.67**.
[104] See **9.10–9.12**.
[105] See **9.29–9.31**.
[106] SOA 2003, s 36(2); maximum on summary conviction: **1.43**.
[107] At pp 5-18, 68, 69, 76 and 77.
[108] But only where the complainant is within the age limit to which s 72 applies: see **2.97**.

Review of lenient sentence	✗	Special provisions of CYPA 1933	✔
Detention of young offender for specified period			✗

See **1.48** et seq.

9.81 Section 36(1)(a), (b) and (c) is identical to s 11(1)(a), (b) and (c) and to s 32(1)(a), (b) and (c); see **4.28** and **4.31–4.36**.

9.82 An example of a case covered by s 36 would be where A masturbates in the presence of B, a mentally disordered person, whose presence A has procured by telling him that he will get into trouble if he is not there.

Causing a person with a mental disorder to watch a sexual act by inducement, threat or deception

9.83 SOA 2003, s 37(1) provides:

'A person (A) commits an offence if—

(a)   for the purpose of obtaining sexual gratification, he intentionally causes another person (B) to watch a third person engaging in an activity, or to look at an image of any person engaging in an activity,

(b)   the activity is sexual,

(c)   B agrees to watch or look because of an inducement offered or given, a threat made or a deception practised by A for the purpose of obtaining that agreement,[109]

(d)   B has a mental disorder,[110] and

(e)   A knows or could reasonably be expected to know[111] that B has a mental disorder.'

An offence under s 37 is triable and punishable[112] in the same way as its counterpart under s 33 and as an offence under s 36 (and its counterpart s 32).[113]

Class of offence	3	SOA 2003, s 72 applies	✔[114]
Notification requirements	✔	SOPO	✔
CJA 2003, Sch 15 applies	✔	Serious specified offence	✔
Review of lenient sentence	✗	Special provisions of CYPA 1933	✔
Detention of young offender for specified period			✗

See **1.48** et seq.

---

[109] See **9.64–9.67**.

[110] See **9.10–9.12**.

[111] See **9.29–9.31**.

[112] See the SGC Definitive Guideline, at pp 5–18, 68, 69, 78 and 79, in the Appendix.

[113] SOA 2003, s 37(2); **9.56**, **9.80** and **9.51**.

[114] But only where the complainant is within the age limit to which s 72 applies: see **2.97**.

9.84   Section 37(1)(a) and (b) is identical to s 12(1)(a) and (b) and to s 33(1)(a) and (b); see **4.38** and **4.43–4.48**.

9.85   Under s 37 it would, for example, be an offence for A, for the purpose of sexual gratification, to get B, a mentally disordered person, to agree to watch X having sexual intercourse with Y by falsely telling B that X wants B to watch. Another example would be where A, for the purpose of sexual gratification, gets B to watch a pornographic DVD of A (or A and B or X) engaging in a sexual activity by threatening B.

OFFENCES BY CARE WORKERS WITH PERSONS WITH A MENTAL DISORDER

9.86   A person with a mental disorder but who nevertheless has the capacity to consent to sexual activity may not be able to make rational decisions about sexual relationships and because of familiarity with, and dependency on, a carer may be likely to be strongly influenced by such a person. Mentally disordered people are, therefore, vulnerable to sexual exploitation by their carers because their sexual autonomy – the right to choose whether or not to engage in sexual activity – is constrained in such a situation.

9.87   Children and mentally disordered people are not the only types of people who may be vulnerable to sexual exploitation by those who are in a relationship of care with them. Examples of others who may be vulnerable in such a way would be physically frail or disabled people, people detained in prison or similar secure institutions and people undergoing therapy. Before SOA 2003, a breach of a relationship of care involving sexual activity had generally involved simply a breach of a disciplinary or professional code of conduct by the carer.[115] The Sex Offences Review[116] concluded that it was not enough to leave the matter to good practice and codes of conduct and recommended that there should be offences of a breach of a relationship of care to prohibit sexual relations between people in various types of relationship (including those involving the care of a mentally disordered person).

9.88   SOA 2003 does not adopt the Review's recommendation, but in ss 38–41 it does create a set of offences to deal with care workers who involve persons with a mental disorder in sexual activity in a range of ways.

9.89   The offences in ss 38–41 are particularly important where the complainant is over the age of legal consent (or, if aged 16 or 17, there is no relationship of trust, as defined by s 21), so that there may not be any other criminal liability for involving him or her in sexual activity.

9.90   The offences mirror the offences under ss 16–19 relating to an abuse of trust in respect of a child. The offences are:

•   sexual activity by a care worker with a person with a mental disorder (s 38);

•   a care worker causing or inciting sexual activity with a person with a mental disorder (s 39);

---

[115]   Except for the offence under MHA 1959, s 128 and the abuse of trust offences introduced by the Sexual Offences (Amendment) Act 2000, referred to in **9.3**, n 4 and **5.2** respectively.

[116]   *SB*, at para 4.8 and Recommendation 32.

- sexual activity by a care worker in the presence of a person with a mental disorder (s 40); and

- a care worker causing a person with a mental disorder to watch a sexual act (s 41).

9.91 There is no need to prove that the 'victim' did not consent or had an 'inability to refuse'. Like the offences under ss 34–37, ss 38–41 deal with ostensibly consensual conduct. Nor is it necessary to prove that the care worker gave an inducement, or made a threat or deception. Where these elements cannot be proved or are difficult to prove and the defendant is a 'care worker', the relevant offence under ss 38–41 should be charged. A prosecution for such an offence will usually take place unless there are public interest factors tending against prosecution which clearly outweigh those tending in favour. Given the seriousness of such an offence a prosecution will normally be required.[117]

9.92 Because of the correspondence between the offences under ss 9–12, ss 16–19 and ss 38–41, much of the description of the present offences will be done by cross-reference. A description of their discrete elements will be followed by a discussion of matters which they share in common.

Sexual activity by a care worker with a person with a mental disorder

9.93 Section 38(1) provides:

'A person (A) commits an offence if—

(a)   he intentionally touches another person (B),

(b)   the touching is sexual,

(c)   B has a mental disorder,[118]

(d)   A knows or could reasonably be expected to know that B has a mental disorder, and

(e)   A is involved in B's care in a way that falls within s 42.'[119]

9.94 If the touching involved penetration in the sense defined in **9.35**, an offence under s 38 is triable only on indictment and the maximum term of imprisonment is 14 years.[120] Otherwise, an offence under s 38 is triable either way and punishable with a maximum of 10 years' imprisonment on indictment.[121] See the SGC Definitive Guideline[122] in the Appendix. These sentences can be compared with the maximum of 5 years' imprisonment which applies to all the offences of abuse of a position of trust under ss 16–19. The effect of s 38(3) and (4) is that under the *Courtie* principle[123] there are two offences under s 38: one requiring proof of a specified type of penetration, and the other proof of a 'non-penetrative' sexual touching. The power under the Powers of Criminal Courts (Sentencing) Act (PCC(S)A) 2000, s 91 to detain young offenders for a specified period applies on conviction of the former offence but not the latter.

---

[117]   *CPS Guidance.*
[118]   See **9.10–9.12**.
[119]   See **9.114–9.122**.
[120]   Section 38(3).
[121]   Section 38(4); maximum on summary conviction: **1.43**.
[122]   At pp 5–18, 68, 69, 74 and 75.
[123]   [1984] AC 463: see **3.170**. There is nothing to rebut the presumption to this effect.

Class of offence	3	SOA 2003, s 72 applies	✔[124]
Notification requirements	See text	SOPO	✔
CJA 2003, Sch 15 applies	✔	Serious specified offence	✔
Review of lenient sentence	See text	Special provisions of CYPA 1933	✔
Detention of young offender for specified period			See text

See **1.48** et seq.

9.95 The notification requirements of SOA 2003, Pt 2 apply to an offender in respect of an offence under s 38 if:

• where the offender was under 18, he or she is or has been sentenced in respect of the offence to imprisonment for a term of at least 12 months;

• in any other case, the offender, in respect of the offence or finding, is or has been:
   – sentenced to a term of imprisonment;
   – detained in a hospital; or
   – made the subject of a community sentence of at least 12 months.[125]

The exceptions under SOA 2003, s 73[126] from liability for aiding, abetting or counselling apply to an offence under s 38 against a person under 16.[127] The provisions of CJA 1988, ss 35 and 36 relating to the Attorney-General's references for a review of a sentence as unduly lenient apply to the offence involving penetration but not the other.[128]

9.96 Section 38(1)(a) and (b) is identical to s 9(1)(a) and (b) and s 30(1)(a) and (b): see **4.9, 4.13, 4.14** and **9.39**. As to mens rea, see **9.123** and **9.124**.

9.97 A need not act for the purpose of sexual gratification. In theory, a care worker who sexually touches a mentally impaired person under his or her supervision as part of a legitimate sex education programme designed to help that person understand and express his or her sexuality commits an offence under s 38. This matter is an important one because it appears that there are some cases, especially that of deaf-blind people who may need sex education because they are displaying inappropriate behaviour or are self-harming, where the only way to provide sex education (and thereby to protect them from abuse or harm) is by the use of touch.[129] A prosecution in such a case could be the subject of a successful challenge under ECHR, Art 8. This would seem to be another instance where the rigour of the law may be avoided by the exercise of prosecutorial discretion against prosecution.

---

124 But only where the complainant is within the age limit to which s 72 applies: **2.97**.
125 Section 80, Sch 3, para 28.
126 See **2.49–2.54**.
127 SOA 2003, s 73(2)(d).
128 As for s 30, this is probably an oversight.
129 Sandra Gidley MP, HC Standing Committee B (September 2003), col 241.

9.98   For statutory exceptions to s 38, see **9.125–9.130.**

Care worker causing or inciting a person with mental disorder to engage in sexual activity

9.99   Section 39(1) provides:

'A person (A) commits an offence if—

(a)   he intentionally causes or incites another person (B) to engage in an activity,
(b)   the activity is sexual,
(c)   B has a mental disorder,[130]
(d)   A knows or could reasonably be expected to know that B has a mental disorder, and
(e)   A is involved in B's care in a way that falls within s 42.'[131]

9.100   The mode of trial and maximum punishment depend on whether the sexual activity caused or incited involved penetration in one of the ways set out in **9.44.** The provisions of s 39(3) and (4) are identical, in terms of mode of trial and maximum punishment, to those under s 38 (**9.94**). See the SGC Definitive Guideline[132] in the Appendix. Because 'causing' and 'inciting' appear to involve separate offences and because of the *Courtie* principle,[133] there are at least two, and arguably four, offences under s 39:

• causing a person with a mental disorder to engage in penetrative sexual activity (in one of the ways specified;

• causing such a person to engage in 'non-penetrative' sexual activity;

• inciting such a person to engage in penetrative sexual activity (as specified above); and

• inciting such a person to engage in 'non-penetrative' sexual activity.

Class of offence	3	SOA 2003, s 72 applies	✔[134]
Notification requirements	See text	SOPO	✔
CJA 2003, Sch 15 applies	✔	Serious specified offence	✔
Review of lenient sentence	See text	Special provisions of CYPA 1933	✔
Detention of young offender for specified period			See text

See **1.48** et seq.

---

[130]   See **9.10–9.12.**
[131]   See **9.114–9.122.**
[132]   At pp 5–18, 68, 69, 74 and 75.
[133]   See **3.170** and **3.182.**
[134]   But only where the complainant is within the age limit to which s 72 applies: see **2.97.**

9.101 The notification requirements of SOA 2003, Pt 2 apply to an offender in respect of an offence under s 39 in the same circumstances as in the case of a s 38 offence (see **9.95**).[135] The provisions of CJA 1988, ss 35 and 36 relating to the Attorney-General's references for a review of a sentence as unduly lenient apply to the offences involving penetration but not the others.[136] The power under PCC(S)A 2000, s 91 to detain a young offender for a specified period applies on conviction of the former offences but not the latter.

9.102 Section 39(1)(a) and (b) is identical to s 10(1)(a) and (b) and s 31(1)(a) and (b); see **4.19, 4.24–4.26** and **9.43**. As to mens rea, see **9.123** and **9.124**.

9.103 There is no need to prove that A acted for the purpose of obtaining sexual gratification. It follows that a care worker who causes or incites the specified conduct can be convicted under s 39, even though the only purpose of his or her conduct was bullying or intimidation or gain. It also follows that a care worker who, for a legitimate sex education or therapy purpose, causes or incites a mentally disordered person to engage in sexual activity commits an offence under s 39. A prosecution in such a case could be the subject of a successful challenge under ECHR, Art 8.

9.104 For statutory exceptions to an offence under s 39 see **9.125–9.130**.

Sexual activity by a care worker in presence of person with mental disorder

9.105 Section 40(1) provides:

'A person (A) commits an offence if—

(a)   he intentionally engages in an activity,
(b)   the activity is sexual,
(c)   for the purpose of obtaining sexual gratification, he engages in it—
  (i)   when another person (B) is present or is in a place from which A can be observed, and
  (ii)   knowing or believing that B is aware, or intending that B should be aware, that he is engaging in it,
(d)   B has a mental disorder,[137]
(e)   A knows or could reasonably be expected to know that B has a mental disorder, and
(f)   A is involved in B's care in a way that falls within s 42.'[138]

An offence under s 40 is triable either way and punishable with a maximum of 7 years' imprisonment on conviction on indictment.[139] See the SGC Definitive Guideline[140] in the Appendix.

Class of offence	3	SOA 2003, s 72 applies	✔[141]

---

[135]   Section 80 and Sch 3, para 28.
[136]   As for s 38, this is probably an oversight.
[137]   See **9.10–9.12**.
[138]   See **9.114–9.122**.
[139]   SOA 2003, s 40(3); maximum on summary conviction: see **1.43**.
[140]   At pp 5-18, 68, 69, 76 and 77.

Notification requirements	See text	SOPO	✔
CJA 2003, Sch 15 applies	✔	Serious specified offence	✘
Review of lenient sentence	✘	Special provisions of CYPA 1933	✔
Detention of young offender for specified period			✘

See **1.48** et seq.

9.106 The notification requirements of SOA 2003, Pt 2 apply to an offender in respect of an offence under s 40 in the same circumstances as in the case of a s 38 offence (see **9.95**).[142]

9.107 Section 40(1)(a), (b) and (c) is identical to s 11(1)(a), (b) and (c) and s 32(1)(a), (b) and (c); see **4.28**, **4.31–4.36** and **9.50**. As to mens rea, see **9.123** and **9.124**.

9.108 Like an offence under s 41, and in contrast to those under s 38 or s 39, an offence under s 40 requires proof that A acted for the purpose of sexual gratification.

9.109 For statutory exceptions to the offence under s 40 see **9.125–9.130**.

Care worker causing person with mental disorder to watch a sexual act

9.110 Section 41(1) provides:

'A person (A) commits an offence if—

    (a)   for the purpose of obtaining sexual gratification, he intentionally causes another person (B) to watch a third person engaging in an activity, or to look at an image of any person engaging in an activity,

    (b)   the activity is sexual,

    (c)   B has a mental disorder,[143]

    (d)   A knows or could reasonably be expected to know that B has a mental disorder, and

    (e)   A is involved in B's care in a way that falls within s 42.'[144]

The provisions relating to trial and punishment[145] are identical to those under s 40: see **9.105**. See the SGC Definitive Guideline[146] in the Appendix.

Class of offence	3	SOA 2003, s 72 applies	✔[147]

---

[141] But only where the complainant is within the age limit to which s 72 applies: see **2.97**.

[142] Section 80 and Sch 3, para 28.

[143] See **9.10–9.12**.

[144] See **9.114–9.122**.

[145] SOA 2003, s 41(3).

[146] At pp 5–18, 68, 69, 78 and 79.

[147] But only where the complainant is within the age limit to which s 72 applies: see **2.97**.

Notification requirements	See text	SOPO	✔
CJA 2003, Sch 15 applies	✔	Serious specified offence	✘
Review of lenient sentence	✘	Special provisions of CYPA 1933	✔
Detention of young offender for specified period			✘

See **1.48** et seq.

9.111 The notification requirements of SOA 2003, Pt 2 apply to an offender in respect of an offence under s 41 in the same circumstances as in the case of a s 38 offence (see **9.95**).[148]

9.112 Section 41(1)(a) and (b) is identical to s 12(1)(a) and (b) and s 33(1)(a) and (b); see **4.38**, **4.43–4.48** and **9.55**. As to mens rea, see **9.123** and **9.124**.

9.113 For statutory exceptions to s 41 see **9.125–9.130**.

Common elements

Care worker

9.114 Sections 38–41 are concerned with the situation where A is involved in the care of B, a person with a mental disorder, in a way which falls within s 42. Once this relationship has ended, the offences cease to apply. For the purposes of ss 38–41, A is B's 'care worker' if s 42(2), (3) or (4) applies.[149] The definition of a care worker is a wide one.

Section 42(2)

9.115 Section 42(2) applies if:

'(a)   B is accommodated and cared for in a care home, community home, voluntary home or children's home[150], and
(b)   A has functions to perform in the home in the course of employment which have brought him or are likely to bring him into regular face-to-face contact with B.'

An example would be where A works at a care home and B is a resident there, provided that they have, or are likely to have, regular face-to-face contact; A could be a cleaner or 'dinner lady'. 'Employment' is defined for the purposes of s 42 by s 42(5) as 'any employment, whether paid or unpaid and whether under a contract of service or apprenticeship, under a contract for services, or otherwise than under a contract'. Thus, a self-employed counsellor or psychotherapist is included, as is a volunteer who assists

---

148   Section 80 and Sch 3, para 28.
149   SOA 2003, s 42(1).
150   'Care home' means an establishment which is a care home for the purposes of the Care Standards Act (CStA) 2000; 'children's home' has the meaning given by CStA 2000, s 1; 'community home' has the meaning given by the Children Act (ChA) 1989, s 53; and 'voluntary home' has the meaning given by ChA 1989, s 60(3): SOA 2003, s 42(5).

at the home, if he or she has regular face-to-face contact with B. The requirement of 'regular face-to-face contact' may be satisfied even where such contact with B has not yet been established if A's functions are likely to bring them into such contact. If, for example, A is appointed to provide counselling in a care home A will be a care worker under s 42(2) from the first day of his employment.

Section 42(3)

9.116 Section 42(3) applies:

'... if B is a patient for whom services are provided—

(a)   by a National Health Service body[151] or an independent medical agency,[152] or

(b)   in an independent clinic or an independent hospital,[153]

and A has functions to perform for the body or agency or in the clinic or hospital in the course of employment [as defined above] which have brought him or are likely to bring him into regular face-to-face contact with B.'

This definition deals with cases where B is not a resident in a care home, children's home, etc. Examples would be where B is a resident in a mental hospital or attends a clinic every week and A is a doctor, nurse or receptionist there whom B sees every week. Another example would be where A is a driver employed to take B to and from the clinic. The comments above about 'in the course of employment' and 'regular face-to-face' are equally applicable here.

Section 42(4)

9.117 Section 42(4) applies if A:

'(a)   ... is, whether or not in the course of employment, a provider of care, assistance or services to B in connection with B's mental disorder, and

(b)   as such, has had or is likely to have regular face-to-face contact with B.'

'Care, assistance or services' is a wide description. It would include a social worker, someone providing training, a complementary therapist, a psychotherapist or a counsellor. It would also include an independent advocate (ie someone trusted to represent people with learning disorders and who to that end enjoys privileged access to them). The responsibilities of an independent advocate do not normally include personal care, but such a person is someone who is in a position of trust and influence vis-à-vis the person he or she represents.

9.118 As indicated above, in the case of s 42(4), A need not provide the personal care, assistance or services in the course of employment (as defined above); a neighbour who, for example, regularly provides personal care to B in B's own home in connection with B's mental disorder is covered.

---

[151] 'National Health Service body' means a Local Health Board, a NHS trust, a Primary Care Trust, or a Special Health Authority: SOA 2003, s 42(5) (as amended by SI 2007/961).

[152] As defined by CStA 2000, s 2: SOA 2003, s 42(5).

[153] Ibid.

9.119 It is irrelevant where the personal care, services or assistance is provided. Section 42(4) applies to people who provide care, etc for mentally disordered people at training centres, day centres and similar facilities, provided that the other requirements of s 42(4) are satisfied.

9.120 Because s 42(4) requires A to provide care, assistance or services to B in connection with B's mental disorder, A will not be a care worker under s 42(4) simply because he or she is a volunteer Meals-on-Wheels deliverer to B or is B's hairdresser; these services are not provided in connection with B's mental disorder. Of course, if the relationship between A and B develops and A begins to provide some form of services in connection with B's mental disorder, A would fall within s 42(4).

9.121 The need for the actual or likely regular contact to be face to face means that someone who provides assistance to B on a regular basis over the telephone or other distant means is not a care worker within s 42.

9.122 An offence does not have to occur on premises where the care relationship is founded.

Mens rea

9.123 In each of the offences A must act intentionally in the specified way. In addition, he or she must know or could reasonably be expected to know that B has a mental disorder.[154] However, the prosecution does not have to prove in the first instance that this mens rea was satisfied at the material time. Instead, if:

'... it is proved that the other person had a mental disorder, it is to be taken that the defendant knew or could reasonably have been expected to know that that person had a mental disorder unless sufficient evidence is adduced to raise an issue as to whether he knew or could reasonably have been expected to know it'.[155]

This provision, and the mens rea itself, have already been discussed in other contexts: see **2.72, 2.61–2.63, 3.65–3.67**. In the light of the definition of a 'care worker', this provision seems sensible.

9.124 It is noteworthy that the sections do not refer to any mental element in respect of B being in A's care within s 42. Given the definitions of the care relationship in s 42 it is not inconceivable that A may not know B is in his or her care. Until the matter is judicially resolved, one must presume that mens rea is required to be proved in this respect and that A is not guilty of an offence under ss 38–41 unless it is proved that he or she knew that he or she had a relationship of care with B.[156] Of course, in the ordinary type of case there will be no difficulty in proving this.

---

[154] See **9.29–9.31**.
[155] Sections 38(2), 39(2), 40(2) and 41(2).
[156] *Sweet v Parsley* [1970] AC 132; *B v DPP* [2000] 2 AC 428; *K* [2002] 1 AC 462.

Exceptions for spouses and civil partners, and pre-existing sexual relationships

9.125 Like the abuse of trust offences, two exceptions are provided from the offences under ss 38–41. The exceptions are set out in ss 43 and 44. Section 43[157] provides:

'(1) Conduct by a person (A) which would otherwise be an offence under any of sections 38 to 41 against another person (B) is not an offence under that section if at the time—

    (a)   B is 16 or over, and
    (b)   A and B are lawfully married or civil partners of each other.

(2) In proceedings for such an offence it is for the defendant to prove that A and B were at the time lawfully married or civil partners of each other.'

Section 44 provides:

'(1) Conduct by a person (A) which would otherwise be an offence under any of sections 38 to 41 against another person (B) is not an offence under that section if, immediately before A became involved in B's care in a way that falls within section 42, a sexual relationship existed between A and B.

(2) Subsection (1) does not apply if at that time sexual intercourse between A and B would have been unlawful.

(3) In proceedings for an offence under any of sections 38 to 41 it is for the defendant to prove that such a relationship existed at that time.'

9.126 The points made in **5.30–5.43** about corresponding provisions in ss 28 and 29 are equally applicable to ss 43 and 44.

9.127 The effect of s 43 is that if a husband who has become a 'care worker' for his wife engages in sexual activity with her he will have the defence under s 43 to a charge under s 38, although he would commit the offence under s 34 if he induces her to engage in the activity by an inducement, threat or deception, and would commit the offence under s 30 if his wife has become unable to refuse.

9.128 It follows from s 44 that, although a care worker who starts an affair with a mentally disordered patient a day after he or she starts a job at a care home can be convicted of an offence under s 38, a care worker who was involved in a sexual relationship with such a person (B) when (ie immediately before) he or she became B's care worker cannot, even if he or she became a care worker in order to have better access to, and influence over, that person. The exception under s 44 does not apply if at *that* time – ie the 'immediately before' time – sexual intercourse between A and B would have been unlawful (ie criminal) (eg because B was under 16 or was A's learning-disabled granddaughter).

9.129 It is no defence that immediately before the offence-creating section came into force, a sexual relationship had developed between A, a care worker, and B, a person in A's care. Where sexual activity between A and B (or involving them) was not criminal before the relevant offence came into force, such activity after the commencement of the

---

[157] As amended by the Civil Partnership Act 2004.

relevant offence is criminal, unless the sexual relationship also existed immediately before A became B's care worker (in which case the second of the two exemptions would be relevant).

9.130 The exceptions in ss 43 and 44 are clearly necessitated by the fact that care may be given by the mentally impaired person's spouse or partner in an established relationship. In such a case that person will be involved in the care of the mentally disordered person for the purposes of the offences under ss 38–41.[158] It would be an unreasonable intrusion into the private life of the couple to criminalise sexual relations between them where, perhaps for many years, they had been married or lived together before dementia, illness or an accident made one of them mentally impaired. The case for the exemptions is particularly strong where A cares for B at home. Concerns that the defence in s 44 would be exploited by falsely claiming a pre-care sexual relationship are partially met by the onus of proof imposed on A in respect of that relationship. However, the influence which the carer may have obtained may make it easy for him or her to persuade the mentally impaired person to support his or her untrue story about a pre-existing relationship.

---

[158] Section 42(4); see **9.117–9.122**.

Chapter 10

PROSTITUTION

10.1 It is trite law that it is not an offence in itself to be a prostitute or to practise prostitution or for the other party to arrange or engage in sexual activity with a prostitute. The criminal law does, however, interfere in cases where, in general terms:

- there is exploitation or abuse in relation to prostitution;

- prostitution causes a nuisance or offensive behaviour (on-street prostitution activities); or

- premises are used for prostitution on a commercial basis (off-street activities, largely relating to brothels).

EXPLOITATION OR ABUSE

10.2 The criminal law has an important role in ensuring that those who introduce people into prostitution and thereafter exploit them in it are dealt with appropriately. For this purpose, a range of offences were available before the Sexual Offences Act (SOA) 2003. The key offences were those under SOA 1956, ss 30 and 31 (man living on the earnings of female prostitution and woman controlling a female prostitute, respectively). There was also the related offence, which could be committed by a man or a woman, of living off the earnings of male prostitution, contrary to SOA 1967, s 5. Other offences, under SOA 1956, ss 22, 23, 28 and 29, respectively, were: procuring a woman to become a prostitute anywhere; procuring a girl under 21 to have unlawful sexual intercourse anywhere; causing or encouraging the prostitution of a girl under 16 for whom the defendant had parental responsibility or care; and causing or encouraging the prostitution of a woman who was a defective. These offences were all repealed by SOA 2003[1] and replaced by two groups of offences: those relating to the abuse of children through prostitution and child pornography; and those relating to the exploitation of prostitution.

ABUSE OF CHILDREN THROUGH PROSTITUTION AND CHILD PORNOGRAPHY

10.3 Children involved in prostitution or pornography are primarily victims of abuse by those who take advantage of them by exploiting them. The Sex Offences Review recommended that the commercial sexual exploitation of children under 18 for

---

[1] See **1.5**.

prostitution or the making of pornography[2] should be an offence and should be dealt with by specific offences rather than simply relying on general offences of sexual exploitation, because this would set an unambiguous standard in society that it was wrong for an adult to buy the sexual services of a child.[3] Perhaps surprisingly, it did not make a similar recommendation in respect of mentally vulnerable adults.

10.4 SOA 2003, ss 47–50 provide the following offences in respect of children under 18:

- paying for sex with a child;

- causing or inciting child prostitution or pornography;

- controlling a child prostitute or a child involved in pornography; and

- arranging or facilitating child prostitution or pornography.

In all these offences the consent of the child is irrelevant.

10.5 The Crown Prosecution Service Guidance on sexual offences and child abuse (*CPS Guidance*)[4] states that, where a child is under 13, prosecutors should charge an offence, if appropriate, under SOA 2003, ss 5–8. See also **10.26**. It adds that, where there are problems in proving that the defendant did not have a reasonable belief that the child was over 18, prosecutors may consider an offence under SOA 2003, s 52 or s 53 (adult prostitution offences) provided that the elements of such an offence can be proved (eg the activity was done for or in expectation of gain). A prosecution will usually take place unless there are public interest factors tending against prosecution which clearly outweigh those tending in favour. The offences under SOA 2003, ss 47–50 are very serious offences in which the public interest normally requires a prosecution.[5]

Paying for sex with a child

10.6 SOA 2003, s 47 deals with paying for sex with a child. This was not previously an offence in itself. Section 47 provides different maximum punishments depending on which of three factual conditions, set out in s 47(3), (4) and (5), is satisfied. It follows that there are three separate offences under s 47, distinguished by these conditions, because there is nothing to rebut the presumption to this effect under the principle in *Courtie*.[6] The conditions relate to the gravity of the sexual activity involved and the degree of vulnerability of children at different ages.

10.7 Each of the three offences has the same core of requirements, set out in s 47(1):

'A person (A) commits an offence if—

---

[2]   Apart from the prohibition on the production of indecent photographs and pseudo-photographs of children under the Protection of Children Act (PoCA) 1978, the criminal law had not specifically targeted this area before SOA 2003.

[3]   *Setting the Boundaries: Reforming the Law on Sexual Offences* (Home Office, 2000) (*SB*), at para 7.6 and Recommendations 50 and 51.

[4]   See **1.56**.

[5]   *CPS Guidance*, at pp 53–54.

[6]   [1984] AC 463; see **3.170**.

    (a)   he intentionally obtains for himself the sexual services of another person (B),

    (b)   before obtaining those services, he has made or promised payment for those services to B or a third person, or knows that another person has made or promised such a payment, and

    (c)   either—

        (i)   B is under 18, and A does not reasonably believe that B is 18 or over, or

        (ii)   B is under 13.'

Class of offence	See text	SOA 2003, s 72 applies	✔[7]
Notification requirements	See text	SOPO[8]	✔[9]
CJA 2003,[10] Sch 15 applies	✔	Serious specified offence	✔, except offence under s 47(5)[11]
Review of lenient sentence	✔	Special provisions of CYPA 1933[12]	✔
Detention of young offender for specified period			✔, except offence under s 47(5)

See **1.48** et seq.

10.8 The notification requirements under SOA 2003, Pt 2 apply in respect of an offence under s 47 if the victim or other party (as the case may be) was under 16, but, where the offender is under 18 at the time of sentencing, only if a sentence of imprisonment for at least 12 months is or has been imposed.[13]

The core elements

Intentionally obtaining sexual services

10.9 Notwithstanding that SOA 2003, s 47(1)(b) speaks in the alternative of payment being made or promised by a third party, the requirement in s 47(1)(a) that A must *intentionally*[14] *obtain* for himself the sexual services of B suggests that there must be words or conduct on A's part (which may be the payment or promise of payment by A referred to in s 47(1)(b)) which, as he intended, results in the services being obtained, and that it is not enough simply for A to receive sexual services without effort on his part. This view is supported by the decision of the Court of Appeal in *Hayat*[15] in another context (offence of obtaining credit by a bankrupt) which is reinforced here by the word 'intentionally'. The contrary view (simple receipt enough) may seem to be supported by the House of Lords' decision in *Attorney-General's Reference (No 1 of*

---

[7]   See **2.97**.

[8]   Sexual offences prevention order.

[9]   See **18.35**, **18.36**.

[10]   Criminal Justice Act (CJA) 2003.

[11]   See **10.20**.

[12]   Children and Young Persons Act (CYPA) 1933.

[13]   SOA 2003, s 80, Sch 3, para 29.

[14]   See **2.56–2.60**.

[15]   (1976) 63 Cr App R 181.

1988)[16] in yet another context (dealing on the Stock Exchange 'having knowingly obtained' information), but this decision can be distinguished because the reference to 'obtained' related to a circumstance of the actus reus and not its central element and '*knowingly* obtained' is very different in sense from '*intentionally* obtains'.

10.10   Section 47(1)(c) indicates that B must be under 18[17] at the time that B's sexual services are obtained. A's age is irrelevant to liability.

10.11   It is surprising that A does not commit the offence if he obtains B's sexual services for a third party for actual or promised payment. However, if B is under 16, A would commit an offence contrary to s 8 or s 10 if he exerted a capacity to control or influence B's acts.[18] In addition, an offence of arranging child prostitution contrary to s 50[19] may well be committed where A obtains B's sexual services for a third party for payment.

10.12   It will be noted that in s 47 the sexual services of B must actually be 'obtained', which seems to mean actually provided and not merely promised by B or someone else. Where sexual services are merely promised for payment, there could be a conviction for arranging child prostitution, contrary to s 50.

Sexual services

10.13   'Services' is not defined by SOA 2003 but it would seem to refer to doing an activity or permitting that activity to be done. It is uncertain whether the definition of 'sexual' in s 78 applies directly to 'sexual services'. Section 78[20] defines 'sexual' in relation to 'penetration, touching or any other activity', and not in relation to 'services', but if 'services' refers to doing an activity, or permitting it to be done, it is arguable that it is an activity which may take one of the three forms referred to by s 78. In any event, even if this argument is rejected, it is submitted that a court would take a similar approach to that under s 78. To do so would also reflect the law as it was developed by the courts in relation to 'indecent' in the repealed offences of indecent assault.[21] It would be surprising if the courts defined 'sexual' in s 47 in different terms.

10.14   On this basis, 'services' are sexual if a reasonable person would consider that, whatever the circumstances and any person's purpose in relation to it, the activity involved is because of its nature sexual (as eg in the case of the penile penetration of a vagina, anus or mouth). Where this test is not satisfied, 'services' are sexual if a reasonable person would consider that because of its nature the activity involved may be sexual and because of its circumstances or the purpose of any person in relation to it (or both) it is sexual. This can be exemplified as follows. The activity of dressing in clothing would not be considered by a reasonable person to be, by its nature and regardless of the circumstances and any person's purpose in relation to it, sexual. However, a reasonable person might consider that because of its nature it could be a sexual activity and, if the activity consisted of a 17-year-old girl dressing in a provocative fashion as a schoolgirl for the admitted delectation of A, a schoolgirl-fetishist, the reasonable person might consider that, in the light of these circumstances and A's purpose in relation to the

16   [1989] 1 AC 971.
17   As to proof of age, see **3.131**, **3.132**.
18   See **3.179** and **4.19**.
19   See **10.33**.
20   See **2.31** et seq.
21   *Court* [1989] AC 28.

activity, it is sexual. If it is found that the reasonable person would so regard it, the services are sexual; otherwise they are not. Cases such as this are liable to be the exception.

Payment or promise of payment

10.15 What converts the conduct referred to in the first requirement (s 47(1)(a)) from an offence under s 8 or s 10 (or no offence at all if B is aged 16 or 17) is the requirement in s 47(1)(b) that, before obtaining B's sexual services:

- A must have made or promised payment for those services to B or to a third person (eg B's pimp or parent); or

- another person must have made or promised such a payment to B or a third person, and A must know[22] this.

There is no requirement that the payment or promised payment should be a cause of the services being obtained. This would be important, for example, where the payment was made to a third party unknown to B and A obtained the services from B by seducing her. The requirement that A must know of a third party payment or promise of payment is welcome. It would have been unfortunate if a person who had otherwise lawful sex with a 16- or 17-year-old in ignorance of payment, etc for it by a third party could be guilty of a serious offence punishable with 7 years' imprisonment.

10.16 'Payment' is widely defined by s 47(2). It means 'any financial advantage, including the discharge of an obligation to pay or the provision of goods or services (including sexual services) gratuitously or at a discount'. Thus, 'payment' includes paying a rent bill, or waiving a debt owed to A, or providing drugs or tattooing free of charge or at a reduced cost, or getting one's friend with whom B is infatuated to have sex with B. The reference to payment by the provision of sexual services is important in respect of paedophile rings whose members provide each other on a reciprocal basis with the sexual services of children. It is implicit in s 47(1)(b) that it is irrelevant that the promise of payment by A or a third party would be unenforceable on grounds of illegality.

Mens rea as to age

10.17 Unless B is under 13, it must be proved that A did not reasonably believe[23] that B was 18 or over. Thus, it will not in itself excuse A that he mistakenly believed that B (actually aged 16) was aged 18 if it is proved that A did not have reasonable grounds for his mistaken belief. The juxtaposition of the terms in s 47(1)(c)(i) and (ii) makes it clear[24] that, where it is proved that B was under 13[25] at the time his or her sexual services were obtained, the presumption that mens rea is required[26] is rebutted. Thus, where B was under 13, the offence is one of strict liability as to age.

---

22 See **2.61, 2.62.**
23 See **2.67–2.71.**
24 See **4.16.**
25 As to proof of age, see **3.131, 3.132.**
26 *B v DPP* [2000] 2 AC 428.

The three offences

Penetration of child under 13

10.18 The most serious offence under SOA 2003, s 47 is provided by s 47(3) and (6). The effect of s 47(3) and (6) is that, where the core requirements are proved to have been committed by A against a person under 13[27] and it is proved that the offence involved:

(a) penetration of B's anus or vagina[28] with a part of A's body or anything else;

(b) penetration of B's mouth with A's penis;[29]

(c) penetration of A's anus or vagina with a part of B's body or by B with anything else; or

(d) penetration of A's mouth with B's penis,

A commits an offence triable only on indictment and punishable with a maximum of life imprisonment. This offence is a Class 2 offence. It corresponds to the offences of rape of a child under 13 or of assault of a child under 13 by penetration, contrary to s 5 or s 6. As to sentencing, see the Sentencing Guidelines Council (SGC) Definitive Guideline[30] in the Appendix.

Child under 16

10.19 Section 47(4) makes it an offence punishable with a maximum of 14 years' imprisonment on conviction on indictment, if it is proved that A satisfied the core requirements in relation to a person under 16. If penetrative activity (as defined in **10.18**) was involved the offence is triable only on indictment[31] and covers the case where the penetrative activity involved a victim aged 13–15. This corresponds to the equivalent provision for penetrative sexual activity by an adult with a child under 16, contrary to s 9. Other types of sexual activity with a child of any age under 16 are triable either way and punishable with a maximum of 14 years' imprisonment on conviction on indictment[32] if the core requirements are satisfied. The offence under s 47(4) is a Class 3 offence. It corresponds to those relating to sexual assault on a child under 13 and non-penetrative sexual activity by a person of 18 or over with a child under 16 (ss 7 and 9). As to sentencing, see the SGC Definitive Guideline in the Appendix.[33]

Child under 18

10.20 Unless s 47(3) or (4) applies, A commits an offence under s 47(5) if he has satisfied the core requirements in s 47(1) and B was under 18 at the time that the sexual services were obtained from B. An offence under s 47(5) is triable either way and punishable with a maximum of 7 years' imprisonment on conviction on indictment.[34]

---

[27] As to proof of age, see **3.131** and **3.132**.
[28] See **3.100–3.102**.
[29] See **3.100** and **3.102**.
[30] At pp 5–18 and 116–118.
[31] SOA 2003, s 47(4)(a).
[32] SOA 2003, s 47(4)(b). Maximum on summary conviction: see **1.43**.
[33] At pp 5–18 and 116–118.
[34] Maximum on summary conviction: see **1.43**.

The offence is a Class 3 offence. As to sentencing, see the SGC Definitive Guideline in the Appendix.[35] The distinction in gravity drawn by this offence and the one in **10.19** is questionable. The prostitution of the child (with all that that involves) is the gravamen of the offence. A distinction based on whether or not the child was over the age of consent would seem irrelevant.

Causing or inciting child prostitution or pornography; controlling a child prostitute or a child involved in pornography; arranging or facilitating child prostitution or pornography

10.21 SOA 2003, ss 48, 49 and 50 provide offences to deal with these matters respectively. Most of the features of these offences are identical, and most of the terminology has already been discussed earlier in this book.

Causing or inciting child prostitution or pornography

10.22 SOA 2003, s 48(1) provides:

'A person (A) commits an offence if—

(a) he intentionally[36] causes or incites another person (B) to become a prostitute, or to be involved in pornography, in any part of the world, and

(b) either—

    (i) B is under 18,[37] and A does not reasonably believe that B is 18 or over, or

    (ii) B is under 13.'[38]

As elsewhere in the Act, it would seem that 'causing' and 'inciting' are separate offences.[39] In addition, the references to prostitution and pornography are to the causing or incitement of two different types of conduct and therefore to distinct offences in respect of them.[40] On these bases, there are four offences under s 48:

- causing a child to become a prostitute;

- inciting such conduct;

- causing a child to be involved in pornography; and

- inciting such conduct.

10.23 In any event, the safe course is to include in an indictment separate counts for more than one of these forms of conduct if it is uncertain which can be proved.

---

[35] At pp 5–18 and 116–118.
[36] See **2.56–2.60**.
[37] As to proof of age, see **3.131, 3.132**.
[38] Ibid.
[39] See **3.182,** n 284.
[40] Ibid, which applies mutatis mutandis.

Causing or inciting

10.24 What was said about 'cause or incite' in **3.174, 3.185** and **3.186** is equally applicable to s 48. Thus, A causes B to become a prostitute, or to be involved in pornography, if he recruits B to this effect; ie if by force, fraud, abuse of power or otherwise, he brings about B's entry into prostitution or child pornography (temporarily or on a longer-term basis, and whether or not B works for him or a third party) which B would not have embarked on spontaneously or of his or her own volition. If A causes his 16-year-old girlfriend to become a prostitute or involved in pornography in order to pay their household bills, A can be convicted under s 48. If his attempts to persuade her fail, he can be convicted on the basis of his incitement. Merely providing the opportunity, for example, by the provision of premises, where B can engage in prostitution or child pornography of his or her own volition, without any pressure or encouragement of any kind by A, does not constitute an offence under s 48. This accords with the case-law relating to the repealed offence of procuring a woman to become a prostitute contrary to SOA 1956, s 22.[41] It is irrelevant where in the world prostitution or pornography takes place or is intended to take place.

10.25 Clearly, the offences of causing or inciting B to become a prostitute cannot be committed if B is already a prostitute.[42] On the other hand, A would commit an offence under s 48 if he caused or incited a child who had been a prostitute, but had ceased to be so, to become a prostitute or if he caused or incited a sexually promiscuous child who had not previously acted for payment to become a prostitute. Although 'become' is not involved in the reference to involvement in pornography, it is submitted that the provision is likely to be interpreted so as not to cover cases where the child is already so involved. Where a child is already involved in prostitution or pornography, the offences under ss 49 and 50 are the appropriate ones to consider.

Overlap

10.26 There is a clear overlap between the offences under s 48 of causing or inciting *child prostitution* and those under s 10 of causing or inciting a child under 16 to engage in sexual activity. The principal differences are that the s 48 offence protects children under 18 and that it only applies if the sexual services (activity) caused or incited is to be provided for payment or a promise of payment. At the Committee stage in the House of Commons, the Government minister expressed the wish that the s 10 offence should be charged, wherever possible, instead of that under s 48 because it is specifically designed to protect children under 16.[43] There is nothing, however, to this effect in the *CPS Guidance*. As to children under 13, see **10.5**.

Controlling child prostitution or pornography

10.27 SOA 2003, s 49(1) provides:

> 'A person (A) commits an offence if—
>
> (a)   he intentionally controls any of the activities of another person (B) relating to B's prostitution or involvement in pornography in any part of the world, and

---

[41]   *Christian* (1913) 23 Cox CC 541; *Broadfoot* [1976] 3 All ER 753.
[42]   For a contrary view, see the explanatory notes to SOA 2003.
[43]   Beverley Hughes, MP, HC Committee, Standing Committee B (September 2003), col 267.

(b) either—
    (i)   B is under 18, and A does not reasonably believe that B is 18 or over, or
    (ii) B is under 13.'

There appear to be two offences under s 49(1): controlling child prostitution and controlling child pornography.[44]

Control

10.28 Common examples of 'controlling' for the purposes of ss 49 and 53[45] below will be the use of physical violence (or the threat of it) or mental coercion such as a threat to deprive a prostitute of her child or of the drugs to which she is addicted. However, it was held by the Court of Appeal in *Massey* that for these purposes:[46]

"'[C]ontrol' includes but is not limited to one who forces another to carry out the relevant activity. "Control" may be exercised in a variety of ways. It is not necessary or appropriate for us to seek to lay down a comprehensive definition of an ordinary English word. It is certainly enough if a defendant instructs or directs the other person to carry out the relevant activity or to do it in a particular way. There may be a variety of reasons why the other person does as instructed. It may be because of physical violence or threats of violence. It may be because the defendant has a dominating personality and the woman who acts under his direction is psychologically damaged and fragile. It may be because the defendant is an older person, and the other person is emotionally immature. It may be because the defendant holds out the lure of gain, or the hope of a better life. Or there may be other reasons.'

The court added that in order to prove that A controlled the relevant activity of B it is not necessary to prove the absence of free will on B's part.

10.29 'Control' implies a fairly close connection between the alleged 'controller' and the child prostitute or child pornography participant. It clearly catches pimps or the like. It can also catch those who exercise indirect control via an intermediary. It may be difficult to prove against those who run a string of child-prostitutes, etc through intermediaries.

10.30 It will be noted that the 'control' offences relate to controlling 'any of the activities' of B relating to B's prostitution or involvement in pornography, as opposed to controlling the whole of such activities. It is irrelevant where in the world the prostitution or pornography takes place.

10.31 Examples of the 'control' offences would be where A instructs B, a child prostitute, to meet particular clients, or to wear particular clothes when she works, or to charge a particular price, or where A directs B to appear in a pornographic film or to pose in a particular way for a pornographic photographer. Other examples would be controlling the prostitute's travel or arrangements relating to that person's prostitution or taking bookings from clients for the prostitute's services which the prostitute is directed to fulfil. On the other hand, the activity of someone who simply takes bookings for a child prostitute on her behalf and relays them to her for *her to decide* whether to undertake them, or who *advertises* her professional services, would not in itself constitute 'controlling', although it would amount to 'arranging or facilitating' within SOA 2003, s 50. Such conduct could, however, provide one of a number of factors

---

[44] See **10.22**.
[45] 'Control' bears the same meaning in both sections: *Massey* [2008] 1 Cr App R 378, at [17].
[46] Ibid, at [20].

evidencing control. Because the defendant's control must relate to B's activities relating to B's prostitution or involvement in pornography, control of other aspects of B's life is not an offence under s 49, even though that control frees B for prostitution, as where A looks after B's child so that she can go 'on the game'. Where two child prostitutes work together consensually (eg for mutual protection), that would not in itself constitute a 'controlling' by one of the other in relation to the other's prostitution. It would be different, of course, if one prostitute was directing the other's prostitution activities. People in other trades who provide services for a child prostitute that may assist him or her in prostitution do not, of course, control him or her. However, if what they do makes the prostitution of the child easier or promotes it, there would be a 'facilitation' of the child's prostitution under s 50 although the requirement that it be intentional would normally be difficult to prove.

10.32 It would be irrelevant that B's activities as a child prostitute, or in pornography, are controlled for part of the time by a third party and for part of the time by the defendant.[47]

Arranging or facilitating child prostitution or pornography

10.33 SOA 2003, s 50(1) provides:

'A person (A) commits an offence if—

(a)   he intentionally arranges or facilitates the prostitution or involvement in pornography in any part of the world of another person (B), and

(b)   either—

   (i)   B is under 18, and A does not reasonably believe that B is 18 or over, or
   (ii)   B is under 13.'

It would seem that 'arranging' and 'facilitating' are separate offences[48] and that, for the same reasons as in s 48,[49] there are four offences under s 50(1):

- arranging child prostitution;

- facilitating child prostitution;

- arranging child pornography; and

- facilitating child pornography.

Arranging or facilitating

10.34 What was said about 'arranging' or 'facilitating' in **4.63** et seq is equally applicable here. Section 50 covers, for example, making arrangements by telephone for a client to meet a child prostitute or for a child to appear in a pornographic film (arranging), or driving a child prostitute to a hotel where she (or he) will offer her services as a prostitute, advertising the services of a child prostitute, providing premises for use for child prostitution or child-minding for a girl to take part in a pornographic film-shoot (facilitating). It is submitted that s 50 only applies to cases where the child is

---

[47]   Explanatory notes to SOA 2003.
[48]   See **3.182**, n 284 is equally applicable here mutatis mutandis.
[49]   See **10.22**.

already involved in prostitution or child pornography. It will be noted that unlike s 48 'to become' is missing from the section, and this would seem to be a crucial distinction. In the case of arranging or facilitating an under-16-year-old child's prostitution, there is an overlap with the offence under SOA 2003, s 14 (see **4.57**). It is irrelevant where in the world the prostitution or pornography takes place. Indeed, the prostitution or involvement in pornography arranged or facilitated need not even occur.

'Prostitute' and 'involvement in pornography'

10.35 SOA 2003, s 51(2) provides that:

> 'In [ss 48–50] a "prostitute" means a person (A) [sic] who, on at least one occasion and whether or not compelled to do so, offers or provides sexual services[50] to another person in return for payment or a promise of payment to A or a third person; and "prostitution" is to be interpreted accordingly.'

This definition corresponds with the common law definition of 'prostitute' referred to in **10.59**. 'Payment' in this context has the same meaning as in s 47(2).[51]

10.36 SOA 2003, s 51(1) provides that:

> 'For the purposes of sections 48 to 50, a person is involved in pornography if an indecent image of that person is recorded; and similar expressions, and "pornography", are to be interpreted accordingly.'

'Image' is defined widely as:[52]

> '"Image" means a moving or still image and includes an image produced by any means and, where the context permits, a three-dimensional image.'

Thus, the essence of pornography is the *recording* of an indecent image. It follows that a person who is involved in an indecent performance which is not recorded but is watched 'live' or viewed via a webcam is not involved in pornography; nor is someone whose decent image is recorded but later computer-manipulated into an indecent image. In the former type of case, however, causing or inciting a child under 16 to engage in such conduct would be an offence under SOA 2003, s 8 or s 10 depending on whether the child was under 13 or 16, and in the latter the less serious offence of making an indecent pseudo-photograph of a child under PoCA 1978, s 1(1)(a) would be committed. The definition of 'image' is wider than that of 'photograph' or 'pseudo-photograph' for PoCA 1978, since it includes an image (including a three-dimensional one) produced by any means. It is strange that the serious offences in ss 48–50 extend to the involvement of a child in indecent image-making of a non-photographic or pseudo-photographic kind, when the making of such an image is not in itself an offence at all.

No need for view to gain

10.37 Unlike the offences in SOA 2003, ss 52 and 53 dealing with exploitation for prostitution, and contrary to the Sex Offences Review's recommendation,[53] none of the

---

[50] See **10.13**, **10.14**.
[51] SOA 2003, s 51(3); see **10.16**.
[52] For example, a video, film or photograph; see **4.44**.
[53] See **10.3**.

offences under ss 48–50 requires proof that the defendant has acted for or in the expectation of gain for themself or a third person. To require proof of this would have been an unnecessary additional hurdle in these offences. In respect of their prostitution aspect, it is surely enough that the defendant has been involved in the child's prostitution whatever the defendant's motivation (which could simply be ruining a young life for sexual gratification). In the case of the pornographic aspect, it would not only have been unnecessary but it would have been potentially wrong to limit the offences to financial gain. As was pointed out in the House of Lords:[54]

> 'The common currency of paedophiles often is not money; it is the disgusting material that feeds their sick minds.'

The offences are clearly aimed at the prevention of child abuse. Whether or not there is an element of gain is irrelevant to this; the conduct is undoubtedly abusive.

Mens rea for three offences

Intentionally cause, incite, control, arrange or facilitate

10.38 By the respective parts of paras (a) of SOA 2003, ss 48(1), 49(1) and 50(1), it must be proved that A intentionally[55] caused or incited, controlled, or arranged or facilitated, the conduct mentioned in those paragraphs in any part of the world.

10.39 Thus, for example, if A, who thinks that B, aged 17, is already a prostitute, causes her to become a prostitute, he cannot be convicted of intentionally causing her to become a child prostitute. He could, however, be convicted of attempting to control a child prostitute on appropriate evidence. Likewise, A will not be guilty of the 'control' offence under s 49 if he is ignorant that B is a prostitute and/or that the activities which he controls relate to prostitution. In such a case, he would not intend to control any of B's activities relating to B's prostitution, as required by s 49(1). The same would be true mutatis mutandis where B's involvement is not in prostitution but in child pornography.

As to age

10.40 By the respective paras (b) of ss 48(1), 49(1) and 50(1), it must be proved that B was under 18,[56] and that A did not reasonably believe that B was 18 or over. In cases under s 48 or s 49 relating to prostitution, where the prosecution is confident that it can prove that A acted for, or in expectation of, gain but is not confident that it can prove that A did not reasonably believe that B (who was actually aged 13 or over) was 18 or over, A may also be charged with the corresponding, but less serious, offence under s 52 or s 53; in respect of these sections, the age (actual and supposed) of the person caused or incited to become a prostitute or controlled as a prostitute is immaterial.[57] Where it is proved that B is under 13 at the material time,[58] the offence is one of strict liability as to age. This is the effect of para (b) whose wording is identical to that of s 47(1)(c).

[54] Baroness Noakes, HL Deb, vol 648, cols 176–177.
[55] See **2.56–2.60**.
[56] As to proof of age, see **3.131, 3.132**.
[57] See **10.46, 10.47**.
[58] See **10.17**.

Trial and punishment

10.41 An offence under SOA 2003, s 48, s 49 or s 50 is triable either way and punishable with a maximum of 14 years' imprisonment on conviction on indictment.[59] As to sentencing, see the SGC Definitive Guideline in the Appendix.[60] It is noteworthy that, as far as child pornography is concerned, the maximum is higher than for offences under PoCA 1978, of taking, making or distributing, etc indecent photographs or pseudo-photographs of children.[61]

Class of offence	3	SOA 2003, s 72 applies	✓[62]
Notification requirements	See text	SOPO	✓
CJA 2003, Sch 15 applies	✓	Serious specified offence	✓
Review of lenient sentence	✓	Special provisions of CYPA 1933	✓
Detention of young offender for specified period			✓

See **1.48** et seq.

10.42 The notification requirements in SOA 2003, Pt 2 apply to an offender in respect of the above offences but, where the offender is under 18 at the time of sentencing, only if a sentence of imprisonment for at least 12 months is or has been imposed.[63] An offence contrary to ss 48, 49 or s 50 is a 'lifestyle offence' within the Proceeds of Crime Act (PCA) 2002,[64] in respect of which a confiscation order may be made under Pt 2 of that Act if the necessary requirements are satisfied or a financial reporting order may be made under the Serious Organised Crime and Police Act 2005, s 76. An offence under ss 48–50 is a serious offence for the purposes of making a serious crime prevention order under the Serious Crime Act (SCA) 2007, Pt 1.[65]

EXPLOITATION OF PROSTITUTION

10.43 The Sex Offences Review also recommended that there should be gender-neutral offences punishing those who exploited others by receiving money from prostitutes of either sex, those who manage or control the activities of prostitutes of either sex, for money or reward, and those who recruit men or women into prostitution (whether or not for gain).[66] SOA 2003, ss 52 and 53 contain offences of:

- causing or inciting prostitution for gain; and

---

59   SOA 2003, ss 48(2), 49(2) and 50(2). Maximum on summary conviction: see **1.43**.
60   At pp 5–18 and 120–123.
61   See **8.4** et seq.
62   See **2.97**.
63   SOA 2003, s 80 and Sch 3, paras 29A–29C.
64   PCA 2002, s 75, Sch 2, para 8.
65   SCA 2007, s 2(2)(a), Sch 1, para 4(1)(b)–(d).
66   *SB*, at para 7.7 and Recommendation 52.

• controlling prostitution for gain,

which implement with some variation the second and third recommended offences. The first recommended offence was not implemented, but SOA 2003 inserted a new section (s 33A), discussed later at **10.162**, which deals with some people (brothel-keepers, managers, etc) who may receive earnings from prostitutes. Otherwise, those who receive the earnings of prostitution do not thereby commit an offence.

10.44 Although the offences under ss 52 and 53 are not limited to cases where the 'victim' is 18 or over, they are aimed at such a case: the more serious offences under ss 48, 49 and 50 specifically cover cases where the victim is under 18. However, where the prosecution is not confident that it can prove that the defendant charged under SOA 2003, s 48 or s 49 did not reasonably believe that the child was aged 18 or over, the corresponding offence under s 52 or s 53 can also be charged as a back-up.

10.45 It will be noted that there is no offence of arranging or facilitating adult prostitution. Thus, those who simply provide an adult prostitute with goods, services or premises for use for the purposes of prostitution do not commit either offence, or any other offence under SOA 2003, whereas if the prostitute was under 18 they can be convicted under s 49. In some cases they would have been guilty of the repealed offence of living on the earnings of prostitution, contrary to SOA 1956, s 30.[67]

10.46 SOA 2003, s 52(1) provides:

'A person commits an offence if—

    (a)   he intentionally causes or incites another person to become a prostitute in any part of the world, and

    (b)   he does so for or in the expectation of gain for himself or a third person.'

As in other parts of the Act, it would seem that 'causing' and 'inciting' are separate offences.

10.47 SOA 2003, s 53(1) provides:

'A person commits an offence if—

    (a)   he intentionally controls any of the activities of another person relating to that person's prostitution in any part of the world, and

    (b)   he does so for or in the expectation of gain for himself or a third person.'

10.48 An offence under s 52 or s 53 is triable either way and punishable with a maximum of 7 years' imprisonment on conviction on indictment.[68] See the SGC Definitive Guideline[69] in the Appendix.

Class of offence	3	SOA 2003, s 72 applies	✗
Notification requirements	✗	SOPO	✓[70]

---

[67]   See, for example, *Shaw v DPP* [1962] AC 220; *Stewart v DPP* (1986) 83 Cr App R 327.
[68]   SOA 2003, ss 52(2) and 53(2); maximum on summary conviction: see **1.43**.
[69]   At pp 5–18 and 126–127.

CJA 2003, Sch 15 applies	✔	Serious specified offence	✘
Review of lenient sentence	s 52 ✔ s 53 ✘	Special provisions of CYPA 1933	✔
Detention of young offender for specified period			✘

See **1.48** et seq.

10.49   An offence contrary to s 52 or s 53 is a 'lifestyle offence': see **10.42**. An offence under s 52 or s 53 is a serious offence for the purposes of making a serious crime prevention order under SCA 2007.[71]

Elements

10.50   The elements of these offences correspond to those under s 48 or s 49 described above,[72] except that they apply whatever the age of the other party,[73] that they require the accused to act for purposes of gain for him- or herself or a third person, and that the offences are not concerned with causing or inciting, or controlling, someone's involvement in pornography.

10.51   The requirement that the defendant must act for or in the expectation of gain for him- or herself or a third party is incorporated because the Government thought that causing, inciting or controlling adult prostitution did not merit criminality without this element.[74] Encouraging a hard-up woman, for example, to pay off her debts by prostitution does not constitute an offence. The particular vulnerability of children clearly merits a lower threshold of criminality. 'Gain' is widely defined by s 54(1):

'In sections 52 and 53 "gain" means—

(a)   any financial advantage, including the discharge of an obligation to pay or the provision of goods or services (including sexual services) gratuitously or at a discount; or

(b)   the goodwill of any person which is or appears likely, in time, to bring financial advantage'.

The provision in (a) is the same as the definition of payment in ss 47(2) and 51(3) discussed in **10.16**. Examples are where A causes or incites B to become a prostitute, or controls B's prostitution, so as to take for himself from B or B's clients B's earnings in whole or part, or so that B can use her earnings to pay off his debts or buy his drugs. The reference to 'sexual services' would cover the case of A controlling a number of women prostitutes, where the gain he derives from them is their engaging in sexual intercourse with him. The reference to 'goodwill' in (b) was included to cover those situations in which one person may undertake one of the prohibited activities (as where A incites B to work as a prostitute for C) in the hope that it will please C so that C may

---

[70]   SOA 2003, s 104, Sch 5, para 63.
[71]   SCA 2007, s 2(2)(a), Sch 1, Pt 1, para 4(2)(e) and (f).
[72]   See **10.24** and **10.28–10.32**.
[73]   'Prostitute' and 'prostitution' in ss 52 and 53 have the same meaning as in s 51(2) : SOA 2003, s 54(2); see **10.35**.
[74]   Lord Falconer of Thoroton, HL Deb, vol 649, col 59.

give him a share of the profits, or drugs, or access to other prostitutes.[75] Proof of such a hope may present evidential difficulties, but may be possible where, for example, A tells a third party why he has acted as he has.[76] It will be noted that there is no requirement that the anticipated gain materialises. If A persuades B to work as a prostitute in the expectation that she will share her earnings with A (or a third party), it is irrelevant that B never shares her earnings with anyone.

STREET OFFENCES

10.52 Street prostitution impacts significantly on the community in the area. Amongst other things, it brings with it sexual acts in public, abuse from kerb-crawlers, drug dealing, litter from hypodermic needles, condoms and telephone cards and anti-social behaviour. The prevention of such things is the justification for the offences discussed in this part.

10.53 The offences in this part are provided by legislation other than SOA 2003, although (with the exception of the last offence, which was already expressly gender neutral) they were all made gender neutral by amendments made by that Act.[77] They are as follows:

- loitering or soliciting for purposes of prostitution;

- kerb-crawling by 'punters' and persistent soliciting by 'punters'; and

- placing of advertisements relating to prostitution.

This part concludes by a consideration of the use of anti-social behaviour orders and binding-over orders in civil proceedings to prevent the activities of street prostitutes and their clients.

Loitering or soliciting for purposes of prostitution

10.54 This is governed by the Street Offences Act (StOffA) 1959. Before that Act loitering or soliciting for prostitution was governed by the Vagrancy Act (VA) 1824, s 3 and a range of local legislation. This statutory regime had proved ineffective by the early 1950s, when large numbers of street prostitutes were working in some parts of London and some other big towns. The reasons were the need in some of the statutes to prove 'riotous or indecent behaviour' (VA 1824, s 3) or 'annoyance' to passers-by or residents (as in the case of a number of local Acts) and the fact that the maximum penalty under many of the provisions was only £2.00.

10.55 The Wolfenden Committee[78]considered that the state of affairs was unacceptable and recommended a new offence of general application which did not require proof of annoyance and would be subject to a system of higher penalties. The Committee's

---

75　Lord Falconer of Thoroton, HL Deb, vol 648, cols 178 and 195.

76　Lord Falconer of Thoroton, ibid, col 195.

77　SOA 2003, s 56 and Sch 1, paras 2, 3 and 4. In *DPP v Bull* [1995] 1 Cr App R 413, it was held that the first offence was limited to loitering, etc by women prostitutes. The offences in the second bullet were expressly (until amended) confined to soliciting by men of women prostitutes.

78　*Report of the Committee on Homosexual Offences and Prostitution*, Cmnd 247 (1957).

recommendations were put into effect by StOffA 1959, which repealed the local legislation. The offence in VA 1824, s 3 was not repealed until the Statute Law (Repeals) Act 1989.

10.56 StOffA 1959, s 1(1)[79] provides:

> 'It shall be an offence for a common prostitute (whether male or female) to loiter or solicit in a street or public place for the purposes of prostitution.'

10.57 A person guilty of an offence under s 1(1) is liable on summary conviction to a fine of an amount not exceeding level 2 on the standard scale, or, for an offence committed after a previous conviction, to a fine of an amount not exceeding level 3 on that scale.[80] 'An offence committed after a previous conviction' clearly refers to a previous conviction for an offence contrary to s 1(1). As will be seen, 'soliciting' and 'loitering' are two ways, active and passive respectively, of doing the same thing. They do not, therefore, appear to constitute separate offences but are separate ways of committing the one offence.

Class of offence	n/a	SOA 2003, s 72 applies	✗
Notification requirements	✗	SOPO	✗
CJA 2003, Sch 15 applies	✗	Serious specified offence	✗
Review of lenient sentence	✗	Special provisions of CYPA 1933	✗
Detention of young offender for specified period			✗

10.58 Although those under 18 who engage in prostitution are subject to the above offences penalising the activities of a prostitute, Home Office Circular 20/2000 states that they are almost invariably victims and should be treated as such. Criminal justice action should only be taken against them (as opposed to those who abuse them or seek to exploit them) if all the relevant local agencies are satisfied that the child is involved in prostitution of his or her own free will, and attempts to divert the child out of prostitution have failed.

---

[79] As amended.

[80] StOffA 1959, s 1(2) (as substituted). Up to 95% of those involved in street prostitution in England and Wales are problematic drug-users and many are homeless: *Paying the Price*: Consultation Paper on Prostitution (Home Office, 2004) at pp 47, 49. Controversial provisions in the Criminal Justice and Immigration (CJI) Bill (2007–2008) for orders for rehabilitation were dropped because of pressure of parliamentary time. Under these provisions, persons convicted under StOffA 1959, s 1 would have been offered help to find alternative lifestyles through an order to promote rehabilitation, in lieu of any other penalty, under which they would have been required to undertake counselling, including drug or alcohol rehabilitation courses, on pain of being dealt with for the original offence if they failed to comply.

Common prostitute

10.59 The classic definition of 'common prostitute' was given by the Court of Criminal Appeal in *De Munck*,[81] a case concerned with the offence of procuring a woman to become a common prostitute, contrary to the Criminal Law Amendment Act (CLAA) 1885, s 2(2) (repealed). The Court said:[82]

> 'The Court is of opinion that the term "common prostitute" in the statute is not limited so as to mean only one who permits acts of lewdness with all and sundry, or with such as hire her, when such acts are in the nature of ordinary sexual connection. We are of opinion that prostitution is proved if it be shown that a woman offers her body commonly for lewdness for payment in return. There was ample evidence that this girl did that, and that the appellant knew what she was doing and procured her for this particular conduct.'

10.60 As was said by the Court of Appeal in *Morris-Lowe*,[83] a common prostitute is:[84]

> '... someone who is prepared for reward to engage in acts of lewdness with all and sundry, or with anyone who may hire her for that purpose.'

Referring to the word 'common' the Court of Appeal said:[85]

> 'It is clear to us that the word is not mere surplusage. We do not pause to consider whether the performance by a woman of a single act of lewdness with a man on one occasion for reward constitutes the woman a prostitute. But we are of the view that it does not make her a woman who offers herself commonly for lewdness. That must be someone who is prepared for reward to engage in acts of lewdness with all and sundry, or with anyone who may hire her for that purpose.'

10.61 The acts of lewdness referred to above are not limited to cases where a person offers his or her body for lewdness in a passive way, ie submits to something being done to his or her body. They also include acts, such as masturbation or whipping, where that person takes an active role. This was held by the Court of Criminal Appeal in *Webb*.[86] It stated that, in the passage in *De Munck* quoted above, 'a woman who offers her body commonly for lewdness':[87]

> '... means no more and was intended to mean no more than offers herself, and it includes, at any rate, such a case as this where a woman offers herself as a participant in physical acts of indecency for the sexual gratification of men.'

10.62 A person cannot be a prostitute unless, at the very least, he or she is in the presence of his or her client at some point and his or her offer to the client must involve direct physical contact of a sexual nature between them. This was held by the Court of Appeal in *Armhouse Lee Ltd v Chappell*[88] where the court concluded that women providing a telephone sex-chat-lines service were not prostitutes. It follows from

---

81 [1918] 1 KB 635.
82 [1918] 1 KB 635, at pp 637–638.
83 [1985] 1 All ER 400 (attempting to procure a woman to become a common prostitute, the substantive offence being contrary to SOA 1956, s 22 (repealed)).
84 Ibid, at p 402.
85 Ibid.
86 [1964] 1 QB 357 (procuring a woman to become a common prostitute, and knowingly living on the earnings of prostitution, contrary to SOA 1956, s 30 (repealed)).
87 Ibid, at p 366.
88 (1996) *The Times*, August 7.

Armhouse Lee that someone who offers to self-masturbate, or to have intercourse with a third party, in the presence of a paying client is not a prostitute.

10.63 In *McFarlane*[89] the Court of Appeal held that the crucial feature in defining prostitution is the making of an offer of sexual services for reward, and that therefore a 'clipper', someone who commonly offers her body for sexual services for reward and pockets the reward in advance, never intending to provide the services, is a prostitute. It said:[90]

> 'If it were a defence to soliciting for prostitution under s 1 of [StOffA 1959] that the accused woman was acting as a "clipper" and not as a "hooker", proof of such offences would be extremely difficult. It would be necessary to prove not merely the offer of sexual services in a public place, but that the services were actually provided, or were at the time of the offering intended to be provided. The mischief being simply the harassment and nuisance to members of the public on the streets, the distinction between "clippers" and "hookers" is immaterial.'

10.64 'Common prostitute' dates back to VA 1824, and is widely regarded as stigmatising and offensive. A provision in the CJI Bill (2007–2008) to remove the term 'common' from StOffA 1959, s 1 was dropped because of pressure on parliamentary time.

Soliciting

10.65 'Soliciting' can not only be done by spoken words but also by physical conduct expressing (e g holding up an advertisement) or implying an invitation to prostitution. For example, in *Horton v Mead*,[91] D, who had artificially reddened his face and lips, had, whilst in public lavatories and in the street, smiled at men, pursed his lips and wriggled his body. He did not, however, at any material time speak to or touch anyone, nor did he attempt to do so. The Divisional Court held that this behaviour amounted to persistently soliciting for immoral purposes in a public place, contrary to VA 1898, s 1(1)(b) (repealed) (which became SOA 1956, s 32 (repealed)). The relevance of this decision is increased by the fact that it was held in *Burge v DPP*[92] that 'soliciting' in SOA 1956, s 32 had exactly the same meaning as in StOffA 1959, s 1.

10.66 According to the majority in *Horton v Mead*, it is not necessary that anyone to whom the solicitation was addressed should have been aware of it. It was not proved in that case that anybody solicited had seen D's conduct. Lord Alverstone CJ and Pickford J held that it was not necessary that anyone intended to be solicited should have had his notice attracted to the solicitation and that it was unnecessary that it should reach the mind of the person. Phillimore J, who agreed that there had been persistent soliciting by D, approached the matter differently. He avoided having to decide whether the person solicited had to be aware of the solicitation because he held that it could be inferred that the men solicited had been aware. According to the view taken by the majority, if D made a solicitation towards a blind man, not knowing that he was blind, D would solicit him. A contrary view from that of the majority in *Horton v Mead* may be contained in

---

[89] [1994] 2 All ER 283 (knowingly living on earnings of prostitution).
[90] Ibid, at p 288. *McFarlane* was distinguished in *Armhouse Lee*.
[91] [1913] 1 KB 154. Also see *Field v Chapman* [1953] CLY 787 (defendant stood beside and in front of men in public lavatory, smiling at them: held persistent soliciting for immoral purposes).
[92] [1962] 1 All ER 666.

Hilbery J's judgment in *Smith v Hughes*,[93] whose facts are set out in **10.81**, where prostitutes had signalled to men passing by in the street intending to solicit them. He said that the signals:[94]

> '... did effect solicitation of the men when they reached those men. At that moment the person in the street to whom the signal was addressed was solicited ...'

One thing is clear. Even if someone has to be aware of the solicitation, he is not required to understand the meaning of the message conveyed; it is irrelevant that he believes that the message is an innocent one.

10.67 In *Weisz v Monahan*[95] the Divisional Court held that an advertisement for her services by a prostitute, which was displayed in a case outside a shop, did not constitute soliciting by her for the purposes of StOffA 1959, s 1(1). Lord Parker CJ, with whom the rest of the Divisional Court agreed, said that:[96]

> '... soliciting in that connexion involves the physical presence of the prostitute and conduct on her part amounting to an importuning of prospective customers. An advertisement is more in the nature of a notice, and though in one sense it may be said to be soliciting custom, certainly something much more than that is needed in the commission of the offence of soliciting by a prostitute.'

Weisz v Monahan was distinguished in *Behrendt v Burridge*,[97] where a female prostitute had sat, scantily clad, at a downstairs bay window of a terrace house; the window was illuminated by a red light. At no time was she observed to wave, shout, rap on the window or make any sign towards or actively communicate from the window with any person in the street. The Divisional Court held that she had been soliciting, contrary to s 1(1). Boreham J, with whom the rest of the court agreed, said:[98]

> 'This young woman, sitting on a stool scantily clad, in a window bathed in red light and in an area where prostitutes were sought, might just as well have had at her feet an advertisement saying: "I am a prostitute. I am ready and willing to give the services of a prostitute and my premises are now available for that purpose." It is clear, in my judgment, that she was soliciting in the sense of tempting or alluring prospective customers to come in for the purpose of prostitution and projecting her solicitation to passers by.'

Loitering

10.68 There is no binding authority on the meaning of 'loitering' in StOffA 1959, s 1(1). Decisions about the term in other, different statutory contexts must be treated with caution. In *Williamson v Wright*,[99] where the High Court of Justiciary was concerned with the offence of loitering in a street for the purposes of betting, contrary to the Street Betting Act 1906, s 1, Lord Anderson said that the meaning of loitering was that 'loitering is just travelling indolently and with frequent pauses. That, in my

---

93   [1960] 2 All ER 859.
94   Ibid, at p 861.
95   [1962] 1 All ER 664.
96   Ibid, at p 665; followed in *Burge v DPP* [1962] 1 All ER 666n (persistently soliciting for immoral purposes, contrary to SOA 1956, s 32 (repealed)).
97   [1976] 3 All ER 285.
98   Ibid, at p 288.
99   1924 SLT 363.

judgment involves an idea of a certain persistence or repetition'.[100] Lord Hunter stated that, '"loitering" ... means something more ... than slowing down or stopping on a single occasion'.[101] Lord Alness, the Lord Justice-Clerk, said that, '"loitering" ... connotes the idea of lingering'.[102]

10.69 Reference may also be made to *Rawlings v Smith*,[103] which was concerned with the subsequently abolished offence of loitering with intent to commit a felony, contrary to VA 1824, s 4. Lord Hewart CJ said:[104]

> 'It seems to me that it would be difficult, almost to the point of impossibility, to contend ... that one single act could be held to show that a person was loitering or frequenting. The expression seems to involve the notion of something which to some degree, at any rate, is continuous or repeated.'

10.70 In *Bridge v Campbell*,[105] another case concerned with loitering with intent to commit a felony, the Divisional Court held that loitering could be done by means of a motor vehicle. There can be no real doubt that this equally applies to the present offence.

10.71 'Loitering' is a wider term than 'soliciting' because it covers the case where the common prostitute does not make the 'approach' but simply waits to be approached by 'punters', but it is narrower in that it requires the element of lingering or repeated slowing or stopping.

Soliciting or loitering need only occur on one occasion

10.72 Soliciting or loitering (as defined above) is not required to occur on two or more occasions. A provision in CJI Bill (2007–2008) to require the conduct to be 'persistent' (defined as taking place on two or more occasions in any 3-month period) was dropped because of pressure of parliamentary time.

Street or public place

10.73 Despite the title of StOffA 1959, the Act applies to public places as well as to streets.

Street

10.74 'Street' is given an extended definition by StOffA 1959, s 1(4) which provides that:

> 'For the purposes of this section "street" includes any bridge, road, lane, footway, subway, square, court, alley or passage, whether a thoroughfare or not, which is for the time being open to the public; and the doorways and entrances of premises abutting on a street (as hereinbefore defined), and any ground adjoining and open to a street, shall be treated as forming part of the street.'

---

[100] Ibid, at p 366.
[101] Ibid, at p 367.
[102] Ibid, at p 367.
[103] [1938] 1 KB 675.
[104] Ibid, at p 686.
[105] (1947) 63 TLR 470.

Three points may be made about this definition:

- the use of 'includes' indicates that it is not exhaustive;

- the places referred to may be in private ownership, and, although those in the first part of the definition must be 'open to the public', those in the second part need not; and

- in relation to 'abutting' and 'adjoining', the case-law in respect of both is not unanimous. Some judges have required contiguity (which would mean that the doorways, entrances or ground would touch or be in physical contact with the street);[106] others have favoured a more liberal requirement, such as close proximity.[107] The subject-matter of these cases varies, none of them involving a statutory provision similar to the present one and, as has been judicially noted,[108] their meaning depends on the subject-matter. The subject-matter of the present offence clearly indicates that the narrower approach is the appropriate one.

Public place

10.75 'Public place' is not defined by StOffA 1959 or any case-law. In *Elkins v Cartlidge*,[109] where the phrase 'road or other public place' in the Road Traffic Act (RTA) 1930 was in issue, the Divisional Court held that the two things were to be treated as ejusdem generis. It will be noted, however, that 'other' is missing from the phrase used in StOffA 1959 and it is submitted that the ejusdem generis rule therefore does not apply and this will be assumed in what follows.

10.76 Case-law on the meaning of 'public place' does provide guidance as to the meaning of that term but, once again, it must not be forgotten that judicial definitions must be understood in the context of the evils which they are intended to avert.[110] In *Wellard*,[111] where the Court for Crown Cases Reserved affirmed the conviction of D for indecent exposure, contrary to common law and to the Offences Against the Person Act 1861, s 29 (repealed), which had occurred in a marsh, not visible from a public road, where people went without hindrance when they liked, although they had no legal right to do so, Grove J stated that: 'A public place is one where the public go, no matter whether they have a right to go or not.' All members of the court agreed that, whether or not the common law offence required the exposure to be in a public place, what had occurred had occurred in a public place.

10.77 In the context of road traffic legislation it has been held that a 'public place' means a place to which members of the public are admitted or have access at the

---

[106]   *Barnett v Covell* (1903) 68 JP 93, at p 94, per Lord Alverstone CJ (abutting); *R (on the prosecution of Lambeth BC) v SE Rly Co* (1910) 74 JP 137, at p 139, per Kennedy LJ (abutting); *New Plymouth BC v Taranaki Electric Power Board* [1933] AC 680, at p 682, per Lord Macmillan (adjoining); *Re Ecclesiastical Comrs for England's Conveyance* [1936] Ch 430, at p 440, per Luxmoore J (adjoining); *Buckinghamshire CC v Trigg* [1963] 1 All ER 403, at p 406, per Lord Parker CJ (abutting and adjoining).

[107]   *Wakefield Local Board of Health v Lee* (1876) 1 Ex D 336, at p 343, per Grove J (abutting), and at p 342, per Cleasby B (adjoining); *Lightbound v Higher Bebington Local Board* (1885) 16 QBD 577, at p 585, per Bowen LJ (adjoining).

[108]   *Wakefield Local Board of Health v Lee*, ibid, at p 343, per Grove J; *Lightbound v Higher Bebington Local Board*, ibid, at p 584, per Bowen LJ.

[109]   (1931) 23 Cr App R 49.

[110]   *Collinson* (1931) 23 Cr App R 49, at p 50, per Lord Hewart CJ.

[111]   (1884) 14 QBD 63, at pp 66–67.

material time, whether on payment or otherwise.[112] The absence of a physical obstruction or of a notice forbidding entry does not of itself mean that the public have access.[113] It is irrelevant that the public could have had access; the question is whether they have actually had access to the place in question.[114] If they have, the fact that it has been in defiance of an express prohibition is irrelevant.[115]

10.78 Cases on the road traffic legislation hold that access must be by virtue of being a member of the public or a section of the public, and not by virtue of some special qualification or other reason personal to entrants not possessed by members of the public in general.[116] On this basis, a railway station is a public place because the public in general have access to it, and so is a public house, even though children are excluded from it in specified circumstances, because a section of the public (those not so excluded) have access. On the other hand, a members' club's premises are not a public place because access is limited to those possessed of a special qualification (membership of the club).[117] Likewise, business premises are not a public place if access is limited to employees and others who enter by virtue of their employment. On the other hand, if customers have access to those premises the premises will be a public place because those customers will not cease to be members of the public and become a special class because they use the premises as customers.[118]

10.79 As was pointed out by Lord Coleridge CJ in *Wellard*,[119] what is a public place may vary from time to time; the question is whether the place was public at the material time. In *Collinson*,[120] a road traffic case, for example, a field to which the public was temporarily admitted on payment was held to be a 'public place' at that time.

10.80 Assuming that the above applies to 'public place' in StOffA 1959 the following are further examples of a 'public place' for that purpose: a public park, an amusement arcade, the 'public' rooms of a hotel, a car park which is open to the members of the public (on payment or otherwise). These places, however, will only be 'public' when they are open to the public. When they are closed, so that the public does not have access, or if access is for a time restricted to people with some special qualification personal to them (as where a hotel has been hired 'exclusively' for a wedding reception), they will cease for that period of time to be a public place.

In a street or public place

10.81 As *Behrendt v Burridge*, referred to in **10.67**, indicates, a person can solicit 'in a street' from within a building and presumably this is equally true in the case of a public place where the soliciting is from a building which is not a public place. The point was directly in issue in *Smith v Hughes*,[121] where two prostitutes had solicited men passing in the street by attracting their attention, inviting them into a house and indicating the price. The solicitation had been made from a first-floor window, or from behind a closed ground-floor window or half-open ground-floor window 3 feet behind 4-foot-high

---

[112] *Collinson*, n 110 above.
[113] *Spence* [1999] RTR 353.
[114] Ibid.
[115] Assumed in *DPP ex parte Taussik* [2000] 9 *Archbold News* 2.
[116] *DPP v Vivier* [1991] 4 All ER 18; *Waters* (1963) 47 Cr App R 149.
[117] *DPP v Vivier*, ibid. See also *Kane* [1965] 1 All ER 705, at p 708.
[118] *May v DPP* [2005] EWHC 1280 (Admin).
[119] (1884) LR 14 QBD 63, at p 66.
[120] (1931) 27 Cr App R 49.
[121] [1960] 2 All ER 859.

railings separating the premises from the street. The Divisional Court held that on these facts the two prostitutes had been soliciting in a street. Lord Parker CJ based his decision on the ground that in each case the solicitation was projected to and addressed to somebody walking in the street. Hilbery J said that in each case what had been done was intended to solicit men passing in the street. They did effect solicitation of the men to whom they were addressed when they reached them in the street. Donovan J agreed with both judgments.

For the purposes of prostitution

10.82 That the common prostitute solicited or loitered for prostitution can be implied from his or her dress, appearance and behaviour or from other circumstances (including the place in question). An example is provided by *Knight v Fryer*.[122] In an area noted for prostitutes, D, a convicted prostitute, from time to time during an afternoon, walked to the kerb of the road, looked into cars driven by lone males and then returned to the doorway where she had been standing. A magistrates' court upheld D's contention that there was no case to answer on a charge of, being a common prostitute, loitering in a street for the purpose of prostitution because the prosecution had failed to prove that she had been loitering for this purpose. Remitting the case for the hearing to continue, the Divisional Court held that the justices could have inferred the purpose of the loitering from the circumstances. It was unnecessary for the prosecution to adduce positive evidence to show D's purpose.

Cautions

10.83 Under a non-statutory system of cautioning recommended by the Wolfenden Committee and governed by Home Office Circular,[123] a person aged 18 or over[124] who has not previously been convicted of loitering or soliciting for the purposes of prostitution is not charged with an offence under StOffA 1959, s 1(1) unless that person has been cautioned by the police on at least two occasions and such caution has been formally recorded.

10.84 A person who wishes to have a caution expunged on the ground that he or she was not loitering or soliciting in a street or public place for the purpose of prostitution may apply to the court under StOffA 1959, s 2 for the caution to be expunged. This procedure appears to have fallen into disuse and no longer serves a useful purpose. Provisions to repeal s 2, contained in CJI Bill (2007–2008), were dropped because of pressure on parliamentary time.

10.85 The fact that StOffA 1959, s 2 (below) recognises the existence of the above system of cautioning does not carry with it the implication that a police officer has power to stop and detain a prostitute for the purpose of implementing the system, nor does a police officer have any other power to do so.[125] If the prostitute is unco-operative the system cannot operate.

---

[122] [1976] Crim LR 322. See also *Field v Chapman* [1953] CLY 787.

[123] No 109/1959, superseded by HO 20/2000 (see **10.58**) in relation to those under 18. A child under 18 may be given a reprimand or warning if the terms of the Crime and Disorder Act (CDA) 1998, s 65 (as amended) are satisfied.

[124] By CDA 1998, s 65(8), a caution may not be given to a person under 18.

[125] *Collins v Wilcock* [1984] 3 All ER 374.

Soliciting by 'punters'

10.86 Following the decision of the Divisional Court in *Crook v Edmondson*[126] in 1966 that soliciting by men of women prostitutes did not constitute the offence of persistently soliciting for immoral purposes, contrary to SOA 1956, s 32 (repealed by SOA 2003), the Criminal Law Revision Committee (CLRC) recommended in 1984 that there should be three offences to deal with such conduct, which was prevalent in some areas and a cause of nuisance and of fear to women, as well as being highly offensive. These three recommended offences were:

- an offence for a man to use a motor vehicle in a street or public place for the purpose of soliciting a woman for prostitution;

- an offence for a man in a street or public place persistently to solicit a woman or women for the purpose of prostitution; and

- an offence for a man to solicit a woman for sexual purposes in a manner likely to cause her fear.[127]

The first (in an amended form) and second recommended offences were implemented by SOA 1985, ss 1 and 2. The third recommended offence has never been enacted. The offences under ss 1 and 2 are now gender neutral.

Kerb-crawling

10.87 SOA 1985, s 1(1), provides:

'A person commits an offence if he solicits another person (or different persons) for the purpose of prostitution—

(a)   from a motor vehicle while it is in a street or public place; or

(b)   in a street or public place while in the immediate vicinity of a motor vehicle[128] that he has just got out of or off,

---

[126]   [1966] 2 QB 81.

[127]   *Sixteenth Report: Prostitution in the Street*, Cmnd 9329 (1984).

[128]   'Motor vehicle' has the same meaning as in the RTA 1988: SOA 1985, s 1(3) (as substituted), i e 'motor vehicle' means, subject to the Chronically Sick and Disabled Persons Act 1970, s 20 (which makes special provision about invalid carriages, within the meaning of that Act), a mechanically propelled vehicle intended or adapted for use on roads: RTA 1988, s 185(2), except that by RTA 1988, s 189(1) the following are to be treated as not being a motor vehicle:
(a) a mechanically propelled vehicle being an implement for cutting grass which is controlled by a pedestrian and is not capable of being used or adapted for any other purpose,
(b) any other mechanically propelled vehicle controlled by a pedestrian which may be specified by regulations made by the Secretary of State for the purposes of s 189 and the Road Traffic Regulation Act 1984, s 140, and
(c) an electrically assisted pedal cycle of such a class as may be prescribed by regulations so made.
Whether or not the definition in s 185 is satisfied depends on whether a reasonable person looking at the vehicle would say that one of its uses would be use on a road, whether or not it is suitable for such use: *Burns v Currell* [1963] 2 QB 433 (go-kart not a motor vehicle); applied in *DPP v Saddington* (2001) 165 JP 122 ('Go-ped' a motor vehicle). See also *DPP v King* [2008] EWHC 447 (Admin) ('Mantis City' electric scooter a motor vehicle).
A motor vehicle does not cease to be a mechanically propelled vehicle for the purposes of RTA 1988 if it has broken down or been immobilised unless there is no reasonable prospect of it ever being made mobile again: *Binks v Dept of the Environment* [1975] RTR 318. See also *Newberry v Simmonds* [1961] 2 All ER 318. As to auto-assisted cycles, see *Lawrence v Howlett* [1952] 2 All ER 74.

persistently or in such a manner or in such circumstances as to be likely to cause annoyance to the person (or any of the persons) solicited, or nuisance to other persons in the neighbourhood.'

An offence under s 1(1) is triable summarily only and punishable with a fine not exceeding level 3 on the standard scale.[129] The power under the Powers of Criminal Courts (Sentencing) Act 2000, s 146 to disqualify from driving for any offence is of obvious relevance to the present offence. A disqualification and the publicity of a conviction are no doubt more effective deterrents than a low-level fine.

Class of offence	n/a	SOA 2003, s 72 applies	✗
Notification requirements	✗	SOPO	✗
CJA 2003, Sch 15 applies	✗	Serious specified offence	✗
Review of lenient sentence	✗	Special provisions of CYPA 1933	✗
Detention of young offender for specified period			✗

Soliciting

10.88 'Soliciting' doubtless has the same meaning as it does in StOffA 1959, s 1[130] and SOA 1985, s 2.[131] A driver who merely accepts the solicitation of a prostitute and invites the prostitute into his car does not thereby solicit the prostitute, because 'soliciting' implies begging a favour, an element of importuning or asking, but the fact that the prostitute makes the first approach does not in itself mean that the driver cannot thereafter 'solicit' the prostitute by subsequent importuning, etc.[132]

For the purpose of prostitution

10.89 The reference to a person soliciting another person (or different persons) for the purpose of prostitution is a reference to his or her soliciting *that* person for the purpose of obtaining *that* person's services as a prostitute.[133] The words italicised indicate that the offence cannot be committed by a prostitute, but only by a would-be client. The words italicised also indicate that soliciting a person to obtain the services of a third party as a prostitute is not an offence under SOA 1985, s 1. It is, of course, not necessary that the person solicited is actually a prostitute.

10.90 SOA 1985 does not define 'prostitution' or 'prostitute' for the purposes of offences under it. 'Prostitute' would seem to bear the meaning (in a gender-neutral way)

[129] SOA 1985, s 1(2) (as amended).
[130] See **10.65**.
[131] See **10.97**.
[132] *DPP v Ollerenshaw* (1992) *The Independent*, January 6, cited in Rook and Ward *Sexual Offences Law & Practice* (Sweet & Maxwell, 3rd edn, 2004) (*Rook & Ward*), at p 371.
[133] SOA 1985, s 4(1).

evolved by courts in relation to other offences relating to prostitution where the parent statute leaves the term undefined,[134] and 'prostitution' should also be understood accordingly.

10.91 It may be noted that the offence under SOA 2003, s 1 applies, despite the title of the offence (given by the Act), to soliciting in a street or a public place. 'Street' is defined by SOA 1985, s 4(4) in identical terms to the definition of that term given by StOffA 1959, s 1(4).[135] What was said about 'public place' in relation to StOffA 1959 is equally applicable to the present offence.[136]

Location

10.92 The solicitation of another person (or different persons) for the purpose of prostitution must be from a motor vehicle whilst it is in a street or public place, whether in motion or stationary, *or* be in a street or public place *in the immediate vicinity of a motor vehicle that the defendant has just got out of* (as eg in the case of a motor car) *or off* (as eg in the case of a motor cycle). The words italicised involve a question of fact and degree. Those who solicit for prostitution on a pedal cycle or in the vicinity of it, as a newspaper report in 2007 shows can occur,[137] fall outside the offence under s 1 (although if their solicitation is persistent they may be convicted of an offence under s 2). If a person who has just got out of or off a motor vehicle leaves the immediate vicinity and then solicits for the purpose of prostitution he or she may likewise be convicted under s 2. The defendant need not be the driver of the vehicle in question. For example, he or she could be, or could have been, a passenger on a bus.

Persistence or likelihood of annoyance or nuisance

10.93 The soliciting must be done (a) persistently or (b) in such manner or such circumstances as to be likely to cause annoyance to the person (or any of the persons) solicited, or nuisance to other persons in the neighbourhood. The Divisional Court in *Dale v Smith*[138] held, in the context of the offence of persistently importuning for immoral purposes, contrary to SOA 1956, s 32 (repealed), that 'persistently' required a degree of repetition, either of invitations to one person or to different persons, but that two invitations, one each to two different people, can be sufficient to amount to 'persistently importuning'. See also *Darroch v DPP*,[139] referred to in **10.98**.

10.94 In respect of (b), the Divisional Court in *Paul v DPP*[140] held that it is not necessary to have witnesses to the effect that a nuisance has been caused, and that in determining the likelihood of nuisance of the prescribed kind, the magistrates are entitled to use their local knowledge of the area. In this case there was evidence of kerb-crawling by D, stopping near a known prostitute, talking to her and her getting into the vehicle, but there was no evidence that anyone had actually been caused a nuisance. The magistrates' court had taken into account its local knowledge that the area was frequented by prostitutes, that there was a constant stream of cars soliciting them and that it was a heavily populated residential area and the residents were likely to

---

[134] See **10.59** et seq.
[135] SOA 1985, s 4(4); see **10.74**.
[136] See **10.75** et seq.
[137] *The Times*, 1 March 2007.
[138] [1967] 2 All ER 1133. Applied in *Tuck* [1994] Crim LR 375 (another case under SOA 1956, s 32).
[139] (1990) 91 Cr App R 378.
[140] (1989) 90 Cr App R 173.

be affected. Upholding D's conviction under SOA 1985, s 1, the Divisional Court held that there were matters which the justices were entitled to take into account in considering whether the circumstances were likely to cause a nuisance; such matters were within their local knowledge. The use of the word 'likely' in s 1(1) indicated that it was not intended by Parliament that it should be necessary to call evidence that a specific member of the public had been caused nuisance or annoyance.

10.95 Because annoyance to the person solicited need not be likely, an offence may be committed under s 1 even though such person is unlikely to be caused annoyance, as where solicitation is of a plain-clothes police officer in a red light district, if it is likely to cause nuisance to others in the neighbourhood.[141]

Persistent soliciting

10.96 SOA 1985, s 2(1)[142] provides:

> 'A person commits an offence if in a street or public place he persistently solicits another person (or different persons) for the purpose of prostitution.'

It will be noted that, unlike an offence under SOA 1985, s 1, the offence under s 2 can only be committed by persistent soliciting. Like an offence under s 1, the present offence is triable summarily only and punishable with a fine not exceeding level 3 on the standard scale.[143]

Class of offence	n/a	SOA 2003, s 72 applies	✗
Notification requirements	✗	SOPO	✗
CJA 2003, Sch 15 applies	✗	Serious specified offence	✗
Review of lenient sentence	✗	Special provisions of CYPA 1933	✗
Detention of young offender for specified period			✗

10.97 The reference to a person soliciting another for the purpose of prostitution is a reference to soliciting that person for the purpose of obtaining that person's services as a prostitute.[144] In *Darroch v DPP*,[145] a case concerned with the offence under s 2, the Divisional Court held that 'it is necessary for the prosecution to establish that a defendant of whom it is said that he has been soliciting a prostitute, had given some positive indication by physical acts or words to a prostitute that he requires her services'.[146] Consequently, it held, the defendant's conduct in simply driving around a red light area (on three occasions) could not amount to acts of soliciting; on the other hand, the magistrates' court had been justified in concluding that an act of beckoning to

---

[141] This was presumably why the Divisional Court in *Hughes v Holley* (1988) 86 Cr App R 130 (a binding over case), without deciding the point, considered (at p 138) that a submission that there would not be an offence on such facts was wrong.

[142] As amended.

[143] SOA 1985, s 2(2) (as amended).

[144] SOA 1985, s 4(1) (as amended).

[145] (1990) 91 Cr App R 378.

[146] Ibid, at p 383.

a prostitute could so amount in the circumstances (namely that 4 days earlier the defendant had been found in the company of a prostitute in a stationary motor car in the same red light district).

10.98 'Persistently' is to be approached in the same way as outlined in respect of SOA 1985, s 1. In *Darroch v DPP* the defendant's conviction of an offence under s 2 was quashed by the Divisional Court because there was only the one act (referred to above) constituting soliciting and (as the court recognised) there must be at least two acts of soliciting for there to be persistent soliciting. It will be noted that, unlike s 1, s 2 does not contain the alternative to 'persistence' of likelihood to cause annoyance or nuisance.

10.99 The offence applies to soliciting in a street or public place. 'Street' is defined by SOA 1985, s 4(4) in identical terms to the definition of that term given by StOffA 1959, s 1(4).[147] What was said about 'public place' in relation to the 1959 Act is equally applicable to the present offence.[148]

Advertisements relating to prostitution

10.100 Placing advertisements relating to prostitution may constitute the offence of outraging public decency,[149] an offence under the Obscene Publications Act 1959, PoCA 1978 or the Indecent Displays (Control) Act 1981,[150] depending on the circumstances. However, this is unlikely because these offences require proof of indecency or obscenity, and adverts relating to prostitution tend to be suggestive of the availability of sexual services rather than indecent or obscene. Certainly, this has been the case in respect of advertisements commonly displayed in telephone boxes in central London and certain other areas. These advertisements can be offensive and an inappropriate influence on young people. They can hide important public service information and cause serious litter problems. The cost of removing them can be significant.

10.101 In 2001 it was estimated by British Telecom that the number of such advertisements being so placed had risen from 14 million pa to 50 million.[151] The existing criminal offences under the legislation relating to criminal damage, indecent displays, environmental protection and town and country planning had proved inappropriate to deal with the problem for a variety of reasons, and civil action by way of injunction was a slow and resource-intensive process (albeit effective when used against individual 'carders').

10.102 An offence similar to that set out in the Criminal Justice and Police Act (CJPA) 2001, s 46, below, was one of the options put forward in 1999 in a Home Office consultation document, *New Measures to Control Prostitutes Cards in Phone Boxes*, although the government did not then favour it. Section 46 was inserted by way of an amendment moved by a private member of the House of Lords, with Government support in the light of the response to the consultation document.

10.103 CJPA 2001, s 46(1) provides:

---

147   SOA 1985, s 4(4); see **10.74**.
148   See **10.75** et seq.
149   See **13.86** et seq.
150   See **10.234**.
151   *The Independent*, 8 April 2001. For a discussion of the problem as it was in 1999, see *New Measures to Control Prostitutes Cards in Phone Boxes*: Consultation Document (Home Office, 1999), at paras 10–19.

'A person commits an offence if—

(a)   he places on, or in the immediate vicinity of, a public telephone an advertisement relating to prostitution, and

(b)   he does so with the intention that the advertisement should come to the attention of any other person or persons.'

The offence is triable summarily only.[152] A person guilty of it is liable to imprisonment for a term not exceeding 6 months[153] or to a fine not exceeding level 5 on the standard scale, or to both.[154]

Class of offence	n/a	SOA 2003, s 72 applies	✗
Notification requirements	✗	SOPO	✗
CJA 2003, Sch 15 applies	✗	Serious specified offence	✗
Review of lenient sentence	✗	Special provisions of CYPA 1933	✗
Detention of young offender for specified period			✗

10.104   Experience suggests that s 46 has had limited success in curbing the problem. So has the practice of British Telecom of blocking the lines of numbers shown on prostitutes' advertisements, where they are reported by members of the public, because this has simply tended to persuade prostitutes to use mobile phone numbers and telephone companies that do not put call-bars on their numbers.[155]

Placing

10.105   'Placing' is a wider term than 'affixing'. It would be satisfied by any form of positioning, including throwing down a batch of leaflets or cards in the immediate vicinity of a public telephone.

Advertisement relating to prostitution

10.106   CJPA 2001, s 46(2) provides:

'For the purposes of this section, an advertisement is an advertisement relating to prostitution if it—

(a)   is for the services of a prostitute, whether male or female; or

(b)   indicates that premises are premises at which such services are offered.'

In any proceedings for an offence under s 46(1), any advertisement which a reasonable person would consider to be an advertisement relating to prostitution is presumed to be

---

[152]   CJPA 2001, s 46(4).

[153]   As from a day to be appointed this maximum term of imprisonment is increased to a maximum term of 51 weeks (see CJA 2003, s 281(4), (5), (7) (not yet in force)), although this does not affect the penalty for any offence committed before that day (CJA 2003, s 281(6)(b) (not yet in force)). At the date at which this book states the law no such day had been appointed.

[154]   CJPA 2001, s 46(4).

[155]   *The Independent*, 8 April 2001.

such an advertisement unless it is shown not to be.[156] It remains to be seen whether 'shown' imposes a persuasive burden in respect of rebutting the presumption or whether it will be read down to impose only an evidential burden to avoid incompatibility with the European Convention on Human Rights (ECHR), Art 6(2).[157] Section 46(2) is intended to get round the problems inherent in proving that an advertisement, for example, of a massage service, relates to prostitution.

10.107 CJPA 2001 does not define 'prostitution' and 'prostitute' for the purposes of s 46. 'Prostitute' would seem to bear the meaning (in a gender-neutral way) evolved by the courts in relation to other offences relating to prostitution where the parent statute leaves the term undefined,[158] and 'prostitution' should also be understood accordingly.

On, or in the immediate vicinity of, a public telephone

10.108 'On, or in the immediate vicinity of' would seem to be a question of fact. It could be found, for example, that a card placed on a wall (or elsewhere) 5 yards from a public telephone is in the immediate vicinity of the telephone.

10.109 By CJPA 2001, s 46(5):

'"public telephone" means—

(a) any telephone which is located in a public place and made available for use by the public, or a section of the public, and

(b) where such a telephone is located in or on, or attached to, a kiosk, booth, acoustic hood, shelter or other structure, that structure; and

"public place" means any place to which the public have or are permitted to have access, whether on payment or otherwise, other than—

(a) any place to which children under the age of 16 years are not permitted to have access, whether by law or otherwise, and

(b) any premises which are wholly or mainly used for residential purposes.'

Thus, any telephone made available to the public (or a section of it) and situated on private land, such as a railway station or shopping centre, is a public telephone, but one in a public house or night club is not (because they are places to which children are not permitted by law to have access). And neither is one in a hostel or hall of residence (because the premises are wholly or mainly used for residential purposes).

10.110 The Secretary of State has power, by order[159] to apply s 46 in relation to any public structure[160] of a description specified in the order as it applies in relation to a public telephone (as defined above). No such order had been made at the date that this book states the law.

---

[156] CJPA 2001, s 46(3).

[157] See **5.41, 5.42**.

[158] See **10.59** et seq (*common* prostitute).

[159] This power to make an order is exercisable by statutory instrument: CJPA 2001, s 47(4). No order may be made unless a draft has been laid before, and approved by a resolution of, each House of Parliament: ibid, s 47(5).

[160] For this purpose, 'public structure' means any structure that (a) is provided as an amenity for the use of the public or a section of the public, and (b) is located in a public place; and 'public place' and 'public telephone' have the same meaning as in s 46: CJPA 2001, s 47(2).

With the intention that the advertisement should come to the attention of any other person or persons

10.111 The offence may be construed as limited to a direct intent (ie aim or purpose)[161] that the advertisement should have this effect. If, however, the offence is construed as including oblique intention,[162] that intention could be difficult to prove. Suppose, for example, a person who reversed a card advertising prostitutes so as to conceal its message and replaced it so reversed on the wall of a telephone box to avoid litter would raise interesting questions for a magistrates' court. Clearly, that person's purpose would not be that the advertisement came to the attention of other person(s). Such person (D) could only be found to have oblique intent in the relevant respect if the magistrates found that:

- the coming to the attention of other(s) was a virtual certainty (barring some unforeseen intervention) as a result of D's actions; and

- D appreciated that such was the case.[163]

Anti-social behaviour orders

10.112 The CDA 1998, s 1[164] gives magistrates' courts in civil proceedings the power to make an anti-social behaviour order (ASBO) to deal with public disorder, harassment, nuisance and other kinds of anti-social behaviour. The conduct of street prostitutes and their clients or would-be clients (such as kerb-crawlers) may satisfy the requirements for an ASBO and ASBOs have been made against such persons.[165] Such an order may also be made in criminal proceedings on conviction of an offence[166] and in county court proceedings.[167]

10.113 An ASBO is akin to an injunction. It prohibits the defendant from doing anything described in the order. Breach of an ASBO without reasonable excuse is an offence.

10.114 To assist in the operation of the rules on ASBOs, the Government has issued non-statutory guidance.[168] Although not technically binding, the guidance is intended for use by all involved with ASBOs; a failure to do so might form part of an application for judicial review. In any event, the spirit of the guidance was set out by ministers during the House of Commons Committee stage of the Bill, and thus forms part of the statutory intent for the purposes of any *Pepper v Hart* argument.[169]

10.115 What follows relates to ASBOs made in civil proceedings in a magistrates' court.

---

[161] *Mohan* [1976] QB 1.
[162] *Woollin* [1999] 1 AC 82.
[163] *Nedrick* [1986] 3 All ER 1 at p 4, approved in *Woollin*.
[164] As amended.
[165] For criticism of making ASBOs against street prostitutes, see Jones and Sagar 'Crime and Disorder Act 1998: Prostitution and the Anti-social Behaviour Order' [2001] Crim LR 873.
[166] CDA 1998, s 1C; see **10.136**.
[167] CDA 1998, s 1B.
[168] Available at:
       www.crimereduction.homeoffice.gov.uk/antisocialbehaviour/antisocialbehaviour55.htm.
[169] *Pepper (Inspector of Taxes) v Hart* [1993] 1 All ER 42.

Who can apply for an order?

10.116 An application for an ASBO can only be made by a relevant authority,[170] namely:

(a)   the council for a local government area;

(b)   in relation to England, a county council;

(c)   the chief officer of police of any police force maintained for a police area;

(d)   the chief constable of the British Transport Police Force;

(e)   any person registered under the Housing Act (HA) 1996, s 1 as a social landlord who provides or manages any houses or hostel in a local government area; or

(f)   a housing action trust established by order in pursuance of the HA 1988, s 62.[171]

An application under s 1 is made by a written complaint to a magistrates' court in the form specified in the Magistrates' Courts (ASBOs) Rules 2002,[172] Sch 1.

Conditions for making an application

10.117   CDA 1998, s 1(1) provides:

'An application for an order under this section may be made by a relevant authority if it appears to the authority that the following conditions are fulfilled with respect to any persons aged 10 or over, namely—

(a)   that the person has acted, since the commencement date [1 April 1999][173], in an anti-social manner, that is to say, in a manner that caused or was likely to cause harassment, alarm or distress to one or more persons not of the same household as himself; and

(b)   that such an order is necessary to protect relevant persons from further anti-social acts by him.'

---

[170]   CDA 1998, s 1(1).

[171]   CDA 1998, s 1(1A). Provision is made by CDA 1998, s 1E for consultation of another specified relevant authority or authorities (council of local government area and chief officer of police) before a relevant authority applies for an ASBO; the details depend on the nature of the applicant relevant authority. The Secretary of State has power to add to the list of relevant authorities: CDA 1998, s 1A. The Environment Agency and Transport for London have been specified as relevant authorities for the purpose of CDA 1998, s 1: see CDA 1998 (Relevant Authorities and Relevant Persons) Order 2006, SI 2006/2137.

[172]   SI 2002/2784: CDA 1998, s 1(3).

[173]   CDA 1998 (Commencement No 3 and Appointed Day) Order 1999, SI 1999/3263. Nothing in CDA 1998, s 1 affects the operation of the Magistrates' Courts Act (MCA) 1980, s 127(1) (time limit of 6 months with which to lay an information or issue a written charge or make a complaint from time of offence or matter complained of): confirmed by CDA 1998, s 1(5A). However, this does not render inadmissible evidence of events that took place more than 6 months before an application for an ASBO both for the purposes of proving that a person acted in an anti-social manner within the 6-month period and that such an order is necessary: *Chief Constable of West Mercia Constabulary v Boorman* (2005) 169 JP 669.

Section 1(1)(a)

10.118 Where it cannot be shown that a potential victim was present, CDA 1998, s 1(1)(a) cannot be satisfied.[174]

10.119 '*Harassment*', '*alarm*' and '*distress*' in s 1(1)(a) are ordinary words of the English language, and since the context does not show that they are being used in an unusual sense, it would seem that their meaning is a question of fact for the magistrates.[175] The 'harassment, alarm or distress' need not be serious, although its seriousness or otherwise will be a relevant factor when the court decides whether or not to make an ASBO, and it must be to one or more persons not of the same household[176] as the defendant. Thus, if D's soliciting causes distress to the other members of D's household, an ASBO cannot be made. Harassment, etc need not actually be caused, it need only be likely[177] to be caused by the anti-social behaviour. In the absence of evidence from an alleged 'victim', whether or not the defendant's behaviour was likely to cause harassment or the like will be a matter which can be inferred from evidence of the defendant's behaviour given by a police officer or officer of one of the other relevant authorities if the defendant's conduct and the circumstances make it reasonable to do so. Thus, the unwillingness of any witness or witnesses to give evidence because of the fear of reprisals[178] will not prevent an ASBO being made.

10.120 Where harassment, alarm or distress is caused by the conduct of a number of people, including the defendant, s 1(1)(a) does not require proof that the defendant's conduct on its own should have been of a sufficiently aggravated nature to cause harassment, alarm or distress, nor that he or she should in some way have shared responsibility with the others for their aggravated conduct. Section 1(1)(a) is concerned simply with a defendant's conduct and its effect, whether looked at on its own or with the conduct of others. This was held by the Divisional Court in *Chief Constable of Lancashire v Potter*.[179] In that case the Chief Constable had applied for an ASBO against P as a result of her activities as a street prostitute in a residential area over 3 months where, as the magistrate found, there was a 'substantial problem' with the activities of street prostitutes in those areas, to which P's conduct had contributed. However, the magistrate dismissed the application because he held that P's conduct could not be aggregated with the conduct of the other prostitutes when considering whether she had acted in a manner that caused or was likely to cause harassment, alarm or distress, and that it had not been proved that her conduct on its own had caused or was likely to have such an effect. The Divisional Court upheld the Chief Constable's appeal against the dismissal. It stated:[180]

> 'Street prostitution in residential areas, whatever the extremes of behaviour by individual prostitutes, is clearly capable, when considered as a whole and depending on the circumstances, including the number, regularity and degree of concentration of activity, of causing or being likely to cause harassment, alarm or distress to others in the area. It is a question of fact whether any individual prostitute, by her contribution to that activity and its

---

[174] *R (Gosport BC) v Fareham Magistrates' Court* (2007) 171 JP 102.

[175] *Brutus v Cozens* [1973] AC 854.

[176] See **6.52**.

[177] Ie more probable than not: *Chief Constable of Lancashire v Potter* [2003] EWHC 2272 (Admin), at [32].

[178] The provisions relating to special measures referred to in **14.25** et seq apply with modifications to applications in magistrates' courts for ASBOs as they apply in relation to criminal proceedings: CDA 1998, s 1I.

[179] [2003] EWHC 2272 (Admin).

[180] Ibid, at [41].

overall effect, has caused a "problem" which is caught by s 1(1)(a). Proof of such a fact need not depend on the attribution to her of proved "aggravated conduct" of other prostitutes that might, considered on its own, constitute harassment, alarm or distress.'

However, it added that:[181]

'... not all prostitution on the streets of a residential area falls foul of the Act, especially when the conduct relied upon by an applicant is that of a single prostitute or a small number of prostitutes or where, however few or many there are, there is no significant concentration of their activities in a particular area to mark it out as "red light district". It is all a matter of fact and degree.'

Section 1(1)(b)

10.121 In terms of the condition in CDA 1998, s 1(1)(b), persistent and serious anti-social behaviour on the part of the defendant is required before it can be necessary to make an ASBO to protect relevant persons from further anti-social acts by the defendant.[182]

10.122 *'Relevant persons'* in s 1(1)(b) means the following, by reference to the list in **10.116**. In relation to a relevant authority falling:

• within (a) it means persons within the local government area of that council;

• within (b) it means persons within the county of the county council;

• within (c) it means persons within the police area;

• within (d) it means persons who are within or likely to be within a place specified in the Railways and Transport Safety Act 2003, s 31(1)(a)–(f) in a local government area, or persons who are within or likely to be within the vicinity of[183] such a place; and

• within para (e) or (f) it means: persons who are residing in or are otherwise on or likely to be on premises provided or managed by that authority; or persons who are in the vicinity of or likely to be in the vicinity of such premises.[184]

The order

10.123 CDA 1998, s 1(4) provides that if it is proved that the conditions mentioned in s 1(1) above are fulfilled, the court may make an ASBO prohibiting the defendant from doing anything described in the order.[185] In *R (McCann) v Crown Court at Manchester*[186] the House of Lords held that condition in s 1(1)(a) (anti-social behaviour) must be proved beyond reasonable doubt, but that condition s 1(1)(b)

181 Ibid, at [46].
182 *Moat Housing Group South Ltd v Harris* [2005] 4 All ER 1051.
183 The words 'in the vicinity of' appear to have been accidentally omitted when the relevant provision was amended by SI 2004/1573, art 12.
184 CDA 1998, s 1(1B).
185 Where a court makes an ASBO in respect of an under-18-year-old it may also make an individual support order under CDA 1998, s 1AA, if the requirements of s 1AA are satisfied.
186 [2003] 1 AC 787.

(ASBO necessary) involves an exercise of judgment and evaluation and does not involve a standard of proof. In determining whether the conditions in s 1(1) are fulfilled the court can take into account hearsay evidence admissible under the Civil Evidence Act 1995.[187] It can also take into account evidence of bad character untrammelled by the conditions for doing so in criminal proceedings under CJA 2003, s 101.

10.124   No order should be made without notice to the other party unless there is very good reason for departing from this rule.[188]

10.125   The prohibitions that may be imposed by an ASBO are those necessary for the purpose of protecting persons (whether relevant persons or persons elsewhere in England and Wales) from further anti-social acts by the defendant.[189] The prohibitions ordered must be necessary, not too wide and sufficiently specific and clear.[190] If a prohibition is not, it can be struck out on an appeal or an application to vary. However, until it is struck down in one of these two ways, an ASBO containing a prohibition which is not necessary or is too wide or is not sufficiently specific or clear is not invalid.[191] If a prohibition lacks sufficient clarity it may be impossible to prove that it has been broken or provide a reasonable excuse for breach.

10.126   An ASBO has effect for a period (not less than 2 years)[192] specified in the order or until further order.

10.127   The applicant or the defendant may apply by complaint to the court which made an ASBO for it to be varied or discharged by a further order.[193] However, except with the consent of both parties, no ASBO shall be discharged before the end of the period of 2 years beginning with the date of service of the order.[194]

Breach of ASBO

10.128   If without reasonable excuse[195] a person does anything which he is prohibited from doing by an ASBO, he is guilty of an offence[196] and liable on conviction on indictment, to imprisonment for a term not exceeding 5 years or to a fine, or to both.[197] A conditional discharge may not be ordered.[198]

---

[187]   *R (McCann) v Crown Court at Manchester* [2003] 1 AC 787.
[188]   *Moat Housing Group South Ltd v Harris* [2005] 4 All ER 1051.
[189]   CDA 1998, s 1(6).
[190]   *B v Chief Constable of the Avon and Somerset Constabulary* [2001] 1 All ER 562, at p 573, per Lord Bingham CJ; *Boness* (2005) 169 JP 621.
[191]   *DPP v T* [2006] 3 All ER 471, not following *R(W) v DPP* (2005) 169 JP 435.
[192]   CDA 1998, s 1(7).
[193]   CDA 1998, s 1(8).
[194]   CDA 1998, s 1(9).
[195]   Where a breach of an ASBO is alleged, ignorance, forgetfulness or misunderstanding may be capable of constituting a reasonable excuse; accordingly, the issues of fact (and the value judgment as to reasonableness) are matters for the jury in the Crown Court: *Nicholson* [2006] 1 WLR 2857.
[196]   In proceedings for an offence under CDA 1998, s 1(10), a copy of the original ASBO, certified as such by the proper officer of the court which made it, is admissible as evidence of its having been made and of its contents to the same extent that oral evidence of those things is admissible in those proceedings: CDA 1998, s 1(10C). The following may bring proceedings for the offence: a council which is a relevant authority, the council for the local government area in which a person in respect of whom an ASBO has been made resides or appears to reside, and (where it was the applicant for the ASBO) Transport for London: CDA 1998, s 1(10A).
[197]   CDA 1998, s 1(10). For maximum on summary conviction, see **1.43**.
[198]   CDA 1998, s 1(11).

Class of offence	3	SOA 2003, s 72 applies	✗
Notification requirements	✗	SOPO	✗
CJA 2003, Sch 15 applies	✗	Serious specified offence	✗
Review of lenient sentence	✗	Special provisions of CYPA 1933	✗
Detention of young offender for specified period			✗

See **1.49**.

10.129 Where breaches of ASBOs do not involve harassment, alarm or distress, community penalties should be considered in order to help the offender learn to live within the terms of the order to which he or she was subject. Where there is no community penalty, custodial sentences which are necessary to maintain the authority of the court can be kept as short as possible.[199] Where a breach of an ASBO consists of the commission of an offence, the sentence passed should be calculated by reference to the 5-year maximum for breach of the order and not by reference to the statutory maximum for the offence.[200]

Related orders

Individual support orders

10.130 Where a court makes an ASBO in respect of a defendant who is under 18, it must consider whether the specified individual support conditions are fulfilled. If it is satisfied that those conditions are fulfilled, the court must make an order ('an individual support order' (ISO)):

- requiring the defendant to comply, for a period not exceeding 6 months, with such requirements as are specified in the order, for example, as to participation in activities or educational arrangements; and

- requiring the defendant to comply with any directions given by the responsible officer with a view to the implementation of such requirements.

The individual support conditions are:

(a) that an ISO would be desirable in the interests of preventing any repetition of the kind of behaviour which led to the making of the ASBO;

(b) that the defendant is not already subject to an ISO; and

(c) that arrangements for implementing ISOs are available in the relevant area.[201]

---

[199] *Lamb* [2006] Crim LR 256.
[200] *Braxton* [2005] 1 Cr App R (S) 167; *Tripp* [2005] EWCA Crim 2253; *Lamb*, ibid (not following *Morrison* [2005] EWCA Crim 2237, to the contrary). See also *Stevens* [2006] All ER (D) 23 (Feb).
[201] CDA 1998, s 1AA.

When amendments made by CJIA 2008, s 124 are in force, a court will also be able to make an ISO where it has previously made an ASBO in respect of a defendant under 18, provided that the application is made by the relevant authority which applied for the ASBO, that the ASBO is still in force and that the defendant is still under 18. On such an application the court must consider whether the above conditions are satisfied. If they are it must make an ISO. When CJIA 2008, s 124 is in force, (a) will be amended so as to read that an ISO would be desirable in the interests of preventing any repetition of the kind of behaviour which led to the making of the ASBO or an order varying that order (when the order results from further anti-social behaviour by the defendant).

Intervention orders

10.131   The provisions relating to intervention orders are designed to deal with the case where a person against whom an ASBO is made is a drug addict who needs help to prevent a repetition of the behaviour which led to the ASBO. If, in relation to a person who has attained 18, a relevant authority:

- makes an application for an ASBO;

- has obtained from an appropriately qualified person a report relating to the effect on the person's behaviour of the misuse of controlled drugs or of some other prescribed factor; and

- appropriate activities will be available,

the relevant authority may apply to the court which is considering the application for the ASBO for an intervention order.

10.132   If the court makes the ASBO, and is satisfied that the relevant conditions are met, it may also make an intervention order. The relevant conditions are:

- that an intervention order is desirable in the interests of preventing a repetition of the behaviour which led to the behaviour order being made ('trigger behaviour');

- that appropriate activities relating to the trigger behaviour or its cause are available for the defendant;

- that the defendant is not subject to another intervention order or to any other treatment relating to the trigger behaviour or its cause; and

- that arrangements for implementing intervention orders are available.

10.133   An intervention order:

- requires the defendant to comply, for a period not exceeding 6 months, with such requirements as are specified in the order; and

- requires the defendant to comply with any directions given by a person authorised to do so under the order.

An intervention order or directions given under the order may require the defendant:

- to participate in the activities specified in the requirement or directions at a time or times so specified; and

- to present him- or herself to a person or persons so specified at a time or times so specified.[202]

Public nuisance injunctions

10.134 Local authorities can make use of their power under the Local Government Act 1972, s 222(1) to bring legal proceedings for the protection of the interests of local inhabitants by applying for injunctions to restrain anti-social behaviour associated with offences under StOffA 1959 and SOA 1985 that constitutes a public nuisance.[203] Such an injunction can prohibit the individual enjoined from entering the area where the nuisance has been committed for a period specified by it or until it is varied or discharged and may also contain other prohibitions (eg not to solicit or loiter for prostitution) designed to restrain the type of anti-social behaviour which has caused the public nuisance during the period of the injunction. Birmingham City Council has taken the lead in using public nuisance injunctions (PNIs) against street prostitutes. Breach of a PNI is punishable (as a civil contempt of court[204]) by imprisonment for a maximum of 2 years and/or an unlimited fine,[205] although persons who are committed to prison will be released from prison before they otherwise would if they successfully purge their contempt by apologising for the contempt, acknowledging the need for punishment for it, demonstrating remorse and contrition and undertaking to obey the PNI in the future.[206] The civil rules of evidence apply to an application for a PNI. The standard of proof to obtain a PNI appears to be the civil standard (on the balance of probabilities[207]) and hearsay evidence and evidence of bad character may be adduced in accordance with the civil rules of evidence. The lower standard of proof than is required for securing a conviction for a street offence or an ASBO (and the more liberal rules about hearsay evidence and bad character evidence than apply for a prosecution) mean that a PNI may be easier to obtain in circumvention of the safeguards of the criminal law. This is a matter open to criticism.[208]

---

[202] CDA 1998, s 1G.

[203] A public nuisance is an act not warranted by law, or an omission to discharge a legal duty, whose effect is to endanger the life, health, property or comfort of the public, or the obstruction of the public in the exercise or enjoyment of rights common to all members of the public: *Rimmington; Goldstein* [2006] 1 AC 459.

[204] The contempt of court must be proved beyond reasonable doubt: *Re Bramblevale Ltd* [1969] 3 All ER 1062.

[205] Contempt of Court Act 1981, s 14(1).

[206] Ibid; *Vowles v Young* (1803) 9 Ves 172; *Anon* (1808) 15 Ves 174; *Wilson v Bates* (1838) 3 My & Cr 197 at 201; www.respect.gov.uk/members/article.aspx?id=7938.

[207] The civil standard of proof is proof on the balance of probabilities. It has sometimes been said that the more serious the allegation, the higher will be the required degree of proof: but the House of Lords has confirmed in *R(D) v Life Sentences Review Commissioners for Northern Ireland* [2008] UKHL 33 that the civil standard of proof never varies. There can be only one 'balance of probabilities' test. What may vary is the quality or quantity of evidence required to satisfy the court that a given fact is likely to be true. A particularly serious or shocking allegation may require cogent evidence before a court would be prepared to believe it, even on a balance of probabilities, but this is because such an allegation may simply be harder to believe. See also *Re B (Children)* [2008] UKHL 35.

There can be exceptions, as in relation to an application for an ASBO where it has been held that the criminal standard of proof applies: see **10.123**.

[208] See Sagar 'Public Nuisance Injunctions Against On-Street Sex Workers?' [2008] Crim LR 353.

Acceptable behaviour contracts

10.135 Voluntary acceptable behaviour contracts can also be used to prohibit anti-social behaviour associated with offences under StOffA 1959 and SOA 1985. They are cheap and can be effective.

ASBOs on conviction

10.136 These are governed by CDA 1998, s 1C. Where a person ('the offender') is convicted of an offence and the court by or before which he or she is convicted, or the Crown Court on committal for sentence, considers that:

- the offender has acted, since 1 April 1999, in an anti-social manner, ie in a manner that caused or was likely to cause harassment, alarm or distress to one or more persons not of the same household as the offender; and

- an ASBO is necessary to protect persons in any place in England and Wales from further anti-social acts by the offender,

it may make an order which prohibits the offender from doing anything described in the order.[209]

10.137 The court may make such an order if the prosecutor asks it to do so or of its own initiative.[210] Such an order may not be made except:

- in addition to a sentence imposed in respect of the relevant offence; or

- in addition to an order discharging the offender conditionally.[211]

10.138 Proceedings under CDA 1998, s 1C are civil in nature, so that hearsay evidence is admissible; but a court must be satisfied to the criminal standard that the offender has acted in the anti-social manner alleged.[212]

Interim ASBOs

10.139 On an application for an ASBO (including a prosecution application under CDA 1998, s 1C) or if the court is minded to make an ASBO under s 1C, the court may make an interim ASBO.[213]

Binding over

10.140 A person who comes before a magistrates' court, by whatever route, may be the subject of a binding-over order.[214] Thus, such an order can be made against someone

---

[209] CDA 1998, s 1C(1), (2). When an amendment made by CJIA 2008, s 124 is in force, a court making an ASBO under CDA 1998, s 1C will be able to make an ISO (see **10.130**) if the individual support conditions are satisfied.

[210] CDA 1998, s 1C(3).

[211] CDA 1998, s 1C(4).

[212] *W* [2006] 3 All ER 562, at [35]–[37] and [41]. See also *R (W) v Acton Youth Court* (2005) 170 JPN 316.

[213] CDA 1998, s 1D.

[214] The power to bind over is not limited to magistrates' courts, since courts of record with a criminal jurisdiction (eg the Crown Court) have the power to make binding-over orders of their own motion

who has been arrested for an offence or for a breach of the peace or against a person who has been summoned or requisitioned after the laying of an information or written charge or the making of a complaint. However, as will be seen, a binding over will rarely be made to deal with the activities of street prostitutes and punters.

10.141   Binding over can be done either:

- on a complaint under MCA 1980, s 115; or

- by a court acting of its own motion under the power vested in magistrates under the common law and under the Justices of the Peace Act (JPA) 1361 to bind over someone already before the court.

A binding-over order requires that a person should enter into a recognisance with or without a surety or sureties for a period on pain of forfeiture of the specified sum(s) if he fails to comply with the order. A recognisance is an undertaking whereby a person binds himself to pay a specified penalty if he breaks the terms of the binding-over order.

10.142   The powers to bind over are exercisable 'not by reason of any offence having been committed, but as a measure of preventive justice';[215] indeed, they do not depend on the actual or suspected commission of an offence.[216] Binding over is not a punishment, although where a court acts under its powers to bind over of its own motion, binding over may be used as a sentencing option against a convicted offender in addition to a penalty, such as a fine, or as a sole order.

10.143   The powers to bind over are anomalous and uncertain in definition. Their application is wide-ranging. They have been used, for example, not only to retrain political demonstrators from engaging in or repeating violence, but also to restrain the conduct of prostitutes and kerb-crawling motorists looking for them, and to restrain various types of disorderly conduct or indecent behaviour in public,[217] but as said below the power is more limited than it was.

10.144   Formerly, there was power to bind over a person whose behaviour did not amount to a breach of the peace or involve an imminent breach, but was found to be *contra bonos mores*. Indeed, the statutes under which binding-over orders are made still provide that the court may bind a person over to keep the peace or to be of good behaviour. However, as a result of the decision of the European Court of Human Rights in *Hashman and Harrup v UK*,[218] orders are no longer to be made in these terms. The explanation is as follows.

10.145   The leading English case on binding over to be of 'good behaviour' is *Hughes v Holley*,[219] decided before the commencement of SOA 1985, where the Divisional Court

---

215   (Blackstone 4 *Commentaries* 251–255; *Percy v DPP* [1995] 3 All ER 124, at p 129), and judges of the High Court and Court of Appeal as justices of the peace can exercise the personal binding-over powers of justices. *Veater v G* [1981] 2 All ER 304, at p 307, per Lord Lane CJ. The powers to bind over to come up for judgment and to bind over a parent or guardian to take proper care of a child or young person are outside the scope of this book.

216   See, for example, *Hughes v Holley* (1988) 86 Cr App R 130, at p 138, per Glidewell LJ; *Nicol v DPP* (1995) 160 JP 155 (both cases under MCA 1980, s 115).

217   Various examples are given in *Binding Over: The Issues*: Law Com Consultation Paper No 103 (1987), at para 5.2.

218   (2000) 30 EHRR 241.

219   (1988) 86 Cr App R 130.

held that such an order could be made where it was proved that the defendant had acted contra bonos mores and there was a real risk that he or she might repeat that conduct. It defined conduct contra bonos mores as conduct 'contrary to the good way of life' and added:[220]

> 'What is a good way of life is for the magistrates to decide ... contra bonos mores is conduct which has the property of being wrong rather than right in the judgment of the vast majority of contemporary fellow citizens.'

The facts of the case were that a kerb-crawler had solicited for the purposes of prostitution a plain clothes policewoman in a red light area. On a complaint under the JPA 1361 the magistrates bound him over to be of good behaviour for 12 months. It was argued before the Divisional Court that, since the kerb-crawler's conduct did not constitute an offence at the material time, his conduct could not be contra bonos mores. The court dismissed the appeal; the magistrates had been justified in concluding that there was material on which they could properly exercise their power to bind over.

10.146 In *Hashman and Harrup v UK* the European Court of Human Rights held that the power to bind over to be of good behaviour was insufficiently defined to satisfy the 'quality of law' standard, ie insufficiently precisely defined to enable the person concerned to foresee to a degree reasonable in the circumstances what would be likely to breach the order. In this case, H1 and H2, two hunt saboteurs, had respectively blown a horn and shouted at hounds. They were bound over to keep the peace and be of good behaviour after it had been found that, although no breach of the peace had been proved, their behaviour had been contra bonos mores.

10.147 With one dissentient, the European Court of Human Rights held that the binding-over orders constituted a violation of ECHR, Art 10 (freedom of expression) because behaviour contra bonos mores was so broad – indeed it was not described at all – that it did not comply with the requirement in Art 10(2) that any interference with freedom of expression must be 'prescribed by law' (ie satisfy the 'quality of law' standard). The court did not accept that it must have been evident to H1 and H2 what they were being ordered not to do for the period of their binding over.

10.148 It follows that, although a bind over to be of good behaviour remains available under the statutes, a court would be acting incompatibly with ECHR rights if it made such an order and the order would be liable to be quashed.

10.149 Pre-*Hashman and Harrup* case-law is to the effect that it is not possible to include specific conditions in a binding-over order to keep the peace or to be of good behaviour.[221] Thus, the appellate courts have declared invalid conditions directing the person bound to keep away from a specified nightclub for 12 months,[222] or forbidding the person bound over to teach or try to teach anyone under 18 for 3 years.[223] Following *Hashman and Harrup*, however, the courts have adopted the informal approach of

---

[220] Ibid, at p 139.
[221] *Ayu* [1958] 3 All ER 636; *Goodlad v Chief Constable of South Yorkshire* [1979] Crim LR 51; *Randall* (1986) 8 Cr App R (S) 433.
[222] *Lister v Morgan* [1978] Crim LR 292.
[223] *Randall*, n 221 above.

making binding-over orders which are specifically worded.[224] Such an approach was recommended in a Home Office consultation paper in 2003:[225]

> 'It is recommended that: Courts should not specify "to keep the peace" or "to be of good behaviour" rather that the individual is bound over to do or refrain from doing specific activities ... This recommendation allows the various statutes to be interpreted as defining the nature of the obligation to be imposed in general terms whilst allowing the court to specify the conduct required providing it comes within the general nature of keeping the peace or good behaviour.'

This approach permitted a binding-over order to be against a street prostitute or kerb-crawler provided the order specified with sufficient certainty what it required.

10.150 In 2007, however, the *Consolidated Criminal Practice Direction*[226] was amended to more limited effect so as to give practical guidance on the practice of imposing binding-over orders. As amended, the *Direction* provides:

> 'III.31.2 Before imposing a binding over order, the court must be satisfied that a breach of the peace involving violence or an imminent threat of violence has occurred or that there is a real risk of violence in the future. Such violence may be perpetrated by the individual who will be subject to the order or by a third party as a natural consequence of the individual's conduct.
>
> III.31.3 In light of the judgment in *Hashman and Harrup*, courts should no longer bind an individual over "to be of good behaviour". Rather than binding an individual over to "keep the peace" in general terms, the court should identify the specific conduct or activity from which the individual must refrain.'

As a result, a binding-over order will rarely be made in respect of the conduct of a prostitute, loitering or soliciting for the purpose of prostitution or kerb crawling or persistent solicitation for such purpose by would-be punters. It will be an exceptional case where such conduct satisfies Practice Direction III.31.2.

OFF-STREET PROSTITUTION

10.151 The following offences under SOA 1956, ss 33–36, are considered under this heading:

- keeping a brothel;

- keeping a brothel used for prostitution;

- lessor or landlord letting premises for use as a brothel;

- tenant or occupier permitting premises to be used as a brothel; and

---

[224] See *Bind Overs: A Power for the 21st Century* (Home Office, 2003), at para 7.3.7. See also Bulletin (CPS) *06/2000 – Bind Overs and the European Convention on Human Rights* (1999).

[225] *Bind Overs: A Power for the 21st Century*, at paras 7.3.3 and 7.3.4.

[226] The *Consolidated Criminal Practice Direction* is a consolidation, with amendments, of existing Practice Directions, Practice Statements and Practice Notes as they affect proceedings in the Court of Appeal (Criminal Division), the Crown Court and the magistrates' courts. It can be found at: www.justice.gov.uk/criminal/procrules_fin/contents/practice_direction/pd_consolidated.htm.

- tenant or occupier permitting premises to be used for prostitution.

Also considered are the statutory offences of:

- allowing a person under 16 to be in a brothel; and

- knowingly permitting prostitutes to meet and remain in a refreshment house,

and the common law offences of:

- keeping a disorderly house; and

- keeping a bawdy house.

OFF-STREET PROSTITUTION: OFFENCES RELATING TO BROTHELS

Keeping a brothel

10.152   SOA 1956, s 33, provides that:

> 'It is an offence for a person to keep a brothel, or to manage, or act or assist in the management of, a brothel.'

An offence under s 33 is triable summarily only and punishable as follows:

- in the case of an offence committed after a previous conviction for an offence under SOA 1956, ss 33, 34, 35 or s 36, a maximum term of imprisonment of 6 months,[227] or a fine not exceeding level 4 on the standard scale, or both;

- otherwise, a maximum of 3 months' imprisonment, or a fine not exceeding level 3 on the standard scale, or both.[228]

Class of offence	n/a	SOA 2003, s 72 applies	✗
Notification requirements	✗	SOPO	✗
CJA 2003, Sch 15 applies	✔[229]	Serious specified offence	✗
Review of lenient sentence	✗	Special provisions of CYPA 1933	✗
Detention of young offender for specified period			✗

---

[227]   SOA 1956, s 37(1), (2), Sch 2, para 33. As from a day to be appointed this maximum term of imprisonment is increased to a maximum term of 51 weeks (see CJA 2003, s 281(4), (5), (7) (not yet in force)), although this does not affect the penalty for any offence committed before that day (s 281(6)(b) (not yet in force)). At the date at which this book states the law no such day had been appointed.

[228]   SOA 1956, s 37(1), (3), Sch 2, para 33.

[229]   The listing of an offence under s 33 in CJA 2003, Sch 15 would seem to be by mistake for the either-way offence under SOA 1956, s 33A which is not so listed. As for CJA 2003, Sch 15, see **1.52**.

10.153   An offence under SOA 1956, s 33 is a 'lifestyle offence': see **10.42**. It is a continuing offence, and therefore an information or written charge is not bad for duplicity where it charges the offence as being committed between specified dates[230] or on specified dates which were not consecutive.[231] The structure of s 33 suggests that it contains three offences – keeping a brothel, managing a brothel and acting or assisting in the management of a brothel.[232]

10.154   Section 33 is important where the brothel is one where people go to engage in sexual activity without payment for it, or it cannot be proved that payment is made. Where it can be proved that payment is made, the more serious offence of keeping a brothel used for prostitution under SOA 1956, s 33A applies to those whose conduct falls within s 33. As to what constitutes a brothel, see **10.187** et seq.

10.155   Keeping a brothel also constitutes the common law offence of keeping a bawdy house and may, depending on the circumstances, amount to keeping a disorderly house.[233]

Keeping a brothel

10.156   There appears to be no authority in English law on the meaning of keeping a brothel, but there is persuasive authority from New Zealand that 'keeping' involves having 'conduct of the business conducted therein'[234] or 'control or a share of control over the brothel'.[235] Analogy with the case-law on the offences of keeping a disorderly house and keeping a bawdy house indicates that 'keeping' does not require that the defendant is an owner or tenant of the premises but that he or she must have control over them and be involved in their use as a brothel.[236]

Managing a brothel

10.157   In *Jones and Wood v DPP*[237] the Divisional Court approved the following suggestion by Judge Chapman in *Abbott v Smith*:[238]

> 'What is required, in my view, is some sort of evidence indicating the taking of an active part in the running of the business as a business, something suggesting control … I do not say that only a person in the position of a director, or a representative or agent of a director can be a manager, but there must, as I see it, be something "a cut above" purely menial or routine duties, such as cleaning the stairs or answering the door.'

In *Abbott v Smith*, D lived with her children, including her 16-year-old daughter, C, in one room in a house which was used as a home by another family and also (through the activities of prostitutes there) as a brothel (as explained later). D was convicted of managing a brothel and C of assisting in its management. On appeal to the Crown Court at Liverpool, Judge Chapman allowed their appeals. D did not collect rents and

---

[230]   *Anderton v Cooper* (1981) 72 Cr App R 232 (13 February to 15 March of the same year).
[231]   *Ex parte Burnby* [1901] 2 KB 458 (26, 28, 29 and 31 January and 1, 4, 5 and 6 March of same year: offence under Licensing Act (LA) 1872, s 15, precursor to SOA 1956, s 34).
[232]   See **3.182**, n 284.
[233]   See **10.224** et seq.
[234]   *Mickle* [1978] 1 NZLR 720, at p 723.
[235]   *Barrie* [1978] 2 NZLR 78, at p 81. Both these cases are cited in *Rook & Ward*, at p 324.
[236]   See **10.228**.
[237]   (1993) 96 Cr App R 130 at 132.
[238]   [1965] 2 QB 662, at pp 665–666.

received no payment from the landlord or a rake-off from the tenants. There was, however, evidence that on one occasion, when one of the prostitutes arrived after midnight, unaccompanied, and called D's name, D opened the front door. Not long after, when two women, not known to be prostitutes, came to the premises with two men, one of the women shouted D's name; it was not known who opened the door. C was associating on terms of intimacy with two of the prostitutes who lived in the house and with two who resorted to it. Judge Chapman concluded that there was no evidence from which it could reasonably be inferred that D was at the material time managing a brothel (or that C was assisting in its management). There was in reality no evidence of activities, menial or otherwise, in connection with the brothel as a brothel, but – said Judge Chapman – even if D or C could be said to be concerned with the brothel as a brothel it was far short of taking any part in the management.

Acting or assisting in the management of a brothel

10.158 It is not a necessary condition for the offence of assisting in the management of a brothel that the defendant had actually exercised some control over the brothel or carried out some specific act of management. This was held in *Jones and Wood v DPP*,[239] where the Divisional Court upheld the conviction for 'assisting in the management of a brothel' of J and W who lived with a male prostitute who operated a brothel at another address. J and W were aware of this and had assisted the male prostitute by taking numerous advertisements of the services of the male prostitute and a female prostitute who 'traded' at the brothel to local newsagent shops and arranging for them to be displayed, in J's case paying for them with his own money. J and W had both frequently driven the male prostitute to the brothel and on shopping and other trips. Both had visited the premises frequently and carried out numerous odd jobs there, often when customers were on the premises. In addition to these findings of fact, the Crown Court (from which the appeal had come) had inferred that J and W were at all times ready, willing and able to assist the male prostitute in any way that was necessary (short of actually providing sexual services themselves) in the successful operation of the brothel and that their roles were not limited to 'menial' or 'routine' duties. The Crown Court was satisfied that this was a joint enterprise between all three men. The Divisional Court rejected an argument that J and W were not guilty of assisting in the management of the brothel because the facts found by the Crown Court did not amount to exercise of any control over the business by J and W Beldam LJ, with whom Laws J agreed, stated:[240]

> 'The submission put forward is that the facts found by the Crown Court do not amount to the exercising of any control over the business by the two defendants but ... that is a requirement of managing the business. They were charged with giving help to a person who was running the business as a business and who was the person exercising some control over it. It is difficult to imagine an activity more helpful to a person managing a brothel than taking his advertisements to the local newsagents, arranging their insertion in shop windows, and paying for them.

> In my judgment, it is not a necessary condition of the offence of assisting in the management that the person has to exercise some sort of control over the management. That is the requirement of managing. Equally it seems to me it is not necessary to show that there was a specific act of management for that would be acting in the management. Assisting is a wider concept. No doubt not every one who carries out some menial task at a brothel, like cleaning

---

[239] (1993) 96 Cr App R 130.
[240] Ibid, at p 132.

the stairs as a daily woman, would be said to be assisting in the management but that was not this case. In my judgment, it was a question of fact for the Crown Court. There was sufficient substance in the acts which they found proved to support the holding that the appellants were, "assisting in the management of a brothel".'

10.159 Merely to act as a prostitute at a brothel does not constitute acting or assisting in the management of a brothel unless there is something more which helps a person in the management of the brothel (in which case there will be an assisting). An example is provided by *Elliott v DPP*,[241] where women working in two 'massage parlours' discussed the nature of the sexual services provided by them and negotiated the price for them. It was held that they were assisting in the management of a brothel, even though there had been a receptionist at the premises. The Divisional Court stated that this conduct went considerably further than menial tasks, such as cleaning the premises and removing the rubbish, which could be done without participating in the management. Likewise, in *DPP v Curley and Farrelly*,[242] the Divisional Court held that a prostitute who kept an appointment system for the brothel, answered the telephone, decided to a large extent the prices of the services, paid the rent and opened and locked the premises assisted in the management of the brothel.

10.160 A borderline case is *Gorman v Standen*,[243] where two women, a stepmother (C) and a stepdaughter (G), were charged respectively with keeping a brothel and assisting in the management. C was the tenant of the premises where she lived with G and a daughter of 15. During an 8-day period at least 19 different men resorted to the premises in company with either C or G or both. When police raided the premises at the end of the period they found C naked in bed with one man and G, also naked, in bed with another. When G was subsequently shown a statement by C, G said 'It's my fault – she is frightened of me. If I told her to go upstairs and sleep with a man she would do it'. The Divisional Court upheld C and G's convictions. In relation to G, Lord Parker CJ, with whom the other two judges simply agreed, said:[244]

> 'The mere fact that a woman participates in the activities being conduced in the brothel does not make her a person assisting in the management of a brothel. "Assisting in the management of a brothel" seems to me to contemplate in the ordinary way the case of a man who runs a brothel not living there himself; he keeps and manages it but he has on the premises a woman who assists in the management ... But where, as here, the two women are living together in the same premises in the relationship of stepmother and stepdaughter and where, as the evidence shows, albeit it is thin, that it is the stepdaughter who has a part, at any rate, of the say of what goes on at that house, then, as it seems to me, it is possible to find that she was assisting in the management.'

Mens rea

10.161 It is submitted that there is nothing to rebut the presumption[245] that an offence is not committed under SOA 1956, s 33 unless it is proved that the defendant had mens rea (ie knowledge)[246] as to the facts constituting the premises in question a brothel.

---

[241] (1989) *The Times*, January 19.
[242] [1991] COD 186.
[243] [1964] 1 QB 294.
[244] Ibid, at p 303.
[245] See, for example, *B v DPP* [2000] 2 AC 428; *K* [2002] 1 AC 462.
[246] See **2.61** et seq.

Keeping a brothel used for prostitution

10.162   SOA 1956, s 33A(1), inserted by SOA 2003, provides:

> 'It is an offence for a person to keep, or to manage, or act or assist in the management of, a
> brothel to which people resort for practices involving prostitution (whether or not also for
> other practices).'

This offence is triable either way[247] and punishable on conviction on indictment with a
maximum of 7 years' imprisonment.[248] For the SGC Definitive Guideline,[249] see the
Appendix.

Class of offence	3	SOA 2003, s 72 applies	✗
Notification requirements	✗	SOPO	✗
CJA 2003, Sch 15 applies	✗	Serious specified offence	✗
Review of lenient sentence	✗	Special provisions of CYPA 1933	✗
Detention of young offender for specified period			✗

See **1.49**.

10.163   The fact that an offence under s 33A is, unlike the related summary offence
under s 33, not listed as a 'specified offence' in CJA 2003, Sch 15 or as a 'lifestyle
offence' in PCA 2002, Sch 2, may be due to legislative oversight. An offence under s 33A
is a serious offence for the purposes of making a serious crime prevention order under
SCA 2007, Pt 1.[250] The structure of s 33A suggests that it contains three offences –
keeping a brothel, managing a brothel and acting or assisting in the management of a
brothel.[251]

10.164   The elements of the offences under s 33A are identical to those for the offence
under s 33 except that an offence under s 33A is limited to brothels to which people
resort for practices involving prostitution (whether or not also for other practices, such
as gambling or drinking). For the purposes of s 33A, 'prostitution' has the meaning
given by SOA 2003, s 51(2).[252] The meaning of 'brothel' is dealt with in **10.187** et seq.
Otherwise, the common elements of both offences have already been explained.

10.165   SOA 1956, s 33A was added to reflect an awareness that the element of
'control' required for an offence under SOA 2003, s 52 or s 53 may not easily be proved
where someone deriving income from a brothel, or multiple brothels, may have
distanced himself from the day-to-day running of the premises. The alternative, of
retaining the offence of living on the earnings of female prostitution contrary to SOA
1956, s 30 (repealed by SOA 2003), would – even if made gender neutral – have
continued to cover quite innocent third parties who knowingly lived off the earnings of

---

247   SOA 1956, s 37(1), (2), Sch 2, para 33A.
248   SOA 1956, s 37(1), (3), Sch 2, para 33A. For maximum on summary conviction, see **1.43**.
249   At pp 5–18, 128–129.
250   SCA 2007, s 2(2)(a), Sch 1, Pt 1, para 4(1).
251   See **3.182**, n 284.
252   SOA 1956, s 33A(2). See **10.35**.

prostitution (eg a long-term partner of a prostitute supported by her earnings or the student who receives maintenance from his prostitute-mother).[253]

Lessor or landlord letting premises for use as a brothel

10.166   SOA 1956, s 34 provides:

> 'It is an offence for the lessor or landlord of any premises or his agent to let the whole or part of the premises with the knowledge that it is to be used, in whole or in part, as a brothel, or, where the whole or part of the premises is used as a brothel, to be wilfully a party to that use continuing.'

The offence is triable summarily[254] only and punishable as follows:

- in the case of an offence committed after a previous conviction for an offence under SOA 1956, s 33, 34, 35 or s 36, a maximum term of imprisonment of 6 months,[255] or a fine not exceeding level 4 on the standard scale, or both;

- otherwise, a maximum of 3 months' imprisonment, or a fine not exceeding level 3 on the standard scale, or both.[256]

There are two offences under s 34: letting premises knowing that they are to be used as a brothel, and being wilfully a party to the continuing use of leased premises as a brothel.[257]

Class of offence	n/a	SOA 2003, s 72 applies	✗
Notification requirements	✗	SOPO	✗
CJA 2003, Sch 15 applies	✗	Serious specified offence	✗
Review of lenient sentence	✗	Special provisions of CYPA 1933	✗
Detention of young offender for specified period			✗

10.167   An offence under s 34 is a 'lifestyle offence': see **10.42**.

10.168   The meaning of 'brothel' is explained in **10.187**.

Lessor or landlord or his agent

10.169   'Lessor' or 'landlord' seem to bear their normal legal meaning. An example of a case where a person could be convicted of the first offence under SOA 1956, s 34 on the basis of acting as agent of a lessor would be where he acts as a negotiator employed

---

253   Baroness Scotland of Asthal, HL Deb, vol 654, col 1638.
254   SOA 1956, s 37(1), (2), Sch 2, para 34.
255   As from a day to be appointed this maximum term of imprisonment is increased to a maximum term of 51 weeks (see CJA 2003, s 281(4), (5), (7) (not yet in force)), although this does not affect the penalty for any offence committed before that day (s 281(6)(b) (not yet in force)). At the date at which this book states the law no such day had been appointed.
256   SOA 1956, s 37(1), (3), Sch 2, para 34.
257   *Donovan v Gavin* [1965] 2 QB 648, at p 657, per Sachs J.

by a firm of estate agents instructed to act for the lessor in letting the premises. An example of a person who was convicted, as agent, of the second offence under the predecessor to s 34 is the porter in *Durose v Wilson*, referred to in **10.208**.

Letting whole or part of premises with knowledge that it is to be used wholly or partly as a brothel

10.170 These words require no explanation, save to say that the meaning of 'knowledge' is dealt with in **2.62**.

Wilfully being a party to continuing use as a brothel

10.171 There is no direct authority on the meaning of this requirement. In *Durose v Wilson* the defendant porter's conduct involved a positive act of participation in the continuing use of the premises as a brothel. On the other hand, in *Donovan v Gavin*,[258] referred to in **10.202**, the defendant lessor merely acquiesced in such continuing use by his prostitute tenants. In neither case, however, was the element of 'wilfully being a party' the subject of the appeal or discussed by the Divisional Court. Whilst a positive act of participation in the continuing use of the premises as a brothel undoubtedly suffices, it is less clear that mere negative acquiescence, for example, simply standing by without objecting to a breach of a covenant against immoral use, does. *Stone's Justices' Manual*[259] takes the view that it does not, referring to *Bell v Alfred Franks & Bartlett Co Ltd*,[260] where it was held that mere acquiescence in a breach of covenant did not amount to a 'consent' to it for the purposes of the Landlord and Tenant Act 1954, s 23(4). Support can be derived also from *Re Maidstone Building Provisions Ltd*,[261] where Pennycuick V-C held that in order to be a party to the carrying on of the business of a company in a fraudulent manner contrary to the Companies Act 1948, s 332 (repealed), a person must have taken some positive steps; mere inertia was not enough (so that the failure of a company secretary and financial adviser to advise the directors that the company was insolvent and should not trade did not constitute being a party to the carrying on of the business of the company).[262] On the other hand, analogy with the law relating to complicity in crime, whereby if D has a right of control over E and deliberately fails to take an opportunity to prevent E committing an offence, and knows that this is capable of assisting or encouraging the commission of the principal offence,[263] D can be convicted as a party to that offence, suggests that a person who has a right of control over premises used as a brothel is a party to their continuing use. *Rook & Ward*[264] consider that the better view is probably that expressed in *Stone's*. There is much, however, to be said in favour of the second view.

10.172 Modern case-law indicates that 'wilfully' almost certainly requires proof that the defendant was at least reckless as to the continuing use as a brothel.[265]

---

[258] [1965] 2 QB 648.
[259] 2008 edn, at para 8-28010.
[260] [1980] 1 All ER 356.
[261] [1971] 3 All ER 363.
[262] Also see *Miles* [1992] Crim LR 657 (misdirection to direct jury in respect of offence of fraudulent trading, contrary to Companies Act 1985, s 458, that 'concurring in the trade involved in the business of the company' could constitute 'being a party to the carrying on of the business of the company').
[263] *Tuck v Robson* [1970] 1 All ER 1171; *Cassady v Reg Morris (Transport) Ltd* [1975] RTR 470; *J F Alford Transport Ltd* [1997] 2 Cr App R 326.
[264] At p 334.
[265] *Sheppard* [1981] AC 394; *A-G's Reference (No 3 of 2003)* [2004] 2 Cr App R 366. See Card, Cross and Jones *Criminal Law* (OUP, 18th edn, 2008), at para 6.29.

Tenant or occupier permitting premises to be used as brothel

10.173 SOA 1956, s 35(1) provides:

'It is an offence for the tenant or occupier, or person in charge, of any premises knowingly to permit the whole or part of the premises to be used as a brothel.'

The offence is triable summarily.[266] The provisions relating to maximum punishment[267] are identical to those relating to SOA 1956, s 34: see **10.166**.

10.174 For the meaning of 'knowledge' and 'brothel' see **2.62** and **10.187** respectively.

Permit

10.175 'Permit' has been held by the House of Lords in *Vehicle Inspectorate v Nuttall*[268] to be capable of having at least two types of meaning, a narrow meaning, 'allow', 'agree to' or 'authorise', and a wider one 'fail to take reasonable steps to prevent', its meaning in any particular offence depending on its context. No guidance was given as to how a court is to approach the question of context. A similar approach to the wider meaning in *Nuttall* was taken by the Court of Appeal in *Brock and Wyner*,[269] to the effect that 'permit' requires proof of unwillingness to prevent the prohibited activity in question which could be inferred from failure to take reasonable steps readily available to prevent it. 'Reasonable steps' in this context, the Court of Appeal held, are to be judged in the light of the defendant's level of knowledge of the prohibited activity, but the fact that the defendant believed he or she had taken reasonable steps was irrelevant. *Brock v Wyner* was concerned with the offence of knowingly permitting specified drug activities on premises, contrary to the Misuse of Drugs Act (MDA) 1971, s 8.

10.176 The similarity between the nature of offences under SOA 1956, s 35 and under MDA 1971, s 8 suggests that the wider approach in *Nuttall* and *Brock and Wyner* is applicable to s 35.

Tenant or occupier

10.177 SOA 1956 does not define these terms. It would seem that 'tenant' means a tenant in occupation and does not cover a landlord who is him- or herself a lessee of the premises on which his or her sub-lessee/tenant runs a brothel. On this basis, a tenant who sublets the whole of the premises used as a brothel cannot be convicted of an offence under s 35, although he could be liable under s 34.[270] On the other hand, if he simply gave a licence in respect of the premises used as a brothel by the licensee, retaining exclusive possession, he could be convicted under s 35 if he permitted such use.

10.178 The fact that 'the occupier' is expressed in the alternative to 'the tenant' suggests that 'the occupier' bears the same meaning as has been given in *Tao*[271] and subsequent cases in respect of the offence of being the occupier of premises permitting

---

[266] SOA 1956, s 37(1), (2), Sch 2, para 35.
[267] SOA 1956, s 37(1), (3), Sch 2, para 35.
[268] [1999] 3 All ER 833.
[269] [2001] 1 WLR 1159.
[270] See **10.215**.
[271] [1977] QB 141.

specified drug-related activities there, contrary to MDA 1971, s 8. In *Tao* the Court of Appeal held that 'the occupier' is not limited to a person who is a tenant or has some other legal estate in the premises; it includes anyone who has the requisite degree of control over the premises to exclude from them persons who might otherwise use them for the purposes forbidden by s 8. Thus, a student who had a study bedroom in a college hostel was held in *Tao* to be the occupier of it because his contractual licence gave him such exclusivity of possession, whether or not he was entitled to exclude the college authorities. The Court of Appeal indicated that it followed from the test of exclusive possession that someone who took a room in a hotel or a cabin on a ship is 'the occupier', and that so is a squatter who unlawfully entered and was in unlawful occupation of a house or part of it.

10.179   The fact that 'the occupier' in MDA 1971, s 8 is not to be given a legalistic definition was confirmed in *Read v DPP*,[272] where the Divisional Court rejected a submission that, in order to be 'the occupier', a person had to have the legal right to exclude others. In *Read v DPP*, D was the cohabitee of his girlfriend in whose name the tenancy of a council house was; he had no proprietary interest in the property. The court held that D was the occupier for the purposes of s 8 since he had possession so as to enable him to exclude those who wished to smoke cannabis there (one of the specified purposes under s 8). A similar approach was followed by the Court of Appeal in *Coid*,[273] which also shows that a person can intermittently be an occupier. In that case D lived for most of the time with his girlfriend in her house, of which she was the tenant, and was living there at the material time, although sometimes he lived with his sister because of the volatility of his relationship with his girlfriend. Rejecting D's claim that the trial judge had misdirected the jury, the court held that the fact that one person could be identified as an occupier, even as a tenant or holder of a legal title, did not preclude another person also being 'the occupier'. There could be more than one occupier and at different times the same person could be an occupier and then cease to be an occupier.

10.180   Reference may also be made to *Mogford*,[274] decided before *Tao*, where Nield J ruled at trial that two sisters, aged 20 and 17, who lived at their parents' house and who permitted cannabis to be smoked there, contrary to the precursor to MDA 1971, s 8, in their parents' absence on holiday were not occupiers. In *Tao* the Court of Appeal approved this ruling, but not its reasoning (which was based on the absence of legal possession by the sisters). Presumably, the court considered or assumed that the girls did not have sufficient control to be occupiers. Nield J had stated that mere power to invite guests to the house did not amount to control of the nature and degree required to be the occupier.

10.181   It would seem that one co-occupier may permit another co-occupier to use premises as a brothel,[275] so that two co-occupiers of premises who both practise prostitution there could be convicted under SOA 1956, s 35 of permitting the premises to be used as a brothel. The more natural charge, however, would be under s 33.

10.182   If the above case-law is applicable to s 35, there will be very few people who are not 'occupiers' but are 'in charge' of the premises.

---

272   [1997] CLYB 1202.
273   [1998] Crim LR 199.
274   (1970) 63 Cr App R 168.
275   *Ashdown* (1974) 59 Cr App R 193 (MDA 1971, s 8).

Position of lessor or landlord

10.183   SOA 1956, s 35(3) provides that, where the tenant or occupier is convicted of an offence under s 35[276] and either:

(a)   the lessor or landlord, after having the conviction brought to his or her notice, fails or failed to exercise his statutory rights,[277] where a tenant or occupier is convicted under s 35, in relation to the lease or contract under which the premises are or were held by the person convicted; or

(b)   the lessor or landlord, after exercising his or her statutory rights so as to determine that lease or contract, grants or granted a new lease or enters or entered into a new contract of tenancy of the premises to, with or for the benefit of the same person, without having all reasonable provisions to prevent the recurrence of the offence inserted in the new lease or contract,

then, if subsequently an offence under s 35 is committed in respect of the premises during the subsistence of the lease or contract referred to in (a) or (where (b) applies) during the subsistence of the new lease or contract, the lessor or landlord is deemed to be a party to that offence unless he shows[278] that he took all reasonable steps to prevent the recurrence of the offence.[279]

Allowing a person under 16 to be in a brothel

10.184   CYPA 1933, s 3(1) provides:

> 'If any person having responsibility for a child or young person who has attained the age of four years and is under the age of sixteen years, allows that child or young person to reside in or to frequent a brothel, he shall be liable on summary conviction to a fine not exceeding level 2 on the standard scale, or alternatively ... or in addition thereto, to imprisonment for any term not exceeding six months[280].'

---

[276]   Or was convicted of the corresponding offence under the CLAA 1885, s 13 before the commencement of SOA 1956.

[277]   Ie the statutory rights of a lessor or landlord under SOA 1956, Sch 1 to require the tenant to assign the lease or other contract to a person approved by the lessor or landlord, and (if the tenant fails to do so within 3 months) to determine the lease or other contract: SOA 1956, s 35(3). These rights do not exist where a tenant or occupier is convicted under ss 33, 33A or s 36.

[278]   The comments in **10.106** are equally applicable here.

[279]   For criticism of these provisions, see CLRC Working Paper *Offences Relating to Prostitution and Allied Offences* (1982), at para 2.42.

[280]   As from a day to be appointed this maximum term of imprisonment is increased to a maximum term of 51 weeks (see CJA 2003, s 281(4), (5), (7) (not yet in force)), although this does not affect the penalty for any offence committed before that day (s 281(6)(b) (not yet in force)). At the date at which this book states the law no such day had been appointed.

Class of offence	n/a	SOA 2003, s 72 applies	✗
Notification requirements	✗	SOPO	✗
CJA 2003, Sch 15 applies	✗	Serious specified offence	✗
Review of lenient sentence	✗	Special provisions of CYPA 1933	✓
Detention of young offender for specified period			✗

See **1.54**.

Person having responsibility for a child or young person who has attained the age of 4 and is under 16[281]

10.185 'Responsibility' in this context may be shared by more than one person.[282] As a matter of law, the following are presumed to have responsibility for a child or young person for these purposes:

(a)   any person who either has parental responsibility[283] for that child or young person or is otherwise legally liable to maintain him; and

(b)   any person who has care of that child or young person,[284] such as a teacher or babysitter.

A person who is presumed to be responsible for a child or young person by virtue of (a) is not to be taken to have ceased to be responsible for him by reason only that he or she does not have care of him.[285] A person not presumed to have responsibility for a child or young person may nevertheless be found as a question of fact to have it.[286]

Allowing to reside in or frequent a brothel

10.186 For the meaning of 'brothel', see **10.187**. 'Allowing' would seem to have the same meaning as 'permitting': see **10.175**. 'Reside in' presumably means 'live at' or 'have a home at'; 'frequent' presumably means 'visit or make use of often'.

Meaning of 'brothel'

10.187 SOA 1956 does not define 'brothel'; the meaning of the term must be derived from case-law. That case-law is framed in terms of sexual practices offered by women to men and the discussion which follows is on that basis, but, by SOA 1967, s 6:

---

[281]   As to proof of age, see **3.131, 3.132**.
[282]   *Liverpool Society for the Prevention of Cruelty to Children v Jones* [1914] 3 KB 813.
[283]   Within the meaning of the Children Act 1989, s 3.
[284]   CYPA 1933, s 17(1).
[285]   CYPA 1933, s 17(2).
[286]   *Liverpool Society for the Prevention of Cruelty to Children v Jones*, n 282 above.

'Premises shall be treated for the purposes of sections 33 to 35 of the Act of 1956 as a brothel if people resort to it for the purpose of lewd homosexual practices in circumstances in which resort thereto for lewd heterosexual practices would have led to its being treated as a brothel for the purposes of those sections.'

Whether premises constitute a brothel is a question of fact and degree.[287]

10.188   The authorities on the meaning of 'brothel' were reviewed by Lord Parker CJ in *Gorman v Standen*,[288] who went on to define a brothel as:[289]

'... a house resorted to or used by more than one woman for the purpose of fornication.'

It is not necessary that the use of the premises should have caused a nuisance to neighbours[290] or that indecency or disorderly conduct should be apparent from outside them.[291] The following paragraphs explain Lord Parker's useful, but not wholly accurate, definition.

Resorted to or used by more than one woman

10.189   Premises frequented by men for acts of fornication (see below) with only one woman who operates as a prostitute there are not a brothel,[292] however many men may visit her there for sex, whether the woman is the tenant and occupier or not.[293] Thus, none of the offences relating to brothels mentioned above is committed where only one prostitute operates as such on the premises.

10.190   However, provided two women use the premises for the purpose of fornication, the fact that one is the tenant and occupier does not prevent the premises being a brothel,[294] nor does the fact that the two women are never present on the premises at the same time. This latter point was established in *Stevens and Stevens v Christy*,[295] where the Divisional Court held that premises (a small, two-storey terraced house) used by a team of prostitutes, although on any individual day only one prostitute was present, constituted a brothel. It held that if there was joint use of premises by prostitutes as part of a team, premises could properly be called a brothel, even though only one prostitute plied her trade there at a given time. It would appear from this that premises are not a brothel if the prostitutes concerned are operating totally independently of each other and not as a team.

10.191   In relation to the present requirement, the question is whether it is satisfied in respect of particular premises. This is a matter dealt with in **10.198** et seq.

---

[287]   *Stevens and Stevens v Christy* (1987) 85 Cr App R 249; *Donovan v Gavin* [1965] 2 QB 648, at p 659.
[288]   [1964] 1 QB 294.
[289]   Ibid, at p 303.
[290]   *Parts of Holland, Lincolnshire JJ* (1882) 46 JP 312.
[291]   *Rice and Wilson* (1866) LR 1 CCR 21.
[292]   *Singleton v Ellison* [1895] 1 QB 607; *Caldwell v Leech* (1913) 109 LT 188; *Mattison v Johnson* (1916) 85 LJKB 741; *Gorman v Standen* [1964] 1 QB 294, at p 303, per Lord Parker.
[293]   *Caldwell v Leech*, n 292 above.
[294]   *Gorman v Standen*, n 292 above.
[295]   (1987) 85 Cr App R 249.

10.192   The fact that premises are a brothel if two or more prostitutes work together is liable to encourage them to work separately, thereby increasing the risk to them. There is much to be said for a Government proposal in 2006 to amend the law so that the two could work together.[296]

For the purposes of fornication

10.193   It is not necessary that the women resort to the premises for the purposes of prostitution, but they must resort there for the purposes of fornication; if they do it is irrelevant that they do not do so for payment. (Thus, premises to which women resort for sexual activity with men without payment, such as swingers' clubs, can be brothels.) The leading authority for this statement is *Winter v Woolfe*,[297] where a magistrates' court had dismissed a charge under the forerunner to SOA 1956, s 33 against the occupier of a dance room, to which students and women resorted on Sunday afternoons for 'lewd and improper acts', on the ground that the dance room was not a brothel because there was no evidence that the women were paid for what they did. The Divisional Court held that the magistrates had been wrong to dismiss the charge on this ground. Avory J said:[298]

> 'There was evidence ... that ... men were resorting to those premises for the purpose of committing fornication with women who resorted there for the same purpose ... That of itself is quite sufficient to justify the inference that these premises were being used for the purposes of prostitution [sic].'

It follows that the legal meaning of 'brothel' is wider than the popular conception of that term. Unless 'free' fornication on the premises involves exploitation or abuse or some other pressing need to interfere, it would not seem to be the law's business to do so. It is interesting to note that 'prostitution' in the above quotation is used in a sense different from its normal legal meaning, which does require a reward for sexual activity.

10.194   *Winter v Woolfe* was referred to with approval in *Kelly v Purvis* (below) where Ackner LJ, as he then was, giving the judgment of the Divisional Court, stated obiter that it showed that to constitute premises as a brothel it is not essential to prove 'that they are used for the purpose of prostitution, which involves payment for services rendered'; a brothel, he said, is also constituted where the women do not charge for 'sexual intercourse'.[299]

10.195   *Winter v Woolfe* can be said to have gained statutory recognition in SOA 2003, which added a new offence (s 33A) to SOA 1956 of keeping a brothel used for the purpose of prostitution. An argument that *Winter v Woolfe* was wrongly decided would be doomed to failure.

10.196   Although proof that the persons concerned were prostitutes is not required, evidence that they were is admissible – and can be important in respect of the present requirement – if that fact is within the personal knowledge of the witness who makes the assertion.[300]

---

[296]   Home Office Press Release, 17 January 2006.
[297]   [1931] 1 KB 549.
[298]   Ibid, at pp 554–555.
[299]   [1983] 1 All ER 525, at p 528.
[300]   *Korie* [1966] 1 All ER 50.

10.197 Although Lord Parker CJ in *Gorman v Standen* referred to women resorting to the premises for the purposes of fornication, it was held by the Divisional Court in *Kelly v Purvis* that a brothel is a place resorted to by members of opposite sexes where the women offer themselves to participate in physical acts of indecency for sexual gratification; sexual intercourse is not required. In that case there was evidence that in a licensed massage parlour masturbation was offered as an additional service for a fee. There was no doubt therefore that the premises were used for the purposes of prostitution,[301] but there was no evidence that sexual intercourse was offered. The Divisional Court concluded that the massage parlour was a brothel.

Premises

10.198 Although Lord Parker CJ in *Gorman v Standen* used the term 'house', the authorities on the meaning of 'brothel' generally use the term 'premises'.

10.199 There is no authoritative definition of the word in the present context. Its normal, legal meaning is, of course, the subject-matter of the habendum in a lease, and this covers any sort of property of which a lease is granted, for example, buildings or land with a building on part of it or land which is not built upon provided that it has a defined boundary.[302] The popular sense of 'premises' is more restricted,[303] and merely includes buildings or land with buildings on it. 'Premises' has been given an extended meaning in some contexts and has been held to include structures, other than buildings, which have an element of permanence in the site which they occupy and have functions similar to those buildings,[304] for example, houseboats which occupy permanent moorings which they do not leave or a static caravan. Indeed, in one case, there is an obiter dictum that 'premises' can include a 'ship or anything of that kind'.[305]

10.200 It is submitted that, in the present context, 'premises' should bear not only its normal meaning but also include structures of the type referred to above which occupy a permanent site. To adopt the popular meaning would impair the effectiveness of the provision.

10.201 For the purposes of the definition of 'brothel', 'premises' does not simply mean the whole of a building or other structure (hereafter simply 'building'). A room or flat within a building can be premises for this purpose, so that if two prostitutes use the same room or flat the premises (ie the room or flat) are clearly a brothel.[306]

10.202 Where separate rooms or flats in a building are independently let to different prostitutes for separate occupation and are used only by one prostitute, the building itself will constitute the premises, and thus a brothel, if the individual rooms or flats

---

[301] See **10.59** et seq.

[302] See *Andrews v Andrews & Mears* [1908] 2 KB 567, at p 570 ('premises' in workmen's compensation legislation); *Whitley v Stumbles* [1930] AC 544; *Bracey v Read* [1963] Ch 88 (landlord and tenant legislation).

[303] *Bracey v Read*, ibid. This meaning of 'premises' was adopted in two cases concerning the supply of water to 'premises' under the terms of a statute: *Metropolitan Water Board v Paine* [1907] 1 KB 285 and *Bristol Water Works Co v Uren* (1885) 15 QBD 637.

[304] See *West Mersea UDC v Fraser* [1950] 2 KB 119 (houseboat can be 'premises' in the context of the statutory right to demand a water supply provided that there is an element of permanence in the site which it occupies).

[305] *Andrews v Andrews & Mears*, n 302 above, at p 570, per Buckley LJ.

[306] Stephen *Digest of the Criminal Law* (Macmillan, 5th edn, 1894), at p 142; see also *I Hawkin's Pleas of the Crown* (3rd edn, 1739), at c 74: both referred to as representing the law by Watkins LJ in *Stevens and Stevens v Christy* (1987) 85 Cr App R 249.

occupied by the prostitutes and used by them for their trade are sufficiently close to each other to form in effect what might be called a nest of prostitutes.[307] This was stated by Sachs J (with whom Lord Parker CJ and Browne J agreed) in *Donovan v Gavin*,[308] which was concerned with an offence under the second part of SOA 1956, s 34. There a house was occupied as follows. There was a self-contained flat, occupied by the defendant. The remaining rooms in the house on the ground, first and second floors were let to different tenants on weekly terms. Some of the tenancies had existed for a substantial period. Each room was let as a separate unit, the bathroom and lavatory on the first floor being the only room in the house which could be used by all the tenants. At the material time, three rooms on the ground floor were let separately to three prostitutes, A, B and C. The front door of the house lay between the rooms occupied by A and B. It led to a communal passageway used by the defendant, A, B and C and all the other tenants. C's room was across the corridor from A's. Each of the tenant's rooms, including A, B and C's, had a door on to the communal passageway. Each tenancy had come into existence separately and at different times. It was specifically found that the lettings to A, B and C had genuinely been made and not as a subterfuge to avoid SOA 1956, s 34. During the material 5-day period 38 men were seen to enter the house, either with or after being admitted by A, B or C. A and C had regularly joined together to solicit men in the nearby streets. On 4 of the 5 days they had together solicited men from the window of A's room, and on one occasion from the front door of the house. On one occasion C used A's room for business, in the absence of A. On the occasion that A and C solicited from the front door, A's room was used for intercourse with a man who had been enticed to enter; there was no evidence with which woman the intercourse took place or whether both women had participated in it. On one occasion when A solicited from the window of her room on her own and attracted a man, C admitted the man to the house and intercourse took place with A in A's room. B solicited on her own and only used her own room for the purpose of her own prostitution. The defendant knew that the women were prostitutes and were doing the things referred to above, and at the material time was wilfully a party to that conduct.

10.203   The Divisional Court held that the mere fact that individual rooms in the house were originally let under separate tenancies, independently effected, for separate occupation did not of itself preclude the court from holding that the house was a brothel. Sachs J, with whom Lord Parker CJ and Browne J agreed, said that such a finding did not depend on it being established that the original lettings were effected as a subterfuge to escape the consequences of the relevant section. Sachs J continued:[309]

'There is indeed a class of separate independent tenancies in which I go further, when, as here, considering cases arising under the second part of s 34. I have in mind the class where in a single house individual rooms occupied by common prostitutes and used by them for their trade are sufficiently close to each other to constitute in effect what might be called a nest of prostitutes, be that nest large or small. In that particular class of case, the fact that the rooms were originally the subject of independent lettings for exclusive occupation may be of no weight at all, though in other types of cases the fact that there were independent lettings may be of considerable weight. In what might be called the "nest" type of cases, the result may well be the same whether technically the prostitute is occupying the room as a lodger, as a tenant or without making any payment at all.

The present case falls into that class and is one where, on the facts as found with regard to user, there can be no weight attached to the fact that they were originally independent

[307]   Or 'nest of rooms really used as a brothel': *Abbott v Smith* [1965] 2 QB 662n, at p 664.
[308]   [1965] 2 QB 648.
[309]   Ibid, at p 659.

lettings. The user of at any rate A's and C's rooms ... coupled with the respondent's knowledge of it are such that it does not matter what was the precise form under which those two women held their rooms.'

Lord Parker CJ took the view that a nest of prostitutes is only a brothel if the prostitutes (or at least two of them as in *Donovan v Gavin*) collaborate in their prostitution or, possibly, if the landlord has taken an active part by way of managing or assisting in the management of the business of prostitution. As yet, there is no judicial support for this view.

10.204 Reference may also be made to *Abbott v Smith*,[310] which was approved in *Donovan v Gavin*. The offence in question was managing a brothel, contrary to SOA 1956, s 33. The upper floors of a large terrace house going to seed were let off in single-room apartments, though not structurally converted for the purpose; in other words it was a house in multiple occupation. The lettings were separate in that each occupier had a right of exclusive occupation of his or her room, but there was no more structural separation of one room in the building from another than there ever had been. The staircase was common and so were the toilets and washing facilities. Two of the occupants were prostitutes. They and three other women, one of whom was also a known prostitute, who were not residents used the house for the entertainment of men, the reasonable inference being that that entertainment was sexual in character. There was no evidence that any one room had ever been used by more than one woman, simultaneously or successively, for this purpose.

10.205 A magistrate held that the *house* constituted a brothel. On appeal to the Crown Court at Liverpool, Judge Chapman agreed. Rejecting the argument that the sole criterion of what constituted 'premises' or 'house' for the purpose of the definition of a brothel was whether there had been an entity which was the subject of a separate letting for exclusive occupation, Judge Chapman concluded that it would be unreal to regard the house as other than a single entity, albeit a warren occupied by a large number of people with separate rights as regards the rooms severally let to them. As the evidence showed that the house was resorted to by more than one woman for the purposes of sexual lewdness with more than one man, it constituted a brothel.

10.206 In rejecting the contention that the exclusive criterion for what constitutes 'premises' for the purposes of a 'brothel' is whether there is an entity which is the subject of a separate letting for separate occupation, Judge Chapman said:[311]

'This would mean that if the owner of a large house let off every room in it to a separate woman known by him to be a prostitute and knowing that she was going to use the room for prostitution, he could not be convicted for keeping or managing a brothel. Frankly I find this submission somewhat startling.'

10.207 *Durose v Wilson*[312] is often claimed to support the approach taken in *Donovan v Gavin* and *Abbott v Smith*[313] but, as explained below, it was decided on a different ground.

---

310   [1965] 2 QB 662n.

311   [1965] 2 QB 662n, at p 664.

312   (1907) 71 JP 263. See Sim *Prostitution and the Law* (Faber & Faber, 1977), at pp 124–127 for a detailed analysis of this case.

313   [1965] 2 QB 662.

10.208 In *Durose v Wilson* the offence charged was wilfully being a party to the continued use of the premises, or part as a brothel, contrary to the second half of what is now SOA 1956, s 34. The premises consisted of one large building divided into 18 self-contained flats, each of which was let to a different tenant. There was only one door to the street, and one common staircase. Each tenant (12 of whom operated there nightly as prostitutes) had a key to his or her flat but none had a key to the front door, which was left open all day until locked at midnight by D, the porter at the block of flats, and thereafter opened on request by D who waited outside in the street and admitted prostitutes and their clients, knowing the purpose of their visits. D also used to call cabs for them when they left. D did not collect the rents but had authority to evict undesirable tenants. It was not proved that any one flat was used by more than one prostitute. A magistrates' court concluded that the whole building constituted one set of premises, a nest of rooms really used as a brothel. This finding was upheld by the Divisional Court, which rejected the argument that the relevant premises were not the building as a whole but the individual flats. Lord Alverstone CJ said that it was 'a case of considerable difficulty; and, but for the fact that there was a distinct finding by the magistrate on a question of fact, he was not prepared to say that he would have affirmed the conviction'. He thought that it was open to the magistrate on the evidence, if he was so convinced, to find as a fact that the case was not one where each flat was being used for prostitution by the woman who was the tenant of it, but one where it could be inferred that a tenant lent the keys of her flat to a non-resident woman to enable her to take a man in, in which case more than one woman would have been using that flat for prostitution. AT Lawrence J, who also had difficulty with the case, seems to have made the same inference because he agreed that if it had been the case that each flat used was only used by one woman for prostitution the building would not have been one set of premises used as a brothel.

10.209 Thus, *Durose v Wilson* did not decide that a building with self-contained flats, each with its own tenant, used solely by the woman for the purposes of prostitution was a brothel, the ground given by the magistrate. Instead, the decision was that, since it could be inferred that some of the flats were used for prostitution by more than one person, part of the building was used as a brothel and therefore the building was a brothel. Without this inference it is clear that Lord Alverstone and AT Lawrence J doubted that the building would be a brothel.[314] It is odd that they considered that the inference could be drawn, given that the magistrate had expressly found that it had not been proved that any one flat was used by more than one prostitute and that he expressly found that all the women using the building for prostitution lived in it.

10.210 The decisions in *Donovan v Gavin* and *Abbott v Smith* can be contrasted with that of the Divisional Court in *Strath v Foxon*,[315] where the offence charged was that of letting the whole or part of premises with knowledge that it is to be used, in whole or part, as a brothel, contrary to the first part of what is now SOA 1956, s 34. In that case, premises comprised three floors. The first and second floors were let to prostitute A and the third to prostitute B. The lettings, by the lessor's agent who knew that the women were prostitutes, were made on the same occasion. Access to the premises was via the same street door and there was a common staircase on which a substantial door fitted with a Yale lock divided the whole of the third floor from the lower ones, and, therefore, the third floor was completely self-contained. A and B each had a key to the street door,

---

314 In *Caldwell v Leech* (1913) 23 Ex CC 510, at p 518, Avory J was of this view. He said: 'So both [Alverstone LCJ and AT Lawrence J] expressed a doubt whether, if in that case it had been clear that each woman was using her own flat for this purpose, there could properly have been a conviction.'
315 [1956] 1 QB 67.

and B to the Yale lock. A kitchen on the second floor was used by both A and B. Otherwise, the first and second floors were used exclusively by A and the third only by B. Acknowledging that premises cannot be regarded as a brothel if they are used by only one prostitute, the Divisional Court said that the only question was whether the two flats were separate premises. It concluded that they were and that therefore the building as a whole was not a brothel, stating:[316]

'... the ... magistrate, after hearing the evidence, and making a personal inspection of the premises, has found that there were separate lettings of the two flats, and no common user other than a joint user of the kitchen. There was evidence to justify his findings, and this court cannot therefore interfere with his decision.'

The court indicated that the answer would have been different if the arrangements had been a subterfuge to evade s 34.

10.211 It is clear from all three judgments in *Donovan v Gavin* that the question of whether premises are a brothel must be answered by looking at the position at the *material* time. The offence under the first part of SOA 1956, s 34, for example, is concerned with the time of the letting of the premises and under the second part the time of the use alleged to be as a brothel.

OFF-STREET PROSTITUTION: OTHER OFFENCES

Tenant or occupier permitting premises to be used for prostitution

10.212 SOA 1956, s 36, as amended by SOA 2003, provides:

'It is an offence for the tenant or occupier of any premises knowingly to permit the whole or part of the premises to be used for the purposes of habitual prostitution (whether any prostitute involved is male or female).'

It will be noted that the offence differs from that under s 35 in that it is not concerned with permitting premises to be used as a brothel. It can be committed where only one prostitute is permitted to use the premises for habitual prostitution.

10.213 The offence is triable summarily.[317] The provisions relating to maximum punishment[318] are identical to those relating to s 34: see **10.166** and the box therein, which is equally applicable to s 36.

Tenant or occupier

10.214 An offence under s 36 can only be committed by the tenant or occupier. Unlike an offence under s 35 it cannot also be committed by a 'person in charge' of the premises, whatever that term may mean.

10.215 In *Siviour v Napolitano*,[319] a case concerned with an offence under the CLAA 1885, s 13(2), the predecessor of SOA 1956, s 36, the Divisional Court held that 'lessee'

---

[316] Ibid, at pp 72–73.
[317] SOA 1956, s 37(1), (2), Sch 2, para 36.
[318] SOA 1956, s 37(1), (3), Sch 2, para 36.
[319] [1931] 1 KB 636.

within the meaning of s 13(2) (which referred to a tenant, lessee or occupier knowingly permitting use of the premises for prostitution) referred to a lessee in occupation and did not cover a landlord who was himself a lessee. In that case, D was the lessee of premises consisting of four floors and a basement. He used the ground floor and basement as a shop and sublet the first and second floors respectively to two women who were prostitutes. The entry to the flats was not through the shop but through a separate entrance, and (otherwise than as landlord) D had no right to enter the flats and did not co-occupy them. The Divisional Court therefore concluded that D was not the 'lessee' of the flats within the meaning of s 13(2). In the light of the fact that SOA 1956 is a consolidating Act this decision is of particular relevance in considering SOA 1956, s 36. As *Rook & Ward*[320] point out, it would seem to follow that a tenant who sublets the entirety of the demised premises cannot be convicted of an offence under s 36, although he or she might be liable for an offence under s 34 (landlord knowingly letting for use as brothel). They note that it would be otherwise if the tenant were merely to allow a licensee to use the premises, retaining exclusive possession; the tenant could be convicted under s 36 even if he or she did not him- or herself use the premises.

Knowingly permitting the whole or part of premises to be used for the purposes of habitual prostitution

10.216   For the meaning of 'knowingly' see **2.62**, for the meaning of 'permit' see **10.175** and **10.176** and for the meaning of 'premises' see **10.198** et seq.

10.217   In *Mattison v Johnson*[321] it was held that 'permit' in the forerunner of SOA 1956, s 36 implied a permission given by the tenant or occupier of the premises to another person or persons to engage in habitual prostitution on them; a prostitute who is the sole occupier of the premises and uses them for her own habitual prostitution cannot be convicted of 'permitting' the premises to be so used. Nor, it was held by the High Court of Justiciary in *Girgawy v Strathern*,[322] can tenants or co-occupiers of premises who habitually invite prostitutes to come to the premises to commit acts of prostitution with them, apparently because they cannot be said to permit themselves to use premises for the purpose of prostitution, although they will if they permit friends to come to the premises to engage in habitual prostitution with prostitutes there.

10.218   'Prostitution' is to be construed by reference to the meaning given to 'prostitute' by the courts in other statutory contexts: see **10.90**. 'Habitual prostitution' seems to mean constantly repeated prostitution, which is a question of fact.

Knowingly permitting prostitutes to meet and remain in house of refreshment

10.219   Under the Metropolitan Police Act (MPA) 1839, s 44:

'Every person who shall have or keep any house, shop, room, or place of public resort within the metropolitan police district, wherein provisions, liquors, or refreshments of any kind shall be sold or consumed, (whether the same shall be kept and retailed therein or procured elsewhere) and who shall ... knowingly permit or suffer prostitutes or persons of notoriously

[320]   At p 338.
[321]   (1916) 85 LJKB 741.
[322]   1925 SLT 84.

bad character to meet together and remain therein, shall for every such offence be liable to a penalty of not more than level 1 on the standard scale'.[323]

As indicated by the description of the penalty, the offence is triable summarily only.

Class of offence	n/a	SOA 2003, s 72 applies	✗
Notification requirements	✗	SOPO	✗
CJA 2003, Sch 15 applies	✗	Serious specified offence	✗
Review of lenient sentence	✗	Special provisions of CYPA 1933	✗
Detention of young offender for specified period			✗

10.220 The offence can only be committed within the Metropolitan Police District (ie Greater London, excluding the City of London, the Inner Temple and the Middle Temple).[324] There is a corresponding offence in respect of the City of London,[325] but the corresponding offence which applied outside London under the Town Police Clauses Act 1947, s 35 has been repealed.[326]

10.221 As to 'place of public resort', 'knowingly' and 'prostitute', see **10.75** et seq, **2.62** and **10.59** et seq (common prostitute), respectively. The defendant must know that the prostitutes who meet and remain on the premises are prostitutes.[327]

Permit or suffer

10.222 For the meaning of 'permit' see **10.175**. 'Suffer' was defined by Darling J in *Rochford RDC v Port of London Authority* as follows:[328]

'If a person is in a position to prevent a thing without committing a legal wrong and does not do so, then in the common use of language that person suffers that thing. Of course, one cannot be said to suffer a thing which one cannot prevent, or which by law one ought not to prevent. But these appellants are in a position in which both physically and legally they could prevent this ... and they have not done so, and, therefore, in my opinion, they may properly be said to have "suffered" it.'

This is not far removed from the wider definition of 'permit' referred to in **10.175**. Indeed, 'permit' and 'suffer' have generally been treated by the courts as synonymous.[329] In view of this apparent synonymity it is not easy to understand why both words are employed in the section. On the other hand, it might be argued that the two words were

---

[323] Penalty increased by virtue of CJA 1982, ss 37, 38 and 46.
[324] London Government Act 1963, s 76(1).
[325] City of London Police Act 1839, s 28.
[326] By SOA 2003.
[327] *Somerset v Wade* (1884) 1 QBD 574.
[328] (1914) 83 LJKB 1066.
[329] For example, *Bond v Evans* (1888) 21 QBD 249, at p 257, per Stephen J; *Somerset v Wade* [1894] 1 QB 574, at p 576, per Mathew J; *Ferguson v Weaving* [1951] 1 KB 814, at p 820, per Lord Goddard CJ; *Thomas* (1976) 63 Cr App R 65, at p 68.

not intended to be synonymous in s 44. If they do have different meanings, it is difficult to see what this could be unless 'permit' is limited to its narrow meaning of authorise, agree to or allow.[330]

Vicarious liability

10.223 In *Allen v Whitehead*[331] the licensee of a refreshment house delegated control of it to an employee who, in the licensee's absence and contrary to his express instructions, allowed prostitutes to enter. The licensee was convicted of 'knowingly suffering prostitutes to meet together in his house and remain therein', contrary to the MPA 1839, s 44, the acts and mens rea of the delegate employee being imputed to him. In *Linnett v Metropolitan Police Comr*[332] it was held that one co-licensee was vicariously liable under s 44 where his co-licensee, to whom he had delegated the management of a refreshment house owned by their employer, had knowingly permitted disorderly conduct there.

Disorderly houses

10.224 A person who keeps a disorderly house commits a common law offence.[333] Although a brothel can fall within the definition of a disorderly house, the offence is particularly important in respect of conduct which does not render the premises a brothel, such as indecent performances, 'peep shows' and sado-masochistic activities.

10.225 As a common law offence keeping a disorderly house is triable only on indictment and punishable with imprisonment or a fine at the discretion of the court, or both, subject to a requirement that the punishment imposed should not be excessive.[334] In *Moores v DPP*,[335] the common law offence was treated as an either-way offence, but whether this was correct was not in issue before the Divisional Court and not discussed by it.

10.226 In some instances, keeping a disorderly house may amount to the common law offence of public nuisance,[336] although this is less likely than previously in the light of the definition of public nuisance approved by the House of Lords in *Rimmington;*

---

[330]   See **10.175**.

[331]   [1930] 1 KB 211.

[332]   [1946] KB 290.

[333]   3 Co Inst 205; *Higginson* (1762) 2 Burr 1232; *Tan* [1983] QB 1053, at p 1059. The Disorderly Houses Act 1751, s 8, which supplemented the common law offence by providing that anyone who appeared, acted or behaved him or herself as master or mistress, or as the person having the management of any bawdy house or other disorderly house was deemed to be the keeper of it and liable to be convicted as such, notwithstanding that he or she was not the real owner or keeper of it, was repealed by the Statute Law (Repeals) Act 2008, s 1, Sch 1, Pt 3.

[334]   *Morris* [1951] 1 KB 394. In *Goldstein* [1971] Crim LR 300, consecutive sentences of 9, 9 and 12 months' imprisonment and a fine of £1,000 were upheld in respect of three charges of keeping a disorderly house at which obscene shows were staged, the second offence occurring after the defendant had been cautioned and told that he would be charged in respect of the first offence and the third when he was on bail in respect of the first two charges. The defendant's takings were £500 a day. He had one previous conviction for keeping a disorderly house, one for exhibiting an indecent advertisement and five for breaches of club licences. There had been no coercion of the women performers or corruption of the audience, but the court held that the gravamen of the offence was the outrage to public decency and it was difficult to imagine more depraved exhibitions.
     In *Payne* (1980) 2 Cr App R (S) 161, a sentence of 18 months' imprisonment was reduced to 6 months. The Court of Appeal described the case as a bad case of brothel keeping (for which offence the maximum is 6 months' imprisonment) and said that it was difficult to see how a longer term could be imposed.

[335]   [1992] QB 125.

[336]   *Quinn and Bloom* [1962] 2 QB 245. A public nuisance is not a necessary ingredient of the disorderly house

Goldstein.[337] If keeping a disorderly house did constitute a public nuisance and was charged as such the offence would be triable either way because public nuisance is so triable by virtue of MCA 1980, s 17 and Sch 1, para 1. The maximum penalty on summary conviction of an offence triable either way by virtue of MCA 1980, s 17 and Sch 1 is currently 6 months' imprisonment or a fine not exceeding the statutory maximum, or both.[338]

10.227   The following may be noted in relation to keeping a disorderly house:

Class of offence	3	SOA 2003, s 72 applies	✗
Notification requirements	✗	SOPO	✗
CJA 2003, Sch 15 applies	✗	Serious specified offence	✗
Review of lenient sentence	✔	Special provisions of CYPA 1933	✗
Detention of young offender for specified period			✔

See **1.48** et seq.

Keeping

10.228   Keeping requires control over the premises and involvement in their use as a disorderly house. A person can keep premises as a disorderly house, even though he or she is not the owner or tenant of them.[339] On the other hand, a landlord of premises who has let them to a tenant who, as the landlord knows, intends to use them for prostitution or has so used them, has been held to be not guilty of, respectively, keeping a disorderly house and keeping a bawdy house (below) because in the cases concerned they had no control over the premises, except for the power to terminate the tenancies, and were not involved in the use of the premises for immoral purposes.[340]

Disorderly house

10.229   'Disorderly house' is not defined by statute. It is clear that a brothel may (but not necessarily) be a disorderly house, and that other types of premises may also be. The latter point was recognised in *Tan*[341] by the Court of Appeal, which observed that many forms of conduct may fall within the scope of keeping a disorderly house. The court added that establishing a universal definition is both undesirable and impossible.

10.230   According to *Stephen's Digest*[342] disorderly houses are common betting houses, common gaming houses and disorderly places of entertainment. The Court of Criminal

---

offence: *Rice and Wilton* (1866) LR 1 CCR 21 (no evidence that disorderly conduct (use of house for prostitution) perceptible from the exterior of house); *Quinn and Bloom* [1962] 2 QB 248, at pp 254–155.

[337]   [2006] 1 AC 459. The definition is set out at n 203 above.

[338]   MCA 1980, s 32(1). When CJA 2003, s 282(1) is in force MCA 1980, s 32(1) will be amended in respect of an offence committed thereafter so that the maximum term of imprisonment will be 12 months.

[339]   *Williams* (1711) 1 Salk 384.

[340]   *Stannard* (1863) 9 Cox CC 405; *Barrett* (1863) Le & Ca 263.

[341]   [1983] QB 1053.

[342]   7th edn, 1926, at p 258.

Appeal in *Berg*[343] did not disagree with this list, but emphasised that it was not exhaustive. In *Moores v DPP*[344] Bingham LJ referred to indecency, illegal pugilism or cock fighting as forms of disorderly recreation which could render premises a disorderly house if members of the public resorted to them for such purposes.[345]

10.231 A rather vague universal definition can be derived from the decision of the Court of Criminal Appeal in *Berg*, which (according to the Court of Appeal in *Tan*) provides clear authority that:

(1)   there must be some element of keeping open house, albeit the premises need not be open to the public at large;

(2)   the house must not be regulated by the restraints of morality, or must be unchaste or of bad repute; and

(3)   it must be so conducted as to violate law and good order.

10.232 Further consideration of element (3) in the context of, and limited to, a charge alleging an indecent performance was given in *Quinn and Bloom*,[346] where premises were used for striptease shows during a specified period, some of the acts being seriously indecent and, in some respects, revolting. Rejecting the argument that, since the audience did not take part in any indecent behaviour, the premises could not be a disorderly house, the Court of Criminal Appeal upheld the defendants' convictions for keeping a disorderly house. Subject to two comments, the court upheld a definition advanced by the prosecution:

> 'A disorderly house is a house conducted contrary to law and good order in that matters are performed or exhibited of such a character that their performance or exhibition in a place of common resort (a) amounts to an outrage of public decency[347] or (b) tends to corrupt or deprave or (c) is otherwise calculated to injure the public interest so as to call for condemnation and punishment.'

The two comments were that this definition had to be taken as limited to indecent performances and that although the elements specified in (a), (b) and (c) were expressed as alternatives, they should not be regarded as mutually exclusive.

10.233 Consideration of the elements established in *Berg* was also given in *Tan*, where the Court of Appeal had to consider how a jury should be directed where a charge is based on premises being used for the purpose of providing sexual services. In *Tan* the two defendants, with the aid of various types of equipment, had on a 'one-to-one basis' and in private subjected clients, at their own risk and with their full consent, to a variety of forms of humiliation, flagellation, bondage and torture, often accompanied by masturbation. The availability of the services at the premises used was advertised extensively, including by advertisement in 'contact magazines'. Having stated that there could be no doubt that there was evidence on which the jury could find that the premises

---

[343]   (1927) 20 Cr App R 38.
[344]   [1992] QB 125.
[345]   The breadth of the offence has been said to be justified by the consideration that disorderly houses present temptations to idleness and the drawing together of a number of disorderly persons: *Rogier* (1823) 1 B & C 272.
[346]   [1962] 2 QB 245.
[347]   See **13.86** et seq.

were not regulated by restraints of morality (element (2) in *Berg*, see **10.231**) the court went on to consider the defendants' argument that the premises were not so conducted as to violate law and good order (since what occurred between the defendants and each client was not in itself a criminal offence) (element (3)) and there was not the necessary element of open house (element (1)). The court rejected both contentions. Lawful activities which so surpass what is acceptable could become unlawful, as shown by *Quinn and Bloom* in the case of a striptease performance; it was for the jury to set the standard. As to the element of open house, there was clearly a public invitation to resort to the premises to indulge in the practices offered and that invitation was clearly part of the conduct of the premises. It was open to the jury to find that both elements were satisfied.

10.234 The court had no hesitation in rejecting the submission that where a single prostitute provided sexual services to a single client at a time in private in certain premises, such premises were incapable in law of being a disorderly house. If this was correct it would be open to anyone, provided that the perverted practices were conducted in private with one client at a time, to advertise them without restriction. Although a prosecution in such a case was novel, the case fell squarely within the scope of the existing offence. The court observed that:[348]

'... acceptance of the submission would involve results that fly in the face of common sense. Premises would, for example, be incapable of being a disorderly house if there was a large notice in neon lights over the door containing an open invitation to be whipped or subjected to any form of perversion, with the tariff set out. Yet the law would be powerless to intervene, save, perhaps, under the Indecent Displays (Control) Act 1981, so long as the service itself was provided successively to those resorting to the premises and this would be so, notwithstanding that the adjoining premises had similar notices and provided similar services. To hold that the law was powerless in such a case, but could act in the case of a much more discreet invitation so long as there was in addition to the prostitute and her client a watcher or watchers, offends against common sense.'

10.235 The Court of Appeal held that, where the charge is based on the use of premises to provide sexual services, the judge should, adopting the definition in *Quinn and Bloom*, direct the jury that:[349]

'... in order to convict, the jury must be satisfied that the services provided are open to those members of the public who wish to partake of them and are of such a character and are conducted in such a manner (whether by advertisement or otherwise) that their provision amounts to an outrage of public decency or is otherwise calculated to injure the public interest to such an extent as to call for condemnation and punishment. They should further be directed that the fact, if it be a fact, that the services are provided by a single prostitute to one client at a time and without spectators does not prevent the house being a disorderly house.'

10.236 Because the jury must be satisfied that the sexual services provided on premises are of such a character and conducted in such a manner that their provision amounts to an outrage to public decency or is otherwise calculated (ie likely) to injure the public interest to such an extent as to call for condemnation and punishment, not every type of sexual service will be sufficient.

---

[348] [1983] QB 1053, at p 1063.
[349] Ibid, at p 1058.

10.237 Whether the conduct in question amounts to an outrage to public decency, etc for the purposes of the definitions in *Quinn and Bloom* and *Tan* is a matter of evaluation by the jury as ordinary reasonable citizens putting aside as far as possible any particular prejudices.[350] There are obvious issues here in terms of ECHR, Art 7. In *DPP v Curley and Farrelly*,[351] where a disorderly house offence under DHA 1751, s 8 (repealed)[352] was charged, the Divisional Court held that the justices were entitled to conclude that there was insufficient evidence to find a prima facie case that the brothel was a disorderly house because the services provided (which were less exotic than in *Tan*) did not outrage public decency and were not otherwise calculated to injure the public interest to such an extent as to call for condemnation and punishment. The court, however, did conclude that the magistrates had been wrong to conclude that there was insufficient evidence that the defendants had assisted in the management of a brothel, contrary to SOA 1956, s 33.[353] This reinforces the point that the threshold for the statutory offences relating to brothels is lower than for the common law offence of keeping a disorderly house.

10.238 In *Quinn and Bloom*[354] the two defendants were charged with keeping a disorderly house. The allegation against them was that the performance of a striptease artiste at their club had been obscene. In their defence, they sought to put in evidence a film of the performance. This film had, however, been taken from a special performance some months after the one which formed the basis of the charge, and had been made with a view to its use at the trial. The court, not surprisingly, excluded it. A different performance, months after the event complained of, could not be assumed to be similar to the acts complained of, especially when it had been made for the specific purpose of demonstrating the supposedly innocent nature of the act; but in giving the judgment of the Court of Criminal Appeal, Ashworth J said: 'this objection goes not only to weight, as was argued, but to admissibility: it is not the best evidence.' With respect, the real issue was simply one of relevance. The film in question was almost worthless. Ashworth J's reference to the concept of 'best evidence' involved the unnecessary resurrection of what in reality was already a long-dead rule.

Habitual or persistent keeping

10.239 In *Moores v DPP*[355] the Divisional Court held that 'keeping a disorderly house' requires habitual or persistent keeping of a house which is a disorderly house. In that case D, the licensee of a public house, was charged with keeping a disorderly house after plain clothes police officers had witnessed two short performances featuring a male exotic stripper. The magistrates found that the first performance was not indecent but that the second consisted of persistent indecency throughout. The Divisional Court allowed D's appeal against conviction because there had not been the requisite habitual or persistent use of the premises for (in this case) indecent performances. Bingham LJ said:[356]

> '[T]he mischief at which the common law offence is aimed is the mischief of keeping a house to which members of the public resort for purposes of the disorderly recreation, if one can so describe it, which is available there ... The essence of the mischief is the continuity which exists where the use of premises for a given unlawful purpose becomes notorious.'

[350] *Quinn and Bloom* [1962] 2 QB 245, at p 256.
[351] [1991] COD 186.
[352] By Statute Law (Repeals) Act 2008.
[353] See **10.152**.
[354] [1962] 2 QB 245.
[355] [1992] QB 125. The Divisional Court did not comment on the fact that the offence had been tried summarily.
[356] Ibid, at p 132.

The court added that 'persistently' could not be established by a reference to persistent indecency throughout one performance.

10.240 It seems that Bingham LJ regarded the present requirement as an element of the concept of 'keeping' and also as an element of the legal character of disorderliness. Hodgson J who entirely agreed with Bingham LJ concentrated in his relatively brief judgment on the present requirement as an element of 'keeping'.

10.241 In *Brady; Ram*[357] the Court of Appeal held that the prosecution can call evidence, or rely on the evidence of the defence, to show that what happened during the period which was the subject of the charge was merely the continuation of a prior user. In this way evidence of indecency at a time outside that named in the charge can be used to show that an indecency at the time charged was merely a continuation of a prior user (ie involved a persistent user as a disorderly house).

Mens rea

10.242 In *Moores v DPP*[358] the Divisional Court held that it must be proved that the defendant knew that the house or room was being used for disorderly purposes.

Keeping a bawdy house

10.243 There is a distinct common law offence of keeping a bawdy house.[359] What is said in **10.225–10.227** about trial and punishment in relation to keeping a disorderly house is equally applicable to the present offence.

10.244 In *Singleton v Ellison* Wills J, giving the judgment of the Divisional Court said:[360]

> 'A brothel is the same thing as a "bawdy house" … In its legal acceptation it applies to a place resorted to by persons of both sexes for the purpose of prostitution.[361] It is certainly not applicable to the … case where one woman receives a number of men.'

The offence does not appear to have been prosecuted in modern times. It appears to have been made redundant by the statutory offences relating to brothels, especially SOA 1956, ss 33 and 33A, quite apart from its overlap with the offence of keeping a disorderly house.

---

[357] [1964] 3 All ER 616n. The court accepted without deciding that an element of persistence was required.
[358] [1992] QB 125.
[359] *Barrett* (1863) Le & Ca 263.
[360] [1895] 1 QB 607, at p 608. See also *Gorman v Standen* [1964] 1 QB 294, at p 301, per Lord Parker CJ.
[361] It will be noted that 'fornication' has been substituted for 'prostitution' in the modern definition of 'brothel': see **10.187** and **10.188**. Presumably, if 'brothel' and 'bawdy house' are identical terms this substitution also applies to the latter.

REFORM

10.245 The problems inherent in prostitution cannot be solved by legal measures. For example, women who are driven to prostitution by drugs, debt or abuse are unlikely to be deterred by the risk of conviction for street prostitution. They need support and counselling to leave prostitution.

10.246 Nevertheless, it may be that the law could do more. Some possible reforms have already been mentioned in this chapter. In addition, a number of options were considered in *Paying the Price: A Consultation Paper on Prostitution* published by the Home Office in 2004:[362]

- Criminalising the purchase or attempted purchase of sexual services and the de-criminalisation of the scale of such services on or off the street, as is the case in Sweden and some other countries. The criminalisation of those who pay for prostitute use was rejected by the Wolfenden Committee[363] on the false assumption that 'the great majority of prostitutes ... choose this life because they find in it a style of living which is easier, freer and more profitable than would be provided by any other occupation'.[364] This is an option which the Government is currently investigating further.

- The introduction of managed areas ('red light areas') to control street-based prostitution, where those involved in prostitution and their clients are permitted to trade, regularly monitored by the police, and provided with drop-in health services and other facilities. This is a model which operates in a number of Dutch cities. In 2006, the Government announced that it had ruled out this option on the ground that there was no evidence that it would reduce exploitation, improve the safety of those involved or make local communities safer.

- The introduction of a brothel licensing system to provide a safer environment for staff and clients and an access-point for health and other services and to monitor and control safe sex practices. Brothel licensing operates in the Netherlands, Greece and some Australian states. The Consultation Paper reported that there are considerable difficulties with this option. Brothel-licensing systems have resulted in an increase in organised crime associated with prostitution, have not resulted in a safer working environment or safer sex and have not resulted in a decrease in the illegal sex industry on or off the street.

- The introduction of a scheme of registration of individuals to work in prostitution which could be used to regulate those working in brothels (licensed or not) or in a managed area. The objective of such a scheme is to ensure regular checks for sexually or drug-transmitted diseases but the Consultation Paper reported that there was evidence that voluntary, accessible checks can be the most effective way to safeguard public health and that there is a danger that mandatory testing produces a two-tier system of registered and non-registered prostitutes, with the latter having very limited healthcare access. In Germany and Greece, where

---

[362] See Ch 9 of the Paper.
[363] See n 78 above.
[364] For a critique, see Dempsey 'Rethinking Wolfenden: Prostitute-Use, Criminal Law, and Remote Harm' [2005] Crim LR 444.

registration systems operate, the great majority of prostitutes are unregi
2005, the Government announced that it had ruled out this option.

Chapter 11

TRAFFICKING

11.1 The trafficking of persons for sexual purposes has become an increasingly important issue, with analogies being drawn to the slave trade.[1] The comparison is undoubtedly accurate and demonstrates the misery of the trade. Trafficking is a complicated body of behaviour that can involve the trafficking of persons to a country, from a country or indeed within a country. As it is largely a covert activity it is difficult to gauge how many victims there are of trafficking but in 2001 it was estimated that between 142 and 1,420 women a year were the victims of trafficking *into* the country for the purposes of sex work.[2] In 2007 a scoping report suggested that over 300 children may have been trafficked *into* the UK for prostitution between March 2005 and December 2006,[3] although the figures are conceivably higher. In 2005 the Court of Appeal estimated the number of trafficking victims at over 1,700.[4] Government figures quoted in *The Guardian* on 18 July 2007 say that 85% of women in brothels now come from outside of the UK whereas in 1997 85% were from within the UK.

11.2 Trafficking can be viewed at best as an exploitative practice where people are deceived as to the employment or money that can be made in a country.[5] Some have argued that it does not require legal regulation because the victims are agreeing to work as prostitutes and thus could be dealt with under legislation governing the controlling and facilitation of prostitution[6] but it is now largely accepted that this is a false argument. Quite separate to the deception argument noted above, it is known that many victims of trafficking are subject to violence and sexual attacks in order to coerce them into the sex industry. Whilst there are undoubtedly parallels to prostitution they are now more commonly thought of as separate behaviours with trafficking being the trading of persons as commodities, thus reinforcing the parallel to slavery.

11.3 The Sex Offences Review concluded that special legislation was necessary.[7] To leave trafficking to the existing offences was inadequate. Trafficking treated people as commodities and solely as a means to service clients and earn large amounts of money for others, with scant regard for the human rights of those trafficked. Like pimping and procuring, trafficking people in order to exploit them as sex workers was unacceptable in a civilised society. This was true even where the person trafficked came willingly. The

---

[1] An analogy recognised by the Government when it established the UK Human Trafficking Centre: see Home Office Press Release 'New Centre Channels Expertise to end "Modern Day Slavery"', 3 October 2006. This analogy was taken further when the Government chose to sign the European Convention on Human Trafficking on the day commemorating the bicentenary of the abolition of slavery.

[2] Sex Offences Review *Setting the Boundaries: Reforming the Law on Sexual Offences* (Home Office, 2000) (*SB*), at p 105.

[3] Child Exploitation and Online Protection centre *A Scoping Project on Child Trafficking in the UK* (CEOP, 2007).

[4] *Maka* [2006] 2 Cr App R (S) 101, at [7].

[5] *SB*, para 7.5.4.

[6] Ibid.

[7] *SB*, at para 7.5.4.

Review therefore recommended that there should be an overarching offence to deal with trafficking a person for the purpose of commercial sexual exploitation.[8]

11.4   The principal mechanism under which trafficking is dealt with is now the Sexual Offences Act (SOA 2003), ss 57–60. Sections 57–59 create offences relating to the trafficking of persons into, out of or within the UK for the purposes of sexual exploitation. The three offences cover:

- trafficking *into* the UK[9] for the purposes of sexual exploitation (s 57);

- trafficking *within* the UK for the purposes of sexual exploitation (s 58); and

- trafficking *out of* the UK for the purposes of sexual exploitation (s 59).

11.5   The offences refer to the trafficking of someone of any age; they are not limited to the trafficking of children. Indeed, they do not distinguish in terms of maximum sentence between children and adults and neither does the Sentencing Guidelines Council (SGC) Definitive Guideline (see the Appendix). That said, in *Maka*[10] the Court of Appeal appears to consider age a factor that can be taken into account when determining the sentence. This decision was made prior to the Definitive Guideline but it is to be hoped that the courts will continue to consider this factor.

11.6   The offences, not surprisingly in a sexual offences Act, are limited to sexual trafficking, although they are not restricted to trafficking for prostitution. An offence or offences to deal with other trafficking for the purposes of domestic servitude or other purposes would be a useful addition to the legal armoury.

11.7   Of the three offences, that under s 57 appears to have been prosecuted the most.[11] At one level this may be unsurprising as it could reasonably be expected that more people would be trafficked into the UK than out of it, but one may also believe that trafficking *within* the UK would be more prevalent. The conduct may well be, but the statistics appear to demonstrate that s 58 is not being used particularly frequently, something the subject of discussion in the Action Plan.[12]

COMMON ELEMENTS

11.8   All three sections have a number of common features, namely:

- the requirement that the defendant intentionally arranges or facilitates trafficking;[13]

---

[8]   *SB*, at para 7.5.14; Recommendation 49.
[9]   The Interpretation Act 1978, Sch 1 would apply here meaning that the UK is defined as 'Great Britain and Northern Ireland' and not, for example, any of the dependent territories, such as the Isle of Man, Channel Islands, etc.
[10]   [2006] 2 Cr App R (S) 101.
[11]   Crime Statistics 2006/7. By July 2007 about 30 prosecutions had been brought: *The Guardian*, 18 July 2007.
[12]   *UK Action Plan on Tackling Human Trafficking* (Home Office/Scottish Executive, March 2007), at pp 7, 21; see **11.34**.
[13]   The word 'trafficking' does not appear in the content of the provisions although it appears in the marginal notes of ss 57-59 inclusive. It is clear from the content of those sections that trafficking, in this context, means the movement of persons.

- the delineation of where the offence can be committed;

- the defendant must either intend to do anything, or believe another person will do something, to or in respect of the other party (B) that will amount to the commission of a relevant offence.

Intentionally arranges or facilitates

11.9 All three offences require the offender intentionally to arrange or facilitate the arrival into the UK,[14] departure from the UK[15] or travel within the UK.[16] Intention is discussed elsewhere[17] and it is clear from the wording of SOA 2003 that recklessness will not suffice. The terms 'arrange' and 'facilitate' are used elsewhere in the Act and have already been discussed.[18] As elsewhere in the Act, 'arranging' and 'facilitating' seem to create two separate offences.[19] It is quite clear that the thing arranged or facilitated need not occur; the arrangement or facilitation of it suffices in itself. The prosecution is not required to prove any use of force, coercion, deception or abuse of power,[20] although where they are present it is likely that they will form additional counts on an indictment. Similarly the absence of 'consent' by the victim need not be proven, not least because it would be difficult to do so. The width of 'arrange' and 'facilitate' means that all those involved in the trafficking chain, and not just the originator and person who ultimately 'receives' the victim, are caught by the offences. Thus someone who supplies a vehicle intending that it be used for the purpose of trafficking would come within this offence, and not simply be a secondary party to it. It should be noted the arranging or facilitating is in respect of the trafficking and not the sexual exploitation. Accordingly, for example, where A provides an aeroplane ticket from the UK to B, knowing that B will be met off the aeroplane and taken to a brothel, this would amount to arranging trafficking out of the UK.

11.10 Contrary to the recommendation of the Sex Offences Review, the arranging or facilitating by A need not be done 'for the purposes of gain'. Although those who traffic human beings for sexual exploitation will almost invariably do so for gain, it could have been difficult to prove that an individual did so.

Where can the offence be committed?

11.11 In order to combat the international aspect of trafficking s 60(2)[21] provides that ss 57–59 apply to anything whether done inside or outside the UK. There are no constraints on the nationality of the offender.

Would involve the commission of a relevant offence

11.12 In all three sections, the defendant must:

---

14 Section 57.
15 Section 59.
16 Section 58.
17 See **2.56–2.60**.
18 See **4.63–4.66**.
19 See **4.63**
20 Although such factors, if present, will act as aggravating factors: see SGC Definitive Guideline, in the Appendix, at p 131.
21 Substituted by the UK Borders Act 2007.

(a)   intend to do anything to or in respect of B in specified circumstances[22] in any part of the world, which if done will involve the commission of a relevant offence; or

(b)   believe that another person is likely to do something to or in respect of B in specified circumstances[23] in any part of the world.

A 'relevant offence' is defined in SOA 2003, s 60(1) as:

(a)   an offence under SOA 2003, Pt 1;

(b)   an offence under the Protection of Children Act (PoCA) 1978, s 1(1)(a);[24]

(c)   an offence listed in the Criminal Justice (Children) (Northern Ireland) Order 1998, Sch 1;[25]

(d)   an offence under the Protection of Children (Northern Ireland) Order 1978, art 3(1)(a);[26]

(e)   anything done outside England and Wales and Northern Ireland which is not an offence within any of paras (a)–(d) but would be done in England and Wales or Northern Ireland.[27]

This list covers most of the conduct that a person subject to sexual exploitation is likely to suffer and to this extent it is to be welcomed. The reference in (e) to 'anything done outside England and Wales and Northern Ireland', coupled with the provision above that the jurisdiction of a court in England and Wales extends to things done anywhere in the UK, means that something done and/or intended, etc to be done in Scotland can satisfy the requirements of the offences, just as they can if done and/or intended, etc to be done elsewhere. This is so, whether or not what occurs is an offence under the Criminal Justice (Scotland) Act (CJ(S)A) 2003, s 22, the provision in Scotland dealing with trafficking for prostitution etc which has similar extra-territorial jurisdiction provisions.[28]

TRAFFICKING INTO THE UK

11.13   Section 57(1)[29] provides:

'A person commits an offence if he intentionally arranges or facilitates the arrival or entry into the United Kingdom of another person (B) and either—

---

22   This will be dependant on each offence: ie it will be after arrival in the UK for s 57 or after B's departure for s 59, etc.

23   Note 22 applies mutatis mutandis.

24   Ie taking, permitting to be taken or making an indecent photograph or pseudo-photograph of a child.

25   SI 1998/1504 (NI 9). The Sexual Offences (Northern Ireland Consequential Amendments) Order 2008, SI 2008/1779, will, when brought into force, add: '(ba) an offence under any provision of the Sexual Offences (Northern Ireland) Order;' (SI 2008/1769).

26   SI 1978/1047 (NI 17). This, in effect, is that which is contained in PoCA 1978, s 1(1)(a).

27   What is notable about this is that it does not have to constitute an offence in the foreign country where it is intended the act will take place.

28   It is likely, of course, that, where appropriate, acts in Scotland within the CJ(S)A 2003, s 22 would be tried by the Scottish courts.

29   As amended by UK Borders Act 2007.

(a)   he intends to do anything to or in respect of B, after B's arrival but in any part of the world, which if done will involve the commission of a relevant offence, or

(b)   he believes that another person is likely to do something to or in respect of B, after B's arrival but in any part of the world, which if done will involve the commission of a relevant offence.'

Class of offence	3	SOA 2003, s 72 applies	✗
Notification requirements	✗	SOPO[30]	✔[31]
CJA 2003,[32] Sch 15 applies	✔	Serious specified offence	✔
Review of lenient sentence	✔	Special Provisions of CYPA 1933[33]	✔
Detention of young offender for specified period			✔

See **1.48** et seq.

11.14 An offence under s 57 is triable either way and is punishable by a maximum sentence of 14 years imprisonment.[34] See also the SGC Definitive Guideline[35] in the Appendix. An offence contrary to s 57 is a 'lifestyle offence' within the Proceeds of Crime Act 2002, Sch 2, in respect of which a confiscation order may be made under that Act or a financial reporting order under the Serious Organised Crime and Police Act 2005, s 76. It is also a serious offence for the purposes of a serious crime prevention order under the Serious Crime Act (SCA) 2007, Pt 1.[36]

11.15 A will arrange the arrival into the UK of B if, for example, he makes arrangements for transport for B's journey or if he recruits B in B's country of origin. He will facilitate B's arrival if he gives B a forged passport, undertakes the transport or adapts the transport. Because A's intent in s 57(1)(a) or (b) may relate to a relevant offence being committed anywhere in the world, A will commit a s 57 offence if, for example, he makes arrangements to bring B into the UK as an interim destination with the intention of sending B on to another country so that B can be subjected to a relevant offence (eg forcing B into prostitution) there by him (A). This would be a case covered by s 57(1)(a). An example of a case covered by s 57(1)(b) would be where A intentionally facilitates the arrival in the UK of B, believing that C will force B into prostitution in the UK or elsewhere.

11.16 The facts of *Attorney-General's Reference (Nos 129 and 132 of 2006)*,[37] a sentencing appeal, also raise a potential use of this offence, although in that case the offenders were convicted of a conspiracy to commit a s 57 offence rather than the specific offence. One of the offenders in that case placed Internet adverts seeking prostitutes abroad wishing to work in the UK. She also telephoned pre-existing contacts.

---

[30]   Sexual offences prevention order.
[31]   SOA 2003, ss 104, 106 and Sch 5, para 63.
[32]   Criminal Justice Act (CJA) 2003.
[33]   Children and Young Persons Act (CYPA) 1933.
[34]   Section 57(2). Maximum on summary conviction: see **1.43**.
[35]   At pp 5–18, 130–131.
[36]   SCA 2007, s 2(2)(a), Sch 1, para 2(2).
[37]   [2007] 2 Cr App R (S) 530.

When a potential prostitute responded she was passed to another offender and she would be brought to the UK. Had it been possible to identify an individual who had been brought into the UK as a result of these adverts, etc this could have amounted to an offence under s 57. In any event the facts of that case illustrate that preparatory work may also contravene the Act if combined with inchoate liability.

TRAFFICKING WITHIN THE UK

11.17 SOA 2003, s 58(1) provides:

'A person commits an offence if he intentionally arranges or facilitates travel within the United Kingdom by another person (B) and either—

(a)   he intends to do anything to or in respect of B, during or after the journey and in any part of the world, which if done will involve the commission of a relevant offence, or

(b)   he believes that another person is likely to do something to or in respect of B, during or after the journey and in any part of the world, which if done will involve the commission of a relevant offence.'

The details in the box set out in **11.13** apply mutatis mutandis to s 58 as they apply to s 57. The provisions on trial and punishment,[38] lifestyle offence and serious offence relating to s 57 also apply to s 58: see **11.14**.

11.18 Section 58 covers a wide range of behaviour, including the transition of a person who is to be trafficked from the entry point to the UK to another part of the UK or, indeed, to an exit port so long as there is a belief that someone will sexually exploit the person in any part of the world. It would also apply where a person is moved from one area of the UK (eg Newcastle) to another area of the UK (eg London).[39] It should be noted the arranging or facilitation is in respect of the travel and not the sexual exploitation (which is covered by belief). Accordingly where A provides a train ticket to London to B, believing that at London she will be met and taken to a brothel, this could amount to arranging. In *Maka*,[40] a sentencing appeal, the victim was sold by the defendant to other men who raped her and forced her to work as a prostitute. Each sale involved her being transported to a different area of the UK and amounted to a separate offence under s 58.

11.19 The meaning of 'travel' is not defined in the Act and it must presumably apply regardless of how short a distance is travelled. Very little is known as to the extent of internal trafficking and this is something that the Government has committed to researching.[41]

TRAFFICKING OUT OF THE UK

11.20 SOA 2003, s 59(1) provides:

---

[38]   Section 58(2).

[39]   As the provision applies to the UK, it covers the movement of persons between the constituent countries within the UK, for example, moving someone from England to Northern Ireland.

[40]   [2006] 2 Cr App R (S) 101.

[41]   *UK Action Plan on Tackling Human Trafficking* (Home Office/Scottish Executive, March 2007), at p 21.

'A person commits an offence if he intentionally arranges or facilitates the departure from the United Kingdom of another person (B) and either—

(a)   he intends to do anything to or in respect of B, after B's departure but in any part of the world, which if done will involve the commission of a relevant offence, or

(b)   he believes that another person is likely to do something to or in respect of B, after B's departure but in any part of the world, which if done will involve the commission of a relevant offence.'

The details in the box set out in **11.13** apply mutatis mutandis to s 59 as they apply to s 57. The provisions on trial and punishment,[42] lifestyle offence and serious offence relating to s 57 also apply to s 59: see **11.14**.

11.21   Section 59 is the mirror of the offence (s 57) of bringing a person *into* the UK. It applies where a person is being taken out of the UK for the purposes of sexual exploitation, presumably outside the UK. The fact that s 59 refers to being taken out of the UK would mean that putting someone on a ferry from Wales to Northern Ireland would not suffice, although this would, of course, constitute an offence within the meaning of s 58.

ENFORCEMENT

11.22   Law enforcement has reacted to trafficking by transforming the way that it detects and investigates this area. Within the UK a new national centre, the UK Human Trafficking Centre (UKHTC) was established in Sheffield with a remit for leading the law enforcement response in this area. The Centre works closely with local police forces, the Serious and Organised Crime Agency and international agencies[43] to create intelligence-led strategies. The Child Exploitation and Online Protection Centre (CEOP) has a remit in this area for child victims of trafficking and it works closely with UKHTC as regards its operations. CEOPs expertise in high technology allows it to identify situations where trafficking is being facilitated across cyberspace.

Forfeiture

11.23   The Violent Crime Reduction Act 2006, s 54 and Sch 4 amended SOA 2003, by inserting ss 60A-60C to provide for the forfeiture and detention of land vehicles, ships and aircraft used in trafficking, restoring a power that had inadvertently been repealed.[44]

Definitions

11.24   The provisions apply to land-vehicles, ships and aircraft. Section 60C(1) provides, inter alia, the definitions of these terms:

---

42   Section 59(2).
43   Including the Secret Intelligence Service (aka MI6), which is starting to be used in this area.
44   Nationality, Immigration and Asylum Act 2002, s 146 broadly speaking allowed a court to order the forfeiture of a vehicle where it was thought that it was *intended* to be used for trafficking. Section 146 was repealed by SOA 2003 because it was thought that existing powers under, for example, the Powers of Criminal Courts (Sentencing) Act 2000 would suffice. However, this neglected the fact that it allowed for detention and forfeiture only after conviction and not prior to the conviction.

- 'aircraft' includes hovercraft;

- 'land vehicle' means any vehicle other than a ship or aircraft; and

- 'ship' includes every description of vessel used in navigation.[45]

Both ss 60A and 60B deal with the rights of an owner and s 60C(2) states that a reference in ss 60A and 60B to an owner of a vehicle, ship or aircraft also includes a reference to being any of a number of persons who jointly own the vehicle, ship or aircraft.

Forfeiture

11.25 SOA 2003, s 60A deals with the forfeiture of a land vehicle, aircraft or ship. It applies only where a person is convicted on indictment for an offence under ss 57–59.[46]

11.26 By s 60A(2), a court can order the forfeiture of a land vehicle used or intended to be used in connection with the offence if the convicted person:

'(a)　owned the vehicle at the time the offence was committed;
(b)　was at that time a director, secretary or manager of a company[47] which owned the vehicle;
(c)　was at that time in possession of the vehicle under a hire-purchase agreement;
(d)　was at that time a director, secretary or manager of a company which was in possession of the vehicle under a hire-purchase agreement; or
(e)　was driving the vehicle in the course of the commission of the offence.'

11.27 By s 60A(3), a ship or aircraft may be forfeited under circumstances corresponding to (a)–(d) above[48] or where he or she was at that time a charterer of the ship or aircraft or committed the offence whilst acting as captain[49] of the ship or aircraft. There are two restrictions. Where the offender was not the owner or a director, secretary or manager of a company which owned the ship or aircraft, forfeiture may be ordered only where:

- at the time the offence was committed, the owner of the ship or aircraft, or a director, secretary or manager of a company which owned it, knew or ought to have known, of the intention to use it in the course of the commission of an offence under ss 57–59,[50] and

- in the case of a ship its gross tonnage is less than 500 tons[51] or in the case of an aircraft (which is not a hovercraft) the maximum weight at take-off in accordance with its airworthiness certificate is less than 5,700 kg.[52]

---

[45]　In *Goodwin* [2006] 1 Cr App R 354 the Court of Appeal held that a jet ski was not used 'in navigation' under similar provisions in the Merchant Shipping Act 1985. It is likely that this decision would apply equally here.
[46]　Section 60(A)(1).
[47]　In *Boal* [1992] QB 591 this was held to mean someone with real power in the company and not just merely someone described as a manager.
[48]　Section 60C(3).
[49]　Section 60C(1) defines 'captain' as meaning the master of a ship or the commander of an aircraft.
[50]　Section 60A(5).
[51]　Section 60A(6).
[52]　Section 60A(7).

11.28 Where a person who claims to have an interest in the vehicle, ship or aircraft applies to a court to make representations on the question of forfeiture, the court may not make an order under s 60A unless that person is given an opportunity to make representations.[53]

Detention

11.29 SOA 2003, s 60B deals with detaining the vehicle, ship or aircraft after arrest but before conviction. It is doubtless intended that if a person is convicted a court would ordinarily make an order under s 60A, but s 60B ensures that the vehicle, ship or aircraft cannot be disposed of in the meantime. Section 60B(1) states:

'If a person has been arrested for an offence under sections 57 to 59, a constable or senior immigration officer[54] may detain a relevant[55] vehicle, ship or aircraft—

(a) until a decision is taken as to whether or not to charge the arrested person with that offence,

(b) if the arrested person has been charged, until he is acquitted, the charge against him is dismissed or the proceedings are discontinued, or

(c) if he has been charged and convicted, until the court decides whether or not to order forfeiture of the vehicle, ship or aircraft.'

11.30 Section 60B(3) provides that a person (other than the arrested person) may apply to the court for the release of the vehicle, ship or aircraft. The relevant person must apply to the court[56] on the grounds that:

- he or she owns the vehicle, ship or aircraft;

- he or she was immediately before the detention of the vehicle, ship or aircraft, in possession of it under a hire-purchase agreement; or

- he or she is a charterer of the ship or aircraft.

11.31 On such an application, the court can release the vehicle, ship or aircraft (subject to such security or surety as it considers satisfactory) on the condition that if the arrested person is convicted and a forfeiture order under s 60A is made it will be made available to the court.[57] This is obviously an important provision where the person charged is not the owner of the vehicle, ship or aircraft but it will be important for the court to consider carefully the level of security or surety, although the court will presumably also have regard to any representations that are likely to be made by the owner under s 60A(8).

---

53   Section 60A(8).

54   Defined in s 60B(6) as an immigration officer (appointed or employed as such under the Immigration Act 1971) not below the rank of chief immigration officer.

55   Ie a land vehicle, ship or aircraft which the constable or officer concerned has reasonable grounds for believing could, on conviction of the arrested person for the offence for which he or she was arrested, be the subject of an order for forfeiture under s 60A (**11.25** et seq).

56   The application must be made to a magistrates' court where a person has not been charged, or has been charged but proceedings have not yet commenced; otherwise it must be made to the court where proceedings are being heard: s 60B(5)(a).

57   Section 60B(4).

EUROPEAN CONVENTION ON HUMAN TRAFFICKING

11.32 It is clear that the majority of trafficking involving the UK remains international.[58] As a result of this it is perhaps not surprising that it is an issue that has been raised in international agreements. The UN passed the Protocol to Prevent, Suppress and Punish Trafficking in Persons,[59] which was signed by the UK in 2000 and ratified in 2006.[60] The Protocol commits governments to a series of actions although it does not create any specific actionable rights in domestic laws.

11.33 Within Europe the issue of trafficking and sexual exploitation has become prominent, with at least one EU Framework Decision being passed.[61] This Framework seeks to provide a minimum standard of law in each Member State of the EU and includes the creation of criminal law provisions to penalise those who facilitate trafficking. More recently the Council of Europe has published the European Convention on Human Trafficking (ECHT) which the UK after considerable political pressure signed in March 2007, although it has not yet been ratified.[62] This Convention provides a number of substantive rights to victims of traffickers and obliges Member States to establish frameworks that help detect, investigate and prosecute those who traffic human beings for the purposes of sexual exploitation.

11.34 At the time the ECHT was signed, the Government produced an action plan[63] with the aim of tackling this menace. One of the principal features of the plan was to recognise that trafficking involved not only adults but also children[64] and to recognise that altering the substantive law was not sufficient but law enforcement had to adapt. A further development of the action plan was the recognition that using the criminal law is only one part of a strategy to stop trafficking and in December 2007 the Government produced guidance on safeguarding children who may have been trafficked.[65] This guidance is an addendum to the general *Working Together* multi-agency guidance and is designed to provide a coordinated response by all multi-agency partners to identify children who may have been trafficked and take steps to ensure their welfare is safeguarded.

11.35 The plan recognises that one of the difficulties with criminal law in this area is that there are undoubtedly difficulties in the gathering of evidence. In common with many sexual offences, victims of trafficking are often subject to violence and threats and may be reluctant to give evidence against their traffickers. There was also the difficulty that victims of trafficking are often considered to be illegal entrants to the UK and thus subject to deportation. The signing of the ECHT will allow victims to stay in the UK for a period of at least 30 days to recover and reflect on whether they wish to assist the authorities.[66] This period of recovery and reflection was why the UK was slow to sign

---

[58] See *Human Trafficking: Update* 21st report from the Joint Committee on Human Rights in the 2006/7 Parliamentary Session, HC 1056/HL Paper 179.
[59] Supplementing the UN Convention Against Trans-national Organized Crime.
[60] The Protocol was signed on 14 December 2000 and ratified on 9 February 2006.
[61] Council Framework Decision on Combating Trafficking in Human Beings, Decision 2002/629/JHA.
[62] The Convention on Action against Trafficking in Human Beings (to state its formal title) came into force (at international level) on 1 February 2008 following the ratification by 10 Member States (not yet including the UK). In its response to the Joint Committee on Human Rights report (n 58 above), the Government stated it was committed to ratifying the treaty 'as soon as possible' but gave no indication as to timescales.
[63] *UK Action Plan on Tackling Human Trafficking* (Home Office/Scottish Executive, March 2007).
[64] Ibid, at p 6.
[65] *Working Together to Safeguard Children who may have been Trafficked* (Home Office, 2007).
[66] ECHT, Art 13.

the Treaty. The UK is not yet under an obligation to legislate to give the ECHT domestic effect. Even if this is done, it is highly questionable whether 30 days will be a sufficient period to gather appropriate evidence. It is likely that where a victim agrees to support a prosecution he or she will be allowed to remain in the UK to give evidence. There is a risk that this could cause undue emotional pressure to a victim, with leave to remain becoming a bargaining tool.

Chapter 12

PREPARATORY OFFENCES

12.1   The Sexual Offences Act (SOA) 2003, ss 61–63 provide offences of:

- administering a substance with intent;

- committing an offence with intent to commit a sexual offence; and

- trespassing with intent to commit a sexual offence.

These offences are preparatory offences. Other examples in the Act are the offences of arranging or facilitating the commission of a child sexual offence, contrary to s 14 (in some of its applications), meeting a child, etc following sexual grooming, etc, contrary to s 15, and installing equipment, etc with intent to enable an offence of voyeurism to be committed, contrary to s 67. They bite at an earlier point of time than the law of attempt in relation to the intended sexual offence (and therefore catch people who are thwarted or give up before getting as far as an attempt), since – for there to be an attempt to commit that offence – there must be an 'act which is more than merely preparatory to' its commission.[1] The width of the offences under ss 61–63 is of obvious attraction to prosecutors: why, for example, charge attempted non-consensual sexual touching if one can charge (and prove) an assault with intent to touch sexually without consent and avoid the potentially difficult task of proving the commission of an act more than merely preparatory to a non-consensual sexual touching? The offences under ss 61-63 can be supported on the ground that the sexual motivation of the offender can be reflected in the charge brought, and thereby an opportunity is provided to identify and treat those inclined to sexual offending who might well actually commit a sex offence in the future. The offences under ss 61–63 can also be supported on the basis that, where a sexual offence is clearly intended, the trauma can be as great for the victim as if the intended sexual offence was actually attempted.[2]

12.2   The law can, of course, bite at an earlier stage than the commission of one of the offences under ss 61–63 because, like the other preparatory offences in SOA 2003, the offence of attempt can be committed in relation to them.

ADMINISTERING A SUBSTANCE WITH INTENT

12.3   SOA 2003, s 61(1) provides:

> 'A person commits an offence if he intentionally administers a substance to, or causes a substance to be taken by, another person (B)—

---

[1]   Criminal Attempts Act (CAA) 1981, s 1(1).
[2]   *Setting the Boundaries: Reforming the Law on Sexual Offences* (Home Office, 2000) (*SB*), at para 2.13.1.

(a) knowing that B does not consent, and

(b) with the intention of stupefying or overpowering B, so as to enable any person to engage in a sexual activity that involves B.'

Class of offence	3	SOA 2003, s 72 applies	✔[3]
Notification requirements	✔	SOPO[4]	✔
CJA 2003,[5] Sch 15 applies	✔	Serious specified offence	✔
Review of lenient sentence	✔	Special provisions of CYPA 1933[6]	✔
Detention of young offender for specified period			✘

See **1.48** et seq.

12.4 An offence under s 61 is triable either way and punishable with a maximum of 10 years' imprisonment on conviction on indictment.[7] See the Sentencing Guidelines Council (SGC) Definitive Guideline,[8] in the Appendix.

12.5 The point has already been made on a number of occasions in this book that offences under SOA 2003 overlap with other offences under that Act. There is some overlap between SOA 2003, s 61 and other offences but this time the overlap is with offences under another Act, those of unlawfully applying or administering to, or attempting to cause to be administered or taken by, any person, any chloroform, laudanum or other stupefying or overpowering drug, matter or thing, with intent thereby to commit or to assist another to commit any indictable offence, contrary to the Offences against the Person Act (OAPA) 1861, s 22, for which the maximum punishment is life imprisonment.

12.6 It would seem that there are two separate offences under s 61(1): one requiring administration of a substance and the other causing a substance to be taken.[9] Where there is one administration with intent to enable more than one person to engage in sexual activity only one offence is committed.[10]

12.7 Section 61 replaces in a gender-neutral way that under SOA 1956, s 4,[11] which provided that it was an offence to give to, or cause to be taken by, a woman any drug, matter or thing with intent to stupefy or overpower her so as to enable any man to have unlawful sexual intercourse with her. It is also wider in that it relates to all sexual activity

---

[3] But only where the victim is within the age limit to which s 72 applies: see **2.97**.
[4] Sexual offences prevention order.
[5] Criminal Justice Act 2003.
[6] Children and Young Persons Act 1933.
[7] SOA 2003, s 61(2); maximum on summary conviction: **1.43**.
[8] At pp 5–18, 88–89.
[9] See **3.170**.
[10] By analogy with *Shillingford, Vanderwall* [1968] 2 All ER 200, a case concerned with SOA 1956, s 4.
[11] SOA 1956, s 4 was repealed by SOA 2003: see **1.5**.

and not just sexual intercourse.[12] It is therefore not to be regarded merely as aimed at responding to the growing problem of drug-assisted rape, although this was the primary purpose in its enactment.

Actus reus

12.8 This is simple: administering a substance to, or causing a substance to be taken by, another person without that person's consent. Although the offence is aimed at the administration (or causing to be taken) of drugs (such as GHB (gammahydroxylbutri-ate) or Rohypnol),[13] spiked drinks (such as vodka in lemonade or beer), or any other substance which would render the victim less liable to resist, without the victim's knowledge or consent, it does not need to be proved that the substance was in fact a stupefying or overpowering agent, or that it was administered (or taken) in a sufficient quantity to have such effect.

12.9 By analogy with the interpretation given to these terms in OAPA 1861, ss 23 and 24 (administering, etc poison, etc so as to endanger life, etc or with intent to injure, etc), 'administers' and 'taken' are to be construed in the Crown Court by the judge and not left as a question of fact to the jury.[14]

12.10 In *Kennedy (No 2)*,[15] where the House of Lords was concerned with an offence under OAPA 1861, s 23, it was held that administration 'is committed where D administers the noxious thing directly to V, as by injecting V with the noxious thing, holding a glass containing the noxious thing to V's lips, or (as in *R v Gillard*[16]) spraying the noxious thing in V's face'.[17] There is no necessity when 'administer' is in issue to postulate any form of entry into the victim's body, whether through any orifice or through absorption.[18] The House of Lords also held that the 'causing to be taken' offence under OAPA 1861, s 23 'covers the situation where the noxious thing is not administered to V but taken by him, provided D causes the noxious thing to be taken by V and V does not make a voluntary and informed decision to take it. If D puts a noxious thing in food which V is about to eat and V, ignorant of the presence of the noxious thing, eats it D commits the offence'.[19] In *Gillard*[20] the Court of Appeal stated that 'taking', for the purposes of 'causing to be taken' in OAPA 1861, s 24, requires ingestion into the digestive system. These statements would seem equally applicable to the offence under SOA 2003, s 61.

12.11 'Causes to be taken' therefore covers directly causing to be taken, as by slipping a date-rape drug into the complainant's drink, or indirectly causing to be taken, as by persuading an innocent associate of the victim to do the slipping in. It also covers the case where the defendant has deceived the complainant as to the substance in question. The complainant's act of taking in these cases would not break the chain of causation

---

[12] The offence is also wider than that under SOA 1956, s 4, because under s 4 the intended intercourse had to be unlawful (ie extra-marital): *Chapman* [1959] 1 QB 100.

[13] See **3.79**.

[14] *Gillard* (1988) 87 Cr App R 189, at p 194.

[15] [2008] 1 Cr App R 256.

[16] (1988) 87 Cr App R 189.

[17] [2008] 1 Cr App R 256, at [10].

[18] *Gillard* above; *Walford* (1899) 34 L Jo 116, per Wills J. The contrary view, that a thing is not administered until it is ingested, taken by trial judges in *Cadman* (1825) Carrington's Supplement 237 and *Harley* (1830) 4 C & P 369, would seem to be wrong.

[19] [2008] 1 Cr App R 256, at [12].

[20] (1988) 87 Cr App R 189, at pp 193–194.

because it would not be an informed act;[21] nor, for the same reason, would the act of the innocent associate.[22] A person who supplies a drug to A for use contrary to s 61, as A intends, will be liable as a secondary party if A administers it or causes it to be taken, and in any event of an inchoate offence.

12.12 SOA 2003, s 61(1)(a) indicates that the complainant must not consent to the substance being administered to him or her, or caused to be taken by him or her. On the other hand, it is not an element of the offence that the complainant does not consent to the intended sexual activity. As elsewhere in Pt 1 of the Act, 'a person consents if he agrees by choice, and has the freedom and capacity to make that choice'.[23] Unlike rape and related offences, however, there are no rebuttable or conclusive presumptions as to the absence of consent. It follows from the definition of consent that a man who plies a woman with excess alcohol, which she knowingly and willingly consumes, and thereby intentionally lowers her resistance to the sexual activity which he intends to have thereby does not commit this offence. This is so, even though the woman was unaware of the man's intent to engage in sexual activity once she was stupefied or overpowered. Of course, if the woman who consented to the administration was, in fact, stupefied or overpowered, and thereby was unable to consent, sexual activity with her by the man or someone else would constitute one of the non-consensual offences under SOA 2003, ss 1-4, described in Chapter 3.

12.13 It is submitted that it is not enough for a person to consent to a substance being administered; he or she must consent to *the* substance administered. If, however, he or she does so it appears irrelevant that he or she was mistaken as to its dosage.

Mens rea

12.14 The defendant (A) must intentionally[24] administer, or cause to be taken, a substance by another person (B). When A does so, A must know[25] that B does not consent (ie does not consent to the administration or taking of the substance in question), and must intend to stupefy or overpower B, so as to enable any person to engage in a sexual activity[26] that involves B. 'Stupefy' means 'make stupid, torpid, or insensible; numb, deaden'; 'overpower' means 'reduce to submission'.[27] It is not enough to intend something less than this, for example, to relax B's inhibitions and make B more amenable to the sexual activity. It is submitted that the natural meaning of the wording of s 61 is that A must intend not only to stupefy or overpower B but also thereby to enable any person to engage in sexual activity involving B.[28]

12.15 It will be noted that the intended sexual activity may be by *anyone* (including B the complainant, or the defendant A). Thus, for example, it could consist of A or C having intercourse with B, of B masturbating himself or of A or C stripping B and

---

21   *Harley*, n 18 above.
22   *Kennedy (No 2)* [2008] 1 Cr App R 256.
23   See **3.13** et seq.
24   See **2.56–2.60**.
25   'Know' here includes wilful blindness; see **2.61–2.62**.
26   See **2.31–2.48**.
27   *The New Shorter Oxford English Dictionary*.
28   Support may be found in the case-law relating to the further intent in relation to offences under the Forgery and Counterfeiting Act 1981: see *Utting* (1988) 86 Cr App R 164; *Tobierre* (1987) 82 Cr App R 212. Contrast *Cato* (1976) 62 Cr App R 41, in respect of the offence under OAPA 1861, s 23, in relation to which offence the natural meaning would seem to be different.

taking indecent photographs of B.[29] It will also be noted that there are no geographical limits on where the intended activity is to take place. It does not appear to be necessary that the victim should be stupefied at the time of the intended sexual activity. A 'white slaver' who gives a woman a soporific drug, intending to put her in a trunk and ship her out of the country to an overseas client commits the present offence, even though the woman will have recovered from the drug by the time of the intended sexual activity.

12.16 Of course, the intended sexual activity need not occur or be attempted, with the result that A can be convicted if the victim of his date-rape drug collapses in the presence of a friend and is taken to hospital before A can proceed.

12.17 It will often be easier to prove the necessary intent if A has embarked on sexual activity after the administration or causing to be taken. Proof of such intent may also be assisted by evidence that A was in possession of condoms or a sex aid.[30]

12.18 If the intended sexual activity does take place A should, of course, be charged with the relevant intended sexual offence. As a matter of good practice, A should, however, also be charged with the offence under s 61. In the event of an acquittal of an offence under ss 1–4, for example, because the relevant sexual activity could not be proved, it would remain possible to convict under s 61 if its terms were proved.

COMMITTING AN OFFENCE WITH INTENT TO COMMIT A SEXUAL OFFENCE

12.19 SOA 2003, s 62 deals with criminal liability for committing an offence with intent to commit a relevant sexual offence. The origins of s 62 lie in the proposal made by the Sex Offences Review (see **1.4**) for the enactment of two offences to fill gaps in the law: assault with intent to commit rape or sexual assault by penetration, and abduction with such intent or with intent to commit a serious sexual offence (rape, sexual assault by penetration, sexual assault or adult sexual abuse of a child).[31] The Government, however, preferred a broader provision along the lines of s 62 on the ground that:[32]

> 'An offender deflected from carrying out [an intended] sex offence will, under existing law, normally only be charged with the offence that has been committed. However, it is important that the criminal law should fully recognise any sexual motivation of an offender and that he or she should be charged with a substantive offence and, if found guilty, managed as an offender.'

It is management of the offender as a sex offender which is the purpose behind the provision. Otherwise it might be difficult to justify, given the existence of liability for the preliminary offence which has to be established for the offence under s 62 to be proved.

12.20 Section s 62(1) is a relatively short offence-creating provision:

---

29   *Guidance on Part 1 of the Sexual Offences Act 2003* (Home Office, 2003), at para 273.
30   Stevenson, Davies and Gunn *Blackstone's Guide to the Sexual Offences Act 2003* (Oxford University Press, 2004), at para 9.2.1.
31   *SB*, at paras 2.15, 2.17.
32   *Protecting the Public: Strengthening Protection Against Sex Offenders and Reforming the Law on Sexual Offences*, Cm 5668 (2002) (*PP*), at para 47.

'A person commits an offence under this section if he commits any offence with the intention of committing a relevant sexual offence.'

Class of offence	See text	SOA 2003, s 72 applies	✔[33]
Notification requirements	See text	SOPO	✔
CJA 2003, Sch 15 applies	✔	Serious specified offence	✔
Review of lenient sentence	See text	Special provisions of CYPA 1933	See text
Detention of young offender for specified period			See text

See **1.48** et seq. The special provisions of CYPA 1933 only apply where the intended offence was one against someone under 18.

12.21 The notification requirements of SOA 2003, Pt 2 apply to an offender in respect of an offence under s 62 in specified circumstances.[34] These are:

- where the offender was under 18, he or she is or has been sentenced in respect of the offence to imprisonment for a term of at least 12 months;

- in any other case where:
  - (a) the intended offence was an offence against a person under 18; or
  - (b) the offender, in respect of the offence or finding, is or has been sentenced to a term of imprisonment, detained in a hospital, or made the subject of a community sentence of at least 12 months.

12.22 Where the offence committed with intent to commit a relevant sexual offence is kidnapping or false imprisonment, an offence under s 62 is a Class 2 offence, triable only on indictment and punishable with a maximum of life imprisonment (the maximum for a common law offence).[35] In the case of any other offence committed with the relevant intent, an offence under s 62 is a Class 3 offence, triable either way and punishable with a maximum of 10 years' imprisonment on conviction on indictment.[36] See the SGC Definitive Guideline[37] in the Appendix. By virtue of the principle in *Courtie*[38] there are two separate offences under s 62: one requiring proof of kidnapping or false imprisonment; and the other proof of any other offence. The provisions of CJA 1988, ss 35 and 36 relating to the review of unduly lenient sentences apply to sentences for the former offence,[39] as do those relating to the detention of a young offender for a specified period.

12.23 Although it can be conceded that kidnapping and false imprisonment are likely to be particularly common types of offence committed with the relevant intent, one has

33 But only where the intended offence relates to a person within the age limit to which s 72 applies: see **2.97**.
34 SOA 2003, s 80 and Sch 3, para 31.
35 SOA 2003, s 62(3).
36 SOA 2003, s 62(4). Maximum on summary conviction: see **1.43**.
37 At pp 5–18, 84–85.
38 [1984] AC 463. There is nothing to rebut the presumption to this effect.
39 CJA 1988, s 35(3)(b).

to ask why special trial and punishment treatment has been reserved for them alone. The answer cannot simply be that, as common law offences, 'simple' kidnapping and false imprisonment are indictable only and carry a maximum of life imprisonment.[40] The same mode of trial and punishment applies, for example, to 'simple' attempted murder.[41] Why should someone who attempts to kill another with intent to commit necrophilia (a relevant offence) only be liable to 10 years' imprisonment?

12.24 Section 62(2) defines a 'relevant sexual offence' which must be *intended* as any offence under Pt 1 (ss 1–79) of the Act ('including an offence of aiding, abetting, counselling or procuring such an offence').[42] The effect is that committing *any* offence with intent to commit any offence under the Act described in Chapters 2–13 (including the present offences) is an offence under s 62(1). The intended relevant sexual offence need not, of course, be committed or even attempted. If it is committed, the defendant should be charged with committing it and with the offence under s 62.

12.25 Although the *commission* of any offence can suffice as the preliminary offence under s 62(1), even an inchoate offence (which shows how wide a preparatory offence s 62 is), it is hard to envisage that most of the 8,000 or so offences which currently exist could be committed with intent to commit a relevant offence. This is particularly true in the case of the thousands of regulatory offences. Besides kidnapping or false imprisonment, a typical example of an offence committed with intent to commit a relevant offence would be a common assault or battery, or stalking, contrary to the Protection from Harassment Act 1997. Other examples would be committing criminal damage by breaking into the intended complainant's car in order to conceal oneself in the back until the intended complainant gets into it and can be raped; committing criminal damage by using an indelible marker to write an invitation to sexual activity on the wall of a public lavatory;[43] and a parent wilfully neglecting to feed a child intending to starve it into submission to sexual activity.

12.26 The offence committed may be a minor one as, for example, where the offender commits a road traffic offence such as a parking offence, with intent to expose himself to passers-by. The intent converts the parking offence (which offences are all summary only and, with one exception,[44] not imprisonable) into an indictable offence with a maximum of 10 years' imprisonment when tried on indictment.[45]

12.27 The preliminary offence committed with the above intent need not be directed at the complainant. It would be committed, for example, where A takes someone's car without consent, contrary to the Theft Act (TA) 1968, s 12, for the purpose of driving 20 miles to a local 'lovers' lane' to engage in voyeurism. Likewise, if A steals some condoms from C in order to commit a relevant sexual offence on B, A will commit an offence under s 62.

12.28 It is implicit in the wording of s 62 that the requisite intent is limited to a direct (purposive) intent and that A must commit the preliminary offence for the purpose of

---

[40]   *Morris* [1951] 1 KB 394, approved in *Verrier v Director of Public Prosecutions* [1967] 2 AC 195.
[41]   CAA 1981, s 4.
[42]   SOA 2003, s 62(2).
[43]   As in *Jones* [2007] 2 Cr App R 267 (appeal did not relate to conviction under s 62).
[44]   The offence of obstructing a street, contrary to the Town Police Clauses Act 1847, s 28 (punishable with 14 days' imprisonment).
[45]   Under the SGC Definitive Guideline, at 85, the starting point, however, in sentencing for an offence under s 62 should be commensurate with that for the preliminary offence actually committed, with an enhancement to reflect the nature and severity of the intended sexual offence: see the Appendix.

committing a relevant sexual offence. It follows that, if A, who intends to rape B tomorrow, assaults X (or even B) in a road rage incident on his way to work, A does not commit the offence under s 62. The same point may be made in relation to the offences under ss 61 and 63. On the other hand, A would commit an offence under s 62 if he committed an offence of speeding in order to get to the home of his intended rape-victim before she left for work.

12.29 It is submitted that, if A commits a preliminary offence for the purpose of pursuing a particular type of conduct, for example, sexual intercourse with B, hoping that B will consent (or that B is 16 or over), but firmly intending to have sexual intercourse with B even if B does not consent (or is under 16), that amounts to committing the preliminary offence with intent to commit rape (or sexual activity with a child under 16, as the case may be).[46]

12.30 If a preliminary offence is not immediately connected with the commission of the alleged intended sexual offence as a *step* in its commission, as where A obtains by fraud a train ticket from Leicester to London with the alleged intention of taking the underground to Walthamstow and raping his ex-wife in her flat there, it may be difficult to prove that he committed the offence of fraud with that intent. As Rook and Ward state:[47] '[I]n general, the more remote A's conduct is from the commission of the [intended sex] offence, the harder it will be to prove that he intended to commit such an offence.' Nevertheless, evidence of things found in his possession, for example, B's address and a street plan relating to it, sex aids and condoms, or of communications with B or of other relevant matters could be used to prove the necessary intention in such a case.

12.31 It would seem that if some of a jury are satisfied that A intended to commit a particular offence (e g rape) but the rest are only satisfied that he intended to commit a less serious offence (e g sexual assault) which the former necessarily involves, A would be proved to have intended to commit a relevant offence, and that if the whole jury is satisfied that A must have intended to commit either relevant offence X or relevant offence Y, but are not satisfied as to which of these, they could properly convict A of an offence under s 62.[48]

12.32 As a matter of good practice there should be two counts in an indictment where the relevant preliminary offence is indictable: the first alleging the preliminary offence, and the second alleging that it was committed with intent to commit a relevant offence. This will simplify matters if the jury is satisfied about the preliminary offence but not that it was committed with the intention of committing a relevant offence.[49]

Common law offence of assault with intent to rape

12.33 The offences under s 62 replace assault with intent to commit buggery contrary to SOA 1956, s 16.[50] For some reason, the common law counterpart to assault with intent to commit buggery, assault with intent to rape, was not put into statutory form by OAPA 1861 when the former offence was. Strictly, assault with intent to rape may

---

[46]   Support for this may be derived from *Walkington* (1979) 68 Cr App R 427; *A-G's References (Nos 1 and 2 of 1979)* (1979) 69 Cr App R 266.

[47]   Rook and Ward *Sexual Offences Law & Practice* (Sweet & Maxwell, 3rd edn, 2004) at p 385.

[48]   See Archbold *Criminal Pleading, Evidence and Practice* (Sweet & Maxwell, 2008 edn), at para 20.193.

[49]   See ibid, at para 20.196.

[50]   This offence was repealed by SOA 2003: see **1.5**.

continue to exist as a common law offence,[51] although, if it does, it 'has become unusable because of arguments about its status, and it has for all practical purposes ceased to exist'.[52] This is untidy. It is unfortunate that the Act does not provide that if an offence of assault with intent to rape exists it is abolished. Because it has not been expressly abolished, the maximum of life imprisonment available for a common law offence might make a zealous prosecutor think that it was worth taking the chance and prosecuting the offence.

TRESPASS WITH INTENT TO COMMIT A SEXUAL OFFENCE

12.34 Before SOA 2003 a person committed the offence of burglary, contrary to the TA 1968, s 9(1)(a), if he entered any building or part of a building as a trespasser with intent (inter alia) to rape any person in the building or part of the building trespassed in. Burglary is not an offence to which the notification requirements, introduced by the Sex Offenders Act 1997, apply. The Sex Offences Review[53] concluded that burglary with intent to rape should be regarded as a sex offence, because the essence of the offence was the sexual intent rather than the burglary, and not continue to be in the 1968 Act. It recommended that there should be a sex offence of trespass with intent to commit a serious sex offence (rape, sexual assault by penetration, sexual assault or adult sexual abuse of a child). The White Paper, which emphasised (as in the case of the offence of committing an offence with intent to commit a sex offence) the importance that the criminal law should fully recognise any sexual motivation of an offender and that he or she should be charged with a substantive offence and, if guilty, managed as a sex offender, proposed an offence of trespass with intent to commit a (ie any) sex offence.[54]

12.35 The reference to an intent to rape in the TA 1968, s 9 was removed by the SOA 2003.[55]

12.36 SOA 2003, s 63 implements the proposal in the White Paper. Section 63(1) provides:

---

[51] It was undoubtedly an offence at common law to assault with intent to rape. Whether or not assault with intent to rape continues to exist as a common law offence depends on whether it was a distinct specific offence or punishable as a variant of a common law offence of assault with intent to commit a felony. If the latter offence existed as a specific offence at common law, it ceased to exist when the distinctions between felonies and misdemeanours were abolished by the Criminal Law Act (CLA) 1967 and the provision in OAPA 1861, s 38, that assault with intent to commit a felony punishable with 2 years' imprisonment, was repealed. No less an authority than Professor Sir John Smith concluded that the better opinion is that there was no general common law offence of assault with intent to commit a felony and that assault with intent to rape survives as a common law offence, not having been abolished by OAPA 1861 or by the repeal of the above provision in OAPA 1861, s 38, which he regarded as offence-creating (see [1990] Crim LR 326 and Smith and Hogan *Criminal Law* (Ormerod (ed)) (OUP, 12th edn, 2008): the relevant passage now appears at p 723). Sir John was influenced in particular by the fact that the draftsman of the 1861 Act, CS Greaves, treated the common law offence of assault with intent to rape as continuing to exist thereafter (*Russell on Crime* (ed Greaves) (4th edn, 1865) vol III, at p 927).
In *P* [1990] Crim LR 323, Pill J concluded that the offence did not survive the enactment of CLA 1967. This was also the opinion of the Criminal Law Revision Committee in its *Fifteenth Report: Sexual Offences*, Cmnd 9213 (1984), at para 4.3, and of Spencer 'Assault with Intent to Rape – Dead or Alive?' [1986] Crim LR 110. However, in *J* (1986), an unreported Crown Court case referred to at [1990] Crim LR 326, Turner J decided that the offence still existed and in *Lionel* (1982) 4 Cr App R (S) 291, on an appeal against sentence for assault with intent to rape, the assumption that the offence exists was not challenged.
[52] *SB*, at para 2.13.1.
[53] *SB*, at para 2.16; Recommendation 12.
[54] *PP*, at para 47.
[55] Sections 139 and 140 and Schs 6 and 7.

'A person commits an offence if—

- (a)   he is a trespasser on any premises,
- (b)   he intends to commit a relevant sexual offence on the premises, and
- (c)   he knows that, or is reckless as to whether, he is a trespasser.'

Class of offence	3	SOA 2003, s 72 applies	✔[56]
Notification requirements	See text	SOPO	✔
CJA 2003, Sch 15 applies	✔	Serious specified offence	✔
Review of lenient sentence	✘	Special provisions of CYPA 1933	See text
Detention of young offender for specified period			✘

See **1.48** et seq. The special provisions of CYPA 1933 only apply where the intended offence was one against someone under 18.

12.37 The offence under s 63 is triable either way and punishable with a maximum of 10 years' imprisonment on conviction on indictment.[57] See the SGC Definitive Guideline[58] in the Appendix. The notification requirements under SOA 2003, Pt 2 apply to s 63 in the same specified circumstances which apply in respect of s 62: see **12.21**.

12.38 There is no equivalent under the Act to the offence of aggravated burglary, punishable with life imprisonment, where the trespasser has with him a firearm, explosive or offensive weapon.

Actus reus

Being a trespasser

12.39 The actus reus simply consists of being a trespasser on any premises. By basing liability on being *on* premises as a trespasser with the specified further intent, s 63 avoids a problem inherent with the old offence of burglary with intent to rape, namely that A had to have entered as a trespasser with the necessary ulterior intent at the time of that entry. It catches people who enter lawfully but become trespassers with the necessary intent, as well as those who enter as trespassers for some non-sexual purpose and subsequently, whilst on the premises, form the specified further intent – as where A enters what he believes are empty premises in order to steal but, finding B inside the premises, decides to rape B.

12.40 Trespass is a concept of the civil law. In civil law a person enters as a trespasser if he or she intentionally, recklessly or negligently enters premises in the possession of

---

56   But only where the intended offence relates to a person within the age limit to which s 72 applies: see **2.97**.
57   SOA 2003, s 63(3)
58   At pp 5–18, 86–87.

another and enters without a right by law or permission to do so.[59] However, a negligent entry does not suffice for an offence under s 63.[60]

12.41 Rights of entry are granted by statute to certain people for certain purposes. For instance, a police officer entering a building with a search warrant authorised under some statute is not a trespasser if he enters with the intention of searching pursuant to such a warrant, but he is if he enters with the intention of raping someone inside the premises or for some other purpose.

12.42 It appears that permission to enter for a particular purpose may be given by someone (X) other than the person (Y) in possession of the premises if that person (X) has Y's authority (express or implied) to do so. In the famous case of *Collins*,[61] the Court of Appeal said that it was unthinkable that an 18-year-old girl was unable to give such permission in the circumstances, whatever the position in the law of tort. Although the statement was made in respect of the offence of burglary it must be equally applicable to the offence under SOA 2003, s 63. The issue is of some importance because members of a family, lodgers and employees, for example, are impliedly (and often expressly) authorised to invite other people generally, or particular classes of persons or particular persons to enter (eg the family home, lodging house or business premises). Thus, if a lodger is authorised by her landlord to invite women, but not men, to her room and Jill and Jack come to her room at her invitation, Jill is not a trespasser but Jack is. Such an authority can, of course, be withdrawn or altered in terms of who may be invited. In addition, it would be most unlikely to be found that a very young child had any implied authority. If a family member, lodger, employee, and so on, does not have authority or acts in excess of a limited authority, and the entrant knows or is reckless as to this, he or she could be convicted under s 63 if he or she had the necessary intent.

12.43 Permission may be express or implied. For instance, in the case of pubs, there is an implied permission for members of the public to enter for the purposes of partaking of food or drink. A person who enters premises with a right or permission to do so for some innocent purpose, intending to commit a relevant sexual offence, enters the premises in excess of his or her permission and is a trespasser.[62] Thus, if A enters a pub, not for the purpose of partaking of drink or food there, but for the purpose of sexual activity with a child in the pub, A enters as a trespasser, and so would A if he secured permission to enter B's premises by deceiving the occupier into believing that he is a prospective purchaser come to view when his true purpose for the entry is to rape her.

12.44 Someone who, with an innocent intent, enters premises lawfully, but who becomes a trespasser by staying on after the lapse of a reasonable time after the termination or cessation of his permission to be there, or by exceeding the purpose for which he is permitted or has a right to be on the premises, thereby becomes a trespasser.[63] If, as such a trespasser, he intends to commit a sexual offence, he can therefore be convicted of an offence under s 63. An example would be where B invited A

---

[59]   See *Winfield and Jolowicz on Tort* (Sweet & Maxwell, 17th edn, 2006), Ch 13.
[60]   See **12.51**.
[61]   [1973] QB 100.
[62]   *Jones; Smith* (1976) 63 Cr App R 47. See also *Taylor v Jackson* (1898) 78 LT 555; *Farrington v Thomas and Bridgland* [1959] VR 286; *Barker* (1983) 7 ALJR 426.
[63]   *Hillen and Pettigrew v ICI (Alkali) Ltd* [1936] AC 65. See also *Wood v Leadbitter* (1845) 13 M & W 838; *Minister of Health v Bellotti* [1944] KB 298; *Robson v Hallett* [1967] 2 QB 939.

in for a drink after a night out but asked A to leave when A makes amorous overtures; if A stayed, intending to have intercourse with B without B's consent, A would commit an offence under s 63.

12.45 A permission to enter or be on premises may not necessarily extend to every part of the premises. Thus, a person may lawfully enter premises, but then enter a part without permission. For example, he may be a lawful guest at a meal in a private house but enter a bedroom without permission. In doing so he becomes a trespasser.[64]

Premises

12.46 Although 'premises' in a popular sense often means buildings or land with buildings on it,[65] in a legal sense 'premises' means the subject matter of the habendum in a lease. This covers any sort of property of which a lease can be granted: a building (or part of a building) or land with a building on part of it or land without a building on it provided that it has a defined boundary,[66] such as a yard, garden, school playing field or other defined piece of land in the open air. It is submitted that premises should be given this wider meaning. It is noteworthy that Parliament, having chosen to divorce the type of conduct from burglary (where 'building' is employed), used different language and that the mischief of the offence is the same whether the trespasser is inside a building or lurking in a park with the relevant intent. Section 63(2) provides that 'premises' includes a structure or part of a structure. By s 63(2), structure includes 'a tent, vehicle, or vessel or other temporary or movable structure'. The vehicle is not required to be mechanically propelled: caravans, for example, are covered. A 'structure' is not required to be inhabited: a motor car, for example, is therefore a structure. An 'other temporary or movable structure' would be, for example, a booth or kiosk at an open-air venue.

12.47 It would seem that, like 'part of a building' in burglary, a 'part of a structure' does not necessarily mean a separate room: it also includes a physically marked out area in a structure from which the defendant is plainly excluded, whether expressly or impliedly.[67]

Mens rea

Intent to commit relevant sexual offence

12.48 The defendant must intend[68] to commit on the premises a 'relevant sexual offence' (ie any offence in SOA 2003, Pt 1, including an offence of aiding, abetting, counselling or procuring such an offence).[69] The defendant's intended sexual offence does not, of course, have to be committed or even attempted.[70] Indeed, it would be irrelevant that it could not be effected on the occasion in question because no one was on the premises, unknown to the defendant. It would also be irrelevant that the defendant's intention is conditional, in the sense that he or she intends to commit a relevant sexual offence on the premises if the occasion arises, for example, if he or she

---

[64]   *Hillen and Pettigrew v ICI (Alkali) Ltd* ibid; *Walkington* (1979) 68 Cr App R 427.
[65]   *Bracey v Read* [1963] Ch 88.
[66]   *Andrews v Andrews & Mears* [1908] 2 KB 567, at p 570 ('premises' in workmen's compensation legislation); *Whitley v Stumbles* [1930] AC 544; *Bracey v Read*, ibid (landlord and tenant legislation).
[67]   *Walkington*, n 64 above.
[68]   See **2.56–2.60**, in particular **2.58**.
[69]   SOA 2003, s 63(2) states that 'relevant sexual offence' has the same meaning as s 62; see **12.24**.
[70]   If the intended offence is committed or attempted, that offence is the appropriate offence to prosecute rather than the offence under s 63.

finds a young child on whom to indulge his or her paedophile desires. What is said in **12.31** is equally applicable to the present offence.

12.49 It seems clear that the intended victim need not be in the premises at the time of the defendant's trespass and, therefore, if the defendant is a trespasser on premises intending to rape their occupant when she returns home but he is apprehended before she does, he can be convicted under s 63. On the other hand, since he has to intend to commit the sexual offence on the premises, he does not commit the offence if he intends to drag a woman to his house to rape her.

12.50 Proof of the above intent will be aided by evidence of what the defendant says or does to the victim or intended victim or of items such as condoms or sex aids in the defendant's possession at the time he or she commits the trespass.

Knowledge or recklessness as to being trespasser

12.51 The defendant must know that, or be reckless[71] as to whether, he or she is a trespasser, ie he or she must be aware that there is a risk that he or she is on premises in the possession of another without a right by law or permission to be there for the purpose for which he or she is there, and it is, in the circumstances known to him or her, unreasonable to take that risk.

12.52 These two elements of mens rea need not exist at the inception of the trespass on the premises. It is enough that the defendant subsequently forms the necessary state of mind whilst he or she is still a trespasser on the premises. Thus, somebody invited to a party, who enters a bedroom to steal but then decides to have sexual intercourse with a woman who has 'passed out' on a bed, can be convicted of the present offence.

---

[71] See **2.73**.

Chapter 13

OFFENCES AGAINST PUBLIC DECENCY

13.1   The Sexual Offences Act (SOA) 2003, ss 66–71 create offences relating to:

- exposure;

- voyeurism;

- intercourse with an animal;

- sexual penetration of a corpse; and

- sexual activity in a public lavatory.

Some of these provisions supplant older statutory offences repealed by the 2003 Act. Others proscribe conduct that might not previously have been criminal at all or provide specific statutory offences in respect of conduct that might previously have been prosecuted only as an act outraging public decency at common law.[1] There is also some overlap here with offences under the Public Order Act (POA) 1986, because conduct that offends against public decency may in some cases prejudice public order, and in the past behaviour such as voyeurism or sexual misconduct in public lavatories was sometimes prosecuted under that Act.

13.2   The offence of outraging public decency has not been abrogated, and remains useful to prosecutors in circumstances where statutory offences may be inapplicable or difficult to establish.[2] In particular, cases involving sexual activity in public may continue to attract such charges, given that a proposal to make this a specific offence under SOA 2003 was dropped by the Government as a result of opposition in the House of Lords.

13.3   Now that SOA 2003 is in force, there is no longer much incentive for prosecutors to charge public order offences when dealing with sexual misconduct. The continued use of such charges cannot entirely be ruled out, however, and there may also be circumstances in which displays of public nudity, etc might have much more to do with public order than with sex. Brief reference will therefore be made to the offences created by POA 1986, ss 4A and 5.[3]

---

[1]   There may also be some overlap with offences under local by-laws; but it is now unlikely that public nuisance could have any application in such cases: see *Rimmington; Goldstein* [2006] 1 AC 459 and **13.23**.

[2]   See **13.86** et seq.

[3]   See **13.102** et seq.

EXPOSURE

13.4 Conduct involving unlawful or indecent exposure of the human body can be divided into

- behaviour in which the offender sets out to shock, insult, embarrass or offend others; and

- behaviour in which, although the causing of such offence may be foreseeable, it is not specifically intended.

Behaviour of the former kind can in turn be divided into that (such as 'flashing') which is sexually motivated and that (such as 'streaking') which typically involves no real sexual intent or purpose and may well be perceived as a public order matter rather than as a sexual offence.

13.5 As far as statutory offences are concerned, there has long been a distinction between exposure of the genitals and other forms of indecency, such as 'mooning'.[4] Men who deliberately expose their genitals to women or children are in practice the principal concern of the laws governing exposure. Although such conduct is sometimes dismissed as a minor nuisance or embarrassment, research shows that it can have a traumatic effect on some victims, especially when the offender is erect and/or masturbating.[5]

13.6 Moreover, not all 'flashers' fit the stereotype of a pathetic and harmless old man. Research shows that some such offenders are aggressive and that many rapists previously committed 'nuisance' offences such as indecent exposure or voyeurism. One study estimated that 80% of rapists began with non-contact behaviour, and another linked 30% of rapists and child molesters in a sample to engagement in nuisance offences.[6]

The old law

13.7 Prior to commencement of SOA 2003, a man who indecently exposed his 'person' (ie penis[7]) could be prosecuted for one of two specific offences or for a more general public order or indecency offence. The specific offences (now repealed) were as follows:

- Under the Vagrancy Act (VA) 1824, s 4, it was an offence, punishable with up to 3 months' imprisonment, for a man 'wilfully, openly, lewdly and obscenely' to expose his person, in public or private, with intent to insult a female. The commission of a second offence qualified the offender as an 'incorrigible rogue' for which he could be imprisoned for up to one year under ss 5 and 10 of the Act.

---

4   This involves baring the buttocks to onlookers or passers-by, and is likely to be perceived as insulting.
5   In the latter case, if the victim is a child, liability may also be incurred under SOA 2003, s 11. See, for example, *Smith* [2007] EWCA Crim 1873.
6   *Setting the Boundaries: Reforming the Law on Sexual Offences* (Home Office, 2000) (*SB*), at para 8.2.4.
7   *Evans v Ewels* [1972] 1 WLR 671.

- Under the Town Police Clauses Act (TCPA) 1847, s 28, it was an offence for a man to expose his person, 'to the annoyance, obstruction or endangerment' of residents or passers-by. This was punishable by just 14 days' imprisonment.

The reform proposals

13.8 The Sex Offences Review (see **1.4**) recommended the abolition of both offences and their replacement by a new offence involving exposure of the penis when D knew or ought to have known that he might cause fear, alarm or distress to another person.[8] Contrary to its general approach that offences should avoid gender-specific liability, the Review concluded that exposure by women should not be covered by the new offence, since (apart from being rare in such a context) it could not in practice be as frightening or distressing to victims as male exposure. It was suggested that offensive female exposure could be dealt with, where necessary, under public nuisance or public order law; but this suggestion was rejected, and the new provision is not gender specific.

The modern law

13.9 By SOA 2003, s 66(1):

'A person commits an offence if—

    (a)   he intentionally exposes his genitals, and
    (b)   he intends that someone will see them and be caused alarm or distress.'

The offence is triable either way and by s 66(2) is punishable on indictment with a maximum of 2 years' imprisonment.[9] See the SGC Definitive Guideline[10] in the Appendix.

Class of offence	3	SOA 2003, s 72 applies	✗
Notification requirements	See **13.10**	SOPO[11]	✔
CJA 2003,[12] Sch 15 applies	✔	Serious specified offence	✗
Review of lenient sentence	✗	Special provisions of CYPA 1933[13]	✔
Detention of young offender for specified period			✗

See **1.48** et seq.

13.10 The notification requirements apply if:[14]

---

[8]   *SB*, at para 8.2; Recommendation 54.
[9]   Maximum on summary conviction: **1.43**.
[10]   At pp 5–18, 96 and 97.
[11]   Sexual offences prevention order.
[12]   Criminal Justice Act (CJA) 2003.
[13]   Children and Young Persons Act (CYPA) 1933.
[14]   SOA 2003, s 80 and Sch 3, para 33.

'(a) where the offender was under 18, he is or has been sentenced, in respect of the offence, to imprisonment for a term of at least 12 months;

(b) in any other case—
  (i) the victim was under 18, or
  (ii) the offender, in respect of the offence or finding, is or has been—
    (a) sentenced to a term of imprisonment,
    (b) detained in a hospital, or
    (c) made the subject of a community sentence of at least 12 months.'

Application to female offenders

13.11 Contrary to the recommendation of the Sex Offences Review, s 66(1) creates a gender-neutral offence of exposure that can (at least in theory) be committed by women as well as men. In practice, the main significance of this change is symbolic. Women do not tend to indulge in 'flashing'; and although female nudity in public may sometimes shock or cause offence, the Review was almost certainly correct in surmising that it is unlikely to cause comparable alarm or distress. It would, however, be difficult to justify a modern law that provided for the prosecution and conviction of a man in circumstances where a woman behaving in more or less the same fashion could not be convicted of a corresponding offence. Even if women rarely behave in such a way, it would be wrong for the law to discriminate between the sexes in those cases where they do.

Actus reus

13.12 'Genitals' are not specifically defined in the Act and the term must accordingly bear its plain English meaning, namely the sexual organs of reproduction. The externally visible male sexual organs are of course the penis and scrotum (containing the testicles); whereas the externally visible female organs are found in the vulva, which includes the labia majora, labia minora, clitoris, and vestibule of the vagina. Under the Interpretation Act 1978, s 6, the plural form generally includes the singular; and clearly the deliberate exposure of any one genital organ (eg the penis alone) may suffice for liability. In the case of a female defendant, however, public nudity will not necessarily involve any obvious exposure of the vulva, which may sometimes remain concealed by pubic hair, etc. Whether this is so will of course depend on the circumstances.

13.13 Although under the new law there is no need for anyone actually to see the exposed genitals or to be alarmed or distressed if doing so, a prosecution is unlikely unless the act is at least seen,[15] and evidence that persons were alarmed or distressed may have some (albeit limited) value in determining whether that was D's intent. This will most obviously be the case if it is proved that he continued to flaunt his genitals in response to expressions of shock or distress, but even here knowledge cannot necessarily be equated with intent.[16]

13.14 Exposure of the buttocks or the female breasts, which are not organs of reproduction, cannot amount to an offence under s 66, however offensively they are

---

[15] If D was seen by X exposing himself in the direction of Y, who appears not to have noticed, this may be enough, even if X could not from his restricted viewpoint see D's genitals: cf *Hunt v DPP* [1990] Crim LR 812.

[16] See **13.19**.

displayed. Such behaviour may occasionally involve a public order offence[17] or an offence of outraging public decency, depending on all the circumstances.[18]

Intent to cause alarm or distress

13.15 It is clear that a person who carelessly exposes his genitals does not commit an offence under s 66, nor does he commit such an offence even through deliberate exposure unless he acts with the specific intent required by s 66(1)(b). If, for example, therefore, a person unwittingly causes alarm by stripping off in a mixed sauna (perhaps because that is normal practice in his own country) he will commit no offence; and nor will a man commit the offence by deliberately exposing himself to a new girlfriend whom he mistakenly supposes would welcome such behaviour. Furthermore, because this is a crime of 'specific intent' (at least in respect of the ulterior intent of causing alarm or distress) the *Majewski* rule[19] cannot apply and no offence is committed where D's intoxication prevents him from being aware of the obvious alarm etc that his conduct will cause.

13.16 'Alarm' and 'distress' are terms borrowed from public order law. They are 'ordinary English words' which must ultimately be construed by the court or jury, but must be distinguished from terms such as 'offence' and 'annoyance' as used in VA 1824 and the TPCA 1847. In *R (R) v DPP*,[20] the Court scoffed at the idea that an experienced police officer could suffer, or be intended to suffer, 'harassment, alarm or distress' under POA 1986, s 4A, when D rudely called him a 'wanker'. Toulson J said:

> 'They [ie the terms harassment, alarm or distress] are relatively strong words befitting an offence which may carry imprisonment or a substantial fine.

> The word "distress" in this context requires emotional disturbance or upset. The statute does not attempt to define the degree required. It does not have to be grave but nor should the requirement be trivialised. There has to be something which amounts to real emotional disturbance or upset ... [D] doubtless intended to be insulting and annoying, but I do not see on what material the magistrates could have inferred that he intended to cause the officer real emotional disturbance or upset.'

13.17 It would therefore seem that in an exposure case a court or jury must consider whether D intended to cause a 'real emotional disturbance or upset', and it would be wrong to direct a jury that this can be equated with a mere intent to annoy or cause mild offence. In contrast, intent to humiliate might well suffice, because a sense of humiliation is an obvious form of emotional upset or distress.

Intent and purpose

13.18 As noted at **2.56** et seq, 'intent' is usually capable of bearing a meaning that is wider than direct intent, ie aim or purpose. It may in other words be open to a jury to 'find' that a defendant obliquely intended a consequence that was merely a side-effect of

---

[17] See **13.102**.

[18] See **13.86**.

[19] See **2.75**. Arguably, the physical act of exposure is also a matter of specific intent, but that depends on whether the Court of Appeal was right to distinguish (obiter) in *Heard* [2008] QB 43 between 'ordinary' and 'purposive' mens rea: see *Heard*, at [8], and **2.83**.

[20] [2006] EWHC 1375 (Admin) at [12], distinguishing *DPP v Orum* [1988] 3 All ER 449.

his real purpose, if he knew that this consequence was inevitable.[21] In relation to the mens rea specified in s 66(1)(b), however, Parliament must have intended a more restricted meaning, because the clause that eventually became s 66 was repeatedly amended, first, by removing recklessness as to such consequences as an alternative mens rea, and then by removing knowledge also. The obvious inference to be drawn is that D's knowledge that someone would be alarmed or distressed by his actions does not suffice: D will be guilty under s 66 only if this was his specific aim or purpose.

13.19 Proof of such intent will not always be easy. Cases may arise in which it can easily be proved that D 'must have known' he was causing alarm, etc, but in which his purpose (if any) is harder to discern.

13.20 D's intent must be to cause alarm or distress *by means of* the exposure. If, for example, D takes out his penis and threatens to urinate over E, who is lying on the ground, D's purpose may be to alarm E only by virtue of the threatened assault, which would not suffice under s 66; but he might also intend to cause her alarm or distress by visually shocking her with his penis, which would suffice. There is no need to prove that his aim or purpose was to obtain sexual gratification. The act may be done in order to inflict humiliation or revenge.

Exposure by naturists, streakers, demonstrators, etc

13.21 As the Sexual Offences Bill made its way through Parliament, concerns were expressed that the new offence of exposure might be used to curtail the activities of bona fide naturists or sunbathers whose conduct may occasionally offend[22] others. These concerns were not alleviated until the clause that became s 66 was amended to ensure that only those who deliberately set out to cause alarm or distress will be caught by its terms.

13.22 This does not mean that naturists or nudists have nothing to fear from the law. Those who risk causing offence to others by practising naturism in public parks, streets or beaches (other than designated nude beaches) or in private gardens that are not shielded from public view, may face other charges, as indeed may 'streakers', 'mooners' or women who expose their breasts in public.

Alternative charges

13.23 The indecent[23] exposure of any part of the body, whether by a man or, possibly, a woman, and whether to a man or to a woman, may constitute the common law offence of outraging public decency, if there is a real possibility that two or more members of the general public are able to see the exposure and might be disgusted or outraged by it.[24] Such charges are rarely considered appropriate in cases of mere indecent exposure, however.[25] Statutory offences, where available, are usually preferred, and until recently

---

21   See *Woollin* [1999] AC 82; *Matthews* [2003] 2 Cr App R 461.
22   Whether such offence could seriously be equated with alarm or distress is another question.
23   An act is 'indecent' if it offends against generally accepted standards of propriety. It need not be obscene or overtly sexual.
24   *Knuller (Publishing, Printing and Promotions) Ltd v DPP* [1973] AC 435; *Mayling* [1963] 2 QB 717. For further consideration of the offence of outraging public decency, see **13.86**.
25   The offence of public nuisance is unlikely to have any relevance in this context following the ruling of the House of Lords in *Rimmington; Goldstein* [2006] 1 AC 459, in which it was held (a) that such an offence must involve the infliction of harm on the community as a whole or on a significant section of it; and (b)

the common law offence was triable only on indictment, which was a major disincentive to using it given that exposure cases are not, on the whole, considered to be particularly serious.

13.24 There was a public outcry in July 2007 when it was reported that two young women were to be prosecuted for outraging public decency by flashing their breasts at a police surveillance camera on Worthing seafront. When they exercised their right to demand trial by jury, the case was dropped. The behaviour of the women in question was widely considered to be, at worst, deserving of a small fine, and in other contexts (eg sunbathing) a woman exposing her breasts in public would be most unlikely to 'disgust or outrage' anyone, even if some might not wholly approve of such behaviour.

13.25 Public nudity or exposure may involve other legal consequences. Indecent exposure may in some circumstances give rise to liability under POA 1986.[26] Liability may also arise under local by-laws. The Public Health Act 1936, s 231(1)(d), which empowers local authorities to make by-laws regulating the wearing of costumes by bathers, was prospectively repealed by the Local Government and Public Involvement in Health Act 2007,[27] but by the Local Government Act (LGA) 1972, s 235:

> '... the council of a district, the council of a principal area in Wales and the council of a London borough may make byelaws for the good rule and government of the whole or any part of the district, principal area or borough, as the case may be, and for the prevention and suppression of nuisances therein.'

Such by-laws must not be unreasonable or repugnant to the general law,[28] and must not merely duplicate laws made under other enactments,[29] but some such overlap is permissible and is often unavoidable.[30]

VOYEURISM

13.26 Until the enactment of SOA 2003, s 67, there was no distinct offence of voyeurism in English law, although some particular manifestations of it could be dealt with by means of a prosecution under POA 1986, s 4 or s 5,[31] or by binding over proceedings. In contrast, many states in the US have long had provisions specifically relating to voyeurism.[32]

---

that such prosecutions ought not to be brought if there is a suitable statutory alternative. *Rimmington* was not cited in *Kavanagh* [2008] EWCA Crim 855, a sentencing case in which the court did not question the validity of K's conviction for committing a public nuisance by making sexually explicit telephone calls to a large number of women, notably those working in a gym overlooked by his flat.

26   See **13.102**.
27   Section 241 and Sch 18, Pt 7. No commencement date had been set as this book went to press.
28   'A byelaw is a local law and may be supplementary to the general law; it is not bad because it deals with something that is not dealt with by the general law. But it must not alter the general law by making that lawful which the general law makes unlawful; or that unlawful which the general law makes lawful': *White v Morely* [1899] 2 KB 34.
29   LGA 1972, s 235(3).
30   *Thomas v Sutters* [1900] 1 Ch 10; *DPP v Gawecki* [1993] Crim LR 202; *Owen v DPP* [1994] Crim LR 192.
31   See *Vigon v DPP* (1998) 162 JP 115.
32   For examples, see *SB*, at paras 8.3.2–8.3.7.

13.27 The Sex Offences Review reported that it had been impressed by evidence linking a range of offending behaviour, from the major sex crimes to voyeurism.[33] Persons who discover that they have been spied upon when they had a reasonable expectation of privacy may feel a loss of personal safety and integrity. Voyeurism, the Review concluded, was more than just an unpleasant nuisance, and should be made criminal.[34]

13.28
   SOA 2003, s 67 creates three distinct offences of voyeurism, namely:

- observation of a private act (s 67(1));

- operating equipment to enable another to observe a private act (s 67(2)); and

- recording another person doing a private act (s 67(3)).

A further preparatory offence is created by s 67(4).[35] Each offence is triable either way and by s 67(5) is punishable on indictment with a maximum of 2 years' imprisonment.[36] See the SGC Definitive Guideline[37] in the Appendix.

Class of offence	3	SOA 2003, s 72 applies	✘
Notification requirements	See text	SOPO	✔
CJA 2003, Sch 15 applies	✔	Serious specified offence	✘
Review of lenient sentence	✘	Special provisions of CYPA 1933	✔
Detention of young offender for specified period			✘

See **1.48** et seq. The notification requirements apply in the same circumstances as for offences of exposure, contrary to s 66.[38]

Observing

13.29 By s 67(1), a person commits an offence if:

'(a)   for the purpose of obtaining sexual gratification, he observes another person doing a private act, and

(b)   he knows that the other person does not consent to being observed for his sexual gratification.'

---

[33]   Ibid. Reference was made to a study which showed that 14% of child molesters and 20% of rapists had committed voyeurism.

[34]   *SB*, at Recommendation 55.

[35]   See **13.52**.

[36]   Maximum on summary conviction: see **1.43**.

[37]   At pp 5-18, 98 and 99.

[38]   SOA 2003, s 80 and Sch 3, para 34. See para **13.10**.

13.30 This offence can be committed either by directly observing the private act or by looking at an image produced in any way[39] (eg via a hidden camera). Examples might include using a peephole to view a neighbour taking a bath; or peeping through curtains at someone having sexual intercourse inside, provided in each case that the act is committed for the purpose of sexual gratification. No offence is committed under this subsection where those viewed consent to being observed for that purpose. Nor can anyone commit this offence merely by viewing pre-recorded images.[40] Section 67(1) requires contemporaneous viewing of the acts in question. If it did not, s 67(3) would be redundant. Note that consent may be given to one person but not to another. If A secretly spies upon a sexual act that B is performing to please C, he may be caught by s 67(1)(b) assuming he knows that B does not consent to being observed *by him*. But no offence would be committed where A, an 'innocent dog walker' happens to derive sexual pleasure from a chance encounter with a naked or sexually active B, who can have 'no reasonable expectation of privacy from that kind of chance encounter'.[41]

Operating equipment

13.31 By s 67(2), a person commits an offence if:

'(a) he operates equipment with the intention of enabling another person to observe, for the purpose of obtaining sexual gratification, a third person (B) doing a private act, and

(b) he knows that B does not consent to his operating equipment with that intention.'

13.32 An example would be where A places and operates a hidden webcam in B's room without her knowledge and with intent to allow others (eg on the internet) to view B getting undressed or engaging in sexual behaviour. Section 67(2) is limited to cases where the observation of a contemporaneous private act is intended. If images are also recorded, there will also be an offence under s 67(3).

13.33 The specified intention here is ulterior. It does not matter whether any other person does in fact get to observe any private act, or indeed whether he gets to see B at all. Nor does the viewer commit any offence under s 67(2), although if he has encouraged or procured the offence he may be liable as a secondary party.

13.34 Does s 67(2) apply where A installs a webcam to relay images of B doing private acts, but designs it to be activated unknowingly by B herself (eg by movement sensors, or by B switching on a bedroom light)? Can it be said that A is 'operating equipment' in such a case? It is submitted that it can, because B's own activation of the webcam is not a conscious or voluntary act.

Recording

13.35 By s 67(3), a person (A) commits an offence if:

'(a) he records another person (B) doing a private act,

---

39 Section 79(7). 'Image' includes moving or still images, however produced: s 79(4).
40 Other charges may sometimes be possible. In December 2005 two council workers at a CCTV control centre pleaded guilty to an offence of misconduct in public office after viewing CCTV images of a woman undressing in her own home. The camera operator who had trained his instrument on the woman's house pleaded guilty to an offence under s 67.
41 *Bassett* [2008] EWCA Crim 1174 at [9].

(b)   he does so with the intention that he or a third person will, for the purpose of
       obtaining sexual gratification, look at an image of B doing the act, and
(c)   he knows that B does not consent to his recording the act with that intention.'

13.36 This offence is concerned with recording a private act for later viewing by A or by
a third person. Section 67(3)(b) effectively excludes sound-only recordings from the
ambit of the offence. The specified intention in s 67(3) is ulterior. It does not matter for
the purpose of liability whether A or anyone else actually gets to view the recording, and
no offence is committed by someone who later does so, although such a person (or
indeed a distributor) may incur secondary liability if he is found to have procured or
encouraged its making.

13.37 A simple example of an offence under s 67(3) might involve A secretly recording
B having sex.[42] It would be difficult in such circumstances for A to deny that he acted
with some kind of sexual gratification in mind, even if that gratification is not his own;
but other cases of intrusive recording or photography may be less clear. Paparazzi who,
without the consent of their subject, take long-range photographs of private acts (eg of
a celebrity sunbathing naked in her garden) may perhaps infringe s 67(3), but proof of
intent under s 67(3)(b) may be difficult. Arguably, such images are merely the stuff of
celebrity gossip magazines. Even if the pictures are later sold to a 'top shelf' magazine, it
does not follow that this must have been the original intent.

13.38 For the same reason, an ex-boyfriend or husband who has made supposedly
private and consensual intimate videos of his partner (or of himself and his partner
together) may not necessarily commit any offence under s 67(3) even if he later places
them on a pornographic website. To secure a conviction, it would have to be proved that
this (or something similar) was his intent all along. Intent formed only when the
relationship goes sour cannot suffice, and in that respect the law fails to give protection
where arguably it is required.[43]

Elements common to offences under s 67(1)–(3)

A private act

13.39 Central to the definitions of each of the offences under s 67(1), (2) and (3) is the
concept of a 'private act'. No offence can be committed under any of those provisions
unless the complainant was doing such an act at the relevant time.

13.40 Section 68(1) defines a 'private act' for the purposes of s 67:

'(1) For the purposes of section 67, a person is doing a private act if the person is in a place
which, in the circumstances, would reasonably be expected to provide privacy, and—

(a)   the person's genitals, buttocks or breasts[44] are exposed or covered only with
       underwear,
(b)   the person is using a lavatory,[45] or
(c)   the person is doing a sexual act that is not of a kind ordinarily done in public.'

---

[42]   As in *Turner* [2006] 2 Cr App R (S) 327. See also *IP* [2005] 1 Cr App R (S) 578.
[43]   A provision criminalising the distribution or publication of such images might address the problem, but
        there is no such provision in the Act. The explanatory notes for the Act overlook this difficulty (at para 129).
[44]   These must be female breasts: *Bassett* [2008] EWCA Crim 1174.
[45]   This presumably must be construed to mean use for urination or defecation.

13.41 The first part of this test is concerned with the place at which and circumstances in which the complainant is observed or filmed, etc. He must be in a place where, *in the circumstances,* he could reasonably expect to have privacy. An act done in a bedroom with the curtains drawn will ordinarily satisfy that test, but one done with the curtains open and the lights on, in full view of the street, might not. An act done at midnight in a forest might well satisfy the test, but one done in the same spot during the day while hikers and dog walkers file past might not.

13.42 Communal changing rooms, saunas or showers require careful consideration. In one sense, of course, they are not 'private', but privacy, which is not defined in the Act, is a relative concept, and those using single-sex showers, etc would not expect to be filmed or spied on by persons of the opposite sex or indeed by anyone of either sex who has set up a concealed camera for that purpose.[46] Their privacy would be infringed in either case. The same appears to be true where A does not merely happen to enjoy what he sees in (say) a communal shower or changing area, but deliberately lurks or lingers there for the purpose of watching other users.[47] Similar (albeit not identical) considerations apply in respect of a changing cubicle in a shop, even if there is a notice on the wall indicating that video surveillance is in operation, or indeed in a private naturist club. In either case, some element of privacy is still expected. In contrast, those who go naked or topless on public beaches must expect to be watched (and perhaps photographed) by others, who may legitimately enjoy seeing them thus exposed.

13.43 In addition, the prosecution must prove that when observed or filmed, etc the complainant was doing one of the things specified in s 68(1)(a)–(c). Some voyeuristic acts will fall outside the scope of the offence. If, for example, A is a foot fetishist and spies on B as she tries on shoes, A does not thereby commit a s 67 offence, even if he sets up a hidden camera in a shoe shop for the purpose of viewing or recording customers who would object if they knew what he was doing. Similarly, if, as in *Ammouchi,*[48] a sentencing appeal relating to the offence of outraging public decency, A spies on B from just outside her window and masturbates as he does so, but she is not doing any of the specified things, there can again be no offence under s 67.

13.44 In *Hamilton,*[49] D used a camera hidden in a rucksack to record a number of 'up-skirt' videos of women and girls, usually while standing behind them at supermarket checkouts and placing the rucksack on the floor with the camera pointing upwards. Only one of his victims was ever identified: she was aged 14 at the time, and this led to a conviction under the Protection of Children Act 1978, s 1. He stopped making the videos in 2001, so no question arose of any prosecution under SOA 2003, s 67, but it was noted that such a prosecution would in any case have been problematic, because none of the complainants were in a private place when he filmed them. They did not of course imagine for one moment that his camera was pointing up their skirts (and only underwear (if anything) covered their buttocks or genitals from the camera's view) but that would not in itself have been enough to satisfy the test laid down in s 68. He was successfully prosecuted for outraging public decency,[50] but given the secretive nature of his activities one may question whether this was a wholly appropriate charge. If s 67

---

[46] *Bassett,* n 41 above, at [12].
[47] Ibid. See also *Swyer* [2007] EWCA Crim 204.
[48] [2007] EWCA Crim 842. This was a sentencing appeal relating to a conviction for outraging public decency at common law.
[49] [2008] 1 Cr App R 171. See Gillespie 'Up-skirts and Down-blouses: Voyeurism and the Law' [2008] Crim LR 370.
[50] See **13.86**. See also *Choi* (1999) 5 *Archbold News* 3.

were amended so as to include illicit up-skirt filming, even when done in public, it would arguably provide a more appropriate charge to bring in cases such as this.

13.45 Other difficulties might conceivably arise concerning the concept of a private act. Assume that A has used a zoom lens to photograph B, sunbathing in her private garden. It can be seen that B was wearing a bra and pants, but some dispute might arise as to whether these garments were underwear or swimwear (ie a bikini). If the former, then A has committed the actus reus of the offence, but in the latter case he has not – unless perhaps the bikini bottoms were cut so high as to leave her buttocks at least partially exposed.

13.46 Questions may also arise as to what kinds of sexual act are 'not ordinarily done in public'. Kissing is or may be, whereas masturbation clearly is not, but some kinds of 'petting', for example, may be difficult to classify in such terms, and it would be for the court or jury to decide any difficult cases as issues of fact. Different courts or juries might of course come to different conclusions in respect of the same type of behaviour.

Absence of consent and knowledge thereof

13.47 Another common feature of all the three offences is that A must *know* that B does not consent to what A is doing, or does not consent to it being done with that intention or purpose. Consent to being watched by a partner is not the same as consent to being watched by a stranger or neighbour; nor is consent to being watched the same as consent to being filmed; and consent to the making of a 'private and personal' recording is not the same thing as consent to it being made for publication on the internet. If it can be proved that A never intended to honour the terms on which B's consent was given, A may be guilty of an offence under s 67. The burden of proof is on the prosecution, and the recording itself may offer few clues as to the limits of B's consent, or indeed as to A's intent at the time.[51]

13.48 Since one cannot 'know' something which is not true, this absence of consent is part of the actus reus and must be proved by the prosecution. No real problem will arise where it is clear that A has installed a camera or drilled a spy-hole without B's knowledge. One cannot consent if one has no idea of what is happening, and (in theory at least) it would be no defence if B, on discovering or being informed of the offence, expresses only amusement or pleasure.

13.49 If B, an exhibitionist, realises that he is being observed by A or that A has installed a camera to record him, and only then performs a sexual act, A will not thereby commit any of the above offences, but if he supposes that B is unaware of him he may be guilty of an attempt to commit such an offence, and in some cases he will already be guilty of a preparatory offence under s 67(4).[52]

Purpose of sexual gratification

13.50 To be guilty of a s 67 offence, A, when observing B doing a private act, or intending to enable himself or another to view a video, etc of B doing a private act, must

---

[51]   In the adult video and photographic industry, actors or models may indicate their consent by signing a 'model release form', but this is unlikely in the case of an explicit 'home movie'.

[52]   See **13.52**.

act for the purpose of sexual gratification.[53] A bona fide researcher who secretly photographs a private act, knowing that the subject did not consent to being photographed, would not commit the present offence, however unethical his research work may be. Likewise, a police officer who observes a private act for the purpose of an investigation would not commit it, nor would an investigative journalist who is seeking to provide material to support a story that premises are being used as a brothel. Incidental sexual gratification would not count.

13.51 Proof of the sexual gratification purpose may be difficult. The Sex Offences Review took the view that such an element ought not to be absolutely necessary for the offence. However, it recognised the risk that an offence of observation which did not require D to act for sexual gratification could intrude into the work of a free press, which was not its intent.[54]

The preparatory offence

13.52 Section 67(4) provides an offence preparatory to that under s 67(1) and punishable on the same basis:

> 'A person commits an offence if he installs equipment, or constructs or adapts a structure or part of a structure, with the intention of enabling himself or another person to commit an offence under [s 67(1)].'

A structure in this context is not limited to a building, or part of a building such as a changing room, cubicle or tanning booth. By s 68(2), it also includes a tent (including a tented cubicle at a market stall), vehicle or vessel or other temporary or movable structure, such as a portable lavatory.

13.53 Examples of offences under s 67(4) might include installing a hidden camera in a hotel room or making a peephole in the partition between two lavatory cubicles, knowing in each case that the subjects would not consent to being so observed.[55] Actual use need not be proved.

13.54 There is, however, a potential problem, in that for some reason the preparatory offence does not apply to would-be offenders under s 67(2) or (3). If A's camera is discovered before it can be used, but it has been designed to automatically capture and record images for later viewing, rather than to enable contemporaneous viewing via a live link, there can be no offence under s 67(4). On the other hand, the installation of an automatic recording device in such circumstances would almost certainly give rise to liability for an attempt to commit an offence under s 67(3). Where two or more parties are involved, there may also be liability for statutory conspiracy. But this would have been unnecessary if s 67(4) had been drafted less restrictively.

---

53 For an appropriate definition of 'sexual', see **2.31** et seq. SOA 2003, s 78 (**2.32**) which helps to determine whether *conduct or activity* can be defined as 'sexual' does not directly assist in determining whether any *gratification* derived is 'sexual'. In practice, however, this is unlikely to cause any great difficulty in voyeurism cases.
54 *SB*, at para 8.3.10.
55 See *Hodgson* [2008] EWCA Crim 1180, where D set up a pinhole camera to spy on the women's toilets at his workplace.

SEXUAL INTERCOURSE WITH AN ANIMAL

13.55 The offence of buggery, contrary to SOA 1956, s 12(1), was repealed by SOA 2003. An offence under s 12 could (inter alia) take the form of sexual intercourse, per vaginam or per anum, between a man or woman and an animal. The animal could be the active or passive party.

13.56 Bestiality is generally regarded as profoundly disturbed and distasteful behaviour, and was once a capital offence, but it became accepted in modern times that the maximum penalty of life imprisonment[56] was unduly harsh. The Criminal Law Revision Committee (CLRC) recommended in 1984 that buggery with an animal should in future be known as bestiality and become a summary offence, but also recommended that there should be a more serious either-way offence of procuring bestiality by another person.[57]

13.57 Although it could be argued that bestiality should no longer be criminal, save where criminal damage or cruelty to animals is involved, the Sex Offences Review disagreed, concluding that:[58]

> 'It was an act that offended against the dignity of animals and of people ... An offence of bestiality would seek to protect animals but we thought that it was primarily a sex offence reflecting some profoundly disturbed behaviour. These are not simply the acts of loneliness and propinquity. There is evidence of a linkage between abuse of animals and other forms of sexual offending ... In some instances severe physical mutilation of horses has been accompanied by sex with them. We felt that society had a profound abhorrence for this behaviour and that it should continue to be a criminal offence ... but with a much-reduced penalty ... We also agree with the CLRC that there should be a more serious offence of compelling sexual activity with animals ...'

13.58 The Review's recommendation that bestiality should remain criminal is adopted by SOA 2003. The recommendation as to compelling others to take part in sexual activity with animals is effected within the general offences in ss 4 and 8 of causing sexual activity.[59]

13.59 SOA 2003, s 69 creates two offences, one involving active penile penetration of a living animal and one involving penile penetration by such an animal. Other forms of sexual activity (such as bestial masturbation) fall outside its scope, but where it is considered that the animal has been abused, liability may arise under the Animal Welfare Act (AWA) 2006. Penetration of a protected animal[60] may cause suffering to that animal contrary to s 4 of that Act, and even if there is no such suffering, inducing abnormal sexual behaviour patterns in protected animals may involve a 'welfare offence' under s 9. Injury or destruction of another person's animal may involve liability under the Criminal Damage Act 1971.

---

[56]   SOA 1956, Sch 2.
[57]   *Fifteenth Report: Sexual Offences* (1984), at paras 12.1–12.9; Recommendations 63 and 64.
[58]   *SB*, at para 8.5.3; Recommendation 57.
[59]   See **3.167** et seq and **3.179** et seq.
[60]   As defined in the AWA 2006, s 2. This includes all vertebrate domestic or farm animals (including birds and fish) and wild ones if captive or under human control.

13.60 Offences under SOA, s 69, are triable either way and punishable on indictment with a maximum of 2 years' imprisonment on conviction.[61] See the SGC Definitive Guideline[62] in the Appendix.

Class of offence	3	SOA 2003, s 72 applies	✗
Notification requirements	See **13.61**	SOPO	✔
CJA 2003, Sch 15 applies	✔	Serious specified offence	✗
Review of lenient sentence	✗	Special provisions of CYPA 1933	✗
Detention of young offender for specified period			✗

See **1.48** et seq.

13.61 Notification requirements apply if:[63]

'(a) where the offender was under 18, he is or has been sentenced in respect of the offence to imprisonment for a term of at least 12 months;
(b) in any other case, the offender, in respect of the offence or finding, is or has been—
(i) sentenced to a term of imprisonment, or
(ii) detained in a hospital.'

Active sexual penetration of an animal

13.62 Section 69(1) states:

'A person commits an offence if—

(a) he intentionally performs an act of penetration with his penis,
(b) what is penetrated is the vagina or anus of a living animal, and
(c) he knows that, or is reckless as to whether, that is what is penetrated.'

Given that the basis of the offence is not one of cruelty to animals, it is not obvious why it is limited to living animals. The conduct is equally deviant if the animal is dead. When the Bill was debated, Lord Lucas could see no qualitative difference between sexual intercourse with a live or dead animal:

'... particularly when you have well-known [sic] sexual practices on the borderline such as avisodomy, which is the practice of breaking a hen's neck at the moment before penetration so that you benefit from the spasms that the animal undergoes afterwards ...'[64]

Passive sexual penetration by an animal

13.63 Section 69(2) provides:

---

61 SOA 2003, s 69(3). Maximum on summary conviction: see **1.43**.
62 At pp 5–18, 100 and 101.
63 SOA 2003, s 80 and Sch 3, para 35.
64 HL Deb, vol 649, col 81.

'A person (A) commits an offence if—

    (a)   A intentionally causes, or allows, A's vagina or anus to be penetrated,

    (b)   the penetration is by the penis of a living animal, and

    (c)   A knows that, or is reckless as to whether, that is what A is being penetrated by.'

Causing and allowing involve active or passive cooperation on A's part. A would 'cause' the animal's behaviour if he encourages or assists it to penetrate him. But A only 'allows' such penetration if he consents to it. If he does not (or legally cannot) consent, any other person who causes the penetration can be convicted of an offence under s 4 or s 8.[65]

13.64 The requirement that the penetration must be by the animal's penis would seem to exclude felching (penetration by the use of a whole small animal) from the offence. It would certainly do so if the animal lacks a penis. There is little moral difference between felching and causing or allowing penetration by an animal's penis; if anything, the former is more objectionable, if only because it may be fatal to the animal. The issue was raised by Lord Lucas in the House of Lords. He claimed that felching was a fairly common and well-attested variety of sexual activity with animals; but the Government's view was that it was extremely rare and not worth addressing in legislation.[66]

SEXUAL PENETRATION OF A CORPSE

13.65 Until the enactment of SOA 2003, s 70, sexual intercourse or interference with a corpse[67] had never been the subject of any specific criminal offence. But such behaviour does occasionally occur, notably where D has sex with the body of a victim he has just murdered.[68]

13.66 The Sex Offences Review concluded that, although there was no firm evidence of the nature or extent of the problem, it was sufficiently serious to be criminally culpable, and that there should be an offence specifically targeted at it. Such conduct is not simply repugnant but is so deviant as to be unacceptable; human remains should be shown respect, and molestation of them may deeply distress relatives and friends. Moreover, the Review's fundamental principle was that sexual activity should be consensual, which is impossible in such cases.[69]

13.67 It was recommended that there should be a general offence of sexual interference with human remains.[70] The s 70 offence is, however, limited to sexual *penetration* of a

---

[65]   See **3.167** et seq and **3.179** et seq. Cf *Bourne* [1939] 1 KB 687.

[66]   HL Deb, vol 649, cols 81–82. Felching must almost inevitably constitute an offence under the AWA 2006, s 4. A more difficult case might involve A causing or allowing an animal to lick his genitals or anus, or performing such acts on an animal. There is no obvious sexual offence here, unless it is done in such circumstances as to outrage public decency. See **13.86**.

[67]   This is usually referred to as necrophilia, although strictly speaking that term refers only to a sexual attraction to corpses.

[68]   One of the most common motives for such an offence is a desire for an unresisting and unrejecting 'partner', offenders often being afraid of rejection by the living: see Rosman and Resnick (1989) *Bulletin of the American Academy of Psychiatry and the Law* 17, at p 153.

[69]   *SB*, at paras 8.6.4 and 8.6.5.

[70]   *SB*, at para 8.6.6; Recommendation 58.

corpse. Unlike comparable offences in New Zealand[71] and Canadian law,[72] it does not cover any other forms of disrespect, abuse or mutilation.[73]

13.68 Despite objecting to the criminalisation of felching on the ground that it is rare,[74] the Government considered that the present offence was necessary despite its admission that necrophilia is also rare.[75]

13.69 *Protecting the Public* said this about cases in which D is suspected of killing his victim:[76]

> '... the first priority will clearly be to charge murder or manslaughter. Where there is evidence of sexual penetration of the body after death, it is important that the sexual deviance of the offending behaviour is properly recognised by a separate indictment of sexual interference with human remains. This will ensure that a defendant who is found guilty on both charges is sentenced accordingly and is treated and monitored as a sex offender both in prison and after release.'

13.70 SOA 2003, s 70(1) provides:

> 'A person commits an offence if—
>
> (a) he intentionally performs an act of penetration with a part of his body or anything else,
> (b) what is penetrated is a part of the body of a dead[77] person,
> (c) he knows that, or is reckless as to whether, that is what is penetrated, and
> (d) the penetration is sexual.'

The offence is triable either way and punishable by 2 years' imprisonment following conviction on indictment.[78] See the SGC Definitive Guideline[79] in the Appendix.

Class of offence	3	SOA 2003, s 72 applies	✗
Notification requirements	See text	SOPO	✔
CJA 2003, Sch 15 applies	✔	Serious specified offence	✗

---

71 (NZ) Crimes Act 1961, s 150.

72 Criminal Code, RSC 1985, s 182(b).

73 Such conduct might in some circumstances involve an act outraging public decency, contrary to common law: cf *Anderson* (unreported) 26 October 2007, in which D urinated on the body of a woman as she lay dying and was duly convicted of that offence. It would surely have made no difference had she already been dead at the time. As to the limits of the common law offence, see **13.86** et seq.

74 See **13.63** and **13.64**.

75 Lord Falconer of Thoroton, HL Deb, vol 649, col 84.

76 *Protecting the Public: Strengthening Protection Against Sex Offenders and Reforming the Law on Sexual Offences*, Cm 5668 (2002), at para 80.

77 In *Airedale NHS Trust v Bland* [1993] AC 789, Lords Keith, Goff and Browne-Wilkinson agreed (obiter) that 'brain stem death' is the legal definition of death; and the same view was taken both in *Mail Newspapers v Express Newspapers* [1987] FSR 90 and in *Re A* [1992] 3 Med LR 303. See also [1976] 2 *British Medical Journal* 1187; (1995) 29 *Journal of the Royal College of Physicians* 381. A patient who can breathe unaided, albeit in a 'persistent vegetative state' (as in *Bland*) has not suffered 'brain stem death'. See Price (1997) 23 *Journal of Medical Ethics* 170.

78 SOA 2003, s 70(2). As to the maximum on summary conviction, see **1.43**.

79 At pp 5–18, 102 and 103.

Sexual Offences

Review of lenient sentence	✗	Special provisions of CYPA 1933	✗
Detention of young offender for specified period			✗

See **1.48** et seq. The notification requirements apply in the same circumstances as for offences contrary to SOA 2003, s 69.[80]

13.71 Penetration of the corpse is required. 'Lesser' acts will not suffice for this offence. The penetration must be sexual, but need not necessarily involve penetration by a penis. Digital penetration will do, for example, as will penetration by an implement or article. The penetration need not be of the deceased's mouth, vagina or anus. The requirement that it must be sexual, however, means that it is difficult to conceive that a penetration of any other part of the body would be sexual, unless it involves the offender's penis.[81]

13.72 The definition of penetration in the Act[82] says that penetration is a continuing act from entry to withdrawal. This suggests that if it could be proved that a person (B) died during intercourse and A, aware of the risk that B might have died, continued, A could be convicted of the present offence. It is submitted, however, that the wording of s 70 can be read as indicating otherwise. The other offences in the Act involving penetration say that it is an offence where a person 'intentionally penetrates', which given the definition of penetration would cover an initially accidental penetration which becomes intentional before withdrawal. In comparison, s 70 speaks of a person intentionally *performing an act of penetration* of a part of a body of a dead person. Read literally, and even allowing for the special definition of penetration, these words arguably require B to be dead at the time of initial penetration.

13.73 The wording of s 70(1)(c) clearly covers the case of the perverted pathologist or mortuary attendant who knows that he is penetrating a human corpse; but the inclusion of the alternative of recklessness means that if A penetrates B's corpse suspecting but not knowing for certain that B is dead, he can be convicted of the offence.

SEXUAL ACTIVITY IN A PUBLIC LAVATORY

13.74 When SOA 2003 was debated in the House of Lords, much concern was focused on the issues raised by sexual activity in public lavatories, whether or not behind closed doors. It was generally agreed that such activity should not be permitted because of the nuisance, annoyance and embarrassment it may cause to others. Hitherto, the only provisions *specifically* dealing with such behaviour were discriminatory because they only dealt with sexual activity in a public lavatory between men (a practice generally known as 'cottaging'). When private homosexual acts between consenting adult males were decriminalised by SOA 1967, it was specifically provided that conduct was deemed not to be 'in private' if it took place:

- when more than two persons participated or were present; or

---

[80] SOA 2003, s 80 and Sch 3, para 35. See **13.61**.
[81] It will be noted that s 70(1)(b) refers to penetration of 'part of [a person's] body'. This might in theory include a dismembered part.
[82] See **3.100** and **3.101**.

- in a public lavatory.[83]

Preparatory conduct to such activity was dealt with by the offence of persistent importuning by a man for immoral purposes, contrary to SOA 1956, s 32. These provisions were all repealed by SOA 2003.[84]

13.75 No offence of sexual activity in a public lavatory was originally included in the Bill that became SOA 2003. It was envisaged that offensive behaviour of that type could if necessary be prosecuted as an offence under POA 1986 or as a common law offence of outraging public decency, but neither of those solutions was ideal, and the Bill was amended at the Report stage in the House of Lords by the insertion of a specific offence which became s 71.

13.76 SOA 2003, s 71(1) provides:

'A person commits an offence if—

(a) he is in a lavatory to which the public or a section of the public has or is permitted to have access, whether on payment or otherwise,
(b) he intentionally engages in an activity, and
(c) the activity is sexual.'

An offence under s 71 is triable only summarily and punishable by a maximum of 6 months' imprisonment or a fine not exceeding level 5 on the standard scale[85] or both.[86] See the SGC Definitive Guideline[87] in the Appendix.

Class of offence	n/a	SOA 2003, s 72 applies	✗
Notification requirements	✗	SOPO	✗
CJA 2003, Sch 15 applies	✗	Serious specified offence	✗
Review of lenient sentence	✗	Special provisions of CYPA 1933	✗
Detention of young offender for specified period			✗

As a summary offence, it cannot be the subject of a criminal attempt.[88] In an appropriately serious case, however, a prosecution might instead be brought for committing (or attempting to commit) an act outraging public decency.

---

[83] SOA 1956, s 12(1B); SOA 1967, s 1(2).
[84] By s 140 and Sch 7.
[85] Currently £5,000: CJA 1982, s 37.
[86] SOA 2003, s 71(3).
[87] At pp 5–18, 94 and 95.
[88] Criminal Attempts Act 1981, s 1(4).

Sexual activity

13.77 For the purposes of s 71:[89]

> '... an activity is sexual if a reasonable person would, in all the circumstances but regardless of any person's purpose, consider it to be sexual.'

This covers only explicitly sexual activity. Behaviour which is ambiguous in its nature and circumstances is not caught. The offence does not require activity between more than one person. Self-masturbation will suffice. Nor does it require proof that the activity was indecent[90] or proof of the particular type of sexual activity involved, which might be difficult if the conduct occurred behind closed doors. It will be enough if the court can safely infer, on the basis of the evidence, that some kind of sexual activity must have been taking place.

13.78 There is no need to prove that anyone was disgusted, harassed, alarmed or distressed by the sexual activity or indeed that anyone else saw or heard the activity or was likely to do so. In theory, D might be convicted merely on the basis of his admission[91] that he masturbated alone in an empty public lavatory.[92]

13.79 The absence of a requirement that anyone was disgusted, harassed, alarmed or distressed by the sexual activity might be thought to raise the possibility of convictions involving entrapment, but although entrapment is not a defence as such, any significant element of police entrapment would lead to a prosecution being stayed as an abuse of process.[93]

Public lavatory

13.80 Whether the sexual act in question was committed in, or merely in proximity to, a lavatory may involve a difficult question of fact. Is an open plan or L-shaped changing room or shower area that includes lavatory cubicles and/or urinals (e g in a sports centre) a lavatory, or must the lavatory area be regarded as separate and distinct from the rest?

13.81 A further difficulty may arise in determining whether, if it is indeed a lavatory, it is one to which 'the public or a section of the public has or is permitted to have access, whether on payment or otherwise' as specified in s 71(1)(a). This may again be a question of fact and degree.[94] If the public or any section of it have access to a lavatory by express or implied permission (e g to enter a customers' lavatory in a café or railway station), it is irrelevant that the owner has the right to refuse entry or restrict who may enter.[95] It would also be irrelevant that a couple, by using the lavatory for an unauthorised purpose, are trespassers. If the public or a section of the public is not

---

[89] Section 71(2). This definition is different from the general definition of 'sexual' in SOA 2003, s 78 (see **2.32**) because it excludes activity which a reasonable person would think was sexual only if he knew of the purpose of the person engaging in it.

[90] As to the difference between indecent conduct and sexual conduct, see **2.33**.

[91] He may not even be aware of the incriminating nature of such an admission. A boast will suffice if it is self-incriminating.

[92] If D's doctor asks him for a semen sample, and directs him discreetly to the men's toilets on the hospital ward, where, behind a locked door, D discreetly obliges him, are both then guilty of an offence under s 71? A prosecution would hardly be in the public interest, but as a matter of law the answer may well be 'yes'.

[93] See generally *Looseley* [2002] 1 Cr App R 360.

[94] *Waters* (1963) 47 Cr App R 149.

[95] *Lawrenson v Oxford* [1982] Crim LR 185.

permitted to have access to a lavatory, it can nevertheless satisfy s 71(1)(a) if there is nothing to prevent access by the public or a section thereof.[96]

13.82 A lavatory will only fall within s 71(1)(a) if the class of people who have, or are permitted to have, access is sufficiently wide to be described as 'the public' or a 'section of the public'. In another context (incitement to racial hatred by publication or distribution to a section of the public) it has been held that a family is not a section of the public but that a 'section of the public' must be an identifiable group, 'in other words, members of a club or association'.[97] With respect, members of a club or association (if they represent a section of the public at all) clearly represent just one example of an identifiable group. The phrase may therefore cover any identifiable group whose connection is not merely a personal, familial or domestic relationship. The employees of X Ltd would thus constitute a section of the public, as would a cinema audience, so that a staff lavatory at X Ltd's premises or a customers' toilet at a cinema falls within the scope of s 71.

13.83 Arguably, members of a private club or association do not represent a section of the public at all. A club is 'private' in this sense, provided there is a membership procedure which involves a genuine process of personal selection, so that entry into membership is not a formality with which any member of the public (or qualified member of the public, eg graduates or women) can comply[98] and thereby obtain membership. This at least was the majority view of the House of Lords in *Charter v Race Relations Board*,[99] a case concerned with whether or not there was a provision of facilities and services to a section of the public under the legislation relating to racial discrimination. On this basis, a lavatory at a gaming club would be within s 71(1)(a) whereas a lavatory at the Athenaeum would not.

13.84 The wording of s 71(1)(a) implies that it is sufficient that the public or any section of the public has or is permitted to have access to the lavatory at the material time. Thus, a lavatory which is open for public use at certain times but closed at others is within s 71(1)(a) when it is open but not when it is closed.[100]

Mens rea

13.85 The requirement that D must intentionally engage in the activity in question does not amount to much. It would be very rare, indeed, that a person could accidentally engage in an activity of a relevant type. Nor would a person intentionally engage in such an activity with D if he was physically compelled to do so. In such a case it is unlikely that D would be charged under s 71; a charge for one of the non-consensual sexual offences would be more appropriate.

---

[96]   *Knox v Anderton* (1982) 76 Cr App R 156.
[97]   *Britton* [1967] 2 QB 51.
[98]   Unless there is some 'obvious disqualification as might cause the manager of ... a restaurant to exclude' the applicant: *Charter v Race Relations Board* [1973] AC 868, at p 887, per Lord Reid.
[99]   [1973] AC 868.
[100] *Sandy v Martin* [1974] Crim LR 258.

OUTRAGING PUBLIC DECENCY

13.86 Some kinds of sexual misconduct do not easily fit within the scheme of SOA 2003. D's behaviour may, for example, cause shock or offence if observed, but without satisfying the specific requirements of any of the new offences of voyeurism, exposure, sexual penetration of a corpse or sex in a public lavatory. For example, public exposure of breasts or buttocks cannot satisfy the terms of s 66; sexual behaviour in a public changing room may be more offensive than similar behaviour in a closed lavatory cubicle, but cannot then be caught by s 71; and the voyeuristic 'up-skirt' filming of women in public may be as offensive as any other voyeuristic activity, but it lacks the 'privacy' element specified by s 67.

13.87 This being the case, the common law offence of outraging public decency may be called upon to fill such loopholes, much as it did under the old law.

Class of offence		3	SOA 2003, s 72 applies	✗
Notification requirements	✗		SOPO	✓[101]
CJA 2003, Sch 15 applies	✗		Serious specified offence	✗
Review of lenient sentence	✗		Special provisions of CYPA 1933	✗
Detention of young offender for specified period				✓

See **1.48** et seq.

13.88 CJA 2003, s 320 made the offence triable either way by amending the list of either-way offences in the Magistrates' Courts Act 1980, Sch 1.[102] The penalty on indictment is at large.[103] On summary conviction it may be punished by imprisonment for up to 6 months or a fine not exceeding the prescribed sum or both. It is not directly addressed by the SGC's Definitive Guideline on sentencing, but some of the guidance relating to the SOA 2003 offences described in this chapter may be applicable mutatis mutandis to comparable examples of the common law offence.[104]

Elements of the offence

13.89 The elements of the offence were reviewed at length by the Court of Appeal in *Hamilton*.[105] Some parts of the Court's analysis are not controversial and are supported by a wealth of earlier authority, but the Court also addressed issues on which there was a dearth of authority.

---

[101] SOA 2003, ss 104, 106, Sch 5, para 4A (inserted by SI 2007/296).
[102] This was put into effect by CJA 2003, and not by SOA 2003, because outraging public decency is not limited to sexual activity.
[103] *Morris* [1951] 1 KB 394.
[104] See the Appendix at pp 102–103. See also *Cosco* [2005] EWCA Crim 405.
[105] [2008] 1 Cr App R 171. See Gillespie 'Up-skirts and Down-blouses: Voyeurism and the Law' [2008] Crim LR 370.

13.90 As a matter of strict law, it is no defence to a charge of outraging public decency that the conduct alleged might also have amounted to a statutory offence.[106] Prosecutors must, however, consider whether resort to the common law offence can be justified in terms of the principles laid down by the House of Lords in *Rimmington; Goldstein*.[107] A charge of outraging public decency is unlikely to be appropriate unless it would be difficult or impossible to convict D of an appropriate statutory offence.

Lewd, obscene or disgusting behaviour

13.91 It is well established that the conduct in question must be not only indecent or improper, but 'lewd, obscene or disgusting',[108] so as to be capable of causing public outrage. Such acts need not be sexual,[109] but in most cases they will be sexual and it is with sexual offences that we are currently concerned.[110]

13.92 In *Hamilton* the Court of Appeal held that:[111]

'(i) An obscene act is an act which offends against recognised standards of propriety and which is at a higher level of impropriety than indecency ... A disgusting act is one "which fills the onlooker with loathing or extreme distaste or causes annoyance"... It is clear that the act done by the appellant was capable of being judged by a jury to be a lewd, obscene or disgusting act. It is the nature of the act that the jury had to consider and it was clear in our view that the jury were entitled to find that it was lewd, obscene or disgusting, even if no one saw him doing it.

(ii) It is not enough that the act is lewd, obscene or disgusting and that it might shock people; it must, as Lord Simon made clear in *Knuller*,[112] be of such a character that it outrages minimum standards of public decency as judged by the jury in contemporary society. As was pointed out, "outrages" is a strong word. It is not necessary to establish that any particular member of the public is outraged, as this court said in *Mayling*[113] and *Choi*;[114] and it must follow that this requirement does not mean that anyone has to see the act whilst it is being carried out.'

13.93 It appears that the test is an objective one that turns on how the act is likely to be perceived. D's secret intent or motive cannot for these purposes make criminal an act that would not otherwise be criminal.[115] Nor is it a defence for D to argue that he lacked any intent to outrage or that he failed to realise his behaviour might be visible to others. As with other examples of public nuisance, it suffices if D merely ought to have been aware of the risk.[116] Finally, it is not necessarily a defence to show that those who

---

[106] *May* (1990) 91 Cr App R 157.

[107] [2006] 1 AC 459, at [30], per Lord Bingham; see n 26. This is reflected in *CPS Guidance on Miscellaneous Offences: Offences against Morals and Decency.*

[108] *Sedley's Case* (1675) Strange 168; *Harris* (1871) 1 CCR 242; *Stanley* [1965] 2 QB 327; *Mayling* [1963] 2 QB 717; *Knuller (Publishing, Printing and Promotions) Ltd v DPP* [1973] AC 435.

[109] See *Lynn* (1788) 2 Durn & E 733 (disinterring a corpse); *Gibson* (1990) 91 Cr App R 341 (exhibiting earrings made from aborted human foetuses). In *Anderson* (unreported) 26 October 2007, D was sentenced to 3 years' imprisonment for outraging public decency by urinating on a woman who had collapsed and lay dying in the road.

[110] As to the possible application of this offence to publications of a sexual nature, see *Knuller (Publishing, Printing and Promotions) Ltd v DPP* [1973] AC 435.

[111] [2008] 1 Cr App R 171, at [30].

[112] *Knuller (Publishing, Printing and Promotions) Ltd v DPP* [1973] AC 435.

[113] [1963] 2 QB 717.

[114] [1999] EWCA Crim 1279.

[115] *Rowley* (1991) 94 Cr App R 94.

[116] *Rose v DPP* [2006] 1 WLR 2626. See also *Shorrock* [1994] 2 QB 279.

actually saw the act were neither shocked nor offended,[117] although where a large number of people appear to have watched in amused tolerance (as where spectators at a sports stadium cheer the performance of a 'streaker') this may be evidence that D's behaviour cannot have been particularly offensive.[118]

13.94 Public nudity has in the past been capable of causing outrage or disgust so as to trigger this offence, even when there is no overtly sexual behaviour involved,[119] but old cases may not always provide a reliable guide to what would today be considered outrageous. As previously noted,[120] the proposed prosecution of two young women who had flashed their breasts at a police surveillance camera provoked more public outrage than the act itself. The main objection was that prosecution would amount to a waste of public money, given that such conduct was perceived as nothing more than mildly offensive.

Misconduct in public and the 'two person' rule

13.95 However offensive the behaviour in question, the offence cannot be committed unless there is a 'public element' involved. This means that the conduct must occur in circumstances where it is at least possible for two or more persons to see (or perhaps hear) it. This is sometimes referred to as the 'two person rule', and was confirmed in *Mayling*.[121] But satisfying the 'two person rule' may not in itself be sufficient, because it has also been held that the conduct in question must, if not itself committed in a public place, be at least potentially visible to members of the public. In *Walker*,[122] D was initially convicted of this offence for exposing himself to his daughter and another child in his own house, but his conviction was quashed on the basis that nothing was done in public or visible to the public. Laws J referred to *Mayling* and added:

> 'In our judgment there is a further requirement. It is dictated by the very purpose for which the offence exists, namely, as Lord Simon said [in *Knuller v DPP*] that reasonable people might venture out in public without the risk of outrage to certain minimum standards of decency. The requirement is that the offence be committed in a place where there exists a real possibility that members of the general public might witness what happens. It does not mean that the very spot where the act is done must itself be a place of public resort, though that, no doubt, is the paradigm case. But it must be a place where the public are able to see what takes place there. In *Smith v Hughes*[123] the balcony of a private house was held to be sufficient. That is wholly in line with the requirement which we have sought to describe, since the balcony was open to public view.'[124]

The Court in *Hamilton* agreed with that analysis, but added (obiter) that acts done within public hearing might be a valid alternative to those done in public view.

13.96 The facts of *Hamilton* gave rise to a further difficulty in connection with the 'two person' rule. Previous authorities had considered cases in which at least one person had indeed seen or observed the act complained of. If one person had actually seen it and

---

[117] *May* (1990) 91 Cr App R 157.
[118] Cf the Canadian case of *Springer* (1975) 31 CR (NS) 48.
[119] *Crunden* (1809) 2 Camp 89 (nude bathing).
[120] See **13.24**.
[121] [1963] 2 QB 717. See also *Watson* (1847) 2 Cox CC 376; *Farrell* (1862) 9 Cox CC 446.
[122] [1996] 1 Cr App R 111.
[123] [1960] 1 WLR 830.
[124] [1996] 1 Cr App R at p 114. In *Wellard* (1884) 14 QBD 63, it was held that private land could be a public place for this purpose, provided that the public are not in fact excluded from it. Huddleston B said: 'The beach at Brighton is not public property, yet an exposure there is punishable ...'

others might potentially have seen it, then the two person rule was satisfied. But in *Hamilton* the appellant had used a hidden camera to film up the skirts of various women without anyone being aware of it at the time. His acts did not come to light until some months later, when the images were found by police officers executing a warrant to search his home. Could the offence be committed in such circumstances?

13.97 There is some authority that it cannot. In *Rose v DPP*,[125] D and his girlfriend engaged in oral sex in the foyer of a bank in the middle of the night. Nobody else was around at the time, but the foyer was well lit and any passers-by would have been able to see into the foyer had they chosen to look. The interior of the foyer was the subject of 24-hour CCTV surveillance, and the act came to light when the branch manageress viewed the security footage the next day. The question stated for the opinion of the Divisional Court was whether the subsequent viewing of an event captured on CCTV could be sufficient to satisfy the requirements of the offence of outraging the public decency. The Court held that:[126]

> 'There is no common law offence … if persons commit an act of the kind that was committed in the present case but it is not seen by anyone who is not participating in it. The only evidence of anyone seeing this act was of one person seeing it, and, on the authorities … that is not a sufficient public element for the offence to be established.
>
> There is … considerable force in [the] submission that the viewing privately of a private recording of an act which had not previously been seen by any person is insufficient to constitute the offence. That is because the offence is committed when it is committed. It would be curious if the offence was completed by a private viewing of a recording and if it could make a difference, for example, as to whether the bank manageress was in the company of somebody else when she saw the video or not, or whether she showed it to someone else afterwards or not.'

13.98 In *Hamilton*, however, the Court of Appeal took a different view:[127]

> 'In our view it is necessary to have regard to the purpose of the two person rule; it goes solely to the necessity that there be a public element in the sense of more than one being present and capable of being affected by it. There is in our view no reason to confine the requirement more restrictively and require actual sight or sound of the nature of the act. The public element in the offence is satisfied if the act is done where persons are present and the nature of what is being done is capable of being seen; the principle is that the public are to be protected from acts of a lewd, obscene or disgusting act which are of a nature that outrages public decency and which are capable of being seen in public …
>
> Looking therefore at the purpose of the two person rule, it can, in our view, be satisfied if there are two or more persons present who are capable of seeing the nature of the act, even if they did not actually see it. Moreover, the purpose of the requirement that the act be of such a kind that it outrages public decency goes, as we have said, to setting a standard which the jury must judge by reference to contemporary standards; it does not in fact require someone in fact saw the act and was outraged. In most cases, there will be no evidence against a defendant unless the act is seen by someone; but that does not mean that where an act is in fact done which is lewd, obscene or disgusting and is of a nature that outrages public decency and is done where it is proved that people are present and capable of seeing its nature, it is not an offence.'

---

[125]   [2006] 2 Cr App R 421.
[126]   Ibid, at [28]–[29].
[127]   [2008] QB 24 at [39]–[40].

13.99 The Court of Appeal subsequently certified the following question of law for possible consideration by the House of Lords:[128]

> 'Is a person capable of outraging public decency at common law if he commits an act of a lewd, obscene or disgusting character in a public place, but the said act, though capable of being seen or heard by more than one person, is neither seen nor heard by anyone at the time of its commission?'

The House of Lords refused leave to appeal.

13.100 The offence of outraging public decency is primarily concerned with protecting public order and/or preventing public nuisance, rather than with protecting individuals from abuse or exploitation; but when the offence is used (or misused) to fill statutory loopholes, this is not always apparent. The secret and undetected up-skirt filming of women in a supermarket appears first and foremost to involve an abuse of their individual rights, but in *Hamilton* the common law offence was charged on such facts, because nothing else could be made to fit.

13.101 The width and flexibility of the offence make it one of uncertain scope. As long ago as 1976, the Law Commission recommended its abolition.[129] This makes it all the more surprising that no serious attempt was made to supplant it by enacting a specific public indecency offence in SOA 2003.

PUBLIC ORDER OFFENCES

13.102 As previously noted, the provisions of POA 1986 are now of greatly reduced importance in the context of sexual or indecent behaviour and they accordingly are not examined in any detail here. In particular, now that we have specific legislation dealing with sexual activity in public lavatories, one would no longer expect to see the widespread charging of such offences in that context.

13.103 One can, however, envisage some acts of indecency in respect of which a public order offence might still seem more appropriate than a charge brought under SOA 2003 or the common law. A charge under POA 1986, s 5 ('insulting or disorderly behaviour ... within the sight of a person likely to be caused harassment, alarm or distress') might, for example, be considered appropriate in an exposure case, in preference to a charge under SOA 2003, s 66, where D's conduct was not intended to cause alarm or distress, but was objectively likely to do so.

13.104 Similarly, a charge under s 66 could not succeed if D's behaviour did not include exposure of his genitals; but if it could be proved that he intentionally caused harassment, alarm or distress to others (e g by 'mooning' disrespectfully at a passing funeral cortege) a charge under POA 1986, s 4A could be made out instead. If D's behaviour demonstrates racial or religious hostility (e g he exposed himself to a group of Muslim women, out of hostility to Muslims generally) this could give rise to the racially or religiously aggravated version of the appropriate s 4A or s 5 offence.[130]

---

128 [2007] All ER (D) 161 (Oct).
129 *Report on Conspiracy and Criminal Law Reform* Law Com No 76 (HMSO, 1976), at para 3.143.
130 See Crime and Disorder Act 1998, ss 28–31.

Chapter 14

PROTECTION OF COMPLAINANTS IN SEXUAL OFFENCE CASES

14.1 The complainant[1] in a prosecution for an alleged sexual offence is protected by a number of evidential, procedural and reporting rules that are not applicable to witnesses generally. Some of these are available exclusively to such complainants. Others protect both complainants and other 'vulnerable witnesses'. This chapter examines:

- anonymity of complainants in reports or publications;

- prohibition on cross-examination by D in person;

- eligibility of complainants to special measures directions; and

- restrictions on the admissibility of evidence (or of questions in cross-examination) concerning a complainant's sexual history or experience.

COMPLAINANTS, DEFENDANTS AND FAIR TRIALS

14.2 The protective rules noted above reflect the belief that complainants in sex cases are inherently vulnerable witnesses who may otherwise fail to come forward in the first place or fail to give their evidence effectively. Underlying this is the belief that too many such offences are not reported, and that too many of those that are reported fail to result in prosecution or conviction.[2] There is of course some truth in this,[3] although the problem is not unique to sex offences. The difficulty is that each of the special rules designed to protect complainants potentially impacts on the defendant (D)'s own right

---

[1] A 'complainant' is defined in the Sexual Offences (Amendment) Act (SO(A)A) 1992, s 1(2), as the person against whom the offence charged was allegedly committed. This person may not have made any complaint, and may even deny that the offence was committed. In the Youth Justice and Criminal Evidence Act (YJCEA) 1999, s 63(1), a complainant is defined for the purposes of that Act as the person against *or in respect of* whom the alleged offence was committed. A complainant might on that basis be a defence witness or even a co-defendant (as where A is charged with an offence of sex with an adult relative, B, who is charged in turn with an identical offence in respect of A). But a witness who merely supports the prosecution case by giving evidence of a similar offence allegedly committed against them is not a complainant: *Maynard* [2006] EWCA Crim 1509, (obiter) at [23].

[2] This is particularly evident in the consultation paper, *Convicting Rapists and Protecting Victims* (Office for Criminal Justice Reform, 2006), in which one of the suggestions was that juries should be required to hear 'expert evidence' to disabuse them of common 'rape myths and misconceptions'.

[3] In 2002, the conviction rate in cases of alleged rape was 5.6% of cases reported (compared with 32% in 1977) but the 5.6% figure reflects higher reporting rates and takes no account of convictions for lesser offences, or cases in which complainants retracted their allegations (Home Office Research Study 293 (2005), at p 25). In 2004, the conviction rate hit an all time low of 5.3%: HM Crown Prosecution Service Inspectorate and HM Inspectorate of Constabulary *Report on the Joint Review of the Investigation and Prosecution of Rape Offences* (2007).

to a fair trial. The more protection that is afforded to complainants (or to any other prosecution witnesses) the more difficult it may be for D, if innocent, to expose the falsity of the evidence against him. This is true even of the rule protecting the anonymity of the complainant in publications or reports, as the Court of Appeal recently acknowledged in *Blackwell (No 2)*.[4]

14.3 There is no accurate way of knowing the proportion of sexual offence allegations that are false. A true allegation may result in acquittal, or be dropped before trial, whereas a false allegation may result in conviction.[5] The oft-quoted assertion that false complaints are no more common in sex cases than in any others, although adopted as an article of faith by many campaigners, has no solid evidential basis.[6] Moreover, the frequency of false complaints in respect of other offences is rarely so important. A false report of theft, made for the purpose of advancing a fraudulent insurance claim, is unlikely to result in proceedings against any alleged thief, but the same cannot be said of a false complaint of sexual assault or rape in which a named person is accused.

14.4 Although it may be impossible to determine the frequency of false allegations in prosecutions for sexual offences, it is clear that the protection of complainants must be balanced with appropriate safeguards for defendants. This does not necessarily mean there should be a return to the practice of routinely warning juries of the dangers of convicting on the uncorroborated testimony of a complainant.[7] It does, however, mean we should question the legitimacy of measures that restrict the right of the defence to ask questions or adduce evidence concerning the background to the case or the credibility of the complainant.

14.5 Critics sometimes protest that at trials for sexual offences the complainant is treated as if she were the one on trial. Many a prosecution witness would, however, report a similar experience, which is common in adversarial trials; but the complainant is not of course on trial. Unlike D, she does not face imprisonment and disgrace if she 'loses'. If, however, the principal evidence before the court takes the form of the complainant's word against the defendant's, then the complainant's evidence and credibility will inevitably be questioned. Someone must be lying, and we cannot assume it must be D. As the Court of Appeal reminded us in *Brown*:[8]

> 'Where ... a defendant is accused of rape, the trial cannot be conducted on the assumption that he is a rapist and the complainant a victim, since the whole purpose of the proceeding is to establish whether that is so or not.'

14.6 If the complainant's credibility is in issue, then in many cases so too is her character. At one time, D's character was (with some exceptions) well protected, whereas

4   [2006] EWCA Crim 2185. See Woolchover and Heaton-Armstrong 'Debunking Rape Myths' (2008) 158 NLJ 117.
5   See for example *Blackwell* (above); *C* [2008] Crim LR 394; *H (No 2)* [2005] EWCA Crim 1828.
6   See Rumney 'False Allegations of Rape' [2006] CLJ 128, at p 143. In one of the most recent studies, undertaken for the Home Office by London Metropolitan University's Child and Woman Abuse Studies Unit in 2005 (Home Office Research Study 293), 8% (216 out of 2,643) of reported rape cases were recorded as 'false' by the police, but applying different criteria the authors of the study revised this figure to 3%. In that same year HH Judge James Tabor told a workshop set up to explore the reasons for the low conviction rate that he had tried 24 rape cases in the past 2½ years, and that four of the complainants involved later pleaded guilty to perverting the course of justice on the basis that their complaints had been false (see *The Guardian*, 17 October 2005).
7   Warnings of possible witness unreliability should now be given only in the circumstances indicated by the Court of Appeal in *Makanjuola* [1995] 1 WLR 1348.
8   [1998] 2 Cr App R 364.

the complainant's character (and in particular her sexual history) was scarcely protected at all. The position now is largely reversed. The Criminal Justice Act (CJA) 2003 made evidence of D's bad character or previous convictions much easier to introduce, but made it harder to expose the characters of complainants or other witnesses; and evidence or questioning concerning the complainant's sexual history is further restricted by YJCEA 1999, s 41.

14.7 None of the measures designed to assist and protect the complainant appear to have had any obvious impact on overall conviction rates. In rape cases, there has been a big increase in the reporting of alleged offences and an increase in the proportion of complaints brought to trial, but no corresponding increase in the number of convictions. Indeed, the conviction rate has fallen.

ANONYMITY IN REPORTS OR PUBLICATIONS

14.8 Measures protecting the public identification of complainants were first introduced in SO(A)A 1976, on the basis of recommendations made by the Heilbron Committee.[9] These were originally confined to cases involving alleged 'rape offences'.[10] The Committee argued that:

> 'Public knowledge of the indignity which [the complainant] has suffered in being raped may be extremely distressing ... and ... can operate as a severe deterrent to bringing proceedings ...'

14.9 SO(A)A 1992, s 1, now provides:

> '(1) Where an allegation has been made that an offence to which this Act applies has been committed against a person, no matter relating to that person shall during that person's lifetime be included in any publication, if it is likely to lead members of the public to identify that person as the person against whom the offence is alleged to have been committed.[11]
>
> (2) Where a person is accused of an offence to which this Act applies, no matter likely to lead members of the public to identify a person as the person against whom the offence is alleged to have been committed ("the complainant")[12] shall during the complainant's lifetime be included in any publication.
>
> (3) This section—
>
> (a) does not apply in relation to a person by virtue of subsection (1) at any time after a person has been accused of the offence, and
> (b) in its application in relation to a person by virtue of subsection (2), has effect subject to any direction given under section 3.
>
> (3A) The matters relating to a person in relation to which the restrictions imposed by subsection (1) or (2) apply (if their inclusion in any publication is likely to have the result mentioned in that subsection) include in particular—

9   Cmnd 6352 (1975), at paras 163–174.
10   This term was defined by SO(A)A 1976, s 7(2).
11   This is not so imprecise a test as to be incompatible with the European Convention on Human Rights (ECHR), Art 10: *O'Riordan v DPP* [2005] EWHC 1240 (Admin).
12   See n 1 above.

(a)   the person's name,
(b)   the person's address,
(c)   the identity of any school or other educational establishment attended by the person,
(d)   the identity of any place of work, and
(e)   any still or moving picture of the person.

(4) Nothing in this section prohibits the inclusion in a publication of matter consisting only of a report of criminal proceedings other than proceedings at, or intended to lead to, or on an appeal arising out of, a trial at which the accused is charged with the offence.'

14.10 If any matter is published or included in a relevant programme in contravention of these provisions, the editors and publishers, etc responsible may be guilty of an offence and liable on summary conviction to a fine not exceeding level 5 on the standard scale.[13]

Relevant offences

14.11 The offences to which SO(A)A 1992 applies are listed in s 2, as amended. They include all offences under the Sexual Offences Act (SOA) 2003, Pt 1, except those under ss 64, 65, 69 and 71, together with corresponding service offences, inchoate offences and secondary participation. Because prosecutions may still be brought for offences committed prior to commencement of SOA 2003, the list also includes any offence of rape, burglary with intent to rape, offences under the Mental Health Act (MHA) 1959, s 128, Indecency with Children Act (ICA) 1960, s 1, Criminal Law Act (CLA) 1977, s 54 and SOA 1956, ss 2–7, 9–12 (save where the complainant is alleged to have committed corresponding offences[14]) and 14–17.

Disapplication of the rule

14.12 By SO(A)A, s 3, the prohibition in s 1 can be displaced or relaxed on application by D:

(1)   where the court or judge is satisfied that it is necessary to name the complainant for the purpose of inducing other possible witnesses to come forward and that the defence is likely to be substantially prejudiced if this is not done;

(2)   where the judge is satisfied that the prohibition would impose a substantial and unreasonable restriction upon the reporting of proceedings and that it is in the public interest to remove or relax it; or

(3)   where an appellate court is satisfied that this is required for the purpose of obtaining evidence in support of the appeal and that the applicant is otherwise likely to suffer substantial injustice.

14.13 By s 3(4), a complainant may not be named or identified 'by reason only of the outcome of the trial'. An acquittal does not ordinarily prove that the complaint was unfounded, and complainants would lose much of their protection if acquittal resulted in loss of anonymity. There is a case for more flexibility, however. In *Blackwell (No 2)*[15]

---

[13]   SO(A)A 1992, s 5(1). Proceedings for an offence under s 5 may not be instituted except by or with the consent of the Attorney-General: s 5(4).
[14]   SO(A)A 1992, s 4.
[15]   [2006] EWCA Crim 2185.

the court could not name a complainant, even though they found her to be a serial fantasist and attention seeker whose lies had caused the appellant to spend several years in prison:[16]

> 'The power under section 3(4) does not apply in this case and there is no other relevant power. The judgment we have delivered gives rise to the concern that there may in the future be another case in which this complainant makes similar allegations against another man. If that were to happen, it would be in the interests of justice that the alleged attacker should be able to find out about and use in his defence the information ... referred to in this judgment. Parliament does not appear to have contemplated the risk of a complainant acting as this complainant is alleged to have done. We are concerned that there appears to be no means by which we can displace the complainant's entitlement to anonymity in the interests of justice for any person against whom she may make allegations in the future.'

Other reporting restrictions

14.14 The restrictions imposed by SO(A)A 1992, s 1, do not prohibit the identification of witnesses who are not complainants, even if such persons also claim to have been the victims of sexual offences committed by D. There are, however, certain other provisions that may apply (either automatically or by order of the court) so as to protect them. These are not specific to sexual offences; readers requiring detailed coverage must refer to general works on criminal procedure.

No anonymity for adult defendants

14.15 An adult defendant[17] enjoys no right to anonymity,[18] although SO(A)A 1976 did originally provide for it until conviction.[19] An acquitted defendant's identity now remains in the public domain, whereas the complainant remains protected unless prosecuted for perjury or perverting the course of justice. This causes resentment, but the rule has its defenders, including Liz Kelly, who argues:[20]

> 'The idea that those accused of sexual crimes should be privileged can only be sustained if one takes a position that either these crimes are of an entirely different order than any other and/or that there is a far higher rate of false accusations'

14.16 With respect, it is precisely because sex crimes are considered special cases that the complainant's anonymity is protected. There is, however, a practical problem in granting defendants anonymity, because this might prevent other witnesses from coming forward with evidence to corroborate the prosecution case. To quote Kelly again:

> 'There are a number of well-publicised cases ... where, following a charge being laid, other victims came forward. In each of these cases we are talking about serial rapists ... who had found a successful way of targeting women – one recent example was a successful Disc

---

[16] Ibid, at [29]. She was eventually named by Lord Campbell-Savours, who used parliamentary privilege to name her during a debate on rape legislation. Some newspapers then followed suit.

[17] As to juvenile defendants, see the Children and Young Persons Act (CYPA) 1933, s 39. Guidance as to the factors that must be taken into account by a court when determining whether to make or discharge a s 39 order in respect of a juvenile defendant was provided in the context of a rape case by the Divisional Court in *Central Criminal Court, ex p S* [1999] Crim LR 159. See also *Central Criminal Court, ex p W* [2001] 1 Cr App R 2 and *Consolidated Criminal Practice Direction* (**1.49**), at para III.30.8.

[18] D's identity may, however, need to be protected (even after conviction) in order to protect those of any closely related complainants.

[19] This was removed in 1988 and omitted from the 1992 Act.

[20] Memorandum to House of Commons Select Committee on Home Affairs, February 2003.

Jockey. If he had been granted anonymity the scale of his offending would never have been known, and he might not even have been convicted.'

14.17 The Home Affairs Select Committee suggested a compromise by which:[21]

'... the anonymity of the accused [would] be protected only for a limited period between allegation and charge ... this strikes an appropriate balance between the need to protect potentially innocent suspects from damaging publicity and the wider public interest in retaining free and full reporting of criminal proceedings.'

This suggestion has never been acted upon.

CROSS-EXAMINATION BY DEFENDANTS IN PERSON

14.18 In most criminal cases, D may choose to conduct all or any aspects of his own defence, including the cross-examination of prosecution witnesses. In prosecutions for sexual offences, however, D is largely prohibited from doing this. Restrictions were first introduced by CJA 1988, s 34A, which protected child witnesses in cases of alleged physical or sexual assault. More extensive restrictions were added by YJCEA 1999, ss 34–40, which are supplemented by Criminal Procedure Rules (CPR) 2005,[22] Pt 31.

14.19 YJCEA 1999, s 34, now provides:

'No person charged with a sexual offence may in any criminal proceedings cross-examine[23] in person a witness who is the complainant, either—

(a)   in connection with that offence, or
(b)   in connection with any other offence (of whatever nature) with which that person is charged in the proceedings.'

14.20 This provision might be criticised as an excessive response to a very limited problem. In a small number of rape cases, defendants had personally conducted painfully prolonged, if ultimately ineffective, cross-examinations of complainants. In *Brown*,[24] trial judges were instructed to deal firmly with abuses (eg by imposing time limits or by curtailing irrelevant and offensive lines of cross-examination), and this might perhaps have sufficed, but media coverage of the cases led instead to the imposition of the present statutory restrictions.

Other witnesses

14.21 Only complainants are protected by s 34, but protection is afforded by s 35 to other 'protected witnesses', including 'children'[25] who are alleged to have witnessed the commission of a sexual offence.[26]

---

21   *Fifth Report 2003*, at para 80.
22   SI 2005/384.
23   There is no prohibition against D calling the complainant as a defence witness. Cf *Paul* [2007] All ER (D) 63 (Dec).
24   [1998] 2 Cr App R 364.
25   Including witnesses aged under 17 or those who were under 17 when they gave their evidence-in-chief or recorded video interviews used as evidence-in-chief under s 27 of the Act.
26   Ie an offence under the Protection of Children Act (PoCA) 1978 or SOA 2003, Pt 1.

14.22 Other witnesses may be cross-examined by D in person, unless the court issues directions forbidding it under ss 36 and 37. This may be done only where it is considered that such directions would be likely to improve the quality of the witness's evidence and would not be contrary to the interests of justice. The court must have particular regard to the views of the witness, his relationship with D, and D's conduct during the proceedings.

Further provisions

14.23 Where unrepresented defendants are prevented from conducting cross-examinations in person, alternative provision may have to be made. Under s 38(2), D must be invited to arrange for a lawyer to act on his behalf. D must then notify the court whether a legal representative is to act for him for that purpose. If D fails to make any such arrangement, s 38(3) provides that:

> '... the court must consider whether it is necessary in the interests of justice for the witness to be cross-examined by a legal representative appointed to represent the interests of the accused.'

14.24 The court may then make such an appointment, the funding for which may be paid out of central funds.[27] The task of a court-appointed cross-examiner may be difficult; and by s 38(5), a person so appointed shall not be responsible to D. Section 39 requires a judge to warn the jury where it appears that a witness's evidence was not tested as fully as it might have been, had cross-examination been carried out by an advocate instructed by D himself.

SPECIAL MEASURES DIRECTIONS

14.25 Complainants and other witnesses in cases involving alleged sexual offences may be embarrassed, fearful or reluctant to testify. In such cases the quality of their evidence may be compromised and where children or handicapped witnesses are involved this may inhibit the provision of intelligible evidence.

14.26 A witness who cannot give intelligible evidence is incompetent,[28] but, where special measures are adopted, evidence can often be secured from witnesses who might otherwise have been unable to communicate effectively with the court. Some measures are of statutory origin (notably the use of live links and the admission of pre-recorded interviews as evidence-in-chief). Others were first introduced by the courts on their own authority.

14.27 YJCEA 1999 consolidated existing measures and introduced others, all but one of which are now in force.[29] The basic thrust of the legislation is laudable, but some provisions concerning child witnesses have been criticised as inflexible and unnecessarily complex.[30]

---

[27] YJCEA 1999, s 40(1). Section 38(4) must be read in conjunction with Crim PR, paras 31.2 and 31.3.
[28] YJCEA 1999, s 53.
[29] No plans exist to bring into force s 28 (pre-recorded cross-examination of witnesses).
[30] See Birch 'A Better Deal for Vulnerable Witnesses' [2000] Crim LR 223. As to the provisions governing child witnesses see Hoyano 'Variations on a Theme by Pigot' [2000] Crim LR 250.

The framework

14.28 The main provisions are contained in YJCEA 1999, Pt 2. These can be divided into:

(1) those that identify witnesses who may be eligible for special measures;

(2) those that identify and define the measures that may be available; and

(3) those governing the circumstances in which directions may (or must) be given, the effect of such directions, and the circumstances in which directions may be varied or discharged.

14.29 YJCEA 1999, s 19(6) provides that the Act does not affect any power to make an order or give leave of any description in cases involving non-eligible witnesses, or those who require special measures for unrelated reasons. A court may still, for example, protect the identity of a witness on grounds of public policy, or order the provision of an interpreter, without reference to the Act.

14.30 Defendants, even if juvenile or mentally disordered, were originally ineligible for any special measures under YJCEA 1999.[31] This inequality gave rise to concerns as to compatibility with the ECHR, Art 6,[32] which were only partly addressed by the willingness of the courts to aid vulnerable defendants by such means as lay within their inherent discretion.[33] An important concession has now been made by the insertion of s 33A into the 1999 Act, enabling vulnerable defendants to testify by live link.[34]

Complainants as eligible witnesses

14.31 Complainants in sex cases may be eligible for special measures either under YJCEA 1999, s 16, on the basis of youth or incapacity, or under s 17, where the court is satisfied that the quality of their evidence is likely to be diminished by reason of fear or distress at testifying. There is no question of a complainant *not* being an eligible witness.[35] By s 17(4):

> 'Where the complainant in respect of a sexual offence is a witness in proceedings relating to that offence (or to that offence and any other offences), the witness is eligible for assistance in relation to those proceedings by virtue of this subsection unless the witness has informed the court of the witness' wish not to be so eligible ...'

14.32 A complainant may have reasons for declining such assistance. She may perhaps prefer to give her evidence in open court, in the belief that her testimony will be more effective that way, and that she has nothing to fear or be ashamed of. Where however the witness is a child, certain directions will be made more or less automatically in accordance with s 21 of the Act.

---

[31] This is stated in both s 16(1) and s 17(1). See also *R (S) v Waltham Forest Youth Court* [2004] 2 Cr App R 335, in which a 13-year-old defendant was denied the benefit of a special measures direction even though apparently scared of testifying in the presence of her co-defendant.

[32] See *R (D) v Camberwell Green Youth Court* [2005] 1 All ER 998.

[33] See *Consolidated Criminal Practice Direction*, at para III.30; *H* [2003] All ER (D) 436 (Mar).

[34] Inserted by Police and Justice Act 2006, s 47.

[35] Assuming the complainant is not also a co-defendant, as could conceivably be the case (see n 1 above). The Act does not appear to contemplate that possibility, however.

Availability of special measures

14.33 The special measures that may be made available to complainants or other witnesses who are eligible under YJCEA 1999, s 16 or s 17 are specified in ss 23–30; but s 28 will not now be brought into force and by s 18(1) measures under s 29 (examination through an intermediary) and s 30 (aids to communication) are appropriate only for witnesses who are eligible under s 16. As far as most adult complainants are concerned, the only measures for which they are eligible are those under ss 23–27.

14.34 Section 18(2) meanwhile recognises that a special measures direction cannot be made in respect of a measure or facility that is not currently available in the relevant area. Some special measures, although ostensibly in force, were not initially available owing in most cases to resource and training issues. Apart from a pilot exercise at two Crown Court centres,[36] the introduction of pre-recorded video testimony for adult complainants in sex cases was thus implemented only in respect of investigations commencing on or after 1 September 2007, and then only in respect of trials on indictment.[37]

---

[36] The ROVI (record of visual interview) pilot scheme ran at the Sheffield and Wood Green Courts from 6 September 2004.

[37] In *R* [2008] EWCA Crim 678, the video-recorded evidence of an adult rape complainant was admitted by mistake at a trial in July 2004. On appeal, it was held that this irregularity was not such as to affect the admissibility of the evidence (given that s 27 was itself 'in force') nor did it prejudice the fairness of the trial.

14.35 The table below, adapted and updated from Ministry of Justice Circular 25/06/07,[38] Appendix 2, shows the availability of special measures as of May 2008.

Availability in criminal proceedings	CROWN COURT		MAGISTRATES' COURTS	
	Section 16 witnesses	Section 17 witnesses	Section 16 witnesses	Section 17 witnesses
Section 23 screening witness from accused	Full availability	Full availability	Full availability	Full availability
Section 24 evidence by live link[39]	Full availability	Full availability	Full availability	Full availability
Section 25 evidence in private	Full availability	Full availability	Full availability	Full availability
Section 26 removal of wigs and gowns	Full availability	Full availability	Not applicable	Not applicable
Section 27 video-recorded evidence-in-chief	Full availability	Available for complainants in sexual offences only	Available only for child witnesses 'in need of special protection'	Not available
Section 28 video-recorded cross-examination	Not available	Not available	Not available	Not available
Section 29 examination through an intermediary	Available nationally from April 2008	Not applicable	Available nationally from April 2008	Not applicable
Section 30 communication aids	Full availability	Not applicable	Full availability	Not applicable

---

[38]   *Complainants in sexual offences tried in the Crown Court.*
[39]   In addition, evidence may now be given by live link in sex cases where the court is satisfied that this is in the interests of the efficient or effective administration of justice: CJA 2003, s 51.

Determining the appropriate special measures

14.36 In the case of an adult complainant (or any other eligible adult witness) the choice of special measures depends on the court or judge, who must (under YJCEA 1999, s 19) consider which measures, if any, would 'maximise ... the quality of the witness's evidence'. The court must 'consider any views expressed by the witness' but is not bound to accede to the witness's preferences.[40]

14.37 In the case of a child complainant or witness, however, s 19 is subject to s 21, which leaves the court far less discretion. The initial presumption (or 'primary rule') under s 21 is that evidence-in-chief will be given by means of a pre-recorded video and that any cross-examination or re-examination will be conducted by live link. The court may ordinarily withhold either measure (under s 21(4)(c)) if it appears that the quality of the child's evidence would not be improved; but where a child witness is deemed to be 'in need of special protection' (and those in proceedings for sexual offences[41] fall into that category, even if they are defence witnesses)[42] the court has no power to consider that question. A video-recorded interview (assuming a suitable one exists) must take the place of evidence-in-chief and any further evidence (by way of cross-examination or re-examination) must be conducted over a live link. If no recording is available, or the court decides under s 27(2) that its admission would 'not be in the interests of justice', testimony must instead be given by live link.

Special measures and competence

14.38 By making special measures directions, a court may enable a young or handicapped complainant to give evidence that he might not otherwise have been able to give at all. A classic illustration of the position as it was before special measures were available can be seen in *Wallwork*,[43] where a child aged 5 was called to testify as to acts allegedly committed against her by her father. At that time little or nothing could be done to assist such witnesses, and in the words of Lord Goddard CJ:

> 'When the poor little thing was put into the witness box, she said nothing and could remember nothing.'

14.39 In contrast, a video-recorded interview would now have been made within a short time of the complaint, and used as the witness's evidence-in-chief; and although it has not proved practicable to video-record cross-examination in advance of the trial, every effort is now made to enable the child to understand and answer questions put to it in cross-examination over a live link. In the case of a handicapped witness who has difficulty in understanding or communicating with lawyers or judges, it may now be possible to provide assistance in the form of a trained intermediary.[44]

---

40   YJCEA 1999, s 19(3).
41   Defined in YJCEA 1999, s 35(3)(a) as including all offences under SOA 2003, Pt 1 or under PoCA 1978. Section 35(3)(a) (as amended) no longer makes any reference to offences under the old sexual offences law, and there are no relevant transitional provisions, but according to *C* [2008] 1 Cr App R 311 (a s 41 case) the implementation of the new law cannot have been intended to deprive witnesses of existing forms of protection in cases governed by the old law.
42   Child witnesses are also deemed to be in need of special protection when they testify in connection with an alleged offence of kidnapping, false imprisonment, child abduction, cruelty or neglect under CYPA 1933, s 1, or any other offence involving an assault, injury or threat of injury to any person. See *McAndrew-Bingham* [1999] 2 Cr App R 293.
43   (1958) 42 Cr App R 153.
44   Although YJCEA 1999 does not preclude the possibility that an intermediary may be an unqualified person who has some experience in communicating with a particular witness, intermediaries will in practice be

14.40 Problems can, however, arise where a young and/or handicapped witness appears competent when the interview is recorded, but proves incapable of understanding or responding to cross-examination in court. Such a problem arose in *Powell*.[45] This case involved a complainant aged 3. She appeared competent (if only just) when a video interview was recorded, and this was played to the jury in accordance with s 27; but when cross-examination was attempted she appeared incapable of understanding or answering questions, however carefully they were put. The trial judge allowed the case to proceed, but the Court of Appeal held that the question of competence should have been reviewed and the case withdrawn from the jury.

14.41 According to the Divisional Court in *DPP v R*,[46] the reason why the trial should have been stopped in *Powell* was that in that state of the evidence no reasonable jury properly directed could have convicted.[47] That might not always be the case where a witness proves incompetent after the video has been played:

> 'If ... by the time the question of competence is raised before the court the video interview has already been admitted, then it is evidence in the case. Section 27(4) does not [permit] the court retrospectively to direct that it be "unadmitted". What is likely to happen ... is that the court may well place little or no weight on the video recorded interview, precisely because it cannot be tested in cross-examination. That will not necessarily be so. It will depend upon the assessment of the evidence as a whole, and of the state of the original interview.'

14.42 This interpretation of *Powell* was obiter, because in *DPP v R* there was no problem of competence. The witness in *R* understood the questions, and gave intelligible answers along the lines of 'I cannot remember'. That made her a poor witness but not (as in *Powell*) an incompetent one.

14.43 An alternative suggested in *DPP v R* appears more obviously correct: If a witness is competent at the time of the recorded interview, but has suffered crippling memory loss since then, the contents of the interview may become admissible at the court's discretion as hearsay under CJA 2003, s 114(1)(d). Where a progressive or degenerative condition is responsible, the witness may be deemed unfit within the meaning of CJA 2003, s 116, and the recording may then be admissible on that basis.[48]

Warnings to juries in special measures cases

14.44 There is a risk, where witnesses are protected by special measures, that this may prejudice the defence. In some cases, special measures may inhibit the cross-examination of the witness. D may appear to be 'demonised' if, for example, a screen or live link is used to shield witnesses from him. YJCEA 1999, s 32 accordingly requires a trial judge to give the jury 'such warning (if any) as the judge considers necessary' to ensure that D is not so prejudiced.

---

trained specialists in communication needs. An Intermediary Registration Board has been established by the Office for Criminal Justice Reform, in order to oversee the registration and accreditation of approved intermediaries. See Plotnikoff and Woolfson 'Making Best Use of the Intermediary Special Measure at Trial' [2008] Crim LR 91.

45   [2006] 1 Cr App R 468.
46   [2007] EWHC 1842 (Admin).
47   Given the scientific evidence in *Powell*, this interpretation must be open to question.
48   Cf *Ali Sed* [2004] EWCA Crim 1294, where the complainant suffered from Alzheimer's disease.

COMPLAINANT'S SEXUAL HISTORY

14.45 In a prosecution for an alleged sexual offence, the defence may wish to cross-examine the complainant concerning her (or his) sexual behaviour or experiences on occasions other than the one that is the subject of the instant proceedings. The defence may also[49] seek to adduce evidence of such behaviour by examining or cross-examining other witnesses. Indeed, D may wish to testify as to his previous or subsequent sexual encounters with the complainant, or as to incidents he has witnessed involving her sexual behaviour. Whether such cross-examination or evidence is admissible is another question.

The relevance of sexual history

14.46 There are several possible reasons why the defence may wish to adduce evidence of this kind. The first is that it may sometimes be relevant to the complainant's character and credibility. Although unmarried sexual contact is now commonplace, and although a young single woman is no longer considered of bad character merely because she is 'unchaste' or promiscuous, some forms of sexual behaviour are still widely condemned. If, for example, the complainant has lied to and deceived her husband and her best friend by conducting a secret affair with her best friend's partner, a jury appraised of this deceit might not consider her to be a particularly trustworthy witness. Furthermore, some forms of sexual behaviour are criminal, and evidence concerning the commission of such offences amounts to evidence of bad character under CJA 2003.[50]

14.47 A second possibility, where consent is in issue, is that sexual history evidence may have some bearing on the issue of whether the complainant did in fact consent. The logic here has nothing to do with one's views on sexual morality. It is based on the argument that individuals are likely to behave on one occasion as they have behaved on other occasions. A promiscuous individual may, for example, be considered more likely to have consented to casual or 'first date' sex than one who had sworn to remain a virgin until marriage; and if the parties have been consensually intimate before, there may be an even more obvious basis for D's claim that sexual activity on the occasion in question was equally consensual. As Lord Hutton observed in *A (No 2)*:[51]

> 'Where there has been a recent close and affectionate relationship ... it is probable that the evidence will be relevant ... [as] evidence of such a relationship will show the complainant's specific mindset towards the defendant, namely her affection for him.'

14.48 This may understate the argument. If as part of the prosecution case it is alleged that A crept into B's bed whilst she slept, how could one possibly avoid injustice to A if the jury were prevented from hearing that A and B had shared that bed for consensual sex on several previous occasions?

14.49 Suppose instead that A meets B when clubbing on a Saturday night. She (B) invites him to her flat 'for a coffee' and sexual intercourse takes place. She later complains of rape, but he insists what happened was consensual. There is evidence that

---

49 Usually this will follow earlier cross-examination, but not of course if the complainant is deceased or too badly injured to testify. Whether Parliament actually considered that possibility is another matter. In 'The Quick and the Dead' (2007) 71 Jo Crim Law 238, Munday considers a similar issue in the context of CJA 2003, s 100.

50 CJA 2003, s 98. See **14.58** et seq.

51 [2002] 1 AC 45, at [152].

B regularly carries condoms in her handbag when clubbing 'just in case' and that she has had 'first date sex' on several occasions in the last year. Such evidence does not prove that she *did* consent to sex with A that night, but if A testifies that she did, it may make his evidence more plausible than it might otherwise have been, because it shows it to be consistent with B's past behaviour. Likewise, if B is a man who complains that A raped him, but A insists that B consented, evidence that B is a practising homosexual would be consistent with A's defence.[52] The logic here is no different from the use by the prosecution of A's previous convictions as evidence of his disposition to commit such offences.

14.50 If there is evidence of a *subsequent* consensual relationship between the parties, evidence of propensity may be augmented by doubts as to whether the genuine victim of a sexual assault would consent to further acts with her attacker. This is not to suggest that such things never happen, particularly in established relationships, but in many contexts such behaviour might be thought highly improbable.[53]

14.51 A third possibility is that the evidence in question has specific relevance to a particular issue in the case, as, for example, where A claims that bruising or injury to B's breasts or genitals was caused not by him but by a sexual encounter with another person earlier that day; or where the defence suggest that B's complaint is malicious and wish to refer to a previous (and perhaps soured) sexual relationship between them (or between B and a third party) as providing a motive for her to fabricate her evidence.[54]

Objections to sexual history evidence

14.52 The extent to which the introduction of 'sexual history' evidence of any kind should be allowed remains a sensitive issue. It is recognised that cross-examination on sexual history can be humiliating to a complainant, and that the fear of it may dissuade genuine victims from coming forward. In the wrong hands, such cross-examination may be gratuitously offensive and yet have minimal relevance either to credibility or to any issue in the case. It is therefore accepted that some controls must be imposed on the use of sexual history evidence. The question is how far such controls should go.

Statutory and common law controls

14.53 The common law provided little protection for complainants. In *Holmes*,[55] it was held that, on an indictment for a rape or indecent assault, if the complainant denied that she had engaged in sexual relations with another man, her answer was final and no evidence could be called to contradict her. This was an application of the wider rule that a witness's answers to cross-examination on collateral issues are final, but it did not spare the complainant from having to answer the initial question.

14.54 Cross-examination of complainants in rape-related cases was more substantially restricted by SO(A)A 1976, s 2, which provided that, except with the leave of the judge, no evidence and no question in cross-examination could be adduced or asked at the trial, by or on behalf of any defendant, about any sexual experience of the complainant

---

52 But see *B* [2007] Crim LR 910.
53 As in *R* [2003] EWCA Crim 2754; and see also *F* [2005] 1 WLR 2848.
54 As in *Martin* [2004] 2 Cr App R 354.
55 (1871) 12 Cox CC 137.

with a person other than that defendant. The judge could give such leave only if satisfied that it would be unfair to that defendant to refuse to allow the evidence to be adduced or the question to be asked.

14.55　The operation of that provision is now primarily a matter of historical interest, but it generated much controversy, as judges struggled to balance the protection of complainants against a defendant's right to deploy his case. Many critics concluded that the judges erred too often on the side of the defence, with the result that complainants were left unprotected from intrusive questioning, even in circumstances where the relevance of that questioning was questionable.[56] The judges, on the other hand, were conscious that defendants have more to lose than complainants, and that any error on their part, in favour of the complainant, might lead to successful appeals against conviction. It was natural, therefore, that they should resolve 'difficult' cases by giving the defence the benefit of any doubt. This was the 'soft option', and meant that s 2 was widely regarded as ineffective.[57]

14.56　In *Funderburk*,[58] it was stated that, although SO(A)A 1976 did not apply to indecent assault or intercourse with underage girls, judges should nevertheless ensure that any cross-examination as to a complainant's sexual history was not abused; but even in rape cases, the restrictions imposed by s 2 had no application to questions concerning matters such as the use of sex toys.[59]

14.57　SO(A)A 1976, s 2 was repealed by YJCEA 1999 and replaced by the much stricter, more elaborate and wider-ranging controls contained in s 41 of that Act. The controls imposed by s 41 appear inflexible, and purport to give little discretion to courts or judges, but this reflects the new orthodoxy, originally advanced by feminist campaigners and now accepted by mainstream lawyers, judges and ministers. According to this new orthodoxy, a complainant's sexual history is not ordinarily relevant to any issue at trial and may be admissible only in exceptional and strictly defined circumstances. In practice, however, the courts may have rather more discretion where D's right to a fair trial would otherwise be prejudiced.[60]

Sexual misconduct as bad character under CJA 2003

14.58　Sexual history evidence cannot ordinarily be equated with evidence of bad character under CJA 2003. A complainant may be of unquestioned good character despite having a varied and colourful sexual history. But clearly some overlap is possible. Where a complainant's sexual history involves misconduct or criminality on her (or his) part, consideration must be given not only to the restrictions imposed by YJCEA, s 41, but also to those imposed by CJA 2003.

14.59　In a criminal prosecution, a witness who is of bad character may be subject to cross-examination as to that character, usually on the basis that this has some bearing on his credibility. If he does not admit this when lawfully questioned, he may in some

---

[56]　See, for example, Temkin 'Sexual History Evidence: the Ravishment of Section 2' [1993] Crim LR 3; Adler
　　　Rape on Trial (Routledge, 1987); Lees *Carnal Knowledge: Rape on Trial* (Hamish Hamilton, 1996).
[57]　See *Speaking up for Justice*, Report of the Interdepartmental Working Group on the treatment of
　　　Vulnerable or Intimidated Witnesses in the Criminal Justice System (Home Office, 1998), at para 9.62 et seq.
[58]　[1990] 2 All ER 482.
[59]　*Barnes* [1994] Crim LR 691.
[60]　See **14.90** et seq.

(but not all) cases be contradicted by evidence adduced for that purpose.[61] But CJA 2003 restricts the circumstances in which evidence of bad character can be raised, and complainants who would have faced such cross-examination at common law may perhaps escape it under the CJA regime.[62]

14.60 Evidence of a person's 'bad character' is defined by CJA 2003, s 98, as:

> '... evidence of, or of a disposition towards, misconduct on his part, other than evidence which
>
> (a)　has to do with the alleged facts of the offence with which D is charged, or
>
> (b)　is evidence of misconduct in connection with the investigation or prosecution of that offence.'

14.61 'Misconduct' is defined in CJA 2003, s 112 as the commission of an offence or other reprehensible behaviour, whether or not it resulted in a conviction.[63] The first part of that test is simple enough, but the second is primarily a matter of subjective judgment. In the context of sexual history evidence, proof that the complainant once committed an offence involving sexual activity with a child or that he was once cautioned for exposure is therefore evidence of bad character. In contrast, adultery, 'swinging' or participation in outré fetish games might or might not be considered 'reprehensible', depending on the circumstances[64] and on the views of the judge who has to make the ruling.

14.62 The admissibility of bad character evidence (or questions designed to elicit it) is governed, in the case of a complainant, or indeed of any person other than D, by CJA 2003, s 100. Such evidence is admissible under s 100(1) if but only if:

(a)　it is important explanatory evidence;

(b)　it has substantial probative value in relation to a matter which is a matter in issue in the proceedings, and is of substantial importance in the context of the case as a whole; or

(c)　all parties to the proceedings agree to the evidence being admissible.[65]

61　This depends on whether any exception to the 'collateral-finality' rule can be established. Where a witness denies a previous conviction, it can easily be proved (in most cases) in accordance with the Criminal Procedure Act 1865, s 6; but if he denies (eg) having been dismissed from a previous job for misconduct, this denial will ordinarily be final. The court cannot allow a trial to be sidetracked by investigation of collateral issues.

62　See, for example, *Goddard* [2007] EWCA Crim 3134.

63　See *Renda* [2006] 1 Cr App R 380 (evidence that D was once found unfit to plead on a charge alleging serious violence was considered to be evidence of bad character).

64　For example, adultery committed by a woman whose husband left her 2 years before might not be considered reprehensible, but adultery at her wedding reception surely would be.

65　Unless admitted by agreement, evidence of the bad character of a person other than a defendant must not be given without leave of the court. A party who proposes to introduce evidence of a non-defendant's bad character or who wishes to cross-examine a witness with a view to eliciting that evidence under s 100 must apply in the form set out in *Consolidated Practice Direction*, Annex D, giving the other parties time to oppose the application. 'Agreement' means agreement of the parties, which is not the same thing as consent of the individual in question. The prosecution may agree to disclosure of the complainant's bad character without his agreement.

'Important explanatory evidence' is evidence 'without which the court or jury would find it impossible or difficult properly to understand other evidence in the case'.[66] It must also have 'substantial value for understanding the case as a whole'. It is possible, for example, that some of the evidence in the case cannot properly be understood unless the jury is made aware that the complainant once worked as a prostitute, served a prison sentence or starred in 'extreme' pornographic videos.

14.63 The most likely way in which a complainant's sexual misconduct on other occasions will have 'substantial probative value in relation to a matter which is a matter in issue in the proceedings', and be of 'substantial importance in the context of the case as a whole' is by having a significant bearing on his or her credibility, in cases where that credibility is crucial.[67] But his credibility will not necessarily suffer substantial damage even where he has been convicted of a criminal offence involving sexual misconduct. It will be a question for the trial judge or court to assess and appellate courts will be slow to interfere with any such decision, assuming that the right test has been applied. In some cases, there may be evidence of behaviour on the part of the complainant that goes beyond issues of credibility and demonstrates a propensity to behave in a particular way. There may, for example, be clear evidence of a propensity to engage in consensual sex and then complain of rape. This would almost certainly be admissible under s 100(1)(b).[68]

14.64 CJA 2003, s 100 cannot therefore be ignored in case where the defence seek to question a complainant (or any other prosecution witness) as to 'reprehensible' sexual behaviour. But as far as the complainant is concerned, the more awkward obstacle confronting any application to adduce sexual history evidence will be YJCEA 1999, s 41, which applies whether the sexual behaviour in question was 'reprehensible' or not.[69]

YJCEA 1999, s 41

14.65 YJCEA, s 41, provides:

'(1) If at a trial a person is charged with a sexual offence, then, except with the leave of the court—

(a) no evidence may be adduced, and
(b) no question may be asked in cross-examination,

by or on behalf of any accused at the trial, about any sexual behaviour of the complainant.

---

[66] CJA 2003, s 100(2).
[67] 'A "Matter in issue in the proceedings" in s 100(1)(b)(i) must be apt to include the creditworthiness of a witness ..., since otherwise it would never be possible to cross-examine a witness as to his or her previous convictions in circumstances where the purpose of doing so was to demonstrate that the witness was unworthy of belief': *S (Andrew)* [2006] 2 Cr App R 31, at [7]. Bad character may be relevant to the credibility of a witness even if it does not involve dishonesty or the telling of lies: *Stephenson* [2006] EWCA Crim 2325, at [27].
[68] Cf *S (Andrew)* [2006] 2 Cr App R 31; but the position is likely to be different where there is no clear evidence that a previous allegation was false at all. Judges will not ordinarily permit cross-examination to suggest that a complainant has made prior false allegations if that would necessitate a detailed collateral investigation into the truth or falsity of the earlier complaint. See *Duckfield* [2007] EWCA Crim 4; *Hamlet* [2007] EWCA Crim 2671.
[69] As the Court observed in *Maynard* [2006] EWCA Crim 1509, at [24], CJA 2003, s 100 may be more important where the witness in question is not a complainant in the instant proceedings.

(2) The court may give leave in relation to any evidence or question only on an application made by or on behalf of an accused, and may not give such leave unless it is satisfied—

(a)   that subsection (3) or (5) applies, and
(b)   that a refusal of leave might have the result of rendering unsafe a conclusion of the jury or (as the case may be) the court on any relevant issue in the case.

(3) This subsection applies if the evidence or question relates to a relevant issue in the case and either—

(a)   that issue is not an issue of consent; or
(b)   it is an issue of consent and the sexual behaviour of the complainant to which the evidence or question relates is alleged to have taken place at or about the same time as the event which is the subject matter of the charge against the accused; or
(c)   it is an issue of consent and the sexual behaviour of the complainant to which the evidence or question relates is alleged to have been, in any respect, so similar—
        (i)   to any sexual behaviour of the complainant which (according to evidence adduced or to be adduced by or on behalf of the accused) took place as part of the event which is the subject matter of the charge against the accused, or
        (ii)   to any other sexual behaviour of the complainant which (according to such evidence) took place at or about the same time as that event,
        that the similarity cannot reasonably be explained as a coincidence.

(4) For the purposes of subsection (3) no evidence or question shall be regarded as relating to a relevant issue in the case if it appears to the court to be reasonable to assume that the purpose (or main purpose) for which it would be adduced or asked is to establish or elicit material for impugning the credibility of the complainant as a witness.

(5) This subsection applies if the evidence or question—

(a)   relates to any evidence adduced by the prosecution about any sexual behaviour of the complainant; and
(b)   in the opinion of the court, would go no further than is necessary to enable the evidence adduced by the prosecution to be rebutted or explained by or on behalf of the accused.

(6) For the purposes of subsections (3) and (5) the evidence or question must relate to a specific instance (or specific instances) of alleged sexual behaviour on the part of the complainant (and accordingly nothing in those subsections is capable of applying in relation to the evidence or question to the extent that it does not so relate).

(7) Where this section applies in relation to a trial by virtue of the fact that one or more of a number of persons charged in the proceedings is or are charged with a sexual offence—

(a)   it shall cease to apply in relation to the trial if the prosecutor decides not to proceed with the case against that person or those persons in respect of that charge; but
(b)   it shall not cease to do so in the event of that person or those persons pleading guilty to, or being convicted of, that charge.

(8) Nothing in this section authorises any evidence to be adduced or any question to be asked which cannot be adduced or asked apart from this section.'

14.66 YJCEA, s 42(1) defines some of the above terms:

'(a)   "relevant issue in the case" means any issue falling to be proved by the prosecution or defence in the trial of the accused;

(b)   "issue of consent" means any issue whether the complainant in fact consented to the
        conduct constituting the offence with which the accused is charged (and accordingly
        does not include any issue as to the belief of the accused that the complainant so
        consented);

(c)   "sexual behaviour" means any sexual behaviour or other sexual experience, whether or
        not involving any accused or other person, but excluding (except in section 41(3)(c)(i)
        and (5)(a)) anything alleged to have taken place as part of the event which is the
        subject matter of the charge against the accused; and

(d)   subject to any order made under subsection (2), "sexual offence" shall be construed in
        accordance with section 62.'

'Sexual behaviour' to which s 41 applies

14.67 As previously noted, the restrictions imposed under s 41 are more extensive than
those contained within SO(A)A 1976. They do not apply to the prosecution,[70] but in
their application to the defence they apply to a wider range of offences,[71] and to all
kinds of sexual behaviour or sexual experience on the part of the complainant,
including previously excluded matters such as self-masturbation,[72] and even previous or
subsequent sexual relations with D himself.[73] The restrictions apply, not just at trial, but
at every possible stage of the proceedings, including appeals.[74] Passive experiences are
included, even when suffered as a defenceless victim.[75] Thus, whereas the prosecution
may choose to reveal that a complainant was sexually abused by third parties when she
was a child, it would not ordinarily be open to the defence to reveal this.

14.68 The prohibitions in s 41 go well beyond restrictions on cross-examination of the
complainant. No other witness can be questioned by the defence concerning the
complainant's sexual behaviour: D cannot ordinarily refer even to his own sexual
experiences with her.

14.69 The only sexual behaviour excluded for the purposes of the s 41 prohibition is
'anything alleged to have taken place as part of the event which is the subject matter of
the charge'.[76] The defence must be allowed to deny the prosecution's case, and offer their
own account of what they say transpired, even if that account involves lurid descriptions
of the complainant's sexual behaviour. Any restriction on that right would fatally
undermine the fairness of the proceedings.

---

[70]   The fact that they do not apply to the prosecution arguably offends against the 'equality of arms' principle,
       but in *Soroya* [2007] Crim LR 181 the Court suggested that the Police and Criminal Evidence Act 1984, s 78,
       'is perfectly apt to be deployed' in cases where this inequality might otherwise produce an adverse effect on
       the fairness of the proceedings.

[71]   YJCEA 1999, s 62 originally listed these as being: rape; burglary with intent to rape; offences under SOA
       1956, ss 2–12 and 14–17; offences under MHA 1959, s 128, and offences under ICA 1960, s 1 or CLA 1977,
       s 54, together with inchoate versions of any of those offences. It now applies to any offence under SOA 2003,
       Pt 1 (ss 1–79) and related inchoate offences. As to the continued application of s 41 to offences charged
       under the old law, see *C* [2008] 1 Cr App R 311 (see **14.37**).

[72]   Contrast *Barnes* (see **14.56**).

[73]   It was argued in *K* [2008] EWCA Crim 434 that s 41 does not apply to cross-examination concerning an
       abortion, because this is not sexual behaviour, even though it must result from sexual behaviour. The Court
       in *K* did not find it necessary to decide the point in the context of that case, because the fact in question was
       of minimal relevance anyway; but it is submitted that, in some contexts at least, such questioning may be a
       way of introducing evidence of sexual behaviour by inference, and in such a case it must indeed fall within
       the ambit of s 41.

[74]   See YJCEA 1999, s 42(3).

[75]   *E (Dennis Andrew)* [2004] EWCA Crim 1313.

[76]   Exempted by s 42(1)(c); see **14.66**.

14.70 Problems may, however, arise when courts are asked to distinguish between behaviour that is alleged to have taken place as 'part of the event' and behaviour that is merely alleged to have taken place 'at or about the same time as' that event. Faced with an allegation that he sexually assaulted his stepdaughter one weekend when her mother was away, D may deny that the incident she described occurred, but claim that he aggrieved her that weekend by rejecting her sexual advances to him. This is in one sense his version of 'what really happened', but what he describes may be a very different event from the one described by his stepdaughter. In doubtful cases the defence must raise the issue with the court before proceeding. If the court agrees that the behaviour in question was 'part of the event', no leave to proceed is needed; but failing that, the defence would have to obtain leave under s 41(2) and (3)(b).

14.71 Conduct that is not obviously sexual may be closely linked to conduct that is. Getting into a car, exchanging telephone numbers or inviting a date to 'come in for a coffee' are not in themselves sexual acts, but in some circumstances they might be perceived as preliminaries to sexual acts, and thus fall within the s 41 restrictions.[77]

14.72 Section 41 does not, in terms, prevent the defence from asking the complainant about matters of sexual preference or orientation. Evidence that the complainant is homosexual might perhaps be considered relevant if, for example, a question arises as to whether he consented to a homosexual act with D. It is unlikely, however, that mere evidence of orientation could be adjudged sufficiently relevant to justify admission. In contrast, 'Have you ever had (or sought, or fantasised about) sex with other men?' is clearly a question about sexual behaviour, and s 41 applies to such questions whatever the gender of the complainant.[78]

14.73 A major problem area is that of lies allegedly told in connection with some other alleged sexual experience. If the defence wish to allege that the complainant has previously lied or fabricated evidence in connection with some other sexual incident or offence, is that governed by s 41? There is no simple answer to that question, and we must defer consideration of it until some of the more basic issues have been clarified.[79]

Questions or evidence for which leave may be given under s 41

14.74 Where proposed defence evidence or questioning does indeed concern the complainant's sexual history, YJCEA 1999, s 41(2) provides that it may be allowed only where the court is satisfied:

(a)   that it falls within either s 41(3) or s 41(5); *and*

(b)   is further satisfied that exclusion might lead to an unsafe verdict.

One might think that (b) should be sufficient justification in itself, as it was under the old law. The perceived failure of the old law was, however, blamed on the over-willingness of judges to allow questions or evidence in the 'interests of justice'. Reformers were determined that judges would no longer be trusted to decide such cases according to the interests of justice. Instead, they would be required to identify specific

---

[77]   See *Mukadi* [2004] Crim LR 373 in which the Court recognised that the complainant's behaviour in getting into a car with a man who accosted her before exchanging telephone numbers with him might be perceived as sexual behaviour on her part.

[78]   *Beedal* [2007] EWCA Crim 23; sub nom *B* [2007] Crim LR 910.

[79]   See **14.93**.

grounds that might justify a 'lifting of the veil'. Those specific grounds would be specified in the legislation, and no other grounds would be recognised.

14.75 Section 41 reflects the reformist view, but the inflexibility of its 'pigeon-hole' approach to admissibility was quickly identified as problematic.[80] In *A (No 2)*, the first reported case on s 41, the House of Lords recognised that, if that section were construed in the normal way, it would potentially interfere with D's right to a fair trial under ECHR, Art 6, and that the only way to avoid incompatibility with Art 6 was for some element of flexibility to be read into it judicially, in accordance with the power given to the courts by the Human Rights Act (HRA) 1998, s 3. This was a necessary ruling, but unfortunately it can be difficult to determine when the courts will consider the exercise of this power to be necessary. Practice in the trial courts has been inconsistent. Many trial judges clearly have reservations as to the exclusion of relevant defence evidence, and are amenable to arguments for its inclusion, but others are more sympathetic to the s 41 approach.[81] In most reported appeals, full effect has been given to the terms of s 41. It is, however, clear that 'judicial redrafting' will sometimes be necessary, not just in the circumstances that arose in *A (No 2)*, but in other circumstances as well.[82]

Questions or evidence which may satisfy s 41(2) and (3)

Gateways and prohibitions

14.76 Perhaps the first thing to note about YJCEA 1999, s 41(3) is that the various gateways it provides are subject to the prohibitions imposed by s 41(4) and (6), as well as to the initial requirement prescribed by s 41(2)(b). By s 41(4), nothing that appears to the court to be wholly or primarily designed to discredit the complainant as a witness can ever be admissible by virtue of s 41(3), although such evidence may sometimes be admissible using the s 41(5) gateway. Allegations of sexual behaviour that do not relate to specific incidents (eg questions or evidence relating to a general reputation for promiscuity, etc) are meanwhile prohibited under s 41(6). Of these two restrictions, the one imposed by s 41(4) is potentially the more troublesome and requires further consideration.[83]

Issues of consent and other issues

14.77 'Relevant issues' under s 41(3) are divided into 'issues of consent' (excluding mistaken belief in consent) and 'issues other than consent', such as mistaken identity, mistaken belief in consent and outright denials that sexual activity, etc occurred). Any attempt by the defence to adduce sexual history evidence concerning the complainant will be subject to s 41(2)(b), (4) and (6), but where the evidence does not bear on any issue of consent, s 41(3)(a) adds no further requirement. Where, however, it does relate to an issue of consent, the defence must surmount further hurdles raised in s 41(3)(b) or (c).

---

[80] This should have come as no surprise, but those responsible for the drafting of s 41 appear not to have heeded the Canadian experience, in which a somewhat similar attempt to restrict the admissibility of such evidence was found to be an obstacle to fair trials. See *Seaboyer* (1991) 2 SCR 577. See also Kibble 'The Sexual History Provisions: Charting a Course between Inflexible Legal Rules and Wholly Untrammelled Judicial Discretion' [2000] Crim LR 274; Kibble 'Judicial Discretion and the Admissibility of Prior Sexual History Evidence under Section 41' [2005] Crim LR 263.

[81] Kibble 'Judicial Perspectives on the Operation of Section 41' [2005] Crim LR 190.

[82] *Hamadi* [2007] EWCA Crim 3048.

[83] See **14.93**.

14.78 If, for example, A claims that he never touched his stepdaughter B, and that she is accusing him of sexual assault out of spite because he stopped her from visiting her boyfriend, C, for underage sex, there is no issue of consent involved, so s 41(3)(a) applies and s 41(3)(b) and (c) are not engaged.[84] Section 41(6) raises no problems on these facts, but if A wants to cross-examine B about her sexual relationship with C, the judge must first be satisfied that excluding it might lead to a wrongful verdict (s 41(2)(b)) and in addition the judge must be satisfied under s 41(4) that the 'purpose or principal purpose' of the evidence or questioning is not 'to establish or elicit material for impugning the credibility of [B] as a witness'.[85]

14.79 The above scenario may be contrasted with one in which A is charged with raping his ex-wife B, and claims that she had consented to have sex with him both on this and on previous occasions since their divorce. If he suggests that her complaint of rape was motivated by a dispute over money, all the obstacles identified in **14.78** still apply if he seeks to adduce evidence of their previous sexual encounters, but *in addition* he must satisfy the court that either the test set out in s 41(3)(b) or that set out in s 41(3)(c) is satisfied.

14.80 It is difficult to see why extra obstacles should be raised against the introduction of sexual history evidence merely because it relates to an issue of consent (rather than, say, to an outright denial, or to mistaken belief in consent). Defendants may run alternative defences of consent and mistaken belief in consent, and in such cases the adoption of different tests can greatly complicate the judge's task, both in deciding whether to admit sexual history evidence and in directing the jury upon its relevance if he does so.[86] It would be wrong, however, to suggest that s 41(3)(a) provides a 'loophole' which the defence can exploit merely by alleging mistaken belief in consent rather than actual consent. All paths to the admission of sexual history evidence are guarded (notably by s 41(2)(b) and (4)), even if some paths are guarded more tightly than others.[87] There will moreover be many cases in which a defence of mistaken belief is simply not tenable on the evidence.[88]

Sexual behaviour 'at or about the same time as the event which is the subject matter of the charge'

14.81 Under s 41(3)(b) the complainant's previous or subsequent sexual behaviour may be admissible even in relation to an issue of consent if it allegedly occurred 'at or about the same time as' the alleged offence. The explanatory notes published with YJCEA 1999 state that this is intended to include only behaviour occurring 'no more widely than 24 hours before or after the offence'.[89] In *Viola*,[90] a rape case decided under SO(A)A 1976, it was held that counsel ought to have been allowed to cross-examine the complainant as to whether she had engaged in sexual intercourse with two other men a

---

[84]   For a further example of facts falling within s 41(3)(a), see *A (No 2)* [2002] 1 AC, at [79], per Lord Hope (see **14.75**) (cross-examination as to alternative explanations for the complainant's physical condition). See also *Mokrecovas* [2002] 1 Cr App R 226.

[85]   As to the potential impact of s 41(4) in such cases, see *Martin* [2004] 2 Cr App R 354 and **14.94**.

[86]   See Elliott 'Consent and Belief in Trials for Sexual Offences' [2000] NLJ 1150. As to defences based on belief in consent, see *Barton* (1986) 85 Cr App R 5.

[87]   See *Bahador* [2005] EWCA Crim 396, at [13].

[88]   See *DPP v Morgan* [1976] AC 182; *Winter* [2008] EWCA Crim 3, at [29]. For a discussion of the mistaken belief issue, see McEwan 'I Thought She Consented: Defeat of the Rape Shield or the Defence that Shall not Run?' [2006] Crim LR 969.

[89]   See also *A (No 2)* [2002] 1 AC 45, at [40], per Lord Steyn; *Pemberton* [2007] EWCA Crim 3201, at [10].

[90]   [1982] 1 WLR 1138, at 1143.

few hours before the alleged rape, and/or with another man the following day; and also as to whether yet another man had been found sleeping naked in her flat that morning. Section 41(3(b) might similarly allow such questioning.

14.82 Evidence of sexual behaviour within this 24-hour period will not necessarily be admissible, however. As with any of the 'gateways' under s 41(3), the requirements of s 41(2), (4) and (6) must also be considered, and in some cases evidence of sexual behaviour just a few minutes before the alleged offence may lack any real probative value. In *Stephenson*,[91] for example, the complainant admitted willingly kissing D at a party immediately prior to the alleged rape, and the judge reminded the jury of this in summing up. In those circumstances, the judge was right not to allow further evidence to be called in order to show that the complainant had kissed two other men earlier that evening.

14.83 As previously noted,[92] it may well be difficult to distinguish between behaviour that is allegedly 'part of the event that is the subject matter of the charge' and behaviour that is merely alleged to have occurred 'at or about the same time' as the alleged offence. The distinction might not ultimately matter if the court or judge is willing to admit the evidence in any event.

Sexual behaviour in which similarity cannot reasonably be explained as a coincidence

14.84 Sexual history evidence or questioning may also be permitted under s 41(3)(c). This provision, which was added to the original Bill only in response to pressure from critics, is not governed by temporal limitations,[93] but in order for it to apply, the complainant's alleged sexual behaviour must involve similarities to the instant case which cannot simply be dismissed as coincidental. At first sight, this might appear to be a very difficult gateway for the defence to exploit, and Baroness Mallalieu did little to dispel that illusion during a House of Lords debate on the addition of this clause when she tried to explain it with the aid of an improbable illustration involving a girl who repeatedly makes rape allegations after re-enacting the balcony scene from Shakespeare's *Romeo and Juliet*.

14.85 The actual operation of s 41(3)(c) may not be so bizarre, but the test is deliberately strict. Assume that the defence has evidence suggesting that the complainant's behaviour or experience on a previous or subsequent occasion was similar to her alleged behaviour in the instant case. One must ask whether the similarities could reasonably be explained away as coincidental; and not merely whether they make it any more likely that the complainant consented. If, for example, A is accused of raping his colleague B in a hotel where they were staying on business, the fact that B previously had consensual sex with another colleague when staying at the same hotel could easily be explained as a 'mere coincidence', and so the test would not be satisfied.

14.86 Although the *Romeo and Juliet* illustration found its way into the Act's Notes for Guidance, s 41(3)(c) does not in fact require conduct that is 'rare or bizarre'[94] and although any evidence or questioning admitted under that provision must be both

---

91   [2002] EWCA Crim 1231. See also *Mokrecovas* [2002] 1 Cr App R 226.
92   At **14.70**.
93   *Tahed* [2004] EWCA Crim 1220; sub nom *T* [2004] 2 Cr App R 551.
94   *A (No 2)* [2002] 1 AC 45, at [135], per Lord Clyde.

highly relevant (in order to satisfy s 41(2)(b)) and have some bearing on the issue of consent, evidence may still satisfy the test without going so far as to prove the complainant must have consented. In *A (No 2)*, Lord Clyde said:[95]

> 'The essentials for the application of the provision are that there should be a similarity in any respect between the two incidents of sexual behaviour which cannot reasonably be explained as a coincidence. It is only a similarity that is required, not an identity. Moreover the words "in any respect" deserve to be stressed. On one view any single factor of similarity might suffice to attract the application of the provision, provided that it is not matter of coincidence. That the behaviour was with the same person, the defendant, must be at least a relevant consideration ... The language seems ... to be looking for some characteristic or incident of the complainant's sexual behaviour ... which bears some kind of connection or relationship with the behaviour which on a reasonable view is not a mere matter of chance.'

14.87 This approach was adopted in *Tahed*,[96] where T was convicted of raping and indecently assaulting the complainant, J, inside a climbing frame in a children's play area. The rape was allegedly committed in a rear-entry standing position and the indecent assault, charged under SOA 1956, involved oral sex. At trial, T was not permitted to prove that he and J had enjoyed consensual intercourse inside the same climbing frame, using the same standing sexual position, a few weeks earlier, nor was he permitted to prove that they had frequently engaged consensually in oral sex. The Court of Appeal quashed T's convictions on the basis that this evidence ought to have been permitted under s 41(3)(c)(i). The relationship had been volatile and it was possible that T raped J in a place where they previously had enjoyed consensual sex, but the court considered it necessary to give s 41(3)(c) 'a broad interpretation when to do otherwise would lead to an unfair trial'.[97]

The 'fair trial' judicial gateway: behaviour between the parties

14.88 If *Tahed* had been decided under SO(A)A 1976, s 2, there could have been no question of excluding evidence as to previous (or subsequent) sexual behaviour between the parties; but YJCEA 1999, s 41 contains no specific provision concerning such matters. This is a remarkable omission given that many would consider it to be essential background evidence.[98] Section 41(3)(c) is capable of applying to some such cases, but in *A (No 2)* the courts have stopped well short of holding that this provision will always be applicable. As Lord Steyn explained in *A (No 2)*:[99]

> 'Making due allowance for the words "in any respect" in section 41(3)(c), the test "that the similarity cannot reasonably be explained *as a coincidence*" is inapt to allow evidence to be admitted or questioning to take place that, for example, ... the complainant and the accused had sexual relations on several occasions in the previous month. While common sense may rebel against the idea that such evidence is never relevant to the issue of consent, that is the effect of the statute.'

---

95   Ibid.
96   [2004] EWCA Crim 1220; reported sub nom *T* [2004] 2 Cr App R 551. See also *R* [2003] EWCA Crim 2754.
97   Contrast *White* [2004] EWCA Crim 946, in which W was not permitted to prove that the complainant had worked as a prostitute, even though the essence of his case was that her complaint of rape arose out of an argument over payment after they had had consensual intercourse. There was nothing, said the Court, to engage s 41(3)(c). With respect, there is no way in which the fact that she worked as a prostitute could be dismissed as a mere coincidence. It had an obvious bearing on the credibility of W's defence and the jury should have been made aware of it.
98   See Birch 'Rethinking Sexual History Evidence: Proposals for Fairer Trials' [2002] Crim LR 531; see also Kibble 'Judicial Perspectives on the Operation of s 41' [2005] Crim LR 190.
99   [2002] 1 AC 45, at [43].

14.89 Arguably, s 41(3)(c) is not really that inapt, even on normal principles of statutory interpretation. No reasonable court or jury, on learning that A and B had regularly engaged in acts of sex before or since, could easily dismiss such evidence as 'mere coincidence'. According to the House of Lords, however, such evidence can be squeezed within s 41(3)(c) only by invoking ECHR, Art 6, and HRA 1998, s 3. To quote Lord Steyn again:[100]

> 'It is ... possible under section 3 [of HRA 1998] to read section 41, and in particular
> section 41(3)(c), as subject to the implied provision that evidence or questioning which is
> required to ensure a fair trial under article 6 of the Convention should not be treated as
> inadmissible. The result of such a reading would be that sometimes logically relevant sexual
> experiences between a complainant and an accused may be admitted under section 41(3)(c).
> On the other hand, there will be cases where previous sexual experience between a
> complainant and an accused will be irrelevant, eg an isolated episode distant in time and
> circumstances. Where the line is to be drawn must be left to the judgment of trial judges.'

Implications of the ruling in A (No 2)

14.90 In a passage with which other members of the Appellate Committee expressly concurred, Lord Steyn said:[101]

> 'It is of supreme importance that the effect of the speeches today should be clear to trial
> judges who have to deal with problems of the admissibility of questioning and evidence on
> alleged prior sexual experience between an accused and a complainant. The effect of the
> decision today is that under section 41(3)(c) of the 1999 Act, construed where necessary by
> applying the interpretative obligation under section 3 of the Human Rights Act 1998, and
> due regard always being paid to the importance of seeking to protect the complainant from
> indignity and from humiliating questions, the test of admissibility is whether the evidence
> (and questioning in relation to it) is nevertheless so relevant to the issue of consent that to
> exclude it would endanger the fairness of the trial under article 6 of the convention. If this
> test is satisfied the evidence should not be excluded.'

14.91 Some commentators have sought to downplay the significance of this dictum. Seizing on the initial reference to cases involving 'sexual experience between an accused and a complainant', Kelly, Temkin and Griffiths argue that:[102]

> '... the rules of precedent should ensure that the formula the House of Lords has tacked
> onto s 41(3)(c) applies only in the case of a previous sexual relationship with the accused.'

14.92 The Court of Appeal in *White*[103] appears to have taken the same view; but (with respect) the Court of Appeal in *Hamadi*[104] was surely right to hold that the whole of s 41 must be interpreted, wherever possible, in such a way as to respect D's right to a fair trial. That consideration may be particularly important when dealing with the ostensibly absolute prohibitions imposed by s 41(4) and (6).[105]

---

[100] Ibid, at [45].
[101] Ibid, at [46].
[102] Section 41: an evaluation of the new legislation limiting sexual history evidence in rape trials. Home Office online report, 20/06: http://www.homeoffice.gov.uk/rds/onlinepubs1.html.
[103] [2004] EWCA Crim 946.
[104] [2007] EWCA Crim 3048, at [21].
[105] See *Martin* [2004] 2 Cr App R 354; *Hamadi*, n 104 above.

The purpose test: s 41(4)

14.93 Admissibility under any of the three s 41(3) gateways depends not just on the content of the evidence, etc, but on what the court perceives to be its purpose. Evidence that appears to satisfy the requirements of s 41(2) and (3) may still fall foul of s 41(4) if its 'purpose or main purpose' appears to be that of impugning the credibility of the complainant as a witness; but in the context of sexual offences the distinction between evidence bearing upon the facts in issue and evidence bearing upon the credibility of the complainant has long been recognised as troublesome. In *Funderburk*,[106] the Court of Appeal agreed with a passage in the 6th edition of *Cross on Evidence*[107] in which it was said that the distinction 'may in some circumstances be reduced to vanishing point'.

14.94 *Martin*[108] provides a good illustration. M denied the complainant's allegation of indecent assault and alleged that she had a grudge against him because of an earlier incident between them in which she had fellated him, only for him to reject her as soon as she had finished. If true, this would indeed provide evidence of bias, but bias is generally perceived to be a collateral matter going to credibility. One solution to the problem might be to construe s 41(4) very narrowly, so that it forbids only outdated arguments to the effect that, 'the complainant is a sexually promiscuous person, and is therefore not a credible witness'. But the Court in *Martin* did not adopt that approach. Instead it reasoned that the attack on the complainant's credibility was a purpose, but not the 'main' purpose of the evidence. 'It could be said that the proposed evidence went to his credibility rather than simply to hers.'[109] Had the Court not reached that conclusion, it would have considered using HRA 1998, s 3, to 'read down' s 41(4) and prevent it from prejudicing the fairness of the trial.[110]

Questions or evidence which may satisfy s 41(2) and (5)

14.95 If the prosecution choose to adduce evidence concerning the complainant's sexual behaviour (or lack of it) on other occasion(s), it is only right that the defence should be permitted to challenge or contradict this. If, for example, the complainant asserts in chief that she was a virgin, or that she would never consent to extramarital sex, it would be unfair to deny the defence any right to question or contradict that assertion; but the defence must still obtain leave, before so doing, and may even then go no further than is necessary to rebut or explain the prosecution evidence.

14.96 In some cases, it may be necessary to adduce some very personal and embarrassing evidence in order to rebut or explain the prosecution evidence. In *F*,[111] the complainant alleged that F, her stepfather, sexually abused her as a child. The prosecution led evidence of a later adult relationship between them, explaining it as a continuation of the oppressive abuse that had occurred when she was a child. The Court held that F ought to have been allowed to rebut this by showing the jury sexually explicit 'home video' evidence that appeared to show the complainant as a willing, happy and enthusiastic participant.

---

106   [1990] 2 All ER 482.
107   Butterworths, 1985. See now 11th edn (OUP, 2007) at p 358.
108   [2004] 2 Cr App R 354.
109   Ibid, at [36].
110   Ibid, at [38].
111   [2005] 1 WLR 2848.

14.97 Following *A (No 2)* s 41(5) must be interpreted where necessary in such a way as to uphold the right to a fair trial. In *Hamadi*, the Court held that:[112]

> '... there may be cases in which the accused ought to be allowed to call evidence to explain or rebut something said by a prosecution witness in cross-examination about the complainant's sexual behaviour which was not deliberately elicited by defence counsel and is potentially damaging to the accused's case. For that reason we would accept that subs (5) has to be read in [a] broader sense than its language might otherwise suggest in order to accommodate such cases.'

The specific instance requirement: s 41(6)

14.98 YJCEA 1999, s 41(6), which requires any evidence or cross-examination to deal with specific instances if it is to be admitted under s 41, has not given rise to as many problems as s 41(4). In most cases, it is entirely reasonable to prohibit vague and generalised assertions or evidence; but once again, the inflexibility of an absolute rule may in some cases threaten to exclude perfectly valid and relevant issues. If, for example, the complainant (B) testifies in chief to the effect that, as a heterosexual male, he was repelled by A's homosexual advances, and would never have consented to them, s 41(2) and (5) might ordinarily permit the defence to cross-examine B as to any specific incidents that tend to contradict him on that issue. What then if the defence wish instead to adduce medical evidence suggesting that B must frequently (but not on any specific occasions) have engaged in 'anal receptive' intercourse during his life? As the Court noted (obiter) in *Beedal*,[113] s 41(6) might threaten to prevent the use of such evidence, unless a more flexible interpretation is adopted on the authority of *A (No 2)*.

14.99 One troublesome case is *White*, in which it was suggested that s 41(6):[114]

> '... only possesses intellectual coherence if it is taken to require that there must be something about the circumstances of a specific episode of alleged sexual conduct by a complainant which has potential probative force.'

With respect, probative force is already required by s 41(2), (3) and (5). If the evidence in question identifies a 'specific instance' of sexual behaviour (e g that the complainant was arrested for soliciting in the street on a given date), that should suffice for s 41(6). Whether it satisfies the wider requirements of s 41 is then another matter.

Lies concerning other sexual experiences

14.100 One particularly difficult question raised by s 41 concerns evidence that the complainant has made false or dubious allegations of rape, etc on other occasions. The Government insisted during the Report stage of the Bill that nothing therein would restrict D's right to discredit the complainant on the basis of her 'untruthful conduct on prior occasions',[115] and that such matters would never be subject to s 41 at all. Telling lies about sexual incidents that never really happened is not 'sexual behaviour' within the meaning of s 41.[116]

---

[112] [2007] EWCA Crim 3048, at [21]. See also *Beedal* [2007] EWCA Crim 23.

[113] [2007] EWCA Crim 23, at [19].

[114] [2004] EWCA Crim 946, at [16]; see **14.87**.

[115] Lord Williams of Mostyn, *Hansard* (Lords) vol 598, col 34, 8 March 1999.

[116] See also the explanatory note to the Act, at para 150.

14.101 That, however, has proved to be a massive oversimplification. One need only posit a scenario in which the defence wish to question the complainant about a previous allegation of rape which they allege was falsely made following a sexual encounter to which she in fact consented. She may, however, insist that she was indeed raped on that previous occasion. Any attempt to pursue this line of questioning would inevitably focus on whether she consented or not, and s 41 would accordingly be engaged. Moreover, this would arguably amount to an attack on the complainant's credibility, and might then fall foul of s 41(4).

14.102 In *RT*,[117] in which T was charged with raping his niece, nothing in s 41 was held to prevent the complainant from being asked why she had originally said nothing of this incident even when other alleged offences were being investigated. She had mentioned being 'touched' by her brother and by her grandfather, but did not originally mention T. In the conjoined case of *MH* it was held that the complainant could properly be questioned about certain lies that she had told on other occasions, including lies concerning being raped and having the foetus aborted by her mother using a knitting needle. The Court of Appeal was nevertheless anxious that this would not open the door to unfounded allegations of 'false complaints':[118]

> 'It is open to a judge to guard against abuse of the system. The defence, wishing to put questions about alleged previous false complaints, will need to seek a ruling from the judge that s 41 does not exclude them. It would be professionally improper for those representing the defendant to put such questions in order to elicit evidence about the complainant's past sexual behaviour as such under the guise of previous false complaints. But in any case the defence must have a proper evidential basis for asserting that any such previous statement was (a) made and (b) untrue. If those requirements were not met, then the questions would not be about lies but would be "about [the] sexual behaviour of the complainant" within the meaning of s 41(1). The judge is entitled to seek assurances from the defence that it has a proper basis for asserting that the statement was made and was untrue. That may not provide a watertight guarantee that in every single case evidence about the complainant's past sexual behaviour will be excluded, but it would normally prevent the sort of danger to which we have referred.'

14.103 Later cases suggest that the courts may be slow to give leave in such cases. In *E*,[119] E's daughters, aged 6 and 4, were interviewed by police officers and made allegations of sexual abuse against him. They were placed into the care of foster parents and made further complaints to them. They were interviewed again 15 months after their first interview. The first complainant then alleged that her mother, aunt and uncle, together with another aunt and the aunt's son, had all committed similar offences against her. She had claimed that yet another aunt and two other people had physically abused her. The second complainant contended that some of people who had physically abused the first complainant had physically abused her. E was charged on the basis of the allegations made at the first interview; but nobody was ever interviewed or charged as a result of the second interview. E sought leave to cross-examine the complainants about their complaints of sexual abuse in this second interview, but leave was refused, because there was no proof that these later complaints were false. E's submission was

---

[117]   [2002] 1 Cr App R 254. See also *Garaxo* [2005] EWCA Crim 1170.
[118]   [2002] 1 Cr App R 254, at [41].
[119]   [2004] EWCA Crim 1313.

that, 'by their extensive nature they were simply implausible'. That ought surely to have been good enough to satisfy the test suggested in *RT and MH*, but the Court of Appeal ruled otherwise.[120]

14.104 Some cases have given s 41(4) an alarmingly wide ambit in this context. In *Winter*,[121] W sought to adduce evidence to show that the complainant had lied to the police as to an affair she had been conducting with another man, S, behind her partner's back. He was not allowed to do so. The Court of Appeal attempted to justify this by reasoning that such evidence was inadmissible under s 41(4), because it was designed to impugn the complainant's credibility. With respect, W was not attempting to argue that her infidelity or any other sexual behaviour affected her credibility. The argument was that her willingness to lie to the police damaged her credibility, and that, in the circumstances, her credibility was crucial to the prosecution case.

14.105 The same faulty reasoning was applied in *Singh*,[122] in which counsel for S was forbidden to prove at a retrial that one of the complainants had lied at the original trial, by falsely claiming that she was a virgin prior to the alleged rape. S's original conviction had been quashed for that very reason. The Court of Appeal held that the evidence in question:[123]

'... appears to us clearly to be evidence or questions about her sexual behaviour deployed for the purpose of impugning her credibility ... As the prosecution did not rely on her virginity s 41(5) did not apply; s 41(3) cannot apply because s 41(4) blocks reliance on that sub-section when the main purpose of introducing the material is to impugn credibility.'

With respect, perjury is not sexual behaviour, even if it involves telling lies about sexual behaviour. Section 41 should have had nothing to do with it.

Procedure on applications under s 41

14.106 By s 43 of the Act:

'(1) An application for leave shall be heard in private and in the absence of the complainant.

In this section "leave" means leave under section 41.

(2) Where such an application has been determined, the court must state in open court (but in the absence of the jury, if there is one)—

(a)   its reasons for giving, or refusing, leave, and
(b)   if it gives leave, the extent to which evidence may be adduced or questions asked in pursuance of the leave,

and, if it is a magistrates' court, must cause those matters to be entered in the register of its proceedings.'

---

[120]   See also *Duckfield* [2007] EWCA Crim 4; *Hamlet* [2007] EWCA Crim 2671; *V* [2006] EWCA Crim 1901. See also Kibble's commentary on *C* [2008] Crim LR 394, at p 396.
[121]   [2008] EWCA Crim 3.
[122]   [2003] EWCA Crim 485.
[123]   Ibid, at [7].

This is supplemented by detailed rules contained in Crim PR, Pt 36, a key provision of which is that the application must be made in writing not more than 28 days after the prosecution have made disclosure.[124]

TREATMENT OF COMPLAINANTS WHO MAKE FALSE ALLEGATIONS

14.107   A remarkable feature of many reported cases in which false allegations of rape, etc have been made is the leniency shown to those who admit or plead guilty to such falsity. In some cases, this may be because the complainant was emotionally disturbed or mentally ill; but as the Court of Appeal pointed out in *C*, false complaints of rape can do enormous damage and must be treated as a serious matter:[125]

> 'A false allegation can have dreadful consequences, obviously and immediately for an innocent man who has not perpetrated the crime. But also, and this is not to be overlooked, because every occasion of a proved false allegation has an insidious effect in public confidence in the truth of genuine complaints, sometimes allowing doubt to creep in where none should in truth exist. There cannot be very many cases, although this may be one of them, where the offence of attempting to pervert the course of justice, on the basis of a false allegation of rape, certainly one which is set out in detailed formal form statement or pursued to the door of the court, should not be prosecuted for what it is. It is only in the rarest of cases that a police caution sufficiently addresses either the criminality of a false allegation of serious sexual crime or (and this is no less important) the possibility of the need for appropriate treatment which will address the problems which have led the complainant to fabricate the allegations she has made.'[126]

---

[124]   One of the major criticisms made by Kelly, Temkin and Griffiths in their Home Office Report on the working of the s 41 regime (see **14.91**) was that these rules (then part of the Crown Court Rules) were frequently ignored or overlooked, not just by counsel, but in many cases by judges as well. It is clear that some judges remain (understandably) reluctant to exclude evidence which they consider to be relevant and probative to the defence case, and these judges may be less than enthusiastic in their enforcement of s 41 or associated rules. See *The Guardian*, 1 April 2008.

[125]   [2008] Crim LR 394; [2007] EWCA Crim 2551, at [26]. See also *H and G* [2002] EWCA Crim 1880 where deluded allegations led to the death in jail of one of the two falsely accused men. See *H (No 2)* [2005] EWCA Crim 1828.

[126]   As to the position where the false complainant is only just old enough to be criminally responsible and unable to appreciate the enormity of her crime, see *O* [2008] All ER (D) 246 (Jun).

Chapter 15

SENTENCING DANGEROUS SEX OFFENDERS

15.1 In this chapter and the following three, we deal with various statutory provisions designed to protect the public or members of the public from the risk of harm by sex offenders:

- the dangerous offender sentencing provisions under the Criminal Justice Act (CJA) 2003;[1]

- the provisions relating to disqualification from working with, etc children and vulnerable adults (Chapter 16);

- the provisions relating to notification requirements (Chapter 17); and

- the provisions relating to various preventative orders (Chapter 18).

APPLICATION OF DANGEROUS OFFENDER PROVISIONS

Offences committed on or after 4 April 2005

15.2 CJA 2003, Pt 12, Ch 5 (ss 224–236), established a new regime of custodial sentences for dangerous offenders (dangerous offender provisions), which only applies to offences committed on or after 4 April 2005.[2] The previous regime relating to sentencing dangerous offenders[3] continues in effect for the purposes of offences committed before that time.[4] Accordingly, a defendant being sentenced for offences committed both before and after 4 April 2005 must be sentenced by reference to the two different regimes. In *Lang*[5] the Court of Appeal held that it will generally be preferable to pass sentence on the later offences by reference to the dangerous offender provisions,

---

[1] Quite apart from these sentencing provisions, a court may make a sexual offences prevention order (SOPO) as part of disposal. Such an order prohibits the offender from doing anything described in it; prohibitions must be limited to those necessary to protect the public or particular members of the public from serious sexual harm from the offender. We deal with such orders in **18.30** et seq.

[2] CJA 2003, s 336(3); CJA 2003 (Commencement No 8 and Transitional and Saving Provisions) Order 2005, SI 2005/950, art 2(1), Sch 1, para 18.

[3] Ie custodial sentences imposed under the Powers of Criminal Courts (Sentencing) Act (PCC(S)A) 2000, s 79 where the offender would not otherwise warrant such a sentence, longer than commensurate custodial sentences under PCC(S)A, s 80, extended sentences under PCC(S)A 2000, s 85 and automatic life sentences for a second 'serious offence' under PCC(S)A 2000, s 109. The repeal of these provisions by CJA 2003 is of no effect in relation to an offence committed before 4 April 2005: CJA 2003 (Commencement No 8 and Transitional and Saving Provisions) Order 2005, SI 2005/950, Sch 2, para 5(2)(c). For special provisions relating to sexual offences committed before 30 September 1998, see PCC(S)A 2000, s 86.

[4] CJA 2003 (Commencement No 8 and Transitional and Saving Provisions) Order 2005, SI 2005/950, Sch 2, para 5(1).

[5] [2006] 2 Cr App R (S) 13, at [3].

imposing no separate penalty for the earlier offences. It admitted that this may not be possible if the later offences are less serious than the earlier ones.

15.3   The dangerous offender provisions do not apply to an offence charged as being committed during a period which straddles 4 April 2005, ie charged as committed between a date before 4 April 2005 and a day on or after it, unless the court is satisfied that the offence was committed on or after that date.[6] Otherwise, unless the court is satisfied that the offence was committed before 4 April 2005, in which case the previous regime operates, the only custodial option available is a custodial sentence outside the dangerous offender provisions or the previous regime. Even if it is not open to the court to impose a sentence under ss 225–228 in respect of an offence because it is unsure whether the offence was committed before or after 4 April 2005, if a qualifying offence or offences is committed after that date, offences committed before might have some bearing on the issue of dangerousness and the determination of the minimum term, both of which are dealt with later.[7]

Types of sentence

15.4   The regime under the dangerous offender provisions consists of:

• life imprisonment (or custody or detention) (CJA 2003, ss 225 and 226);

• imprisonment (or detention) for public protection (CJA 2003, ss 225 and 226); and

• extended sentence of imprisonment (or detention) (CJA 2003, ss 227 and 228).

Like a life sentence, a sentence for public protection is indeterminate.

15.5   Each of the three groups of provisions contains separate provisions for offenders aged 18 or over at the time of conviction[8] and offenders under 18 at that time. In the case of offenders who were under 18 when the offence was committed but 18 or over when convicted it is not a breach of the European Convention on Human Rights (ECHR), Art 7(1) to sentence them to a more severe sentence than would have been possible if they had been convicted at age 17; the fact that they would have been liable to a less severe sentence at 17 is a 'powerful factor', but not a sole or determining factor, in determining sentence.[9]

15.6   Under the provisions relating to sentences for public protection and extended sentences, as CJA 2003 was enacted, a court was obliged to impose a sentence for public protection or an extended sentence if the conditions specified for that sentence were satisfied. This obligation gave rise to various difficulties in terms of the application of the provisions. It was also identified (when coupled with the effects of either type of

---

6   *Harries* [2007] Crim LR 820. The provisions of CJA 2003 (Commencement No 8 and Transitional And Saving Provisions) Order 2005, Sch 2, para 5(3) (offence committed over a period of 2 or more days, or at some time during such a period, to be taken to have been committed on the last of those days) have no application to ss 225–228) and do not empower a court to impose a sentence under ss 225–228 on an individual as though the offence had been committed on or after 4 April 2005 where the dates in the relevant count straddle that date: *Howe* [2007] 2 Cr App R (S) 47; *Maunder* [2007] EWCA Crim 1254; *Pressdee* [2008] 1 Cr App R (S) 120; *Harries* [2007] Crim LR 820. See the commentary by Thomas at [2007] Crim LR 397.
7   *Harries* [2007] Crim LR 820.
8   *Robson* [2007] 1 Cr App R (S) 301, at [13].
9   *Bowker* [2007] Crim LR 904.

sentence) as resulting in many prisoners staying in prison for longer periods than they otherwise would and, thus, as being a major driver of the shortage of prison accommodation and the consequent overcrowding problem. The overcrowding prevented many of the thousands of prisoners detained under a sentence for public protection from accessing the programmes they needed to complete in order to convince the Parole Board that they were no longer dangerous and could be released on licence.[10] Consequent on the recommendations of Lord Carter's *Review of Prisons: Securing the Future*,[11] published in December 2007, the Government initiated fundamental changes designed to reduce the number of persons sentenced to one of these sentences, which were enacted in Criminal Justice and Immigration Act (CJIA) 2008. The most important of these amendments is the replacement of the duty, referred to above, to impose a sentence for public protection or an extended sentence, as the case might be, by a power to do so. Other amendments restrict the eligibility of an offender for one of these sentences by introducing a new threshold. The amended provisions came into force on 14 July 2008. They apply to persons sentenced on or after that date even in respect of offences committed before that date[12] (but on or after 4 April 2005).

SPECIFIED OFFENCE

15.7 A critical and recurring term in CJA 2003, ss 225–228 is 'specified offence'.

15.8 An offence is a 'specified offence' for the purposes of CJA 2003, Pt 12, Ch 5 if it is a specified violent offence (ie an offence specified in CJA 2003, Sch 15, Pt 1) or a specified sexual offence (ie an offence specified in CJA 2003, Sch 15, Pt 2).[13] All specified offences carry a maximum of 2 years' imprisonment or more.

Specified violent offences

15.9 CJA 2003, Sch 15, Pt 1 lists the following offences: manslaughter; kidnapping; false imprisonment; an offence under the Offences Against the Person Act (OAPA) 1861, ss 4, 16, 18, 20, 21, 22, 23, 27, 28, 29, 30, 31, 32, 35, 37, 38 or s 47; an offence under the Explosive Substances Act 1883, s 2 or s 3; an offence under the Infant Life (Preservation) Act 1929, s 1; an offence under the Children and Young Persons Act 1933, s 1; an offence under the Infanticide Act 1938, s 1; an offence under the

---

10   In *R (Walker) v Secretary of State for the Home Department* [2008] EWCA Civ 30, it was held (1) that the Secretary of State's conduct in failing to provide an adequate opportunity to access the programmes was in breach of his public law duty because its direct consequence was that a proportion of prisoners under indeterminate sentences for public protection would avoidably be kept in prison for longer than necessary either for punishment or for protection of the public, contrary to the intention of Parliament; (2) that, however, such prisoners who had completed their minimum term were not, in the current circumstances of the cases, unlawfully detained; and (3) that if detention continued beyond that term it was likely to result in a breach of ECHR, Art 5(4), and would cease to be justified under Art 5(1)(a) when the stage was reached when it was no longer necessary for public protection or if such a long time elapsed without a meaningful review that detention became disproportionate or arbitrary.

11   Available at www.justice.gov.uk/publications/securing-the-future.htm.

12   Since the amendments are in the offender's favour (and therefore their retrospective application is not unfair to the offender) it is permissible to construe them as having retrospective effect: *L'Office Cherifien des Phosphates v Yamashita-Shinnihon Steamship Co Ltd* [1994] 1 AC 486. The ECHR, Art 7 does not prevent the retrospective application of the criminal law in the offender's favour: *Kokkinakis v Greece* (1993) 17 EHRR 397; *G v France* (1995) 21 EHRR 288. The CJIA 2008 (Commencement No 2 and Transitional and Saving Provisions) Order 2008, SI 2008/1586, Art 2(3), Sch 2, para 2, confirms that the amendments do not apply to a person sentenced before 14 July 2008.

13   CJA 2003, s 224(1), (3).

Firearms Act (FA) 1968, ss 16, 16A, 17(1), 17(2) or s 18; an offence under the Theft Act
(TA) 1968, ss 8, 9 (when committed with intent to inflict grievous bodily harm on a
person, or do unlawful damage to a building or anything in it), s 10 or s 12A (when
involving an accident which caused the death of any person); an offence of arson under
the Criminal Damage Act 1971, s 1 or an offence under s 1(2) other than an offence of
arson; an offence under the Taking of Hostages Act 1982, s 1; an offence under the
Aviation Security Act 1982, ss 1, 2, 3 or s 4; an offence under the Mental Health Act
(MHA) 1983, s 127; an offence under the Prohibition of Female Circumcision Act 1985,
s 1; an offence under the Public Order Act 1986, ss 1, 2 or s 3; an offence under CJA
1988, s 134; an offence under the Road Traffic Act 1988, s 1 or s 3A; an offence under
the Aviation and Maritime Security Act 1990, ss 1, 9, 10, 11, 12 or s 13; an offence under
the Channel Tunnel (Security) Order 1994, SI 1994/570, Pt II; an offence under the
Protection from Harassment Act 1997, s 4; an offence under the Crime and Disorder
Act 1998, s 29 or s 31(1)(a) or (b); an offence (other than one involving murder) under
the International Criminal Court Act 2001, s 51 or s 52; an offence under the Female
Genital Mutilation Act 2003, ss 1, 2 or s 3; an offence under the Domestic Violence,
Crime and Victims Act (DVCVA) 2004, s 5;[14] an offence of (a) aiding, abetting,
counselling, procuring or inciting[15] the commission of an offence specified in CJA 2003,
Sch 15, Pt 1, (b) conspiring to commit an offence so specified or (c) attempting to
commit an offence so specified; or attempt, or conspiracy, to commit murder.

Specified sexual offences

15.10 CJA 2003, Sch 15, Pt 2, lists the offences under the following provisions: the
Sexual Offences Act (SOA) 1956, ss 1, 2, 3, 4, 5, 6, 7, 9, 10, 11, 14, 15, 16, 17, 19, 20, 21,
22, 23, 24, 25, 26, 27, 28, 29, 32 or s 33;[16] MHA 1959, s 128; the Indecency with Children
Act 1960, s 1; SOA 1967, s 4 or s 5; the TA 1968, s 9 (when committed with intent to
commit rape); the Criminal Law Act 1977, s 54; the Protection of Children Act 1978,
s 1; the Customs and Excise Management Act 1979, s 170 (in relation to goods
prohibited to be imported (indecent or obscene articles)); CJA 1988, s 160; SOA 2003,
ss 1–19, 25, 26, 30–41, 47–50, 52, 53, 57–59, 61–67, 69 or 70; or an offence of (a) aiding,
abetting, counselling, procuring or inciting[17] the commission of an offence specified in
CJA 2003, Sch 15, Pt 2, (b) conspiring to commit an offence so specified or (c)
attempting to commit an offence so specified.

SERIOUS OFFENCE

15.11 Sentences under CJA 2003, s 225 or s 226 of imprisonment (or custody or
detention) for life or of imprisonment for public protection apply only to offenders
convicted of a 'serious offence'. CJA 2003, s 224(2) provides that:

> 'An offence is a "serious offence" for the purposes of [Ch 12, Pt 5] if and only if—
>
> (a)   it is a *specified offence*, and
> (b)   it is, apart from s 225, *punishable* in the case of a person aged 18 or over by—

---

14   Inserted by the DVCVA 2004.
15   When the Serious Crime Act (SCA) 2007, Pt 2, is in force, the reference to incitement will have effect as a
     reference to the offences of encouraging or assisting crime contrary to Pt 2: SCA 2007, s 63(1), Sch 6.
16   In respect of s 33, see **10.152**, n 229.
17   See n 15 above.

> (i)   *imprisonment for life* [or, in the case of a person aged at least 18 but under 21, custody for life],[18] or
>
> (ii)   *imprisonment* [or, in the case of a person aged at least 18 but under 21, detention in a young offender institution,][19] *for a determinate period of 10 years or more.*'[20]

IMPRISONMENT (OR CUSTODY OR DETENTION) FOR LIFE

Imprisonment or custody for life for serious offences: persons aged 18 or over

15.12   CJA 2003, s 225(1) and (2) provides:

'(1) This section applies where—

> (a)   a person aged 18 or over is convicted of a serious offence[21] committed after the commencement of this section [4 April 2005][22], and
>
> (b)   the court is of the opinion that there is a significant risk to members of the public of serious harm occasioned by the commission by him of further specified offences.

(2) If—

> (a)   the offence is one in respect of which the offender would apart from this section be liable to imprisonment for life, and
>
> (b)   the court considers that the seriousness of the offence, or of the offence and one or more offences associated with it, is such as to justify the imposition of a sentence of imprisonment for life,

the court must impose a sentence of imprisonment for life [or in the case of a person aged at least 18 but under 21, a sentence of custody for life][23].'[24]

Thus, for a sentence of life imprisonment to be imposed under s 225, five conditions must be satisfied:

- the offender must be 18 or over at the time of conviction;

- the offender must have been convicted of a '*serious offence*', punishable with life imprisonment;

- the offence must have been committed on or after 4 April 2005;

---

[18]   The words in square brackets inserted apply in relation to any time before the coming into force of the Criminal Justice and Court Services Act (CJCSA) 2000, s 61, by CJA 2003 (Sentencing) (Transitory Provisions) Order 2005, SI 2005/643, art 3(1), (3)(a).

[19]   The words in square brackets inserted apply in relation to any time before the coming into force of CJCSA 2000, s 61, by CJA 2003 (Sentencing) (Transitory Provisions) Order 2005, SI 2005/643, art 3(1), (3)(b).

[20]   Emphasis added.

[21]   See **15.11**.

[22]   See **15.2**, **15.3**.

[23]   Words in square brackets inserted apply in relation to any time before the coming into force of CJCSA 2000, s 61, by CJA 2003 (Sentencing) (Transitory Provisions) Order 2005, SI 2005/643, Art 3(1), (4)(a).

[24]   An offence the sentence for which is imposed under s 225 is not to be regarded as an offence the sentence for which is fixed by law: CJA 2003, s 225(5).

- the court must be of the opinion that there is a significant risk to members of the public of 'serious harm' occasioned by the commission by the offender of further *specified* offences[25];[26] and

- the court must consider that the seriousness of the offence, or of the offence and one or more offences associated with it,[27] is such as to justify the imposition of a sentence of imprisonment (or custody) for life.

The fourth condition is common to all the types of sentence under ss 225 and 226. It refers to the 'criteria of dangerousness'.

15.13 In relation to the last condition, the Court of Appeal in *Lang*[28] inclined to the view that Parliament intended to adopt the previous criteria for the imposition of a discretionary life sentence (very serious offence plus good grounds for believing that the offender may remain a serious danger to the public for a period which cannot be reliably estimated)[29] rather than a new, more restrictive criterion for seriousness relating it solely to the offence (rather than also to the dangerousness of the offender). However, in *Kehoe*[30] the Court of Appeal subsequently decided that the pre-CJA 2003 case-law no longer afforded guidance on when a life sentence should be imposed. It said:[31]

> 'When ... an offender meets the criteria of dangerousness, there is no longer any need to protect the public by passing a sentence of life imprisonment for the public are now properly protected by the imposition of the sentence of imprisonment for public protection. In such cases, therefore, the cases decided before the CJA 2003 came into effect no longer offer guidance on when a life sentence should be imposed. We think that now, when the court finds that the defendant satisfies the criteria for dangerousness, a life sentence should be reserved for those cases where the culpability of the offender is particularly high or the offence itself particularly grave.'

15.14 In *Frota*, where CJA 2003, s 225 was in issue, the Court of Appeal stated that the distinction between a life sentence and a sentence of imprisonment for public protection:[32]

> '... is a fine one, but it is not an insignificant one and it requires careful consideration in each case. It includes, as we have said, a dual consideration of the dangerousness of the offender as well as the gravity of the offence or offences. The effect of the distinction is particularly important, in our judgment, with young offenders such as these for if they are released from a sentence of imprisonment for public protection they will have the prospect of being able to demonstrate after 10 years on licence that the licence conditions are no longer warranted and necessary in their case and they can, if successful in so arguing, have the prospect of a life free of any restriction on their autonomy and their liberty. With a life prisoner that is never

---

25 See **15.7** et seq.
26 See **15.71** et seq.
27 'Associated' in relation to offences is to be read in accordance with PCC(S)A 2000, s 161(1): CJA 2003, s 305(1), ie an offence is associated with another if:
   • the offender is convicted of it in the proceedings in which he or she is convicted of the other offence, or (although convicted of it in earlier proceedings) is sentenced for it at the same time as he or she is sentenced for that offence; or
   • the offender admits the commission of it in the proceedings in which he or she is sentenced for the other offence and requests the court to take it into consideration in sentencing him or her for that offence.
28 [2006] 2 Cr App R (S) 13, at [8]. See also *Folkes* [2006] 2 Cr App R (S) 345.
29 *A-G's Reference (No 32 of 1996)* [1997] 1 Cr App R (S) 261; *Chapman* [2000] 1 Cr App R 77.
30 [2008] EWCA Crim 819.
31 Ibid, at [17].
32 [2007] EWCA Crim 2602, at [15].

present. There is therefore arguably an incentive appropriate to be offered to young offenders to that effect, provided the seriousness of the offence does not call for and justify a life sentence.'

15.15 If the five conditions are satisfied the court *must*[33] impose a sentence of imprisonment for life; it has no discretion to do otherwise. If the first four conditions are satisfied but the fifth is not, the court may impose a sentence of imprisonment (or detention) for public protection under CJA 2003, s 225(3).

Minimum term

15.16 In accordance with PCC(S)A 2000, s 82A(2),[34] the court must fix a 'minimum term' to be served before the offender can be considered for release on licence under the 'early release provisions' of C(S)A 1997, s 28.[35] However, by s 82A(4),[36] where the offender is aged 21 or over, the court must decline to do so if, given the seriousness of the offence, or of the combination of the offence and one or more offences associated with it, it considers that no such order should be made. In such a case the judge should state this in open court when passing sentence.[37] As to the minimum term and its determination, see **15.44–15.47**; as to release on licence, see **15.48–15.50**.

Detention for life for serious offences committed by those under 18

15.17 CJA 2003, s 226(1) and (2) provides:

'(1) This section applies where—

(a) a person aged under 18 is convicted of a serious offence committed after the commencement of this section [4 April 2005],[38] and

(b) the court is of the opinion that there is a significant risk to members of the public of serious harm occasioned by the commission by him of further specified offences.

(2) If—

(a) the offence is one in respect of which the offender would apart from this section be liable to a sentence of detention for life under [PCC(S)A 2000], section 91,[39] and

---

[33] Subject to MHA 1983, s 37(1A)(c) (as amended), which provides that in the case of an offence the sentence for which would otherwise fall to be imposed under CJA 2003, s 225(2), nothing in s 225(2) prevents a court making a hospital order under MHA 1983, s 37(1). A sentence falls to be imposed under CJA 2003, s 225(2) if the court is obliged to pass a sentence for life under that provision: CJA 2003, s 305(4)(c) (as substituted) (substitution by CJIA 2008, Sch 26, Pt 2, paras 59, 72(a) not in force at time of going to press).

[34] Section 82A was inserted by CJCSA 2000, s 60(1) (as amended). Section 82A applies to a sentence passed on or after 30 November 2000: CJCSA 2000, s 60(3).

[35] As amended. An offender so released by the Secretary of State will be released on the direction of the Parole Board: C(S)A 1997, s 28.

[36] As amended by CJA 2003. For an order to be made under s 82A(4) the offence, or combination of offences, must fall into the category of dreadful and exceptional cases where the gravity of the offence, or the combination, required the offender to be detained for the rest of his or her life: *Lawson* [2006] 2 Cr App R (S) 197, at [11].

[37] *Consolidated Criminal Practice Direction*, IV. at para 47.3. (The *Consolidated Criminal Practice Direction* is a consolidation, with amendments, of existing Practice Directions, Practice Statements and Practice Notes as they affect proceedings in the Court of Appeal (Criminal Division), the Crown Court and the magistrates' courts. It can be found at www.justice.gov.uk/criminal/procrules_fin/contents/practice_direction/pd_consolidated.htm.)

[38] See **15.2, 15.3**.

[39] As to PCC(S)A 2000, s 91, see n 42 below.

(b)   the court considers that the seriousness of the offence, or of the offence and one or
more offences associated with it, is such as to justify the imposition of a sentence of
detention for life,

the court must impose a sentence of detention for life under that section.'[40]

Thus, for a sentence of detention for life under s 226, six conditions must be satisfied:

• the offender must be under 18 at the time of conviction;

• the offender must have been convicted of a *'serious offence'*;[41]

• the offence must carry a maximum sentence of detention for life under PCC(S)A
2000, s 91;[42]

• the offence must have been committed on or after 4 April 2005;

• the court must be of the opinion that there is a significant risk to members of the
public of serious harm occasioned by the commission by the offender of further
specified offences[43];[44] and

• the court must consider that the seriousness of the offence, or of the offence and
one or more offences associated[45] with it, is such as to justify a sentence of
detention for life (as to which see **15.13**).

If the six conditions are satisfied, the court *must*[46] impose a sentence of detention for
life. If the first five conditions are satisfied but the sixth is not, the court may impose a
sentence of detention for public protection or an extended sentence, as explained below.
Detention for life under s 226 should not be imposed unless it is essential to do so.[47] If a
life sentence could not have been imposed under the pre-2003 scheme, a life sentence
under the new scheme will be inappropriate.[48]

15.18 If a court imposes a sentence of detention for life under CJA 2003, s 226, it must,
in accordance with PCC(S)A 2000, s 82A, fix a 'minimum term' to be served before the
offender can be considered for release on licence.[49] There is no exception to this
obligation. As to the 'minimum term' and its determination, see **15.44–15.47**; as to
release on licence, see **15.48–15.50**.

---

[40]   An offence the sentence for which is imposed under s 226 is not to be regarded as an offence the sentence for
which is fixed by law: CJA 2003, s 226(5).
[41]   See **15.11**.
[42]   See **1.55**.
[43]   See **15.7** et seq.
[44]   See **15.71** et seq.
[45]   See n 27 above.
[46]   Subject to MHA 1983, s 37(1A)(c) (as amended), which provides that in the case of an offence the sentence
for which would otherwise fall to be imposed under CJA 2003, s 226(2), nothing in s 226(2) prevents a court
making a hospital order under MHA 1983, s 37(1). A sentence falls to be imposed under CJA 2003, s 226(2)
if the court is obliged to pass a sentence of detention for life under that provision: CJA 2003, s 305(4)(d) (as
substituted) (substitution by CJIA 2008, Sch 26, Pt 2, paras 59, 72(a) not in force at time of going to press).
[47]   *Costello* [2007] 1 Cr App R (S) 286.
[48]   Ibid.
[49]   PCC(S)A 2000, s 82A(2).

Consecutive or concurrent sentences?

15.19 It is long established that a sentence of imprisonment may not be imposed to run consecutively to a sentence of life imprisonment (or custody or detention).[50]

15.20 It is also long established that, whilst a sentence of life imprisonment consecutive to an existing sentence of imprisonment (or custody or detention) is not unlawful, such a sentence should not be imposed.[51] Instead, a court sentencing an offender to imprisonment (or custody or detention) for life and to imprisonment (whether determinate or not) should order the latter sentence to be concurrent with the life sentence and increase the notional determinate sentence[52] to take account of the overall criminality.[53]

15.21 The same approach should be adopted where an offender who is already serving a sentence of imprisonment (or custody or detention) is being sentenced to imprisonment for life.[54]

15.22 The Court of Appeal[55] has stated obiter that it will not interfere where a consecutive sentence has been imposed under the regime relating to sentences of life imprisonment under CJA 2003, Pt 12, Ch 5, where the life sentence was justified, unless the practical result is manifestly excessive,[56] or for some reason gives rise to real problems of administration. This, however, is questionable where a sentence of imprisonment is imposed to run consecutively to a life sentence. The Court prefaced its remarks by saying that there was nothing unlawful in the imposition of such a consecutive life sentence, but (as stated in **15.19**) this is not the case.

IMPRISONMENT (OR DETENTION) FOR PUBLIC PROTECTION

15.23 For all practical purposes, imprisonment or detention for public protection is exactly the same as a life sentence: both are sentences for an indeterminate period, subject to the provisions of the Crime (Sentences) Act (C(S)A) 1997, Pt 2, Ch 2 as to the release of prisoners and duration of licences. The only discernible differences between a life sentence and imprisonment or detention for public protection are, first, that in the case of a sentence for imprisonment or detention for public protection, the Parole Board may, on application 10 years after release, direct the Secretary of State to order that a licence shall cease to have effect; and, secondly, in relation to such a sentence no order can be made that the early release provisions of C(S)A 1997, s 28 shall not apply.[57]

15.24 As CJA 2003, s 225 was originally enacted, where a life sentence was not required in respect of an offender convicted of a serious offence, the court *was obliged* by CJA 2003, s 225(1) and (3) to impose a sentence of imprisonment for public protection on

---

50   *Foy* (1962) 46 Cr App R 290.
51   *Jones* [1962] AC 635.
52   See **15.44**.
53   *Lang* [2006] 2 Cr App R (S) 13, at [20]; *O'Brien* [2007] 1 Cr App R (S) 442, at [58]–[60], [70].
54   This is based on *Haywood* [2000] 2 Cr App R (S) 418, a case concerned with an automatic life sentence under PCC(S)A 2000, s 109 (repealed).
55   *C* [2007] 2 Cr App R (S) 627, at [19], [20].
56   Or unduly lenient in the case of a reference by the Attorney-General under CJA 1988, s 36.
57   These points were noted in *Lang* [2006] 2 Cr App R (S) 13, at [8].

someone who otherwise satisfied the conditions for a life sentence. There *was* also a *mandatory* element under s 226 in respect of sentences of detention in respect of a young offender in such circumstances. The obligations in these circumstances no longer exist.

Imprisonment (or detention) for public protection for serious offences: persons aged 18 or over

15.25 As amended,[58] CJA 2003, s 225 provides:

> '(1) This section applies where—
>
>   (a)   a person aged 18 or over is convicted of a serious offence[59] committed after the commencement of this section [4 April 2005],[60] and
>
>   (b)   the court is of the opinion that there is a significant risk to members of the public of serious harm occasioned by the commission by him of further specified offences.
>
> ...
>
> (3) In a case not falling within subsection (2), the court may impose a sentence of imprisonment for public protection [or, in the case of a person aged at least 18 but under 21, a sentence of detention in a young offender institution for public protection][61] if the condition in subsection (3A) or the condition in subsection (3B) is met.
>
> (3A) The condition in this subsection is that, at the time when the offence was committed, the offender had been convicted of an offence specified in Schedule 15A.
>
> (3B) The condition in this subsection is that the notional minimum term is at least two years.'

15.26 Thus, for a sentence of imprisonment for public protection to be imposed under s 225 five conditions must be satisfied:

- the offender must be 18 or over at the time of conviction;[62]

- the offender must have been convicted of a *'serious offence'* not falling within s 225(2); the serious offence will not fall within s 225(2) *unless* it is punishable with life imprisonment *and* the court considers that the seriousness of the offence, or of the offence and an associated offence(s),[63] is such as to justify a life sentence;

- the serious offence must have been committed on or after 4 April 2005;

- the court must be of the opinion that there is a significant risk to members of the public of 'serious harm' occasioned by the offender by the commission by him or her of further specified offences[64];[65] and

---

58   By CJIA 2008, s 13(1).

59   See **15.11**.

60   See **15.2**, **15.3**.

61   Words in square brackets in s 225(3) inserted in relation to any time before the coming into force of CJCSA 2000, s 61 by CJIA 2008 (Transitory Provisions) Order 2008, SI 2008/1587, Art 2(1), (2)(a).

62   *Robson* [2007] 1 Cr App R (S) 301.

63   See n 27 above.

64   See **15.7** et seq. Section 225 does not require any kind of nexus between the facts of the particular offence and the finding of dangerousness; once an offender has been convicted of a serious offence, whatever the

- *either*, at the time when the offence was committed, the offender had been convicted of an offence specified in Sch 15A;[66] *or* the notional minimum term is at least 2 years.

15.27 The last condition, inserted by CJIA 2008, provides a new restriction on the eligibility for a sentence of imprisonment (or detention) for public protection.

15.28 This condition has no counterpart in respect of a life sentence under CJA 2003, s 225. The list of offences in Sch 15A corresponds, with some additions, to the list of 'serious offences' specified in PCC(S)A 2000, s 109 (automatic life sentences) which was repealed by CJA 2003.[67]

15.29 CJA 2003, Sch 15A, Pt 1[68] specifies the following offences under the law of England and Wales as the ones which enable a court to impose on an offender, on a subsequent conviction for a serious offence, a public protection sentence although the seriousness of the offence before the court does not justify a notional term of 2 years: murder; manslaughter; an offence under OAPA 1861, s 4 or s 18; SOA 1956, s 1 or s 5; the FA 1968, ss 16, 17(1) or s 18; the TA 1968, s 8 (where, at some time during the commission of the offence, the offender had in his or her possession a firearm or an imitation firearm within the meaning of the FA 1968); an offence under SOA 2003, ss 1, 2, 5, 6 and, if the offender was liable on conviction on indictment to imprisonment for life,[69] ss 4, 8, 30, 31, 34, 35, 47 or s 62. Schedule 15A, Pt 1 also specifies an attempt, conspiracy or incitement to commit one of the above substantive offences; an offence under SCA 2007, Pt 2 (not yet in force) in relation to which a listed offence is the offence (or one of the offences) which the person intended or believed would be committed; or aiding, abetting, counselling or procuring the commission of one of the specified substantive offences. Schedule 15A, Pt 2, specifies corresponding offences under the law of Scotland, Pt 3 corresponding offences under the law of Northern Ireland and Pt 4 corresponding offences under Service law.

15.30 In respect of the reference in the condition in CJA 2003, s 225(3B) to 'the notional minimum term' of at least 2 years:

> 'The notional minimum term is the part of the sentence that the court would specify under section 82A(2) of [PCC(S)A 2000] (determination of tariff) if it imposed a sentence of imprisonment for public protection [or, in the case of a person aged at least 18 but under 21,

---

facts and nature, a finding of dangerousness can be made on the basis of material which has no close relationship with the offence for which the sentence is passed: *Green* [2008] Crim LR 66.

[65]   See **15.71** et seq.

[66]   Where on any date on or after 14 July 2008, a person is convicted in England and Wales of an offence specified in that Schedule, and the court by or before which he is so convicted states in open court that he has been convicted of such an offence on that date and subsequently certifies that fact, the certificate is evidence for the purposes of ss 225(3A) and 227(2A) (see **15.52**) that he was so convicted on that date: CJA 2003, s 232 (as amended by CJIA 2008, s 18(2)). It will be noted that the certificate is evidence, and not conclusive proof. If the requisite statement is not made in open court, the conviction can be proved by other means.

[67]   See n 3 above.

[68]   Inserted by CJIA 2008, s 13(2), Sch 5.

[69]   Imprisonment for life in this context includes custody for life and detention for life: CJA 2003, Sch 15A, para 53.

a sentence of detention in a young offender institution for public protection][70] but was required to disregard the matter mentioned in section 82A(3)(b) of that Act (crediting periods of remand)[71].'[72]

In other words, the court should follow the usual practice in setting the tariff for a sentence of imprisonment (or detention) for public protection,[73] save that it should not credit periods of time on remand in custody in arriving at the minimum term. Thus, where the offender does not have a previous conviction for a Sch 15A offence, the condition in s 225(3B) is satisfied if the notional determinate sentence is not less than 4 years because, as explained in **15.44** and **15.45**, this will produce the notional minimum term within the terms of s 225(3C).

15.31 The effect of the threshold introduced by the last bullet point in **15.26** is to exclude from the operation of the sentence for public protection provisions cases where the 'serious offence' in question is in itself relatively minor but is the latest in a line of similar relatively minor offences. Unless at least one of these offences is a Sch 15A offence, a sentence for public protection would be most unlikely to be an option because it would be most unlikely that the alternative requirement (notional minimum term of at least 2 years for the offence in question) would be satisfied. A corresponding point can be made in respect of an extended sentence under CJA 2003, Pt 12, Ch 5, whether or not the specified offence in question is a 'serious offence'. The result is that there may be some persistent offenders who cannot be made subject to a sentence under the dangerous offender provisions although they do present a significant risk of serious harm by the commission of further specified offences. As Thomas has pointed out,[74] in such a case the court will have to resort to combining a commensurate term with a sexual offences prevention order (SOPO)[75] or a 'criminal ASBO [anti-social behaviour order]'.[76]

15.32 If the five conditions set out in **15.26** are satisfied the court *may* impose a sentence of imprisonment (or detention) for public protection. Where the offender has a previous conviction for a Sch 15A offence, and the other conditions are satisfied, the court can impose such a sentence (with a short minimum term) on a person convicted of a 'serious offence' of a trifling nature.

15.33 If the five conditions are satisfied, the court will have to decide whether a sentence commensurate with the seriousness of the offence (with or without the addition of a SOPO or a criminal ASBO) would be sufficient to protect the public against future specified offences despite the dangerousness of the offender. If the court decides that it would not be sufficient, it will have to decide whether a sentence for public protection or an extended sentence would be more appropriate. Pending guidance from the Court of Appeal, the following valuable advice by Thomas should be noted:[77]

---

[70]   Words in square brackets in s 225(3) inserted in relation to any time before the coming into force of CJCSA 2000, s 61 by the Criminal Justice Act 2003 (Sentencing) (Transitory Provisions) Order 2005, SI 2005/643, Art 2(1), (2)(b).
[71]   Ie the part of the sentence that the court would order under PCC(S)A 2000, s 82A(2) to be served before the offender can be considered for release on licence under the 'early release provisions' of C(S)A 1997, s 28. See **15.44**.
[72]   CJA 2003, s 225(3C) (inserted by CJIA 2008, s 13).
[73]   Ie in accordance with PCC(S)A 2000, s 82A(3); see **15.44**.
[74]   Thomas 'IPP Amended' [2008] 5 *Archbold News* 7, at p 9.
[75]   See **18.40** et seq.
[76]   See **10.136** et seq.
[77]   Thomas, n 74 above, at p 9.

'The overriding principle should be that the sentencing court should impose the least onerous sentence which is consistent with the proper protection of the public. Given that the court is satisfied of the existence of a significant risk of serious harm in the future what would be the least sentence which would afford the public adequate protection from that risk? Would a community order with appropriate requirements provide adequately for public safety? In many cases the seriousness of the offence will rule out such a course. If a community order is inappropriate either because it will not provide adequately for public protection or because it would inadequately reflect the seriousness of the offence, would a commensurate determinate sentence be sufficient for the purpose of public protection? Only if a commensurate determinate sentence would be insufficient, the court should consider whether an extended sentence, with a commensurate custodial term followed by an extended licence (bearing in mind the different release provisions for extended sentences), would satisfy the need for public protection.

Only if an extended sentence would be inadequate should the court pass to consider the final alternative of a sentence of imprisonment for public protection (this will be available only if the offence is a serious specified offence). It seems likely that one of the major issues in practice will be the dividing line between an extended sentence and [a sentence of imprisonment (or detention) for public protection].'

Minimum term

15.34 A sentence of imprisonment for public protection (or a sentence of detention in a young offender institution for public protection[78]) is a sentence of imprisonment for an indeterminate period, subject to the provisions of C(S)A 1997, Pt 2, Ch 2, as to the early release of prisoners and duration of licences.[79] In accordance with PCC(S)A 2000, s 82A the court must fix a minimum term to be served before the offender can be considered for release on licence. It may not decline to do so on the grounds of the seriousness of the offence or the offence and associated offence or offences.[80] As to the 'minimum term' and its determination, see **15.44–15.47**; as to release on licence, see **15.48–15.50**.

Detention for public protection for serious offences committed by those under 18

15.35 As amended,[81] CJA 2003, s 226 provides:

'(1) This section applies where—

(a) a person aged under 18 is convicted of a serious offence committed after the commencement of this section [4 April 2005],[82] and
(b) the court is of the opinion that there is a significant risk to members of the public of serious harm occasioned by the commission by him of further specified offences.

...

(3) In a case not falling within subsection (2),[83] the court may impose a sentence of detention for public protection if the notional minimum term is at least two years.

---

[78] Words in brackets apply in relation to any time before the coming into force of CJCSA 2000, s 61, by CJA 2003 (Sentencing) (Transitory Provisions) Order 2005, SI 2005/643, Art 3(1), (4)(c).
[79] CJA 2003, s 225(4).
[80] PCC(S)A 2000, s 82A(4A) (inserted by CJA 2003, s 230, Sch 18, para 4).
[81] By CJIA 2008, s 14.
[82] See **15.2**, **15.3**.
[83] See **15.36**.

(3A) The notional minimum term is the part of sentence that the court would specify under section 82A(2) of [PCC(S)A 2000] (determination of tariff) if it imposed a sentence of detention for public protection but was required to disregard the matter mentioned in section 82A(3)(b) of that Act (crediting periods of remand).'

15.36 Thus, for a sentence of detention for public protection to be imposed under s 226 five conditions will have to be satisfied:

- the offender must be aged under 18 at the time of conviction;[84]

- the offender must have been convicted of a 'serious offence'[85] not falling within s 226(2); the serious offence will not fall within s 226(2) *unless* the offence is one carrying a maximum sentence of detention for life under PCC(S)A 2000, s 91,[86] *and* the court considers that the seriousness of the offence, or of the offence and an associated offence(s),[87] is such as to justify a sentence of detention for life;

- the offence must have been committed on or after 4 April 2005;

- the court must be of the opinion that there is a significant risk to members of the public of 'serious harm' occasioned by the commission by the offender of further specified offences[88];[89] and

- the notional minimum term as defined by s 226(3A)[90] is at least 2 years.

The last condition was inserted by CJIA 2008. It will be noted that a previous conviction for a Sch 15A offence does not suffice in the alternative to a notional minimum term of at least 2 years.

15.37 If the above conditions are satisfied, the court may impose a sentence of detention for public protection. As to the exercise of this power, see **15.33**. In relation to a particularly young offender, such a sentence may be inappropriate even where a serious offence has been committed and there is a significant risk of serious harm from further offences.[91] The sentencer should consider whether during the finite custodial term of an extended sentence, the offender will mature and change sufficiently so as to present a manageable risk on licence.[92] Relevant factors include the offender's age and criminal record, whether he has previously received a custodial sentence, the number of specified offences committed, whether any serious harm has been caused and his attitude to the offences.[93]

Minimum term

15.38 A sentence of detention in a young offender institution for public protection is a sentence of detention for an indeterminate period, subject to the provisions of C(S)A

---

84 *Robson* [2007] 1 Cr App R (S) 301.
85 See **15.11**.
86 See **1.55**.
87 See n 27 above.
88 See **15.7** et seq.
89 See **15.71** et seq.
90 See **15.35**, **15.44**.
91 *Lang* [2006] 2 Cr App R (S) 13, at [17].
92 *Ings* [2007] 2 Cr App R (S) 4.
93 *D (Hollie Louise)* [2006] 1 Cr App R (S) 616.

1997, Pt 2, Ch 2, (ss 28–34) as to the release of prisoners on licences.[94] As a result, the court must fix a 'minimum term' which must be served before the offender can be released on licence. As to the 'minimum term' and its determination, see **15.44–15.47**; as to release on licence, see **15.48–15.50**.

Concurrent or consecutive sentences?

15.39 It is not unlawful to make consecutive indeterminate sentences of imprisonment (or detention) for public protection or to make them consecutive to some other term or period of imprisonment, but it is undesirable to do so.[95] As the Court of Appeal in *O'Brien* said:[96]

> 'Common sense suggests that a sentence of life imprisonment or of IPP [imprisonment for public protection] starts immediately on its imposition. Given the difficulties that may be encountered already in determining when a prisoner must be released or is eligible for parole, it seems to us to be much easier not to compound those difficulties by making indeterminate sentences consecutive to other sentences or periods in custody.'

Instead of consecutive sentences, therefore, the judge should order the other sentence of imprisonment to be concurrent with the indeterminate sentence for public protection and increase the notional determinate sentence to take account of the overall criminality.[97] Where a judge is imposing concurrent indeterminate sentences for two or more offences with corresponding concurrent minimum terms, and he or she would have passed determinate custodial sentences consecutive to each other had he or she not passed indeterminate sentences, he or she should reflect in the notional determinate term the totality of the offending either by choosing the same notional term for all the offences or take the most serious and make the notional determinate term reflect the totality of the offending.[98]

15.40 Where an offender already serving a custodial sentence has not been released on licence the court may order an indeterminate sentence to be consecutive to an existing custodial sentence (whether determinate or indeterminate). However, wherever possible it should not do so. Where the existing sentence is a *determinate* one, the court should try to impose a term for the sentence for public protection which is concurrent with the existing determinate sentence but which also takes account of:

(a)   the period still then remaining to be *served* under the existing determinate term, and that should be the period of the sentence still to be served but then halved to take account of the automatic release provisions for determinate sentences;

---

[94]   CJA 2003, s 226(4). See **15.44**.

[95]   *O'Brien* [2007] 1 Cr App R (S) 442, at [59], [70]. Also see *Lang* [2006] 2 Cr App R (S) 13, at [20]. Since such a sentence is not unlawful, permission to appeal should not normally be granted on this ground only because if an appeal succeeds on this point it is unlikely that the length of time which the prisoner will have to serve before being eligible for release on licence will be altered, and there will be no practical point in giving permission to appeal: *O'Brien*, at [70].

[96]   [2007] 1 Cr App R (S) 442, at [59].

[97]   Ibid, at [58]–[61]. The fact that the notional determinate sentence so increased exceeds the statutory maximum for the offence does not offend against that maximum because the notional determinate sentence is nothing more than an explanation by the court of the process by which it arrives at a minimum term; it is not a sentence of imprisonment. See *Delucca and Rhoden* [2007] EWCA Crim 1455, at [20].

[98]   *O'Brien* [2007] 1 Cr App R (S) 442, at [69]. See also *O'Halloran* [2006] EWCA Crim 3148; *Edwards* [2007] 1 Cr App R (S) 646; and *Meade* [2007] 1 Cr App R (S) 762.

(b)   the appropriate *additional* period as the *sentence* for the offence in respect of which the court is minded to impose a sentence of imprisonment for public protection, which should then be halved; and

(c)   the need to ensure that the total of the sentences imposed under stages (a) and (b) above do not offend the principle of totality.[99]

It is imperative that the sentencing judge should bear in mind that the period imposed in the sentence for public protection is the period which the offender *must* serve before he or she is considered for parole and that means that the constituent period to be taken into account for ascertaining the determinate sentence at stage (a) above is the period remaining to be *served* rather than the total sentence imposed.[100]

15.41 It has yet to be decided how a court should approach as a matter of principle imposing a sentence of imprisonment (whether determinate or under the dangerous offender provisions) on an offender who is *already serving a sentence of imprisonment for public protection* and whether in the circumstances of a case such as this some adjustment, if otherwise permissible, might be made to the term which he or she is destined to serve before release may be considered. In *Ashes* the Court of Appeal stated that:[101]

> 'In the ordinary way, in cases in which the appropriate sentence would be a consecutive sentence to the sentence for public protection, there is a serious problem because a sentencing judge considering imposing such a sentence does not know when the existing sentence for public protection will expire as he or she cannot predict when the parole board will agree to release the offender. A further difficulty is that even if the offender might be safe for release at the end of the sentence for public protection, there is no guarantee that he or she will also be safe to be released at the end of any consecutive determinate sentence. Thus problems arise first as to how to shape a sentence which would overcome this difficulty and second in ascertaining the date when the sentence for public protection ends and when the determinate sentence starts.'

The Court of Appeal went on to express the provisional view that:[102]

> '... when dealing on a subsequent occasion with a further offence, the sentencing court should impose an appropriate concurrent sentence, be it determinate, indeterminate or extended, depending on the circumstances. In any event the parole board would be able to take into consideration the subsequent offence in determining whether to release the offender'.

15.42 Where a dangerous offender has been released from an existing custodial sentence on licence under the early release provisions of CJA 2003, Pt 12, Ch 6, a sentencer cannot order a sentence for public protection (or any other custodial sentence) to run consecutively to that sentence on the expiry of it.[103] The sentence must normally be ordered to run concurrently with the original sentence. Although the court has power to order that an offender who was, at the time of committing the offence for which he or she is to be sentenced, on licence under a determinate sentence of imprisonment of less

---

99   *Ashes* [2008] 1 All ER 113, at [5].
100   Ibid, at [6].
101   Ibid, at [7].
102   Ibid, at [9].
103   CJA 2003, s 265. See *Spence* [2007] EWCA Crim 987.

than 12 months[104] or under such a sentence imposed before 4 April 2005, be returned to custody to serve the remainder of that sentence before serving the sentence imposed for the offence,[105] the court should not exercise that power. Instead, it should increase the notional determinate sentence[106] to reflect the remainder of the previous sentence.[107]

15.43 Because there is nothing unlawful about the imposition of a consecutive sentence of imprisonment for public protection, the Court of Appeal will not interfere where a sentence of imprisonment for public protection was justified, unless the practical result is manifestly excessive[108] or for some reason gives rise to real problems of administration.[109]

DETERMINING THE MINIMUM TERM UNDER CJA 2003, S 225 OR S 226

15.44 Unless he or she declines to do so under PCC(S)A 2000, s 82A(4)[110] in the case of a sentence of life imprisonment,[111] the judge must in accordance with s 82A(2) fix a minimum term ('the tariff') to be served before the offender can be considered for release on licence under the early release provisions of C(S)A 1997, s 28(5)–(8). By PCC(S)A 2000, s 82A(3),[112] the minimum term must be such as the court considers appropriate taking into account:

'(a)   the seriousness of the offence, or the combination of the offence and one or more offences associated with it;

(b)   the effect of any direction which it would have given under [CJA 2003, s 240] (crediting periods of remand in custody)[113] if it had sentenced him to a term of imprisonment; and

(c)   the early release provisions as compared with [CJA 2003, s 244(1) (general duty to release on licence fixed-term prisoners, other than ones sentenced under CJA 2003, s 227 or 228, after "requisite custodial period"[114] served, ie half of the sentence if sentence of 12 months or more)].'[115]

In *Lang*, the Court of Appeal expressed the procedure as follows:[116]

'The court, taking into account the seriousness of the offence or the combination of the offence and one or more offences associated with it, must identify the *notional determinate*

---

[104]   Ie under CJA 1991, Pt II. The repeal of CJA 1991, Pt II by CJA 2003 is of no effect in relation to sentences of imprisonment of less than 12 months: CJA 2003 (Commencement No 8 and Transitional and Saving Provisions) Order 2005, SI 2005/950, art 2(1), Sch 2, para 14.

[105]   PCC(S)A 2000, s 116. Section 116 was repealed by CJA 2003 on 4 April 2005, but that repeal has no effect in relation to sentences of less than 12 months or sentences imposed before that date: CJA 2003 (Commencement No 8 and Transitional and Saving Provisions) Order 2005, SI 2005/950, Sch 2, para 29.

[106]   See **15.44**.

[107]   *O'Brien* [2007] 1 Cr App R (S) 442.

[108]   Or unduly lenient in the case of a reference by the Attorney-General under CJA 1988, s 36.

[109]   *C* [2007] 2 Cr App R (S) 627 at [19], [20].

[110]   As amended by CJA 2003.

[111]   See **15.16**.

[112]   As amended by CJA 2003.

[113]   Or under the Armed Forces Act (AFA) 2006, s 246 (equivalent provision for service courts) or under CJA 2003, s 240A (crediting periods of remand on bail) when the relevant amendments are brought into force.

[114]   For 'requisite custodial period' in general, see CJA 2003, s 244(3).

[115]   The minimum term must not include any element reflecting risk to the public: *Bennett* [2006] 2 Cr App R (S) 478.

[116]   [2006] 2 Cr App R (S) 13, at [10].

sentence[117] which would have been imposed if a life sentence or imprisonment for public protection had not been required. This should not exceed the maximum permitted for the offence. Half that term should normally then be taken and from this should be deducted time spent in custody or on remand[118] ... There will continue to be exceptional cases[119] where more than half may be appropriate[120] ... In calculating the minimum term, an appropriate reduction should be allowed for a plea of guilty[121] ... and care should be taken not to incorporate in the notional determinate sentence an element for risk which is already covered by the indeterminate sentence.'

15.45 When the relevant provisions[122] of CJIA 2008, which amend s 82A(3) and insert s 82A(3A)–(3C), are in force, s 82A(3) will have effect in Case A or Case B below subject to and in accordance with s 82A(3C), which increases the court's discretion when determining the tariff under s 82A by giving it discretion to reduce the notional determinate sentence by less than half in two limited cases.

15.46 Case A (s 82A(3A)) is limited to minimum term determinations in respect of life sentences under CJA 2003, ss 225 and 226.[123] Case A is where the offender was aged 18 or over when he or she committed the offence and the court is of the opinion that the seriousness of the offence, or of the combination of the offence and one or more other offences associated with it:

- is exceptional (but not such that the court proposes to make an order under s 82A(4)); and

- would not be adequately reflected by the period which the court would otherwise specify under s 82A(2).

By s 82A(3C), in deciding the effect which the comparison required by s 82A(3)(c) is to have on reducing the period which the court determines for the purposes of s 82A(3)(a) (and before giving effect to s 82A(3)(b)), the court may, instead of reducing that period by one-half, reduce it by such lesser amount (including nil) as the court may consider appropriate according to the seriousness of the offence.

15.47 Case B (s 82A(3B)) is where the court is of the opinion that the period which it would otherwise specify under s 82A(2) above would have little or no effect on time spent in custody, taking into account all the circumstances of the particular offender. Section 82A(3C) provides that, in deciding the effect which the comparison required by s 82A(3)(c) is to have on reducing the period which the court determines for the purposes of s 82A(3)(a) (and before giving effect to s 82A(3)(b)), the court may, instead of reducing that period by one-half, reduce it by such lesser amount (but not by less than one-third) as the court may consider appropriate in the circumstances. This preserves the power, developed by case-law and referred to in *Lang*,[124] of the courts not to apply a one-half reduction where to do so would result in a situation where the

---

[117] Emphasis added. For the meaning of 'associated offence' see n 27 above.

[118] See *Taylor* [2008] EWCA Crim 465.

[119] For example, that the offence was committed whilst the offender was in prison or on licence: *Szczerba* [2002] 2 Cr App R (S) 387, at [33].

[120] See ibid, at [32]–[35]. If the court specifies a higher proportion than half, it should give its reasons: ibid, at [35].

[121] See SGC Definitive Guideline *Reduction in Sentence for a Guilty Plea* (revised 2007), esp at para 5.1.

[122] CJIA 2008, s 19.

[123] PCC(S)A 2000, s 82A(4A) (as amended by CJIA 2008, s 19(1), (4)) (not in force at time of going to press).

[124] See **15.44**.

offender did not serve any extra time in custody. This situation can arise where the offender is already serving a determinate custodial sentence and the minimum term would expire before the offender is eligible for release, because tariffs of indeterminate sentences should not be ordered to be served consecutively with other custodial sentences.

RELEASE ON LICENCE OF OFFENDER SENTENCED UNDER CJA 2003, S 225 OR S 226

15.48 Where a minimum term has been fixed in accordance with PCC(S)A 2000, s 82A, an offender who has served that term may require the Secretary of State to refer his or her case to the Parole Board, who may direct the Secretary of State to release the offender on licence if the Board is satisfied that it is no longer necessary for the protection of the public that he or she be confined.[125] If the Parole Board is not so satisfied, the offender will remain in custody indefinitely, ie even after the maximum term for the offence of which he or she was convicted.

15.49 An offender sentenced to life imprisonment or detention will remain on licence[126] for life.[127]

15.50 An offender sentenced to imprisonment or detention for public protection will remain on licence[128] for at least the qualifying period of 10 years after release, after which he or she can apply to the Parole Board for the licence to cease to have effect. If it is satisfied that it is no longer necessary for the protection of the public, the Parole Board can direct the Secretary of State to order that the offender's licence should cease to have effect.[129] If not terminated on an initial or subsequent application, the licence remains in force until the death of the offender.[130] This is one of the two substantial differences between a life sentence and a sentence of imprisonment for public protection.[131]

EXTENDED SENTENCES FOR SPECIFIED OFFENCES

15.51 CJA 2003, ss 227 and 228 provide for the imposition of an extended sentence on an offender who has been convicted of an offence which is a violent or sexual offence specified in CJA 2003, Sch 15. As amended, CJA 2003, s 227 applies even if the offence in question is a 'serious offence', ie has a maximum sentence of 10 years' imprisonment or more in the case of an offender aged 18 or over, just as s 228 has from its inception. Extended sentences under ss 227 and 228 are fundamentally different from those imposed under the old regime (ie under PCC(S)A 2000, s 85). Section 227 applies where an offender is 18 or over when convicted and s 228 where an offender is under 18 at that

---

[125] C(S)A 1997, s 28 (as amended).
[126] Unless it has been revoked under C(S)A 1997, s 32 (as amended).
[127] C(S)A 1997, s 31(1).
[128] See n 126 above.
[129] C(S)A 1997, s 31A.
[130] C(S)A 1997, s 31(1A).
[131] For the other substantial difference, see PCC(S)A 2000, s 82A(4): see **15.44**.

time.[132] Following another amendment by CJIA 2008, a court is not obliged to impose an extended sentence under CJA 2003, s 227 or s 228 if the other conditions of the relevant section are satisfied.

Extended sentences for specified offences: persons aged 18 or over

15.52 As amended,[133] CJA 2003, s 227 provides:

'(1) This section applies where—

(a)   a person aged 18 or over is convicted of a specified offence committed after the commencement of this section [4 April 2005],[134] and

(b)   the court considers that there is a significant risk to members of the public of serious harm occasioned by the commission by the offender of further specified offences, but

(c)   the court is not required by section 225(2) to impose a sentence of imprisonment for life [or, in the case of a person aged at least 18 but under 21, a sentence of custody for life[135]].

(2) The court may impose on the offender an extended sentence of imprisonment [or, in the case of a person aged at least 18 but under 21, an extended sentence of detention in a young offender institution[136]], if the condition in subsection (2A) or the condition in subsection (2B) is met.

(2A) The condition in this subsection is that, at the time the offence was committed, the offender had been convicted of an offence specified in Schedule 15A.

(2B) The condition in this subsection is that, if the court were to impose an extended sentence of imprisonment [or, in the case of an offender aged at least 18 but under 21, an extended sentence of detention in a young offender institution[137]], the term that it would specify as the appropriate custodial term would be at least 4 years.'[138]

15.53 Thus, for an extended sentence to be imposed under s 227, six conditions must currently be satisfied:

- the offender must be aged 18 or over at the time of conviction;[139]

---

[132]   See **15.5** where the offender was under 18 at the time of the offence but 18 or over at conviction.

[133]   By CJIA 2008, s 15(1)–(4).

[134]   See **15.2, 15.3**.

[135]   Words in square brackets in s 227(1)(c) inserted in relation to any time before the coming into force of CJCSA 2000, s 61 by CJIA 2008 (Transitory Provisions) Order 2008, SI 2008/1587, Art 2(1), (3)(a).

[136]   Words in square brackets in s 227(2) inserted in relation to any time before the coming into force of the Criminal Justice Act 2003 (Sentencing) (Transitory Provisions) Order 2005, SI 2005/643, Art 3(1), (5).

[137]   Words in square brackets in s 227(2B) inserted in relation to any time before the coming into force of CJCSA 2000, s 61 by CJIA 20087 (Transitory Provisions) Order 2008, Art 2(1), (3)(b).

[138]   The Secretary of State may, by order, substitute a different period for that specified in s 227(2B): s 227(6) (inserted by CJIA 2008, s 15(1), (6)). The reason for this power is that the Government intends that the condition in s 227(2B) should be met only if the offence warrants that the offender spend a minimum period of 2 years in custody. This currently requires a custodial sentence of at least 4 years as a result of the release on licence provisions in s 247(2) (release on licence at halfway point). The figure of 4 years would need to be changed if the proportion of sentence required to be served before release on licence was changed: Explanatory notes to CJIA 2008.

[139]   *Robson* [2007] 1 Cr App R (S) 301.

- the offender must have been convicted of a specified offence,[140] which may or may not be a 'serious offence';[141]

- the offence must have been committed on or after 4 April 2005;

- the court must consider that there is a significant risk to members of the public of 'serious harm' occasioned by the commission by the offender of further specified offences;[142]

- the court must not be required by s 225(2)[143] to impose a sentence of imprisonment [detention if offender aged 18 or over but under 21] for life; and

- *either*, at the time the offence was committed, the offender had previously been convicted of an offence specified in Sch 15A;[144] *or* if the court were to impose an extended sentence, the term that it would specify as the appropriate custodial term (see below) would be at least 4 years (ie equivalent in custodial time to a notional minimum term of 2 years).

15.54 The last condition, which corresponds to the restriction on eligibility inserted in CJA 2003, s 225 by CJIA 2008, was also inserted by that Act. Thomas has pointed out[145] that, in the absence of a previous conviction for a Sch 15A offence, the second alternative last condition may prevent the use of extended sentences in less serious cases for which a sentence of imprisonment for public protection would be excessive, but some form of intervention beyond a normal commensurate determinate sentence would be desirable.

15.55 If the six conditions are satisfied the court *may* impose an extended sentence. If the offence in question is a 'serious offence' the court could choose, instead, to impose a sentence of imprisonment (or detention) for public protection or simply a sentence commensurate to the seriousness of the offence. The comments in **15.33** are equally applicable here.

Meaning of 'extended sentence' in s 227

15.56 An extended sentence of imprisonment (or, in the case of an offender aged at least 18 but under 21, an extended sentence of detention in a young offender institution) is a sentence of imprisonment (or detention in a young offender institution) the term of which is equal to the aggregate of two components:

- 'the appropriate custodial term', and

- a further period, 'the extension period', for which the offender is to be subject to a licence and which is of such length as the court considers necessary for the purpose of protecting members of the public from serious harm occasioned by the commission by the offender of further specified offences.[146]

---

[140] See **15.7** et seq.
[141] See **15.11**.
[142] See **15.71** et seq.
[143] See **15.26**.
[144] See **15.26**, including n 66 above.
[145] Thomas 'IPP Amended' [2008] 5 *Archbold News* 7.
[146] CJA 2003, s 227(2C) (inserted by CJIA 2008, s 15(1), (4)). The words in brackets apply in relation to any

15.57 'The appropriate custodial term' is the maximum period which the offender must serve in custody. It means a term of imprisonment, or detention in a young offender institution,[147] not exceeding the maximum term permitted for the offence, which:

- is the *notional determinate term*, ie the term that would otherwise be imposed in the normal way in compliance with CJA 2003, s 153(2) (custodial sentence must be for shortest term commensurate with seriousness of offence, or combination of offence and associated offences); *or*

- where the notional term is a term of less than 12 months (ie the seriousness of the offence would normally warrant a custodial sentence of less than 12 months), is a term of 12 *months*.[148]

Unless the court considers it unjust to do so or in certain other cases, the court must direct that any time that the offender was remanded in custody in connection with the offence or a related offence is to count towards the custodial sentence (ie credit is to be given for it).[149]

15.58 'The extension period' must not exceed 5 years in the case of a specified violent offence,[150] and 8 years in the case of a specified sexual offence[151],[152] The term of an extended sentence passed under s 227 in respect of an offence (ie the custodial period and the period of extended licence) must not exceed the maximum term permitted for the offence.[153]

15.59 The length of the extension period is not designed to reflect the seriousness of the offence but is a measure designed to give greater protection for the public from the commission of further offences. Proportionality with the seriousness of the offence is, of course, of central importance to the notional determinate term for the purposes of fixing the appropriate custodial term, but it should not be a primary factor in determining the length of the extension period. The court must decide what period will be adequate to secure the offender's rehabilitation and to prevent re-offending. In some cases involving less serious sexual offences where the custodial term is relatively short, the court may be able to take advice on the availability and length of treatment programmes and tailor the extension period accordingly. In all cases the court should consider whether a particular extension period can be justified on the evidence available. The objective, where possible, should be to fix the length of the extension period by reference to what can realistically be achieved within it.[154]

---

time before the coming into force of CJCSA 2000, s 61: CJIA 2008 (Transitory Provisions) Order 2008, SI 2008/1587, art 2(1), (3)(c). As to release on licence, see **15.67**, and as for the extension period, see below.

[147] The words in brackets apply in relation to any time before the coming into force of CJCSA 2000, s 61: Criminal Justice Act 2003 (Sentencing) (Transitory Provisions) Order 2005, SI 2005/643, art 3(1), (5).

[148] CJA 2003, s 227(3). The latter provision is, of course, only relevant where the offender has been convicted of a Sch 15A offence on a previous occasion. The fact that the court considers that the appropriate non-extended custodial sentence would have been one of less than 12 months' duration does not as a matter of principle or common sense mean that the offender does not pose a significant risk of serious harm by the commission of further specified offences: *Smith (Stephen Gary)* [2007] 1 Cr App R (S) 607.

[149] See CJA 2003, s 240(3), (4); Remand in Custody (Effect of Concurrent or Consecutive Sentences of Imprisonment) Rules 2005, SI 2005/2054, r 2.

[150] See **15.9**.

[151] See **15.10**.

[152] CJA 2003, s 227(4). It follows that the custodial term may not be increased on grounds of protecting the public.

[153] CJA 2003, s 227(5).

[154] *Nelson* [2002] 1 Cr App R (S) 565.

15.60 The principal difference between a sentence of imprisonment for public protection and an extended sentence passed under CJA 2003, s 227 is that, in the case of the latter, the custodial period and the period of extended licence may not exceed the maximum sentence for the offence.

Extended sentence for specified offences: persons aged under 18

15.61 As amended,[155] CJA 2003, s 228(1) and (2) provides:

'(1) This section applies where—

(a)   a person under 18 is convicted of a specified offence committed after the commencement of this section [4 April 2005],[156] and
(b)   the court considers—
　　(i)   that there is a significant risk to members of the public of serious harm occasioned by the commission by the offender of further specified offences, and
　　(ii)   where the specified offence is a serious offence, that the case is not one in which the court is required by section 226(2) to impose a sentence of detention for life under section 91 of [PCC(S)A 2000].

(2) The court may impose on the offender an extended sentence of detention if the condition in subsection (2A) is met.

(2A) The condition in this subsection is that, if the court were to impose an extended sentence of detention, the term that it would specify as the appropriate custodial term would be at least 4 years.'[157]

15.62 Thus, for an extended sentence to be imposed under s 228, as amended, five conditions must be satisfied:

- the offender must be aged under 18 at the time of conviction;[158]

- the offender must have committed a specified offence,[159] which may or may not be a serious offence;[160]

- the offence must have been committed on or after 4 April 2005;

- the court must consider:
  (a)   that there is a significant risk to members of the public of serious harm occasioned by the commission by the offender of further specified offences;[161] and
  (b)   where the specified offence is a serious offence, that the case is not one in which the court is required by CJA 2003, s 226(2)[162] to impose a sentence of detention for life under PCC(S)A 2000, s 91; and

---

[155]   By CJIA 2008, s 16(1)–(4).
[156]   See **15.2, 15.3**.
[157]   The Secretary of State may, by order, substitute a different period for that specified in s 228(2A): s 228(7) (inserted by CJIA 2008, s 16(1), (6)). See n 138 above.
[158]   *Robson* [2007] 1 Cr App R (S) 301.
[159]   See **15.7** et seq.
[160]   See **15.11**.
[161]   See **15.71** et seq.
[162]   See **15.17**.

- if the court were to impose an extended sentence of detention the term that it would specify as the appropriate custodial term (see below) would be at least 4 years.

The last condition was inserted by CJIA 2008. It will be noted that a previous conviction for a Sch 15A offence does not suffice in the alternative to the 4-year custodial term referred to.

15.63 If the five conditions are satisfied the court *may* impose an extended sentence of detention. The comments in **15.33** are applicable here.

Meaning of 'extended sentence' in s 228

15.64 An extended sentence is a sentence of detention the term of which is equal to the aggregate of:

- 'the appropriate custodial term'; and

- a further period ('the extension period') for which the offender is to be subject to a licence and which is of such length as the court considers necessary for the purpose of protecting members of the public from serious harm occasioned by the commission by the offender of further specified offences.[163]

The appropriate custodial term means such term as the court considers appropriate, which must not exceed the maximum term of imprisonment[164] permitted for the offence.[165]

15.65 Unlike an extended sentence under CJA 2003, s 227, which defines the appropriate custodial term as the term which would be imposed in compliance with CJA 2003, s 153(2), which requires a custodial sentence to be the shortest commensurate with offence-seriousness, or 12 months if that term would be less, s 228(2) seems to imply that the appropriate custodial term in an extended sentence under s 228 may be longer than the shortest term commensurate with the offence, or the offence and associated offences. The matter is not, however, clear-cut because s 228 is not one of the provisions expressly exempted by s 153 from the operation of s 153(2).

15.66 'The extension period' must not exceed 5 years in the case of a specified violent offence, and 8 years in the case of a specified sexual offence.[166] The term of an extended sentence of detention passed under CJA 2003, s 228 in respect of an offence (ie the custodial period and the period of extended licence) must not exceed the maximum term permitted for the offence.[167] This is the principal difference between a sentence of detention for public protection under s 226 and an extended sentence under s 228.

---

[163] CJA 2003, s 228(2B) (inserted by CJIA 2008, s 16(1), (4)). The same provision was previously made by CJA 2003, s 228(2) before its amendment by CJIA 2008.

[164] Any reference in this section to the maximum term of imprisonment permitted for an offence is a reference to the maximum term of imprisonment that is, apart from CJA 2003, s 225, permitted for the offence in the case of a person aged 18 or over: CJA 2003, s 228(6).

[165] CJA 2003, s 228(3) (as amended by CJIA 2008, s 16(1), (5)).

[166] CJA 2003, s 228(4).

[167] CJA 2003, s 228(5).

Release on licence

15.67 By CJA 2003, s 247 (as amended),[168] an offender sentenced to an extended sentence under s 227 or s 228 on or after 14 July 2008 must be released on licence after serving one-half of the 'appropriate custodial term' component.

15.68 An offender sentenced to an extended sentence under CJA 2003, s 227 or s 228 before 14 July 2008 must serve one-half of the 'appropriate custodial term' component of his or her sentence. Thereafter the offender is not entitled to be released until the Parole Board directs the Secretary of State to release him or her, which it may not do unless satisfied that it is no longer necessary for the protection of the public that the offender should be confined.[169] If the offender is not released on such a direction before the end of the custodial term, he or she must be released on licence at the end of that term.[170]

15.69 When released (under either regime), the offender will remain on licence until the end of the extended period.[171] The extension period nevertheless runs from the end of the custodial term specified in the sentence, and not from the date of the release on licence.[172]

Concurrent or consecutive sentences

15.70 It is not unlawful to order an extended sentence under CJA 2003, s 227 or s 228 to run consecutively to another such sentence or to a determinate sentence of imprisonment, or to order a determinate sentence to run consecutively to an extended sentence.[173] Nevertheless, judges should, wherever possible, try to avoid consecutive sentences and should, instead, impose concurrent sentences, adjusting the custodial term to reflect the overall criminality.[174] This cannot be achieved if increasing the custodial term would produce an aggregate sentence (custodial term plus extension period) in excess of the maximum punishment for the offence.[175] In such circumstances, a consecutive extended sentence should be imposed. The difficulties of calculating in advance release dates and licence periods, which used to exist and which led to the Court of Appeal stating that where consecutive sentences were imposed an extended sentence should be ordered to run consecutively to a determinate sentence, and not vice versa,[176] no longer apply.[177] What is said in **15.41** and **15.42** about offenders already serving custodial sentences and in **15.43** about appeals applies mutatis mutandis to extended sentences.

---

[168] By CJIA 2008, s 25.

[169] CJA 2003, s 247(1)–(3). The amendments to s 247 are of no effect in relation to a person sentenced under CJA 2003, s 227 or s 228 before 14 July 2008: CJIA 2008 (Commencement No 2 and Transitional and Saving Provisions) Order 2008, SI 2008/1586, art 2(3), Sch 2, para 2.

[170] CJA 2003, s 247(4).

[171] See **15.56, 15.64**.

[172] *R v S; R v Burt* [2006] 2 Cr App R (S) 224.

[173] *C* [2007] 2 Cr App R (S) 627, at [19].

[174] Ibid. It is advisable to avoid imposing, concurrently with an extended sentence, a non-extended determinate sentence longer than the custodial element of the extended sentence; otherwise the extension period may be subsumed in the longer determinate sentence, thereby defeating the purpose of the extension period: *Brown; Butterworth* [2007] 1 Cr App R (S) 468.

[175] Because of CJA 2003, ss 227(5) and 228(5); see **15.58** and **15.66** respectively.

[176] *Brown; Butterworth* [2007] 1 Cr App R (S) 468, at [24]; *C* [2007] 2 Cr App R (S) 627, at [19].

[177] Until CJA 2003, s 247(2) was amended by CJIA 2008 (see **15.67**), an offender subject to an extended sentence could not be released on licence after serving half of the appropriate custodial term unless the Parole Board was satisfied that it was no longer necessary for the protection of the public that the offender

CRITERIA OF DANGEROUSNESS

15.71 One of the conditions of each of CJA 2003, ss 225–228 is that the court must be of the opinion/consider 'that there is a significant risk to members of the public of serious harm occasioned by the commission by [the offender] of further specified offences'. 'Dangerousness' is used as a convenient shorthand for this; it is so used by CJA 2003, s 229. There is a body of case-law about this condition under CJA 2003, ss 225–228. Two cases provide wide-ranging guidance: *Lang*[178] and *Johnson*.[179] In *Johnson*, which explained and amplified *Lang*, the Court of Appeal stated that, whilst the judgment in *Lang* was expressed in clear and trenchant terms, it was important that it should not be treated as a statute.

15.72 Referring to a sentence of imprisonment for public protection, the Court of Appeal in *Johnson*[180] stated that the sentence is concerned with *future* risk and public protection; although punitive in its effect, it does not represent punishment for past offending.[181] Any such assessment of future risk must be based on the information available to the court; when it is evaluated, the decision is directed not to the past but to the future.[182]

15.73 The inadequacy, suggestibility or vulnerability of the offender may serve to mitigate the offender's culpability, but it may also serve to produce or reinforce the conclusion that the offender is dangerous.[183] In one of the cases dealt with in *Johnson* it was suggested that the sentence was wrong because an inadequate offender had suffered what was described as an 'aberrant moment'. The Court of Appeal commented:[184] 'But, as experience shows, aberrant moments may be productive of catastrophe. The sentencer is right to be alert to such risks of aberrant moments in the future, and their consequences.'

Significant risk ...

15.74 It was stated in *Lang*[185] that significant risk must be shown in relation to two matters:

• there must be a significant risk of the offender committing further *specified* offences;[186] and

---

be confined. Accordingly, if a determinate sentence was passed consecutive to an extended sentence it could be difficult to determine when the custodial element of the extended term ended and the determinate sentence began.

[178] [2006] 2 Cr App R (S) 13.
[179] [2007] 1 Cr App R (S) 674. In *Johnson* the guidance related to the criterion of dangerousness when imposing a sentence of imprisonment for public protection. However, as pointed out in Archbold *Criminal Pleading, Evidence and Practice* (Sweet & Maxwell, 2008 edn), at para 5.306, the guidance undoubtedly applies equally to the assessment of dangerousness in relation to life sentences and extended sentences under CJA 2003, ss 225–228.
[180] [2007] 1 Cr App R (S) 674 at [3].
[181] Ibid, at [2].
[182] Ibid, at [3].
[183] Ibid, at [10].
[184] Ibid.
[185] [2006] 2 Cr App R (S) 13, at [7]. See also *Duncan* [2006] 2 Cr App R (S) 189.
[186] See **15.7** et seq.

- there must be a significant risk of serious harm[187] to members of the public being caused by such offences.

Significant

15.75 'Significant' is a higher threshold than the mere possibility of occurrence and means 'noteworthy, of considerable amount or importance'.[188]

Significant risk of further specified offences

15.76 In assessing the risk of further specified offences being committed, the sentencer should take into account the nature and circumstances of the current offence; the offender's history of offending, including not just the kind of offence but its circumstances and the sentence passed and whether the offending demonstrates any pattern; social and economic factors in relation to the offender including accommodation, employability, education, associates, relationships and drug or alcohol abuse; and the offender's thinking, attitude towards offending and supervision and emotional state.[189]

Significant risk to members of the public of serious harm occasioned by the commission by offender of further specified offences

15.77 'Members of the public' is not limited to members of the public in the UK. 'Serious harm' means death or serious personal injury, whether physical or psychological.[190]

15.78 Although the criteria of dangerousness and the criteria for a SOPO both involve a risk of serious harm to members of the public, 'serious harm' does not bear the same meaning in both. Something can be 'serious harm' for the purposes of the criteria for a SOPO but not for the purposes of the criteria of dangerousness.[191] Consequently, it is permissible for a sentencer to make a SOPO even though he or she does not consider that the harm of which there is a risk is not sufficient to be serious harm for the purposes of the dangerous offender provisions.

15.79 Sentencers must guard against assuming there is a significant risk of serious harm merely because the foreseen specified offence[192] is a serious offence.[193] Although,

---

187 It follows that, because, inter alia, there must be a significant risk of serious harm as defined (**15.77**), a sentence under CJA 2003, ss 225–228 is not appropriate where there is a significant risk (even a high risk) of the offender re-offending and engaging in highly antisocial, unpleasant, distressing, upsetting, even violent, certainly erratic and unpredictable behaviour, which makes him or her substantially more than a social nuisance, because the future harm to which the public is at risk cannot be described as serious within the definition given in the CJA 2003, s 224(3): *Fulton* [2007] 1 Cr App R (S) 110.

188 *Lang* [2006] 2 Cr App R (S) 13, at [17]; *Duncan* [2006] 2 Cr App R (S) 189.

189 *Lang*, at [17]. An offender's inadequacy, suggestibility or vulnerability may mitigate his or her culpability, but conversely may produce or reinforce a conclusion that the criteria of dangerousness are satisfied: *Johnson*, at [10].

190 CJA 2003, s 224(3). In terms of the application of this test, contrast *Mackney* [2007] 1 Cr App R (S) 95 and *Gazzard* [2007] 2 Cr App R (S) 446.

191 *Rampley* [2007] 1 Cr App R (S) 542; *Richards* [2007] 1 Cr App R (S) 734. For an example of a case where the harm was not 'serious' enough to satisfy the criteria of dangerousness but was 'serious' enough for a SOPO, see *Gazzard* [2007] 2 Cr App R (S) 446.

192 Ie the offence(s) which the sentencer believes there is a significant risk of the offender committing.

193 *Lang* [2006] 2 Cr App R (S) 13, at [17].

for example, rape is a specified serious offence it does not follow that a sentence under CJA 2003, ss 225–228 may be imposed in every case; a conclusion that there is a significant risk of serious harm from re-offending must be founded on evidence rather than speculation or mere apprehension of some risk of future harm.[194] Thomas has argued that the question, for example, whether re-offending is likely to cause serious psychological harm to the next as yet unidentified victim seems to be one which requires expert medical or psychological evidence.[195] In relation to an offender under 18, a sentencer must be particularly rigorous before concluding that there is a significant risk of further harm by the commission of further specified offences.[196] It is necessary, when sentencing young offenders, to bear in mind that, within a shorter time than adults, they may change and develop. This and their level of maturity may be highly pertinent when assessing what their future conduct may be and whether it may give rise to significant risk of serious harm.[197]

15.80 The risk to be assessed is to 'members of the public'. In *Lang*, the Court of Appeal stated:[198]

> 'This seems to be an all-embracing term. It is wider than "others", which would exclude the offender himself. We see no reason to construe it so as to exclude any particular group, for example prison officers or staff at mental hospitals, all of whom, like the offender, are members of the public. In some cases, particular members of the public may be more at risk than members of the public generally, for example when an offender has a history of violence to cohabitees or of sexually abusing children of cohabitees, or, as in one of the cases before us, where the offender has a particular problem in relation to a particular woman.'

15.81 In giving its guidance, the Court of Appeal in *Lang* stated that:[199]

> 'If the foreseen specified offence is not serious, there will be comparatively few cases in which a risk of serious harm will properly be regarded as significant. Repetitive violent or sexual offending at a relatively low level without serious harm does not of itself give rise to a significant risk of serious harm in the future. There may, in such cases, be some risk of future victims being more adversely affected than past victims but this, of itself, does not give rise to significant risk of serious harm.'

15.82 It is important to consider whether, even if there is a risk of further offending, there is a significant risk of the defendant's re-offending causing *serious* harm. This was stated by the Court of Appeal in *Swinscoe*.[200] A, who had no convictions for sexual offences, was convicted of sexual assault on a girl aged 8 and had pleaded guilty to engaging in sexual activity with a girl aged 13. There was evidence that A had paedophile tendencies and suffered from a frontal lobe brain injury which affected his judgment, and that, although the older girl was not troubled by A's attentions, the younger girl was very traumatised. The judge imposed a sentence of imprisonment for public protection. The Court of Appeal substituted determinate sentences of imprisonment. It held that there was insufficient evidence to support the conclusion that

---

194   *Xhelollari* (2007) 151 SJ 1265.
195   See Thomas [2007] Crim LR 491.
196   *R (CPS) v SE Surrey Youth Court* [2006] 2 Cr App R (S) 177.
197   *Lang*, at [17].
198   Ibid, at [19].
199   Ibid, at [17].
200   (2006) 150 SJLB 1332.

the type of further offending that could be foreseen was likely to cause *serious* harm, although doubtless the child victim of it would find it a distressing and potentially harmful experience.

15.83 There will not be a significant risk of the defendant's re-offending causing serious harm where a small, uncertain and indirect contribution to such harm may be made by that re-offending. This was held by the Court of Appeal in *Terrell*,[201] where the defendant, aged 21, had been convicted of four counts of making an indecent photograph of a child by downloading the photographs. He had been convicted when aged 16 of 26 such offences. The pre-sentence report assessed the defendant as posing a medium risk of re-offending. The judge considered that he was obliged to impose a sentence of imprisonment for public protection with a minimum term of 5 months concurrent for each count; but for the sentence for public protection he would have imposed a 10-month sentence. The Court of Appeal held that the judge was entitled to conclude that the defendant posed a significant risk of re-offending. However, the judge did not find that the offences which might be committed in the future were different from or graver than those already committed. The risk was of repetition of the same offence committed in the same way. The Court of Appeal said:[202]

> '[I]t cannot reasonably be said … that there is a significant risk of this appellant's re-offending occasioning harm to a child or children whether through perpetuating the market, or through further indecent images being taken, or through a child becoming aware of the indecent purposes to which photographs might be put. The link between the offending act of downloading these indecent images and the possible harm which might be done to children is too remote to satisfy the requirement that it be this appellant's re-offending which causes the serious harm. At worst there would be an indirect and small contribution to a harm which might or might not occur, depending on whether further photographs were taken in part as a result of the appellant's contribution to the market, or depending on whether a child found out about the uses to which they were put as a result. The imprisonment for public protection provisions of the CJA do not apply in the circumstances here, where simply as a matter of generalisation, a small, uncertain and indirect contribution to harm may be made by a repeat of this offender's offending. No significant risk of serious harm of the requisite gravity, occasioned by a repetition of the offending in this case by this offender can reasonably be said to exist.
>
> … The question for us however is whether the quite severe provisions of this part of the CJA are apt here; they are not. This is not a case in which the re-offending at risk involves any particular children, or a progression in terms of contact or gravity of image, or of the offender widening the network. Such circumstances could give rise to the application of these provisions.'

A determinate sentence of 10 months' imprisonment was substituted. It follows from this decision that a sentence under CJA 2003, ss 225–228 can never be justified in a case

---

[201] [2008] 2 Cr App R (S) 292.

[202] Ibid, at [28] and [29]. In *Howe* [2007] 2 Cr App R (S) 47 a sentence for public protection was upheld by the Court of Appeal in a case concerning making indecent photographs of children, the Court holding that the trial judge had been entitled to reach the conclusion that Howe satisfied the statutory criteria. In *Lang* [2006] 2 Cr App R (S) 13 the Court of Appeal regarded *Collard* [2005] 1 Cr App R (S) 155 (a case concerned with the making of a restriction order (now a SOPO)) as an example of the risk of serious psychological harm to a child arising from the downloading of indecent photographs of children not only from what the child was forced to do but also from knowledge that others will see them. In *Terrell* the Court of Appeal said that it would be wrong to treat the decision in *Howe* or the above part of *Lang* as laying down the proposition that downloading indecent images could create a significant risk of serious harm through perpetuating the market or through harm to the child who became aware of the use to which the photographs might be put. They did not seek to do so, and the issue was not argued in *Howe* and did not arise for argument in *Lang*.

of downloading indecent images from the internet, unless there is a risk that the defendant's re-offending will progress to offences which are grave enough to give rise to a significant risk of serious harm to a child or children (eg by committing physical contact offences or actually photographing a child or commissioning photographs).

15.84 In *Terrell* the Court of Appeal accepted, obiter, that, if a SOPO could be imposed, the restrictions under it would be relevant to whether the statutory criteria for a sentence of imprisonment for public protection are satisfied; if such restrictions addressed the degree of risk and seriousness of harm, those criteria might not be satisfied. The Court added that the same effect would be true of other available penalties or orders.

15.85 Where the facts of the offence in question, or indeed any other offences of which the offender has been convicted, are examined, it may emerge that no harm actually occurred.[203] This may be advantageous to the offender. An example is provided by *Isa*,[204] where a sentence of imprisonment for public protection had been imposed on A, aged 39, who had previous convictions for indecent assaults on girls aged under 14 (for which he had served short terms of imprisonment and an extended sentence), after he had been convicted of sexual assault on a girl aged 13. The Court of Appeal substituted a sentence of 12 months' imprisonment. It held that, although the medical report indicated a past diagnosis of schizophrenia and substance abuse which was a major risk factor for future re-offending, and the pre-sentence report indicated that A was often drunk and liable to commit similar offences in that state, repetitive minor offending did not of itself give rise to a risk of serious harm in the future, and this was particularly so where there was no evidence that any of the victims, albeit young, had suffered serious harm.

15.86 In *Johnson*, the Court pointed out that, however, the absence of harm may be entirely fortuitous. It would be incorrect to state that as a matter of law offences which do not result in harm to the victim should be treated as irrelevant; to do so would re-write the statute.[205] Reference may also be made to *Islam*,[206] where the Court of Appeal stated that there was no general requirement for the purposes of CJA 2003, s 225 that actual serious harm had been caused by the instant offence. It said that:[207]

'For the purposes of s 225, the focus of the court is, by reference to past relevant conduct, whether there is a significant risk of serious harm to the public; that is looking to the future. That risk may be established even where the instant serious offence or antecedent relevant offences happened not to have caused serious harm ...'

---

203 See *Johnson* [2007] 1 Cr App R (S) 674, at [10]. The statement in the text takes account of the changes made to CJA 2003, s 229 (see **15.88**) by CJIA 2008.
204 [2006] 2 Cr App R (S) 192. See also *Bailey* [2006] 2 Cr App R (S) 323.
205 *Shaffi* [2006] 2 Cr App R (S) 606, which appeared to suggest the contrary, does not do so and should be read in the context of the particular facts of that case: *Islam* [2007] 1 Cr App R (S) 244; *Johnson* [2007] 1 Cr App R (S) 674.
206 [2007] 1 Cr App R (S) 244, at [21]. For other cases where sentences under the dangerous offender provisions have been upheld although the offence in question had not involved serious harm, see *Bryan and Bryan* [2007] 1 Cr App R (S) 296; *Manir* [2007] 1 Cr App R (S) 576.
207 Ibid.

Assessment of dangerousness

15.87 CJA 2003, s 229 deals with how a court is to assess under any of CJA 2003, ss 225–228 whether there is a significant risk to members of the public of serious harm occasioned by the commission by the offender of further such offences (the assessment of dangerousness).[208]

15.88 Section 229(2) (as amended)[209] provides that the court, in making the assessment of dangerousness:

'(a) must take into account all such information as is available to it about the nature and circumstances of the offence,

(aa) may take into account all such information as is available to it about the nature and circumstances of any other offences of which the offender has been convicted[210] by a court anywhere in the world,

(b) may take into account any information which is before it about any pattern of behaviour of which any of the offences mentioned in paragraph (a) or (aa) forms part, and

(c) may take into account any information about the offender which is before it.'

General points about s 229(2)

15.89 The provisions of s 229(2) add nothing to the approach that the court would normally take, ie to consider all the information available to the court, but it does make it clear that the court's discretion under s 229(2) is not constrained by any initial assumption of dangerousness such as used to apply under s 229(3) (until it was repealed)[211] to adults with a previous conviction or convictions for a relevant offence. It is still necessary, when sentencing young offenders, to bear in mind that, within a shorter time than adults, they may change and develop. This and their level of maturity may be highly pertinent when assessing what their future conduct may be and whether it may give rise to significant risk of serious harm.[212]

15.90 As the Court of Appeal pointed out in *Johnson*,[213] s 229(2) highlights the fact that it is not a prerequisite to a finding of dangerousness that the offender should be someone with previous convictions; a person of good character may properly qualify for a sentence under ss 225–228.

15.91 CJA 2003, s 231 (as amended)[214] provides that where:

• a sentence for public protection under CJA 2003, s 225(3)[215] or an extended sentence under s 227(2)[216] has been imposed on any person;

---

[208] CJA 2003, s 229(1).

[209] By CJIA 2008, s 17(1), (2).

[210] For this purpose, a conviction includes a finding of guilt in service disciplinary proceedings, and a conviction of a service offence: CJA 2003, s 229(2A) (inserted by CJIA 2008, s 17(1), (3)).

[211] By CJIA 2008, ss 17(1), (4), 149, Sch 28, Pt 2.

[212] *Lang* [2006] 2 Cr App R (S) 13.

[213] [2007] 1 Cr App R (S) 674, at [7].

[214] By CJIA 2008, s 18(1).

[215] See **15.25–15.32**.

[216] See **15.52–15.55**.

- the condition as to conviction of a Sch 15A offence in s 225(3A)[217] or (as the case may be) s 227(2A)[218] was met but the condition as to a notional minimum term of at least 2 years in s 225(3B)[219] or (as the case may be) as to an appropriate custodial term of at least 4 years in s 227(2B)[220] was not; and

- any previous conviction of the offender without which the condition in s 225(3A) or (as the case may be) s 227(2A) would not have been met has subsequently been set aside on appeal,

notice of appeal against the sentence may be given at any time within 28 days from the date on which the previous conviction was set aside.

Information

15.92 In s 229(2) the critical, recurring word is 'information'. The court must obtain a pre-sentence report before deciding that the offender is a dangerous offender (ie satisfies the criteria of dangerousness), unless, in the circumstances of the case, it considers such a report unnecessary.[221] Where the offender is under 18, the court must not conclude that a pre-sentence report is unnecessary unless there is one or more previous pre-sentence reports in respect of the offender and the court has had regard to the most recent of them.[222] If the offender in any case is or appears to be mentally disturbed (or the circumstances of the offence or the history of the offender suggest that he or she is), the court must obtain a medical report, unless, in the circumstances of the case, it considers it unnecessary.[223] A pre-sentence report will contain an assessment of the level of risk of serious harm posed by the offender as being low, medium, high or very high, but it will not assess whether such harm will be caused by further specified offences. Sentencers are entitled to reject an expert's report tending to show that the defendant does not pose a significant risk of serious harm, but the reasons for doing so must be explained.[224] The court will be guided, but not bound, by the assessment of risk in pre-sentence, probation and medical reports; if it contemplates differing from that assessment it should give both counsel the opportunity to address the point.[225]

15.93 In *Considine; Davis*,[226] the Court of Appeal held that for the purposes of s 229 information bearing on an assessment of dangerousness is not limited to formal evidence adduced before a jury; evidence as to the offender's guilt for the offence for which he or she is to be sentenced which would have been admissible is 'information' (otherwise a defendant could circumvent admissible evidence being deployed for the present purpose by pleading guilty). Accordingly, relevant information bearing on the assessment of dangerousness can include material adverse to the defendant which was

---

[217] See **15.25**.
[218] See **15.52**.
[219] See **15.25**.
[220] See **15.52**.
[221] CJA 2003, s 156(3), (4). Although it may be obvious where a case falls at an extreme of the spectrum of sexual offending that the offender does or does not pose a significant risk of serious harm to members of the public occasioned by the commission of further specified offences, in most cases the answer will not be obvious and it will be necessary to obtain a pre-sentence report: *A-G's Reference (No 145 of 2006)* [2007] EWCA Crim 692.
[222] CJA 2003, s 156(5).
[223] CJA 2003, s 157(1), (2); *Lang*, n 212 above.
[224] *Rocha* [2007] EWCA Crim 1505.
[225] *Lang* [2006] 2 Cr App R (S) 13, at [17]. See also *B (Samuel)* [2006] 2 Cr App R (S) 472.
[226] [2007] 3 All ER 621.

not substantiated or proved by criminal convictions, such as an alleged history of violence not marked by previous convictions which was disclosed in a pre-sentence report or a document prepared for the purposes of a successful application for an ASBO.[227] The Court of Appeal observed that there will be very few cases in which a fair analysis of all the information in the papers prepared by the prosecution, events at the trial (if there has been one), the judicial assessment of the defendant's character and personality (always a critical feature in the assessment), the material in mitigation drawn to the attention of the court by the defendant's advocate, the contents of the pre-sentence report, and any psychiatric or psychological assessment prepared on behalf of the defendant, or at the behest of the court itself, should not provide the judge with sufficient appropriate information on which to form the necessary judgment in relation to dangerousness. The court should not rely on a disputed fact in forming that judgment unless the dispute can fairly be resolved adversely to the defendant.[228]

Information to be provided by the prosecution

15.94 It was held by the Court of Appeal in *Bryan and Bryan*[229] that where a sentence under CJA 2003, ss 225–228 is a possibility, it is incumbent on the prosecution to furnish the Court with the fullest information in relation to the offender's previous offences. If sufficient information to form a proper view is not furnished, the judge should adjourn sentence until it is; the judge should not impose a sentence under these sections, notwithstanding the inadequacy of the information, and then rely on the 28-day slip rule[230] to reduce the sentence if facts emerge to suggest that it was wrong.[231]

15.95 These statements must not, however, be read as absolutes. Although it is plainly desirable that the prosecution should be in a position to describe the facts of previous specified offences,[232] the Court of Appeal in *Johnson* recognised that this is not always practicable.[233] The Court of Appeal stated that, even if it could have complied with this practice, the prosecution's failure to do so does not make an adjournment obligatory or preclude the making of a sentence under CJA 2003, ss 225–228, where appropriate. In any such case, the instructions of counsel for the defendant should enable him or her to explain the facts of previous offences. If the prosecution is not in a position to challenge those instructions, the court may proceed on the information it has. Equally, there are situations in which the sentence imposed by the court dealing with earlier specified offences may enable the court to draw inferences about their seriousness, or otherwise.[234]

Role of the Court of Appeal

15.96 In *Johnson*, the Court of Appeal gave the following guidance which may be regarded as of general application to sentences under CJA 2003, ss 225–228:[235]

---

227 *Hillman* [2006] 2 Cr App R (S) 565.
228 *Johnson* [2007] 1 Cr App R (S) 674, at [10]. The court is not permitted to embark on a *Newton* hearing to decide whether or not the defendant has committed a discrete, but similar, offence to those already before the court, which has not been prosecuted and which the defendant did not admit, solely for the purpose of making the assessment of dangerousness: ibid, at [34]; *Farrar* [2007] 2 Cr App R (S) 202.
229 [2007] 1 Cr App R (S) 296.
230 Under PCC(S)A 2000, s 155. The period will be 56 days when an amendment made by CJIA 2008 comes into force.
231 *Bryan and Bryan* [2007] 1 Cr App R (S) 296.
232 As suggested in *Lang* [2006] 2 Cr App R (S) 13, at [17].
233 [2007] 1 Cr App R (S) 674, at [10].
234 Ibid.
235 Ibid, at [11].

'[T]his court will not normally interfere with the conclusions reached by a sentencer who has accurately identified the relevant principles, and applied his mind to the relevant facts. We cannot too strongly emphasise that the question to be addressed in this court is ... whether the imposition of the sentence was manifestly excessive or wrong in principle. Notwithstanding the 'labyrinthine' provisions of ss 224–229 of the 2003 Act, and the guidance offered by *Lang*, these essential principles are not affected. They apply with equal force to references by the Attorney-General. In such cases the question is whether the decision not to impose the sentence, in the circumstances, was unduly lenient. In particular ... [t]his court is normally not assisted by reference to previous individual cases where there appears to be some similarity with the instant case. We hesitate to remind advocates that individual sentencing decisions are fact-specific, and that it is rare for reports of sentencing cases to provide guidance about principle, or indeed to treat all the details of the information before the court which are no more than summarised.'

Chapter 16

DISQUALIFICATION FROM WORKING WITH CHILDREN AND VULNERABLE ADULTS

16.1 The account below does not claim to be an exhaustive account of the schemes discussed, which would merit a book in their own right. Instead it concentrates on matters of particular interest to criminal lawyers.

POSITION BEFORE THE IMPLEMENTATION OF SAFEGUARDING VULNERABLE GROUPS ACT 2006

16.2 At the time of going to press, the law relating to disqualification from working with children (ie under-18s) and vulnerable adults operates as follows.

Vetting

16.3 The current system for vetting people who wish to work (paid or unpaid) with children and vulnerable adults operates through standard or enhanced criminal record certificates issued under the Police Act (PA) 1997, ss 113A and 113B respectively by the Criminal Records Bureau (CRB disclosures). The application for a certificate must be made by the individual concerned but it must be countersigned by a person registered for this purpose. Any criminal records certificate will disclose the individual's criminal records history and will indicate if he or she is subject to a disqualification order (below). Enhanced criminal record certificates can only be issued if they are required for the purpose of considering the applicant's suitability for a position involving regular caring for, training, supervising or being solely in charge of, children or a vulnerable adult, or for certain other specified purposes. They contain not only criminal record information but also relevant non-conviction/caution information obtained from the police, the quality of which is variable. By PA 1997, ss 113C–113D, criminal record certificates of either type must, on request, state whether an applicant to work is included in a 'barring list', referred to below. A certificate is only valid on the day of issue; it is not updated by the CRB.

16.4 CRB disclosures give employers information about the applicant which informs their assessment of his or her suitability for such work. Such assessments may be made by people with little experience of handling information about offences and other information disclosed, and can be inconsistent.

Barring lists

16.5   There are three separate 'barring' lists operating under different legislation and with different criteria and procedures:

- List 99, a list maintained by the Department for Children, Schools and Families of those in respect of whom directions under the Education Act (EA) 2002, s 142(1) have been made prohibiting an individual on grounds including misconduct from teaching or similar activities at a school or further education college;

- the Protection of Children Act List (POCA List) maintained by the Department of Health under the Protection of Children Act (PoCA) 1999, s 1 of individuals considered unsuitable on grounds, including misconduct, to work with children. The list includes persons transferred to it from the Consultancy Service Index under PoCA 1999, s 3; and

- the Protection of Vulnerable Adults List (POVA List) maintained by the Department of Health under the Care Standards Act (CStA) 2000, s 81, of individuals whose misconduct renders them unsuitable to work with vulnerable adults.

The barring lists are reactive. Individuals are only considered for barring after harming, or placing at risk of harm, a child or vulnerable adult, or in the case of List 99 for professional misconduct as well, and only certain types of employer have a duty, or even a right, to refer for 'barring' employees whom they dismiss for harming a child or vulnerable adult.

Disqualification orders under CJCSA 2000

16.6   Disqualification orders may be made under the Criminal Justice and Court Services Act (CJCSA) 2000, ss 28-29A[1] disqualifying an individual from working with children.[2] For this purpose, 'work' includes:

- work of any kind, whether paid or unpaid and whether under a contract of service or apprenticeship, under a contract for services, or otherwise than under a contract; and

- an office established by or by virtue of an enactment.[3]

---

[1]   A disqualification order is not a sentence for the purposes of the Rehabilitation of Offenders Act 1974: CJCSA 2000, s 38(1). It is not a 'penalty' for the purposes of the European Convention on Human Rights, Art 7 and therefore it can be made in respect of an offence committed before the commencement of the relevant disqualification order provision: *Field and Young* [2003] 2 Cr App R (S) 175; *G (M)* [2006] 1 Cr App R (S) 174. A disqualification order does not amount to degrading treatment contrary to Art 3 because it does not humiliate or debase an individual by showing a lack of respect for their human dignity nor does it arouse feelings of fear, anguish or inferiority capable of breaking an individual's moral or physical resistance: *G(M)*. A disqualification order does not engage Art 8 because it does not affect employability any more than the conviction to which it relates. Even if it did, the interference is plainly in accordance with domestic law and pursues a legitimate purpose; provided it was proportionate to that end it would not be in breach of Art 8: *G(M)*.

[2]   CJCSA 2000, ss 28(4), 29(4) and 29A(2) respectively.

[3]   CJCSA 2000, s 42(1).

16.7 A disqualification order lasts indefinitely, although provision is made for it to be reviewed.

Disqualification of adults from working with children

16.8 CJCSA 2000, s 28 provides that where either of the conditions below is satisfied in the case of an individual, the court *must* order the individual to be disqualified from working with children.[4] The conditions, set out in s 28(2) and (3) respectively, are:

- the individual is convicted of an offence against a child committed when he or she was aged 18 or over, and a qualifying sentence is imposed by the Crown Court or the Court of Appeal[5] in respect of the conviction; or

- the individual is charged with an offence against a child committed when he or she was aged 18 or over, and a relevant order (ie an order that the individual be admitted to a hospital or a guardianship order under the Mental Health Act (MHA) 1983) is made by such a court in respect of the act or omission charged against him or her as the offence.

16.9 There is an exception to the presumption that an order will be made. An order made under s 28 may not be made if the court is satisfied,[6] having regard to all the circumstances, that it is unlikely that the individual will commit any further offence against a child.[7] However, if the court does not make an order, it must state its reasons and cause them to be recorded in the record of the proceedings.[8]

Disqualification of juveniles from working with children

16.10 CJCSA 2000, s 29 provides that where, in the case of an individual:

- the individual is convicted of an offence against a child committed at a time when the individual was under the age of 18, and a qualifying sentence is imposed by the Crown Court or the Court of Appeal[9] in respect of the conviction; or

- the individual is charged with an offence against a child committed at a time when the individual was under the age of 18, and a hospital order or guardianship order by the Crown Court or the Court of Appeal[10] is made in respect of the act or omission charged against him or her as the offence,

and the court is satisfied,[11] having regard to all the circumstances, that it is likely that the individual will commit a further offence against a child, the court must order the

---

[4] CJCSA 2000, s 28(1) and (4).
[5] CJCSA 2000, s 30(1). Disqualification orders under ss 28–29A may also be made by a court-martial or Courts-Martial Appeal Court (the Court Martial or the Court Martial Appeal Court, when an amendment made by the Armed Forces Act (AFA) 2006 is in force): s 30(1).
[6] It is not necessary for the sentencer to be satisfied to the criminal standard of proof: the civil standard, proof on the balance of probabilities, applies: *MG* [2002] 2 Cr App R (S) 1. See also *Clayton* [2004] 1 Cr App R(S) 201 (CJCSA 2000, s 29).
[7] CJCSA 2000, s 28(5).
[8] CJCSA 2000, s 28(6).
[9] CJCSA 2000, s 30(1). See n 5 above.
[10] Or one of the other courts mentioned in n 5 above.
[11] See n 6 above.

individual to be disqualified from working with children.[12] In the case of juveniles, therefore, there is a presumption against an order being made. If the court makes such an order, it must state its reasons and cause them to be included in the record of the proceedings.[13]

Subsequent application for order under s 28 or s 29

16.11 Where:

(a)   s 28 applies but the court has neither made an order under that section nor complied with the requirements relating to the giving or recording of reasons for not doing so; or

(b)   s 29 applies but the court has not made an order under that section, and it appears to the prosecutor that the court has not considered the making of an order under s 29,

the prosecutor may at any time apply to that court for an order under s 28 or s 29.[14]

16.12 On such an application:

*   in a case falling within (a) above, the court:
    (a)   *must* make an order under s 28 *unless* it is satisfied[15] having regard to all the circumstances, that it is *unlikely* that the individual will commit any further offence against a child; and
    (b)   if it does not make such an order, must comply with the obligations referred to in **16.9** relating to the giving and recording of reasons;

*   in a case falling within (b) above, the court:
    (a)   *must* make an order under s 29 *if* it is satisfied, having regard to all the circumstances, that it is *likely* that the individual will commit a further offence against a child; and
    (b)   if it does so, must comply with the obligations referred to in **16.10** relating to the giving and recording of reasons.[16]

However, this does not enable or require an order under s 28 or s 29 to be made where the court is satisfied that it had considered the making of an order under that section at the time when it imposed the qualifying sentence or made the relevant order.[17]

Disqualification at discretion of court: adults and juveniles

16.13 CJCSA 2000, s 29A provides that where:

*   an individual is convicted of an offence against a child (whether or not committed when he or she was aged 18 or over);

---

12   CJCSA 2000, s 29(1)–(4).
13   CJCSA 2000, s 29(5).
14   CJCSA 2000, s 29B(1).
15   See n 6 above.
16   CJCSA 2000, s 29B(2).
17   CJCSA 2000, s 29B(3).

•   the individual is sentenced by the Crown Court or Court of Appeal;[18] and

•   no qualifying sentence is imposed in respect of the conviction,

the court *may* make a disqualification order if it is satisfied, having regard to all the circumstances, that it is likely that the individual will commit a further offence against a child.[19] If the court makes an order under s 29A, it must state its reasons and cause them to be included in the record of the proceedings.[20]

General

Child

16.14 For the purposes of the provisions of CJCSA 2000 relating to disqualification orders, 'child' means a person under 18.[21] If the court determines, after considering any available evidence, that an individual was, or was not, under 18 at the time when the offence in question was committed, the individual's age at that time must be taken to be that which the court determines it to be.[22]

Offence against a child

16.15 An individual commits an offence against a child if:

(a)   he or she commits any offence mentioned in CJCSA 2000, Sch 4, para 1;

(b)   he or she commits against a child any offence mentioned in Sch 4, para 2;

(c)   he or she commits an offence mentioned in within Sch 4, para 3 in relation to a child.[23]

16.16 These offences against a child include the following:

(a)   The list of offences in Sch 4, para 1 includes an offence under PoCA 1978, s 1; the Criminal Justice Act (CJA) 1988, s 160; or SOA 2003, ss 5-26 or ss 47-50.

(b)   The list of offences in Sch 4, para 2 includes the offences under SOA 2003, ss 1–4, 30–41, 52, 53, 57–61, 66 or s 67.

(c)   The list of offences in Sch 4, para 3, includes:
   −   an offence under SOA 2003, s 62 or s 63 where the intended offence was an offence against a child; or
   −   an offence of aiding, abetting, counselling, procuring or inciting[24] the commission of an offence against a child, or conspiring or attempting to commit such an offence.

---

[18]   CJCSA 2000, s 30(1). See n 5 above.
[19]   CJCSA 2000, s 29A(1), (2).
[20]   CJCSA 2000, s 29A(3).
[21]   CJCSA 2000, s 42(1). As to the determination of age, see **3.131** and **3.132**.
[22]   CJCSA 2000, s 30(4).
[23]   CJCSA 2000, s 26(1). Sch 4 can be amended by the Secretary of State: ibid, s 26(2).
[24]   The reference to the common law offence of inciting the commission of another offence will have effect as a

Qualifying sentence

16.17 By CJCSA 2000, s 30(1), 'qualifying sentence' means:

- a sentence of imprisonment for a term of 12 months or more;

- a sentence of detention in a young offender institution for a term of 12 months or more;

- a sentence of detention during Her Majesty's pleasure;

- a sentence of detention for a period of 12 months or more under the Powers of Criminal Courts (Sentencing) Act 2000, s 91[25] (offenders under 18 convicted of certain serious offences);

- a sentence of detention under CJA 2003, s 226 or s 228;

- a hospital order within the meaning of MHA 1983; or

- a guardianship order under MHA 1983.

Appeals

16.18 An individual may appeal against a disqualification order:

- where the first condition mentioned in CJCSA 2000, s 28 or s 29 is satisfied, as if the order were a sentence passed on him for the offence of which he has been convicted;

- where the second condition mentioned in s 28 or s 29 is satisfied, as if he had been convicted of an offence on indictment and the order were a sentence passed on him for the offence;

- where an order is made under s 29A, as if the order were a sentence passed on him for the offence of which he has been convicted.[26]

Review

16.19 Provision is made for a person subject to a disqualification order to apply to the Care Standards Tribunal established under PoCA 1999 for a review of the order. An individual who was under 18 when he committed the offence against the child can apply after a minimum period of 5 years (but cannot apply within 5 years of a previous application). In the case of any other individual both these periods are 10 years. The Tribunal must direct that the order is to cease to have effect if satisfied that the individual is suitable to work with children; otherwise it must dismiss the application.[27] Provision is made for a chief officer of police or a director of children's services (in

---

reference to offences of encouraging or assisting crime contrary to the Serious Crime Act 2007, Pt 2, as from
the day that the common law offence is abolished: Serious Crime Act 2007, s 63(1), Sch 6, Pt 1, para 40.

[25] Or AFA 2006, s 209 (not in force at time of going to press).

[26] CJCSA 2000, s 31(1).

[27] See CJCSA 2000, ss 32 and 33.

England) or of social services (in Wales) of a local authority to apply for the restoration of a disqualification order which is no longer in force.[28]

Persons disqualified from working with children: offences

16.20 By CJCSA 2000, s 35(1), an individual who is included in List 99 or, otherwise than provisionally, in the POCA List or subject to a disqualification order is guilty of an offence if he or she knowingly[29] applies for, offers to do, accepts or does any work in a regulated position. It is a defence for the individual to prove[30] that he did not know, and could not reasonably be expected to know,[31] that he was disqualified from working with children.[32] 'Regulated position' is defined by s 36. Essentially – but not always – the term covers positions where an individual is likely to have contact with children in a way which will enable him to commit an offence against a child. Under s 36, 'regulated positions' are:

(a)   a position whose normal duties:
  –   include work in a children's hospital, children's home, educational institution or institution for the detention of children, or similar establishments, or work on day-care premises;
  –   include caring for, training, supervising or being in sole charge of children;
  –   involve unsupervised contact with children under arrangements made by a responsible person, such as a parent, guardian or foster parent, or the child's head teacher (or someone acting on that person's behalf);
  –   include caring for children under 16 in the course of the children's employment;

(b)   a position a substantial part of whose normal duties include supervising or training children under 16 in the course of the children's employment;

(c)   various specified positions, such as school governor, membership of (or of an executive of) a local government body discharging educational functions, membership of the Children and Family Courts Advisory and Support Services (CAFCASS) or the Youth Justice Board and various offices whose work relates to children; and

(d)   a position whose normal duties include supervising or managing an individual in his work in a regulated position.

16.21 By CJCSA 2000, s 35(2), an individual is guilty of an offence if he or she knowingly:

(a)   offers work in a regulated position to, or procures work in a regulated position for, an individual who is disqualified from working with children; or

(b)   fails to remove such an individual from such work.

---

[28]   See CJCSA 2000, s 34.
[29]   What is said about this term in **2.62** and **2.63** is equally applicable mutatis mutandis to an offence under CJCSA 2000, s 35(1).
[30]   As to reverse burden provisions, see **5.41** and **5.42**.
[31]   What is said about this term in **2.72** and **2.63** is equally applicable mutatis mutandis to an offence under CJCSA 2000, s 35(1).
[32]   CJCSA 2000, s 35(3).

16.22 An offence under CJCSA 2000, s 35 is triable either way and punishable on conviction on indictment with imprisonment for a maximum of 5 years or a fine or both.[33]

Class of offence[34]	3	SOA 2003, s 72 applies	✗
Notification requirements	✗	SOPO[35]	✗
CJA 2003, Sch 15 applies	✗	Serious specified offence	✗
Review of lenient sentence	✗	Special provisions of CYPA 1933[36]	✗
Detention of young offender for specified period			✗

16.23 CStA 2000, s 89(5)–(7) makes essentially the same provision as CJCSA 2000, s 35(1) in respect of an individual included in the POVA List and employment in a care position relating to vulnerable adults. See **16.20** and **16.22**.

Repeal

16.24 As from a day to be appointed the provisions relating to the 'barring' lists and to disqualification orders and the provisions of PA 1997, ss 113C–113E are repealed by the Safeguarding of Vulnerable Groups Act (SVGA) 2006,[37] and replaced by the provisions of that Act. It is anticipated that the appointed day will be in the second half of 2008.

DISQUALIFICATION UNDER SVGA 2006

16.25 The Bichard Inquiry,[38] set up following the Soham murders of Holly Wells and Jessica Chapman, and whose report was published in 2004, identified systemic failures in the vetting and barring systems referred to in **16.3** and **16.5**, including:

- inconsistent decisions by employers on the basis of information disclosed in criminal record certificates;

- the information disclosed by the CRB was only certain to be accurate on the day of issue;

- inconsistencies between List 99, the POCA List and the POVA List;

- barring was reactive to harmful behaviour, rather than preventative.

SVGA 2006 provides the framework for a new, central vetting and barring scheme for those whose work (paid or unpaid) gives them significant access to children and

---

[33] CJCSA 2000, s 35(6).
[34] See **1.49**.
[35] Sexual offences prevention order.
[36] Children and Young Persons Act (CYPA) 1933.
[37] SVGA 2006, s 63 and Sch 10.
[38] Available at www.webarchive.org.uk/pan/12841/20060926/www.bichardinquiry.org.uk/.

vulnerable people. Provision has been made for those subject to the current restrictions described in **16.2** et seq to be included or considered for inclusion in the new barred lists; see **16.60** et seq. What follows is written on the basis of the law as it will be when SVGA 2006 is fully in force, although regulations have yet to be made prescribing some of the detail.

How the SVGA 2006 scheme works

16.26 Those who are closely working with children or vulnerable adults ('regulated activity', whose definition is referred to in **16.45–16.47**), or applying so to work, are required to make an application to the Secretary of State, in the guise of the CRB, to be 'subject to monitoring'. Monitoring, an ongoing process, will cover everyone engaging in a regulated activity with the permission of a regulated activity provider.[39] An individual who engages in regulated activity without being subject to monitoring, a regulated activity provider who uses in regulated activity an individual who is not subject to monitoring and a regulated activity provider who fails to check whether an individual is subject to monitoring may all be guilty of a summary offence punishable with a fine not exceeding level 5 on the standard scale.[40] By PA 1997, ss 113BA–113BB, inserted by SVGA 2006, an enhanced criminal record certificate must in prescribed cases include information about whether the applicant is barred from regulated activity in relation to children or vulnerable adults, as the case may be (and, if so, the prescribed details), whether he or she is subject to monitoring, and whether the Independent Barring Board (IBB) is considering whether to bar him or her on grounds of his or her behaviour or a risk of harm.[41]

16.27 On receipt of an application to be subject to monitoring, the Secretary of State, using the CRB, then searches the Police National Computer for cautions and convictions and makes inquiries of local police forces to obtain other relevant non-conviction/caution information.

---

[39] A person (P) is a regulated activity provider if: (a) P is responsible (without being subject to another's supervision or direction) for the management or control of regulated activity and he or she makes or authorises the making of arrangements for another person to engage in that activity; (b) P makes arrangements for another person to be a private foster parent and has power to end the arrangements, in which case he or she is a regulated activity provider in relation to such fostering; or (c) P carries on a scheme, under which an individual agrees with P to provide care and support to an adult in need of it, which must be registered under CStA 2000, s 11: SVGA 2006, ss 6(1)–(4), 53(3), (4).
P is not a regulated activity provider if he or she is an individual and the arrangements he or she makes are private arrangements. Arrangements are private if the regulated activity is for, or for the benefit of, P him- or herself, or if the regulated activity is for, or for the benefit of, a child or vulnerable adult who is a member of P's family or a friend of P: SVGA 2006, s 6(5)–(7).

[40] SVGA 2006, ss 8, 10 and 11 respectively. See also ss 12, 13, 19(1) and (3), (4), (6)-(10), and 20.

[41] It is intended that employers engaging individuals in a 'controlled activity' will also in most cases need to ensure that those individuals are subject to monitoring, for example, by obtaining an enhanced criminal record certificate (which will be obligatory in some cases); this requirement will be made by regulations. 'Controlled activity' covers certain activity other than regulated activity. Broadly, it covers support work in general health settings, further education settings and adult social care settings. It also covers work which gives a person the opportunity for access to sensitive records about children and vulnerable adults, including education and social service records: SVGA 2006, ss 21, 22. There is no current intention to prevent a barred individual from engaging in controlled activity. But in part the regulations will be used so as to require employers (and others with responsibility for managing controlled activity) to put in place appropriate safeguards to manage the risks posed by barred individuals.
Power is given for regulations to be made as to who may engage in 'controlled activities', the steps to be taken by a responsible person in connection with permitting another to engage in controlled activity and the circumstances in which a responsible person must not permit another to engage in controlled activity. The regulations may provide that a responsible person who contravenes them is guilty of a summary offence punishable with a fine not exceeding level 5 on the standard scale. See SVGA 2006, s 23.

16.28 Where the CRB's inquiries reveal that a person not already barred satisfies one of the criteria that lead to automatic inclusion in the children's barred list (CBL) or adults' barred list (ABL), it will refer the matter to the IBB so that the person can be included in the relevant barred list (see below). The CRB will also pass details of relevant convictions and cautions together with all information received from local police forces to the IBB, which the IBB (through the use of persons with the appropriate expertise) can then consider in relation to inclusion in a non-automatic barred list on grounds of unsuitability. Where a person is included in the CBL or ABL, he ceases to be subject to monitoring (if he was previously) and is not able to engage in regulated activity. Regulated activity providers, personnel suppliers, local authorities and professional and supervisory bodies are required to provide prescribed details to the IBB.

16.29 At appropriate intervals, the CRB must repeat the searches and inquiries referred to above. If new information comes to light about a person who is subject to monitoring, the CRB will give the information to the IBB as outlined above. The IBB may also have cause to consider including a person in a barred list on the basis of referrals from employers, local authorities, professional bodies and supervisory authorities. An employer may register to be notified if an employee ceases to be subject to monitoring. Where this is the case the employer will then be informed of it by the CRB.[42]

Independent Barring Board

16.30 The Independent Barring Board (IBB)[43] works under the name 'Independent Safeguarding Authority'. By SVGA 2006, s 2(1), the IBB must establish and maintain two barred lists:

(a)   the 'children's barred list' (CBL) listing those barred from engaging in regulated activity with children; and

(b)   the 'adults' barred list' (ABL) listing those barred from engaging in such activity with vulnerable adults.[44]

An individual can be included in both lists.

16.31 For the purposes of SVGA 2006: a 'child' means someone under 18;[45] a 'vulnerable adult'[46] means someone aged 18 or over who:

*   is in residential accommodation or sheltered housing;

*   receives domiciliary care or any form of health care;

*   is detained in lawful custody;

---

[42]   The information in **16.26–16.29** is based on the explanatory notes to SVGA 2006.
[43]   The IBB was established under SVGA 2006, s 1.
[44]   SVGA 2006, s 2(1). The Safeguarding of Vulnerable Groups Act 2006 (Barred List Prescribed Information) Regulations 2008, SI 2008/16, regs 2, 3 and 4 prescribe descriptions of information that the IBB must keep in respect of an individual who is included in a barred list.
[45]   SVGA 2006, s 60(1).
[46]   SVGA 2006, ss 59, 60(1).

- is by virtue of an order of a court under supervision by a person exercising functions for the purposes of CJCSA 2000, Pt 1;

- receives a welfare service of a prescribed description;

- receives any service or participates in any activity provided specifically for persons with special needs;

- is paid directly (or via another on his or her behalf) in pursuance of arrangements under the Health and Social Care Act 2001, s 57; or

- requires assistance in the conduct of his or her own affairs.

Barred lists

16.32 SVGA 2006, Sch 3,[47] Pts 1[48] and 2[49] contain provisions for the determination of whether an individual is included in the CBL or the ABL, respectively, whilst Pt 3[50] sets out necessary provisions common to both the other Parts. Parts 1 and 2 essentially make identical provision, any differences being identified below. They provide for inclusion on four different bases:

- automatic inclusion;

- automatic inclusion subject to the consideration of representations;

- discretionary inclusion on the ground of engagement in relevant conduct; and

- discretionary inclusion on the ground of risk of future harm.

Automatic inclusion

16.33 Where it appears to the Secretary of State that any of the criteria prescribed for *this* purpose under Sch 3, para 24[51] is satisfied in respect of a person, the Secretary of State must refer the matter to the IBB; on such a reference the IBB must include that person in the CBL or ABL, as appropriate.[52] The criteria that may be prescribed under Sch 3, para 24, are that a person has been convicted or cautioned, that an order of a specified type has been made against him, that a person is included in a foreign barred list, or that a foreign order of a specified type has been made against him: see **16.39**. There will be no right for the individual to make representations nor a right of appeal in these cases.

---

47   Given effect by SVGA 2006, s 2(2)–(4).
48   Paras 1–6.
49   Paras 7–12.
50   Paras 13–25.
51   See **16.39**.
52   SVGA 2006, Sch 3, Pt 1, para 1, Pt 2, para 7.

Automatic inclusion subject to consideration of representations

16.34 Where it appears to the Secretary of State that any of the criteria prescribed for *this* purpose under Sch 3, para 24[53] is satisfied in respect of a person, the Secretary of State must refer the matter to the IBB.[54] On such a reference, the IBB must:

•   include the person in the CBL or ABL, as appropriate; and

•   give the person the opportunity to make representations as to why he should be
    removed from the relevant list.[55] The IBB must give that person notice in writing,
    sent by post, that he may make such representations.[56] Representations must be
    made within the period of 8 weeks starting on the day on which the notice is
    deemed[57] to have been received.[58]

If it appears to the IBB that it is not appropriate for the person to be included in the list, it must remove him from the list.[59]

Inclusion on grounds of relevant conduct

16.35 Where it appears to the IBB that the person concerned has (at any time) engaged in 'relevant conduct', and the IBB proposes to include him in the CBL or ABL, as appropriate, the IBB must give him the opportunity to make representations as to why he should not be included in the relevant list.[60] The IBB must give that person notice in writing, sent by post, that he may make such representations. Representations must be made within the period of 8 weeks starting on the day on which the notice is deemed to have been received.[61] The IBB must include the person in the CBL or ABL, as the case may be, if:

•   it is satisfied that the person has engaged in relevant conduct; and

•   it appears to the IBB that it is appropriate to include the person in the list.[62]

These provisions do not apply in the case of the CBL if the relevant conduct consists only of an offence committed against a child[63] before the commencement of SVGA 2006, s 2 and the court, having considered whether to make a disqualification order under CJCSA 2000,[64] decided not to.[65]

---

[53]   See **16.39**.
[54]   SVGA 2006, Sch 3, Pt 1, para 2(1), (2), Pt 2, para 8(1), (2).
[55]   SVGA 2006, Sch 3, Pt 1, para 2(1), (3), Pt 2, para 8(1), (3).
[56]   Safeguarding of Vulnerable Groups Act 2006 (Barring Procedure) Regulations 2008, SI 2008/474, reg 2(1), (2), (3).
[57]   A notice is deemed to have been received by its addressee 48 hours after the date on which it was sent, unless the contrary is proved: ibid, reg 2(1), (4).
[58]   Ibid, reg 2(1), (5). Where a person has not completed making their representations within the 8-week period, the IBB may allow him such further period to make representations as it considers reasonable, if satisfied that he has good reasons for not completing: ibid, reg 2(1), (6).
[59]   SVGA 2006, Sch 3, Pt 1, para 2(1), (4), Pt 2, para 8(1), (4).
[60]   SVGA 2006, Sch 3, Pt 1, para 3(1), (2), Pt 2, para 9(1), (2).
[61]   Safeguarding of Vulnerable Groups Act 2006 (Barring Procedure) Regulations 2008, SI 2008/474, reg 2. See nn 56–58.
[62]   SVGA 2006, Sch 3, Pt 1, para 3(3), Pt 2, para 9(3).
[63]   Offence against a child is to be construed in accordance with CJCSA 2000, Pt 2 (ss 26–42) (see **16.15**): SVGA 2006, Sch 3, Pt 1, para 3(5)(a).
[64]   Ie a disqualification order under CJCSA 2000, ss 28–29A (see **16.6–16.19**): SVGA 2006, s 3(5)(b).

16.36 For the above purposes, 'relevant conduct' is defined as follows:

(a)   conduct which endangers a child or vulnerable adult, as the case may be, or is likely to endanger a child or vulnerable adult, as the case may be;

(b)   conduct which, if repeated against or in relation to a child or vulnerable adult, as the case may be, would endanger that child or vulnerable adult or would be likely to endanger him;

(c)   conduct involving sexual material[66] (including possession of such material) relating to children or vulnerable adults, as the case may be;

(d)   conduct involving sexually explicit images[67] depicting violence against human beings (including possession of such images), if it appears to the IBB that the conduct is inappropriate; and

(e)   conduct of a sexual nature involving a child or vulnerable adult, as the case may be, if it appears to the IBB that the conduct is inappropriate.[68]

For the purposes of (a) and (b), a person's conduct endangers a child or vulnerable adult, as the case may be, if he:

•   harms that other person;

•   causes that other person to be harmed;

•   puts that other person at risk of harm;

•   attempts to harm that other person; or

•   incites another to harm that other person.[69]

A person does not engage in relevant conduct merely by committing an offence prescribed for this purpose.[70]

Inclusion on grounds of risk of harm

16.37 Where it appears to the IBB that a person may:

(a)   harm a child or vulnerable adult, as the case may be;

---

[65]   SVGA 2006, Sch 3, Pt 1, para 3(4).
[66]   Ie indecent images of children or vulnerable adults, or material (in whatever form) which portrays children or vulnerable adults involved in sexual activity and which is produced for the purposes of giving sexual gratification: SVGA 2006, Sch 3, Pt 1, para 4(3), Pt 2, para 10(3).
[67]   'Image' means an image produced by any means, whether of a real or imaginary subject: SVGA 2006, Sch 3, Pt 1, para 4(4), Pt 2, para 10(4).
[68]   SVGA 2006, Sch 3, Pt 1, para 4(1), Pt 2, para 10(1). For the purposes of the last two types of relevant conduct, the IBB must have regard to guidance issued by the Secretary of State as to conduct which is inappropriate: ibid, Sch 3, Pt 1, para 4(6), Pt 2, para 10(6).
[69]   SVGA 2006, Sch 3, Pt 1, para 4(2), Pt 2, para 10(2).
[70]   SVGA 2006, Sch 3, Pt 1, para 4(5), Pt 2, para 10(5).

(b)   cause a child or vulnerable adult, as the case may be, to be harmed;

(c)   put a child or vulnerable adult, as the case may be, at risk of harm;

(d)   attempt to harm a child or vulnerable adult, as the case may be; or

(e)   incite another to harm a child or vulnerable adult, as the case may be,

and it proposes to include that person in the CBL or ABL, as the case may be, the IBB must give him the opportunity to make representations as to why he should not be included in such list.[71] The IBB must give that person notice in writing, sent by post, that he may make such representations. Representations must be made within the period of 8 weeks starting on the day on which notice is deemed to have been received.[72] The IBB must include the person in the appropriate list if it is satisfied that the person falls within (a) to (e), and it appears to it that it is appropriate to include that person in the list.[73]

Restriction on inclusion

16.38 The IBB must not include a person in the CBL or ABL:

*   only on a particular ground if a relevant authority in Scotland has already made a decision to include or not to include the person in its equivalent barred list on the same ground; or

*   if prescribed conditions are met such that it is more appropriate for the person's case to be considered by the relevant authority in Scotland.[74]

Prescribed criteria

16.39 Which of the four procedures referred to in **16.33–16.38** applies will depend on the criteria to be prescribed by statutory instrument. The criteria that may be prescribed for the purposes of the provisions relating to:

*   automatic inclusion; and

*   automatic inclusion subject to representations,[75]

are:

(a)   that a person has been convicted of, or cautioned in relation to, an offence of a specified description;

(b)   that an order of a specified description requiring the person to do or not to do anything has been made against him;

---

[71]   SVGA 2006, Sch 3, Pt 1, para 5(1), (2) and (4), Pt 2, para 11(1), (2) and (4).
[72]   Safeguarding of Vulnerable Groups Act 2006 (Barring Procedure) Regulations 2008, SI 2008/474, reg 2. See nn 56–58.
[73]   SVGA 2006, Sch 3, Pt 1, para 5(1), (3), Pt 2, para 11(1), (3).
[74]   SVGA 2006, Sch 3, Pt 1, para 6, Pt 2, para 12.
[75]   See **16.33**, **16.34**.

(c)   that a person is included in a specified list maintained for the purposes of a country or territory outside the UK; and

(d)   that an order or direction of a specified description requiring the person to do or not to do anything has been made against him for the purposes of a country or territory outside the UK.[76]

For the purpose of determining whether any of the criteria is satisfied in relation to a person, an offence committed before the person concerned reached the age of 18 is to be ignored as is any order or direction made before that time.[77] The criteria which may be prescribed in respect of inclusion in the CBL must not consist only of circumstances in which the person has committed an offence against a child before the commencement of provisions relating to the barred lists if the court had considered whether to make a disqualification order under CJCSA 2000 and had decided not to do so.[78]

Advance notice of barring

16.40 Where a person is convicted of an offence of a specified description for the purposes of (a) in **16.39**, or where an order of a specified description under (b) is made against them, the court must inform him when he is convicted or the order is made that the IBB will include him in the barred list concerned.[79] There is no corresponding obligation on a person giving a caution.

Supplementary

16.41 SVGA 2006, Sch 3 contains a number of procedural provisions relating to the exercise of the IBB's powers,[80] which are outside the scope of this book.

16.42 The IBB must take all reasonable steps to notify an individual when he or she has been included in a barred list.[81]

16.43 The IBB must provide the Secretary of State with prescribed information about an individual who has been barred or whom it is considering barring.[82] The Secretary of State, in the guise of the CRB, will perform the administrative function of actually adding the individual's name to the barred list.

Effect of inclusion in barred list

16.44 A person included in the CBL or the ABL, or the corresponding lists in Scotland or Northern Ireland, is barred from regulated activity relating to children or vulnerable adults, as the case may be.[83]

---

[76]   SVGA 2006, Sch 3, Pt 3, para 24(1).
[77]   SVGA 2006, Sch 3, Pt 3, para 24(4).
[78]   SVGA 2006, Sch 3, Pt 3, para 24(5).
[79]   SVGA 2006, Sch 3, Pt 3, para 25.
[80]   SVGA 2006, Sch 3, Pt 3, paras 13, 15, 16 and 17.
[81]   SVGA 2006, Sch 3, Pt 3, para 14.
[82]   SVGA 2006, Sch 3, Pt 3, para 21.
[83]   SVGA 2006, s 3.

16.45 SVGA 2006, s 5 provides that 'regulated activity' in relation to children and in relation to adults bears the meaning set out in Sch 4, Pts 1 and 2 respectively,[84] as amended from time to time by the Secretary of State.[85] The scope of 'regulated activity', and consequently the bar imposed by inclusion in the CBL or the ABL, is wider than that of the corresponding terminology and restriction under the legislation currently in force. Broadly speaking, regulated activity includes work (paid or unpaid) which involves certain close contact with children or vulnerable adults. More particularly, the provisions can be summarised as follows.[86]

Schedule 4, Pt 1, regulated activity relating to children

16.46 The principal activities are:

(a)   Certain types of specified close contact activity carried out frequently by the same person, or carried out by a person on more than 2 days in a 30-day period or, in most instances, overnight ('the period condition'). Examples would include teaching, supervising, advising or caring for children. Another example would be the moderation of internet chatrooms likely to be used wholly or mainly by children if that activity is carried out on more than 2 days in a 30-day period.

(b)   Any activity carried out frequently by the same person or on more than 2 days in a 30-day period ('the period condition') in a school, nursery, children's home, institution for the detention of children or the like which gives a person the opportunity to have contact with children in pursuance of his or her duties there. Examples would include the activity carried out by a school secretary or a caretaker at a children's home.

(c)   The provision of childminding where there is a requirement to be registered under the provisions of the Childcare Act 2006 or where there would be a requirement to be registered but for the fact that the individual does not provide childcare for a child below the age of 8. Similarly childminders in Wales are also covered, but here the requirement to register arises from the Children Act (ChA) 1989.

(d)   Fostering a child.

(e)   The exercise of functions of CAFCASS support officers and their Welsh equivalent.

(f)   The inspection of specified establishments (eg a school) on behalf of specified organisations (eg OFSTED, Healthcare Commission) and the inspection of specified generalist health establishments on behalf of specified organisations.

(g)   The day-to-day management or supervision on a regular basis of any person carrying out the activities mentioned in (a), (b), (e) and (f) above.

(h)   The exercise of a function of certain specified positions, such as school governor, Children's Commissioner, trustee of a children's charity, operator of the Information Sharing Index set up under ChA 2004.

---

[84]   Supplemented by SVGA 2006, Sch 4, Pt 3.
[85]   SVGA 2006, s 5.
[86]   The summary is based on the explanatory notes to the Act.

Teaching, training, supervising, etc a child in the course of his or her employment will not be regulated activity. However, this will not be the case where the child is under 16 and it is a person's principal responsibility to be engaged in that particular activity in relation to the child.

Schedule 4, Pt 2, regulated activity relating to vulnerable adults

16.47 Broadly, the principal activities are:

(a) Certain types of specified activity, such as teaching, training, advising and caring for vulnerable adults, carried out frequently by the same person, or carried out by a person on more than 2 days in a 30-day period or, in most instances, overnight ('the period condition').

(b) Any activity carried out frequently by the same person or on more than 2 days in a 30-day period ('the period condition') in a care home which gives a person the opportunity to have contact with vulnerable adults as a result of their duties or anything they are allowed to do there.

(c) The day-to-day management or supervision or a regular basis of any person carrying out the activities mentioned in (a) and (b).

(d) The inspection of specified establishments, such as a care home, by a specified organisation, for example, the Healthcare Commission.

(e) The exercise of a function of a specified position such as the directorship of adult social services or trusteeship of a vulnerable adults' charity.

Review

16.48 After the minimum barred period[87] has elapsed, and provided he has made no other such application in the prescribed period ending with the time when he does so, a barred individual may apply to the IBB for permission to apply for a review of his inclusion.[88] The IBB must not grant permission unless it thinks that the applicant's circumstances have changed since he was included in the list or last applied for permission and that the change is such that permission should be granted.[89]

16.49 The minimum barred period depends on the age of a person when the IBB includes him in the CBL or ABL. If he is under 18, the minimum period is one year; if he is 18 or over but under 25, it is 5 years; and if he is 25 or over it is 10 years.[90] The age differential is based on the impact that being barred has on the development of a child under 18, the capacity of young people to change over a shorter period than older people and the fact that the typical circumstances behind relevant types of young offending often involve the most vulnerable young people and/or those more greatly influenced by their environment and peers.[91] If the person concerned is included in the CBL or ABL because he satisfies the criteria prescribed for the purposes of automatic

---

[87] See **16.49**.
[88] SVGA 2006, Sch 3, Pt 3, para 18(1), (2) and (3).
[89] SVGA 2006, Sch 3, Pt 3, para 18(4).
[90] Safeguarding of Vulnerable Groups Act 2006 (Barring Procedure) Regulations 2008, SI 2008/474, reg 9.
[91] Explanatory memorandum to ibid, paras 7.2.4, 7.2.5.

inclusion or inclusion subject to consideration of representations, the minimum barred period starts when he satisfies the relevant criteria; in any other case, the minimum barred period starts when the IBB includes them in the CBL or ABL.[92]

16.50 The prescribed period is as follows:

(a)   In relation to a person under 18, the period is one year.

(b)   In relation to a person who:
   –   is aged 18 or over;
   –   had been eligible before he reached that age to apply for permission pursuant to (a);
   –   did not do so before they reached that age; and
   –   has not done so since they reached that age,
   the period is one year.

(c)   In relation to a person who has not reached the age of 25 but to whom neither (a) nor (b) applies, the period is 5 years.

(d)   In relation to a person who:
   –   is 25 or over;
   –   is not eligible to apply for permission pursuant to (b);
   –   had been eligible before he reached 25 to apply for permission pursuant to (c);
   –   did not do so before he reached that age; and
   –   has not done so since he reached that age,
   the period is 5 years.

(e)   In any other case, the period is 10 years.[93]

Appeal

16.51 SVGA 2006, s 4 provides for an appeal by the barred individual to the Care Standards Tribunal against a decision of the IBB to include[94] or keep[95] him or her in the CBL or ABL.[96] Such an appeal may be made only on a point of law or on a finding of fact made by the IBB.[97] For these purposes, the decision whether or not it is appropriate for an individual to be included in a barred list is not a question of law or fact.[98] Such an appeal may only be made with the permission of the Tribunal.[99] The Government expects that, when informing the barred person of its decision, the IBB will follow current practice on, for example, List 99 decisions, where the Department for Children, Schools and Families' decision letter outlines the factor taken into account in reaching

---

92   Ibid, reg 10.
93   Ibid, reg 11.
94   Ie under SVGA 2006, Sch 3, Pt 1, para 3 or para 5, or Pt 2, para 9 or para 11 (see **16.35, 16.37**).
95   Ie under SVGA 2006, Sch 3, paras 2, 8 (see **16.34**), 17 (unsuccessful representations by person whose whereabouts were unknown to IBB before inclusion in barred list except automatic inclusion under Sch 3, para 1 or para 7) or para 18 (**16.48**).
96   SVGA 2006, s 4(1).
97   SVGA 2006, s 4(2).
98   SVGA 2006, s 4(3).
99   SVGA 2006, s 4(4).

the decision. Regulations are to be made governing the procedure to be followed by the Tribunal in considering appeals under SVGA 2006.[100]

16.52 Appeal against a decision of the Tribunal lies on a point of law to the Court of Appeal (Civil Division) with its permission.[101]

Offences

Barred person engaging in regulated activity

16.53 By SVGA 2006, s 7(1):

'An individual commits an offence if he—

(a)   seeks to engage in regulated activity from which he is barred;
(b)   offers to engage in regulated activity from which he is barred;
(c)   engages in regulated activity from which he is barred.'

Thus, for example, an individual on the CBL commits an offence under s 7(1)(a) if he or she seeks to engage in regulated activity in relation to children, and an individual on the ABL commits an offence against s 7(1)(c) if he or she engages in regulated activity in relation to vulnerable adults. The offence is triable either way and punishable on conviction on indictment with a maximum of 5 years' imprisonment, or a fine, or both.[102] For the purposes of s 7, the requirements[103] about frequency or the period condition are disapplied.[104] Thus, a relevant activity will be regulated activity for the purposes of s 7 even if it is carried out only once. As a result, for example, A who is barred from regulated activity relating to children will commit an offence if A supervises children on a single occasion.

16.54 It is a defence for a person charged with an offence under s 7(1) to prove[105] that he did not know,[106] and could not reasonably be expected to know,[107] that he was barred from that activity.[108] It is also a defence for a person charged with an offence under s 7(1) to prove:

•   that he reasonably thought that it was necessary for him to engage in the activity for the purpose of preventing harm to a child or vulnerable adult (as the case may be);

•   that he reasonably thought that there was no other person who could engage in the activity for that purpose; and

---

100   Explanatory memorandum on the implementation of SVGA 2006 (2008), para 4.4.5. Regulations have already been made about the procedure to be followed where an appeal arises in a case to which the transitional provisions referred to in **16.60** et seq apply: see n 123.
101   SVGA 2006, s 4(9) and (10).
102   SVGA 2006, s 7(2). See **16.22** where the box relating to CJCSA 2000, s 35 applies likewise to an offence under s 7.
103   See **16.46(a), (b)** and **16.47(a), (b)**.
104   SVGA 2006, s 7(5).
105   As to reverse burden provisions, see **5.41, 5.42**.
106   What is said about this term in **2.62** and **2.63** is equally applicable mutatis mutandis to an offence under SVGA 2006, s 7(1).
107   What is said about this term in **2.72** and **2.63** is equally applicable mutatis mutandis to an offence under SVGA 2006, s 7(1).
108   SVGA 2006, s 7(3).

- that he engaged in the activity for no longer than was necessary for that purpose.[109]

This would, for example, cover a barred doctor providing first aid to a child after an accident in the street.

Use of barred person for regulated activity

16.55 By SVGA 2006, s 9(1) and (2):

'(1) A person commits an offence if—

(a)   he permits an individual (B) to engage in regulated activity from which B is barred,
(b)   he knows or has reason to believe that B is barred from that activity, and
(c)   B engages in the activity.

(2) A personnel supplier[110] commits an offence if—

(a)   he supplies an individual (B) to another (P),
(b)   he knows or has reason to believe that P will make arrangements for B to engage in regulated activity from which B is barred, and
(c)   he knows or has reason to believe that B is barred from that activity.'

An offence under s 9 is triable and punishable in the same way as an offence under s 7.[111]

16.56 It is a defence for a person charged with an offence under s 9 to prove:

(a)   that he reasonably thought that it was necessary for the barred person to engage in the activity for the purpose of preventing harm to a child or vulnerable adult (as the case may be);

(b)   that he reasonably thought that there was no other person who could engage in the activity for that purpose; and

(c)   that the barred person engaged in the activity for no longer than was necessary for that purpose.[112]

16.57 If an offence under s 9 is committed by a body corporate and is proved to have been committed with the consent or connivance of, or to be attributable to neglect on the part of:

- a director, manager, secretary or other similar officer of the body; or

- a person purporting to act in such a capacity,

---

[109]   SVGA 2006, s 7(4).
[110]   Ie a person carrying on an employment agency or an employment business, or an educational institution which supplies to another person a student who is following a course at the institution, for the purpose of enabling the student to obtain experience of engaging in regulated or controlled activity: SVGA 2006, s 60(1).
[111]   SVGA 2006, s 9(3). See **16.22** where the box relating to CJCSA 2000, s 35 applies likewise to an offence under s 9. See n 115.
[112]   SVGA 2006, s 9(4).

he or she (as well as the body) commit the offence.[113]

16.58 If an offence under s 9 is committed by a partnership (whether or not a limited partnership) and is proved to have been committed with the consent or connivance of, or to be attributable to neglect on the part of:

- a partner; or

- a person purporting to act as a partner,

he or she (as well as the partnership) commits the offence.[114]

Personnel suppliers: supply, etc of barred individual

16.59 By SVGA 2006, s 19(2):

> 'A person commits an offence if, in the course of acting or appearing to act on behalf of a personnel supplier—
>
> (a)   he supplies an individual (B) to another (P),
> (b)   he knows or has reason to believe that P will make arrangements for B to engage in regulated activity from which B is barred,[115] and
> (c)   he knows or has reason to believe that B is barred from the activity.'

'Personnel supplier' means a person carrying on an employment agency or an employment business, or an educational institution supplying a trainee teacher for teaching practice.[116] An offence under s 19(2) is triable either way and punishable on conviction on indictment with imprisonment for a maximum of 5 years.[117] A person does not commit an offence under s 19 if B has not attained the age of 16.[118] Nor does he commit such an offence if the regulated activity is regulated activity relating to adults, and falls within a specified exemption from the monitoring check requirements.[119]

Transitional provisions

16.60 The arrangements introduced by SVGA 2006 will replace those provided by the legislation described in **16.2–16.24**. Under transitional arrangements made by the Safeguarding of Vulnerable Groups Act 2006 (Transitional Provisions) Order 2008 (TPO),[120] persons included in the list kept under PoCA 1999, s 1 (POCA List), or CStA 2000, s 81 (POVA List), subject to a direction under the EA 2002, s 142 (List 99), or subject to a disqualification order under CJCSA 2000, ss 28, 29 or s 29A are to be included or considered for inclusion by the IBB in the CBL or ABL.

---

[113]   SVGA 2006, s 18(1); see Card, Cross and Jones *Criminal Law* (OUP, 18th edn, 2008), at paras 18.43–18.45. 'Director', in relation to a body corporate whose affairs are managed by its members, means a member of the body: s 18(3). Section 18 also applies to an offence under s 10 or s 11 described in **16.26**, n 40.
[114]   SVGA 2006, s 18(2).
[115]   For the purposes of ss 9(2) and 19(2)(b), the requirements about frequency or the period condition in the definitions of regulated activity are disapplied: SVGA 2006, ss 9(5), 19(8).
[116]   SVGA 2006, s 60(1).
[117]   SVGA 2006, s 19(5). See **16.22** where the box relating to CJCSA 2000, s 35 applies likewise to s 19.
[118]   SVGA 2006, s 20(1).
[119]   SVGA 2006, s 20(2).
[120]   SI 2008/473, made under SVGA 2006, s 62, Sch 8.

Inclusion in the CBL: persons disqualified from working with children

16.61 TPO, art 2 requires the IBB on a reference by the Secretary of State to include in the CBL a person (X) who is:

- otherwise than provisionally, included in the POCA List;

- subject to a disqualification order; or

- included in List 99 on the grounds of unsuitability to work with children,

and who has no representations, appeal or review outstanding under the legislation relating to these matters. The IBB must give X the opportunity to make representations as to why he or she should be removed from the CBL unless X is a person who satisfied the criteria prescribed for the purposes of automatic inclusion without the right to make representations,[121] in which case there is no right to make representations. The IBB must consider any representations made by X and, if it appears to it in the light of them that it is not appropriate for X to be included in the CBL, it must remove X from that list. As already noted, the effect of inclusion in the CBL will be to impose a bar whose scope is wider than the effect of the current restriction; the right to make representations is limited to making representations only in relation to engaging in regulated activity relating to children which does not constitute work in a regulated position within the meaning of CJCSA 2000, s 36.[122] If the IBB decides not to remove an individual from the CBL, the individual has a right of appeal to the Care Standards Tribunal.[123]

Inclusion in the CBL: other persons prohibited from teaching, etc

16.62 Although outside the remit of this book, it may be noted that TPO, art 3 requires the IBB, on a reference by the Secretary of State, to *consider* including in the CBL a person (Y):

- included in the POCA List, having been transferred to it from the Consultancy Service Index under PoCA 1999, s 3 (unless Y is subject to a disqualification order or to a direction under the EA 2002, s 142(1) on grounds of unsuitability); or

- subject to a direction under the EA 2002, s 142(1) given only on grounds relating to Y's misconduct, health or professional incompetence,

---

[121] SVGA 2006, Sch 3 (as amended by TPO, art 2) has effect for the purposes of art 2. Safeguarding of Vulnerable Groups Act 2006 (Barring Procedure) Regulations 2008, SI 2008/474, reg 2 (see **16.37**) applies in relation to such representations as it applies to representations made under SVGA 2006, Sch 3: TPO, art 2(3). The criteria for automatic inclusion in the CBL under the TPO are that the person has been convicted of, or cautioned in relation to, an offence specified in Protection of Vulnerable Groups Act 2006 (Prescribed Criteria) (Transitional Provisions) Regulations 2008, SI 2008/1062, Sch, para 1: ibid reg 2(1). The offences specified in Sch, para 1 include offences under SOA 2003, ss 5–8; offences of rape committed against a child; the offences under SOA 2003, ss 2, 30, 34 or 38 committed against a child, and ss 31–33, 35–37 or 39–41 where the person 'B' referred to in the statutory definition was a child. Regulation 2(1) does not apply in relation to the commission of an offence specified in Sch, para 1 if the offence was committed more than 10 years before the reference to the IBB or if the court, having considered whether to make a disqualification order in relation to that commission of that offence, decided not to.
[122] Referred to in **16.20**.
[123] SVGA 2006, s 4. For the procedural rules relating to such an appeal or an appeal under the corresponding provisions referred to in **16.63**, see the Protection of Children and Vulnerable Adults and Care Standards Tribunal (Children's and Adults' Barred Lists) (Transitional Provisions) Regulations 2008, SI 2008/1497.

and who has no outstanding appeal or review under the legislation relating to these matters. The IBB must consider including Y in the CBL in accordance with SVGA 2006, Sch 3, paras 3–5.[124]

Inclusion in the ABL: persons considered unsuitable to work with vulnerable adults

16.63 TPO, art 4 requires the IBB, on a reference by the Secretary of State, to include in the ABL a person (X) who is, otherwise than provisionally, included in the POVA List, and who has no appeal or review outstanding under the legislation relating to these matters. The IBB must give X the opportunity to make representations as to why X should be removed from the ABL unless X is a person who satisfies the criteria prescribed for the purposes of automatic inclusion, ie the type of inclusion without the right to make representations,[125] in which case there is no right to make representations. The IBB must consider any representations made by X and, if it appears to it in the light of them that it is not appropriate for X to be included in the ABL, it must remove X from that list. As already noted, the effect of inclusion in the ABL will be to impose a bar whose scope is wider than the effect of the current restriction; the right to make representations is limited to making representations only in relation to X's engaging in regulated activity relating to vulnerable adults which does not constitute work in a care position.[126] If the IBB decides not to remove an individual from the ABL, the individual has a right of appeal to the Care Standards Tribunal.[127]

Minimum barred period

16.64 In respect of the review provisions set out in **16.48** et seq, the minimum barred period for those included in the CBL or ABL pursuant to TPO, art 2 takes account both of the time (or the most recent time) that they were subject to a disqualification under the regime from which they transferred (in effect to treat this as time served) and of the minimum period of disqualification that would have applied under that regime (5 years, in the case of someone under 18, 10 years in other cases).[128] For example:

- if X was made subject to a restriction decision[129] under PoCA 1999 in 2006 and was therefore included in the POCA List, and was then aged 36;

- if that restriction decision was the only (or the most recent) 'unsuitability decision' made against him; and

---

[124] As to these paragraphs, see **16.35–16.37**.

[125] SVGA 2006, Sch 3 (as amended by TPO art 4) has effect for the purposes of art 4. Safeguarding of Vulnerable Groups Act 2006 (Barring Procedure) Regulations 2008, SI 2008/474, reg 2 (see **16.34**) applies in relation to such representations as it applies to representations made under SVGA 2006, Sch 3: TPO, art 4(3). The criteria for inclusion in the ABL under the TPO are that the person has been convicted of, or cautioned in relation to, an offence, committed more than 10 years before the reference to the IBB, specified in Protection of Vulnerable Groups Act 2006 (Prescribed Criteria) (Transitional Provisions) Regulations 2008, Sch 1, para 2: ibid, reg 3. The offences under English law specified in Sch, para 2 are those offences under SOA 2003, s 30–41. Corresponding offences under Scottish, Northern Irish and Service law are also specified.

[126] Within the meaning of CStA 2000, s 80(2)(a), (c).

[127] SVGA 2006, s 4. See n 123.

[128] This is a summary of the detailed provisions of Safeguarding of Vulnerable Groups Act 2006 (Barring Procedure) Regulations 2008, SI 2008/474, regs 3–8.

[129] 'Restriction decision' means a decision of (a) the Secretary of State to include the person in the POCA List, or not to remove the person from that list; (b) the Tribunal not to direct the person's removal from that list: ibid, reg 4(2).

- if X is included in the CBL under TPO in 2008 on the second anniversary of his inclusion in the POCA List,

one first establishes the period that he has been subject to the restriction decision (ie 2006–2008 – 2 years), one then subtracts that period from the period of 10 years and one then finds that X becomes eligible to seek a review 8 years after his inclusion on the CBL.

Chapter 17

NOTIFICATION REQUIREMENTS

17.1   The framework of offences in the Sexual Offences Act (SOA) 2003, Pt 1 is only part of that Act's strategy to protect the public from sex offenders; that framework's aim is their punishment (with the deterrent and other effects of punishment). The other part of the strategy is the management of sex offenders in the community. This is dealt with by SOA 2003, Pt 2, below and in Chapter 18.

17.2   The Sex Offenders Act (SOffA) 1997, Pt 1, which was repealed by SOA 2003, created a scheme whereby those convicted of or cautioned[1] for a range of sexual offences against children were required to notify the local police of their names and addresses, and any subsequent changes. People whose addresses have been notified are commonly said to be on the 'Sex Offenders Register'. Initially, talk of a 'Register' was inaccurate because the names of those required to notify were merely identified with a 'flag' on the Police National Computer. However, this has changed with the development of VISOR (Violent and Sex Offender Register) which includes (inter alia) a wide range of information about all sex offenders in addition to the information required to be notified under the notification requirements described in this chapter.

17.3   The information required to be notified by sex offenders against children is invaluable to the police and probation service in two ways: it helps them to monitor such sex offenders living in the community and it helps in the detection of sexual crime because the police will know the whereabouts of potential suspects.[2] VISOR gives the police and probation service better access to the full range of information held on all offenders on the register.

17.4   SOffA 1997, Pt 1 was strengthened by the Criminal Justice and Court Services Act (CJCSA) 2000, s 66 and Sch 5, which, inter alia, reduced the initial notification requirement period, required initial notification in person, provided for the taking of fingerprints or a photograph on initial notification and provided the power to make regulations requiring persons subject to the notification requirements to give notice of their intention to leave the UK.

17.5   In addition, if a restraining order, a new type of order added to SOffA 1997 by CJCSA 2000, was made the notification requirements did not cease as long as the order was in force. Notification requirements could also arise as a result of the making of a sex offender order, a civil order introduced by the Crime and Disorder Act (CDA) 1998, or an interim sex offender order.

---

[1]   Or found not guilty by reason of insanity or to be under a disability and to have done the act charged against him in respect of such an offence.

[2]   *Protecting the Public: Strengthening Protection Against Sex Offenders and Reforming the Law on Sexual Offences*, Cm 5668 (2002) (*PP*), at paras 16–18.

17.6　CJCSA 2000, s 67 required the chief officer of police for the area and the local probation board for that area acting jointly to establish Multi-Agency Public Protection Arrangements (MAPPA) agencies for the purpose of assessing and managing the risks posed in the area concerned by (amongst others) people subject to the notification requirements of SOA 2003, Pt 2. Section 67 of CJCSA 2000 was replaced in essentially the same terms by the Criminal Justice Act (CJA) 2003, s 325.[3]

17.7　SOA 2003, Pt 2 further strengthened the provisions relating to the notification requirements, to give effect, in whole or part, to proposals made by the 2001 Home Office Consultation Paper, *Review of Part 1 of the Sex Offenders Act 1997*.[4]

17.8　Because breach of notification requirements resulting from a conviction, order, etc in a court in one part of the UK[5] can result in criminal proceedings before a court (with jurisdiction) in another part of the UK, reference will have to be made to Scotland and Northern Ireland, as well as to England and Wales.

WHO IS SUBJECT TO THE NOTIFICATION REQUIREMENTS?

17.9　A person for the time being subject to the notification requirements of SOA 2003, Pt 2 is referred to as a 'relevant offender'.[6] The Act distinguishes between two types of relevant offender:

- those becoming subject to notification requirements after 1 May 2004;[7] and

- those subject to notification requirements under Pt 1 of SOffA 1997 before 1 May 2004.

Persons becoming subject to notification requirements on or after 1 May 2004

17.10　By SOA 2003, s 80(1) a person is subject to the notification requirements for the notification period set out in s 82 if:

'(a)　he is convicted of an offence listed in Sch 3;
(b)　he is found not guilty of such an offence by reason of insanity;
(c)　he is found to be under a disability and to have done the act charged against him in respect of such an offence; or
(d)　in England and Wales or Northern Ireland, he is cautioned in respect of such an offence.'[8]

3　This is discussed in **17.133** et seq.
4　Hereafter *Review SOffA*.
5　Or a conviction, etc by a service court (ie a court-martial in respect of an offence committed in the UK or elsewhere by service personnel, or Standing Civilian Court in respect of offences committed outside the UK by associated persons): s 137(1) and (4). Service courts have jurisdiction outside the UK to try all offences under service law outside the UK committed by service personnel, their dependants or other civilians (eg attached MoD staff) subject to service law overseas. When the relevant provisions of the Armed Forces Act (AFA) 2006 are in force, these service courts will be re-named 'the Court Martial and the Service Civilian Court'.
6　SOA 2003, s 80(2).
7　The commencement date for Pt 2: Sexual Offences Act 2003 (Commencement) Order 2004, SI 2004/874.
8　The notification requirements also apply to people subject to a notification order (NO), interim NO, sexual offences prevention order (SOPO) or interim SOPO. This is dealt with in Chapter 18.

17.11 There is no need for a court (or person administering a caution) to 'order' that an offender is subject to the notification requirements because an offender is automatically subject to them; there is no discretion as to whether the offender is subject to the requirements or as to the notification period. It has however been stated that ordinarily a court should deal expressly with the registration requirements[9] although the failure to do so cannot invalidate a sentence.[10] In addition, the court[11] may issue a certificate under SOA 2003, s 92[12] and the court may make a parental direction where the offender is under 18 at the date of the conviction or finding.[13] As the notification requirement is not part of the sentencing regime this means that it would be wrong to reduce a sentence in order that the offender is subject to the notification requirements for a shorter period of time[14] or even so as to ensure that an offender is not subject to the requirements.[15] Because the notification requirements (and their duration) are automatic there is no appeal against a judicial statement that they apply (or apply for a specified period).[16] In *Odam*[17] the Court of Appeal got round this problem by stating that it was appropriate for it to 'correct any errors made in the sentencing remarks which may have misled the applicant [for leave to appeal out of time]'.[18] The Court did so by declaring that the applicant was not subject to the notification requirements to which the sentencing judge had erroneously stated he was subject,[19] and ordering a copy of the transcript to be given to the applicant to enable him to show the Court's judgment to the police.

Persons subject to SOffA 1997, Pt 1 before 1 May 2004

17.12 SOA 2003, s 81(1) deals with such persons. It does not apply to someone whose notification period ended before 1 May 2004.[20]

17.13 SOA 2003, s 81(1) provides that a person is, from the commencement of Pt 2 until the end of the notification period, subject to the notification requirements of Pt 2 if, before the commencement of Pt 2:

'(a)   he was convicted of an offence listed in Sch 3;
(b)   he was found not guilty of such an offence by reason of insanity;
(c)   he was found to be under a disability and to have done the act charged against him in respect of such an offence; or
(d)   in England and Wales or Northern Ireland, he was cautioned in respect of such an offence.'

17.14 SOA 2003 did not take the opportunity automatically to remove notification requirements imposed in respect of convictions, findings or cautions in respect of consensual homosexual acts in private with 16- or 17-year-olds[21] which ceased to be punishable as buggery or gross indecency in consequence of the Sexual Offences (Amendment) Act (SO(A)A) 2000. The reason seems to have been difficulty of

---

9   *Attorney-General's Reference (No 72 of 1999)* [2000] 2 Cr App R (S) 79. See further **17.32** and **17.35**.
10   *Longworth* [2006] 2 Cr App R (S) 401.
11   Or person administering a caution.
12   See **17.122.**
13   See **17.106, 17.107.**
14   *Attorney-General's Reference (No 50 of 1997)* [1998] 2 Cr App R (S) 155.
15   *DPP v Clutterbuck* [2007] 2 Cr App R (S) 72.
16   *Longworth* n 10 above.
17   [2008] EWCA Crim 1087.
18   Ibid at [9].
19   See **17.24** et seq.
20   SOA 2003, s 81(2).
21   17-year-olds only in Northern Ireland.

implementation. At the time of the conviction, finding or caution, attention might not have been given to whether the act was consensual because it was an offence in any event. SOA 2003, s 93 and Sch 4, however, provide a procedure whereby men who are subject to the notification requirements as a result of a conviction, finding or caution for buggery or gross indecency[22] can apply to the Secretary of State for exemption from those requirements on the basis of the abolition of criminal liability for consensual homosexual acts with 16- or 17-year-olds. The procedure does not apply to Scotland.[23] Exemption will be granted if the Secretary of State decides that it appears that the other party to the relevant act was 16[24] or over at the time of the offence and consented to the act; it is irrelevant whether or not the act was in private. The application is made on an application form. It is followed by a confidential check on the available records but evidence must not be sought by the Secretary of State from any witness. Having considered the representations in the application form and any available records, the Secretary of State will notify the applicant of the written decision. The decision will not be made public. A successful applicant is exempt from the notification requirements from the beginning of the day on which the Secretary of State records his decision in writing. With the permission of the High Court, the applicant may appeal to that Court against a dismissal of the application. The Court will not receive oral evidence. There is no appeal from the High Court's decision.

17.15 By and large, s 81(1) does not apply to a conviction, finding or caution before 1 September 1997,[25] the commencement date of SOffA 1997, Pt 1.[26] However, in respect of a conviction or finding, s 81(3) and (4) replicates the partially retrospective provisions of that Part so that:

- s 81(1)(a) applies to a conviction for a Sch 3 offence before 1 September 1997 if, at the beginning of that day, the person convicted:
  - had not been dealt with in respect of the offence;
  - was serving a sentence of imprisonment[27] or a term of service detention,[28] or was subject to a community order,[29] in respect of the offence;[30]
  - was subject to post-release supervision;[31] or

---

[22] Or a conviction, etc for incitement, conspiracy or attempt to commit such an offence or secondary liability in respect of it: SOA 2003, s 93, Sch 4.
[23] SOA 2003, s 142(3)(a).
[24] In Northern Ireland, 17 or over.
[25] SOA 2003, s 81(3)–(5).
[26] Sex Offenders Act 1997 (Commencement) Order 1999, SI 1997/1920.
[27] In the case of young offenders, SOA 2003, s 131 (as amended) (qv) lists a range of sentences and periods of detention applicable to them to which Pt 2 (including the present provision) applies as it applies to an equivalent sentence of imprisonment, for example: a period of detention under a detention and training order, or a secure training order; or a sentence of detention in a young offender institution; or a sentence of custody for life; or a sentence of detention for public protection; or an extended sentence of detention.
[28] The reference to service detention will be repealed when AFA 2006, Sch 16 is in force.
[29] 'Community order' is defined by SOA 2003, s 133 (as amended by CJA 2003). The term includes a community order within the meaning of the Powers of Criminal Courts (Sentencing) Act (PCC(S)A) 2000 as that Act had effect before the passing of CJA 2003, namely: a curfew order; a community rehabilitation order; a community punishment order; a community punishment and rehabilitation order; a drug treatment and testing order; a drug abstinence order; an attendance centre order; a supervision order; or an action plan order.
[30] A person who would have been within this provision but for the fact that at the beginning of 1 September 1997 he was unlawfully at large or absent without leave, on temporary release or leave of absence, or on bail pending an appeal, is treated as being within this provision: SOA 2003, s 81(6).
[31] Ie supervision in pursuance of an order made for the purpose or, in the case of a person released from prison on licence, in pursuance of a condition contained in their licence: SOA 2003, s 133.

–   was detained in a hospital or was subject to a guardianship order,[32] following the conviction.[33]

•   Section 81(1)(b) and (c) applies to a finding in respect of a Sch 3 offence before 1 September 1997 if, at the beginning of that day, the person in question:
    –   had not been dealt with in respect of the finding; or
    –   was detained in a hospital,[34] following the finding.[35]

17.16 Section 81(7) makes special provision for persons who, immediately before the commencement of Pt 2, were subject to the following orders, listed in s 81(8). It provides that such a person is subject to the notification requirements of Pt 2 from its commencement until the order is discharged or otherwise ceases to have effect. The orders listed are:

•   a restraining order under SOffA 1997, s 5A. Section 5A(4) provided that, if a court made this order against an offender in respect of an offence to which SOffA 1997, Pt 1 applied, the offender did not cease to be subject to the notification requirements of SOffA 1997, Pt 1, whilst the order had effect;

•   a sex offender order or an interim sex offender order under CDA 1998, s 2 or s 2A respectively (or the Scottish or Northern Irish counterpart of these orders).[36] A person subject to such an order was subject to the notification requirements of SOffA 1997, Pt 1.

17.17 Despite their partially retrospective effect, the notification requirements have been held to be preventative rather than punitive in nature and therefore do not constitute a 'penalty' for the purposes of the European Convention on Human Rights (ECHR), Art 7.[37] The notification requirements undoubtedly act as an interference with the right to respect of private life within the meaning of Art 8 but they are clearly prescribed by law and for a legitimate aim. In *Forbes v Secretary of State for the Home Department*[38] the Court of Appeal held that the imposition of notification requirements on a person convicted of importing prohibited indecent material involving photographs of children was not disproportionate and therefore not incompatible with Art 8.

Where must the conviction, finding or caution have occurred for the purposes of s 80 or s 81?

17.18 Although this text is concerned with the operation of the notification requirements in England and Wales, it must be emphasised that the provisions relating to the requirements apply to Scotland and Northern Ireland as well, and that a requirement to notify police in England and Wales (e g of a changed address) may exist under s 80(1) or s 81(1) because of a conviction, finding or caution in Scotland or Northern Ireland. The notification requirements under those sections do not, on the

---

32   Ie a guardianship order under MHA 1983, s 37 or the corresponding Scottish or Northern Irish legislation: SOA 2003, s 133.
33   SOA 2003, s 81(3).
34   As defined in SOA 2003, s 133.
35   SOA 2003, s 81(4).
36   See **18.30–18.32**.
37   *Ibbotson v UK* (1998) 27 EHRR CD 332; *Adamson v UK* (1999) 28 EHRR CD 209.
38   [2007] 1 Cr App R (S) 418.

other hand, arise where the conviction is in a court outside the UK, whether that court is, for example, in the Isle of Man or Thailand.

An offence listed in Sch 3

17.19 SOA 2003, Sch 3 lists more than 90 sexual offences under English, Scots or Northern Irish law in respect of which notification requirements arise on conviction, etc. Many offences in Sch 3 are subject to age and/or sentence conditions which trigger the notification requirements. Age conditions relate to the age of the victim or of the offender at the time of the offence. Age conditions relating to a victim are expressed as a maximum, normally 18. Age conditions in respect of an offender are expressed either as a minimum, again normally 18, or as an upper age limit (which may be implied not expressed). The term 'sentence condition' (or 'threshold', as it is sometimes called) is used in a loose sense to cover any condition relating to the way in which the defendant is dealt with in respect of an offence or in respect of a finding of not guilty by reason of insanity or a finding that a person is under a disability and did the act charged against him in respect of the offence (a 'relevant finding'[39]). Most upper age conditions are associated with a sentence condition.

17.20 The list of substantive offences in Sch 3 includes those listed in Sch 1 to SOffA 1997 (most of which were repealed by SOA 2003 in the case of English or Northern Irish offences), as well as all the offences in SOA 2003, Pt 1, besides those under ss 52 and 53 (exploitation of prostitution), ss 57–59 (trafficking) and s 71 (sexual activity in a public lavatory).

17.21 Schedule 3 lists the following offences under English law:

- an offence under SOA 1956, ss 1 (rape), 5 (intercourse with a girl under 13), 28 (causing etc prostitution, etc of girl under 16); the Indecency with Children Act (ICA) 1960, s 1 (indecent conduct towards young child); the Criminal Law Act (CLA) 1977, s 54 (inciting girl under 16 to have incestuous sexual intercourse); SOA 2003, s 1 or s 2 (rape, assault by penetration), ss 4-6 (causing sexual activity without consent, rape of child under 13, assault of child under 13 by penetration), ss 8–12 (causing or inciting child under 13 to engage in sexual activity, child sex offences committed by adults), s 15 (sexual grooming, etc), ss 30–37 (offences against persons with a mental disorder impeding choice, inducements, etc to persons with mental disorder), s 61 (administering substance with intent);

- an offence under SOA 1956, s 6 (intercourse with girl under 16) or SO(A)A 2000, s 3 (abuse of position of trust), *if the offender was 20 or over*;

- an offence under SOA 1956, s 10 (incest by a man) or s 16 (assault with intent to commit buggery), *if the victim or (as the case may be) other party was under 18*;

- an offence under SOA 2003, s 13 (child sex offences committed by children or young persons), *if the offender is or has been sentenced, in respect of the offence, to imprisonment for a term of at least 12 months*;

---

[39]   SOA 2003, s 132(9).

- an offence under SOA 1956, s 12 (buggery) or s 13 (indecency between men), *if the offender was 20 or over, and the victim or (as the case may be) other party was under 18;*

- an offence under SOA 1956, s 14 or s 15 (indecent assault) if:
  - *the victim or (as the case may be) other party was under 18; or*
  - *the offender, in respect of the offence or finding, is or has been:*
    - *(a) sentenced to imprisonment for a term of at least 30 months; or*
    - *(b) admitted to a hospital subject to a restriction order;*

- an offence under SOA 2003, ss 16–19 (abuse of position of trust) *if the offender, in respect of the offence, is or has been:*
  - *sentenced to a term of imprisonment;*
  - *detained in a hospital; or*
  - *made the subject of a community sentence of at least 12 months;*

- an offence under SOA 2003, s 64 or s 65 (sex with adult relative) *if:*
  - *where the offender was under 18, he is or has been sentenced in respect of the offence to imprisonment for a term of at least 12 months;*
  - *in any other case, the offender, in respect of the offence or finding, is or has been sentenced to a term of imprisonment, or detained in a hospital;*

- an offence under SOA 2003, s 3 (sexual assault), s 66 (exposure) or s 67 (voyeurism) *if:*
  - *where the offender was under 18, he is or has been sentenced, in respect of the offence, to imprisonment for a term of at least 12 months;*
  - *in any other case:*
    - *(a) the victim was under 18; or*
    - *(b) the offender, in respect of the offence or finding, is or has been sentenced to a term of imprisonment, detained in a hospital, or made the subject of a community sentence of at least 12 months;*

- an offence under SOA 2003, ss 38–41 (care workers) *if:*
  - *where the offender was under 18, he is or has been sentenced, in respect of the offence, to imprisonment for a term of at least 12 months;*
  - *in any other case, the offender, in respect of the offence or finding, is or has been sentenced to a term of imprisonment, detained in a hospital, or made the subject of a community sentence of at least 12 months;*

- an offence under SOA 2003, s 62 or s 63 (committing an offence, or trespassing, with intent to commit sexual offence) *if:*
  - *where the offender was under 18, he is or has been sentenced, in respect of the offence, to imprisonment for a term of at least 12 months;*
  - *in any other case:*
    - *(a) the intended offence was an offence against a person under 18; or*
    - *(b) the offender, in respect of the offence or finding, is or has been sentenced to a term of imprisonment, detained in a hospital, or made the subject of a community sentence of at least 12 months;*

- an offence under SOA 2003, s 7 (sexual assault on child under 13) or s 14 (arranging or facilitating commission of child sex offence) or s 25 or s 26 (familial child sex offences) or ss 48-50 (paying for child sex and child prostitution), *if the offender was 18 or over, or is or has been sentenced, in respect of the offence, to imprisonment for a term of at least 12 months*;

- an offence under SOA 2003, s 47 (paying for sexual services of a child) if:
  - *the victim or (as the case may be) other party was under 16; and*
  - *the offender:*
    - *(a) was 18 or over; or*
    - *(b) is or has been sentenced in respect of the offence to imprisonment for a term of at least 12 months;*

- an offence under the Protection of Children Act (PoCA) 1978, s 1 (indecent photographs etc of children) *if indecent photographs, etc showed persons under 16* or the Customs and Excise Management Act (CEMA) 1979, s 170 (in relation to goods prohibited to be imported under the Customs Consolidation Act 1876, s 42) (indecent or obscene articles), *if the prohibited goods included indecent photographs of persons under 16*[40] or CJA 1988, s 160 (possession of indecent photographs, etc of child) *if indecent photographs, etc showed persons under 16, and*:
  - *the conviction, finding or caution was before 1 May 2004; or*
  - the offender:
    - *(a) was 18 or over; or*
    - *(b) is sentenced in respect of the offence to imprisonment for a term of at least 12 months;*

- an offence under SOA 2003, s 69 or s 70 (intercourse with animal, sexual penetration of corpse) *if*:
  - *where the offender was under 18, he is or has been sentenced in respect of the offence to imprisonment for a term of at least 12 months;*
  - *in any other case, the offender, in respect of the offence or finding, is or has been:*
    - *(a) sentenced to a term of imprisonment; or*
    - *(b) detained in a hospital;* and

- when an amendment made by the Criminal Justice and Immigration Act (CJIA) 2008 is in force,[41] an offence under CJIA 2008, s 63 (possession of extreme pornographic images) *if the offender was 18 or over and is sentenced in respect of the offence to imprisonment for a term of at least 2 years.*[42]

Schedule 3 also makes the like provision for corresponding offences under Scots or Northern Irish law. It also specifies that an offence under military law (Service law) of which the corresponding civil offence is one of the sexual offences under English law is an offence in respect of which notification requirements arise on conviction, etc.[43] A reference to an offence in the list includes a reference to an attempt, conspiracy or

---

[40] For the purposes of the reference to this offence: (a) a person is to be taken to have been under 16 at any time if it appears from the evidence as a whole that he was under that age at that time; (b) PoCA 1978, s 7 (Chapter 8) and the corresponding Scottish and Northern Irish provisions apply in England and Wales, Scotland and Northern Ireland respectively: Sch 3, para 97.

[41] CJIA 2008, s 148(1), Sch 26, Pt 2, para 58(1), (2).

[42] *Age and sentence conditions have been shown in italics.* A reference in Sch 3 to a person's age is: (a) in the case of an indecent photograph, a reference to the person's age when the photograph was taken; (b) in any other case, a reference to his age at the time of the offence: Sch 3, para 95. In Sch 3 'community sentence' has, in relation to England and Wales, the same meaning as in PCC(S)A 2000 (ie a community order under CJA 2003, s 177, or one or more youth community orders: PCC(S)A 2000, s 33(2) (as amended)) or the corresponding Northern Irish provision: Sch 3, para 96. As to 'imprisonment' see n 27 above.

[43] See Sch 3, paras 93 and 93A (inserted by AFA 2006, but not brought into force at the time of writing).

incitement[44] to commit one of the above offences, and to liability for one of the above offences as aider, abettor, counsellor or procurer.[45]

17.22 Schedule 3 can be amended by statutory instrument[46] subject to the affirmative procedure.[47] At the time of going to press this power has been exercised on a number of occasions.

17.23 The age and sentence conditions for quite a number of offences mean that offenders who were under 18 (an upper age condition) *at the time of the offence* are only subject to the notification requirements if they have been sentenced to a custodial sentence of at least 12 months. If, in the case of such an offence, for example, an offender has only received a community sentence[48] after conviction, or if he has been reprimanded or finally warned, the offence is not within Sch 3. Broadly, the effect is that only those under-18s who commit a sexual offence of the most serious type (e g rape) or a lesser type of offence which is so serious in its circumstances as to warrant a 12-month custodial sentence are covered. This excludes completely offenders under 12 who cannot be sentenced to detention.[49] The intention is to provide public protection against those young sex offenders who are dangerous and to avoid stigmatising further those who are essentially in need of help.

17.24 One of the sentence conditions for some of the offences listed in Sch 3 'is that the offender is or has been made the subject of a community sentence of at least 12 months'. These words were in issue in *Odam*[50] where such a sentence condition applied to the offence in question in the specific circumstances. D was convicted of exposure.[51] On 15 June 2007 D was sentenced to a community order whose only requirement was to carry out 120 hours of unpaid work. The judge did not indicate the length of the community order itself. The record indicated that the unpaid work requirement had to be completed *by* 14 June, ie (as the Court of Appeal indicated) one day short of a 12-month period commencing on 15 June. In his sentencing remarks, the judge said that D would be subject to the notification requirements for 5 years. D completed the unpaid work within 4½ months of sentence. Noting that by CJA 2003, s 200(3) a community order containing only an unpaid work requirement comes to an end when work has been completed, the Court of Appeal held:[52]

> 'In those circumstances . . . the applicant was not sentenced, as it turns out, to a community order of at least 12 months. His community order lasted in fact some 4 and a half months

---

44 The Serious Crime Act (SCA) 2007, s 63, Sch 6, para 63 inserts a new paragraph – para 94A (not in force at the time of writing) – which states that: 'A reference in a preceding paragraph to an offence ("offence A") includes a reference to an offence under Part 2 of the Serious Crimes Act 2007 in relation to which offence A is the offence (or one of the offences) which the person intended or believed would be committed'. This is necessary since SCA 2007, Pt 2 will, when implemented, abolish the common law offence of incitement and replace it with offences of encouraging or assisting crime.

45 Schedule 3, para 94. In respect of an attempt, conspiracy or incitement, it will be noted that the reference is only to an attempt, etc to commit one of the substantive offences in Sch 3 and not a reference to, for example, an attempt to incite the commission of such an offence: *Parnell* [2005] 1 WLR 853. For a limitation in respect of a secondary party to some offences in Scotland, see Sch 3, para 94(b).

46 SOA 2003, ss 130(1), 138(1).

47 Section 138(1) and (2). For the purposes of the notification requirements (other than those arising via a SOPO or a foreign travel order (FTO), discussed in Chapter 18), an amendment to Sch 3 does not apply to convictions, findings or cautions before the amendment takes effect: s 130(2).

48 Schedule 3, para 96. Also see para 93(2).

49 Unless, and until, an order is made under PCC(S)A 2000, s 100(2)(b)(ii).

50 [2008] EWCA Crim 1087.

51 Contrary to SOA 2003, s 66; **13.9.**

52 [2008] EWCA Crim 1087 at [8] and [18].

only . . . The judgment of this court is that, given the nature of the sentence imposed on you, there was no power to require you to notify your details to the police in accordance with [SOA 2003].'

17.25 While the Court of Appeal may have been correct to hold that D was not someone who had been sentenced to a community sentence of at least 12 months, it is submitted that its reason was incorrect. The sentence condition refers to a person who 'is or has been made subject to a community sentence of at least 12 months'. The 'is' alternative would seem to relate to the situation where the notification requirements arise simultaneously with a conviction etc or the fulfilment of a sentence condition; and 'has been' to the case where a SOPO is made on complaint by the police in respect of a defendant who (in the context of a sexual offence) has in the past been convicted of, and sentenced for, a Sch 3 offence before SOffA 1997, Pt 1 came into force (in which case the notification requirements will apply from the date of service of the SOPO).[53] In any event, the natural interpretation of 'is or has been made subject to a community sentence of at least 12 months' is that if either of the alternatives 'is' or 'has been' is satisfied, the sentence condition is also satisfied. As noted in **17.27**, the notification requirements run from the date of sentence (the 'relevant date') where a sentence condition has to be fulfilled. It is at that point that the question whether the defendant is made subject to a community sentence of at least 12 months must be answered. If the defendant is so sentenced, the sentence condition is satisfied and the notification requirements apply. There is nothing in Sch 3 (or elsewhere in the Act) to warrant the Court of Appeal's conclusion that D had been *sentenced* to a community sentence of $4^1/_2$ months. If the judge had expressly indicated the length of the community order as 12 months (or more) the Court of Appeal's decision that D had not been sentenced to a community sentence of at least 12 months would clearly have been wrong.

17.26 Although the Court of Appeal's reason for reaching its conclusion was wrong, it is submitted that the conclusion it reached was correct. Given that the community order only contained an unpaid work requirement, that the judge required that work to be done in one day less than 12 months running from the relevant date and given the terms of CJA 2003, s 200(3), it would seem that the judge had impliedly sentenced D to a community sentence of one day less than 12 months, with the result that the sentence condition was not fulfilled and the Court of Appeal's decision that D was not subject to the notification requirements was correct, albeit for the wrong reasons.

17.27 SOA 2003, s 132 provides that, where a sentence condition applies to an offence under Sch 3:

(a)   a person is to be regarded as convicted of such an offence, or

(b)   (as the case may be) a relevant finding in relation to such an offence is to be regarded as made,

at the time when that condition is met.[54] The importance of this is that the date of conviction or of a relevant finding is the date when the notification requirements (if they arise) begin to run. It means that if D is convicted on 1 October of a Sch 3 offence subject to a sentence condition but sentencing is adjourned or deferred until 20 October, at which time a community sentence is passed which meets the condition for the offence

---

53   See **18.89**.
54   SOA 2003, s 132(1)–(3).

in question, the notification requirements will run from 20 October (the 'deemed date of conviction') and, for instance, D must comply with the initial notification requirement under s 83 within 3 days of 20 October. This special provision is rendered necessary because, where a Sch 3 offence is subject to a sentence condition, it cannot be known until sentence is passed whether or not the condition is satisfied and therefore whether the offence triggers the notification requirements.

17.28 If an offender is convicted of an offence for which there is no sentence condition but sentence is adjourned, it could happen that he is subsequently given an absolute discharge. Until then he will have been subject to the notification requirements, but thereafter he will cease to be so.

Conviction

17.29 This term in SOA 2003, s 80(1) (and elsewhere in Pt 2) includes a conviction[55] for an offence in respect of which the offender receives a conditional discharge or, in Scotland, a probation order is made;[56] the provisions which state that a conviction with such an order is deemed not to be a conviction for any other purpose are disapplied[57] by s 134 in relation to convictions after the commencement of Pt 2[58] in respect of the notification requirements. Under the previous legislation a discharge (conditional or absolute) could not trigger the notification requirements.[59]

17.30 The effect of the absence of absolute discharges from s 134 is to prevent a conviction followed by an absolute discharge constituting a conviction for present purposes. It seems somewhat anomalous that a police caution triggers notification requirements when a conviction followed by an absolute discharge does not.

17.31 'Conviction' also includes a finding in summary proceedings, where the court makes a hospital or guardianship order under the Mental Health Act 1983, s 37(3) (or its Scottish or Northern Irish counterpart), that a mentally ill or severely mentally disordered defendant did the act or made the omission charged.[60]

17.32 A notice of requirement to register with the police and certificate of conviction may be given by the court to the offender and to the Crown Prosecution Service (CPS), police and to the prison service, local authority or probation service as appropriate.[61]

Persons under a disability

17.33 The reference in SOA 2003, ss 80(1)(c) and 81(1)(c) to a person found to be under a disability and to have done the act charged against him in respect of a Sch 3 offence includes a reference to his having been found:[62]

'(a) unfit to be tried for the offence;
(b) to be insane so that his trial for the offence cannot or could not proceed; or

---

55   Including a conviction by a court martial or Standing Civilian Court: s 137(1)(a): see n 5 above.
56   Or a community supervision order imposed under Service law.
57   The disapplication does not apply to absolute discharges.
58   Or before or after that date in the case of a community supervision order: s 134(3).
59   See Gillespie 'Discharging Sex Offenders' [2002] Crim LR 53 and *Longworth* [2006] 2 Cr App R (S) 401.
60   SOA 2003, s 135(1), (2).
61   *Guidance on Part 2 of the Sexual Offences Act 2003* (Home Office, 2004) (*Guidance Pt 2*), at Annex C.
62   SOA 2003, s 135(3).

(c)   unfit to be tried and to have done the act charged against him in respect of the offence.'

17.34 If a person found to be under a disability, etc later becomes capable of being tried, and is tried, an unexpired notification period automatically brought into force by the disability finding ends at the conclusion of the trial.[63] Of course, if the person is convicted of a Sch 3 offence at that trial a new notification requirement and period may come into force. The ending of the original notification period in this type of case does not retrospectively invalidate the notification requirements. If an original requirement was broken before its cessation, a prosecution for its breach may still be brought.

17.35 A notice and certificate of the type referred to in **17.32** also applies to 'findings' and should be given as above.

Cautions

17.36 By SOA 2003, s 133,[64] the reference in ss 80(1)(d) and 81(1)(d) (and elsewhere in Pt 2) to a person being cautioned in England and Wales or Northern Ireland for a Sch 3 offence means:

(a)   cautioned after the person concerned has admitted the offence. This refers to someone given a 'simple caution'[65] or a conditional caution[66] or (when the relevant provisions[67] are in force) a youth conditional caution; or

(b)   in England and Wales, reprimanded or finally warned within the meaning given by CDA 1998, s 65, which replaced the system of police cautions for young offenders (persons under 18) in England and Wales.

It is only in the case of the more serious offences listed in Sch 3 that cautions can result in notification requirements.

17.37 Before being cautioned, reprimanded or warned the offender must be informed of the notification requirements.[68] An adult can only be given either a simple or conditional caution where he admits the offence and gives his consent to being cautioned,[69] and the same will be true when an adolescent is given a youth conditional caution.[70] A reprimand or warning can only be given if the adolescent offender admits

---

[63]   SOA 2003, s 82(5). This is a better formulation than that of its predecessor under SOffA 1997, which stated that if the person found under the disability, etc was subsequently tried for the offence 'the finding, and any order made in respect of the finding, shall be disregarded for the purposes of' SOffA 1997, s 1 (the counterpart to s 80). It was arguable that this meant not only that the notification requirement following the finding of disability did not prevent a new requirement if there was a conviction at the new trial, but also that the first requirement had to be disregarded for the purposes of a prosecution for breach of it during its currency, a somewhat absurd result.

[64]   As amended by CJIA 2008, s 148, Sch 26, Pt 2, para 56(1), (2). This amendment came into force on 14 July 2008: CJIA 2008 (Commencement No 2 and Transitional and Saving Provisions) Order 2008 (CO 2), SI 2008/1586, art 2(1), Sch 1.

[65]   Ie the informal cautioning scheme governed by Home Office circular 30/2005.

[66]   CJA 2003, Pt 3.

[67]   CDA 1998, ss 66A–66H (inserted by CJIA 2008, s 48, Sch 9, paras 1, 3) will, when in force, introduce youth conditional cautions.

[68]   *Guidance Pt 2*, at pp 9–10.

[69]   The admission must be freely made (see *R (R) v Durham Constabulary)* [2005] 1 WLR 1184, at p 1207, per Baroness Hale, and *Commissioner of the Police of the Metropolis ex parte P* (1995) 8 Admin LR 6).

[70]   CJA 2003, s 23(5)(b), (c); CDA 1998, s 66B(6)(b), (c) (inserted by CJIA 2008, Sch 9, para 3).

guilt[71] but there is no requirement that the offender consents to this disposal.[72] A notice of requirement to register with the police and certificate of caution (reprimand or formal warning) may be given to the person cautioned and signed by that person and the appropriate adult (if appropriate).[73]

17.38 The extension of notification requirements to those who are cautioned is undoubtedly controversial since the authorities have decided that they are not going to prosecute the offender. This means that the evidence will never be tested by the courts and, in relation to simple cautions, reprimands and final warnings, it is possible that the evidence will not even be considered by the CPS.

17.39 The justification put forward by the Government was that there is a variety of different reasons why a caution may be administered, including the reluctance of a victim to testify[74] or personal mitigating circumstances relating to the offender. Notwithstanding this the issue remains controversial, not least because someone who is subject to a caution is likely to be subject to the notification requirements for longer than someone who is subject to a conditional discharge, and yet in the latter instance no admission of guilty need necessarily have been made and, of course, the evidence has been tested in court.

NOTIFICATION PERIOD

17.40 The notification period for someone subject to a notification requirement under SOA 2003, s 80(1) or s 81(1) is the period in the right-hand column of the following Table[75] set out in s 82(1) opposite the description applicable to them. The Table is different in some respects from that under SOffA 1997.[76]

TABLE	
Description of relevant offender	*Notification period*
A person who, in respect of the offence, is or has been sentenced to imprisonment for life, to imprisonment for public protection under CJA 2003, s 225[77] or to imprisonment for a term of 30 months or more[78]	An indefinite period beginning with the relevant date

---

71 CDA 1998, s 65.
72 *R (R) v Durham Constabulary*, n 69 above.
73 *Guidance Pt 2*, at Annex D.
74 Although if this is true then it is difficult to see how the evidence against the offender can be said to meet the 'evidential test' in the *Code for Crown Prosecutors*, something it is supposed to do for all forms of caution.
75 As amended by Violent Crime Reduction Act (VCRA) 2006, s 57.
76 Where the notification requirement arises as a result of a NO (described in **18.3** et seq), references to an 'order' in the Table are read as references to any corresponding disposal made in relation to the defendant in respect of an offence or finding by reference to which the NO was made: s 98(3)(c).
77 See **15.25** et seq.
78 Or to an indeterminate custodial sentence in Northern Ireland when SI 2008/1216, Sch 5, para 10(1) is in force.

A person who, in respect of the offence, has been made the subject of an order under the Criminal Procedure (Scotland) Act 1995, s 210F(1) (order for lifelong restriction)	An indefinite period beginning with that date
A person who, in respect of the offence or finding, is or has been admitted to a hospital subject to a restriction order	An indefinite period beginning with that date
A person who, in respect of the offence, is or has been sentenced to imprisonment for a term of more than 6 months but less than 30 months	10 years beginning with that date
A person who, in respect of the offence, is or has been sentenced to imprisonment for a term of 6 months or less	7 years beginning with that date
A person who, in respect of the offence or finding, is or has been admitted to a hospital without being subject to a restriction order	7 years beginning with that date
A person within s 80(1)(d) (caution, etc)	2 years beginning with that date
A person in whose case an order for conditional discharge or, in Scotland, a probation order, is made in respect of the offence	The period of conditional discharge or, in Scotland, the probation period
A person of any other description	5 years beginning with the relevant date

17.41 The meaning of 'relevant date' for the purposes of the table is the date of the conviction, finding or caution.[79] As explained in **17.27**, where the Sch 3 offence in question is subject to a 'sentence condition' a person is to be regarded as convicted or made the subject of a finding when that condition is met.

17.42 Reference is made in the Table to 'imprisonment' but it should be noted that for young offenders, a range of sentences and periods of detention apply as SOA 2003, Pt 2 applies to an equivalent sentence of imprisonment, eg a period of detention under a detention and training order or secure training order (now abolished), a sentence of detention in a young offender institution, a young offenders institution or a young offenders centre, or a sentence of custody for life.[80]

17.43 The calculation of the notification period where an offender is subject to an extended sentence[81] is not completely clear. Two cases concerned with extended sentences under PCC(S)A 2000, s 85 (repealed) give different indications. In *S (Graham)*[82] the Court of Appeal concluded that where a person was the subject of an extended sentence, the custodial term should be the length of sentence for the purposes of calculating the notification requirement. However, in *Wiles*[83] a different constitution of the Court of Appeal reached the opposite conclusion in respect of the duration of a

---

79   Section 82(6).
80   See SOA 2003, s 131.
81   PCC(S)A 2000, s 85 (now repealed) and CJA 2003, s 227 (see **15.52** et seq).
82   [2001] 1 Cr App R 7.
83   [2004] 2 Cr App R (S) 467.

disqualification order, and thought that the overall sentence (ie the custodial term plus the period of licence) was relevant in deciding the duration of the notification period. Although *Wiles* was concerned with the disqualification of children,[84] the two sets of provisions should be treated the same since they both provide preventative ancillary arrangements dependent on sentence. Whilst awaiting a definitive ruling on this it would appear that the courts consider that *Wiles* applies to the determination of the notification period relating to sentences under s 85.[85] The position where an extended sentence is passed under CJA 2003 should be governed by *Wiles*. Certainly the phrasing of s 227 of that Act lends credence to this argument since it talks about a '*sentence of imprisonment the term of which is equal to the aggregate of* the appropriate custodial term and the extension (licence) period,[86] thereby making it clear that the sentence of *imprisonment* is the total sentence. This has obvious relevance to SOA 2003, s 82, which does not refer to a term of custody but rather a term of imprisonment.

Juvenile offenders

17.44 The logic that operates in respect of the duration of notification requirements does not apply in the case of adolescent offenders. Detention and training orders (DTOs) require a judge to set a sentence, only some of which will be served in custody with the balance being served under supervision.[87] In *Slocombe*[88] the Court of Appeal held that there was a significant difference between a DTO and ordinary sentence of imprisonment in that the custodial period for a DTO was set by a court and could not be extended without a further order of court. Accordingly the Court held that only the custodial period set at the time of sentence should be relevant to the notification period under s 82. It is difficult to reconcile this decision with *Wiles* although it is conceded that there is some logic behind the difference. That said, it is perhaps best explained as another example of how the benefit of doubt is given to adolescent offenders because of the concern that arises from them being made subject to the notification requirements.

17.45 Another important point to note about juvenile offenders is that if an offender is under 18 *on the relevant date*, ie *the time of the conviction, finding or caution,* the notification periods of 10, 7, 5 and 2 years for an adult are halved.[89] For example, a custodial sentence of less than 6 months' imprisonment requires an adult to notify for a period of 7 years[90] but an adolescent would notify for a period of 3½ years. Where, however, a sentence is for the equivalent of imprisonment for more than 30 months, the notification period lasts indefinitely. The Court of Appeal has reminded judges that they should not artificially impose a lesser sentence so as to escape that consequence.[91]

Where offender subject to notification requirements is convicted, etc

17.46 If an offender already subject to notification requirements is convicted or receives a finding or caution for a Sch 3 offence, he or she does not become subject to a new set of notification requirements. An offender cannot be subject to more than one

---

84   Under C(S)A 1997, s 28; see **15.48**.
85   See, for example, *Broad* [2007] EWCA Crim 2146.
86   CJA 2003, s 227(2).
87   See PCC(S)A 2000, s 100.
88   [2006] 1 Cr App R 33.
89   SOA 2003, s 82(2). Where the notification period is for an indeterminate period of time then no change is made.
90   See **17.40**.
91   *H* [2007] EWCA Crim 2622.

set of requirements (eg in terms of initial or periodic notification). Instead, the single period of notification is as set out in **17.47** and **17.48** (which deals, inter alia, with the special case of partly concurrent sentences).

17.47 Leaving aside consecutive sentences and partly concurrent sentences of imprisonment, the position is as follows. The offender must comply with the notification requirements for the notification period which ends the latest. For example, D has a notification period of 5 years which is due to end on 1 December 2010. On 1 August 2009 he is convicted of another offence and sentenced to 12 months' community punishment. Therefore another 5-year notification period applies to him and he must comply with the requirements until that period expires on 1 August 2014. Another example: E is subject to the requirements for an indefinite period because of a previous conviction which resulted in a 30-month prison sentence. Some time after the end of his sentence, on 1 June 2009, he is cautioned for another relevant offence. This would mean that his notification period runs until 1 June 2011, but because he is already subject to the requirements for an indefinite period he will have to comply with the requirements indefinitely.[92]

Consecutive or partly concurrent sentences

17.48 SOA 2003, s 82(4) makes special provision about the notification period for cases where a relevant offender within s 80(1)(a) or s 81(1)(a) is or has been sentenced in respect of two or more Sch 3 offences to consecutive terms of imprisonment or to partly concurrent sentences.[93] Terms are partly concurrent when they are passed on different occasions. In respect of each the rule is that s 82(1) applies as if the term of imprisonment:

'(a)   in the case of consecutive terms, is equal to the aggregate of those terms;
(b)   in the case of partly concurrent terms (X and Y, which overlap for a period Z), is equal to X plus Y minus Z.'

An example of (a) would be where A is sentenced to 2 years' imprisonment for crime X and a consecutive sentence of 12 months' imprisonment for crime Y. The aggregate term is therefore 3 years' imprisonment with the result that the notification period lasts indefinitely.

17.49 An example of (b) would be where A is sentenced to 12 months' imprisonment for crime X and 4 months into this term he is sentenced to 2 years' imprisonment for crime Y, to be served concurrently with the sentence for crime X. The arithmetic in (b) means that s 82(1) has effect as if A had been sentenced to a 28-month term with the result that the notification period is 10 years.

Disability

17.50 Where a relevant offender, the subject of a finding of a disability within s 80(1)(c) or s 81(1)(c) and of notification requirements, is subsequently tried for the offence, the notification period relating to the finding ends at the conclusion of the trial.[94] Where, at

---

[92]   *Guidance Pt 2*, at p 12.
[93]   SOA 2003, s 82(4).
[94]   Section 82(5).

that trial, the person is convicted, a new notification period (assuming any sentence condition is satisfied) of the relevant duration will apply.

Cautions

17.51 Read literally the Table in s 82(1) provides that, although the notification period for someone cautioned for an offence listed in Sch 3 on or after 1 May 2004 is 2 years, the notification period for a person cautioned before that date for such an offence, a 5-year period under SOffA 1997, remained of that duration. It is arguable that this is not what Parliament intended.[95]

NOTIFICATION REQUIREMENTS: INITIAL NOTIFICATION

17.52 By SOA 2003, s 83(1) a relevant offender[96] (ie someone subject to the notification requirements) must, within the period of 3 days[97] beginning with the relevant date (the date of conviction, finding or caution),[98] notify to the police the information listed in s 83(5). Where a sentence condition applies to the offence in question in respect of the offender, he is regarded as convicted (or a finding is regarded as made) when the sentence condition is met.[99]

17.53 By s 83(6), the above period does not include any time when the relevant offender[100] is:

(a)   remanded in or committed to custody by a court or (prospectively)[101] kept in service custody;

(b)   serving a prison sentence or service detention;

(c)   detained in a hospital; or

(d)   outside the UK.

17.54 It will be noted that 'remand in custody' in s 83(6) does not include being held in police detention, or being remanded or committed to local authority accommodation under the Children and Young Persons Act (CYPA) 1969, s 23, and placed and kept in secure accommodation. However, if a person so detained failed to make his initial notification during the 3-day period he would not – it is submitted – commit the offence

---

95   See Gillespie 'Changing Register' (2005) 155 NLJ 84.
96   See **17.10** and **17.13**.
97   'Day' is ambiguous. It could bear two meanings in the context of Pt 2: the beginning of a period of time commencing with one midnight and ending the next or a 24-hour period. The preferable view that it has the former meaning in the Act was supported by Paul Goggins MP, HC Committee, Standing Committee B (October 2003), col 338. Thus, if a requirement arises at 2 pm on a Thursday the period will run from the previous midnight. The concept of 'working days' does not appear in the Act.
98   SOA 2003, s 82(6). Or date of service of a sex offender order (or interim sex offender order); this is the effect of s 82(6)(d). As to the beginning of the initial notification period for those orders see Chapter 18.
99   SOA 2003, s 132(3).
100 The defendant in the case of a NO: SOA 2003, s 98(3)(a).
101 When an amendment made to SOA 2003, s 83(6) by CJIA 2008, s 148, Sch 26, Pt 2, para 54(1) is in force. The amendment does not apply to Scotland.

of failing to comply with the initial notification requirement under s 91(1)(a)[102] because he would have a 'reasonable excuse' for not doing so.

17.55 One effect of s 83(6) is that if a relevant offender is at once taken into custody after being sentenced to imprisonment immediately after conviction for a Sch 3 offence he is not required to do the impossible and notify the police of the listed information within 3 days of conviction. Instead, the requirement will be to notify the information within 3 days of his release.[103] On the other hand, if sentence is deferred for 3 weeks on conviction for an offence in respect of which there is not an applicable sentence condition, the offender will have to notify the information within 3 days of conviction; it would be irrelevant that he is ultimately sentenced to imprisonment.

17.56 Another effect of s 83(6) is that an offender, who has been convicted of a Sch 3 offence and sentenced to a community sentence, and who goes on a fortnight's holiday in France the next day, will have to notify the police of the listed information within the balance of the 3 days on his return.

17.57 The initial notification requirement does not apply to a relevant offender[104] in respect of a conviction, finding or caution relating to a Sch 3 offence after the commencement of the SOA 2003 if:

(a)   immediately before the *conviction, finding or caution*, the offender was subject to the notification requirements of Pt 2 as a result of another conviction, finding or caution or court order, such as a sex offender order, NO or SOPO[105] ('the earlier event');

(b)   at that time, the offender had made a notification under s 83(1) in respect of the earlier event; and

(c)   throughout the initial notification period under s 83(1), the offender remains subject to the notification requirements as a result of the earlier event.[106]

Thus, such a person does not need to give an initial notification again in respect of the later conviction, etc, provided that throughout the 3-day period referred to in s 83(1) he was subject to the notification requirements as a result of 'the earlier event'. The same applies where a NO is made in respect of a conviction, finding or caution.[107]

17.58 Not surprisingly, the initial notification requirement under s 83(1) does not apply to a relevant offender in respect of a conviction, finding or caution, or restraining order

---

102   See **17.112** et seq.
103   Lest it is thought that 3 days is too long in the case of a serious sex offender, it must be remembered that the most serious offenders are required to report to their supervising probation officer within 24 hours of their release from prison. In some cases they may be required to live in an approved hostel. Non-compliance with either condition can result in an immediate return to prison. Thus, the most serious sex offenders should be known to the authorities within 24 hours of release and can be dealt with immediately if they are not.
104   See **17.9.**
105   These orders are discussed in Chapter 18.
106   SOA 2003, s 83(2).
107   Section 83(4) repeats in this respect s 83(2) save that 'NO' replaces the italicised reference to the subsequent conviction, etc in (a) above.

or sex offender order (or interim sex offender order), before the commencement of SOA 2003, Pt 2[108] if he has complied with the initial notification requirements under SOffA 1997.[109]

Information to be notified

17.59 By SOA 2003, s 83(5), the information that must be notified is:

'(a) the relevant offender's date of birth;
(b) his national insurance number;
(c) his name on the relevant date and, where he used one or more other names on that date, each of those names;
(d) his home address on the relevant date;
(e) his name on the date on which notification is given and, where he uses one or more other names on that date, each of those names;
(f) his home address on the date on which notification is given;
(g) the address of any premises in the United Kingdom at which, at the time the notification is given, he regularly resides or stays;
(h) any prescribed information.'[110]

Paragraphs (c)-(f) address slightly different points in that they are designed to tackle those offenders who change their name or address between the relevant date, ie the date of conviction (or sentence), and the date of initial notification. 'Any prescribed information' in (h) means information prescribed by regulations made by the Secretary of State.[111] The press has reported that the Government has indicated that the first piece of prescribed information will be the e-mail addresses of an offender and also user-names for social networking sites.

17.60 In s 83 and the rest of Pt 2, 'home address' means:

(a) the address of the relevant offender's sole or main residence in the UK; or

(b) where the relevant offender has no such residence, the address or location of a place in the UK where they can regularly be found and, if there is more than one such place, such one of those places as the person may select.[112]

The equivalent to part (b) was not found in SOffA 1997 and is of obvious importance where the relevant offender is itinerant or homeless or of no fixed abode or where he or she lives abroad and has no residence in the UK. It does not refer simply to the address or location of places the offender regularly visits to reside or stay; such addresses have to be notified under s 83(5)(g) anyway.[113] Instead, it refers to places where the offender can regularly be found (eg a park bench or the location of a cardboard box where he can be found each night, or his 'regular' pub or their place of work). It is, therefore, not

---

[108] Ie a relevant offender within SOA 2003, s 81(1).
[109] SOA 2003, s 83(3).
[110] As amended by the insertion of (h) by CJIA 2008, s 142(1)(a); s 142 came into force on 14 July 2008: CO2, art 2, Sch 1, para 45. CJIA 2008, s 142 does not apply to Scotland: s 142(11).
[111] SOA 2003, s 83(5A) (inserted by CJIA 2008, s 142(1)(b)). Such regulations (and those made under SOA 2003, ss 84–86 and 130) must be made by statutory instrument and be subject to the affirmative resolution procedure: SOA 2003, s 138(1) and (2) (s 138(2) as amended by CJIA 2008, s 142(10)). CJIA 2008, s 142 only applies to England and Wales and Northern Ireland (s 142(11)) and came into force on 14 July 2008.
[112] SOA 2003, s 83(7).
[113] SOA 2003, s 83(5)(g).

possible for a relevant offender charged with failing to comply with a notification requirement to escape liability on the ground of no fixed address.

17.61 Failure without reasonable excuse to comply with the requirement to notify personal details is an offence; so is giving false information when notifying details.[114]

NOTIFICATION REQUIREMENTS: CHANGES

17.62 A relevant offender cannot be prevented from changing his or her name or address by the notification requirements' provisions, although other means are potentially available for achieving this (at least in relation to a change of address, including post-release licence conditions and SOPOs).

17.63 By SOA 2003, s 84(1), a relevant offender who:

(a)   uses a name which has not been notified to the police;

(b)   changes his or her home address;

(c)   has resided or stayed, for a qualifying period, at any premises in the UK whose address has not been notified to the police; or

(ca) has been the subject of any prescribed change of circumstances;

(d)   is released from custody pursuant to a court order or from imprisonment, service detention or detention in a hospital,

must within 3 days, beginning with the change, notify the details of that change to the police.[115] In the event of 'any prescribed change of circumstances' (para (ca)),[116] the duty is to notify the prescribed details.[117] In addition, the relevant offender must notify to the police the information listed in s 83(5) (see **17.59**). The disregards under s 83(6), referred to in **17.53**, in respect of periods of remand, etc to custody, imprisonment, etc, detention in a hospital or absence from the UK apply to the determination of the 3-day period.[118]

17.64 The 'qualifying period' referred to in (c) is a period of 7 days, or two or more periods, in any 12-month period, which together amount to 7 days;[119] under SOffA 1997 the period was 14 days.[120] The requirement to notify staying at premises for a qualifying period is obviously designed to tackle those who go on holiday (although separate

---

[114] See **17.112** et seq.
[115] SOA 2003, s 84(1).
[116] (ca) inserted by CJIA 2008, s 142(3). 'Prescribed change of circumstances' means any change occurring in relation to any matter in respect of which information is required to be notified by virtue of s 83(5)(h) (**17.59**), and of a description prescribed by regulations made by the Secretary of State: s 84(5A)(a) (inserted by CJIA 2008, s 142(2), (5)). CJIA 2008, s 142 came into force on 14 July 2008 and does not apply to Scotland (s 142(11)).
[117] 'The prescribed details', in relation to a prescribed change of circumstances, means such details of the change as may be so prescribed: SOA 2003, s 84(5A)(b) (inserted by CJIA 2008, s 142(2), (5)).
[118] SOA 2003, s 84(5).
[119] SOA 2003, s 84(6).
[120] SOffA 1997, s 2(7).

provision exists in respect of those who seek to leave the UK[121]). It follows from (c), for example, that if A, whose home address is in London, goes to Blackpool to stay in a guesthouse for a fortnight, A must notify this change after he has been there for 7 days, and must do so within 3 days from that point of time.

17.65 The requirement to notify changes is particularly important in respect of a change of address; some relevant offenders do not have long-term stable accommodation and have to move frequently. Unless they are notified of a change of address, the police will assume that the relevant offender is still resident at the last notified address until they make a periodic visit to it or discover the offender living elsewhere.

17.66 The wording of the Act potentially creates a loophole through which a person could evade the requirement to notify changes. SOA 2003 states that a person must notify the details where he stays *at* premises for the qualifying period and not *away* from notified premises. Accordingly, if an offender moves address every 6 days there is no obligation on him to notify his whereabouts, so long as he does not return within a period of 12 months.[122]

17.67 The composite qualifying period is designed to tackle those situations where an offender stays for short periods of time within 12 months. Accordingly if an offender A stays for 3 days at address X in January A does not need to notify his stay. If A returns for another 3 days in March he still does not need to notify the address because his total stay is only 6 days. If A returns for a further 3 days in June then he must notify his details within 3 days of the first day of that stay. This means that he could do so upon departure from address X. For all future visits to address X within that 12-month period there is no obligation to notify the police (regardless of the duration of the stay) because the premises have now been notified.

17.68 The ability to make retrospective notification may cause some concern. For example, if a sex offender stays at a holiday park for 8 days in the school holidays, he does not need to notify the police of his residence there until the end of the qualifying period of 7 days, and he then has 3 days to do so. Suppose that the offender only makes notification at the end of the 3-day period. The offender has by then left the park and, other than allowing the police to identify the offender if any crime took place in the park during his stay, there is little else that can be done. The solution to this, and also to cases where the police believe that allowing a dangerous offender to stay away for 7 days would be too risky, would be to apply for a SOPO preventing the offender from staying away for a shorter period of time (even one night) without notifying the police.[123] Specific evidence of risk would be required to obtain this order.

17.69 In some cases, it may be more convenient for a person to make use of the advance notification provision in s 84(2). By s 84(2),[124] a notification under s 84(1) may be given before the name is used, the change of home address or the prescribed change of circumstances occurs, or the qualifying period ends, but in that case the relevant offender must also specify the date when the event is expected to occur. However, if the event to which an advance notification relates occurs more than 2 days before the expected date specified in it, the notification does not affect the duty imposed by

---

121 See **17.80** et seq.
122 Which would obviously bring them within s 84(6)(b).
123 See **18.55** et seq.
124 As amended by CJIA 2008, s 142(2), (4) which does not apply to Scotland.

s 84(1).[125] Moreover, s 84(4) provides that if advance notification is given and the event to which it relates has not occurred by the end of the 3-day period beginning with the expected date specified:

(a)   the notification does not affect the duty imposed by s 84(1) (s 84(4)(a)); and

(b)   the relevant offender must, within a 6-day period beginning with the expected date specified, notify the police that the event did not occur within the 3-day period beginning with the date specified (s 84(4)(b)).

The following example has been given. Offender A intends to move house and informs the police that the change is anticipated to occur on 10 July. In the event, if the change of address occurs on:

•   7 July – this is more than 2 days before the date given at the advance notification and therefore the advance notification is insufficient. A must notify this change as he would any other, ie within the period of 3 days of the change having occurred;

•   8 July – since this is 2 days before the date notified in advance, the advance notification is sufficient and A has complied with the requirements;

•   12 July – since this is within 3 days beginning with the date notified in advance, the advance notification is sufficient and the offender has complied with the requirements;

•   if, by the end of 12 July, the change of address has still not occurred the offender must notify the police on or before 15 July that the change did not take place.[126]

Failure without reasonable excuse to comply with the requirement in s 84(4)(b) is an offence.[127]

17.70 The disregards under s 83(6)[128] in respect of periods of remand, etc to custody, imprisonment, etc, detention in a hospital or absence from the UK apply to the determination of the periods under ss 84(1) and 84(4).[129]

17.71 Failure without reasonable excuse to comply with the requirement to notify changes is an offence; so is giving false information when notifying a change.[130]

NOTIFICATION REQUIREMENTS: PERIODIC RE-NOTIFICATION

17.72 Perhaps the most notable change to the notification requirements brought about by SOA 2003, Pt 2 is the introduction of the requirement to re-notify personal details periodically. Under the scheme initiated by SOffA 1997 an offender notified his or her

---

125   SOA 2003, s 84(3).
126   *Guidance Pt 2*, at pp 14–15.
127   See **17.112** et seq.
128   See **17.53**.
129   SOA 2003, s 84(5).
130   See **17.112** et seq.

details initially and then only needed to re-notify when a change occurred. This led to some concern as to whether it allowed offenders to escape their liability to notify as the police would not necessarily easily detect when a person had moved away from his notified addresses. Research suggested that there was an extremely high compliance rate with the notification requirements,[131] far higher than in comparable countries. However, notwithstanding this compliance rate, concern as to the possibility of non-compliance persisted, culminating in the introduction by SOA 2003 of the requirement periodically to re-notify.

17.73 The basic rule is contained in SOA 2003, s 85(1) which provides that:

> 'A relevant offender must, within the applicable period[132] after each event within [s 85(2)], notify to the police the information set out in section 83(5), unless within that period he has given a notification under section 84(1).'

As to the 'applicable period', see further **17.74**. The information set out in s 83(5) is those details required on initial notification.[133] The events prescribed by s 85(2) are:

'(a)   the commencement of this Part (but only in the case of a person who is a relevant offender from that commencement);
(b)   any notification given by the relevant offender under section 83(1) or 84(1); and
(c)   any notification given by him under subsection (1).'

17.74 'Applicable period' means:

'(a)   in any case where [s 85(6)][134] applies to the relevant offender, such period as may be prescribed by regulations made by the Secretary of State, and
(b)   in any other case, the period of one year.'[135]

Section 85(6) applies to the relevant offender if the last home address notified by him under s 83(1) or 84(1) or 85(1) was the address or location of such a place as is mentioned in s 83(7)(b). The effect of this is that where the last home address notified by the relevant offender is within s 83(7)(b) (referred to in **17.60**), namely, where the offender has no UK residence, the address or location of a place in the UK where he can regularly be found, the applicable period for periodic notification will be a period yet to be prescribed by regulations made by the Secretary of State by statutory instrument subject to the affirmative procedure. In all other cases the period will be one year.

17.75 As a result of s 85(1) an offender with a UK residence must ordinarily re-notify the police one year after the last notification given. Accordingly if an offender became subject to the notification requirements on 1 June then they will ordinarily have to re-notify the police by 1 June next year. The exception to this is where a change has been notified. For example, an offender who became subject to the requirements on 1 June, but then notified that he stayed at a set of premises for a qualifying period on 1 October, is liable next to notify the police on 1 October and not 1 June. The reason for this is that

---

131   Plotnikoff and Woolfson *Where Are They Now? An evaluation of sex offender registration in England and Wales*: Police Research Series Paper 126 (Home Office, 2000).
132   Words substituted by CJIA 2008, s 142(7). CJIA 2008, s 142 came into force on 14 July 2008 and does not apply to Scotland (s 142(11)).
133   See **17.59**
134   Inserted by CJIA 2008, s 142(9). CJIA 2008, s 142 came into force on 14 July 2008 and does not apply to Scotland (s 142(11)).
135   SOA 2003, s 85(5) inserted by CJIA 2008, s 142(9).

whenever a notification is made, including a notification of change, the full details of s 83(5), set out in **17.59**, need to be given and accordingly a full check can be made then. A person will continue to be required to make periodic notifications at the same time every year unless, of course, a change is notified in which case the requirement runs from the date of the notification of change on a rolling basis.

17.76 An offender can give his or her periodic notification in advance of the end of the applicable period. If he or she does so the date of that notification becomes the start date for the next applicable period.

17.77 Special provision is made where the applicable period under s 85(1) would otherwise end whilst a relevant offender is:

- remanded in or committed to custody by a court or (prospectively)[136] kept in service custody;

- serving a prison sentence or a term of service detention;

- detained in a hospital; or

- outside the UK.[137]

In such a case, the period under s 85(1) is to be suspended until the offender's release or return, following which notification must be given within a 3-day period beginning with that occurrence.[138] Thus, if A, remanded in custody in respect of *any* offence at the time when the period referred to in s 85(1) would otherwise end, is then convicted of that offence and sentenced to 18 months' imprisonment, that period is treated as continuing up to the end of a 3-day period after his release from prison after service of his sentence of imprisonment.

17.78 To ensure that the offender does not accidentally forget the periodic requirement it was suggested that the police should remind him of it annually.[139] This raised some concern as to whether it could accidentally disclose the identity of the relevant offender where, for example, he lived in accommodation with shared mail facility. It is, therefore, for the offender to ensure that he remembers to re-notify the details.

17.79 Failure without reasonable excuse to comply with the requirement to re-notify personal details is an offence; so is giving false information when notifying details.[140]

NOTIFICATION REQUIREMENTS: TRAVEL OUTSIDE THE UK

17.80 SOA 2003, s 86 is the relevant provision. The detail of any requirements in this respect is dependent on regulations made by statutory instrument subject to the

---

136   When an amendment made by CJIA 2008, s 148, Sch 26, Pt 2, para 55 is in force. This amendment does not apply to Scotland.
137   SOA 2003, s 85(3) and (4).
138   SOA 2003, s 85(3).
139   *Review SOffA*, at p 23.
140   See **17.112** et seq.

affirmative procedure[141] made by the Secretary of State. But for the present type of notification requirement, offenders found missing from their notified address could successfully maintain that they were abroad at the time and thus not in breach of the requirement to notify a change of address, because the requirements mentioned above only relate to addresses and changes of address in the UK. In addition, but for the present requirement, the police would not be able to warn law enforcement agencies overseas that sex offenders are travelling to their country (which the police do either as a matter of course or depending on the risk) nor apply for a foreign travel order[142] to prohibit travel abroad.

17.81 Section 86(1) provides that the Secretary of State may make regulations requiring relevant offenders who leave the UK (whether indefinitely or for a specified period), or any description of such offenders:

- to give a notification under s 86(2) before they leave; and

- if they subsequently return to the UK, to give a notification under s 86(3).

17.82 A notification under s 86(2) must disclose:

- the date on which the offender will leave the UK;

- the country[143] (or, if there is more than one, the first country) to which the offender will travel and his point of arrival (determined in accordance with the regulations) in that country;

- any other information prescribed by the regulations which the offender holds about his departure from or return to the UK or his movements whilst outside the UK.[144]

17.83 A notification under s 86(3) must disclose any information prescribed by the regulations about the offender's return to the UK.[145]

17.84 Inter alia, the Sexual Offences Act 2003 (Travel Notification Requirements) Regulations 2004[146] require a notification under s 86(2) to be made if the relevant offender intends to leave the UK for a period of 3 days or longer.[147] Where a relevant offender knows the information required to be disclosed by s 86(2)(a) and (b) more than 7 days before the date of his intended departure, he must give a notification which sets out that information and as much of the additional information referred to below as he holds (a) not less than 7 days before that date, or (b) as soon as reasonably practicable but not less than 24 hours before that date, if and only if he has a reasonable excuse for not complying with the 7-day requirement.[148] Where a relevant offender does not know the information required to be disclosed by s 86(2)(a) and (b) more than 7 days before

---

[141] See SOA 2003, s 138(1) and (2).
[142] See **18.135** et seq.
[143] 'Country' includes 'territory' (e g a dependency): SOA 2003, s 133.
[144] SOA 2003, s 86(2).
[145] SOA 2003, s 86(3).
[146] SI 2004/1220.
[147] Ibid, reg 5(1).
[148] Ibid, reg 5(2).

the date of his intended departure (the special case), he must give, not less than 24 hours before that date, a notification which sets out that information and as much of the additional information as he holds.[149]

17.85 In addition to the information required by s 86(2)(a) and (b), a relevant offender must disclose, where he holds such information, the following additional information:

- where he intends to travel to more than one country outside the UK, his intended point of arrival[150] in each such additional country;

- the identity of any carrier or carriers he intends to use for the purposes of his departure from and return to the UK, and of travelling to any other point of arrival;

- details of his accommodation arrangements for his first night outside the UK;

- in a case in which he intends to return to the UK on a particular date, that date; and

- in a case in which he intends to return to the UK at a particular point of arrival, that point of arrival.[151]

17.86 Where a relevant offender has given a notification under s 86(2), and at any time prior to his intended departure from the UK, the information disclosed in that notification becomes inaccurate or incomplete as a statement of all the information mentioned in s 86(2)(a) and (b) and the additional information[152] which he currently holds, he must give a further notification under s 86(2).[153] Such further notification must be given not less than 24 hours before the relevant offender's intended departure from the UK.[154]

17.87 Where a relevant offender who is required to give a notification under s 86(2):

- has left the UK; and

- subsequently returns to the UK,

he must give a notification under s 86(3) of the date of his return to the UK and his point of arrival in the UK within 3 days of his return to the UK.[155] However, a relevant offender need not give a notification under s 86(3) where he gave a relevant notification

---

[149] Ibid, reg 5(3).
[150] For the purposes of SOA 2003, s 86(2)(b) and of the Regulations, a relevant offender's point of arrival in a country is to be determined as follows. Where relevant offenders will arrive in a country by rail, sea or air, their point of arrival is the station, port or airport at which they will first disembark. Where relevant offenders will arrive in a country by any means other than those just mentioned, their point of arrival is the place at which they will first enter the country: reg 4.
[151] Regulation 6.
[152] Ie that whose disclosure is required by reg 6.
[153] Regulation 7(1).
[154] Regulation 7(2).
[155] Regulations 8(1) and (2) and 9.

under s 86(2) which disclosed the date of his intended return to the UK, and disclosed his point of arrival, provided his return to the UK was on that date and at that point of arrival.[156]

17.88 A relevant offender giving notification under s 86(2) or (3) must inform the person to whom he gives the notice of his name and other names he is using, his home address and his date of birth, as currently notified under Pt 2 of the Act.[157]

17.89 A relevant offender giving further notification under s 86(2) of a change in information must inform the person to whom he gives the notification of the police station at which he first gave a notification in respect of the journey in question under s 86(2).[158] This allows the police to ensure that all those involved in the management of the offender know the change to the travel arrangements.

17.90 Failure without reasonable excuse to comply with any foreign travel notification requirements made by regulation is an offence; so is notifying false information when making a notification.[159]

METHOD OF NOTIFICATION

17.91 By SOA 2003, s 87(1), a person must give an initial notification, a notification of change, or a periodic re-notification, by:

- attending at such police station in his local police area[160] as the Secretary of State may by regulations prescribe[161] or, if there is more than one, at any of them; and

- giving an oral notification to any police officer, or to any person authorised ('an authorised person') for the purpose by the officer in charge of the station.[162]

---

[156] Regulation 8(3).

[157] Regulation 10(4).

[158] Regulation 10(5).

[159] See **17.112** et seq.

[160] 'Local police area' means, in relation to a person: (a) the police area in which his 'home address' (see **17.60**) is situated; (b) in the absence of a home address (as where the person lives outside the UK or is of no fixed abode), the police area in which the home address last notified is situated; (c) in the absence of a home address and of any such notification, the police area in which the court which last dealt with the person in a way mentioned in SOA 2003, s 88(4) is situated: s 88(3). In relation to England and Wales, police area has the meaning given to it by the Police Act 1996, s 101(1) (Interpretation Act 1978, s 5 and Sch 1), namely: the police area of one of the 43 local police forces in England and Wales.

By s 88(4), the ways mentioned in s 88(3) are: (a) dealing with a person in respect of a Sch 3 offence or an insanity or disability finding in respect of such an offence; or (b) dealing with a person in respect of an offence of breach of a risk of sexual harm order or of an interim risk of sexual harm order (see **18.202**) or a finding in respect of such an offence; or (c) making, in respect of a person, a NO, interim NO, SOPO, interim SOPO, sex offender order or interim sex offender order. The reference to either type of sex offender order is a transitional provision covering people subject to the notification requirements via such an order before the commencement of Pt 2.

[161] By statutory instrument subject to annulment by either House of Parliament: SOA 2003, s 138(1) and (3). Sexual Offences Act 2003 (Prescribed Police Stations) Regulations 2005, SI 2005/210, reg 2 and Sch 1, prescribe the police stations for this purpose.

[162] A person giving a notification under SOA 2003, s 84(1):
(a) in relation to a prospective change of 'home address'; or
(b) in relation to premises referred to in s 84(1)(c),
may give the notification at a police station that would fall within s 87(1) if the change in home address had already occurred or (as the case may be) if the address of those premises were his home address: s 87(2).

Any notification under s 87 must be acknowledged in writing in such form as the Secretary of State may direct.[163]

17.92 It is not possible for a notification of change to be given by post. The reason for requiring notification in person is that this gives greater confidence that the offender is giving his true address because he has to be physically in the area in order to visit the police station.[164] Because a notification must be given at a prescribed police station in the relevant offender's local police area, a person subjected to notification requirements in one area will be obliged to give a notification (e g a notification of change) in another area if he has moved there by the relevant time to notify.

17.93 Where an initial notification, notification of change or periodic re-notification is given, the relevant offender must, if requested by the police officer or authorised person, allow that officer or person to take his fingerprints, or to photograph[165] any part of him, or to do both,[166] for the purpose of verifying the identity of the relevant offender.[167] The Act does not require the destruction of any fingerprints or photographs once the offender's identity has been established. Failure without reasonable excuse to allow fingerprints or photographs to be taken is an offence.[168]

17.94 It was stated in *Protecting the Public*[169] that the Government was exploring new biometric technologies, such as iris scanning, to eliminate any possibility of evading the system. Since a photograph (which is deemed to include any process by means of which an image may be produced[170]) can be of *a part* of a person, it is submitted that an iris scan of the eye would satisfy these requirements and an offender would have to comply with a request to submit to such procedure.

17.95 A notification of travel outside the UK is required by the Sexual Offences Act 2003 (Travel Notification Requirements) Regulations 2004 to be made in the same way as the other notifications,[171] except that for the purpose of giving a notification before leaving in the special case[172] referred to in **17.84** or in the case of a change of circumstances (**17.86**) the prescribed police station at which the notification is made need not be in the notifier's local police area.[173]

Verification

17.96 SOA 2003, ss 94 and 95 introduce a new power to enable electronic verification of information notified pursuant to the initial notification requirement, the requirement to notify changes or the periodic re-notification requirement under the Act (or pursuant to the initial notification requirement or the requirement to notify changes under SOffA 1997). The police will, however, continue to verify in person information notified.

---

[163] SOA 2003, s 87(3).
[164] *Review SOffA*, at p 22.
[165] 'Photograph' includes any process by means of which an image may be produced: SOA 2003, s 88(2).
[166] SOA 2003, s 87(4).
[167] SOA 2003, s 87(5).
[168] See **17.112** et seq.
[169] *PP*, at para 23.
[170] SOA 2003, s 88(2).
[171] SI 2004/1220, reg 10(1), (3).
[172] See reg 5(3).
[173] Regulation 10(2).

17.97 SOA 2003, s 94[174] empowers a chief officer of police, the National Policing Improvement Agency and the Serious Organised Crime Agency (SOCA) to supply to the Secretary of State or a Northern Ireland Department (*or a person providing services to the Secretary of State or Department in connection with a relevant function*) information for verification purposes. The reference to 'a person providing services to the Secretary of State' is to a relevant official of the Driver and Vehicle Licensing Authority, the UK Passport Service or the Department for Work and Pensions. These agencies have been identified because the majority of sex offenders will provide information of the relevant types when they apply for a driving licence, for a passport (or a renewed one) or for a social security benefit or pension. Section 95[175] provides for the verification report to be sent to a chief officer of police or SOCA, who may use it for any purpose related to the prevention, detection, investigation or prosecution of *any* offence, but for no other purpose. Any discrepancy revealed by the report will be investigated by the local police.[176]

YOUNG OFFENDERS: PARENTAL DIRECTIONS

17.98 The rules about notification requirements generally apply in respect of a relevant offender who was under 18 *at the time of the offence*, although except in respect of the most serious offences only if the young offender has been sentenced to a custodial sentence of 12 months or more. However, consistent with the notion of parental responsibility and to ensure that young offenders attend to give any notification under the notification requirements, SOA 2003, s 89 provides for the making of a parental direction against an individual with parental responsibility.

17.99 The following individuals can have parental responsibility[177] for a child:

- both parents, if married to each other at the time of the child's birth;

- the mother, where they were not so married;

- the father, where they were not so married, if he acquires parental responsibility (and has not ceased to have it) under ChA 1989;

- a step-parent[178] if he or she acquires parental responsibility (and has not ceased to have it) under ChA 1989;

- a guardian or guardians;

- a person in whose favour a residence order is in force.[179]

---

[174] As amended by the Serious Organised Crime and Police Act 2005 and the Police and Justice Act 2006.

[175] As amended by the Serious Organised Crime and Police Act 2005.

[176] Paul Goggins MP, HC Committee, Standing Committee B (October 2003), col 394.

[177] 'Parental responsibility' has the same meaning as in the Children Act (ChA) 1989 or the corresponding Northern Irish legislation, and 'parental responsibilities' (the term used in Scotland) has the same meaning as in Pt 1 of the Children (Scotland) Act 1995: s 133. In ChA 1989, 'parental responsibility' means all the rights, duties, powers, responsibilities and authority which by law a parent of a child has in relation to the child and his property: ChA 1989, s 3(1).

[178] Ie a person who is married to, or in a civil partnership with, a parent holding parental responsibility.

[179] See ChA 1989, ss 2, 5(6), and 12(2).

17.100   On the other hand, a foster parent or grandparent with de facto care of the child does not have parental responsibility. Where more than one individual has parental responsibility the order must be made against one of them, described by s 89 (and hereafter) as 'the parent'. Because a parental direction can only be made against an individual, it cannot be made against a local authority with care of a child under a care order, even though the order gives it parental responsibility.[180]

17.101   When a parental direction is made:

- the notification obligations that would otherwise be imposed on the young offender are treated instead as obligations on the parent; and

- the parent must ensure that the young offender attends at the police station with him or her, when a notification is being given.[181]

Parental directions do not require the parent's consent but it would be appropriate for the court to seek the views of the parent before making a direction.

17.102   A failure without reasonable excuse by the parent to give the necessary notification pursuant to a parental direction is an offence. In addition, a notifying parent commits an offence if, without reasonable excuse, he or she fails to ensure that the young offender attends with him or her.[182] In either case, the young offender does not commit an offence.

17.103   A parental direction takes immediate effect and applies:

- until the young offender attains 18;[183] or

- for such shorter period as the court may, at the time the direction is given, direct.[184]

A parental direction can be made as part of the disposal in a criminal case or on an application by the police.

As part of disposal

17.104   SOA 2003, s 89(1) provides that, where a relevant offender[185] within s 80(1)(a)–(c) or s 81(1)(a)–(c)[186] is under 18 (or under 16 in Scotland) *when dealt with by the court in respect of a Sch 3 offence or finding in relation to such an offence*, the court *may* make a parental direction in respect of an individual ('the parent') having parental responsibility (parental 'responsibilities' in Scotland) for the young offender.

17.105   Because a direction can only be made against persons under 18 (16 in Scotland) when the court deals with them in respect of the conviction or finding, a direction cannot be made by an English court against someone who was 17 when convicted of the

---

[180]   ChA 1989, s 33(3).
[181]   SOA 2003, s 89(2).
[182]   See **17.112** et seq.
[183]   16 if the direction is given by a court in Scotland.
[184]   SOA 2003, s 89(3).
[185]   As defined by SOA 2003, s 80(2): s 133. See **17.9**.
[186]   See **17.10** and **17.13**.

Sch 3 offence, if that person is 18 when sentenced. Whether or not the court makes a parental direction will depend on whether it thinks it appropriate to do so.

Applications by police

17.106 SOA 2003, s 89(4) provides that a chief officer of police[187] may, by complaint[188] to a magistrates' court, apply for a parental direction in respect of a relevant offender ('the defendant'):

- who resides in the chief officer's police area, or who the chief officer believes is in or is intending to come to that police area; and

- who the chief officer believes is under 18.

17.107 This would be suitable where an adolescent is made the subject of the notification requirements after a reprimand or final warning has been administered to him. However, it is clearly not limited to these circumstances and it could, for example, be used as an alternative to prosecuting an offender after he fails to notify a change or make a periodic notification. In these circumstances the police may legitimately believe that it would be more appropriate to seek a parental direction which would place the emphasis onto the parent. No application can be dealt with where the offender is aged 18 or over[189] and the magistrates' court has discretion as to whether to impose such an order.[190]

Variation, renewal or discharge

17.108 Various people can apply to the 'appropriate court' for an order varying, renewing or discharging a parental direction.[191] The 'appropriate court' is the Crown Court where the parental direction was made by the Court of Appeal, otherwise it means the court that made the direction.[192] An application to the Crown Court must be made in accordance with rules of court;[193] otherwise it is made by complaint to the magistrates' court.[194]

17.109 The following people can apply for an order to vary, renew or discharge an order:

- the young offender;

- the parent;

- the chief officer of police for the area in which the young offender resides;

---

[187] It is clear from *R (Chief Constable of West Midlands Police) v Birmingham Magistrates' Court* [2003] ACD 18 that it is possible for a chief constable to delegate this power to another named officer. Although this case related to an anti-social behaviour order, its reasoning is equally applicable to the other orders in Pt 2.
[188] See **18.70**.
[189] SOA 2003, s 89(1).
[190] Accordingly their decision is reviewable only where it can be shown that they have acted illegally, irrationally or in a procedurally improper way.
[191] SOA 2003, s 90(1).
[192] SOA 2003, s 90(5).
[193] No relevant rules have been made.
[194] SOA 2003, s 90(3).

- a chief officer of police who believes the young offender is in, or is intending to come, to his police area; and

- where the direction was made on an application under s 89(4), the chief officer of police who made the application.[195]

17.110 After hearing the applicant and any other person listed above, the court may make any order varying, renewing or discharging the direction, as it considers appropriate.[196] An example of a case where an application for a variation is likely to be made is where a parental direction is made against a father who subsequently dies or divorces the mother and the young offender goes to live with his mother. A case where an application for a discharge is likely to be made is where the parent can no longer control the young offender and thus cannot ensure that the young offender attends with the parent to make the requisite notifications. In such a case the court may, and arguably should, decide that the liability for failure should revert to the offender himself, in which case it will discharge the parental direction. Alternatively it may decide that the order should be varied so as to apply to another person with parental responsibility.

17.111 An application for renewal would be made where the direction is for a fixed time and it is decided that renewing it would be desirable so that it does not expire.

OFFENCES RELATING TO NOTIFICATION

17.112 The notification requirements are backed up by penal sanction. There are two types of offences:

- a failure to comply with a notification requirement (or an associated requirement for fingerprinting or photographing or, where a parental direction has been made, to ensure that the young offender attends when a notification is given); and

- notifying false information when giving notification.[197]

Both types of offence are defined by s 91(1). An offence under s 91 is triable either way and punishable with a maximum of 5 years' imprisonment on conviction on indictment.[198]

Class of offence[199]	3	SOA 2003, s 72 applies	✘
Notification requirements	✘	SOPO	✘
CJA 2003, Sch 15 applies	✘	Serious specified offence	✘

---

[195] SOA 2003, s 90(2).

[196] SOA 2003, s 90(4).

[197] SOA 2003, s 91(1).

[198] SOA 2003, s 91(2). For maximum on summary conviction: see **1.43**. There is no sentencing guideline in respect of these offences. For sentencing cases, see *Daly* [2008] 1 Cr App R (S) 105; *Adams* [2004] 2 Cr App R (S) 78; *Spencer* [2004] EWCA Crim 3216; *Bowman* [2006] 2 Cr App R (S) 268; *Clarke* [2003] 1 Cr App R (S) 6.

[199] See **1.49**.

Review of lenient sentence	✘	Special provisions of CYPA 1933	✘
Detention of young offender for specified period			✘

17.113 Proceedings for an offence under s 91 may be commenced in any court with jurisdiction in any place where the defendant resides or is found.[200]

Failing to notify, etc

17.114 SOA 2003, s 91(1)(a) provides that a person commits an offence if he or she fails, without reasonable excuse, to comply with:

- s 83(1) (initial notification requirement);

- s 84(1) (requirement to notify changes);

- s 84(4)(b) (requirement to notify non-occurrence of events in respect of which advance notice has been given);

- s 85(1) (requirement periodically to re-notify);

- s 87(4) (requirement to allow fingerprints to be taken or to be photographed when notification given);

- s 89(2)(b) (requirement, when a parental direction has been made, that the parent ensures that the young offender attends with them when notification given by the parent); or

- any requirement imposed by regulations made under s 86(1) (notification requirements in respect of travel outside the UK).

17.115 It has been held in other offences that whether there is a reasonable excuse depends on whether a reasonable person would think the excuse reasonable in the circumstances,[201] but as a matter of law there are limitations (imposed by the courts) as to what a reasonable person might think.[202] This is likely to be the approach taken by the courts in relation to the present provision. In terms of other offences of 'failing', the limits of what a reasonable person would think a reasonable excuse have been particularly well developed in respect of offences of failing to supply a specimen under the drink-drive legislation. It is submitted that the case-law there can be applied by analogy to the present offences. According to that case-law, a reasonable person would not think it a reasonable excuse that the defendant mistakenly believed that the requirement to notify was invalid.[203] On the other hand, the fact that the defendant was physically or mentally incapable of complying (or there is a substantial risk to his health or safety if he complies) with the duty to notify in the order is capable of amounting to a reasonable excuse.[204] This would, for example, cover cases where the defendant is in hospital following an accident or is confined to bed by illness or injury. Likewise, if the

---

[200] SOA 2003, s 91(4).
[201] *Bryan v Mott* (1975) 62 Cr App Rep 71.
[202] Ibid; *Evans v Hughes* [1972] 3 All ER 412.
[203] *Downey* [1970] RTR 257; *Reid* [1973] 3 All ER 1020.
[204] *Lennard* [1973] 2 All ER 831.

offences are construed as ones of strict liability, it would seem that the fact that the defendant is mentally incapable of understanding what he is required to do (as where he is a recent immigrant with little understanding of English) can amount to a reasonable excuse.[205] An alleged linguistic difficulty, however, must be scrutinised very carefully.[206]

17.116 It remains to be seen whether there could be a reasonable excuse if the failure was due to difficulty in complying or the disruptive effect of complying, as when one of the defendant's children or parents was ill or his employer would not give him time off to report, or (in the case of an offence relating to s 89(2)(b)) that the parent has taken all reasonable steps to get the young offender to attend at the police station with him.

17.117 If a person initially has a reasonable excuse for a failure to make a notification under s 83(1), s 84(1) or s 85(1) or under regulations made under s 86(1), but subsequently the reasonable excuse ceases, and he still fails to make the notification, he commits an offence under s 91(1)(a) on the day on which he first fails without reasonable excuse to comply with the requirement in question.[207]

17.118 The defendant has an evidential burden of raising reasonable excuse.[208]

17.119 An offence under s 91(1)(a) is a continuing offence in respect of a failure, without reasonable excuse, to make a notification; it continues to be committed from the first day of that failure and continues throughout the period of 'the failure' (without reasonable excuse). This is important because a person must not be prosecuted under s 91 more than once in respect of the same failure,[209] so that there can only be one prosecution under s 91 for a 6-month continuing failure without reasonable excuse.

17.120 Of course, if a person is convicted of an offence under s 91(1)(a) and then fails again to make a notification under the same provision, he commits a new offence and may be prosecuted again. The non-compliance offences have rarely been committed; the compliance rate has been around 97%.[210]

Proof by certificate

17.121 A conviction of an offence under s 91(1)(a) will depend on proof that there was a notification requirement which in turn will depend on whether there has been a conviction, finding or caution in respect of a Sch 3 offence. Proof of such a conviction, etc by certificate is dealt with by s 92.

Court certificate

17.122 The first type of certificate is a court certificate. If a court by or before any date the person is convicted of a Sch 3 offence, or is the subject of a finding of not guilty by reason of insanity or a finding of disability in respect of such an offence:

(a)   states in open court:

---

[205]   *Chief Constable of Avon and Somerset Constabulary v Singh* [1988] RTR 107.
[206]   *DPP v Whalley* [1991] RTR 661.
[207]   SOA 2003, s 91(3).
[208]   *Polychronakis v Richards & Jerrom Ltd* [1998] Env LR 347; *O'Boyle* [1973] RTR 445; *Mallows v Harris* [1979] RTR 404.
[209]   SOA 2003, s 91(3).
[210]   *PP*, at para 19.

(i) that on that date he has been convicted, found not guilty by reason of insanity or found to be under a disability and to have done the act charged against him; and

(ii) that the offence in question is a Sch 3 offence; and

(b) certifies those facts, whether at the time or subsequently,

the certificate is, for the purposes of Pt 2, evidence of those facts.[211]

Police certificate

17.123 Where someone on any date is cautioned, reprimanded or finally warned in England, Wales or Northern Ireland in respect of a Sch 3 offence, and the constable:

(a) informs the person that he has been cautioned, etc on that date and that the offence in question is a Sch 3 offence; and

(b) certifies those facts, whether at the time or subsequently, in such forms as the Secretary of State prescribes,

the certificate is, for the purposes of Pt 2, evidence of those facts.[212]

Notifying false information

17.124 SOA 2003, s 91(1)(b) provides that a person commits an offence if he notifies to the police information that he knows to be false in purported compliance with:

- s 83(1) (initial notification requirements);

- s 84(1) (requirement to notify changes);

- s 85(1) (requirement periodically to re-notify); or

- any requirement imposed by regulations under s 86(1).

The information must actually be false because one cannot know, as opposed to believe, that a thing is false unless it is false, but it is not required to be false in a material particular.

USE OF THE INFORMATION

17.125 Although the requirement to notify was established in SOffA 1997 no detail was given as to how this information should be used. This position has largely been replicated by SOA 2003 although other legislative changes and government policy provides some assistance.

---

[211] SOA 2003, s 92(2).
[212] SOA 2003, s 92(3), (4).

Information about release or transfer

17.126 Ensuring that a relevant offender is tracked and complies at the relevant time with the notification requirements can be complicated if he is removed from society whilst serving a prison sentence or service detention, or is detained in a hospital. SOffA 1997 did not explain how this would be achieved but the Act was eventually amended to allow the Secretary of State to make regulations requiring notice to be given by the person responsible for such an offender to persons prescribed in the regulations (eg a chief constable) of any occasion when an offender is released or a different person becomes responsible for the offender (eg when transferred between prisons). No regulations were ever drafted but a similar provision is now contained within SOA 2003, s 96(2). Again, no regulations have been made even though it was stated in 2001 that work on the regulations was 'well under way'.[213] The notice requirements were conceived for a reason and it is submitted that regulations should be made.

Risk assessment

17.127 It is clear that the police will ordinarily conduct a risk assessment on an offender who notifies his details to the police, and indeed will conduct further risk assessments as required.[214] In the majority of situations an offender will co-operate with the risk assessment process, not least because it is in his interests to do so as this will affect the way that he is managed. However, during the review of SOffA 1997 concern was raised that the police had no power of entry to a suspect's house: an offender could legitimately refuse to co-operate with the police. The Review concluded that there was no need for such a power[215] but the matter returned to prominence in 2005 when a Private Member's Bill was unsuccessfully introduced to provide such a power.[216]

17.128 The Private Member's Bill was resisted by the Government and the Association of Chief Police Officers (ACPO), both of which argued that the Bill was unnecessary and disproportionate.[217] The Bill was, however, supported by the Metropolitan Police Commissioner.[218] In early 2006 there was a reversal in Government thinking and policy, culminating in the passing of the VCRA 2006, s 58. This section inserts a new section, s 96B, into SOA 2003[219] which allows a senior police officer[220] of the relevant police force[221] to apply to a justice of the peace for a warrant to enter premises to conduct a risk assessment on a relevant offender[222] and to search the premises for that purpose.[223]

17.129 The warrant can only be granted where a justice of the peace is satisfied that:

---

[213] *Review SOffA*, at p 4.
[214] *PP*, at para 22.
[215] *Review SOffA*, at p 38.
[216] SOA 2003 (Amendment) Bill.
[217] See Thorp and Berman *The Sexual Offences Act 2003 (Amendment Bill)*: House of Commons Research Paper 05/19, at p 23.
[218] Ibid.
[219] SOA 2003, s 96B.
[220] Ie an officer of the rank of superintendent or above: SOA 2003, s 96B(10).
[221] Ie the police force maintained for the police area in which the premises in respect of which the application is made or the warrant is issued are situated: ibid.
[222] SOA 2003, s 96B(9).
[223] SOA 2003, s 96B(1). See Home Office Circular 17/2007.

- the address of each set of premises specified in the application is either the address last notified to the police as his home address by a relevant offender, or there are reasonable grounds to believe that a relevant offender resides or may regularly be found there;

- the relevant offender is not in custody by order of a court, serving a sentence of imprisonment, detained in hospital or outside the UK;

- it is necessary for a constable to enter and search the premises for the purpose of assessing the risks posed by the relevant offender; and

- on at least two occasions a constable has sought entry to the premises in order to search them for that purpose and has been unable to gain access.[224]

The warrant must specify the one or more sets of premises to which it applies.[225]

17.130   As can be seen in **17.129**, the justice of the peace does not have to be satisfied that there are reasonable grounds for suspecting that the relevant offender is in breach of the notification requirements. The power under s 96B is intended to enable the police to gather all the information they need about a relevant offender for the purposes of assessing the risk he poses, even if he is in apparent compliance with the notification requirements and there are insufficient grounds to believe that he has committed another sexual offence.[226]

17.131   Section 96B is undoubtedly an interference with the offender's rights under ECHR, Art 8(1).[227] However, the Government would (rightly) seek to argue that the interference is justified under Art 8(2). Justices of the peace will be required to think carefully about granting warrants under this section. As noted, ACPO was initially concerned that this would be a disproportionate interference,[228] but it will be for a justice to consider this in each case. Where a justice is persuaded that the offender poses a risk of harm and the offender has not voluntarily complied with the risk assessment, it may be proportionate to grant a warrant. Early research indicated that the vast majority of offenders comply with risk assessments,[229] but the fact that some do not must give rise to concern by the authorities. The power under s 96B, if exercised properly, will assist in the assessment and management of offenders.

Managing sex offenders

17.132   CJCSA 2000, s 67(2) placed a statutory duty on the chief constable and local probation board to establish procedures to assess and manage, inter alia, sexual or

---

[224]   SOA 2003, s 96B(1), (2), (3), (4).

[225]   SOA 2003, s 96B(5). The warrant may authorise the constable executing it to use reasonable force if necessary to enter and search the premises: s 96B(6). The warrant may authorise entry to and search of premises on more than one occasion if, on the application, the justice of the peace is satisfied that it is necessary to authorise multiple entries in order to achieve the purpose of assessing the risks posed by the relevant offender: s 96B(7).

[226]   Home Office Circular 17/2007, para 6.

[227]   Right to respect for private and family life, home and correspondence.

[228]   See **17.128**.

[229]   Plotnikoff and Woolfson *Where are they now? An Evaluation of Sex Offender Registration in England and Wales*: Police Research Series Paper 126 (Home Office, 2000).

violent offenders. These arrangements (known as MAPPA) had to be kept under review[230] and an annual report had to be published that explained how the agency had discharged its duty.[231]

17.133 CJA 2003 repealed CJCSA 2000, s 67 and replaced the arrangements made under it. The relevant provision is CJA 2003, s 325. The replacement is, in essence, simply an extension of the former procedures. The statutory duty is on the 'responsible authority' for each area, ie the chief constable, local probation board and the Government minister exercising function in relation to prisons (the latter, in essence, meaning the Prison Service) acting jointly.[232] Bringing the Prison Service on board was considered appropriate because the communication between the Prison Service, probation service and the police was not always ideal. This was particularly so where a sex offender had been later sentenced to imprisonment for a non-sex offence. When released the police and probation service were not always informed.

17.134 Although the statutory duty is placed on the three bodies referred to above, the MAPPA itself has always involved other authorities. CJA 2003, s 325(3) places a reciprocal 'duty to co-operate' between the responsible authority and:

- every youth offending team established for an area any part of which falls within the relevant area;

- the ministers of the Crown exercising functions in relation to social security, child support, war pensions, employment and training;

- every local education authority[233] any part of whose area falls within the relevant area;

- every local housing authority[234] or social services authority[235] any part of whose area falls within the relevant area;

- every registered social landlord[236] which provides or manages residential accommodation in the relevant area in which relevant offenders reside;

- every health authority or strategic health authority any part of whose area falls within the relevant area;

- every primary care trust or local health board any part of whose area falls within the relevant area;

- every NHS trust[237] for any part of whose area falls within the relevant area; and

---

[230] CJCSA 2000, s 67(3).
[231] CJCSA 2000, s 67(4), (5).
[232] CJA 2003, s 325(1), (2). If there is no local probation board for the areas, a relevant provider of probation services acts in lieu of such a board: ibid, s 325(2) (as amended).
[233] For the meaning of this see the Education Act 1996.
[234] This term has the same meaning as in the Housing Act (HA) 1985: CJA 2003, s 325(9).
[235] Ie a local authority for the purposes of the Local Authority Social Services Act 1970: ibid.
[236] This term has the same meaning as in the HA 1996, Pt 1: ibid.
[237] This term has the same meaning as in the National Health Service Act 2006: ibid.

- every person who is designated by the Secretary of State by order for the purposes of s 325(3) as a provider of electronic monitoring services.[238]

17.135 The actual arrangements required are not set out in CJA 2003 but they include the exchange of information, with the Act providing the authorities with the power to exchange this information.[239] This power is in addition to any pre-existing powers but would mean that the sharing of information would not be considered to be a breach of either the Data Protection Act 1998 or the Human Rights Act 1998 so long as it is necessary and proportionate to do so. CJA 2003 requires each MAPPA to create a memorandum of understanding between all the parties that sets out what the duty to co-operate involves.[240]

17.136 The Secretary of State has the power to issue guidance to the responsible authorities on how to discharge their functions.[241] In March 2003 such guidance was issued which clarified matters. The first point is that the duty to co-operate applies only in respect to the management of offenders and not, for example, the review of the multi-agency arrangements.[242] The guidance also reinforces the fact that the duty is reciprocal,[243] ie that each MAPPA has a duty to co-operate with the agencies and not just the other way around. This could be particularly important where the relevant authorities are, for example, housing an offender who is considered to be dangerous.

Functions of a MAPPA

17.137 The Guidance for MAPPAs states that there are four functions of a MAPPA:

(a) the identification of offenders;

(b) the sharing of relevant information;

(c) the assessment of the risk of serious harm; and

(d) the management of that risk.[244]

Each of these functions is simple to state but perhaps less easy to put into practice. Not all are relevant to this chapter, or indeed this book,[245] but certainly the identification, assessment and management of offenders should be considered briefly. The identification of offenders is perhaps the key task and the establishment of VISOR[246] has undoubtedly assisted this. Offenders are classified into three broad categories:

- *Category 1 offenders* are registered sex offenders, ie those subject to the notification requirements.

---

[238] CJA 2003, s 325(6).
[239] CJA 2003, s 325(4).
[240] CJA 2003, s 325(5).
[241] CJA 2003, s 325(8).
[242] *The MAPPA Guidance* Probation Circular 54/2004, at para 180.
[243] Ibid, at para 181.
[244] Ibid, at para 34.
[245] A comprehensive discussion of the position is presented in Cobley *Sex Offenders: Law, Policy and Practice* (Jordans, 2nd edn, 2005).
[246] See **17.2**.

- *Category 2 offenders* are violent offenders and other sex offenders, for example, those convicted of a non-Sch 3 offence or an offender convicted of an offence prior to SOffA 1997.

- *Category 3 offenders* are all other offenders requiring MAPPA supervision, ie those convicted of other offences who may cause serious harm to the public.[247]

17.138 Each offender is risk assessed in order to discharge function (c). Common risk assessment tools are used, normally *OASys* or *Risk Matrix 2000*,[248] and the results of this will be discussed by the MAPPA. The risk assessment allows offenders to be sorted into one of three categories which alters the way in which they are managed:

- Level 1: ordinary risk management;

- Level 2: local inter-agency risk management;

- Level 3: MAPPP – Multi-Agency Public Protection Panels.[249]

17.139 Level 1 ordinary risk management means, in essence, that an offender will be managed without specific reference to the MAPPA. The police will continue to monitor and assess the offender through the notification requirements and the probation service will continue to be involved, where appropriate, depending on the conditions of any licence or community sentence.

17.140 Level 2 risk means that a more defined plan of action is required. It ordinarily means that more than the statutory partners[250] are required to monitor and manage the offender. An offender who has access to children may well be deemed a level 2 risk because it is quite possible that social services will be required to participate in the monitoring of those children to discharge their duty under ChA 1989. Level 2 risk offenders may also include situations where special housing may be needed or where an offender has a history of mental or other health problems.

17.141 The highest level of risk management is level 3, which is referred to a MAPPP. This is a specific panel that is constituted by members of the statutory agencies and, where necessary, other agencies. The Panel will meet to discuss the specific offender and produce a plan of action that relates specifically to the offender. Level 3 offenders will ordinarily be the lowest in number and the resource implications of such management can be high since it could involve, for example, surveillance or other proactive forms of control. Any application by the police for a SOPO[251] or FTO[252] is likely to be made following discussion by the relevant MAPPP.

---

247 *MAPPA Guidance*, n 242 above, at para 52.
248 See *Assessment and Management of Sex Offenders*: Probation Circular 17/2007 (Home Office, July 2007). *Risk Matrix 2000* is the more complex and relies on psychological profiling and statistical analysis to identify the potential risk an offender poses. *OASys* is more a process allowing continual risk assessment and management to be made.
249 *MAPPA Guidance*, n 242 above, at para 109.
250 Ie police, prison service and probation service.
251 See **18.55** et seq.
252 See **18.135** et seq.

Community disclosure

17.142 The issue that is perhaps most controversial concerns the circumstances under which the responsible authority, usually through the MAPPP, is able to disclose the identity of a sex offender. SOffA 1997 was silent as to whether the police would be able to disclose to the community the identities of sex offenders, something that was controversial at the time, and this position was replicated under SOA 2003. Disclosure is perhaps one of the most misunderstood issues since it happens relatively frequently. Moreover, disclosure is usually between authorities, for example, a school being told about a sex offender in the area, and not direct to a community.[253]

17.143 Following the murder of Sarah Payne, an 8-year-old schoolgirl, the *News of the World* established a campaign for 'Sarah's Law', which it described as a UK version of Megan's Law in the US. The precise details of Sarah's Law have never been fully set out although it would appear that, at the very least, Sara Payne (the mother of Sarah) never intended it to be a regime applying to all offenders but simply to those considered to be the most serious.[254] The Government has consistently rejected general disclosure,[255] expressing fear as to whether it would undermine notification compliance or incite violence. In respect of the latter, it is noteworthy that, when the *News of the World* has on a number of occasions displayed the photographs of convicted child sex offenders, this has occasioned violence. This, and other isolated incidents, led the Supreme Court of Ireland to argue that notification requirements were, contrary to what the European Court of Human Rights has held, punitive.[256] The most prominent example of violence purportedly caused by community disclosure is that of the riots in the Paulsgrove Estate in Portsmouth. These riots are often cited as being a reason why routine community disclosures should not occur; but research has suggested that the riots were not sparked by the media disclosing the identity of sex offenders residing in the estate but rather that they were caused by the mismanagement of the sex offenders by the police.[257]

17.144 Interim guidance,[258] viewed favourably by the Court of Appeal in *Chief Constable of the North Wales Police ex parte Thorpe*,[259] about the sharing of information with someone with a legitimate interest indicated that information should only be revealed where the risk to the public or a section of it outweighed the offender's right to a private life. Further guidance is given by paras 78–95 of the *MAPPA Guidance*,[260] which applies not only to sex offenders but also to other dangerous offenders. Both pieces of guidance take into account the relevant law, including the ECHR.[261]

---

[253] The latter would now be empowered through the MAPPA reciprocal duty to co-operate: **17.134**.

[254] Payne *A Mother's Story* (Hodder & Stoughton, 2004), at p 94.

[255] *Review SOffA*, at p 4.

[256] *CC v Ireland* [2006] IESC 33; cf *Adamson v United Kingdom* (1999) 28 EHRR CD 209 and *R v United Kingdom* (2007) 44 EHRR SE 17.

[257] Williams and Thompson 'Vigilance or Vigilante: The Paulsgrove Riots and Policing Paedophiles in the Community' (2004) 77 Police Journal 99.

[258] *Managing Information Acquired under the Provisions of the Sex Offenders Act 1997*: Home Office Circular 39/1997, Appendix A.

[259] [1999] QB 396; discussed by Mullender [1998] PL 384 and Power [1999] Crim LR at pp 11–16. See also *Local Authority in the Midlands ex parte LM* [2000] 1 FLR 612.

[260] Home Office Probation Circular 25/2003.

[261] The relevant law was discussed by Ward *Criminal Sentencing: The New Law* (Jordans, 1997), at paras 5.44–5.50. The only significant change since that discussion has been the replacement of the Data Protection Act (DPA) 1984 by the DPA 1998.

17.145 Despite the fact that the police do manage offenders, pressure has continued to grow for the introduction of 'Sarah's Law', in part because much of the disclosure takes place away from the gaze of the general public.[262] The then Home Secretary, John Reid, announced that the Government would attempt to identify circumstances under which disclosure would be considered.[263] The Government stated that it did not intend there to be general disclosure[264] but that more detail should be given as to the circumstances when disclosure takes place. This was then followed by a commitment to introduce a legal duty to be placed on MAPPAs that would require them to consider disclosure in every case.[265]

17.146 This proposal was taken forward by CJIA 2008, s 140[266] which inserted ss 327A and 327B and Sch 34A into CJA 2003. CJA 2003, s 327A:

- requires the responsible authority for each area to consider whether to disclose information in its possession about the relevant convictions, cautions or findings of any child sex offender managed by it to any particular member of the public. A 'child sex offender' is any person who has been convicted of an offence listed in Sch 34A (below), or been found not guilty of such an offence by reason of insanity, or been found to be under a disability and to have done the act charged in respect of it, or been cautioned in respect of such an offence.[267] 'Information about the relevant convictions of a child sex offender' refers to information about convictions, findings or cautions in respect of a Sch 34A offence or about anything under the law of a country or territory outside England and Wales which in the responsible authority's opinion corresponds to any conviction, finding or caution of a Sch 34A offence (however described);[268]

- creates a presumption that the responsible authority should disclose information where it has reasonable cause to believe that a child sex offender poses a risk of causing serious harm to any particular child[269] or children or to children of any particular description, and that the disclosure of that information to the particular member of the public is necessary to protect the child or children at risk from serious harm (see **17.148**) caused by the offender;

- empowers the responsible authority to disclose[270] such information about the sex offender's previous convictions as it considers appropriate to disclose to the member of the public concerned, and to impose conditions (to prevent further dissemination) on the member of the public to whom the information is disclosed; and

- requires the responsible authority for each area to compile and maintain a record about its decisions relating to the discharge of its functions under CJA 2003,

---

262 See Gillespie 'Smoke and Mirrors' (2007) 157 NLJ 565.
263 *Review of the Protection of Children From Sex Offenders* (Home Office, July 2007).
264 Ibid, at p 10.
265 Ibid, at p 11.
266 In force 14 July 2008: CJIA 2008 (Commencement No 2 and Transitional and Saving Provisions) Order 2008, art 2(1), Sch 1, para 43.
267 CJA 2003, s 327B(3), (4). 'Cautioned' includes 'reprimanded or warned' under CDA 1998, s 65: CJA 2003, s 327B(9).
268 CJA 2003, s 327B(5).
269 Ie someone under the age of 18: CJA 2003, s 327B(2).
270 Any disclosure under CJA 2003, s 327A must be made as soon as is reasonably practicable in the circumstances: s 327A(6).

s 327A, including its reasons for deciding to disclose or not to disclose information, the information disclosed, any conditions imposed and the name and address of the person to whom it is disclosed.

17.147 All the offences listed in CJA 2003, Sch 34A are offences under English law and are listed in SOA 2003, Sch 3 (set out in **17.21**) with the addition italicised below, but are not subject to any age or sentence condition prescribed for the purposes of Sch 3. Where an offence can be committed in respect of an adult, it must, for the purposes of Sch 34A, be committed (or be intended to be committed) against a person under 18. The offences listed in Sch 34A fall into two groups, those repealed by SOA 2003 and those which still exist. They are offences:

- under any of SOA 1956, ss 1, 5, 6, 10, 12–16 or s 28; ICA 1960, s 1; *Theft Act 1968, s 9 (if burglary committed with intent to rape)*; CLA 1977, s 54; and SO(A)A 2000, s 3; and

- under any of SOA 2003, ss 1–19, 25 and 26, 30–41, 47–50, 61–63, 66 or s 67; PoCA 1978, s 1; CJA 1988, s 160; CEMA 1979, s 170 (where prohibited goods included indecent photograph of person under 18); and (when in force) CJIA 2008, s 63 (where extreme pornographic image showing person under 18).

A reference to an offence in Sch 34A also includes inchoate or secondary liability in relation to it or to a corresponding offence under Service law.

17.148 By CJA 2003, s 327B(6), references in s 327A to serious harm caused by a child sex offender are references to serious physical or psychological harm caused by the offender committing any of the non-repealed offences listed in Sch 34A.

17.149 Whether CJA 2003, s 327A will change anything practically is less certain. In *Thorpe*[271] the Court stated there should not be a presumption in favour of disclosure. It is likely that a challenge will be made against the presumption in s 327A on the basis that it is incompatible with the ECHR. *Thorpe* discussed this jurisprudence and there was certainly an implication that a presumption would be contrary to ECHR, Art 8. However, a statutory duty obviously provides 'legality' and the specific reference to 'necessity' (which must encompass proportionality) may mean that it should be possible to comply with Art 8 on a case-by-case basis, especially since the European Court of Human Rights has traditionally given considerable latitude to states in the management of sex offenders.

---

[271] [1999] QB 396; see **17.144**.

Chapter 18

PREVENTATIVE ORDERS

18.1   The Sexual Offences Act (SOA) 2003, Pt 2 introduced the following types of order, all but the last of which impose notification requirements:

- notification orders (NOs) and interim NOs (whose sole effect is to subject someone convicted or cautioned abroad for sex offences of a specified type to the notification requirements);

- sexual offences prevention orders (SOPOs) and interim SOPOs (which prohibit a person convicted or cautioned for a specified sexual offence or offence of violence doing anything described in the order; prohibitions are limited to those necessary to protect the public or particular members of the public from serious sexual harm by the subject);

- foreign travel orders (FTOs) (which prohibit their subject, a person convicted of a specified sexual offence against a child under 16, travelling to a country or countries outside the UK); and

- risk of sexual harm orders (RSHOs) and interim RSHOs (which prohibit their subject, whether or not he has been convicted of any offence, doing anything described in the order on the ground that on two or more occasions the subject has engaged in sexually explicit conduct with a child or children and the order is necessary to protect a child or children from harm by the subject).

18.2   These orders are designed to complement the substantive offences under SOA 2003, Pt 1, by assisting in the management of those who pose a risk of sexual harm and thereby providing protection against that risk. The making of an order is not a conviction, does not in itself result in a penalty and does not go on a criminal record. The orders can all be made by a magistrates' court on application by the police. A SOPO can also be made as part of the disposal after a person has been convicted of a specified sexual offence or offence of violence. A person may simultaneously be subjected to more than one of the different types of order (but not to more than one of a particular type). In cases where a person's behaviour causes or is or is likely to cause harassment, alarm or distress but the requirements for a SOPO or RSHO are not satisfied, it may be possible to deal with that person by an anti-social behaviour order (ASBO) under the Crime and Disorder Act (CDA) 1998 if he is not a member of the same household as the victim.[1]

---

[1]   See **10.112** et seq.

NOTIFICATION ORDERS

18.3   There have been instances where people convicted abroad of sex offences have returned or come to the UK and committed sexual offences here. The notification requirements referred to in Chapter 17 do not automatically apply to sex offenders convicted or cautioned outside the UK. The practical reason is that a person subject to the notification requirements should be made aware that he is subject to them,[2] and it would be unrealistic to expect a foreign court or police officer to warn individuals that they will be subject to the requirements if they ever enter the UK. The provisions of SOA 2003, ss 97–103 go some way towards rectifying the problem. A NO subjects someone, whether a UK citizen or foreign national, convicted of a sex offence outside the UK to the notification requirements under SOA 2003, Pt 2. Once an order has been made, the police are able to track where the sex offender is staying and make arrangements to help to ensure that he does not commit further offences. The NO provisions apply to England and Wales, to Northern Ireland and to Scotland.[3]

18.4   The effectiveness of the NO system depends on the police being aware that an overseas sex offender is in or is travelling to the UK. Intelligence can come from a variety of sources. The 2004 Home Office *Guidance on Part 2 of the Sexual Offences Act 2003* (*Guidance Pt 2*) gives the following examples:

(a)   A British citizen is being released from custody overseas, after conviction for a sexual offence, and the diplomatic service is organising return to the UK.

(b)   A British citizen is returning to the UK after receiving a caution for a sexual offence overseas. During his dealings with the authorities in the foreign country he was assisted by the diplomatic service.

(c)   A British citizen is being repatriated to a UK prison to serve his sentence received overseas for a sexual offence.

(d)   Authorities in the UK have been informed by a foreign country that one of its citizens who has previous convictions for sexual offences is intending to come to the UK.

(e)   An individual comes to the attention of the police, and on investigation of his criminal history it becomes apparent that he has convictions for relevant sexual offences overseas.[4]

Without such intelligence, it will be relatively rare for an offender to come to the attention of the police in this country. Where the offender is from the EU, free-movement regulations mean that minimal passport checks now take place at entry points into the UK. Where the offender is a non-EU citizen, the UK will frequently not have access to the criminal records of other countries and so detecting the individuals may not be possible, despite the stricter passport controls. At an international level there

---

[2]   See **17.11** and **17.37**.

[3]   SOA 2003, s 142(1)–(3) extends the relevant provisions to these countries. Sections 102 (appeals) and 103 (procedural modifications) apply only to Scotland.

[4]   At pp 33–34.

is increased co-operation between countries, most notably within the EU where the development of computer systems allows Member States to check the criminal records of people from across the EU.

NOs: application and grounds

18.5 A NO can only be made by a magistrates' court. An application for an order must be made by the police. Section 97(1) states that: 'A chief officer of police may, by complaint[5] to any magistrates' court whose commission area includes any part of his police area,[6] apply for . . . a notification order'.

18.6 The chief officer[7] may apply for a NO against the defendant if:

(a)   it appears to the chief officer that the three conditions set out in **18.9–18.13** are met with respect to the defendant; and

(b)   the defendant resides in the chief officer's police area or the chief officer believes that the defendant is in, or is intending to come to, that police area.[8]

Whether an application is made in such circumstances may depend on the outcome of a risk assessment.

18.7 An application for a NO may be in the form set out in Sch 1 to the Magistrates' Courts (Notification Orders) Rules (MC(NO)R) 2004,[9] and a summons directed to the defendant requiring him to appear before a magistrates' court to answer an application for such an order may be in the form set out in Sch 2 thereto.[10]

18.8 Where an order is sought on an anticipatory basis there may be problems in ensuring adequate opportunity to make representation. The right to a fair trial under the European Convention on Human Rights (ECHR), Art 6(1) must not be forgotten.

The conditions

18.9 By SOA 2003, s 97(2), the *first condition* is that under the law of a country[11] outside the UK:[12]

•   the defendant has been convicted[13] of a *relevant offence* (whether or not punished for it);

---

5   See **18.70**.

6   In relation to England and Wales, 'police area' has the meaning given to it by the Police Act 1996, s 101(1) (Interpretation Act (IA) 1978, s 5 and Sch 1), namely the police area of one of the 43 local police forces in England and Wales.

7   See **17.106**, n 187.

8   SOA 2003, s 97(1).

9   SI 2004/1052, r 3(1).

10   Ibid, r 3(2).

11   Or territory (e g a dependency): SOA 2003, s 133.

12   Outside Great Britain and Northern Ireland: IA 1978, s 5 and Sch 1.

13   Including a 'spent' conviction. The Rehabilitation of Offenders Act 1974 does not apply in proceedings under SOA 2003, Pt 2: 1974 Act, s 7(2)(bb), as amended by SOA 2003, Sch 6, para 19. As to proof of a foreign conviction, see **18.71**.

- a foreign court has made in respect of that offence a finding equivalent to a finding that the defendant is not guilty by reason of insanity, or to a finding that he is under a disability and did the act charged against him; or

- the defendant has been cautioned in respect of a relevant offence.[14] (The definition of 'cautioned' in s 133 (see **17.36**) means that the foreign caution must equate to one in this country, for example, in terms of the defendant's admission of guilt or the requirement of an informed consent to being cautioned.)

18.10 By SOA 2003, s 99(1), a *'relevant offence'* means an act which:

- constituted an offence[15] under the law of the country concerned; and

- would have constituted an offence listed in SOA 2003, Sch 3[16] if it had been done in any part of the UK.

The latter requirement is to be taken as met unless, not later than 3 days before the hearing date for the application for the NO,[17] the defendant serves on the applicant a notice:

- stating that, on the facts as alleged, the condition is not met;

- explaining why; and

- requiring the applicant to prove that the condition is met.[18]

If the defendant serves such a notice, the applicant must prove that the requirement is satisfied. Moreover, even if such a notice is not served, the court may, if it thinks fit, permit the defendant to require the applicant to prove the requirement.[19]

18.11 Where the act involved in a relevant offence would have constituted a Sch 3 offence only because the disposal made by the foreign court would satisfy a sentence condition under Sch 3 in respect of the UK equivalent, the date of conviction or finding in respect of a relevant offence is taken as the date when the relevant sentence condition is met. This is the effect of SOA 2003, s 132(4)–(7). The rule corresponds to that in relation to the commencement of notification requirements, described in **17.27**.

18.12 By SOA 2003, s 97(3), the *second condition* is that:

- the first condition is met because of a conviction, finding or caution which occurred on or after 1 September 1997 (commencement of the Sex Offenders Act (SOffA) 1997, Pt 1); *or*

---

14   SOA 2003, s 97(2).
15   An act punishable under the law in force in a country outside the UK constitutes an offence under that law for this purpose however described in that law: s 99(2).
16   See **17.19–17.28**. Except an offence in Scotland which satisfies the requirements in Sch 3, para 60 (ie an offence in Scotland not otherwise listed in Sch 3 where the court disposing of the case determines that there was a significant sexual aspect to the offender's behaviour in committing the offence): s 99(1)(b).
17   MC(NO)R 2004, SI 2004/1052, r 4.
18   SOA 2003, s 99(3).
19   SOA 2003, s 99(4).

- the first condition is met because of a conviction or finding which occurred before that date, but the person was dealt with in respect of the offence or finding on or after that date, or has yet to be dealt with in respect of it; *or*

- the first condition is met because of a conviction or finding which occurred before that date, but on that date the person was, in respect of the offence or finding, subject under the law of the country concerned to detention, supervision or any other disposal equivalent to any of those mentioned in the first bullet point[20] in **17.15**.

These provisions reflect the partially retrospective arrangements of s 81[21] in respect of the application of the notification requirements to people convicted, etc in the UK before Pt 2's commencement.

18.13 By SOA 2003, s 97(4), the *third condition* is that the notification period[22] set out in s 82[23] in respect of a notification requirement under s 80 or s 81 in respect of a relevant offence has not expired.[24] Thus, an order may not be made where the notification period, calculated from the date of conviction, etc abroad, has expired. For example, where someone was given a 3-month sentence for a sex offence following a conviction on 1 March 2005 in a French court for a relevant offence, the court may not make a NO against him 7 years (the applicable notification period) or more after that date.

18.14 It will be noted that the above provisions envisage that the foreign conviction, etc may not have been in the recent past. The 6-month time-limit under the Magistrates' Courts Act (MCA) 1980, s 127, on the hearing of a complaint does not apply to a NO because the 6-month period refers to 6 months 'from the time that the matter of complaint arose' and the requirements for a NO cannot be said to relate to a matter of complaint.

The proceedings

18.15 For the same reasons as given in **18.68** in respect of a SOPO, proceedings for the imposition of a NO are civil in character, not criminal. Nevertheless, for the reasons given in **18.77**, the standard of proof is the criminal standard.

18.16 If it is proved that the three conditions are satisfied, the court must make a NO,[25] regardless of its views as to the propriety of the foreign conviction, etc or its views as to

---

20   Ie SOA 2003, s 81(3). As in the case of s 81(3) itself, the reference to s 81(3) is to be read with s 81(6) and s 131 referred to in the notes to **17.15**: SOA 2003, s 97(3)(c).
21   See **17.12–17.17**.
22   See **17.40–17.51**.
23   As modified by SOA 2003, s 98(2) and (3), namely: the 'relevant date' means the date of the conviction, the date of the finding, or the date of the caution, as the case may be: s 98(2). In s 82: references, except in the Table (para **17.40**), to a person (or relevant offender) within any provision of s 80 are to be read as references to the defendant; the reference in the Table to s 80(1)(d) is to be read as a reference to s 97(2)(d); references to an order are to be read as references to any corresponding disposal in respect of an offence or finding by reference to which the NO was made; the reference to offences listed in Sch 3 is to be read as a reference to relevant offences: s 98(3).
24   SOA 2003, s 97(4).
25   SOA 2003, s 97(5).

whether an order is necessary, for example, to protect the public against serious sexual harm. What is said in **18.68–18.71** is equally applicable mutatis mutandis in respect of NO proceedings.

Effect

18.17 Where a NO is made, the defendant becomes or (as the case may be) remains subject to the notification requirements of SOA 2003, Pt 2 for the notification period set out in s 82.[26] The order does not give rise to any other conditions or prohibitions. If prohibitions to prevent sexual harm are thought to be necessary an application must be made for a SOPO.

18.18 A NO must be in the form set out in Sch 3 to the MC(NO)R 2004.[27] The form sets out briefly the notification requirements and the consequences of breaking them without reasonable excuse. As soon as reasonably practicable after a NO has been made, the designated officer for the court must serve a copy of that order on the defendant. Service must be effected either by giving a copy to the defendant in person or by sending it by post to the defendant's last known address; if a copy is so given or sent, it is deemed to have been received by the defendant, unless he proves that he did not receive it.[28] A copy of the 'Notice of requirement to register' form should also be provided. The process of appeal must be made clear to the offender. A copy of the NO and the notice should be provided to the police.[29] The police should consider passing a copy of the NO to those public protection agencies which need to be informed according to a risk assessment.

18.19 The notification period[30] runs from the 'relevant date', ie the date of the foreign conviction, etc.[31] Thus, if a person was cautioned in a foreign country on 1 July 2008 for a relevant offence, the notification period will expire 2 years from that date (the applicable notification period under s 82). If a NO is made against that person on 1 May 2010 it will only last for the remaining 2 months of the period.

18.20 If a NO is made, the initial notification requirement under s 83 must be complied with within 3 days[32] beginning with the date of service of the NO.[33] Thereafter, subject to s 85, the other notification requirements apply.

18.21 A court which makes a NO in respect of a 'young offender' (ie someone under 18, or 16 in Scotland) may make a parental direction.[34]

---

[26]   SOA 2003, s 98(1).
[27]   Rule 3(3).
[28]   Rule 3(5).
[29]   *Guidance Pt 2*, at pp 29 and 35.
[30]   As modified by SOA 2003, s 98(2), and (3) (above) and (4) (below).
[31]   This is the effect of s 98(2).
[32]   See **17.52**, n 97.
[33]   This is the effect of s 98(4).
[34]   SOA 2003, s 89(1); see **17.98** et seq.

Interim NOs

18.22 An application for an interim NO can be made pending the determination of an application for a NO ('the main application').[35] This will be useful where, for example, papers need to be obtained from abroad before the main application can be determined.

18.23 An application for an interim order:

• may be made in the complaint[36] containing the main application; or

• if the main application has been made, may be made by the person who made it, by complaint to the court to which that application has been made.[37]

18.24 An application for an interim NO may be in the form set out in Sch 1 to the MC(NO)R 2004,[38] and a summons directed to the defendant requiring him to appear before a magistrates' court to answer an application for such an order may be in the form set out in Sch 2 thereto.[39] Since the purpose of an interim SOPO is temporarily to impose the notification requirements pending the determination of the application for the full order, it will not be normal to adjourn the interim proceedings to allow the defendant more time to prepare.[40]

18.25 The court may make an interim NO *if it considers it just to do so*.[41] The court is not required to be satisfied that the three conditions required for a NO have been satisfied, nor even that there is a prima facie case disclosed by the material before it. An interim order subjects the defendant to the notification requirements of Pt 2 for the duration of the order from the date of service of the order,[42] so that the initial notification requirement must be complied with within 3 days of that date. The duration of an interim order is not specified by the Act. Instead, it is a fixed period specified in the order.[43] If it has not already done so, an interim order ceases to have effect on the determination of the application for the main order.[44]

18.26 An interim NO must be in the form set out in Sch 4 to the MC(NO)R 2004.[45] The rules about service are identical to those for a full order.[46]

18.27 The applicant or the defendant may by complaint apply to the court which made the interim order for it to be varied, renewed or discharged.[47] There is no corresponding provision in respect of NOs themselves because the length of the notification requirements to which they give rise is fixed by law. Because the other terms of a notification requirement imposed by an interim order remain fixed, the only variation of such an order which is possible relates to its duration.

---

[35] SOA 2003, s 100(1).
[36] See **18.5** et seq.
[37] SOA 2003, s 100(2).
[38] Rule 3(1).
[39] Rule 3(2).
[40] *Guidance Pt 2*, at p 26.
[41] SOA 2003, s 100(3).
[42] SOA 2003, s 100(5), (6).
[43] SOA 2003, s 100(4)(a).
[44] SOA 2003, s 100(4)(b).
[45] Rule 3(4).
[46] Rule 3(5). See **18.18**.
[47] SOA 2003, s 100(7).

18.28 A court which makes an interim NO in respect of a 'young offender' may make a 'parental direction'.[48]

Appeal

18.29 A defendant may appeal by way of re-hearing[49] to the Crown Court against the making of a NO or an interim NO.[50] Because a court is obliged to make a NO if the three conditions set out in **18.9–18.13** are satisfied, an appeal against a full order must be based on the grounds that one of the three conditions is not satisfied. The ground of appeal against the making of an interim NO is not so limited. Arguably, the renewal of an interim NO constitutes the making of such an order, and therefore is amenable to an appeal by the defendant, but it is difficult to see that a variation of an interim NO constitutes a making of it. The applicant does not have a right of appeal against the dismissal of an application. In the case of irrationality or procedural impropriety, an application could be made for judicial review.

SEXUAL OFFENCES PREVENTION ORDERS

Introduction

18.30 The notification requirements under SOA 2003, Pt 2 simply require a relevant offender to provide initial and periodic notifications and to notify any changes and foreign travel. They do not prohibit the offender from doing things which may pose a risk of sexual harm. Concern that effective action could not be taken where a sex offender posed such a risk led to the introduction of sex offender orders (SOOs) and restraining orders (ROs).

18.31 SOOs, introduced by CDA 1998, s 2, and interim SOOs could be made by a magistrates' court on application by the police on the ground that the person was a sex offender whose behaviour since conviction or caution gave reasonable cause to believe that an order was necessary to protect the public from serious harm. Such an order prohibited the offender from doing anything described in it. It also activated for its duration the notification requirements under SOffA 1997 if they were not already in force, and thereby provided another route to managing offenders via those requirements.

18.32 The Criminal Justice and Court Services Act 2000, s 66 and Sch 5 added s 5A to SOffA 1997, which empowered the Court of Appeal, the Crown Court and youth courts to add a RO to a custodial sentence, or a hospital order or guardianship order, imposed on a person convicted of a sexual offence, if the court was satisfied that it was necessary to do so in order to protect the public in general, or any particular member of the public, from serious harm from the offender. Such an order could prohibit the offender from doing anything described in the order. It also activated the notification requirements under SOffA 1997. The notification requirements lasted as long as the order, if it was longer than the notification period normally applicable in respect of the sentence imposed.

---

48   SOA 2003, s 89(1); see **17.98** et seq.
49   Supreme Court Act (SCtA) 1981, s 79(3).
50   SOA 2003, s 101. There is in comparison no right of appeal against a notification requirement imposed under s 80 or s 81 because such a requirement is not the product of a court order but is automatically imposed in consequence of the 'triggering' conviction, etc.

18.33 These orders were replaced and combined by the SOPO and interim SOPO.[51] SOPOs and interim SOPOs are governed by SOA 2003, ss 104–113. A SOPO or interim SOPO can be made by a court in England and Wales, Scotland or Northern Ireland and is enforceable in one of those countries if broken there.[52]

SOPOs: when can they be made?

18.34 A court can make a SOPO in two types of case:

- where it deals with the defendant in respect of a conviction or finding[53] for an offence listed in Sch 3 or Sch 5 to the Act, or a finding that he is not guilty of such an offence by reason of insanity, or a finding that he is under a disability and has done the act charged against him in respect of such an offence[54]. This type of case is dealt with in **18.40** et seq;

- on a complaint by the police against a person with a conviction, etc for a Sch 3 or Sch 5 offence as described in **18.55** et seq.[55]

18.35 The contents of Sch 3 were referred to in **17.19–17.28**. As a result of SOA 2003, s 106(13) and (14) (both inserted by the Criminal Justice and Immigration Act (CJIA) 2008[56]) which came into force on 14 July 2008,[57] any age or sentence condition in Sch 3 (ie any condition subject to which an offence listed in Sch 3 is so listed that relates to the way the defendant is dealt with in respect of a listed offence, or to the age of any person) is to be disregarded *for the purposes of the provisions relating to SOPOs* in relation to their application in England and Wales and Northern Ireland. Thus, if an offence is listed in Sch 3 the SOPO provisions apply to it regardless of the fact that an age or sentence condition in respect of it is not satisfied. It is submitted that s 106(13) and (14) has retrospective force. In relation to SOPOs made on complaint by the police, the reference to a conviction etc for a Sch 3 offence applies to a Sch 3 offence, for the purposes of the definition of a 'qualifying offender' in s 106, whether committed before or after the commencement of SOA 2003. It would be inconsistent with the retrospectivity of a Sch 3 offence as a pre-condition for a SOPO on police complaint if SOA 2003, s 106(13) and (14) was not given retrospective force in relation to a conviction etc before 14 July 2008. In relation to a SOPO made on conviction etc, it is submitted that SOA 2003, s 106(13) and (14) is also retrospective in its application, so as to apply to disposals on or after 14 July 2008 in respect of Sch 3 offences committed before that date. A SOPO made as part of a disposal is not a sentence (so ECHR, Art 7 is not engaged) and the consequences of reading SOA 2003, s 106(13) and (14) with retrospective effect is not sufficiently unfair that Parliament cannot have intended it not

---

[51] The replacement of ROs and SOOs does not affect the continuance of orders already made.

[52] Section 142(1)–(3) extends ss 104–113 to these countries. Sections 105 (further provision as to police application for a SOPO), 111 (appeals) and 112 (modifications of the provisions discussed below) (all as amended by the Protection of Children and Prevention of Sexual Offences (Scotland) Act (PCPSO(S)A) 2005, s 17) apply only to Scotland. The amendments apply to England, Wales and Northern Ireland: Violent Crime Reduction Act (VCRA) 2006, s 56(1).

[53] See **17.29–17.31**.

[54] SOA 2003, s 104(2), (3). See s 135(3), referred to in **17.33, 17.34**.

[55] SOA 2003, s 104(4)–(6).

[56] CJIA 2008, s 141.

[57] CJIA 2008 (Commencement No 2 and Transitional and Saving Provisions) Order 2008, SI 2008/1586, art 2(1), Sch 1.

so to apply.[58] It is noteworthy that the wording of SOA 2003, s 106(13) and (14) does not amend Sch 3 but introduces a rule of construction. It therefore does not fall foul of s 130 which (save in relation to the definition of 'qualifying offender' in s 106) states that an *amendment* of Sch 3 which removes a threshold (ie age or sentence condition) does not apply to convictions, findings and cautions before the amendment takes effect.[59]

18.36 The Sch 5[60] offences are the offences under SOA 2003, ss 47 (see below), 52 and 53 and 57–59, relating to paying for the sexual services of a child, to exploitation of prostitution, and to trafficking; as well as murder; manslaughter; kidnapping; false imprisonment; outraging public decency; and offences under the Offences against the Person Act 1861, ss 4, 16, 18, 20–23, 27–32, 35, 37, 38, 47; the Explosive Substances Act 1883, ss 2, 3; the Infant Life (Preservation) Act 1929, s 1; the Children and Young Persons Act (CYPA) 1933, s 1; the Infanticide Act 1938, s 1; the Firearms Act 1968, ss 16, 16A, 17, 18; the Theft Act 1968, ss 1, 8, 9(1)(a) (burglary with intent to steal, inflict grievous bodily harm or do unlawful damage), 10, 12A; the Criminal Damage Act 1971, s 1 (if offence of arson), 1(2) (other than offence of arson); the Taking of Hostages Act 1982, s 1; the Aviation Security Act 1982, ss 1, 2, 3, 4; the Mental Health Act (MHA) 1983, s 127; the Child Abduction Act 1984, ss 1, 2; the Prohibition of Female Circumcision Act 1985, s 1; the Public Order Act 1986, ss 1, 2, 3; the Criminal Justice Act (CJA) 1988, s 134; the Road Traffic Act 1988, ss 1, 3A; the Aviation and Maritime Security Act 1990, ss 1, 9, 10, 11, 12, 13; the Protection from Harassment Act (PHA) 1997, ss 2, 4; CDA 1998, ss 29, 31(1)(a) or (b); the Channel Tunnel (Security) Order 1994,[61] Pt II; the Postal Services Act 2000, s 85(3) or (4); the International Criminal Court Act 2001, ss 51, 52; the Communication Act 2003, s 127(1); the Domestic Violence, Crime and Victims Act 2004, s 5; and corresponding offences under the law of Scotland or Northern Ireland and Service law. References to these offences include a reference to inchoate liability or secondary liability for such an offence. This is a bizarre list. Whilst a person who commits many of the offences listed may thereby pose a risk of sexual harm to the public, it is hard to conceive the likelihood of this in respect of other offences. The offence of paying for the sexual services of a child, contrary to SOA 2003, s 47, is subject to the age condition that the victim or (as the case may be) other party was 16 or over at the time of the offence.[62] Section 47 also appears in Sch 3. Now that the age and sentence conditions which apply to it under Sch 3 are to be disregarded for the purposes of a SOPO, the appearance in Sch 5 of SOA 2003, s 47 is otiose.

18.37 Schedule 5, like Sch 3, can be amended by statutory instrument subject to the affirmative procedure.[63]

18.38 For the purposes of a SOPO made by a court as part of the disposal, an amendment to Sch 3 or Sch 5 is not retrospective if it adds an offence, removes a condition or changes a condition adversely to an offender.[64] Thus, for example, if a person was convicted of an offence outside Sch 3 or Sch 5 at the time of conviction and

[58] The 'unfairness principle' of construction in respect of whether or not a provision is retrospective was formulated by the House of Lords in *L'Office Cherifien des Phosphates v Yamashita-Shinnihan Steamship Co Ltd* [1994] 1 AC 486.
[59] SOA 2003, s 130(2) and (4)(b) (**18.37–18.39**).
[60] As amended by SI 2007/296.
[61] SI 1994/570.
[62] SOA 2003, Sch 5, para 62.
[63] SOA 2003, ss 130(1), 138(1), (2).
[64] SOA 2003, s 130(2), (4).

sentence is adjourned, but by the time that the offender is dealt with in respect of that conviction the offence is included in Sch 3 or Sch 5, this cannot trigger the making of a SOPO as part of the disposal.

18.39 For the purposes of an application for a SOPO[65] by the police, any amendment to Sch 3 or Sch 5 which adds an offence, removes a condition or changes one adversely to an offender applies to convictions, findings and cautions before as well as after the amendment takes effect.[66]

SOPO as part of disposal

18.40 Unlike a RO, a SOPO can be made on disposal by a magistrates' court, is not subject to any requirement as to the sentence, etc imposed by the court and can be made against someone convicted, etc in respect of an offence of violence listed in SOA 2003, Sch 5, if there is a risk of him causing serious sexual harm, as well as against a sex offender. On the other hand, the Court of Appeal[67] has stated that the test of necessity for a RO under SOffA 1997, s 5A (as interpreted in *Beaney*[68]) and the corresponding test under the SOPO provisions are substantially the same.

The power

18.41 The power to make a SOPO as part of disposal can be exercised in relation to conduct before SOA 2003 came into force (1 May 2004) of which the defendant has been convicted after that date.[69] As a SOPO is a civil preventative order, and not a penalty, the retrospective application of the power does not contravene ECHR, Art 7. The power to make a RO ceased to be exercisable on 1 May 2004.[70]

18.42 No application is necessary for a court to make a SOPO as part of disposal, although a prosecutor may invite the court to make a SOPO in appropriate cases, either drafting an order or at the very least giving thought to the conditions that are to be imposed.[71] The Crown Court or a magistrates' court must not make a SOPO unless the person to whom it is directed has had an opportunity to consider what order is proposed, and why, and to make representations at a hearing (whether or not that person in fact attends).[72] Courts may also ask pre-sentence report writers to consider the suitability of a SOPO on a non-prejudicial basis.[73]

18.43 In respect of a decision whether or not to make a SOPO, hearsay evidence is admissible under rules which broadly correspond to the rules[74] applicable in civil proceedings in magistrates' courts.[75]

---

[65] Or a FTO.
[66] SOA 2003, s 130(3).
[67] *Monument* [2005] 2 Cr App R (S) 341 at [26].
[68] [2004] 2 Cr App R (S) 441.
[69] SOA 2003, s 106(4); *Monument*, n 67 above.
[70] *Monument*, n 67 above. Thus, there is an exception to the normal rule (IA 1978, s 16), that the repeal of an Act does not affect any 'punishment' in respect of an offence committed before its repeal. Cf *Bradshaw* [2007] EWCA Crim 2971.
[71] *Guidance Pt 2*, at p 38.
[72] Criminal Procedure Rules (Crim PR), SI 2005/384, r 50.2(1).
[73] *Guidance Pt 2*, at p 38.
[74] See Magistrates' Courts (Hearsay Evidence in Civil Proceedings) Rules (MC(HECP)R) 1999, SI 1999/681, rr 3, 4 and 5; see also the Civil Evidence Act (CEA) 1995.
[75] Crim PR, rr 50.6, 50.7 and 50.8.

18.44 SOA 2003, s 104(1)(b), (2) and (3) provide that, where any court[76] is dealing with a defendant in respect of a conviction[77] for an offence listed in Sch 3 or Sch 5 of the Act, or a finding that he is not guilty of such an offence by reason of insanity, or a finding that he is under a disability and has done the act charged against him in respect of such an offence,[78] whatever the sentence passed or order made, the court *may* make a SOPO if it is satisfied that *it is necessary to make such an order, for the purpose of protecting the public or any particular members of the public from serious sexual harm from the defendant*. 'Members of the public' includes a particular member of the public.[79] We discuss the italicised words in **18.46–18.52**.

18.45 The evidence presented at trial is likely to be a key factor in determining the risk of sexual harm (and the need for a SOPO), together with the offender's previous convictions and the assessment of risk presented in the pre-sentence report. The assessment of risk should include reference to the likelihood of the defendant committing a sexual offence, the imminence of that offending and the seriousness of the harm resulting from it.[80]

Serious sexual harm

18.46 '*Protecting the public or any particular members of the public from serious sexual harm from the defendant*' means protecting the public *in the UK* or any particular members of that public from serious physical or psychological[81] harm, caused by the defendant committing one or more offences listed in Sch 3.[82] Protection of people outside the UK, in particular children in sex tourist countries, can be sought by an application for a FTO, described in **18.135** et seq.

18.47 The requirement of a risk of the defendant committing a Sch 3 offence means that, although a person who has been convicted of a Sch 5 offence can be the subject of a SOPO, a SOPO cannot be made unless there is a risk of that person committing a Sch 3 offence. For example, a SOPO cannot be made where a person convicted of a trafficking offence, contrary to SOA 2003, s 57, a Sch 5 offence, is assessed as presenting a high risk of committing another such offence. In such a case, a court wishing to make a prohibitory order would have to consider whether an ASBO could be made.

---

[76] Ie the Court of Appeal, the Crown Court, a magistrates' court or a youth court.
[77] For these purposes, 'conviction' includes a conviction for an offence in respect of which the offender receives a conditional discharge or, in Scotland, a probation order is made; the provisions which state that a conviction with such an order is deemed not to be a conviction for any other purpose are disapplied by SOA 2003, s 134(1). The effect of the absence of absolute discharges from s 134 is to prevent a conviction followed by an absolute discharge constituting a conviction for present purposes.
'Conviction' also includes a finding in summary proceedings, where the court makes a hospital or guardianship order under MHA 1983, s 37(3) (or its Scottish or Northern Irish counterpart), that a mentally ill or severely mentally disordered defendant did the act or made the omission charged: SOA 2003, s 135(1).
[78] The reference to a person being or having been found to be under a disability and to have done the act charged against him in respect of an offence includes a reference to his being or having been found (a) unfit to be tried for the offence, (b) to be insane so that his trial for the offence cannot or could not proceed, or (c) unfit to be tried and to have done the act charged against him in respect of the offence: SOA 2003, s 135(3).
[79] *Yates* [2004] 1 Cr App R (S) 269 (corresponding provision in SOffA 1997, s 5A). The plural includes the singular unless the contrary intention appears: IA 1978, s 6.
[80] *Guidance Pt 2*, at p 37.
[81] An example of a case giving rise to a risk of psychological harm alone could be that of intentional exposure of the genitals, contrary to SOA 2003, s 66: see *Whitton* [2007] 2 Cr App R (S) 67.
[82] SOA 2003, s 106(3).

18.48 The fact that an offender does not pose a risk of 'serious harm' for the purposes of the dangerous offender provisions in CJA 2003, Pt 12, Ch 5 (in particular ss 224–229)[83] does not preclude a court from finding that a SOPO is necessary for the purpose of protecting the public or any particular members of the public from 'serious sexual harm' from the defendant as required by SOA 2003, s 104; the degree of harm required for the former is higher than for the latter. There are three reasons for the distinction. First, the element of risk for the purposes of the dangerous offender provisions has to be significant; there is no equivalent requirement for a SOPO. Secondly, a life sentence can be imposed under the dangerous offender provisions, whereas a SOPO will last for not less than 5 years. Thirdly, the dangerous offender provisions define 'serious harm' as meaning death or serious personal injury, whereas 'serious sexual harm' for the purposes of a SOPO is defined by reference to serious physical or psychological harm (as opposed to injury).[84]

Necessity to make order

18.49 By SOA 2003, s 104(1)(b), a court can only make a SOPO if it is satisfied that it is necessary to make such an order for the purpose of protecting the public or any particular member(s) of the public from serious sexual harm from the offender. A SOPO as a disposal is primarily intended for those who present a serious ongoing risk of danger to the public in general, or any particular member of the public, from serious harm from the offender[85] by their re-offending.[86] In *Halloren*[87] the Court of Appeal held in respect of the corresponding provision relating to a RO:

- that a court can only impose a SOPO if there is material before it from which it can be 'satisfied' that it is so 'necessary'. It is not enough that it is merely desirable.[88] There must be clear evidence showing, for example, in the case of a SOPO as part of a disposal that any other sentencing on its own is unlikely to prevent further offending;[89] and

- that 'satisfied' means that the court has to consider expressly the statutory requirements in what is now s 104(1)(b) and to indicate the basis on which they have been met in the case.

In *Halloren*, A had pleaded guilty to 13 counts of making indecent photographs or pseudo-photographs of a child by downloading images from the internet. He had been sentenced to 8 months' imprisonment, with a RO, unlimited in time, restraining him from owning or using any personal computer capable of connection to the internet or related equipment, otherwise than in the course or furtherance of his work, together with a forfeiture order in respect of the computer. The Court of Appeal allowed A's appeal against the RO and quashed it because there was nothing to indicate that the judge had been satisfied that it was necessary to make an order for the purposes set out in SOffA 1997, s 5A(2), the condition corresponding to SOA 2003, s 104(1)(b).

---

83 See Chapter 15.
84 *Rampley* [2007] 1 Cr App R (S) 542; *Richards* [2007] 1 Cr App R (S) 734.
85 *Yates*, n 79 above (see **18.80, 18.81**).
86 This was recognised in *D* [2006] 2 Cr App R (S) 204 where the court stated at [10] that, when regard was had to the wording in the context of s 104 as a whole, it seemed clear that the focus of SOA 2003, s 104(1)(b), and hence the definition in s 106(3), had to be the risk of future offending.
87 [2004] 2 Cr App R (S) 301.
88 Or 'appropriate': *D*, n 86 above.
89 *Leslie* [2006] EWCA Crim 847.

18.50 *Halloren* was referred to by the Court of Appeal in *Beaney*,[90] where the facts were similar but the RO was upheld by the Court of Appeal. Although it did not dissent from the basic propositions in *Halloren*, the Court of Appeal analysed the evidence in a different way. A had pleaded guilty to 17 counts of making indecent photographs of a child. He had been sentenced to 6 months' imprisonment, with a RO prohibiting him without limit of time from owning or having access to any personal computer or related equipment, or any equipment capable of viewing any form of images, or purchasing or possessing any disks or other medium capable of storing or playing images. The RO did not prevent or prohibit A from viewing lawfully broadcast television programmes, or from using computer equipment for the purpose of any lawful employment, but only at his place of employment. A forfeiture order was made in respect of his computer. The Court of Appeal declined to quash the RO, although it varied it. It noted that, in *Halloren*, the Court had concluded that the RO should be quashed as there was nothing to indicate that the judge had been satisfied that it was necessary to make the order to achieve the specific aims set out in SOffA 1997, s 5A(2). It held, however, that the particular members of the public who might be at risk of serious harm were the children who were forced to pose or to participate in sexual conduct for the purpose of allowing the images to be produced and disseminated. They would have been subjected to that risk not only by the persons responsible for producing and disseminating the images, but also by people like A who simply downloaded images and had viewed them. The serious psychological injury to which they would be at risk would arise from their knowledge that what they were to do would be viewed by others. If people like A continued to download images of this kind, the offences which they committed could properly be said to contribute to the psychological harm which the children in those images would suffer by virtue of their awareness that there were people getting a perverted thrill from watching them forced to pose and behave in this way. In the Court's view, there were sufficient indications in the material before the judge to entitle him to form the view that there was a continuing risk of A continuing to view indecent images of children on the internet so as to justify the conclusion that it was necessary to protect children from serious harm from him. The Court, however, varied the terms of the order so as to prevent it restricting use of computers by other members of A's family or his use of equipment that was not capable of displaying indecent images.

18.51 The general principles in *Halloren* were endorsed and those in *Beaney* qualified by the Court of Appeal in *Collard*,[91] where A, a schoolteacher, had pleaded guilty to seven counts of making indecent photographs or pseudo-photographs of children, and 16 counts of possessing such photographs or pseudo-photographs. Most of the images had been downloaded from the internet. A was sentenced to 2 years' imprisonment, disqualified indefinitely from working with children and subjected to a RO whose terms prohibited him indefinitely from owning, possessing or having any access to any computer or other equipment capable of downloading any material from the internet otherwise than for the purpose of any lawful employment and only at a place of lawful employment. On appeal against the RO, A submitted that:

- there was no material before the Court of Appeal on which it could decide that he qualified for a RO;

- the indefinite period of the RO was manifestly excessive; and

---

90   [2004] 2 Cr App R (S) 441.
91   [2005] 1 Cr App R (S) 155.

- the terms of the RO were too wide.

The Court of Appeal in *Collard* allowed the appeal in part. It held that if the logic of the Court of Appeal in *Beaney* was correct, potentially everyone convicted of the type of offence in question *qualified* for a RO. The Court had no doubt that the reasoning was correct. The reasoning behind both the legislation and the sentencing policy was that participation in indecent or pornographic activity damaged children and that those who downloaded such material from the internet contributed to such damage. *However, it did not follow that the court would be satisfied that it was necessary to make a RO in every case. That was only part of the test the court should consider.* The court should also consider the number of offences, their duration, the nature of the material, the extent of publication, the use to which the material was put, the offender's antecedents, his personal circumstances and the risk of re-offending. The Court of Appeal stated that, where a court was satisfied that there was a real risk of the offender committing further offences and that the further offences would cause serious harm to children, it would be necessary to make a RO. The *terms* of the restraining order must be *tailored* to meet the danger presented by the offender. It must be proportionate to that risk and not oppressive.[92] The court was aware of the ever-increasing legitimate use of the internet, for example, as a source of news, information and entertainment. Employment might require the use of the internet at home as well as in the workplace. A wide prohibition on an offender might have the effect of depriving his wife and children of the benefit of legitimate use of the internet. The Court was satisfied that the sentencing judge was entitled to conclude that A qualified for a RO on looking at the nature and extent of the material, the duration of the offences and his occupation. Given that an order could be discharged, the Court was satisfied that it was appropriate for the order to be indefinite. The Court decided, however, that the terms of the order were too wide and should be curtailed. It would have been sufficient if the order had prohibited the offender from downloading any material from the internet, other than that required for the purpose of any lawful employment or lawful study. The Court therefore varied the RO to that effect.

18.52 In a more recent decision, *Hammond*,[93] where A had pleaded guilty to five counts relating to indecent photographs found on his computer, the Court of Appeal held that a prohibition in the SOPO that A was not to download any material from the internet save that applying to downloading for the purpose of any lawful employment or lawful study was too wide and should be quashed. It pointed out that the prohibition would prevent A from accessing the internet to order a train ticket or to book a holiday. It pointed out that the purpose of a SOPO made on disposal was to prevent a repetition of the offences in question and any term of the order had to be proportionate and designed to achieve that purpose. It substituted a prohibition that A was not to download any photographs or pseudo-photographs of any person under 18.

Deciding whether to make a SOPO

18.53 It was held by the Court of Appeal in *D*[94] that the Court must conduct a risk assessment and consider the likelihood of the defendant committing a further sexual offence listed in SOA 2003, Sch 3 and thereby causing serious physical or psychological

---

[92] As a general rule, a court should not make a SOPO restraining a person from doing things he was neither threatening nor likely to do: *Yates* [2004] 1 Cr App R (S) 269. The mere fact that the offender would be an unsuitable person to work within the vicinity of children is not a sufficient reason in itself for a SOPO restraining him from doing so: ibid.

[93] [2008] EWCA Crim 1358.

[94] [2006] 2 Cr App R (S) 204.

harm to the public or any particular member(s) of the public. Whilst the harm envisaged had to be caused by the defendant, the Sch 3 offence did not necessarily have to be directed against a person specified in the SOPO, provided that that person might suffer some harm, including psychological harm, as a result.

18.54 As to the order and its effect, see **18.80** et seq.

SOPO made on complaint by the police

18.55 The relevant provisions came into force, and the SOO provisions were repealed, on 1 May 2004. However, if an application for a SOO was made before that date but an order made after it, the court only had power to make an order under the SOO provisions.[95] An application for a SOPO may be made to any magistrates' court[96] by a chief officer of police.[97] The fact that the acts in question were before 1 May 2004 (the commencement[98] of s 104) does not prevent an application for a SOPO (and an interim SOPO) being made after commencement.[99]

Making the application

18.56 An application for a SOPO may be prompted not only by concerns which a police force has about a violent or sexual offender in the community, but also by such concerns on the part of the probation service or prison staff. Although it is only the police who are given the power to apply to the court for a SOPO, guidance makes it quite clear that this is a decision that should ordinarily be taken in a multi-agency context, particularly through the MAPPA (Multi-Agency Public Protection Arrangements).[100] The reason is that a SOPO affects the management of the offender in the community for all the various agencies concerned; it is obviously important that they are involved in the assessment process prior to the SOPO being sought. The need for a SOPO will almost certainly arise as a result of a risk assessment and indeed guidance suggests that the possibility of a SOPO is something that should be considered as part of the general monitoring process.[101] Where the offender is under 18, an application for a SOPO should only be considered exceptionally.[102]

18.57 A specific risk assessment should be considered before applying for a SOPO, with the following being taken into account:

- the risk that a sexual offence will be committed;

- the potential harm resulting from such an offence;

- the date, nature and circumstances of the previous conviction or convictions and any pattern which emerges;

---

95 *Bradshaw* [2007] EWCA Crim 2971.
96 SOA 2003, s 104(6). Section 104(6) refers to the application being made to any magistrates' court whose commission areas includes (a) any part of that chief officer's police area; or (b) any place where it is alleged that the defendant acted in such a way as to give reasonable cause to believe that it is necessary for a SOPO to be made. The commission areas were abolished by the Courts Act (CA) 2003, s 109(3) and Sch 10.
97 See **17.106**, n 187.
98 See **2.1**
99 SOA 2003, s 106(4).
100 *Guidance Pt 2*, at p 39 et seq.
101 Ibid, at p 38.
102 Ibid, at p 36.

- the current circumstances of an offender and how these might foreseeably change;

- the disclosure implications if an order is applied for, and how the court process might affect the ability to manage an offender in the community;

- an assessment of the accuracy and relevance of the information about the individual;

- the nature and pattern of the behaviour giving rise to concern, including any predatory behaviour which may indicate a likelihood of re-offending;

- the extent of compliance, or otherwise, with previous sentences, court orders or supervision arrangements; and

- compliance or otherwise with therapeutic help and its outcome.[103]

The risk assessment can be put before the court. It can be seen that the risk assessment is comprehensive and this perhaps reflects the fact that a SOPO is not something that should be applied for routinely: it is designed to be an order that can be tailored to respond to the specific risks of an individual.

18.58 An application by the police for a SOPO must be made by complaint.[104] It may be made in respect of a person residing in the chief officer's police area or who the chief officer believes is in, or is intending to come to, his police area[105] if it appears to the chief officer that:

- the person is a 'qualifying offender'; and

- the person has since the 'appropriate date' (below) acted in such a way as to give reasonable cause to believe that it is necessary for a SOPO to be made.[106]

The behaviour need not have occurred in the chief officer's police area.

18.59 An application for a SOPO may be in the form set out in Sch 1 to the Magistrates' Courts (Sexual Offences Prevention Orders) Rules 2004,[107] and a summons directed to the defendant requiring him to appear before a magistrates' court to answer an application for such an order may be in the form set out in Sch 2 thereto.[108]

18.60 Ordinarily the police should inform the offender as soon as is practicably possible that they intend to seek a SOPO, give their reasons and inform the offender of the need to seek legal advice at the earliest possible opportunity.[109] This will allow the police legal team and the offender (or the offender's legal team) to liaise as to the application. Where it is intended to seek an order relating to an offender under the age

---

[103] Ibid, at pp 40 and 41.
[104] SOA 2003, s 104(5). As to proceedings initiated by complaint, see **18.70**.
[105] See n 6 above.
[106] SOA 2003, s 104(5).
[107] SI 2004/1054, r 4(1).
[108] SI 2004/1054, r 4(2).
[109] *Guidance Pt 2*, at p 40. The exception to this would be where telling the offender would raise an immediate risk (eg cause the offender to 'go underground'). In such circumstances it is likely that an interim SOPO would be sought (see **18.104** et seq).

of 18, the police should contact the social services department and youth offending team for the area before making an application.[110] Where an offender poses a risk to children, the development of prohibitions must be made following reference to Local Safeguarding Children's Boards' procedures and agencies.[111] Where an offender is known to have suffered mental disorder, or appears to be so suffering, advice should be sought through the relevant social services department; any assessment of the need for a SOPO should include consideration by psychiatric services of whether the offender should be referred for admission to hospital under MHA 1983.[112]

18.61 Although the Crown Prosecution Service (CPS) has no formal role in any application, it is responsible for prosecuting any breach. Because the CPS would be unlikely to prosecute a breach of a prohibition which it believed to be uncertain or unlawful,[113] it is advisable for the police to contact the CPS before making the application in cases where the circumstances are unusual or particularly complex, to ensure that any breaches of the SOPO will be capable of being proved as an offence.[114]

Qualifying offender

18.62 A 'qualifying offender' means someone within SOA 2003, s 106(6) or (7).[115]

18.63 A person is within s 106(6) if, whether before or after the commencement of Pt 2 (1 May 2004),[116] he has:

- been convicted[117] of a Sch 3[118] or Sch 5 offence;[119]

- been found not guilty of such an offence by reason of insanity, or to be under a disability and to have done the act charged against him in respect of such an offence;[120] or

- in England and Wales or Northern Ireland, been cautioned[121] in respect of such an offence.

Whereas a person convicted after 1 May 2004 could have been made the subject of a SOPO as part of the disposal, so that the present provisions are a back-up for cases where he was not, the power to make a SOPO on application by the police in respect of those who have been cautioned fills a gap which would otherwise exist in the law.

---

[110] Ibid.
[111] Ibid, at p 41. LSCBs have replaced the Area Child Protection Committees referred to in the *Guidance*.
[112] Ibid, at p 40.
[113] In *B v Chief Constable of Avon and Somerset* [2001] 1 All ER 562 the Divisional Court held that the criminal law required an offender to know clearly and unambiguously what conduct would leave him open to the possibility of penal sanctions.
[114] *Guidance Pt 2*, at p 41.
[115] SOA 2003, s 106(5).
[116] See **2.1**.
[117] See **17.29–17.30**.
[118] Except an offence in Scotland of the type described in n 16 above As to Sch 3 offences, see **18.35**.
[119] Including a 'spent' conviction (see n 13 above) or a conviction which has resulted in a conditional discharge (s 134; see **17.29**) after the commencement of SOA 2003, Pt 2.
[120] See **17.33**, **17.34**.
[121] See **17.36**.

18.64 Persons are within s 106(7) if, under the law of a country[122] outside the UK and whether before or after the commencement of Pt 2:

- they have been convicted[123] of a relevant offence;

- a foreign court has made in respect of a relevant offence a finding equivalent to a finding of not guilty by reason of insanity, or to a finding that they are under a disability and did the act charged against them; or

- they have been cautioned in respect of a relevant offence.

A 'relevant offence' means an act which constituted an offence[124] under the law of the country concerned, *and would have constituted a Sch 3*[125] *or Sch 5 offence if it had been done in any part of the UK.*[126] SOA 2003, s 106(13) and (14) (see **18.35**) apply in respect of a Sch 3 offence. As in the case of a corresponding provision relating to NOs,[127] on a police application for a SOPO, the italicised condition in s 106(9) is rebuttably presumed to be satisfied unless the defendant serves a notice, not later than 3 days before the hearing date for the application for the SOPO, questioning this.[128] The court, however, has power to waive the need for such a notice and permit the defendant to require the applicant to prove that the condition is not satisfied.[129]

18.65 It will be noted that in both s 106(6) and (7) the first 'trigger' for the making of a SOPO is simply a conviction. There is no need for the convicted person to have been sentenced or punished. Thus, a SOPO can be made against a convicted person who has absconded before sentence or before serving his sentence.

18.66 Where a person is not a 'qualifying offender' but it is sought to protect children or any child from harm from him, it may be possible to obtain a RSHO (see **18.171** et seq).

Appropriate date

18.67 The 'appropriate date', in relation to a qualifying offender, means the date (or first date) on which the offender was convicted, found or cautioned as mentioned in s 106(6) or (7) above.[130] By virtue of MCA 1980, s 127(1) (6-month time-limit from time of matter complained of within which complaint must be made), at least part of the behaviour relied on must have taken place in the 6 months prior to the complaint being made. However, this does not render inadmissible evidence of events after the appropriate date that took place more than 6 months before the complaint, for the purposes of proving that a SOPO is necessary.[131]

---

122 Or territory (e g a dependency): SOA 2003, s 133.
123 See n 119 above.
124 However described by the foreign law: s 106(10).
125 Except an offence in Scotland of the type described in n 16 above.
126 SOA 2003, s 106(9).
127 See **18.10**.
128 SOA 2003, s 106(11); MC(SOPO)R 2004, r 5. For full details see **18.10**; the material terms of both sets of provisions are identical.
129 SOA 2003, s 106(12).
130 SOA 2003, s 106(8).
131 *Chief Constable of West Mercia Constabulary v Boorman* (2005) 169 JP 669 (ASBO).

Proceedings on police application

18.68 Proceedings on a police application for the imposition of a SOPO are civil, not criminal, both as a matter of domestic law and for the purposes of ECHR, Art 6, just like applications for ASBOs[132] and football banning orders.[133] Pursuant to the principles laid down by the House of Lords in *R (McCann) v Crown Court at Manchester; Clingham v Kensington and Chelsea Royal London Borough Council*,[134] as regards domestic law, such proceedings are civil for the following reasons. They do not involve a formal accusation of a breach of criminal law, and they are initiated by the civil process of complaint. They require an objective inquiry, and there is no need to prove any element of fault. It is unnecessary to prove criminal liability, the true purpose of the proceedings being preventative and not a condemnation or penalty. The procedure leading to the making of a SOPO is separate from the criminal proceedings for breach of the order. Pursuant to the principles in the above case, as regards Art 6, proceedings on a police application for a SOPO do not constitute the bringing of a criminal charge for the purposes of ECHR, Art 6. Consequently, the protection in Arts 6(2) and (3) which only applies to criminal proceedings does not apply to proceedings for a SOPO.

18.69 The right to fair trial under Art 6(1), however, must not be forgotten. Ensuring sufficient opportunity to make representations when orders are sought in an area distant from where the defendant is not resident may be difficult. The point applies equally well to the other orders dealt with later in this chapter.

18.70 Proceedings by complaint are governed by MCA 1980, ss 51–57, under which (as in the case of criminal proceedings) the court cannot proceed in the absence of the defendant unless he has been given sufficient opportunity to attend. Because the proceedings are civil, the rules of civil evidence, not criminal evidence, apply.[135] Thus, hearsay evidence, admitted under the statutory procedure for the introduction of such evidence in civil cases, is, depending on its persuasiveness, capable of satisfying the proof required[136] as to the defendant's behaviour.[137] It follows that it is not necessary to call witnesses; their written statements may suffice.[138]

18.71 Because proceedings in respect of a police application for a SOPO are civil in nature, the Police and Criminal Evidence Act 1984, s 73 (which permits proof of a conviction in a UK court by certificate in criminal proceedings) has no application. A conviction by any court (including a foreign one) can be proved by the production of a certificate of conviction, and a caution, etc by the production of the relevant record. Depending on the facts, SOA 2003, s 92 (see **17.122** and **17.123**) may be relevant in this respect.

---

[132]   *R (McCann) v Crown Court at Manchester; Clingham v Kensington and Chelsea Royal London Borough Council* [2003] 1 AC 787.

[133]   *Gough v Chief Constable of Derby Constabulary* [2002] 2 All ER 985.

[134]   [2003] 1 AC 787.

[135]   Confirmed in *R (McCann) v Crown Court at Manchester; Clingham v Kensington and Chelsea Royal London Borough Council*, above n 132, in respect of an ASBO.

[136]   By SOA 2003, s 104(1).

[137]   *R (McCann) v Crown Court at Manchester; Clingham v Kensington and Chelsea Royal London Borough Council*, above n 132. As to admissibility of hearsay evidence in the present type of civil proceedings, see CEA 1995 and MC(HECP)R 1999, SI 1999/681.

[138]   Despite the further relaxation in CJA 2003, Part 11, Ch 2, of the rule against hearsay in criminal cases, the law is still stricter about hearsay in criminal cases.

Making a SOPO on application by the police

18.72 If, on a police application, it is proved that the defendant is a qualifying offender,[139] the magistrates' court may (but is not obliged to) make a SOPO in respect of the defendant (A) if satisfied that A's behaviour since the 'appropriate date' (see **18.67**) makes it *necessary to make such an order, for the purpose of protecting the public or any particular members*[140] *of the public from serious sexual harm from A* (SOA 2003, s 104(1)(a)). The italicised words also appear in s 104(1)(b) in relation to making a SOPO as part of a disposal, and reference should be made to **18.46–18.53** in respect of them. Evidence of A's behaviour may come, for example, from the probation service, a head teacher or social services, as well as from the police. As in the case of a SOPO made on disposal, the words italicised refer to protecting the public *in the UK* or any particular members of that public from serious physical or psychological harm caused by A committing one or more Sch 3 offences.[141]

18.73 'Behaviour' in this context embraces not only a course of conduct but also a single act. There is nothing in s 104 to prevent a court making a SOPO on the basis of one act (or only one act which can be proved) if it satisfies the condition in s 104(1)(a). However, there must be an act: the fact that A is a suspected paedophile and is considered to present a significant risk of serious sexual harm to young children is insufficient.

18.74 The behaviour in question does not have to be an illegal act or itself cause sexual harm. It is what the act in question shows about the future behaviour of the defendant which is important. Thus, the behaviour in question by A might be offering sweets to children or frequenting places where children congregate. Another example might be thought to be the sex offender allowed contact with his child on a supervised basis, say, on Saturday afternoons, who regularly turns up for unsupervised contact at other times and creates a risk of serious sexual harm to the child.

18.75 The reference to A's behaviour includes a reference to any behaviour by A occurring before the commencement of Pt 2 (1 May 2004).[142]

18.76 In deciding whether it is 'necessary' to make a SOPO it would seem that the magistrates should, first, decide whether there is a risk of serious sexual harm to the public or any members of the public from the defendant and, secondly, whether an order is necessary to give protection against that risk. If the risk is remote, a court should conclude that a SOPO is not necessary. 'Necessary' makes it clear that simply being a sex offender or a violent offender does not, of itself, entitle the making of the order. A SOPO is not necessary if there are effective alternative ways of achieving the protection sought.

Proof

18.77 It is not an invariable rule that the lower standard of proof normally applied in civil proceedings (proof on the balance of probabilities) must apply. This was held by the House of Lords in *R (McCann) v Crown Court at Manchester; Clingham v*

---

[139]   SOA 2003, s 104(4)(b).
[140]   The plural in s 104(1)(a) includes the singular: IA 1978, s 6(c).
[141]   SOA 2003, s 106(3).
[142]   SOA 2003, s 106(4).

Kensington and Chelsea Royal London Borough Council, an ASBO case. Lord Hope, with whom the rest of the House agreed, stated that:[143]

> 'I think that there are good reasons, in the interests of fairness, for applying the higher standard when allegations are made of criminal or quasi-criminal conduct which, if proved, would have serious consequences for the person against whom they are made.'

Like an ASBO, breach of an order of the present type involves serious consequences (criminal liability and liability to arrest). Like the condition in CDA 1998, s 1(1)(a) (that the defendant has acted in an anti-social manner), the issues of whether the defendant is a qualifying offender and of his alleged behaviour since the appropriate date raise serious questions of fact. On this basis, proof of these issues must satisfy the criminal standard of proof by the applicant, namely beyond reasonable doubt.[144]

18.78 On the other hand, the issue of whether a defendant's behaviour since the appropriate date makes it necessary to make an order for the purpose of protection involves an exercise in judgment or evaluation, rather than a standard of proof.[145]

18.79 Determining the risk of serious sexual harm may depend on the views of expert witnesses, such as psychiatrists, probation officers, housing officers and social workers. The level of risk, and the nature of the danger posed, will, of course, often have been the subject of a risk assessment of the type referred to in **18.57**.

The order and its effect

18.80 A SOPO, whether made as part of disposal or on police application, prohibits the defendant doing anything described in it.[146] SOA 2003, s 107(2), however, provides that the only prohibitions which may be included in the order are those *necessary to protect the public or any particular members of the public from serious sexual harm from the defendant*. 'Members of the public' includes a particular member of the public.[147] 'Necessary' indicates that there must be a need for the specific prohibition and not simply that it is desirable or appropriate. 'Protecting the public ...' has the same meaning as in s 104.[148] 'Serious sexual harm' was dealt with in **18.46–18.48**. Section 107 does not limit the acts which may be prohibited by a SOPO, provided that the prohibitions in it are necessary and proportionate. The court must consider carefully whether the proposed prohibitions will protect the public, etc from serious sexual harm and must ensure that they are no wider than necessary to protect against the risks ascertained by it.[149] Where the order is necessary to protect a particular child (or children) the order could prohibit the defendant from doing things related to the antecedent behaviour involved in relation to the child (or children) in question. To make an order referring to children in general would be disproportionate. If a prohibition is not necessary or is too

---

143 [2003] 1 AC 787 at [82]. Also see *B v Chief Constable of the Avon and Somerset Constabulary* [2001] 1 All ER 562. The decision on proof in respect of what is now s 104(1)(a) must now be read in the light of *McCann*.

144 *Woolmington v DPP* [1935] AC 462.

145 *R (McCann) v Crown Court at Manchester; Clingham v Kensington and Chelsea Royal London Borough Council*, n 132 above.

146 SOA 2003, s 107(1)(a).

147 *Yates* [2004] 1 Cr App R (S) 269; IA 1978, s 6(c).

148 SOA 2003, s 107(7). Ie the meaning given by s 106(3); see **18.72**.

149 *Owen* [2007] EWCA Crim 694.

wide, it can be struck out on appeal or an application to vary. However, until it is struck down in one of these two ways, a SOPO containing a prohibition which is not necessary is not invalid.[150]

18.81 A court should not make an order restraining the defendant from doing things he was neither threatening nor likely to do. This was held in *Yates*,[151] where A appealed against the making, following his conviction for indecent assault, of a RO under SOffA 1997, s 5A, prohibiting him from working with or in the vicinity of children for a period of 20 years. A argued that it had been wrong in principle to impose the order. He submitted that he had not been convicted of any offence against children and that there had been no suggestion that he was attracted to children. Allowing the appeal, the Court of Appeal held that it was not wrong in principle to make an order under SOffA 1997, s 5A where the offence of which the offender had been convicted had not been committed against a child; a child was a 'particular member of the public' for the purposes of s 5A. Whilst A was a most unsuitable person to be working with or in the vicinity of children, there had been no evidence that he was ever likely to do so. The mere fact that an offender would not be suitable for working with or in the vicinity of children was not a sufficient reason for making a RO prohibiting him from doing so. Accordingly, the RO should not have been made.

18.82 A SOPO can only *prohibit* a person doing something. It cannot *require* an offender *to do* something. To some extent this is of no consequence. For example, although an order cannot require a defendant to stay away from or only to talk to children in the presence of a adult in recreation grounds, it can prohibit him from frequenting such grounds or from talking to children in the absence of an adult. Nevertheless, the inability of an order to make a requirement can be of practical importance. For example, an order cannot require a defendant to agree to supervision by a probation officer, to comply with a child protection plan (although non-compliance might involve a breach of a prohibition) or to attend a sex offenders' treatment programme.

18.83 The statute does not limit the discretion of the courts as to the nature of the prohibitions and accordingly courts can act creatively. This could include an order limiting an offender in a more draconian way than is possible under the notification requirements referred to in Chapter 17. It would be possible in appropriate circumstances for a SOPO to include a prohibition that a person should not stay away from notified premises for more than 24 hours without notifying the police of the details of residence, even though under the notification requirements an offender may stay at qualifying premises for up to 7 days without having to notify the police.[152] This can be useful where an offender poses a very high risk and the normal notification requirements would be insufficient to manage him. Similarly a SOPO could prevent someone from leaving the country for any duration without advance notification, even though the notification requirements require notification of a foreign trip only where it will last 3 days or more.[153]

18.84 Where the offending conduct has involved information technology, a common SOPO prohibition relates to access to information technology. The courts have, for example, imposed restrictions on access to information and communication

---

[150] *DPP v T* [2006] 3 All ER 471 (ASBO); not following *R(W) v DPP* (2005) 169 JP 435 (ASBO).
[151] [2004] 1 Cr App R (S) 269. See also *Whitton* [2007] 2 Cr App R (S) 67.
[152] See **17.64**.
[153] See **17.84**.

technologies (ICT) for offenders convicted of offences relating to indecent photographs of children,[154] grooming[155] and inciting a child to engage in sexual activity.[156] Such limitations must, however, be proportionate. Access to ICT is required for many jobs and a complete ban may be an unjustified interference.[157]

18.85 Where the risk is to the offender's own family (or a member of it), a SOPO may restrict unsupervised access to the child or another child of the family. However, parental access is normally the purview of the civil rather than criminal courts. Although a criminal court undoubtedly has jurisdiction to restrict access through a SOPO and the terms of a SOPO can be varied,[158] seeking variation may be problematic. For example, a victim or other child of the family has no power to seek a variation, only the police and offender have such a power. What happens if a child of the family wishes parental contact? In any event requiring an application to the criminal court for contact may unnecessarily complicate matters. In *D*[159] the Court of Appeal held that the most suitable method would be to use the following term:[160]

'[The defendant] shall not, without the order of a judge exercising jurisdiction under the Children Act 1989, communicate or seek to communicate, whether directly or indirectly with [the victim] whilst he remains under the age of sixteen years.'

This would appear an appropriate compromise and ensures that the criminal justice system does not fetter the discretion of a judge considering what is in the best interests of the child.

Duration

18.86 A SOPO comes into effect on the day it is made. It can have effect for a fixed period specified in the order.[161] The fixed period must be not less than 5 years,[162] irrespective of the age or maturity of the defendant, or the levels of risk or seriousness of harm which he poses. Alternatively, a SOPO may be stated to have effect until further order by the court, ie indefinite effect until successfully appealed or discharged.[163] If the order says nothing about its duration, it will be of indefinite duration. An order 'for life' may not be made because it is neither for a fixed period nor 'until further order'.[164] In accordance with the requirements of necessity and proportionality an indefinite order should be imposed only where the evidence shows ongoing risk.[165] In *Hammond*[166] the Court of Appeal held that, when a SOPO was imposed as part of the disposal for an offence listed in SOA 2003, Sch 3, the duration of the SOPO should normally be that of the notification requirements to which the offender was subject for that offence. A fixed-period order can be reduced, discharged or renewed, and an indefinite order can

---

154 *Beaney* [2004] 2 Cr App R (S) 441; *Collard* [2005] 1 Cr App R (S) 155; see **18.50** and **18.51**.
155 *Warren* [2007] EWCA Crim 2733.
156 *Ardener* [2007] 1 Cr App R (S) 569.
157 The usual solution to this is to bar access 'save for the purposes of employment': see *Crowley* [2005] EWCA Crim 3181; *Lewis* [2006] EWCA Crim 2225.
158 SOA 2003, s 108; see **18.98**.
159 [2006] 2 Cr App R (S) 204.
160 Ibid, at [36].
161 SOA 2003, s 107(1)(b).
162 Ibid.
163 Ibid.
164 *Williamson* [2005] EWCA Crim 2151.
165 See *Pravin Jeyaraj* [2007] EWCA Crim 1677, where an indeterminate SOPO was amended to a fixed period because it was not established that an indeterminate length was necessary.
166 [2008] EWCA Crim 1358.

be varied to a fixed term or discharged: see **18.98** et seq. However, there is a restriction[167] on the discharge of any SOPO within its first 5 years.

18.87 Where a court makes a SOPO against someone already subject to a SOPO, the earlier SOPO ceases to have effect.[168] Thus, someone cannot be subject to more than one SOPO at a time. A new SOPO is particularly likely to be imposed on conviction or when an offender moves location into a new police area. Although it is possible for an order to be varied in such a case,[169] it may be that the new location has changed the risk assessment sufficiently to justify a completely new order rather than a revised one. In addition, since a new order will last a minimum of another 5 years, the police must carefully consider the wisdom of seeking a new order rather than varying an existing order, especially where the existing order is likely to lapse within 5 years.

Notification requirements

18.88 By SOA 2003, s 107(3), where a SOPO is made in respect of a defendant (A) who was a 'relevant offender' (ie subject to the notification requirements of SOA 2003, Pt 2)[170] immediately before the making of the SOPO, and A would otherwise cease to be subject to the notification requirements of Pt 2[171] whilst the SOPO (as renewed from time to time) has effect, A remains subject to the notification requirements as long as the SOPO has effect.[172] For example, if an offender was sentenced on 1 June 2004 to 4 months' imprisonment, the duration of registration would ordinarily be 7 years from that date.[173] If, however, on 1 June 2006 the offender was the subject of a 10-year SOPO, the offender is subject to the notification requirements until 1 June 2016. This, coupled with the fact that breach of a SOPO is an either way offence, means that the effect of a SOPO has serious consequences, actual and potential, beyond the prohibitions contained in the SOPO. A will, of course, remain subject to notification requirements imposed on him as a relevant offender after the cessation of a SOPO if those requirements last for longer than the SOPO.

18.89 SOA 2003, s 107(4) deals with the case where a SOPO is made in respect of a defendant (A) who was not a 'relevant offender' immediately before the making of the SOPO, for example, because A had been convicted or cautioned for a non-sexual serious offence of violence or because he had been but his notification period had expired or because his offences pre-dated the introduction of notification requirements under SOffA 1997. It provides that, in such a case, the SOPO subjects D to the notification requirements of SOA 2003, Pt 2 from the making of the order. The notification requirements apply to A from the date of service of the order, the 'relevant date' for the application of the notification period rules,[174] and not from the date of any conviction, etc. This means, for example, that A must comply with the initial notification requirements (under s 83(1)) within 3 days[175] of the date of the service of the order.[176]

---

[167] See **18.102**.
[168] SOA 2003, s 107(6).
[169] See **18.98**.
[170] SOA 2003, s 80(2); see **17.9**.
[171] See **17.52** et seq.
[172] SOA 2003, s 107(3).
[173] SOA 2003, s 82; see **17.40**.
[174] SOA 2003, s 107(5).
[175] See **17.52**, n 97.
[176] SOA 2003, s 107(5).

Parental direction

18.90 A court which makes a SOPO in respect of a 'young offender' (ie someone under 18, or 16 in Scotland) may make a parental direction.[177]

Information

18.91 *On disposal:* When imposing SOPOs as part of a disposal, sentencers should make it clear that they are doing so under SOA 2003, s 104, and the appropriate notices should tally with the judge's order.[178]

18.92 The restrictions contained in the SOPO must be included in the court's committal warrant provided to the Prison Service. The restrictions must also be detailed on the certificate part of the notice to the police (and others) issued by the court.[179]

18.93 *On police application:* It is advisable that, whenever possible, a SOPO should be served in person on the defendant, together with a copy of the 'Notice of requirement to register' form (where appropriate). In the case of defendants under 18, a copy should also be given to their parent or guardian. The process of appeal must be made clear to the individual, so must the consequences of a breach of the order or of the notification requirements.[180]

18.94 *General:* A person subject to a SOPO is entitled to know what he can and cannot do; the prohibition(s) ordered must be sufficiently specific and clear to enable the defendant to comply without difficulty. In making a SOPO, the court should formally notify the defendant that, by reason of SOA 2003, s 107, he is subject to the notification requirements.[181] If a prohibition is not sufficiently specific and clear, it can be struck out on an appeal or an application to vary. However, until it is struck down in one of these two ways, a SOPO containing a prohibition which is too wide or is not sufficiently specific or clear is not invalid.[182] The defendant should be given a 'Notice of requirement to register' form (where appropriate).[183]

18.95 The police will be given a copy of the SOPO. It may be appropriate, particularly for SOPOs made on disposal, for a copy of the 'Notice of requirement to register' form to be given to the police.[184] The *Guidance* recommends that the police consider passing a copy of the SOPO to those public protection bodies which need to be informed according to the risk assessment. It adds that that any disclosure to the wider community should be treated with great sensitivity, on a case-by-case basis, especially if a minor is concerned and reporting restrictions have been imposed.[185] The issue of publicity is an interesting point and one that has caused concern in the past. An application for a SOPO is heard in open court and some police forces had been nervous about the idea of applying for an order, fearing that it might lead to the press disclosing

---

177 SOA 2003, s 89(1); see **17.98** et seq.
178 *Yates* [2004] 1 Cr App R (S) 269, CA.
179 *Guidance Pt 2*, at p 38.
180 Ibid, at p 29.
181 *R(W) v DPP* (2005) 169 JP 435 (ASBO).
182 See n 150 above.
183 *Guidance Pt 2*, at p 42. The form is attached to the *Guidance*.
184 Ibid, at p 42.
185 At pp 29 and 42. Disclosure must also have regard to the Data Protection Act 1998 and the subject's rights under ECHR, Art 8.

the identity of an offender, causing violence.[186] Research has, however, suggested that only in a minority of circumstances was the offender named,[187] with only isolated problematic incidents being reported.[188] In part this is because the police have attempted to take a proactive stance in media-management, including explaining the risks to newspapers.

Human rights

18.96 Like the other orders under SOA 2003, Pt 2 described in this chapter, a SOPO can have ECHR implications because it may restrict the rights to private life, expression or association, in breach of Arts 8, 10 and 11 respectively. However, provided the order (and its terms) are necessary to prevent crime, to protect morals or to protect the rights and freedoms of others and are proportionate to the risk, these Articles will not be contravened on the ground of that restriction.

18.97 As in the case of any other prohibiting order, breach of which renders the person subject to it liable to severe punishment, that person is entitled to know, clearly and unambiguously, what conduct he has to avoid to comply with the order. If the prohibitions in the order are unclear, vague or unintelligible they are liable to be found to contravene the above Articles on this ground.[189]

Variation, renewal and discharge

18.98 SOA 2003, s 108 provides for the variation, renewal or discharge of a SOPO or of a RO or SOO, wherever made.[190]

Application process

18.99 The following can apply for the variation, renewal or discharge of a SOPO, RO or SOO (hereafter 'order'):

- the defendant (A);

- a chief officer of police[191] for the area in which A resides;

- a chief officer of police who believes that A is in, or is intending to come to, his police area;

- where the order was made on a police application (ie by complaint), the chief officer who made the application.[192]

---

[186] Knock *The Police Perspective on Sex Offender Orders*: Police Research Paper 155 (Home Office, 2002), at p 49.
[187] Ibid, at p 51.
[188] Ibid, at p 53.
[189] *B v Chief Constable of the Avon and Somerset Constabulary* [2001] 1 All ER 562.
[190] SOA 2003, s 108(8)(a) extends the provisions of s 108 relating to the variation, renewal or discharge of a SOPO to a RO or SOO.
[191] See **17.106**, n 187.
[192] SOA 2003, s 108(1) and (2). For 'police area' see n 6 above.

Other people with an interest in the terms of the order[193] have no standing to apply and accordingly must seek to persuade either the defendant or the police to do so. Given that the management of an offender is now undertaken in a multi-agency context this may not be problematic as the police are likely to accede to a request of the MAPPA although, as a matter of law, it remains a matter for their discretion.

18.100 In the case of an order made by the Court of Appeal or the Crown Court, the application is to the Crown Court, in accordance with the Crim PR 2005.[194] In the case of an order made by a magistrates' court (or a youth court), it is made to that court by complaint.[195]

18.101 An application for discharge might be made by a defendant who has successfully undergone treatment for his sexual problem (subject to the restriction on discharge of an order within 5 years of its making: see **18.102**). The defendant might apply for the removal of conditions made unnecessary by changed circumstances. The police might apply for a variation of an order if it only restricted A's behaviour in a particular area and it was believed that A was now living, or intending to live in their (different) area, or if an additional group needed protection. If a change sought by the police is major, an application for the discharge of the order and the making of a new order would seem more appropriate. The police might apply for the renewal of an order where the continuing risk assessment indicated that the prohibition in the order needs to be continued after expiry.

Outcome of an application

18.102 Subject to the restrictions set out below, the court, after hearing the applicant and representations from anyone else who could have applied for a variation, etc and wishes to be heard, may make any order, varying, renewing or discharging the main order, that it considers appropriate.[196] The restrictions are that:

- A renewal or variation order may only impose additional prohibitions on the defendant if it is necessary to do so for the purpose of protecting *the public or any particular members of the public*[197] from serious sexual harm from the defendant (and any renewed or varied order may contain only such prohibitions as are necessary for this purpose).[198]

- The court must not discharge an order before the end of the fixed period of 5 years beginning with the day on which it was made, without the consent of the defendant and:
  (a) where the application is made by the police, the chief officer who made that application; or
  (b) in any other case, the chief officer for the area in which the defendant resides.[199]

---

[193] For example, a child of the offender: see *D* [2006] 2 Cr App R (S) 204; see **18.85**.
[194] SI 2005/384, see r 50.5 (order made on disposal).
[195] SOA 2003, s 108(3).
[196] SOA 2003, s 108(4).
[197] The italicised words have the same meaning as they bear in respect of the making of an order.
[198] SOA 2003, s 108(5).
[199] SOA 2003, s 108(6).

It is submitted that the 'renewal' of a fixed-term SOPO must be for the same fixed term, but, by analogy with decisions made on the power to 'vary or discharge' a restraining order under the PHA 1997, s 5, the court has power under SOA 2003, s 108, to vary a SOPO so as to extend it for some other fixed term or until further order.[200]

18.103 Copies of an order dismissing the application, or varying or discharging it, should be given or sent to the defendant.[201] An order renewing a SOPO should be dealt with in the same way as the original order. Copies of any of these orders should also go to all persons who were given notice of the defendant's obligation to comply with the notification requirements.[202]

Interim SOPOs

18.104 SOA 2003, s 109 makes provision for interim SOPOs. The purpose of an interim SOPO is to enable prohibitions to be placed on someone against whom a police application for a full order has been made but not yet been determined and to ensure that he is subject to the notification requirements in Pt 2 in the time before the application for a full order is determined. There is no power to make an interim order on adjournment for sentence but protection from risk can be achieved pending sentence by bail conditions.

18.105 An interim SOPO may be imposed, for example, where the court wishes to have extra information about the risk assessment or indeed has suggested to the parties that further assessments are carried out on the offender. The availability of an interim SOPO may also be useful where an offender has committed an offence abroad as this would provide time to obtain the relevant paperwork.

18.106 Pending the determination of a police application for a SOPO ('the main application'), an application for an interim order:

(a)   may be made as part of the main application; or

(b)   if the main application has been made, may be made by the person who has made it, by complaint to the court to which that application was made.[203]

18.107 An application for an interim SOPO may be in the form set out in Sch 1 to the MC(SOPO)R 2004,[204] and a summons directed to the defendant requiring him to appear before a magistrates' court to answer an application for such an order may be in the form set out in Sch 2 thereto.[205] Since the purpose of an interim SOPO is to provide temporary protection until the application for the full order is determined, it will not be normal to adjourn the interim proceedings to allow the defendant more time to prepare.[206]

[200]   *Shaw v DPP* [2005] EWHC 1215 (Admin), at [14], per Laws LJ; *DPP v Hall* [2006] 3 All ER 170.
[201]   *Guidance Pt 2*, at p 29.
[202]   Ibid.
[203]   SOA 2003, s 109(1), (2); see **18.55**.
[204]   Rule 4(1).
[205]   Rule 4(2).
[206]   *Guidance Pt 2*, at p 26.

18.108   *If it considers it just to do so*, the court may make an interim SOPO.[207] Thus, the court has a discretion as to whether an interim SOPO is made. It is submitted that a court could not consider it just to make an order unless there is some evidence demonstrating a likelihood that the public or any particular member(s) need to be protected from serious sexual harm. An interim SOPO prohibits the defendant doing anything specified in the order.[208] Unlike a SOPO there is no statutory requirement that the prohibitions in an interim SOPO are necessary and proportionate for the purpose of protecting the public or a particular person from harm. However, it is submitted that this must be implicit and that, as in the case of an interim ASBO,[209] the consideration of whether it is just to make an interim order is necessarily a balancing exercise between the need to protect the public and the impact that an order would have on the defendant; the court will need to consider the seriousness of the behaviour, the urgency with which it must be controlled and the degree to which the order would impede the defendant's rights of free movement and association. Because an interim order is made before the court has heard and tested the evidence, it is essential that it ensures that the interim SOPO is justified. Otherwise there may be a contravention of ECHR, Art 8 or Art 11.

18.109   An interim SOPO has effect only for a fixed period, which must be specified in the order.[210] If the main application is determined during that period, the interim order ceases to have effect at that time.[211]

18.110   An interim SOPO made against someone already subject to a SOPO does not terminate the SOPO.

18.111   Where an interim SOPO is made in respect of a defendant (A) who was a 'relevant offender' (ie subject to the notification requirements of SOA 2003, Pt 2) immediately before the making of the interim SOPO, and A would otherwise cease to be subject to the notification requirements of Pt 2 whilst the order has effect, A remains subject to those notification requirements.[212]

18.112   Where an interim SOPO is made in respect of a defendant (A) who was not a 'relevant offender' immediately before the making of the interim SOPO (eg because A had been convicted or cautioned for a non-sexual serious offence of violence):

(a)   the interim SOPO subjects A to the notification requirements of SOA 2003, Pt 2 from the making of the order until it ceases; and

(b)   the notification requirements apply to A from the date of service of the order, the relevant date for the application of the notification period rules,[213] and not from the date of any conviction, etc. This means that A will have to comply with the initial notification requirements within 3 days of the service of the interim order.

18.113   A court which makes an interim SOPO in respect of a 'young offender' may make a 'parental direction'.[214]

---

[207]   SOA 2003, s 109(3).
[208]   Ibid.
[209]   *R (Kenny) v Leeds Magistrates' Court* [2004] 1 All ER 1333.
[210]   SOA 2003, s 109(4)(a).
[211]   SOA 2003, s 109(4)(b).
[212]   SOA 2003, s 109(5), applying with amendments s 107(3).
[213]   SOA 2003, s 109(5), applying with amendments s 107(4) and (5).
[214]   SOA 2003, s 89(1); see **17.98** et seq.

18.114 The applicant for an interim SOPO (or the defendant) may by complaint apply to the court for the variation, renewal or discharge of the order.[215] It is submitted that the order should only be varied or renewed so as to impose an additional prohibition if it is necessary for protection of the public, etc.

Appeal

SOA 2003, s 110

18.115 SOA 2003, s 110 provides for an appeal against the making of a SOPO or an interim SOPO. The court to which appeal lies depends on the circumstances in which the order was made.

18.116 Where a SOPO is made against the defendant as part of disposal after a conviction for, or finding in respect of, a Sch 3 or Sch 5 offence, the *defendant* can appeal against the making of the order as if he was appealing against sentence.[216] Thus, for example, if the SOPO is made following a conviction by a magistrates' court (or youth court), an appeal against the making of the SOPO lies by way of re-hearing[217] to the Crown Court; if the SOPO is made following a conviction in the Crown Court, appeal lies against the making of the SOPO to the Court of Appeal with its leave or a certificate from the trial judge.[218] The Crown Court or Court of Appeal, as the case may be, will have its normal powers to deal with an appeal against sentence when determining an appeal of the present type.

18.117 Where a SOPO or interim SOPO is made by a magistrates' court following a police application, the *defendant* may (under s 110(1)(c) and (2) respectively) appeal by way of re-hearing to the Crown Court against its making. The applicant is not given the right to appeal against a refusal to make an order or against its terms. On such an appeal under s 110(1)(c) or (2), the Crown Court may make such orders as may be necessary to give effect to its determination of the appeal.[219] It may also make such incidental or consequential orders as appear to it to be just.[220] It can therefore remit the case to a magistrates' court for re-hearing. If it considered it just to do so, it could make an incidental order to suspend the operation of the order pending the determination of the appeal.

18.118 An order made by the Crown Court on an appeal against the making of an order on application (other than an order that an application be re-heard by a magistrates' court) is to be treated as if it were an order of the court appealed from (and not an order of the Crown Court).[221] The importance of this is that an order made by the Crown Court on appeal is treated as an order of the magistrates' court which imposed the original order, for the purposes of determining where any subsequent application for variation, renewal or discharge should be heard.

---

[215] SOA 2003, s 109(6).
[216] SOA 2003, s 110(1)(a), (b).
[217] SCtA 1981, s 79(3).
[218] As required by the Criminal Appeals Act 1968, s 11.
[219] SOA 2003, s 110(4).
[220] Ibid.
[221] SOA 2003, s 110(5).

18.119 A *defendant* may also appeal against an order varying, renewing or discharging a SOPO (but not an interim SOPO), or the refusal to make such an order.[222] Where the application for variation, etc was made to the Crown Court, appeal lies to the Court of Appeal,[223] presumably as if it is an appeal against sentence.[224] Otherwise, it lies to the Crown Court.[225] On such an appeal to it, the Crown Court has the same powers as when determining an appeal against the making of the initial order if that order was made on the application of the police.[226] Where the initial order was made by a magistrates' court on convicting the offender, the Crown Court has its usual powers when hearing an appeal against sentence.

Other methods of challenge

18.120 In an appropriate case, there could be an appeal by either side against the making or a refusal of a SOPO or interim SOPO (or an application for variation, etc) by a magistrates' court, or against a determination of an appeal (or an application for variation, etc) by the Crown Court, to the High Court by case stated on the ground that the court's determination of the application was wrong in law or in excess of jurisdiction.[227] Alternatively, in such a case there could be an application for judicial review by either side in an appropriate case.[228] Thus, either order could be challenged in the High Court on grounds including the fact that it is ultra vires, *Wednesbury*[229] unreasonable or not proportionate to the harm sought to be prevented. Judicial review is the least suitable procedure where the defendant concedes that there was sufficient evidence before the court to justify the order being made. In such a case, the High Court does not have before it a statement of the facts on which the decision was based or of the reason for the order. It cannot substitute its discretion for that of the court. Nor can it vary the order so as to accommodate contentions successfully made by the defendant.[230]

Breach

18.121 SOA 2003, s 113 provides that a person commits an offence if, without reasonable excuse, he does anything which he is prohibited from doing by a SOPO or interim SOPO[231] (in whatever part of the UK it was made). It is likewise an offence under s 113, without reasonable excuse, to do anything which a person is prohibited from doing by a RO, SOO or interim SOO[232] made by a court in England and Wales or Northern Ireland. Where the breach is of an interim order the defendant is criminally liable even though no court has yet been satisfied, after hearing and testing all the evidence, that the grounds for a full order have been established.

18.122 An offence under s 113 is triable either way and is punishable by a maximum sentence, when tried on indictment, of 5 years' imprisonment.[233] A court, when passing

---

[222] SOA 2003, s 110(3).
[223] SOA 2003, s 110(3)(a).
[224] See **18.116**.
[225] SOA 2003, s 110(3)(b).
[226] SOA 2003, s 110(4).
[227] MCA 1980, s 111; SCtA 1981, s 28.
[228] SCtA 1981, s 29.
[229] *Associated Provincial Picture Houses v Wednesbury Corporation* [1948] 1 KB 223.
[230] *R (A) v Leeds Magistrates' Court* (2004) *The Times*, March 31 (interim ASBO).
[231] SOA 2003, s 113(1)(a) and (b).
[232] SOA 2003, s 113(1)(c)–(e).
[233] SOA 2003, s 113(2); maximum on summary conviction: **1.43**.

a sentence for this offence cannot make a conditional discharge.[234] It is not immediately clear why this prohibition is imposed since no prohibition applies, for example, to the making of an absolute discharge.

Class of offence[235]	3	SOA 2003, s 72 applies	✗
Notification requirements	✗	SOPO	✗
CJA 2003, Sch 15 applies	✗[236]	Serious specified offence	✗
Review of lenient sentence	✗	Special provisions of CYPA 1933	✗
Detention of young offender for specified period			✗

18.123 As the offence under s 113 is a separate offence the CPS must consider both the evidential and public interest tests before deciding to prosecute and it could, if it considered it appropriate, require the police to deal with the offence by way of administrative punishment.[237] The prosecution will need to establish, beyond reasonable doubt, the making of the order and its terms. This will be done by producing to the court a copy of the order.

18.124 The prosecution will also need to prove that there has been a breach of the order, by the defendant doing something prohibited by the order. In many cases that may be by an admission through a plea of guilty, or by a formal admission under CJA 1967, s 9. If there is not a formal admission or a plea of guilty, the breach will be proved in the normal way through evidence admissible under the rules of criminal evidence. The prosecution does not need to prove that the acts complained of create a danger of serious harm to anybody, or to the public at large.

18.125 The offence is committed simply by a breach of the requirements of the order, subject to that breach not being with reasonable excuse.[238] The burden of showing lack of reasonable excuse is on the prosecution, although the defendant will bear an evidential burden in respect of that defence.[239] Breach of an order which is invalid because the court had no jurisdiction to make it is not an offence; it is not the case that an order is valid until set aside.[240] The same is true in respect of the offences relating to FTOs and RSHOs.

---

[234] SOA 2003, s 113(3).

[235] See **1.49**.

[236] In *Williams (Christopher Peter)* [2007] EWCA Crim 1951, the Court of Appeal thought that careful consideration be given to adding breach of a SOPO to the list of offences in CJA 2003, Sch 15. See **1.52**.

[237] Ie a simple caution or a conditional caution for an adult offender, or a reprimand or final warning or (when in force) youth conditional caution for a juvenile.

[238] See **17.115–17.118**.

[239] *Polychronakis v Richards & Jerrom Ltd* [1998] Env LR 347; *O'Boyle* [1973] RTR 445; *Mallows v Harris* [1979] RTR 404.

[240] *L* (2008) 158 NLJ 297. An order which contains a prohibition which is unnecessary, too wide or insufficiently clear or specific is not thereby invalid: see **10.125**.

18.126 Research relating to SOOs has demonstrated that some police forces were frustrated by the attitude of the CPS to breach of an order.[241] The police argued that since the CPS was not ordinarily involved in the application of an order it sometimes appeared reluctant to institute a prosecution for breach. The same difficulties should arise less frequently in respect of SOPOs since where an order is made at the time of sentence, the CPS may have invited a SOPO to be made, and where it is made on an application by way of complaint, the CPS will probably have been involved if the case is unusual or particularly complex.[242] A prosecution may not succeed where the terms are vague or uncertain and liaising with the CPS should ensure that terms are structured appropriately.

18.127 Although there has been no comprehensive research conducted on the breach of SOPOs, it is known that the rate for breach of SOOs was relatively high.[243] Some police officers allowed repeated breaches to occur before taking action because they believed a court would take repeated breach more seriously than a single occurrence.[244] The difficulty with this approach is that not only is it arguably unethical (in that the police could be considered to be condoning the breaches if they are aware of the breach but do not take action) but it also is difficult to justify in terms of the necessity of an order. If a term was necessary to protect the public from serious sexual harm a breach will ordinarily expose the public to serious harm and the police should take action against the offender.

Sentencing

18.128 There is no Sentencing Guidelines Council (SGC) definitive guideline dealing with the offence under s 113. Research relating to SOOs indicated that in a majority of cases a conviction would lead to a sentence of imprisonment.[245] There is no evidence that this has changed where a breach of a SOPO is concerned.

18.129 A number of cases concerned with breach of a SOO have indicated that that, where the court has to balance the fact that the offending behaviour would in other circumstances be relatively innocuous against the risk that that the offender poses, the latter is the predominant consideration.

18.130 In *Brown*,[246] for example, a SOO had been made against A just before his release from prison for outraging public decency. The terms of the SOO prohibited A, inter alia, from seeking to contact or communicate with anyone under 16, or seeking to associate with or befriend such a person. On the day that A was released from prison, A communicated with a boy of 14 in the street, spending an hour with him and putting his arm over the boy's shoulder. The next day A gave a boy of 13 a £5 note in the street. Soon afterwards, he approached a boy of 14 at a post office and made 'somewhat sexual remarks' to him. A appealed against his concurrent sentence of 3 years' imprisonment imposed following conviction for these breaches of the SOO, to which he had pleaded not guilty. The judge had concluded that, despite the relative harmlessness of A's conduct, the element of risk should be the prime consideration, saying that A

---

[241]   Knock, n 186 above, at p 47.
[242]   See **18.61**.
[243]   Knock, n 186 above, at p 41.
[244]   Ibid, at p 43.
[245]   Ibid, at p 44.
[246]   [2002] 1 Cr App R (S) 1. See also *Norkett* [2003] EWCA Crim 924; *Beech* [2001] EWCA Crim 915. These cases were discussed by Shute 'New Civil Preventative Orders' [2004] Crim LR 417, at pp 435–438.

unquestionably posed a very serious risk to children and that it was his duty to impose a sentence designed to protect them. A appealed, arguing that the 3-year sentence was excessive in the light of the comparatively harmless activities involved in the three breaches. The Court of Appeal, which described A as a 'sexual obsessive', dismissed the appeal. It stated that the quality of the acts constituting the breaches was not the only consideration in determining their seriousness. The breaches were serious principally because of the speed at which they occurred so soon after A's release. That, coupled with the fact that there had been three breaches in 48 hours, gave rise to the wholly justified fear that the breaches would be but a prelude to further and possibly more serious offences. In the course of its judgment, the Court stated that it would have been wholly illogical if the judge had not had the protection of children foremost in his mind.

18.131   *Brown* can be contrasted with *Clark*.[247] A, aged 59, appealed, inter alia, against a 3-year custodial sentence for breach of a SOO. A had a 'perverted interest in pre-pubescent girls'. He had been convicted for attempting to abduct a young girl and attempting to impersonate a police officer. After he had been released on licence a SOO was made that A should not reside at a place where under-16s resided. Subsequently, A was traced to an address where boys under the age of 3 lived and he was arrested for failing to comply with the order. A pleaded guilty at an early stage. On appeal, A submitted that there had been no purposeful contempt of the order and that by living at the property with two boys aged under 3 he was not residing or surrounding himself with his target group of young girls. A also contended that he had been given insufficient credit for his guilty plea. The Court of Appeal allowed the appeal and reduced the sentence to 18 months' imprisonment. It stated:[248]

> 'This was a case where [A] had complied with the order for a year. It was not a case of an immediate purposeful contempt of the order which had been made. Also it can truly be said that residence in those particular premises was not an example of [A's] seeking out his target group. Further it was pointed out that he pleaded guilty and indicated his plea of guilty at the earliest opportunity … [A] sentence of three years' imprisonment on a plea of guilty represents a sentence which is too close to the maximum of five years for the circumstances of this particular case, where there was no suggestion of targeting of girls, or of children in whom [A] had previously shown improper sexual interest.'

18.132   In *Fenton*,[249] A appealed against a sentence of 2½ years' imprisonment imposed for breach of a SOO. A had convictions for rape, indecent exposure and offences of violence, public order and drunkenness. A SOO had been made in 2000 and renewed in 2003, when A was prohibited, inter alia, from using threatening, abusive or insulting words or behaviour towards any female and from being drunk in any place. A breached that order four times before the events forming the subject of the appeal occurred. As to those events, A, who appeared to be drunk, was heard being abusive to young women waiting to enter a public house. When stopped by police officers, he was abusive and continued to be so after being warned about his behaviour. The pre-sentence report described A as having an untreatable, psychopathic anti-social and borderline personality disorder, with drug and alcohol misuse being a significant factor. It was stated that he showed a total disregard and lack of empathy for others and that he had no insight into his offending behaviour, which he invariably denied. He was assessed as

---

247   [2003] 1 Cr App R (S) 6.
248   Ibid, at [6], [7].
249   [2007] 1 Cr App R (S) 597.

presenting a high risk of re-offending with a very high risk of harm to the public. On appeal A argued that, given the trivial nature of the breach in question, his sentence was manifestly excessive.

18.133 Dismissing A's appeal, the Court of Appeal held that the proper approach to cases of this type could be informed by a study of the decisions[250] relating to ASBOs. If the breach did not involve any real or obvious risk to that section of the public whom it was intended should be protected by the order, a community penalty might well be appropriate, although repeated breaches would necessarily result in a custodial sentence, if only to demonstrate that orders of the court were not to be ignored and could not be broken with impunity. Any breach which did create a real or obvious risk to those whom the order was intended to protect had inevitably to be treated more seriously, and multiple or repeated breaches might well justify sentences that might be considered draconian for the specific offence or misconduct in question.

18.134 The Court of Appeal held that the case had a number of features that were extremely worrying:

- There had been multiple and repeated breaches of the order against the background that A felt aggrieved that he should be subject to such restrictions, notwithstanding his background of offending, and did not believe that he had done anything to justify criminal sanction.

- The nature of the breaches and, in particular, the sexually offensive approach to young women whilst drunk showed the existence of the very risk factors that the order had been designed to minimise.

- A's recent behaviour in custody had only served to reveal that he was not prepared to engage in the type of programme that could help him to understand why he continued to be subject to the order, how he might modify his behaviour to live within its terms and, just as important, what he should do to obtain help if he felt that he was at risk of continuing to breach the order.

A's breach of the order had not been trivial, and a substantial custodial sentence had been entirely justified. The sentence of 2½ years was neither wrong in principle nor manifestly excessive.

FOREIGN TRAVEL ORDERS

18.135 The UK has, since the mid-1990s, attempted to tackle child sex tourism. The initial efforts were to create extra-territorial jurisdiction in respect of those who travelled abroad to commit a child sex offence or made arrangements to do so.[251] Whilst this was a strong starting point, the extra-territorial application of the substantive offences was necessarily reactive.

---

[250] *Braxton* [2005] 1 Cr App R (S) 36; *Boness* [2006] 1 Cr App R (S) 120; *Lamb* [2006] 2 Cr App R (S) 11; and *H* [2006] 2 Cr App R (S) 68.
[251] See the Sexual Offences (Conspiracy and Incitement) Act 1996 and SOffA 1997, Pt 2, dealt with in **2.89** et seq.

18.136 Although it was possible to use a RO or SOO to prevent travel within the UK, it was not possible to use it to prevent travel abroad since this would not be necessary to protect members of the public in the UK from harm.[252] Restrictions on foreign travel could only be achieved via standard post-release licence conditions prohibiting leaving the country without permission, or by restrictions imposed as part of a probation order in certain cases. This potentially left a loophole and it was decided to introduce a new civil order, known as the foreign travel order (FTO), contained in SOA 2003, ss 114–122. An alternative solution would have been to remove the territorial restrictions to a SOPO but it was decided not to do this,[253] in part because this would have changed the SOPO beyond its intended purpose.

18.137 The provisions of SOA 2003, ss 114–122 apply to England and Wales, to Northern Ireland and to Scotland.[254] They empower police who suspect that a sex offender is planning a sex tourism trip to apply for an order banning foreign travel. FTOs operate for a maximum of 6 months at a time in a similar way to SOPOs, but are renewable.

Application for FTO

18.138 An application for a FTO must be made by a chief officer of police[255] by complaint[256] to a magistrates' court.[257] A FTO can be applied for at the same time as a SOPO or separately.

18.139 An application for a FTO may be in the form set out in Sch 1 to the Magistrates' Courts (Foreign Travel Orders) Rules 2004,[258] and a summons directed to the defendant requiring him to appear before a magistrates' court to answer an application for such an order may be in the form set out in Sch 2 thereto.[259]

18.140 The proceedings are civil in nature for the same reasons as in the case of a police application for a SOPO.[260]

18.141 The application must be made in respect of a person (the defendant, A) who resides in the chief officer's police area or who the chief officer believes is in or is intending to come to his police area.[261] An application for a FTO may only be made if it appears to the applicant that:

(a) A is a 'qualifying offender' as defined by SOA 2003, s 116 (below);[262] and

(b) A has since the appropriate date[263] acted in such a way as to give reasonable cause to believe that it is necessary for a FTO to be made.[264]

---

[252] CDA 1998, s 2(1)(b) referred to 'the public' which had to be taken to mean the public in the UK.
[253] The restriction is to be found in s 106(3).
[254] Section 142(1)–(3). Sections 120 (appeals) and 121 (procedural modifications) apply only to Scotland.
[255] SOA 2003, s 114(1); see **17.106**, n 187.
[256] See **18.70**.
[257] SOA 2003, s 114(1), (2). See n 96 above.
[258] SI 2004/1051, r 3(1).
[259] Rule 3(2).
[260] See **18.68**.
[261] SOA 2003, s 114(1).
[262] SOA 2003, s 115(4).
[263] Including acts before 1 May 2004, the commencement of Pt 2: s 115(3).
[264] SOA 2003, s 114(1).

Grounds

18.142 A court may make a FTO if it is satisfied that:

(a) the defendant is a 'qualifying offender'; and

(b) the defendant's behaviour since the appropriate date makes it necessary to make such an order, for the purpose of protecting children generally or any child from serious sexual harm from the defendant outside the UK.[265]

The first condition

18.143 There are two types of qualifying offender.

18.144 By SOA 2003, s 116(1), a person is a 'qualifying offender' if, whether before or after 1 May 2004 (the commencement of SOA 2003, Pt 2),[266] he:

- has been convicted[267] of an offence within s 116(2);[268]

- has been found not guilty of such an offence by reason of insanity or to be under a disability and to have done the act charged against him in respect of such an offence;[269] or

- in England and Wales or Northern Ireland, has been cautioned,[270] in respect of such an offence.

The offences within s 116(2) are defined by reference to the list of offences in Sch 3; the age and sentence conditions in Sch 3 apply with the exceptions italicised below. The list of offences is:

- offences under the Protection of Children Act 1978, s 1, the Customs and Excise Management Act 1979, s 170 and CJA 1988, s 160 relating to the making, taking, etc, importation or possession of indecent photographs or pseudo-photographs of children under 16 if the conviction, etc was before the commencement of Pt 2 or, if after, the offender was 18 or over or he is sentenced to at least 12 months' imprisonment (and the equivalent offences in Scotland or Northern Ireland);

- an offence under SOA 2003, s 62 or s 63 (committing an offence, or trespassing with intent to commit a sexual offence) in specified circumstances **(17.21)** *if the intended offence was against someone under 16;*[271]

- a corresponding Service offence;

---

[265] SOA 2003, s 114(3).
[266] See **2.1**.
[267] See **17.29, 17.31**.
[268] Including a 'spent' conviction: see n 13 above.
[269] See **17.33, 17.34**.
[270] SOA 2003, s 133. See **17.36**.
[271] 17 years old in Northern Ireland: s 115(6). As to proof of age, see **3.131, 3.132**.

- any other offence under any other paragraph of Sch 3,[272] *if the victim was under 16*[273] *at the time of the offence.*

For these purposes, any amendment to Sch 3 or Sch 5 which adds an offence, removes a condition or changes one adversely to an offender applies to convictions, findings and cautions before as well as after the amendment takes effect.[274]

18.145 By SOA 2003, s 116(3), a person is *also* a 'qualifying offender' if, under the law of a country outside the UK and whether before or after the commencement of Pt 2:

- he has been convicted of a 'relevant offence' (whether or not he has been punished for it);

- a foreign court has made in respect of a relevant offence a finding equivalent to a finding that he is not guilty by reason of insanity, or to a finding that he is under a disability and did the act charged against him in respect of the offence; or

- he has been cautioned in respect of a relevant offence.

A 'relevant offence' for the purposes of s 116(3) means an act which:

- constituted an offence[275] under the law of the country concerned; and

- *would have constituted an offence within s 116(2) if it had been done in any part of the UK.*[276]

The provisions about proof of the words italicised are the same as apply to the corresponding provision in respect of a NO or SOPO.[277]

18.146 The effect of s 116(2) and (3) is that a FTO can only be made against someone who has a history of sexual offending against, or involving, a child under 16. The reason is that such a person represents the greatest risk of future offending overseas either because of the existence of brothels where child-prostitutes are available or because the absence of effective policing makes some countries attractive destinations for paedophiles.[278]

The second condition

18.147 The second condition for a FTO is that the defendant's *behaviour* since the appropriate date makes it *necessary* to make such an order, for the purposes of protecting children generally or any child from serious sexual harm from the defendant outside the UK.[279] SOA 2003, s 115(2) states that:

---

[272] See **17.19–17.28**.
[273] See n 271 above.
[274] SOA 2003, s 130(3).
[275] However described: s 116(5).
[276] SOA 2003, s 116(4).
[277] SOA 2003, s 116(6), (7); see **18.10** and **18.64**; MC(FTO)R 2004, SI 2004/1051, r 4.
[278] Lord Falconer of Thoroton, HL Deb, vol 648, col 659.
[279] SOA 2003, s 114(3)(b).

'"Protecting children generally or any child from serious sexual harm from the defendant outside the United Kingdom" means protecting persons under 16 generally or any particular person under 16[280] from serious physical or psychological harm caused by the defendant doing, outside the United Kingdom, anything which would constitute an offence listed in Sch 3 if done in any part of the United Kingdom.'

Evidence indicating that this condition is satisfied could consist, for example, of e-mail contact with a person in a foreign country through whom the defendant organises sexual tourism.[281] It will be noted that there is no requirement that the foreign behaviour anticipated should amount to an offence in the country to which the defendant is seeking to travel. Nor is it necessary to prove precisely which offence under Sch 3 the foreign behaviour would constitute. It will be enough to prove that the defendant has arranged to have any sort of sexual contact with a child under 16, because any sort of such contact is covered by at least one of the offences in Sch 3.[282]

18.148   The reference to the appropriate date, in relation to a qualifying offender, means the date or (as the case may be) the first date on which he was convicted, found or cautioned as mentioned in s 116(1) or (3) above.[283] Although the defendant's behaviour must have occurred after the appropriate date, it is irrelevant whether it occurred before or after 1 May 2004 (the commencement of Pt 2).[284] By virtue of MCA 1980, s 127(1) (6-month time-limit from time of matter complained of within which complaint must be made), at least part of the behaviour relied on must have taken place in the 6 months prior to the complaint being made. However, this does not render inadmissible evidence of events after 1 May 2004 that took place more than 6 months before the complaint, for the purposes of proving that a FTO is necessary.[285]

18.149   In deciding whether the defendant's behaviour since the appropriate date makes it *necessary* to make a FTO to protect children under 16 generally or any such child from serious sexual harm from the defendant outside the UK, the court might take into account previous offending behaviour, previous allegations of sex offending in the country to which the defendant intends to travel, the circumstances of the proposed travel and likely contact with other offenders and potential victims in the intended destination. It will also have to consider what alternative measures are potentially available to prevent the defendant causing serious sexual harm to children or a child. These measures could include notifying relevant authorities abroad of the offender's travel plans so that monitoring, reporting or surveillance could be put in place in the destination country. If effective alternative measures are available in the country or countries at risk from the offender it will not be necessary to make a FTO. On the other hand, if alternative measures are not available, or have not proved effective (e g because a previous notification to the police in the foreign country has not been acted on), a court may be satisfied that it is necessary to make a FTO to prevent serious sexual harm to children in that country or more than one country.

18.150   The comments in **18.68–18.71** and **18.77–18.79** about evidence and proof are equally applicable to a FTO.

---

[280]   See n 271 above.
[281]   *Guidance Pt 2*, at p 47.
[282]   Ibid.
[283]   SOA 2003, s 115(5).
[284]   SOA 2003, s 115(3).
[285]   *Chief Constable of West Mercia Constabulary v Boorman* (2005) 169 JP 669 (ASBO).

The order and its effect

18.151   By SOA 2003, s 117(2), an FTO prohibits the defendant from doing whichever one of the following is specified in the order:

(a)   travelling to any country[286] outside the UK, named or described in the order;

(b)   travelling to any country outside the UK other than a country named or described in the order (eg not to travel to any country outside the UK other than the Republic of Ireland); or

(c)   travelling to any country outside the UK.

It will be noted that these prohibitions relate to travel to a foreign country, as opposed to leaving the UK. An order cannot, therefore, prohibit a convicted paedophile from going on an ocean cruise which will not involve a visit to a foreign country.

18.152   The only prohibitions which may be included in the FTO are those necessary for the purpose of protecting children generally or any child from serious sexual harm from the defendant outside the UK.[287] The provisions of s 115(2), referred to in **18.147**, apply equally to s 117(3).[288] The prohibition in a FTO must be proportionate to this need. If the defendant is a paedophile who presents such a high risk of abusing children that he is likely to abuse children wherever he goes a blanket prohibition under (c) could be justified. An order under (c) could also be justified where there are concerns that the defendant intends to mask his ultimate destination. On the other hand, if it is only proved that the defendant paedophile intends to travel to some specified sex-tourism centres, only a prohibition under (a) naming those would normally be justifiable. An order under (a) could also specify a country or countries in a region through which the court considered that the defendant could access his 'target' country. An order under (b) is likely to be made in a case where a worldwide ban is justifiable but there are good reasons outweighing the risk in respect of any particular country to exclude that country (eg employment there or family reasons).

18.153   A FTO does not require the surrender of a passport; nor is the court given the power so to order when making the order. This does not help the enforcement of a FTO.

Duration

18.154   A FTO comes into effect on the day that it is made. By SOA 2003, s 117(1), a FTO has effect for a fixed period of not more than 6 months[289] specified in it. Because of s 117(3), the court must fix such a length of time (subject to the 6-month maximum) as it considers necessary in relation to the risk of serious sexual harm, etc posed by the defendant. A FTO is renewable on a fresh application by the police. The Government believed that in most cases the 6-month period would be enough to prevent a defendant making a particular trip abroad without putting an unfair restriction on his longer-term right to travel.

---

[286]   'Country' includes territory (s 133), such as a dependency. 'Country' includes 'countries': Interpretation Act 1978, s 6(c).
[287]   SOA 2003, s 117(3).
[288]   SOA 2003, s 117(6).
[289]   'Month(s)' are calendar months: IA 1978, s 5 and Sch 1.

18.155 Where a FTO is made in relation to a person already subject to a FTO, the earlier FTO ceases to have effect.[290]

Form and service

18.156 A FTO must be in the form set out in Sch 3 to the MC(FTO)R 2004.[291] Notes to the form set out the requirements of the foreign travel notification regulations (see **17.80** et seq) and state that breach of the obligations without reasonable excuse is an offence. As soon as reasonably practicable after a FTO has been made, the designated officer of the court must serve a copy of that order on the defendant. Any copy of an order required to be sent under the Rules to the defendant must be either given to him in person or sent by post to his last known address and, if so given or sent, is deemed to have been received by him, unless the defendant proves that he did not receive it.[292] The comments in **18.93** and **18.94** are equally applicable mutatis mutandis.

Notification requirements

18.157 People subject to a FTO are likely to be subject to the notification requirements of SOA 2003, Pt 2[293] by virtue of their conviction, finding or caution in respect of a sexual offence against or involving a child (since such a conviction, etc is necessary to make someone a qualifying offender for a FTO). As we saw in **17.9**, someone subject to these requirements is described as a 'relevant offender'. However, some defendants may not be 'relevant offenders': the obvious examples are where the material conviction, etc was before SOffA 1997 or is a foreign one. SOA 2003, s 117(4) deals with such people. It provides that where a defendant is not a 'relevant offender' the FTO causes him, whilst it is in force, to be subject to the notification requirements *as to foreign travel* imposed by regulations made under s 86(1).[294] For these purposes the defendant is to be treated as if he was a 'relevant offender'. Under the foreign travel notification requirement the 'relevant offender' has to notify the police of his intended destination. Such notification would enable the police to apply, for example, for a variation of the FTO so as to apply to that country of destination if it is not already covered by the order.

Human rights

18.158 The UK is not a party to Protocol 4 of the ECHR, Art 2 of which guarantees freedom of movement and the freedom to leave any country, including one's own, although restrictions may be placed by law on such freedoms if necessary in a democratic society for the maintenance of *ordre public*, for the prevention of crime or for the protection of the rights and freedoms of others.

18.159 A FTO, however, may result in interference with the right to respect for private life under ECHR, Art 8, but a properly made and proportionate FTO would seem to be a justified interference under Art 8(2) as necessary for the protection of morals, for the prevention of crime or for the protection of the rights and freedoms of others.

---

[290] SOA 2003, s 117(5).
[291] Rule 3(3).
[292] Rule 3(4).
[293] See **17.52** et seq.
[294] See **17.80** et seq.

18.160   For the reasons given below a FTO is not in itself unlawful under EC law. The freedom to provide services under Art 49 (formerly Art 59) EC has been interpreted to include freedom for the recipient of services to go to another member state to receive services there. In addition, Arts 1 and 2 of Council Directive 73/148/EEC, which has direct effect in English law, confer on nationals of Member States wishing to go to another Member State as recipients of services[295] a right of free movement. However, derogations from the Directive are lawful if they can be justified on public policy grounds,[296] and the power to derogate includes restraining people leaving this country if the restraint can be justified on public policy grounds. This was held by the Court of Appeal in *Gough v Chief Constable of Derbyshire Constabulary*.[297] To be justified on public policy grounds the restraint must not only seek to fulfil a legitimate aim of public policy but it must also be proportionate.[298] In *Gough* the Court of Appeal rejected an argument that the provisions relating to a football banning order were a disproportionate interference with the right conferred by Directive 73/148/EEC. There can be no doubt that the courts would reach the same conclusion about the provisions relating to a FTO in the light of the objectives which a FTO seeks to achieve, of the grounds for a FTO which have to be satisfied, of the limited period of an order, of the fact that it is not necessarily a blanket ban but can be 'targeted' and of the availability of variation or discharge of the order. Of course, whilst the provisions relating to a FTO may comply with the Directive, an individual FTO will not do so if it is disproportionate.

Variation, renewal and discharge

18.161   SOA 2003, s 118 provides for the variation, renewal or discharge of a FTO. Typical instances of an application would be an application for variation by a person subject to a FTO prohibiting travel to Thailand who wishes to go there to see a terminally ill friend and wishes the order to be varied so as to permit this, or an application for renewal of a FTO by the police on the ground that the defendant still poses a risk of serious sexual harm to children abroad.

Application process

18.162   The following can apply for the variation, renewal or discharge of a FTO:

• the defendant;

• a chief officer of police[299] for the area in which the defendant resides;

• a chief officer of police who believes that the defendant is in, or is intending to come to, his police area;[300]

• the chief police officer who made the application for the order.[301]

---

[295]   In *Luisi v Ministero del Tesero* Cases 286/82 and 26/83 [1984] ECR 377, the European Court of Justice held that 'tourists', amongst others, are 'recipients of services' who enjoy the right of free movement under Community law. 'Sex tourists' in a foreign country would seem to be 'tourists'.
[296]   Directive 73/148/EEC, Art 8.
[297]   [2002] 2 All ER 985.
[298]   As to proportionality, see **1.29**.
[299]   See **17.106**, n 187.
[300]   For 'police area' n 6 above.
[301]   SOA 2003, s 118(1), (2).

18.163 An application for variation, renewal or discharge must be made to 'the appropriate court', namely the court which made the order, a magistrates' court for the area in which the defendant resides or, where the application is made by a chief officer of police, any magistrates' court.[302] An application must be made by complaint.[303]

Outcome of an application

18.164 Subject to the restriction set out below, the court, after hearing the applicant and representations from anyone else who could have applied for a variation, etc and wishes to be heard, may make an order, varying, renewing or discharging the main order, that it considers appropriate.[304] The restriction is that a renewal or variation order may only impose additional prohibitions on the defendant if it is necessary to do so for the purpose of protecting *children generally or any child from serious sexual harm from the defendant outside the UK*, and any such order may only contain such prohibitions as are necessary for this purpose.[305]

18.165 The comments in **18.103** about copies of an order apply mutatis mutandis to an order under the present provisions.

Appeal

18.166 A defendant, but nobody else, may appeal by way of re-hearing[306] to the Crown Court:

(a) against the making of a FTO; and

(b) against the making of an order of variation or renewal of a FTO, or the refusal to make an order of variation or discharge.[307]

The Crown Court may make such orders as may be necessary to give effect to its determination of the appeal;[308] it may also make such incidental[309] or consequential order as may appear to it to be just.[310]

Breach

18.167 By SOA 2003, s 122(1), it is an offence for a person, without reasonable excuse, to do anything which he is prohibited from doing by a FTO (in whatever part of the UK it was made).

18.168 The prosecution will need to establish, beyond reasonable doubt, the making of the order and its terms. See further **18.124.**

---

[302] SOA 2003, s 118(5).
[303] SOA 2003, s 118(1).
[304] SOA 2003, s 118(3).
[305] SOA 2003, s 118(4).
[306] SCtA 1981, s 79(3).
[307] SOA 2003, s 119(1).
[308] SOA 2003, s 119(2).
[309] See **18.117.**
[310] SOA 2003, s 119(2). Section 119(3) makes similar provision to that in s 110(5) (**18.118**) about the Crown Court's order being treated as an order from the court appealed from. The points made in **18.120** apply mutatis mutandis to a FTO.

18.169 The offence is committed simply by a breach of the requirements of the order, subject to that breach not being with reasonable excuse. The burden of showing lack of reasonable excuse is on the prosecution, although the defendant will bear an evidential burden in respect of that defence.[311]

18.170 An offence under s 122(1) is triable either way and punishable with a maximum of 5 years' imprisonment on conviction on indictment.[312] It is not open to the court by or before which a person is convicted of this offence to make an order of conditional discharge in respect of it although it can make an absolute discharge.[313]

Class of offence[314]	3	SOA 2003, s 72 applies	✗
Notification requirements	✗	SOPO	✗
CJA 2003, Sch 15 applies	✗	Serious specified offence	✗
Review of lenient sentence	✗	Special provisions of CYPA 1933	✗
Detention of young offender for specified period			✗

RISK OF SEXUAL HARM ORDERS

18.171 These orders are specifically designed to protect children under 16 against inappropriate sexual behaviour by adults,[315] including grooming, irrespective of whether there has been a conviction for a sexual offence. The relevant provisions are SOA 2003, ss 123–129, which apply to England and Wales and Northern Ireland only.[316] There are separate provisions in Scotland for the making and effect of a RSHO or an interim RSHO.[317] A RSHO prohibits the defendant from doing anything described in the order; the prohibitions must be necessary to protect a child or children in general from the defendant. A conviction, finding or caution for breach of a RSHO gives rise to a notification requirement or the extension of an existing one.

18.172 The *Guidance*[318] states that an application for a RSHO should not be used as a substitute to a prosecution for an offence where one is thought to have been committed,[319] and that the RSHO procedure should be used at an earlier stage where the adult's behaviour gives reason to believe that a child is at risk from the defendant and intervention is necessary to protect the child.

---

[311] See **17.115–17.118** and **18.125**.
[312] SOA 2003, s 122(2); maximum on summary conviction: **1.43**.
[313] SOA 2003, s 122(3).
[314] See **1.49**.
[315] Non-criminal inappropriate behaviour by those under 18 has to be dealt with by the intervention by the care agencies, such as social service departments.
[316] SOA 2003, s 142(1)–(3).
[317] PCPSO(S)A 2005, s 2.
[318] *Guidance Pt 2*, at p 50.
[319] Even if an offence is thought to have been committed, there may not be sufficient admissible evidence under the law of criminal evidence to secure a conviction. Here the RSHO procedure may prove useful.

Application for RSHO

18.173   An application for a RSHO must be made by a chief officer of police.[320] Thus, a parent cannot apply for a RSHO in order to protect a daughter of 15 against her unsuitable 18-year-old boyfriend. The application must be made by complaint to a magistrates' court.[321] Consequently, the proceedings are civil in nature for the same reasons as in the case of police application for a SOPO.[322] The application must be made in respect of a defendant (A) aged 18[323] or over who resides in the applicant's police area or who the applicant believes is, or is intending to come to, his police area.[324] By s 123(1), an application may only be made if it appears to the applicant that:

- A has on at least two occasions, whether before or after 1 May 2004 (the commencement of SOA 2003, Pt 2), done an act within s 123(3), namely:

    '(a)   engaging in sexual activity involving a child [under 16][325] or in the presence of such a child;

    (b)   causing or inciting[326] such a child to watch a person engaging in sexual activity or to look at a moving or still image[327] that is sexual;

    (c)   giving such a child anything that relates to sexual activity or contains a reference to such an activity [eg giving a child a condom, sending it a sex toy, a pornographic book or a video about sexual technique]; or

    (d)   communicating with such a child, where any part of the communication is sexual'; *and*

- as a result, there is reasonable cause to believe that it is necessary for a RSHO to be made.[328]

18.174   At first sight the inclusion in s 123(3) of paras (a) and (b) would appear somewhat surprising since the conduct within para (a) is, in effect, a repetition of the offences contained in SOA 2003, ss 9[329] and 11[330] and the conduct within para (b) in essence replicates s 12.[331] The standard of proof on a RSHO application is the criminal standard[332] and so if there is proof that this conduct has occurred on two separate occasions it would seem more appropriate to charge the defendant. However, there may be reasons why a RSHO may be the more appropriate course of action. The first is that SOA 2003 expressly states that the acts can be before the commencement of the Act;[333] an application for a RSHO could be made in situations where the conduct was not then the subject of the criminal law. The second possible reason would be where the defendant had reasonable grounds to believe that the child was over the age of 16. A consequence of the drafting of the four types of act which can trigger a RSHO is that internet chatroom communications by a groomer which induce the child to believe that

---

[320]   SOA 2003, s 123(1); see **17.106**, n 187.
[321]   Ibid. See **18.70**.
[322]   See **18.68**.
[323]   As to proof of age, see **3.131**, **3.132**.
[324]   For 'police area' see n 6 above.
[325]   SOA 2003, s 124(3); 17 in Northern Ireland: s 124(8). 'Child' includes 'children': IA 1978, s 6(c).
[326]   See **3.174** and **3.185**.
[327]   'Image' means an image produced by any means, whether of a real or imaginary subject: s 124(4). Examples are photographs, pseudo-photographs, drawings and cartoon strips.
[328]   SOA 2003, s 123(1).
[329]   Sexual activity with a child: see **4.9**.
[330]   Engaging in sexual activity in the presence of a child: see **4.28**.
[331]   Causing a child to watch a sexual act: see **4.38**.
[332]   *R (McCann) v Manchester Crown Court* [2003] 1 AC 787.
[333]   SOA 2003, s 123(1).

the communicator is also a child so as to gain the child's trust are not a trigger for a RSHO (unlike the offence of grooming under SOA 2003, s 15) if they do not contain any sexual content. On the other hand, unlike the grooming offence, the communication need not be directed towards a particular child, nor need it be proved that the adult intends to engage in sexual activity with the child or, even, to meet it.

18.175 For the purpose of the acts within SOA 2003, s 123(3):

- Sexual activity means an activity that a reasonable person would, in all the circumstances but regardless of any person's purpose, consider to be sexual.[334] This can be contrasted with the definition in s 78 of sexual activity for the purposes of Pt 1 of the Act, where account may be taken of the actor's purpose. The activity of a stranger in removing a young child's clothing in circumstances which do not require this would be sexual under this test. So would that of a doctor who performs an intimate examination of a teenage girl, with consent, knowing that it is completely unnecessary. The conduct is objectively sexual. On the other hand, the activity of a shoe-fetishist who removes a girl's shoe for purposes of sexual gratification, or of a buttock-fetishist who spanks his daughter ostensibly for disciplinary reasons but in reality for sexual gratification, would not be a sexual activity under s 124 because it is not objectively sexual, and the actor's purpose must be discounted.

- A communication (or image) is sexual if:
  (a) any part of it relates to sexual activity (as defined above), for example, where it describes sexual activity engaged in, or to be engaged in, by the defendant; or
  (b) a reasonable person would, in all the circumstances but regardless of any person's purpose, consider that any part of the communication (or image) is sexual.[335]
  Sending an email to a child describing oral sex, or describing it over the telephone, would be a sexual communication, but communicating a double entendre with a sexual purpose would not; the communication is not objectively sexual, and the purpose must be discounted. A pornographic video obviously satisfies (a).

An act within s 123(3) need not be done in relation to the same child on each occasion. Accordingly the police could seek a RSHO where the defendant has communicated sexually with child A on one occasion and child B on another. By virtue of MCA 1980, s 127(1) (6-month time-limit from time of matter complained of within which complaint must be made), at least part of the behaviour relied on must have taken place in the 6 months prior to the complaint being made. However, this does not render inadmissible evidence of events that took place more than 6 months before the complaint, for the purposes of proving that a RSHO is necessary.[336]

18.176 The key factor in assessing whether a RSHO is necessary is whether or not an individual poses a risk of harming a child or children. The assessment process undertaken by the police before making an application will need to consider the degree of risk currently posed by the individual. Where appropriate, the assessment should be carried out in consultation with the probation service, social services, other child

---

[334] SOA 2003, s 124(5).
[335] SOA 2003, s 124(6), (7).
[336] See case cited at n 285 above.

protection agencies and other relevant agencies. Because, unlike the other preventative orders, the individual may not have a criminal record, it may be necessary to use an external independent risk assessor.[337]

18.177   The *Guidance* states that the assessment of how the child's safety can best be assured should be informed by consideration, where relevant, of:

• the nature of the behaviour giving rise to concern and any pattern associated with this;

• the nature and extent of the potential harm;

• an assessment of the accuracy and currency of the information about the individual (including an assessment of the status of those expressing concern and their reasons for doing so);

• the current circumstances of a potential defendant and how these might change, including employment, training, housing, who they live with and where, any addictions, health problems, etc;

• whether, in appropriate cases, the child would be able to give evidence;

• the relevance of any previous convictions or cautions;

• compliance or otherwise with any previous sentences, court orders or supervision arrangements;

• compliance or otherwise with therapeutic help and its outcome;

• if he is a convicted sex offender and fulfils the SOPO criteria, whether that would be a more appropriate order to apply for; and

• the development of plans to address the potential impact of any media coverage on the management by relevant agencies of the person in the community.[338]

18.178   An application for a RSHO may be in the form set out in Sch 1 to the Magistrates' Courts (Risk of Sexual Harm Orders) Rules (MC(RSHO)R) 2004,[339] and a summons directed to the defendant requiring him to appear before a magistrates' court to answer an application for such an order may be in the form set out in Sch 2 thereto.[340]

Grounds

18.179   On an application for a RSHO, the court may make that order if it is satisfied that:

(a) the defendant (A) has on at least two occasions, whether before or after 1 May 2004, done an act within s 123(3) (set out in **18.173**); and

---

[337]   *Guidance Pt 2*, at p 51.
[338]   Ibid.
[339]   SI 2004/1053, r 3(1).
[340]   Rule 3(2).

(b)   it is necessary to make such an order, for the purpose of protecting children under 16[341] generally or any child under 16[342] from harm from A.[343]

18.180   The requirement in (a) of an act on at least two occasions provides some limit on the width of the grounds for a RSHO. Someone who has done a one-off act of which he feels ashamed and does not repeat cannot be subjected to a RSHO, but a repeat actor clearly poses a danger of further repetition and can be subjected to one. It is essential that there is clarity about the risk assessment of defendants.

18.181   'Harm from A' in (b) means physical or psychological harm, caused by the defendant doing acts within s 123(3).[344] Unlike the provision relating to a SOPO or FTO, the court need not be satisfied that an order is necessary to protect from *serious sexual* harm from A. Requirement (b) restricts the operation of requirement (a). A doctor who gives contraceptives to a girl under 16 for clinical reasons, knowing that this would encourage or facilitate sexual intercourse by her with her 15-year-old boyfriend, would not be a secondary party to the offence under s 9 committed when the girl subsequently has intercourse.[345] Nor could the doctor be made subject to an RSHO after providing the girl with contraceptives on two occasions, because the order would not be necessary to protect the girl from harm from the doctor. Likewise, a schoolteacher delivering bona fide sex education classes on two occasions to pupils under 16 makes a communication to the pupils which is sexual but could not be made subject to a RSHO because the order would not be necessary to protect the children from harm from the teacher.

18.182   It is not necessary to prove that the defendant acted in order to gain sexual gratification or with any other sexual motivation. Thus, if A has acted on two occasions in one of the ways specified in (a) (listed in **18.73**) in order to 'train' a child in sexual ways and make it believe that sexual activity with adults is normal, so that A can exploit the child by selling the child's sexual services, a RSHO can be made against A, even though A's motives are financial.

18.183   What was said about evidence and proof in **18.68–18.71** and **18.77–18.79** is equally applicable here.

Effect

18.184   Like a SOPO, a RSHO:

(a)   prohibits the defendant from doing anything described in the order; and

(b)   has effect for a fixed period specified in the order or until further order.[346]

18.185   A RSHO can seriously interfere with the freedom of movement and action, and it could have a disastrous impact on the reputation, of someone who may never have been convicted of (or even cautioned for) a sexually related offence, or indeed of

---

[341]   SOA 2003, s 124(3); 17 years old in Northern Ireland: s 124(8). As to proof of age, see **3.131**, **3.132**.
[342]   Ibid.
[343]   SOA 2003, s 123(4).
[344]   SOA 2003, s 124(2).
[345]   SOA 2003, s 73: see **2.49**.
[346]   SOA 2003, s 123(5). What is said about the corresponding SOPO provision in **18.86** is equally applicable to a RSHO.

any offence. Overall, a RSHO constitutes a significant interference with the right to respect for private life under ECHR, Art 8(1) and potentially with the rights to freedom of expression and of association under Arts 10 and 11. What is said in **18.96** and **18.97** is equally applicable here.

18.186 The only prohibitions that may be imposed are those necessary for the purpose of protecting children under 16 generally or any child under 16[347] from harm from the defendant. The risk assessment will obviously be crucial. The activities prohibited must be tailored to the particular facts and risk. They may relate to activities which, absent those facts and that risk, would be of no significance, for example, not to communicate with a particular child or not to go to a place where children congregate. The prohibitions should be specific in time and place wherever possible so that the defendant understands what will and what will not breach the RSHO.[348] It may be sensible for the police, before making the application, to seek the advice of the CPS about the wording of unusual or complex prohibitions, to ensure that any allegations of breach of them can be proved. Because a RSHO cannot require the defendant to do anything, an order cannot require the defendant to take part in counselling or to receive support. If a prohibition is unnecessary or too wide, or insufficiently specific and clear, it can be struck out on an appeal or an application to vary. However, until it is struck down in one of these two ways, a RSHO containing a prohibition which is not necessary or is too wide or is not sufficiently specific or clear is not invalid.[349]

18.187 A RSHO must be in the form set out in Sch 3 to the MC(RSHO)R 2004.[350] The form makes clear that non-compliance without reasonable excuse with a prohibition in the order is an offence. As soon as reasonably practicable after a RSHO has been made, the designated officer of the court must serve a copy of that order on the defendant. Any copy of an order required to be sent under the Rules to the defendant must be either given to him in person or sent by post to his last known address and, if so given or sent, is deemed to have been received by him, unless the defendant proves that it was not received by him.[351] The process of appeal must be made clear to the defendant. It would be good practice to give the police a copy of the order.[352]

Duration

18.188 The minimum duration of 2 years is less than that for a SOPO (5 years) but it will be noted that an order of indefinite duration can be made. A RSHO of indefinite duration might well be held to be disproportionate unless the case was exceptional. Where a RSHO is made in relation to a person already subject to such an order, the earlier order ceases to have effect.[353] Oddly, a RSHO is not discharged by the making of a SOPO. It is for the police to monitor a RSHO to ensure that it continues to meet the need for protection and is still necessary for that purpose.[354]

---

347 As to Northern Ireland and proof of age, see n 341 above.
348 *Guidance Pt 2*, at p 26. See **18.61**, nn 113, 114.
349 *DPP v T* [2006] 3 All ER 471 (ASBO); not following *R(W) v DPP* (2005) 169 JP 435 (ASBO).
350 Rule 3(3).
351 Rule 3(5).
352 *Guidance Pt 2*, at p 29.
353 SOA 2003, s 123(7).
354 *Guidance Pt 2*, at p 52.

No notification requirements

18.189 A RSHO does not in itself give rise to notification requirements under SOA 2003, Pt 2, presumably because an order does not depend on a conviction or caution for any offence. When the SOA 2003 was passed it would not have been possible to have included a person on the register since at that time it was simply a flag on the Police National Computer system. Given that a person need not have been convicted of any offence prior to a RSHO being imposed, there would not necessarily have been a record to which a flag could have been attached.

Variation, renewal and discharge

18.190 SOA 2003, s 125 provides for the variation, renewal or discharge of a RSHO.

Application process

18.191 The following can apply for the variation, renewal or discharge of a RSHO:

• the defendant (A);

• a chief officer of police[355] for the area in which A resides;

• a chief officer of police who believes that A is in, or is intending to come to, his or her police area;[356]

• the chief police officer who made the application for the order.[357]

18.192 An application for variation, renewal or discharge must be made to 'the appropriate court', namely the court which made the order, a magistrates' court for the area in which A resides, or, where the application is made by a chief officer of police, any magistrates' court for his police area.[358] An application to a magistrates' court must be made by complaint.[359] A variation might be sought, for example, to delete or amend a prohibition which has become unnecessary or inappropriate. An example would be where the child protected by the order has moved from the area which the defendant is prohibited from visiting; in such a case the order could be varied to substitute a new area. A variation might also be sought to impose an entirely new prohibition, as where a new group requiring protection is identified. Where a proposed variation is major, it would be preferable to seek a new order.

Outcome of an application

18.193 Subject to the restrictions set out below, the court, after hearing the applicant and representations from anyone else who could have applied for a variation, etc and

---

[355] See **17.106**.
[356] For 'police area' see n 6 above.
[357] SOA 2003, s 125(1), (2).
[358] SOA 2003, s 125(7). Section 125(7) requires the application in the last instance to be made to a magistrates' court whose commission area includes any part of the police area but commission areas were abolished by the CA 2003, s 109(3) and Sch 10.
[359] SOA 2003, s 125(1).

wishes to be heard, may make an order, varying, renewing or discharging the main order, that it considers appropriate.[360] The restrictions are that:

- A renewal or variation order may only impose additional prohibitions on the defendant (A) if it is necessary to do so for the purpose of protecting 'children generally or any child *from harm* from the defendant' (and any renewed or varied order may contain only such prohibitions as are necessary for this purpose).[361]

- The court must not discharge a RSHO before the end of the fixed period of 2 years beginning with the day on which it was made, without A's consent and:
    - (a) where the application is made by the police, the chief officer who made that application; or
    - (b) in any other case, the chief officer for the area in which A resides.[362]

Copies of an order dismissing the application, or a variation order or order of discharge, should be given in person or sent by post, and a copy sent to the police.[363] An order of renewal should be dealt with in the same way as the original order.

Interim RSHOs

18.194 SOA 2003, s 126 allows the police to apply for an interim RSHO where an application for a RSHO in respect of a defendant has not yet been determined.[364] The purpose of an interim RSHO is to provide temporary protection for a child or children. In view of this it is unlikely that an interim hearing will be adjourned to allow the defendant more time to prepare.[365]

18.195 An application for an interim RSHO:

(a) may be made by the complaint[366] by which the main application is made; or

(b) if the main application has been made, may be made by the person who made it, by complaint to the court to which that application has been made.[367]

18.196 An application for an interim RSHO may be in the form set out in Sch 1 to the MC(RSHO)R 2004,[368] and a summons directed to the defendant requiring him to appear before a magistrates' court to answer an application for such an order may be in the form set out in Sch 2 thereto.[369]

18.197 The court may *if it considers it just to do so*, make an interim RSHO, prohibiting the defendant from doing anything described in the order.[370] The court does not have to be satisfied that an interim order is necessary for the purpose of the

---

[360] SOA 2003, s 125(3).
[361] SOA 2003, s 125(4).
[362] SOA 2003, s 125(5).
[363] *Guidance Pt 2*, at p 52.
[364] SOA 2003, s 126(1).
[365] *Guidance Pt 2*, at p 26.
[366] See **18.70**.
[367] SOA 2003, s 126(2).
[368] Rule 3(1).
[369] Rule 3(2).
[370] SOA 2003, s 126(3).

protection of children (or a child) under 16 from harm from the defendant, but it is submitted that a court could not consider it just to make such an order unless there is some evidence demonstrating a likelihood that children (or a child) need to be protected from harm.[371] It is arguable that the availability of an interim RSHO is open to objection. The grounds for a RSHO are themselves broad, especially in that they can be imposed on someone with no previous convictions, findings or cautions of any kind. The provisions about interim RSHOs extend the ambit of the law even further. Nevertheless, the Joint Committee on Human Rights concluded that overall there were sufficient safeguards under the general applicable law, including the fact that the court would have to act in accordance with ECHR rights unless compelled to do otherwise by primary legislation, against the making of an order in violation of the ECHR.[372] Clearly, given that an interim RSHO is made before the court has heard and tested all the evidence, the court must take great care to ensure that such an order is justified. Since an interim RSHO cannot require the defendant to do anything, it cannot require him to undergo assessment.

18.198   An interim RHSO:

(a)   has effect only for a fixed period specified in the order; and

(b)   ceases to have effect, if it has not already done so, on the determination of the main application.[373]

18.199   An interim RSHO must be in the form set out in Sch 4 to the MC(RSHO)R 2004.[374] The form makes clear that non-compliance without reasonable excuse with a prohibition in the order is an offence. As soon as reasonably practicable after an interim order has been made, the justices' chief executive must serve a copy of that order on the defendant. Any copy of an order required to be sent under these Rules to the defendant must be either given to him in person or sent by post to his last known address and, if so given or sent, is deemed to have been received by him, unless the defendant proves that it was not received by him.[375]

18.200   The applicant or the defendant may by complaint apply to the court that made the interim RSHO for the order to be varied, renewed or discharged.[376]

Appeal

18.201   A defendant may appeal by way of re-hearing[377] to the Crown Court:

• against the making of a RSHO or an interim RSHO; or

• against the making of an order of variation, renewal or discharge of a RSHO (but not of an interim RSHO), or the refusal to make such an order.[378]

---

[371]   The comments in **18.108** are applicable mutatis mutandis here.
[372]   *Twelfth Report for Session 2002–03 Scrutiny of Bills: Further Progress Report* (HL 121; HC 765), at para 2.42.
[373]   SOA 2003, s 126(4).
[374]   Rule 3(4).
[375]   Rule 3(5).
[376]   SOA 2003, s 126(5).
[377]   SCtA 1981, s 79(3).
[378]   SOA 2003, s 127(1).

It will be noted that only the defendant has a right of appeal.[379] On appeal, the Crown Court may make such orders as may be necessary to give effect to its determination of the appeal, and may also make such incidental or consequential orders as appear to it to be just.[380] Although there is no automatic stay of proceedings, the Crown Court could by way of incidental order, suspend the operation of the RSHO or interim RSHO pending the determination of the appeal where this appears just.[381]

Breach

18.202   By SOA 2003, s 128(1):

> 'A person commits an offence if, without reasonable excuse, he does anything which he is prohibited from doing by—
>
> (a)   a risk of sexual harm order; or
> (b)   an interim risk of sexual harm order.'

The offence applies whether the order was made in England and Wales, in Northern Ireland or in Scotland.[382] Where the breach is of an interim order, the defendant is criminally liable even though no court has yet been satisfied that the grounds for a full order have been established.

18.203   An offence under s 128 is triable either way and punishable with a maximum of 5 years' imprisonment on conviction on indictment.[383] It is not open to the court by or before which a person is convicted of one of these offences to make an order of conditional discharge in respect of it.[384]

Class of offence[385]	3	SOA 2003, s 72 applies	✗
Notification requirements	✗	SOPO	✗
CJA 2003, Sch 15 applies	✗	Serious specified offence	✗
Review of lenient sentence	✗	Special provisions of CYPA 1933	✗
Detention of young offender for specified period			✗

18.204   The prosecution will need to establish, beyond reasonable doubt, the making of the order and its terms. See further **18.124**.

---

[379]   Where a decision is considered to be *Wednesbury* unreasonable, not proportionate or ultra vires, an application can be made for judicial review: see **18.120**.

[380]   SOA 2003, s 127(2). Section 127(3) makes similar provision to that in s 110(5) about the Crown Court's order being treated as an order from the court appealed from (see **18.118**).

[381]   *Guidance Pt 2*, at p 30.

[382]   By SOA 2003, s 128(1A) (inserted by VCRA 2006, s 56(2)), in s 128(1), and s 129(5) (see **18.208, 18.209**), the references to a RSHO and to an interim RSHO include references respectively to an order under the PCPSO(S)A 2005, s 2 (RSHOs in Scotland), and to an order under s 5 thereof (interim RSHOs in Scotland); and for the purposes of SOA 2003, s 128 prohibitions imposed by an order made in one part of the UK apply (unless expressly confined to particular localities) throughout that and every other part of the UK.

[383]   SOA 2003, s 128(2); maximum on summary conviction: **1.43**.

[384]   SOA 2003, s 128(3).

[385]   See **1.49**.

18.205 The offence is committed simply by a breach of the requirements of the order, subject to that breach not being with reasonable excuse. The burden of showing lack of reasonable excuse is on the prosecution, although the defendant will bear an evidential burden in respect of that defence.[386]

Notification requirements

18.206 These are dealt with by SOA 2003, s 129[387]. If a person (A):

(a) is convicted[388] of a s 128 offence or of the corresponding offence of breach of a Scottish RSHO or interim RSHO;[389]

(b) is found not guilty of such an offence by reason of insanity;

(c) is found to be under a disability and to have done the act charged against him in respect of such an offence;[390] or

(d) is cautioned[391] in respect of such an offence,[392]

existing notification requirements of Pt 2 will be extended or new notification requirements will come into effect, in accordance with the following provisions.

18.207 Where A was already subject to the notification requirements, A will remain subject to those requirements for the duration of the RSHO (as renewed from time to time), even though the notification requirements would otherwise have ceased.[393] If the original notification period lasts for longer than the RSHO, A remains subject to the notification requirements until the end of that longer period.

18.208 On the other hand, where A was not subject to notification requirements of SOA 2003, Pt 2 immediately before the conviction, finding or caution:

(a) s 129 subjects A to the notification requirements from the time of the conviction, etc in respect of the RSHO until the RSHO ceases to have effect; and

(b) the notification requirements apply to A from the date of the conviction, etc in respect of the RSHO.[394]

This means, for example, that A must comply with the initial notification requirement (under s 83(1)) within 3 days[395] of the conviction, finding or caution in respect of a s 128 offence.

---

[386] See **17.115–17.118** and **18.125**.
[387] As amended by VCRA 2006, s 56(3).
[388] See **17.29–17.31**.
[389] Contrary to the PCPSO(S)A 2005, s 7.
[390] See **17.33, 17.34**.
[391] See **17.36**.
[392] SOA 2003, s 129(1).
[393] SOA 2003, s 129(2).
[394] SOA 2003, s 129(3), (4), (5)(a).
[395] See **17.55**, n 103.

18.209 The same rules about notification requirements apply to a conviction, finding or caution in respect of a breach of an interim RSHO. The only difference is that where the conviction, finding or caution is in respect of a breach of an interim RSHO, the notification requirements run until the full RSHO, if eventually made, ceases to have effect, or, if no full RSHO is made, the interim RSHO ceases to have effect.[396]

APPENDIX

NOTE

This appendix sets out the SGC Definitive Guideline: Sexual Offences Act 2003 page by page as it is available as a pdf file at www.sentencing-guidelines.gov.uk. Throughout this book references have been made to pages in this Guideline. These page numbers appear at the *bottom of each page* as printed in the Appendix.

Sentencing Guidelines Council

Sexual Offences Act 2003

Definitive Guideline

FOREWORD

In accordance with section 170(9) of the Criminal Justice Act (CJA) 2003, the Sentencing Guidelines Council issues this guideline as a definitive guideline. By virtue of section 172 of the CJA 2003, every court must have regard to a relevant guideline. This guideline applies to the sentencing of offenders convicted of any of the sexual offences covered by this guideline who are sentenced on or after 14 May 2007.

The Sexual Offences Act 2003 contains a large number of new or amended offences for which there was no sentencing case law. Following implementation of this Act in May 2004, a number of cases have been considered by the Court of Appeal and guidance from those judgments has been incorporated into this guideline.

The guideline uses the starting point of 5 years for the rape of an adult with no aggravating or mitigating factors (derived from Millberry and others[1]) as the baseline from which all other sentences for offences in this guideline have been calculated. Since the judgment in Millberry, changes introduced by the CJA 2003 have both affected the structure of custodial sentences of 12 months and above and introduced new sentences for those convicted of many of the offences in this guideline where the court considers that the offender provides a significant risk of serious harm in the future.

The sentencing ranges and starting points in this guideline take account of both these changes. Accordingly, the transitional arrangements set out in paragraphs 2.1.7–2.1.10 of the Council guideline New Sentences: Criminal Justice Act 2003 do not apply.

Sexual offences can be committed in a domestic context and so come within the definition of 'domestic violence' used in the Council guideline Overarching Principles: Domestic Violence published in December 2006. In such circumstances, reference should also be made to this guideline to identify additional principles and factors that should also be taken into account in assessing the seriousness of an offence and determining the appropriate sentence.

The Council is indebted to the Sentencing Advisory Panel for its comprehensive advice which followed two public consultations and included a review of work that the Panel had previously undertaken in relation to offences of rape and of child pornography, where its advice had led to guideline judgments from the Court of Appeal. The advice and this guideline are available on www.sentencing-guidelines.gov.uk or from the Sentencing Guidelines Secretariat at 4th floor, 8–10 Great George Street, London SW1P 3AE. A summary of the responses to the Council's consultation also appears on the website.

Chairman of the Council
April 2007

---

1 [2003] 2 Cr App R (S) 31

CONTENTS

Sexual Offences – Contents

Offences – Sexual Offences Act 2003 Section	Part and page(s) of the guideline
1	Part 2A, pages 24, 25 and 26
2	Part 2A, pages 28, 29 and 30
3	Part 2B, pages 32, 33 and 34
4	Part 2C, pages 38, 39, 40 and 41
5	Part 2A, pages 24, 25 and 26
6	Part 2A, pages 28, 29 and 30
7	Part 2B, pages 32, 33 and 34
8	Part 2C, pages 38, 39, 40 and 41
9	Part 3A, pages 52, 53, 54 and Part 7, page 135
10	Part 3A, pages 52, 53, 54 and Part 7, page 136
11	Part 2D, pages 44, 45 and Part 7, page 137
12	Part 2D, pages 46, 47 and Part 7, page 138
14	Part 3A, pages 66 and 67
15	Part 4, pages 82 and 83
16	Part 3A, pages 60 and 61
17	Part 3A, pages 60 and 61
18	Part 3A, pages 62 and 63
19	Part 3A, pages 64 and 65
25	Part 3A, pages 56, 57, 58 and Part 7, page 139
26	Part 3A, pages 56, 57, 58 and Part 7, page 139
30	Part 3B, pages 70, 71 and 72
31	Part 2C, pages 38, 39, 40 and 41
32	Part 2D, pages 44 and 45
33	Part 2D, pages 46 and 47
34	Part 3B, pages 70, 71 and 72
35	Part 3B, pages 70, 71 and 72
36	Part 3B, pages 76 and 77
37	Part 3B, pages 78 and 79
38	Part 3B, pages 74 and 75
39	Part 3B, pages 74 and 75
40	Part 3B, pages 76 and 77
41	Part 3B, pages 78 and 79
45	Part 6A, pages 112, 113 and 114 (section 1 Protection of Children Act 1978 and section 160 Criminal Justice Act 1988)
47	Part 6B, pages 116, 117 and 118
48	Part 6B, pages 120, 121, 122 and 123
49	Part 6B, pages 120, 121, 122 and 123
50	Part 6B, pages 120, 121, 122 and 123
52	Part 6C, pages 126 and 127
53	Part 6C, pages 126 and 127
55	Part 6C, pages 128 and 129 (section 33A Sexual Offences Act 1956)
57	Part 6D, pages 130 and 131
58	Part 6D, pages 130 and 131
59	Part 6D, pages 130 and 131
61	Part 4, pages 88 and 89
62	Part 4, pages 84 and 85
63	Part 4, pages 86 and 87
64	Part 5, pages 92 and 93
65	Part 5, pages 92 and 93
66	Part 5, pages 96 and 97
67	Part 5, pages 98 and 99
69	Part 5, pages 100 and 101
70	Part 5, pages 102 and 103
71	Part 5, pages 94 and 95

Part 1: GENERAL PRINCIPLES

Introduction

1.1   The Sexual Offences Act (SOA) 2003 came into force on 1 May 2004. Part 1 creates a number of new sexual offences. It also includes a large number of pre-existing offences, some of which have been redefined and/or have revised maximum penalties.

1.2   The Criminal Justice Act (CJA) 2003 provides[1] that the seriousness of an offence should be determined by two main parameters: the culpability of the offender and the harm caused, or risked, by the offence, including the impact on the victim(s). The Sentencing Guidelines Council guideline on seriousness[2] provides that the seriousness of an offence is to be determined according to the relative impact of the culpability of the offender and the actual or foreseeable harm caused to the victim. Where there is an imbalance between culpability and harm, the culpability of the offender in the particular circumstances of an individual case should be the primary factor in determining the seriousness of the offence.

1.3   The guideline has been formulated on the basis of the sentencing framework that is currently in force. For these types of offence more than for many others, the sentencing process must allow for flexibility and variability. The suggested starting points and sentencing ranges contained in the offence guidelines are not rigid, and movement within and between ranges will be dependent upon the circumstances of individual cases and, in particular, the aggravating and mitigating factors that are present.

In order to assist in developing consistency of approach, a decision making process is set out at page 17.

1.4   In the guideline published by the Council to support the new sentencing framework introduced by the CJA 2003,[3] in relation to custodial sentences of 12 months or more it is stated that, generally, a court should only make specific recommendations about the requirements to be included in the licence conditions when announcing shorter sentences where it is reasonable to anticipate the relevance of the requirement at the point of release. However, sentencing for a sexual offence is an example of an occasion where the court may sensibly suggest interventions that could be useful, either during the custodial period or on release. The court's recommendation will not form part of the sentence, but will be a helpful guide for the probation service.

1.5   Apart from the offence of rape which, when charged as a primary offence, is confined to male defendants, the SOA 2003 makes no distinction in terms of liability or maximum penalties for male and female offenders. The guidelines are proposed on the basis that they should apply irrespective of the gender of the victim or of the offender, except in specified circumstances where a distinction is justified by the nature of the offence.

---

1   s.143(1)
2   Overarching Principles: Seriousness, published 16 December 2004 – www.sentencing-guidelines.gov.uk
3   New Sentences: Criminal Justice Act 2003, published 16 December 2004 – www.sentencing-guidelines.gov.uk

Seriousness

1.6   The guidelines for sentencing for serious sexual offences have been based on the guideline judgment on rape – Millberry and others[4] – in which the Court of Appeal stated that:

'... there are, broadly, three dimensions to consider in assessing the gravity of an individual offence of rape. The first is the degree of harm to the victim; the second is the level of culpability of the offender; and the third is the level of risk posed by the offender to society.'

1.7   In the subsequent Attorney General's Reference (Nos. 91, 119, 120 of 2002),[5] the Court of Appeal held that 'similar dimensions should apply to other categories of sexual offences', and added that there would also be a need to deter others from acting in a similar fashion.

1.8   These statements established the general principles for assessing the seriousness of sexual offences that are now encapsulated in the provisions of the CJA 2003.

1.9   The maximum penalty and mode of trial prescribed by Parliament for each sexual offence give a general indication of the relative seriousness of different offences and these have also acted as a broad guide for the proposed sentencing starting points.

The harm caused by sexual offences

1.10   All sexual offences where the activity is non-consensual, coercive or exploitative result in harm. Harm is also inherent where victims ostensibly consent but where their capacity to give informed consent is affected by their youth or mental disorder.

1.11   The effects of sexual offending may be physical and/or psychological. The physical effects – injury, pregnancy or sexually transmitted infections – may be very serious. The psychological effects may be equally or even more serious, but much less obvious (even unascertainable) at the time of sentencing. They may include any or all of the following (although this list is not intended to be comprehensive and items are not listed in any form of priority):

- Violation of the victim's sexual autonomy
- Fear
- Humiliation
- Degradation
- Shame
- Embarrassment
- Inability to trust
- Inability to form personal or intimate relationships in adulthood
- Self harm or suicide

---

4   [2003] 2 Cr App R (S) 31
5   [2003] 2 Cr App R (S) 338

The offender's culpability in sexual offences

1.12   According to the Council's guideline on seriousness, culpability is determined by the extent to which the offender intends to cause harm – the worse the harm intended, the greater the offender's culpability. Sexual offences are somewhat different in that the offender's intention may be to obtain sexual gratification, financial gain or some other result, rather than to harm the victim. However, where the activity is in any way non-consensual, coercive or exploitative, the offence is inherently harmful and therefore the offender's culpability is high. Planning an offence makes the offender more highly culpable than engaging in opportunistic or impulsive offending.

1.13   In general, the difficulty of assessing seriousness where there is an imbalance between culpability and harm does not arise in relation to sexual offences. However, some offences in the SOA 2003 are defined in terms of the offender's intention to commit an offence that does not, in fact, take place, for example the 'incitement offences', the 'preparatory offences' and the new offence of 'meeting a child following sexual grooming etc'. In such cases, the level of actual harm to the victim may be lower than in cases involving the commission of a physical sexual offence. Here the level of culpability will be the primary factor in determining the seriousness of the offence, with the degree of harm that could have been caused to an individual victim, and the risk posed to others by the offender, being integral to the sentencing decision.

The culpability of young offenders

1.14   The SOA 2003 makes special provision for young offenders found guilty of certain sexual offences – namely those in the 'ostensibly consensual' category – by providing that offenders aged under 18 will face a maximum penalty of 5 years' detention, as opposed to the maximum 14 years for offenders aged 18 or over. These are dealt with in Part 7 of the guideline.

1.15   The age of the offender will also be significant in the sentencing exercise in relation to non-consensual offences, where no special sentencing provisions have been provided for in the legislation. Its significance is particularly acute in relation to the strict liability offences such as 'rape of a child under 13', where the maximum penalty is life imprisonment, especially if an offender is very young and the disparity in age between the offender and the victim is very small.

1.16   Section 44(1) of the Children and Young Persons Act 1933 provides that every court dealing with a child or young person, as an offender or otherwise, 'shall have regard to the welfare of the child or young person'.

1.17   The youth and immaturity of an offender must always be potential mitigating factors for the courts to take into account when passing sentence. However, where the facts of a case are particularly serious, the youth of the offender will not necessarily mitigate the appropriate sentence.[6]

---

6   R v Paiwant Asi-Akram [2005] EWCA Crim 1543, R v Patrick M [2005] EWCA Crim 1679

The nature of the sexual activity

1.18   The nature of the sexual activity covered by some offences in the SOA 2003 (such as 'rape' and 'assault by penetration') is quite precisely defined whilst others – for example, 'sexual activity with a child', 'sexual activity with a child family member', 'abuse of a position of trust' – are drawn very widely and cover all forms of intentional activity involving sexual touching, including penetration.

- Sexual activity involves varying types and degrees of touching ranging from genital or oral penetration through to non-genital touching of the victim's clothed body.
- Penetrative acts are more serious than non-penetrative acts. The fact that the offender or victim (especially the victim) is totally or partially naked makes the activity more serious.
- The touching may be consensual, ostensibly consensual or non-consensual. Where the victim's ability to consent is impaired by, for example, youth or mental incapacity, this makes the activity, regardless of its nature, more serious.

Aggravating and mitigating factors

1.19   The Council guideline on seriousness sets out aggravating and mitigating factors that are applicable to a wide range of cases. Care needs to be taken to ensure that there is no double counting where an essential element of the offence charged might, in other circumstances, be an aggravating factor.

1.20   Sentencers should refer to paragraphs 1.20–1.27 of the Council guideline. For ease of reference, extracts from the guideline are provided below. The fact that a victim was vulnerable will be of particular relevance in cases involving sexual offences.

THESE FACTORS APPLY TO A WIDE RANGE OF OFFENCES AND NOT ALL WILL BE
RELEVANT TO SEXUAL OFFENCES.

Factors indicating higher culpability:

- Offence committed whilst on bail for other offences
- Failure to respond to previous sentences
- Offence was racially or religiously aggravated
- Offence motivated by, or demonstrating, hostility to the victim based on his or her sexual orientation (or presumed sexual orientation)
- Offence motivated by, or demonstrating, hostility based on the victim's disability (or presumed disability)
- Previous conviction(s), particularly where a pattern of repeat offending is disclosed
- Planning of an offence
- An intention to commit more serious harm than actually resulted from the offence
- Offenders operating in groups or gangs
- 'Professional' offending
- Commission of the offence for financial gain (where this is not inherent in the offence itself)
- High level of profit from the offence
- An attempt to conceal or dispose of evidence
- Failure to respond to warnings or concerns expressed by others about the offender's behaviour
- Offence committed whilst on licence
- Offence motivated by hostility towards a minority group, or a member or members of it
- Deliberate targeting of vulnerable victim(s)
- Commission of an offence while under the influence of alcohol or drugs
- Use of a weapon to frighten or injure victim
- Deliberate and gratuitous violence or damage to property, over and above what is needed to carry out the offence
- Abuse of power
- Abuse of a position of trust

Factors indicating a more than usually serious degree of harm:

- Multiple victims
- An especially serious physical or psychological effect on the victim, even if unintended
- A sustained assault or repeated assaults on the same victim
- Victim is particularly vulnerable
- Location of the offence (for example, in an isolated place)
- Offence is committed against those working in the public sector or providing a service to the public
- Presence of others e.g. relatives, especially children or partner of the victim
- Additional degradation of the victim (e.g. taking photographs of a victim as part of a sexual offence)
- In property offences, high value (including sentimental value) of property to the victim, or substantial consequential loss (e.g. where the theft of equipment causes serious disruption to a victim's life or business)

Factors indicating significantly lower culpability:

- A greater degree of provocation than normally expected
- Mental illness or disability
- Youth or age, where it affects the responsibility of the individual defendant
- The fact that the offender played only a minor role in the offence

---

Personal mitigation

Section 166(1) Criminal Justice Act 2003 makes provision for a sentencer to take account of any matters that 'in the opinion of the court, are relevant in mitigation of sentence'. When the court has formed an initial assessment of the seriousness of the offence, then it should consider any offender mitigation. The issue of remorse should be taken into account at this point along with other mitigating features such as admissions to the police in interview.

The risk of re-offending

1.21 One of the purposes of sentencing set out in the CJA 2003[7] is 'the protection of the public'. Part 2 of the Sexual Offences Act 2003 strengthens the current system of registration for sex offenders and also introduces a number of new orders, some of which are available on conviction and others by application in civil proceedings to a magistrates' court. There are also a number of sentencing options, custodial and non-custodial, open to sentencers where the risk of re-offending is high.

1.22 The arrangements for registration of sex offenders (see also paragraph 1.29 below) follow automatically on conviction, and are not part of the sentencing process. The duty to give reasons for, and to explain the effect of, sentencing is now set out in the CJA 2003.[8]

---

7 s.142(1)
8 s.174

10

1.23 If a victim personal statement has not been produced, the court should enquire whether the victim has been given the opportunity to make one. In the absence of a victim personal statement, the court should not assume that the offence had no impact on the victim. A pre-sentence report should normally be prepared before sentence is passed for any sexual offence, as this may contain important information about the sexually deviant tendencies of an offender and an assessment of the likelihood of re-offending; a psychiatric report may also be appropriate. It is clearly in the interests of public protection to provide effective treatment for sex offenders at the earliest opportunity.

Dangerous offenders

1.24 In relation to custodial sentences, the starting point will be the assessment of dangerousness as set out in section 229 of the CJA 2003; since the majority of the offences in the SOA 2003 are 'specified' offences (as defined in section 224 and listed in schedule 15, part 2). There are three sentencing options for offenders aged 18 or over: discretionary life sentences, indeterminate sentences of 'imprisonment for public protection', and the redefined extended sentences.[9]

1.25 The criterion for the assessment of dangerousness in all cases falling within the provisions for dangerous offenders is whether the court considers that there is a significant risk to members of the public of serious harm occasioned by the commission by the offender of further specified offences.[10] If the criterion is met, the options available depend on whether the offence is a 'serious' offence.

1.26 Where a specified offence carries a maximum penalty of life imprisonment or 10 years' imprisonment or more, it is a 'serious' offence for the purposes of section 225. In such cases, if the risk criterion is met in respect of an adult offender, a life sentence or imprisonment for public protection must be imposed.

1.27 In setting the minimum term to be served within an indeterminate sentence under these provisions, in accordance with normal practice that term will usually be half the equivalent determinate sentence. Such period will normally be reduced by time spent on remand in custody.

1.28 In relation to 'specified' offences that are not 'serious' offences, where the risk criterion is met in relation to an adult offender, under section 227 the court is required to extend the period for which the offender will be subject to a licence on release from custody; the custodial element in such cases must be for a minimum of 12 months. Within the statutory limits, the period of licence must be of such length as the court considers necessary for the purposes of protecting members of the public from serious harm occasioned by the commission of further specified offences.

9 Criminal Justice Act 2003, ss.225–228
10 Ibid. 225(1)

11

Other orders

1.29   There are a number of orders and requirements relevant to those convicted of sexual offences. Some follow automatically on conviction and others can be applied for:

- inclusion of an offender's name on a Sex Offenders' Register – used for risk management by local authorities and other statutory agencies to indicate that an individual may pose an ongoing risk to children – follows automatically on conviction or caution for a sexual offence;[11] and
- notification orders which impose sex offender registration requirements on offenders living in the UK who have been convicted of a sexual offence overseas – available on application by complaint to a magistrates' court.[12]

1.30   A court has a duty to consider making two ancillary orders that require the intervention of the sentencer, namely sexual offences prevention orders (SOPO)[13] and orders disqualifying an offender from working with children:[14]

- sexual offences prevention orders – civil preventative orders that can be made either at the point of sentence in the Crown Court or a magistrates' court, or by complaint to a magistrates' court in respect of someone previously convicted of a sexual offence where that person's behaviour suggests the possibility of re-offending; and
- disqualification orders – an order disqualifying an offender convicted of an offence against a child from working with children, which must (or in defined circumstances may) be imposed unless the court is satisfied that the offender is unlikely to commit a further offence against a child.

When passing sentence for a sexual offence, the court must always consider whether or not it would be appropriate to make a sexual offences prevention order or an order disqualifying the offender from working with children.

Community orders

1.31   The availability of requirements able to be included within a community order, and the suitability of them for an individual offender, will be detailed in a pre-sentence report. Some options of direct relevance to sex offenders are considered below.

Sex offender treatment programmes

1.31.1   These are available both in prisons and in the community. Participation in a programme whilst in custody is voluntary, but programmes in the community can be a mandatory requirement of a community order where a PSR writer has made a recommendation and commented on the suitability of the offender for such a requirement.

- Accredited treatment programmes are targeted at males, who form the overwhelming majority of sex offenders, but individual programmes are devised for female offenders.

---

11 Children and Young Persons Act 1933, schedule 1 – currently subject to a cross-government review, in light of the alternative provisions that now exist to prohibit working with children
12 Sexual Offences Act 2003, s.97
13 Sexual Offences Act 2003, s.104
14 Criminal Justice and Courts Services Act 2000, ss.28 and 29, as amended by the Criminal Justice Act 2003, s.299 and schedule 30

- Treatment programmes are usually only available to those who are given a long community order (normally 3 years), and may not always be available for those sentenced to shorter custodial sentences.

Before imposing sentence, the court should investigate the content and availability of such programmes and will wish to be satisfied that a programme will be able to commence within a realistic timeframe.

Curfews

1.31.2 A curfew requirement, usually associated with electronic monitoring, may be helpful in restricting an offender's right to be out in public at the same time as, for example, schoolchildren. A curfew requirement is most likely to be effective when used in conjunction with a residence requirement requiring an offender to live in approved accommodation where behaviour and compliance can be monitored. Such a requirement can be for between 2 and 12 hours per day and last up to 6 months.

When a court imposes a community order for a sexual offence, it should always consider imposing a requirement to attend a special treatment programme designed to help the offender recognise and control any sexually deviant tendencies.

Financial orders

1.32   In addition to the sentence imposed for the offence(s), the following supplementary penalties should be considered.

Confiscation orders

1.32.1 Depending on the date of the offence, the CJA 1988 or Proceeds of Crime Act 2002 set out the circumstances in which the courts are entitled or required to make a confiscation order to recover some of the proceeds of an offender's crime. The prosecution may suggest consideration of a confiscation order but, where appropriate, the court should consider making such an order of its own volition.

Deprivation orders

1.32.2 The courts should also consider whether, in the particular circumstances of the case, it would be appropriate to make an order depriving an offender of property used for the purposes of crime.[15] This will be a particularly relevant consideration where, for example, someone convicted of a voyeurism or child pornography offence possesses a camera or a computer used to make, store or circulate sexual material connected to the offence, or where a pimp convicted of controlling prostitution uses a car to drive prostitutes to their 'patch'. A Crown Court can also make a restraint order[16] in respect of realisable property held by an offender who is believed to have benefited from criminal conduct, prohibiting them from dealing with it.

---

15 Powers of Criminal Courts (Sentencing) Act 2000, s.143
16 Proceeds of Crime Act 2002, s.41

13

Whenever an offender has profited in some way from the sexual exploitation of others, the court should give serious consideration to the making of a confiscation order to recover the proceeds of the crime.

The court should also, especially in relation to offences involving voyeurism, prostitution, pornography and trafficking, consider whether it would be appropriate to make an order depriving an offender of property used, or intended to be used, in connection with the offence.

Compensation orders

1.32.3 The court must consider making a compensation order, in accordance with the provisions of the Powers of Criminal Courts (Sentencing) Act 2000, in respect of any personal injury, loss or damage occasioned to a victim. Compensation should benefit, not inflict further harm on, the victim. Any financial recompense from the offender for a sexual offence may cause the victim additional humiliation, degradation and distress. The victim's views are properly obtained through sensitive discussion with the victim by the police or witness care unit, when it can be explained that the offender's ability to pay will ultimately determine whether, and how much, compensation is ordered. The views of the victim regarding compensation should be made known to the court and respected and, if appropriate, acknowledged at the time of sentencing. A victim may not want compensation from the offender, but this should not be assumed.

Summary of general principles

(i) Except where otherwise indicated, the offence guidelines all relate to sentencing on conviction for a first-time offender after a plea of not guilty.

(ii) Starting points are based on a basic offence[17] of its category. Aggravating and mitigating factors that are particularly relevant to each offence are listed in the individual offence guidelines. The list of aggravating factors is not exhaustive and the factors are not ranked in any particular order. A factor that is an ingredient of an offence cannot also be an aggravating factor. Sexual offences will often involve some form of violence as an essential element of the offence and this has been included in fixing the starting points. Where harm is inflicted over and above that necessary to commit the offence, that will be an aggravating factor.

(iii) In relation to sexual offences, the presence of generic and offence-specific aggravating factors will significantly influence the type and length of sentence imposed. The generic list of aggravating and mitigating factors identified by the Sentencing Guidelines Council in its guideline on seriousness is reproduced at paragraph 1.20 above but not for each offence. These factors apply to a wide range of offences and not all will be relevant to sexual offences.

(iv) Unless specifically stated, the starting points assume that the offender is an adult. Sentences will normally need to be reduced where the offender is sentenced as a youth, save in the most serious cases (see paragraph 1.17 above).

(v) Specific guidance on sentencing youths for one of the child sex offences that attracts a lower statutory maximum penalty where the offender is under 18 can be found in Part 7.

(vi) There are a large number of new or amended offences in the SOA 2003 for which there is no sentencing case law. The guidelines use the starting point of 5 years for the rape of an adult with no aggravating or mitigating factors (derived from Millberry and others[18]) as the baseline from which all other sentences have been calculated.

(vii) Where a community order is the recommended starting point, the requirements to be imposed are left for the court to decide according to the particular facts of the individual case. Where a community order is the proposed starting point for different levels of seriousness of the same offence or for a second or subsequent offence of the same level of seriousness, this should be reflected by the imposition of more onerous requirements.[19]

(viii) Treatment programmes are not specifically mentioned in the guidelines. A sentencer should always consider whether, in the circumstances of the individual case and the profile of the offending behaviour, it would be sensible to require the offender to take part in a programme designed to address sexually deviant behaviour.

---

17 A 'basic offence' is one in which the ingredients of the offence as defined are present, and assuming no aggravating or mitigating factors
18 [2003] 2 Cr App R (S) 31
19 For further information, see the Council guideline New Sentences: Criminal Justice Act 2003, section B: 'Imposing a Community Sentence – The Approach'

(ix) Reference to 'non-custodial sentence' in any of the offence guidelines (save for those in Part 7) suggests that the court consider a community order or a fine. In most instances, an offence will have crossed the threshold for a community order. However, in accordance with normal sentencing practice, even in those circumstances a court is not precluded from imposing a financial penalty where that is determined to be the appropriate sentence.

(x) In all cases, the court must consider whether it would be appropriate to make any ancillary orders, such as an order banning the offender from working with children, an order requiring the offender to pay compensation to a victim, or an order confiscating an offender's assets or requiring the forfeiture of equipment used in connection with an offence.

The decision making process

The process set out below is intended to show that the sentencing approach for sexual offences is fluid and requires the structured exercise of discretion.

1. Identify dangerous offenders

Most sexual offences are specified offences for the purposes of the public protection provisions in the CJA 2003. The court must determine whether there is a significant risk of serious harm by the commission of a further specified offence. The starting points in the guidelines are a) for offenders who do not meet the dangerous offender criteria and b) as the basis for the setting of a minimum term within an indeterminate sentence for those who do meet the criteria.

2. Identify the appropriate starting point

Because many acts can be charged as more than one offence, consideration will have to be given to the appropriate guideline once findings of fact have been made. The sentence should reflect the facts found to exist and not just the title of the offence of which the offender is convicted.

3. Consider relevant aggravating factors, both general and those specific to the type of offence

This may result in a sentence level being identified that is higher than the suggested starting point, sometimes substantially so.

4. Consider mitigating factors and personal mitigation

There may be general or offence-specific mitigating factors and matters of personal mitigation which could result in a sentence that is lower than the suggested starting point (possibly substantially so), or a sentence of a different type.

5. Reduction for guilty plea

The court will then apply any reduction for a guilty plea following the approach set out in the Council's guideline Reduction in Sentence for a Guilty Plea.

6. Consider ancillary orders

The court should consider whether ancillary orders are appropriate or necessary. These are referred to in some of the offence guidelines.

7. The totality principle

The court should review the total sentence to ensure that it is proportionate to the offending behaviour and properly balanced.

8. Reasons

When a court moves from the suggested starting points and sentencing ranges identified in the guidelines, it should explain its reasons for doing so.

Sentencing ranges and starting points

1. Typically, a guideline will apply to an offence that can be committed in a variety of circumstances with different levels of seriousness. It will apply to a first-time offender who has been convicted after a trial. Within the guidelines, a first-time offender is a person who does not have a conviction which, by virtue of section 143(2) of the CJA 2003, must be treated as an aggravating factor.

2. As an aid to consistency of approach, the guidelines describe a number of types of activity which would fall within the broad definition of the offence. These are set out in a column headed 'Type/nature of activity'.

3. The expected approach is for a court to identify the description that most nearly matches the particular facts of the offence for which sentence is being imposed. This will identify a starting point from which the sentencer can depart to reflect aggravating or mitigating factors affecting the seriousness of the offence (beyond those contained within the column describing the type or nature of offence activity) to reach a provisional sentence.

4. The sentencing range is the bracket into which the provisional sentence will normally fall after having regard to factors which aggravate or mitigate the seriousness of the offence. The particular circumstances may, however, make it appropriate that the provisional sentence falls outside the range.

5. Where the offender has previous convictions which aggravate the seriousness of the current offence, that may take the provisional sentence beyond the range given, particularly where there are significant other aggravating factors present.

6. Once the provisional sentence has been identified by reference to those factors affecting the seriousness of the offence, the court will take into account any relevant factors of personal mitigation, which may take the sentence outside the range indicated in the guideline.

7. Where there has been a guilty plea, any reduction attributable to that plea will be applied to the sentence at this stage. This reduction may take the sentence below the range provided.

8. A court must give its reasons for imposing a sentence of a different kind or outside the range provided in the guidelines.[20]

---

20 Criminal Justice Act 2003, s.174(2)(a)

Part 2: NON-CONSENSUAL OFFENCES

2.1   The offences in this category include 'rape', 'assault by penetration', 'sexual assault' and causing a victim to take part in sexual activity without consent. Some offences are generic; others protect victims who are under 13 or who have a mental disorder impeding choice.

2.2   The SOA 2003 creates a rule of law that there is no defence of consent where sexual activity is alleged in relation to a child under 13 years of age or a person who has a mental disorder impeding choice.[1]

The harm caused by non-consensual offences

2.3   All non-consensual offences involve the violation of the victim's sexual autonomy and will result in harm.

2.4   The seriousness of the violation may depend on a number of factors, but the nature of the sexual behaviour will be the primary indicator of the degree of harm caused in the first instance.

2.5   The principle that offences involving sexual penetration are more serious than non-penetrative sexual assault is reflected in the higher maximum penalty accorded in statute to these offences.

The relationship between the victim and the offender

2.6   The guideline judgment in Millberry and others[2] established the principle that sentencers should adopt the same starting point for 'relationship rape' or 'acquaintance rape' as for 'stranger rape'. The Council has determined that the same principle should apply to all non-consensual offences. Any rape is a traumatic and humiliating experience and, although the particular circumstances in which the rape takes place may affect the sentence imposed, the starting point for sentencing should be the same.

The age of the victim

2.7   The extreme youth or old age of a victim should be an aggravating factor.

2.8   In addition, in principle, the younger the child and the greater the age gap between the offender and the victim, the higher the sentence should be.

2.9   However, the youth and immaturity of the offender must also be taken into account in each case.

2.10   The court in Millberry adopted the principle that a sexual offence against a child is more serious than the same offence perpetrated against an adult and attracts a higher starting point. No distinction was made between children aged 13 and over but under 16, and those aged under 13.

---

1   See, for example, the offences set out in the Sexual Offences Act 2003, ss.5–8 and 30–33
2   [2003] 2 Cr App R (S) 31

2.11   Special weight has subsequently been accorded to the protection of very young children by the introduction of a range of strict liability offences in the SOA 2003 specifically designed to protect children under 13:

- The offences of 'rape of a child under 13', 'assault by penetration of a child under 13' and 'causing a child under 13 to engage in sexual activity' where the activity included sexual penetration carry the maximum life penalty.
- The maximum penalty for the new offence of 'sexual assault of a child under 13' is 14 years, as opposed to a maximum of 10 years for the generic 'sexual assault' offence.

2.12   In keeping with the principles of protection established in the SOA 2003, the Council has determined that:

- higher starting points in cases involving victims under 13 should normally apply, but there may be exceptions;
- particular care will need to be taken when applying the starting points in certain cases, such as those involving young offenders or offenders whose judgement is impaired by a mental disorder; and
- proximity in age between a young victim and an offender is also a relevant consideration.

Victims with a mental disorder

2.13   The SOA 2003 introduces three groups of offences specifically designed to protect vulnerable adults who have a mental disorder. The aim is to protect all victims with a mental disorder, whether or not they have the capacity to consent to sexual activity, but the legislation has been drafted to make a distinction between:

(i)   those persons who have a mental disorder 'impeding choice' – persons whose mental functioning is so impaired at the time of the sexual activity that they are 'unable to refuse';

(ii) those who have a mental disorder (but not falling within (i) above[3]) such that any ability to choose is easily overridden and agreement to sexual activity can be secured through relatively low levels of inducement, threat or deception; and

(iii) those who have a mental disorder, regardless of their ability to choose whether or not to take part in sexual activity, whose actions may be influenced by their familiarity with, or dependence upon, a care worker.

The latter two groups are considered in Part 3 of the guideline, which relates to offences involving ostensible consent.

2.14   The maximum penalty for non-consensual offences involving victims with a mental disorder is high, indicating the relative seriousness of such offending behaviour.

2.15   In line with the thinking relating to the protection of children under 13, the fact that the victim has a mental disorder impeding choice should always aggravate an offence, bearing in mind that it will have been proven that the offender knew, or could reasonably have been expected to know, that the victim had a mental disorder impeding choice.

---

3   That is, it is not of such a character that it 'impedes choice' within the meaning of the SOA 2003

The starting points for sentencing for offences involving victims with a mental disorder impeding choice should be higher than in comparable cases where the victim has no such disability.

The offender's culpability in non-consensual offences

2.16   All the non-consensual offences involve a high level of culpability on the part of the offender, since that person will have acted either deliberately without the victim's consent or without giving due consideration to whether the victim was able to or did, in fact, consent.

2.17   Notwithstanding paragraph 2.11 above, there will be cases involving victims under 13 years of age where there was, in fact, consent where, in law, it cannot be given. In such circumstances, presence of consent may be material in relation to sentence, particularly in relation to a young offender where there is close proximity in age between the victim and offender or where the mental capacity or maturity of the offender is impaired.

2.18   Where there was reasonable belief on the part of a young offender that the victim was 16, this can be taken into consideration as a mitigating factor.

2.19   The planning of an offence indicates a higher level of culpability than an opportunistic or impulsive offence.

2.20   In Millberry, the Court of Appeal established that the offender's culpability in a case of rape would be 'somewhat less' in cases where the victim had consented to sexual familiarity with the offender on the occasion in question than in cases where the offender had set out with the intention of committing rape.

2.21   Save in cases of breach of trust or grooming, an offender's culpability may be reduced if the offender and victim engaged in consensual sexual activity on the same occasion and immediately before the offence took place. Factors relevant to culpability in such circumstances include the type of consensual activity that occurred, similarity to what then occurs, and timing. However, the seriousness of the non-consensual act may overwhelm any other consideration.

2.22   The same principle should apply to the generic offences of 'assault by penetration' and 'sexual assault'. However, it should not apply to the equivalent offences relating to victims who are under 13 or who have a mental disorder impeding choice, given the presumption inherent in these offences that the victim cannot in law consent to any form of sexual activity, save where there is close proximity of age between the offender and the victim, or where the mental capacity or maturity of the offender is impaired.

PART 2A: RAPE AND ASSAULT BY PENETRATION

2A.1   The SOA 2003 has redefined the offence of rape so that it now includes non-consensual penile penetration of the mouth and has also introduced a new offence of 'assault by penetration'. Parliament agreed the same maximum penalty of life imprisonment for these offences.

2A.2   It is impossible to say that any one form of non-consensual penetration is inherently a more serious violation of the victim's sexual autonomy than another. The Council therefore has determined that the sentencing starting points established in Millberry should apply to all non-consensual offences involving penetration of the anus or vagina or penile penetration of the mouth.

- 5 years is intended to be the starting point for a case involving an adult victim raped by a single offender in a case that involves no aggravating factors at all.
- 8 years is the suggested starting point where any of the particular aggravating factors identified in the offence guidelines are involved.

2A.3   In addition:

- where identified aggravating factors exist and the victim is a child aged 13 or over but under 16, the recommended starting point is 10 years;
- for the rape of a child under 13 where there are no aggravating factors, a starting point of 10 years is recommended, rising to 13 years for cases involving any of the particular aggravating factors identified in the guideline.

2A.4   These are starting points. The existence of aggravating factors may significantly increase the sentence. The new sentences for public protection are designed to ensure that sexual offenders are not released into the community if they present a significant risk of serious harm.

Rape

Factors to take into consideration:

1.   The sentences for public protection must be considered in all cases of rape.

   a) As a result, imprisonment for life or an order of imprisonment for public protection will be imposed in some cases. Both sentences are designed to ensure that sexual offenders are not released into the community if they present a significant risk of serious harm.
   b) Life imprisonment is the maximum for the offence. Such a sentence may be imposed either as a result of the offence itself where a number of aggravating factors are present, or because the offender meets the dangerousness criterion.
   c) Within any indeterminate sentence, the minimum term will generally be half the appropriate determinate sentence. The starting points will be relevant, therefore, to the process of fixing any minimum term that may be necessary.

2.   Rape includes penile penetration of the mouth.

3.   There is no distinction in the starting points for penetration of the vagina, anus or mouth.

4.   All the non-consensual offences involve a high level of culpability on the part of the offender, since that person will have acted either deliberately without the victim's consent or without giving due care to whether the victim was able to or did, in fact, consent.

5.   The planning of an offence indicates a higher level of culpability than an opportunistic or impulsive offence.

6.   An offender's culpability may be reduced if the offender and victim engaged in consensual sexual activity on the same occasion and immediately before the offence took place. Factors relevant to culpability in such circumstances include the type of consensual activity that occurred, similarity to what then occurs, and timing. However, the seriousness of the non-consensual act may overwhelm any other consideration.

7.   The seriousness of the violation of the victim's sexual autonomy may depend on a number of factors, but the nature of the sexual behaviour will be the primary indicator of the degree of harm caused in the first instance.

8.   The presence of any of the general aggravating factors identified in the Council guideline on seriousness or any of the additional factors identified in the guidelines will indicate a sentence above the normal starting point.

Rape

THESE ARE SERIOUS OFFENCES FOR THE PURPOSES OF SECTION 224 CJA 2003

1.   Rape (section 1): Intentional non-consensual penile penetration of the vagina, anus or mouth

2.   Rape of a child under 13 (section 5): Intentional penile penetration of the vagina, anus or mouth of a person under 13

Maximum penalty for both offences: Life imprisonment

Type/nature of activity	Starting points	Sentencing ranges
Repeated rape of same victim over a course of time or rape involving multiple victims	15 years custody	13–19 years custody
Rape accompanied by any one of the following: abduction or detention; offender aware that he is suffering from a sexually transmitted infection; more than one offender acting together; abuse of trust; offence motivated by prejudice (race, religion, sexual orientation, physical disability); sustained attack	13 years custody if the victim is under 13	11–17 years custody
	10 years custody if the victim is a child aged 13 or over but under 16	8–13 years custody
	8 years custody if the victim is 16 or over	6–11 years custody
Single offence of rape by single offender	10 years custody if the victim is under 13	8–13 years custody
	8 years custody if the victim is 13 or over but under 16	6–11 years custody
	5 years custody if the victim is 16 or over	4–8 years custody

Sexual Offences – Part 2A

Additional aggravating factors	Additional mitigating factors
1. Offender ejaculated or caused victim to ejaculate	Where the victim is aged 16 or over
	Victim engaged in consensual sexual activity with the offender on the same occasion and immediately before the offence
2. Background of intimidation or coercion	
3. Use of drugs, alcohol or other substance to facilitate the offence	
	Where the victim is under 16
4. Threats to prevent victim reporting the incident	• Sexual activity between two children (one of whom is the offender) was mutually agreed and experimental
5. Abduction or detention	
6. Offender aware that he is suffering from a sexually transmitted infection	• Reasonable belief (by a young offender) that the victim was aged 16 or over
7. Pregnancy or infection results	

An offender convicted of these offences is automatically subject to notification requirements.[4]

---

4   In accordance with the SOA 2003, s.80 and schedule 3

Assault by penetration

Factors to take into consideration:

1.　　The sentences for public protection must be considered in all cases of assault by penetration. They are designed to ensure that sexual offenders are not released into the community if they present a significant risk of serious harm. Within any indeterminate sentence, the minimum term will generally be half the appropriate determinate sentence. The starting points will be relevant, therefore, to the process of fixing any minimum term that may be necessary.

2.　　This offence involves penetration of the vagina or anus only, with objects or body parts. It may include penile penetration where the means of penetration is only established during the trial.

3.　　All the non-consensual offences involve a high level of culpability on the part of the offender, since that person will have acted either deliberately without the victim's consent or without giving due care to whether the victim was able to or did, in fact, consent.

4.　　The planning of an offence indicates a higher level of culpability than an opportunistic or impulsive offence.

5.　　An offender's culpability may be reduced if the offender and victim engaged in consensual sexual activity on the same occasion and immediately before the offence took place. Factors relevant to culpability in such circumstances include the type of consensual activity that occurred, similarity to what then occurs, and timing. However, the seriousness of the non-consensual act may overwhelm any other consideration.

6.　　The seriousness of the violation of the victim's sexual autonomy may depend on a number of factors, but the nature of the sexual behaviour will be the primary indicator of the degree of harm caused in the first instance.

7.　　The presence of any of the general aggravating factors identified in the Council guideline on seriousness or any of the additional factors identified in the guidelines will indicate a sentence above the normal starting point.

8.　　Brief penetration with fingers, toes or tongue may result in a significantly lower sentence where no physical harm is caused to the victim.

Assault by penetration

THESE ARE SERIOUS OFFENCES FOR THE PURPOSES OF SECTION 224 CJA 2003

1.   Assault by penetration (section 2): Non-consensual penetration of the vagina or anus with objects or body parts

2.   Assault of a child under 13 by penetration (section 6): Intentional penetration of the vagina or anus of a person under 13 with objects or body parts

Maximum penalty for both offences: Life imprisonment

Type/nature of activity	Starting points	Sentencing ranges
Penetration with an object or body part, accompanied by any one of the following: abduction or detention; more than one offender acting together; abuse of trust; offence motivated by prejudice (race, religion, sexual orientation, physical disability); sustained attack	13 years custody if the victim is under 13 10 years custody if the victim is 13 or over but under 16 8 years custody if the victim is 16 or over	11–17 years custody 8–13 years custody 6–11 years custody
Penetration with an object – in general, the larger or more dangerous the object, the higher the sentence should be	7 years custody if the victim is under 13 5 years custody if the victim is 13 or over but under 16 3 years custody if the victim is 16 or over	5–10 years custody 4–8 years custody 2–5 years custody
Penetration with a body part (fingers, toes or tongue) where no physical harm is sustained by the victim	5 years custody if the victim is under 13 4 years custody if the victim is 13 or over but under 16 2 years custody if the victim is 16 or over	4–8 years custody 3–7 years custody 1–4 years custody

Sexual Offences – Part 2A

Additional aggravating factors	Additional mitigating factors
1. Background of intimidation or coercion	Where the victim is aged 16 or over
2. Use of drugs, alcohol or other substance to facilitate the offence	Victim engaged in consensual sexual activity with the offender on the same occasion and immediately before the offence
3. Threats to prevent victim reporting the incident	
4. Abduction or detention	Where the victim is under 16
5. Offender aware that he or she is suffering from a sexually transmitted infection	• Sexual activity between two children (one of whom is the offender) was mutually agreed and experimental
6. Physical harm arising from the penetration	• Reasonable belief (by a young offender) that the victim was aged 16 or over
7. Offender ejaculated or caused the victim to ejaculate	Penetration is minimal or for a short duration

An offender convicted of these offences is automatically subject to notification requirements.[5]

---

5   In accordance with the SOA 2003, s.80 and schedule 3

PART 2B: SEXUAL ASSAULT

2B.1   Various activities previously covered by the offence of 'indecent assault' now fall within the definitions of other offences in the SOA 2003:

- Forcible penile penetration of the mouth now comes within the definition of 'rape'.
- Penetration of the vagina or anus with a body part or other object is covered by the offence of 'assault by penetration'.
- All forms of ostensibly consensual sexual activity involving children under 16 (who cannot in law give any consent to prevent an act being an assault) now fall within a range of child sex offences.
- Vulnerable adults subjected to a sexual assault are now protected by the offences of 'sexual activity with a person with a mental disorder impeding choice' and 'causing or inciting a person with a mental disorder impeding choice to engage in sexual activity'.

2B.2   The offence of 'sexual assault' covers all forms of sexual touching and will largely be used in relation to the lesser forms of assault that would have previously fallen at the lower end of the penalty scale.

2B.3   The exact nature of the sexual activity should be the key factor in assessing the seriousness of a sexual assault and should be used as the starting point from which to begin the process of assessing the overall seriousness of the offending behaviour.

2B.4   The presence of aggravating factors can make an offence significantly more serious than the nature of the activity alone might suggest.

- The nature of the sexual activity will be the primary factor in assessing the seriousness of an offence of sexual assault.
- In all cases, the fact that the offender has ejaculated or has caused the victim to ejaculate will increase the seriousness of the offence.

572 *Sexual Offences*

Sexual assault

Factors to take into consideration:

1.   The sentences for public protection must be considered in all cases of sexual assault. They are designed to ensure that sexual offenders are not released into the community if they present a significant risk of serious harm.

2.   The offence of 'sexual assault' covers all forms of sexual touching and therefore covers a wide range of offending behaviour. Some offences may justify a lesser sentence where the actions were more offensive than threatening and comprised a single act rather than more persistent behaviour.

3.   The nature of the sexual activity will be the primary factor in assessing the seriousness of an offence and should be used as the starting point from which to begin the process of assessing the overall seriousness of the offending behaviour.

4.   The presence of aggravating factors can make an offence significantly more serious than the nature of the activity alone might suggest.

5.   For the purpose of the guideline, types of sexual touching are broadly grouped in terms of seriousness. An offence may involve activities from more than one group. In all cases, the fact that the offender has ejaculated or has caused the victim to ejaculate will increase the seriousness of the offence.

6.   An offender's culpability may be reduced if the offender and victim engaged in consensual sexual activity on the same occasion and immediately before the offence took place. Factors relevant to culpability in such circumstances include the type of consensual activity that occurred, similarity to what then occurs, and timing. However, the seriousness of the non-consensual act may overwhelm any other consideration.

7.   Where this offence is being dealt with in a magistrates' court, more detailed guidance is provided in the Magistrates' Court Sentencing Guidelines (MCSG).

Sexual assault

THESE ARE SERIOUS OFFENCES FOR THE PURPOSES OF SECTION 224 CJA 2003

1.   Sexual assault (section 3): Non-consensual sexual touching

Maximum penalty: 10 years

2.   Sexual assault of a child under 13 (section 7): Intentional sexual touching of a person under 13

Maximum penalty: 14 years

Type/nature of activity	Starting points	Sentencing ranges
Contact between naked genitalia of offender and naked genitalia, face or mouth of the victim	5 years custody if the victim is under 13	4–8 years custody
	3 years custody if the victim is aged 13 or over	2–5 years custody
Contact between naked genitalia of offender and another part of victim's body Contact with genitalia of victim by offender using part of his or her body other than the genitalia, or an object Contact between either the clothed genitalia of offender and naked genitalia of victim or naked genitalia of offender and clothed genitalia of victim	2 years custody if the victim is under 13	1–4 years custody
	12 months custody if the victim is aged 13 or over	26 weeks–2 years custody
Contact between part of offender's body (other than the genitalia) with part of the victim's body (other than the genitalia)	26 weeks custody if the victim is under 13	4 weeks–18 months custody
	Community order if the victim is aged 13 or over	An appropriate non-custodial sentence*

* 'Non-custodial sentence' in this context suggests a community order or a fine. In most instances, an offence will have crossed the threshold for a community order. However, in accordance with normal sentencing practice, a court is not precluded from imposing a financial penalty where that is determined to be the appropriate sentence.

Additional aggravating factors	Additional mitigating factors
1. Offender ejaculated or caused victim to ejaculate	Where the victim is aged 16 or over
2. Background of intimidation or coercion	Victim engaged in consensual sexual activity with the offender on the same occasion and immediately before the offence
3. Use of drugs, alcohol or other substance to facilitate the offence	Where the victim is under 16
4. Threats to prevent victim reporting the incident	• Sexual activity between two children (one of whom is the offender) was mutually agreed and experimental
5. Abduction or detention	• Reasonable belief (by a young offender) that the victim was aged 16 or over
6. Offender aware that he or she is suffering from a sexually transmitted infection	Youth and immaturity of the offender
7. Physical harm caused	Minimal or fleeting contact
8. Prolonged activity or contact	

An offender convicted of these offences is automatically subject to notification requirements.[6]

---

6   In accordance with the SOA 2003, s.80 and schedule 3

PART 2C: CAUSING OR INCITING SEXUAL ACTIVITY

2C.1   There are three offences in this category covering a wide range of sexual activity:

- Causing a person to engage in sexual activity without consent
- Causing or inciting a child under 13 to engage in sexual activity
- Causing or inciting a person with a mental disorder impeding choice to engage in sexual activity

2C.2   The maximum penalty for the second and third of these offences is the same whether the sexual activity is caused or incited. This recognises that, with vulnerable victims, incitement to indulge in sexual activity is, of itself, likely to result in harm.

2C.3   Deciding sentence may be complex where an incited offence did not actually take place. Whilst the effect of the incitement is of no relevance to whether or not the offence incited was committed, it is likely to be relevant to the sentence imposed.

2C.4   Accordingly, the starting point should be the same whether or not the sexual activity takes place. Where it does not take place, the harm (and sometimes the culpability) is likely to be less, and the sentence should be reduced appropriately to reflect this.

2C.5   If the activity does not take place because the offender desists of his or her own accord, culpability (and sometimes harm) will be reduced. This should be treated as a mitigating factor for sentencing purposes and does not affect the principle that starting points for 'causing' or 'inciting' an activity should be the same.

2C.6   If the offender is prevented from achieving his or her aim by reasons outside their control, culpability may not be reduced, but it is possible that the harm will be less than if the activity had taken place.

2C.7   Culpability must be the primary indicator for sentencing in such cases, but it would make no sense for courts to pass the same sentence for an incited offence that did not actually take place as it would for the substantive offence itself. In these circumstances, the sentence should be calculated using the starting point for the substantive offence, taking account of the nature of the harm that would have been caused had the offence taken place, and the degree to which an intended victim may have suffered as a result of knowing or believing that the incited offence would take place, but nevertheless reflecting the facts if no actual harm has been caused to a victim.

- The starting point should be the same whether an offender causes an act to take place or incites an act which does not take place.
- A reduction will generally be appropriate where the incited activity does not take place.
- Where an offender voluntarily desists from any action taken to incite a sexual act, or personally and of their own volition intervenes to prevent a sexual act from taking place, this will be an additional mitigating factor.
- Whether or not the sexual activity takes place, the degree of harm done to the victim will be a material consideration when considering the sentence.

2C.8   The offence of 'causing a person to engage in sexual activity without consent' covers situations where, for example, a victim is forced to carry out a sexual act involving his or her own person, such as self-masturbation, or to engage in sexual activity with a third party, or situations in which the victim is forced to engage in sexual activity with the offender.

2C.9   The underlying purpose is to create offences that carry the same level of penalties for what amounts to the same type of offending behaviour, regardless of the gender or sexual orientation of the offender. This is reflected in the recommended starting points for penetrative acts charged within this category.

2C.10 The two main factors determining the seriousness of an offence of causing or inciting sexual activity without consent will be the nature of the sexual activity (as an indication of the degree of harm caused, or likely to be caused, to the victim) and the level of the offender's culpability. Culpability will be higher if the victim is forced to engage in sexual activity with the offender, or with another victim, than in cases where there is no sexual contact between the victim and the offender or anyone else. In all cases, the degree of force or coercion used by the offender will be an indication of the offender's level of culpability and may also exacerbate the harm suffered by the victim.

2C.11 The same sentencing starting points for offences involving non-consensual penetration of the vagina or anus of another person will apply regardless of whether the offender is male or female. There should be no differentiation between the starting point for 'rape' and an offence where a female offender causes or incites a non-consenting male to penetrate her vagina, anus or mouth. Similarly, where a victim is caused or incited to take part in penetrative activities with a third party or where the offender causes or incites other forms of sexual activity, there is no reason to differentiate sentence for male and female offenders.

The starting points for sentencing for sexual activity that is caused or incited by the offender without the consent of the victim(s) should mirror those for similar activity perpetrated within the offences of 'rape', 'assault by penetration' and 'sexual assault'.

Sexual Offences – Part 2C

Causing sexual activity without consent

Factors to take into consideration:

1.   The sentences for public protection must be considered in all cases of causing sexual activity. They are designed to ensure that sexual offenders are not released into the community if they present a significant risk of serious harm. Within any indeterminate sentence, the minimum term will generally be half the appropriate determinate sentence. The starting points will be relevant, therefore, to the process of fixing any minimum term that may be necessary.

2.   The same degree of seriousness applies whether an offender causes an act to take place, incites an act that actually takes place, or incites an act that does not take place only because it is prevented by factors beyond the control of the offender.

3.   The same starting points apply whether the activity was caused or incited and whether or not the incited activity took place, but some reduction will generally be appropriate when the incited activity does not, in fact, take place.

4.   Where an offender voluntarily desists from any action taken to incite a sexual act or personally, and of their own volition, intervenes to prevent from taking place a sexual act that he or she has incited, this should be treated as a mitigating factor.

5.   The effect of the incitement is relevant to the length of the sentence to be imposed. A court should take into account the degree to which the intended victim may have suffered as a result of knowing or believing that an offence would take place.

Sexual Offences

Causing sexual activity without consent

THESE ARE SERIOUS OFFENCES FOR THE PURPOSES OF SECTION 224 CJA 2003

1.   Causing a person to engage in sexual activity without consent (section 4): Forcing someone else to perform a sexual act on him or herself or another person

Maximum penalty: Life imprisonment if the activity involves penetration; 10 years if the activity does not involve penetration

2.   Causing or inciting a child under 13 to engage in sexual activity (section 8): Causing or inciting a person under 13 to perform a sexual act on him or herself or another person

Maximum penalty: Life imprisonment if the activity involves penetration; 14 years if the activity does not involve penetration

3.   Causing or inciting a person with a mental disorder impeding choice to engage in sexual activity (section 31): Intentionally causing or inciting a person with a mental disorder impeding choice to engage in sexual activity.

Maximum penalty: Life imprisonment if the activity involves penetration; 14 years if penetration not involved

Type/nature of activity	Starting points:	Sentencing ranges
Penetration with any one of the following aggravating factors: abduction or detention; offender aware that he or she is suffering from a sexually transmitted infection; more than one offender acting together; abuse of trust; offence motivated by prejudice (race, religion, sexual orientation, physical disability); sustained attack	13 years custody if the victim is a child under 13 or a person with a mental disorder	11–17 years custody
	10 years custody if the victim is 13 or over but under 16	8–13 years custody
	8 years custody if the victim is 16 or over	6–11 years custody
Single offence of penetration of/by single offender with no aggravating or mitigating factors	7 years custody if the victim is a child under 13 or a person with a mental disorder	5–10 years custody
	5 years custody if the victim is 13 or over but under 16	4–8 years custody
	3 years custody if the victim is 16 or over	2–5 years custody

Sexual Offences – Part 2C

Type/nature of activity	Starting points:	Sentencing ranges
Contact between naked genitalia of offender and naked genitalia of victim, or causing two or more victims to engage in such activity with each other, or causing victim to masturbate him/herself	5 years custody if the victim is a child under 13 or a person with a mental disorder 3 years custody	4–8 years custody 2–5 years custody
Contact between naked genitalia of offender and another part of victim's body, or causing two or more victims to engage in such activity with each other Contact with naked genitalia of victim by offender using part of the body other than the genitalia or an object, or causing two or more victims to engage in such activity with each other Contact between either the clothed genitalia of offender and naked genitalia of victim, between naked genitalia of offender and clothed genitalia of victim, or causing two or more victims to engage in such activity with each other	2 years custody if the victim is a child under 13 or a person with a mental disorder 12 months custody	1–4 years custody 26 weeks–2 years custody
Contact between part of offender's body (other than the genitalia) with part of victim's body (other than the genitalia)	26 weeks custody if the victim is a child under 13 or a person with a mental disorder Community order	4 weeks–18 months custody An appropriate non-custodial sentence*

* 'Non-custodial sentence' in this context suggests a community order or a fine. In most instances, an offence will have crossed the threshold for a community order. However, in accordance with normal sentencing practice, a court is not precluded from imposing a financial penalty where that is determined to be the appropriate sentence.

Additional aggravating factors	Additional mitigating factors
1. Offender ejaculated or caused victim to ejaculate	
2. History of intimidation or coercion	
3. Use of drugs, alcohol or other substance to facilitate the offence	
4. Threats to prevent victim reporting the incident	
5. Abduction or detention	
6. Offender aware that he or she is suffering from a sexually transmitted infection	

An offender convicted of these offences is automatically subject to notification requirements.[7]

---

7   In accordance with the SOA 2003, s.80 and schedule 3

PART 2D: OTHER NON-CONSENSUAL OFFENCES

2D.1   Four other offences fall within the general category of non-consensual offences:

- Engaging in sexual activity in the presence of a child
- Engaging in sexual activity in the presence of a person with a mental disorder impeding choice
- Causing a child to watch a sexual act
- Causing a person with a mental disorder impeding choice to watch a sexual act

2D.2   These are offences that relate to lesser forms of offending behaviour than offences that involve physical touching of the victim, but they nevertheless attract maximum penalties of 10 years' imprisonment in recognition of the fact that the victims are particularly vulnerable.

2D.3   The guidelines are predicated on the principle that the more serious the nature of the sexual activity a victim is forced to witness, the higher the sentencing starting point should be.

2D.4   These offences can cover a very wide range of sexual activity and an equally wide range of circumstances in which a victim is subjected to witnessing it.

2D.5   However, any form of sexual activity in the presence of a child or person with a mental disorder impeding choice may well be serious enough to merit a custodial starting point. It is always within the power of the court in an individual case to consider whether there are particular factors that mitigate sentence and should move it back below the custodial threshold.

- The same starting points for sentencing should apply in relation to the various levels of activity falling within the offences of 'engaging in sexual activity in the presence of a child' and 'engaging in sexual activity in the presence of a person with a mental disorder impeding choice'. Similarly, the same starting points should apply in relation to the offences of 'causing a child to watch a sexual act' and 'causing a person with a mental disorder impeding choice to watch a sexual act'.
- An offence involving an offender who intentionally commits a sexual act in the presence of a child or a person with a mental disorder impeding choice in order to obtain sexual gratification will potentially be serious enough to merit a custodial sentence. In an individual case the court will need to consider whether there are particular mitigating factors that move the sentence below the custodial threshold.

Sexual activity in the presence of another person

Factors to take into consideration:

1.   The sentences for public protection must be considered in all cases of engaging in sexual activity in the presence of another person. They are designed to ensure that sexual offenders are not released into the community if they present a significant risk of serious harm.

2.   These offences involve intentionally, and for the purpose of obtaining sexual gratification, engaging in sexual activity in the presence of a person under 16, or a person with a mental disorder, knowing or believing that person to be aware of the activity.

3.   The guidelines are predicated on the principle that the more serious the nature of the sexual activity a victim is forced to witness, the higher the sentencing starting point should be.

4.   These offences will potentially be serious enough to merit a custodial sentence. In an individual case the court will need to consider whether there are particular mitigating factors that move the sentence below the custodial threshold.

Sexual activity in the presence of another person

THESE ARE SERIOUS OFFENCES FOR THE PURPOSES OF SECTION 224 CJA 2003

1.   Engaging in sexual activity in the presence of a child (section 11)

Maximum penalty: 10 years (5 years if offender is under 18)

2.   Engaging in sexual activity in the presence of a person with a mental disorder impeding choice (section 32)

Maximum penalty: 10 years

Type/nature of activity	Starting points	Sentencing ranges
Consensual intercourse or other forms of consensual penetration	2 years custody	1–4 years custody
Masturbation (of oneself or another person)	18 months custody	12 months–2 years 6 months custody
Consensual sexual touching involving naked genitalia	12 months custody	26 weeks–18 months custody
Consensual sexual touching of naked body parts but not involving naked genitalia	26 weeks custody	4 weeks–18 months custody

Additional aggravating factors	Additional mitigating factors
1. Background of intimidation or coercion	
2. Use of drugs, alcohol or other substance to facilitate the offence	
3. Threats to prevent victim reporting the incident	
4. Abduction or detention	

An offender convicted of these offences is automatically subject to notification requirements.[8]

---

8   In accordance with the SOA 2003, s.80 and schedule 3

Causing or inciting another person to watch a sexual act

Factors to take into consideration:

1.   The sentences for public protection must be considered in all cases. They are designed to ensure that sexual offenders are not released into the community if they present a significant risk of serious harm.

2.   These offences include intentionally causing or inciting, for the purpose of sexual gratification, a person under 16, or a person with a mental disorder, to watch sexual activity or look at a photograph or pseudo-photograph of sexual activity.

3.   The guidelines are predicated on the principle that the more serious the nature of the sexual activity a victim is caused to witness, the higher the sentencing starting point should be.

4.   These offences will potentially be serious enough to merit a custodial sentence. In an individual case the court will need to consider whether there are particular mitigating factors that should move the sentence below the custodial threshold.

5.   The same starting points apply whether the activity was caused or incited and whether or not the incited activity took place.

Causing or inciting another person to watch a sexual act

THESE ARE SERIOUS OFFENCES FOR THE PURPOSES OF SECTION 224 CJA 2003

1. Causing a child to watch a sexual act (section 12)

Maximum penalty: 10 years (5 years if offender is under 18)

2. Causing a person with a mental disorder impeding choice, to watch a sexual act (section 33)

Maximum penalty: 10 years

Type/nature of activity	Starting points	Sentencing ranges
Live sexual activity	18 months custody	12 months–2 years custody
Moving or still images of people engaged in sexual activity involving penetration	32 weeks custody	26 weeks–12 months custody
Moving or still images of people engaged in sexual activity other than penetration	Community order	Community order– 26 weeks custody

Additional aggravating factors	Additional mitigating factors
1. Background of intimidation or coercion 2. Use of drugs, alcohol or other substance to facilitate the offence 3. Threats to prevent victim reporting the incident 4. Abduction or detention 5. Images of violent activity	

An offender convicted of these offences is automatically subject to notification requirements.[9]

---

9 In accordance with the SOA 2003, s.80 and schedule 3

47

PART 3: OFFENCES INVOLVING OSTENSIBLE CONSENT

3.1   There are several groups of offences in the SOA 2003 that involve a compliant or willing partner. Any sexual activity involving a person below the age of consent is unlawful notwithstanding any ostensible consent. In addition, there are circumstances where sexual activity takes place with the ostensible consent of both parties but where one of the parties is in such a great position of power over the other that the sexual activity is wrong.

3.2   There are two categories of offence within this broad grouping:

- Part 3A – sexual activity with children under 16 – or under 18 where there is an imbalance of power (for example, within the family unit) or an abuse of trust (for example, between a teacher and a pupil); and
- Part 3B – sexual activity with adults who have the capacity to consent but who, by reason of, or for reasons related to, a mental disorder are susceptible to coercion and exploitation.

PART 3A: OFFENCES INVOLVING CHILDREN

3A.1   In addition to the range of non-consensual sexual offences designed to protect children under 13, there are three further groups of offences that cover all forms of ostensibly consensual sexual activity involving children under 16 and also provide additional protection for older children:

   (i) 'child sex offences' (covering unlawful sexual activity with children under 16) including 'arranging or facilitating the commission of a child sex offence';

   (ii) 'familial child sex offences' (relating to offences committed by members of the child's family or household and primarily intended to ensure that charges can be brought in relation to victims aged 16 or 17); and

   (iii) 'abuse of a position of trust' (another offence that enables the prosecution of sexual activity involving victims aged 16 or 17, in this case where the offender has a relationship of trust with the child, such as that of a teacher or care worker).

3A.2   A 'reasonable' belief that the child was aged 16 or over is a defence to all the child sex offences, provided the child was, in fact, aged 13 or over. With the same proviso, a reasonable belief that the victim was aged 18 or over is a defence to the familial child sex offences and the abuse of trust offences.

3A.3   The maximum penalties for the offences in these groups give some indication of their relative seriousness and of the factors that increase the seriousness of an offence.

3A.4   Conversely, the lower maximum penalties for offenders aged under 18 indicate that the offence is less serious when the age gap between the victim and the offender is relatively narrow. The young age of an offender may often be seen as a mitigating factor for sentencing. This principle has already largely been catered for in the child sex offences by the provision in statute of lower maximum penalties for young offenders, which are designed to take account of their immaturity (see Part 7). However, the extreme youth of an offender and close proximity in age between the offender and the victim are both factors that will still be relevant for the court to consider when deciding sentence.

The significance of family relationships

3A.5   Family relationships, as defined in the SOA 2003 in relation to the offences of sexual activity with a child family member and inciting a child family member to engage in sexual activity, are not restricted to blood relationships and include relationships formed through adoption, fostering, marriage or partnership.

3A.6   Some relationships, such as parents and siblings, are automatically covered. Others, such as step-parents and cousins, fall within the definition of 'family member' only if they live, or have lived, in the same household as the child or if they are, or have been, regularly involved in caring for, training, supervising or being in sole charge of the child.

3A.7   More distant 'relationships', such as lodgers and au pairs, are covered only if they were living in the same household as the child at the time of the offence and were regularly involved in caring for, training, supervising or being in sole charge of the child at that time.

3A.8   These offences bring ostensibly consensual sexual activity between persons over the age of consent (which would not otherwise be unlawful) within the scope of the criminal law.

All children, even those aged 16 or 17, are potentially vulnerable to exploitation within the family unit and the offences attract the same maximum penalty regardless of the age of the victim. The Council's view is that the worst aspect of child sexual abuse within the family is that the offender is one of the very people to whom the child would normally expect to turn for support and protection.

3A.9   Victims aged 16 or 17 may have been 'groomed' by a family member from a very young age before sexual activity takes place. Evidence of grooming can be treated as an aggravating factor for sentencing purposes, as can the extreme youth of a victim. However, the closeness of the relationship in such cases increases the seriousness of the offence regardless of the age of the victim and should be reflected in the sentencing starting points.

3A.10 There is a clear difference between a young person being coerced into sexual activity by an adult who holds a position of trust in his or her life outside the family unit and being coerced into a sexual relationship by someone (adult or child) who holds a position of trust within the family unit.

3A.11 The starting points for sentencing where the child is aged 13 or over but under 16 should be higher than for the equivalent child sex offences, to reflect the inherent abuse of trust. The amount of enhancement should vary to reflect the wide range of 'familial' relationships covered by this offence – on the basis that abuse by a parent is more serious than abuse by, for example, a foster sibling or lodger.

> The starting points for sentencing for the familial child sex offences should be between 25% and 50% higher than those for the generic child sex offences in all cases where the victim is aged 13 or over but under 16; the closer the familial relationship, using the statutory definitions as a guide, the higher the increase that should be applied.

3A.12 Where a victim is over the age of consent, the starting points should only be significant where the offender is a close relative and where the abuse of a familial relationship is most serious. Where the activity is commenced when the victim is already aged 16 or 17 and the sexual relationship is unlawful only because it takes place within a familial setting (e.g. the activity is between foster siblings or involves an au pair or lodger), the starting points for sentencing should be lower than those for 'sexual activity with a child' and should be matched with the starting points for the 'abuse of trust' offences.

> • Where the victim of a familial child sex offence is aged 16 or 17 when the sexual activity is commenced and the sexual relationship is unlawful only because it takes place within a familial setting, the starting points for sentencing should be in line with those for the generic abuse of trust offences.
> • Evidence that a victim has been 'groomed' by the offender to agree to take part in sexual activity will aggravate sentence.

Abuse of a position of trust

3A.13 These offences criminalise sexual activity by adults over 18 with children under 18 in situations where the adults are looking after the children in educational establishments or in various residential settings, or where their duties involve them in the regular unsupervised contact of children in the community.

3A.14 The maximum penalty for the offences of abuse of trust (5 years) is relatively low because the offences are primarily designed to protect young people who are over the legal age of consent (i.e. aged 16 or 17) from being persuaded to engage in sexual activity that would not be criminal except for the offender's position of trust in relation to the victim.

3A.15 In view of the fact that these offences will only be charged where the victim is aged 16 or 17, the sentencing starting points in the guidelines are significantly lower than those for a child sex offence involving the same type of sexual activity. The potential harm caused to victims who have been coerced and manipulated into undesirable sexual relationships has not been underestimated, and evidence of serious coercion, threats or trauma would all be aggravating factors that would move a sentence well beyond the starting point. However, some relationships caught within the scope of these offences, although unlawful, will be wholly consensual. The length of time over which a relationship has been sustained and the proximity in age between the parties could point to a relationship born out of genuine affection. Each case must be considered carefully on its own facts.

> When sentencing for an abuse of trust offence, serious coercion, threats or trauma are aggravating factors that should move a sentence well beyond the starting point.

Assessing the seriousness of sexual offences against children

3A.16 The culpability of the offender will be the primary indicator of offence seriousness, and the nature of the sexual activity will provide a guide as to the seriousness of the harm caused to the victim, for any of the offences in the three categories involving ostensibly consensual activity with children. Other factors will include:

- the age and degree of vulnerability of the victim – as a general indication, the younger the child, the more vulnerable he or she is likely to be, although older children may also suffer serious and long-term psychological damage as a result of sexual abuse;
- the age gap between the child and the offender;
- the youth and immaturity of the offender; and
- except where it is inherent in an offence, any breach of trust arising from a family relationship between the child and the offender, or from the offender's professional or other responsibility for the child's welfare, will make an offence more serious.

Sexual activity with a child

Factors to take into consideration:

1.   The sentences for public protection must be considered in all cases. They are designed to ensure that sexual offenders are not released into the community if they present a significant risk of serious harm.

2.   The culpability of the offender will be the primary indicator of offence seriousness, and the nature of the sexual activity will provide a guide as to the seriousness of the harm caused to the victim. Other factors will include:

- the age and degree of vulnerability of the victim – as a general indication, the younger the child, the more vulnerable he or she is likely to be, although older children may also suffer serious and long-term psychological damage as a result of sexual abuse;
- the age gap between the child and the offender;
- the youth and immaturity of the offender; and
- except where it is inherent in an offence, any breach of trust arising from a family relationship between the child and the offender, or from the offender's professional or other responsibility for the child's welfare, will make an offence more serious.

3.   The same starting points apply whether the activity was caused or incited. Where an offence was incited but did not take place as a result of the voluntary intervention of the offender, that is likely to reduce the severity of the sentence imposed.

Sexual activity with a child

THESE ARE SERIOUS OFFENCES FOR THE PURPOSES OF SECTION 224 CJA 2003

1.   Sexual activity with a child (section 9): Intentional sexual touching of a person under 16

2.   Causing or inciting a child to engage in sexual activity (section 10): Intentionally causing or inciting a person under 16 to engage in sexual activity

Maximum penalty for both offences: 14 years (5 years if offender is under 18)

Type/nature of activity	Starting points	Sentencing ranges
Penile penetration of the vagina, anus or mouth or penetration of the vagina or anus with another body part or an object	4 years custody	3–7 years custody
Contact between naked genitalia of offender and naked genitalia or another part of victim's body, particularly face or mouth	2 years custody	1–4 years custody
Contact between naked genitalia of offender or victim and clothed genitalia of victim or offender or contact with naked genitalia of victim by offender using part of his or her body other than the genitalia or an object	12 months custody	26 weeks–2 years custody
Contact between part of offender's body (other than the genitalia) with part of the victim's body (other than the genitalia)	Community order	An appropriate non-custodial sentence*

* 'Non-custodial sentence' in this context suggests a community order or a fine. In most instances, an offence will have crossed the threshold for a community order. However, in accordance with normal sentencing practice, a court is not precluded from imposing a financial penalty where that is determined to be the appropriate sentence.

Sexual Offences – Part 3A

Additional aggravating factors	Additional mitigating factors
1. Offender ejaculated or caused victim to ejaculate	1. Offender intervenes to prevent incited offence from taking place
2. Threats to prevent victim reporting the incident	2. Small disparity in age between the offender and the victim
3. Offender aware that he or she is suffering from a sexually transmitted infection	

An offender convicted of these offences is automatically subject to notification requirements.[1]

---

1 In accordance with the SOA 2003, s.80 and schedule 3

Sexual Offences – Part 3A

Familial child sex offences

Factors to take into consideration:

1.   The new sentences for public protection must be considered in all cases. They are designed to ensure that sexual offenders are not released into the community if they present a significant risk of serious harm.

2.   The culpability of the offender will be the primary indicator of offence seriousness, and the nature of the sexual activity will provide a guide as to the seriousness of the harm caused to the victim. Other factors will include:

- the age and degree of vulnerability of the victim – as a general indication, the younger the child, the more vulnerable he or she is likely to be, although older children may also suffer serious and long-term psychological damage as a result of sexual abuse;
- the age gap between the child and the offender; and
- the youth and immaturity of the offender.

3.   The starting points for sentencing for the familial child sex offences should be between 25% and 50% higher than those for the generic child sex offences in all cases where the victim is aged 13 or over but under 16; the closer the familial relationship, using the statutory definitions as a guide, the higher the increase that should be applied.

4.   Where a victim is over the age of consent, the starting points assume that the offender is a close relative.

5.   Where the victim of a familial child sex offence is aged 16 or 17 when the sexual activity is commenced and the sexual relationship is unlawful only because it takes place within a familial setting, the starting points for sentencing should be in line with those for the generic abuse of trust offences.

6.   Evidence that a victim has been 'groomed' by the offender to agree to take part in sexual activity will aggravate the seriousness of the offence.

Familial child sex offences

THESE ARE SERIOUS OFFENCES FOR THE PURPOSES OF SECTION 224 CJA 2003

1.   Sexual activity with a child family member (section 25)

2.   Inciting a child family member to engage in sexual activity (section 26)

Maximum penalty for both offences: 14 years (5 years if offender is under 18)

For use in cases where:

(a) the victim is 13 or over but under 16, regardless of the familial relationship with the offender; (b) the victim is 16 or 17 but the sexual relationship commenced when the victim was under 16; or (c) the victim is aged 16 or 17 and the offender is a blood relative.

Type/nature of activity	Starting points	Sentencing ranges
Penile penetration of the vagina, anus or mouth or penetration of the vagina or anus with another body part or an object	5 years custody	4–8 years custody
Contact between naked genitalia of offender and naked genitalia of victim	4 years custody	3–7 years custody
Contact between naked genitalia of offender or victim and clothed genitalia of the victim or offender	18 months custody	12 months–2 years 6 months custody
Contact between naked genitalia of victim by another part of the offender's body or an object, or between the naked genitalia of offender and another part of victim's body		
Contact between part of offender's body (other than the genitalia) with part of the victim's body (other than the genitalia)	Community order	An appropriate non-custodial sentence*

* 'Non-custodial sentence' in this context suggests a community order or a fine. In most instances, an offence will have crossed the threshold for a community order. However, in accordance with normal sentencing practice, a court is not precluded from imposing a financial penalty where that is determined to be the appropriate sentence.

Sexual Offences – Part 3A

For use in cases where the victim was aged 16 or 17 when the sexual relationship commenced and the relationship is only unlawful because of the abuse of trust implicit in the offence.

Type/nature of activity	Starting points	Sentencing ranges
Penile penetration of the vagina, anus or mouth or penetration of the vagina or anus with another body part or an object	2 years custody	1–4 years custody
Any other form of non-penetrative sexual activity involving the naked contact between the offender and victim	12 months custody	26 weeks–2 years custody
Contact between clothed part of offender's body (other than the genitalia) with clothed part of victim's body (other than the genitalia)	Community order	An appropriate non-custodial sentence*

* 'Non-custodial sentence' in this context suggests a community order or a fine. In most instances, an offence will have crossed the threshold for a community order. However, in accordance with normal sentencing practice, a court is not precluded from imposing a financial penalty where that is determined to be the appropriate sentence.

Additional aggravating factors	Additional mitigating factors
1. Background of intimidation or coercion	1. Small disparity in age between victim and offender
2. Use of drugs, alcohol or other substance	
3. Threats deterring the victim from reporting the incident	
4. Offender aware that he or she is suffering from a sexually transmitted infection	
5. Closeness of familial relationship	

An offender convicted of these offences is automatically subject to notification requirements.[2]

---

2 In accordance with the SOA 2003, s.80 and schedule 3

Abuse of trust: sexual activity with a person under 18

Factors to take into consideration:

1.   The sentences for public protection must be considered in all cases. They are designed to ensure that sexual offenders are not released into the community if they present a significant risk of serious harm.

2.   The culpability of the offender will be the primary indicator of offence seriousness, and the nature of the sexual activity will provide a guide as to the seriousness of the harm caused to the victim. Other factors will include:

- the age and degree of vulnerability of the victim – as a general indication, the younger the child, the more vulnerable he or she is likely to be, although older children may also suffer serious and long-term psychological damage as a result of sexual abuse;
- the age gap between the child and the offender; and
- the youth and immaturity of the offender.

3.   These offences will only be charged where the victim is aged 16 or 17. Therefore, the sentencing starting points in the guidelines are only intended for those cases and are significantly lower than those for a child sex offence involving the same type of sexual activity, which should be applied in all other cases.

4.   When sentencing for an abuse of trust offence, evidence of serious coercion, threats or trauma are aggravating factors that should move a sentence well beyond the starting point.

5.   Some relationships caught within the scope of these offences, although unlawful, will be wholly consensual. The length of time over which a relationship has been sustained and the proximity in age between the parties could point to a relationship born out of genuine affection. Each case must be considered carefully on its own facts.

6.   The same starting points apply whether the activity was caused or incited. Where an offence was incited but did not take place as a result of the voluntary intervention of the offender, that is likely to reduce the severity of the sentence imposed.

Abuse of trust: sexual activity with a person under 18

THESE ARE SPECIFIED OFFENCES FOR THE PURPOSES OF SECTION 224 CJA 2003

1.   Abuse of position of trust: sexual activity with a child (section 16): Intentional sexual touching of a child under 18 by a person aged 18 or over who is in a position of trust in relation to the child

2.   Abuse of position of trust: Causing or inciting a child to engage in sexual activity (section 17): Intentional causing or inciting of a child under 18 to engage in sexual activity, by a person aged 18 or over who is in a position of trust in relation to the child

Maximum penalty for both offences: 5 years

The starting points shown below are intended to be used only in relation to victims aged 16 or 17. Where the victim is a child under 16, one of the child sex offences in sections 9 to 13 should normally be charged. If one of the abuse of trust offences has nevertheless been charged, the starting points should be the same as they would be for the relevant child sex offence.

Type/nature of activity	Starting points	Sentencing ranges
Penile penetration of the vagina, anus or mouth or penetration of the vagina or anus with another body part or an object	18 months custody	12 months–2 years 6 months custody
Other forms of non-penetrative activity	26 weeks custody	4 weeks–18 months custody
Contact between part of offender's body (other than the genitalia) with part of the victim's body (other than the genitalia)	Community order	An appropriate non-custodial sentence*

* 'Non-custodial sentence' in this context suggests a community order or a fine. In most instances, an offence will have crossed the threshold for a community order. However, in accordance with normal sentencing practice, a court is not precluded from imposing a financial penalty where that is determined to be the appropriate sentence.

Additional aggravating factors	Additional mitigating factors
1. Background of intimidation or coercion	1. Small disparity in age between victim and offender
2. Offender ejaculated or caused the victim to ejaculate	2. Relationship of genuine affection
3. Use of drugs, alcohol or other substance to facilitate the offence	3. No element of corruption
4. Offender aware that he or she is suffering from a sexually transmitted infection	

An offender convicted of these offences is automatically subject to notification requirements.[3]

---

3   In accordance with the SOA 2003, s.80 and schedule 3

Abuse of trust: sexual activity in presence of a person under 18

Factors to take into consideration:

1.　The sentences for public protection must be considered in all cases. They are designed to ensure that sexual offenders are not released into the community if they present a significant risk of serious harm.

2.　The guidelines are predicated on the principle that the more serious the nature of the sexual activity a victim is forced to witness, the higher the sentencing starting point should be.

3.　These offences will only be charged where the victim is aged 16 or 17. Therefore, the sentencing starting points in the guidelines are only intended for those cases and are significantly lower than those for a child sex offence involving the same type of sexual activity, which should be applied in all other cases.

4.　These offences will potentially be serious enough to merit a custodial sentence. In an individual case, the court will need to consider whether there are particular mitigating factors that should move the sentence below the custodial threshold.

Abuse of trust: sexual activity in presence of a person under 18

THIS IS A SPECIFIED OFFENCE FOR THE PURPOSES OF SECTION 224 CJA 2003

Abuse of trust: sexual activity in the presence of a child (section 18): Intentionally, and for the purpose of obtaining sexual gratification, engaging in sexual activity in the presence of a person under 18 (abuse of trust), knowing or believing that person to be aware of the activity

Maximum penalty: 5 years

Type/nature of activity	Starting points	Sentencing ranges
Consensual intercourse or other forms of consensual penetration	2 years custody	1–4 years custody
Masturbation (of oneself or another person)	18 months custody	12 months–2 years 6 months custody
Consensual sexual touching involving naked genitalia	12 months custody	26 weeks–2 years custody
Consensual sexual touching of naked body parts but not involving naked genitalia	26 weeks custody	4 weeks–18 months custody

Additional aggravating factors	Additional mitigating factors
1. Background of intimidation or coercion	
2. Use of drugs, alcohol or other substance to facilitate the offence	
3. Threats to prevent victim reporting the incident	
4. Abduction or detention	

An offender convicted of this offence is automatically subject to notification requirements.[4]

---

4   In accordance with the SOA 2003, s.80 and schedule 3

Abuse of trust: cause a person under 18 to watch a sexual act

Factors to take into consideration:

1.　　The sentences for public protection must be considered in all cases. They are designed to ensure that sexual offenders are not released into the community if they present a significant risk of serious harm.

2.　　The culpability of the offender will be the primary indicator of offence seriousness, and the nature of the sexual activity will provide a guide as to the seriousness of the harm caused to the victim. Other factors will include:

- the age and degree of vulnerability of the victim – as a general indication, the younger the child, the more vulnerable he or she is likely to be, although older children may also suffer serious and long-term psychological damage as a result of sexual abuse;
- the age gap between the child and the offender; and
- the youth and immaturity of the offender.

3.　　Serious coercion, threats, corruption or trauma are aggravating factors that should move a sentence well beyond the starting point.

4.　　Some relationships caught within the scope of these offences, although unlawful, will be wholly consensual. The length of time over which a relationship has been sustained and the proximity in age between the parties could point to a relationship born out of genuine affection. Each case must be considered carefully on its own facts.

5.　　These offences will only be charged where the victim is aged 16 or 17. Therefore, the sentencing starting points in the guidelines are only intended for those cases and are significantly lower than those for a child sex offence involving the same type of sexual activity, which should be applied in all other cases.

6.　　The guideline is predicated on the principle that the more serious the nature of the sexual activity a victim is forced to witness, the higher the sentencing starting point should be.

7.　　The offence will potentially be serious enough to merit a custodial sentence. In an individual case, the court will need to consider whether there are particular mitigating factors that should move the sentence below the custodial threshold.

Abuse of trust: cause a person under 18 to watch a sexual act

THIS IS A SPECIFIED OFFENCE FOR THE PURPOSES OF SECTION 224 CJA 2003

Abuse of position of trust: causing a child to watch a sexual act (section 19): Intentionally causing or inciting, for the purpose of sexual gratification, a person under 18 (abuse of trust) to watch sexual activity or look at a photograph or pseudo-photograph of sexual activity

Maximum penalty: 5 years

Type/nature of activity	Starting points	Sentencing ranges
Live sexual activity	18 months custody	12 months–2 years custody
Moving or still images of people engaged in sexual activity involving penetration	32 weeks custody	26 weeks–12 months custody
Moving or still images of people engaging in sexual activity other than penetration	Community order	Community order–26 weeks custody

Additional aggravating factors	Additional mitigating factors
1. Background of intimidation or coercion	1. Small disparity in age between victim and offender
2. Use of drugs, alcohol or other substance to facilitate the offence	
3. Threats to prevent victim reporting the incident	
4. Abduction or detention	
5. Images of violent activity	

An offender convicted of this offence is automatically subject to notification requirements.[5]

---

5   In accordance with the SOA 2003, s.80 and schedule 3

Sexual Offences – Part 3A

Arranging a child sex offence

Factors to take into consideration:

1.   The sentences for public protection must be considered in all cases. They are designed to ensure that sexual offenders are not released into the community if they present a significant risk of serious harm.

2.   Sentencers should refer to the individual guideline for the substantive offence under sections 9–13 of the SOA 2003 that was arranged or facilitated.

3.   In cases where there is no commercial exploitation, the range of behaviour within, and the type of offender charged with, this offence will be wide. In some cases, a starting point below the suggested starting point for the substantive child sex offence may be appropriate.

Arranging a child sex offence

THIS IS A SERIOUS OFFENCE FOR THE PURPOSES OF SECTION 224 CJA 2003

Arranging or facilitating commission of a child sex offence (section 14): Intentionally arranging or facilitating the commission of a child sex offence by the defendant or another person, anywhere in the world

Maximum penalty: 14 years

Type/nature of activity	Starting points and sentencing ranges
Where the activity is arranged or facilitated as part of a commercial enterprise, even if the offender is under 18	As this offence is primarily aimed at persons organising the commission of relevant sexual offences for gain, and sometimes across international borders, this is the most likely aggravating factor. Starting points and sentencing ranges should be increased above those for the relevant substantive offence under sections 9–13.
Basic offence as defined in the SOA 2003 assuming no aggravating or mitigating factors.	The starting point and sentencing range should be commensurate with that for the relevant substantive offence under sections 9–13.

Additional aggravating factors	Additional mitigating factors
1. Background of intimidation or coercion 2. Use of drugs, alcohol or other substance to facilitate the offence 3. Threats to prevent victim reporting the incident 4. Abduction or detention 5. Number of victims involved	

An offender convicted of this offence is automatically subject to notification requirements.[6]

---

6 In accordance with the SOA 2003, s.80 and schedule 3

PART 3B: OFFENCES AGAINST VULNERABLE ADULTS

3B.1   The offences in the SOA 2003 that are designed to protect those who have a mental disorder impeding choice are referred to in Part 1.

3B.2   In addition, the Act includes a group of offences designed to protect adults whose mental impairment is not so severe that they are unable to make a choice, but who are nevertheless vulnerable to relatively low levels of inducement, threats or deception.

3B.3   The structure of these offences broadly parallels that of the offences against children, but the maximum penalties for the offences are higher and mirror those for the offences relating to persons with a mental disorder impeding choice. Charges brought under these offences relate to ostensibly consensual activity, but cases will be brought in circumstances where there is clear evidence to suggest that agreement has been secured unlawfully.

3B.4   Although the level of mental impairment of the victim is different between the offences in Part 1 and those in this part, the prosecution is required in all cases to prove that the offender knew of the victim's mental disorder. Thus the victim's capacity to consent will be irrelevant to a finding of guilt, and the level of offender culpability is high.

3B.5   Where a victim is unable to refuse, the sexual activity may, or may not, have been forced upon the victim. Where a victim has the capacity to consent but is vulnerable to coercion, the activity will be ostensibly consensual, but the level of trauma and harm caused, or risked, to the victim may be very high.

3B.6   The level of protection accorded to the victim should be the same, and sentencing starting points for the two groups of offences should also be comparable.

> The starting points for sentencing for a sexual offence should be the same whether the victim has a mental disorder impeding choice, or has a mental disorder and the activity has been procured by inducement, threat or deception.

3B.7   There is a further group of offences designed to protect those with a mental disorder, which consists of four offences relating to sexual activity by care workers. As with the abuse of trust offences protecting children, these offences primarily relate to ostensibly consensual sexual activity with persons over 16 that is only criminal because of the care worker relationship.

3B.8   These offences are primarily designed to be charged where victims have the capacity to choose and where there is no clear evidence of inducement, threat or deception. The maximum penalties, therefore, are lower than those arising from the other two groups of 'mental disorder' offences and it follows that starting points for sentencing should be proportionately lower. The maximum penalties, however, are more significant than those for the range of abuse of trust offences, in recognition of the fact that these offences are designed to protect a particularly vulnerable group of victims, and this has been taken into account in the guideline.

3B.9   The nature of the sexual activity and the degree of vulnerability of the victim will be the main determinants of the seriousness of an offence in these categories. The aggravating factors identified in the Council guideline on seriousness and in Part 1 are relevant to these offences.

3B.10 The period of time during which sexual activity has taken place will be relevant in determining the seriousness of an offender's behaviour but could, depending on the particular circumstances, be considered as either an aggravating or a mitigating factor. The fact that an offender has repeatedly involved a victim in exploitative behaviour over a period of time will normally be an aggravating feature for sentencing purposes. However, in cases involving ostensibly consensual sexual activity with a person over the age of consent who has a low-level mental disorder that does not impair his or her ability to choose, evidence of a long-term relationship between the parties may indicate the existence of genuine feelings of love and affection that deserve to be treated as a mitigating factor for sentencing. As with the abuse of trust offences, each case must be carefully considered on its facts.

Sexual activity with a person who has a mental disorder

Factors to take into consideration:

1.   The sentences for public protection must be considered in all cases. They are designed to ensure that sexual offenders are not released into the community if they present a significant risk of serious harm. Within any indeterminate sentence, the minimum term will generally be half the appropriate determinate sentence. The starting points will be relevant, therefore, to the process of fixing any minimum term that may be necessary.

2.   The starting points for sentencing for a sexual offence should be the same whether the victim has a mental disorder impeding choice, or has a mental disorder that makes him or her vulnerable to inducement, threat or deception.

3.   The same starting points apply whether the activity was caused or incited. Where an offence was incited but did not take place as a result of the voluntary intervention of the offender, that is likely to reduce the severity of the sentence imposed.

Sexual activity with a person who has a mental disorder

THESE ARE SERIOUS OFFENCES FOR THE PURPOSES OF SECTION 224 CJA 2003

1.　　Sexual activity with a person with a mental disorder impeding choice (section 30): Intentional sexual touching of a person with a mental disorder

2.　　Inducement, threat or deception to procure sexual activity with a person with a mental disorder (section 34): Intentional sexual touching of someone with a mental disorder whose agreement has been obtained by the giving or offering of an inducement, the making of a threat or the practice of a deception

3.　　Causing a person with a mental disorder to engage in, or agree to engage in, sexual activity by inducement, threat or deception (section 35): Using inducement, threat or deception to secure the agreement of a person with a mental disorder impeding choice to perform a sexual act on him or herself or another person.

Maximum penalty: Life if activity involves penetration; 14 years if no penetration

Type/nature of activity	Starting points	Sentencing ranges
Penetration with any of the aggravating factors: abduction or detention; offender aware that he or she is suffering from a sexually transmitted infection; more than one offender acting together; offence motivated by prejudice (race, religion, sexual orientation, physical disability); sustained or repeated activity	13 years custody	11–17 years custody
Single offence of penetration of/by single offender with no aggravating or mitigating factors	10 years custody	8–13 years custody
Contact between naked genitalia of offender and naked genitalia of victim	5 years custody	4–8 years custody

Sexual Offences – Part 3B

Contact between naked genitalia of offender and another part of victim's body or naked genitalia of victim by offender using part of his or her body other than the genitalia	15 months custody	36 weeks–3 years custody
Contact between clothed genitalia of offender and naked genitalia of victim or naked genitalia of offender and clothed genitalia of victim		
Contact between part of offender's body (other than the genitalia) with parts of victim's body (other than the genitalia)	26 weeks custody	4 weeks–18 months custody

Additional aggravating factors	Additional mitigating factors
1. Background of intimidation or coercion	1. Relationship of genuine affection
2. Offender ejaculated or caused the victim to ejaculate	2. Offender had a mental disorder at the time of the offence that significantly affected his or her culpability
3. Use of drugs, alcohol or other substance to facilitate the offence	
4. Threats to prevent the victim reporting the incident	
5. Abduction or detention	
6. Offender is aware that he or she is suffering from a sexually transmitted infection	

An offender convicted of these offences is automatically subject to notification requirements.[7]

---

7   In accordance with the SOA 2003, s.80 and schedule 3

Sexual Offences – Part 3B

Care workers: sexual activity with a person who has a mental disorder

Factors to take into consideration:

1.   The sentences for public protection must be considered in all cases. They are designed to ensure that sexual offenders are not released into the community if they present a significant risk of serious harm.

2.   The starting points for sentencing are predicated on the fact that these offences are designed to be charged where victims have the capacity to choose and where there is no clear evidence of inducement, threat or deception.

Care workers: sexual activity with a person who has a mental disorder

THESE ARE SERIOUS OFFENCES FOR THE PURPOSES OF SECTION 224 CJA 2003

1.   Care workers: sexual activity with a person with a mental disorder (section 38): Intentional sexual touching of a person with a mental disorder by someone involved in his or her care

2.   Care workers: causing or inciting sexual activity (section 39): Someone involved in the care of a person with a mental disorder intentionally causing or inciting that person to engage in sexual activity

Maximum penalty: 14 years if activity involves penetration; 10 years if activity does not involve penetration

Type/nature of activity	Starting points	Sentencing ranges
Basic offence of sexual activity involving penetration, assuming no aggravating or mitigating factors	3 years custody	2–5 years custody
Other forms of non-penetrative activity	12 months custody	26 weeks–2 years custody
Naked contact between part of the offender's body with part of the victim's body	Community order	An appropriate non-custodial sentence*

* 'Non-custodial sentence' in this context suggests a community order or a fine. In most instances, an offence will have crossed the threshold for a community order. However, in accordance with normal sentencing practice, a court is not precluded from imposing a financial penalty where that is determined to be the appropriate sentence.

Additional aggravating factors	Additional mitigating factors
1. History of intimidation	1. Relationship of genuine affection
2. Use of drugs, alcohol or other substance to facilitate the offence	
3. Threats to prevent victim reporting the incident	
4. Abduction or detention	
5. Offender aware that he or she is suffering from a sexually transmitted infection	

An offender convicted of these offences is automatically subject to notification requirements.[8]

---

8   In accordance with the SOA 2003, s.80 and schedule 3

Sexual Offences – Part 3B

Sexual activity in the presence of a person with a mental disorder

Factors to take into consideration:

1.   The sentences for public protection must be considered in all cases. They are designed to ensure that sexual offenders are not released into the community if they present a significant risk of serious harm.

2.   The starting points for sentencing for a sexual offence should be the same whether the victim has a mental disorder impeding choice, or has a mental disorder that makes him or her vulnerable to inducement, threat or deception.

3.   The guidelines are predicated on the principle that the more serious the nature of the sexual activity a victim is forced to witness, the higher the sentencing starting point should be.

4.   These offences will potentially be serious enough to merit a custodial sentence. In an individual case, the court will need to consider whether there are particular mitigating factors that should move the sentence below the custodial threshold.

Sexual activity in the presence of a person with a mental disorder

OFFENCES UNDER SECTION 36 ARE SERIOUS OFFENCES FOR THE PURPOSES OF SECTION 224 CJA 2003

OFFENCES UNDER SECTION 40 ARE SPECIFIED OFFENCES FOR THE PURPOSES OF SECTION 224 CJA 2003

1.   Engaging in sexual activity in the presence, secured by inducement, threat or deception, of a person with a mental disorder (section 36): Intentionally, and for the purpose of obtaining sexual gratification, engaging in sexual activity in the presence of a person with a mental disorder, knowing or believing that person to be aware of the activity

Maximum penalty: 10 years

2.   Care workers: sexual activity in the presence of a person with a mental disorder (section 40): Care worker intentionally, and for the purpose of obtaining sexual gratification, engaging in sexual activity in the presence of a person with a mental disorder, knowing or believing that person to be aware of the activity

Maximum penalty: 7 years

Type/nature of activity	Starting points	Sentencing ranges
Consensual intercourse or other forms of consensual penetration	2 years custody	1–4 years custody
Masturbation (of oneself or another person)	18 months custody	12 months–2 years 6 months custody
Consensual sexual touching involving naked genitalia	12 months custody	26 weeks–2 years custody
Consensual sexual touching of naked body parts but not involving naked genitalia	26 weeks custody	4 weeks–18 months custody

Additional aggravating factors	Additional mitigating factors
1. Background of intimidation or coercion	
2. Use of drugs, alcohol or other substance to facilitate the offence	
3. Threats to prevent victim reporting the incident	
4. Abduction or detention	

An offender convicted of these offences is automatically subject to notification requirements.[9]

---

9   In accordance with the SOA 2003, s.80 and schedule 3

Sexual Offences – Part 3B

Causing or inciting a person with a mental disorder to watch a sexual act

Factors to take into consideration:

1.   The sentences for public protection must be considered in all cases. They are designed to ensure that sexual offenders are not released into the community if they present a significant risk of serious harm.

2.   The starting points for sentencing for a sexual offence should be the same whether the victim has a mental disorder impeding choice, or has a mental disorder that makes him or her vulnerable to inducement, threat or deception.

3.   The guidelines are predicated on the principle that the more serious the nature of the sexual activity a victim is forced to witness, the higher the sentencing starting point should be.

4.   These offences will potentially be serious enough to merit a custodial sentence. In an individual case, the court will need to consider whether there are particular mitigating factors that move the sentence below the custodial threshold.

5.   The same starting points apply whether the activity was caused or incited. Where an offence was incited but did not take place as a result of the voluntary intervention of the offender, that is likely to reduce the severity of the sentence imposed.

Causing or inciting a person with a mental disorder to watch a sexual act

OFFENCES UNDER SECTION 37 ARE SERIOUS OFFENCES FOR THE PURPOSES OF SECTION 224 CJA 2003

OFFENCES UNDER SECTION 41 ARE SPECIFIED OFFENCES FOR THE PURPOSES OF SECTION 224 CJA 2003

1.   Causing a person with a mental disorder to watch a sexual act by inducement, threat or deception (section 37): Intentionally causing by inducement, threat or deception, for the purpose of sexual gratification, a person with a mental disorder to watch sexual activity or look at a photograph or pseudo-photograph of sexual activity

Maximum penalty: 10 years

2.   Care workers: causing a person with a mental disorder to watch a sexual act (section 41): Intentionally causing, for the purpose of sexual gratification, a person with a mental disorder to watch sexual activity or look at a photograph or pseudo-photograph of sexual activity

Maximum penalty: 7 years

Type/nature of activity	Starting points	Sentencing ranges
Live sexual activity	18 months custody	12 months–2 years custody
Moving or still images of people engaged in sexual activity involving penetration	32 weeks custody	26 weeks–12 months custody
Moving or still images of people engaging in sexual activity other than penetration	Community order	Community order– 26 weeks custody

Additional aggravating factors	Additional mitigating factors
1. Background of intimidation or coercion	
2. Use of drugs, alcohol or other substance to facilitate the offence	
3. Threats to prevent victim reporting the incident	
4. Abduction or detention	
5. Images of violent activity	

An offender convicted of these offences is automatically subject to notification requirements.[10]

---

10 In accordance with the SOA 2003, s.80 and schedule 3

PART 4: PREPARATORY OFFENCES

4.1   The characteristic feature of this group of offences is that the offender intended to commit a sexual offence that was not, in fact, carried out, either because the act was interrupted or because of a change of mind.

4.2   In some circumstances, an offender may be charged with both the preparatory and the substantive offence.

4.3   The new offence of 'meeting a child following sexual grooming etc' has been included within this category.

The following offences are covered in this section:

- Sexual grooming
- Committing another offence with intent
- Trespass with intent
- Administering a substance with intent

Sexual grooming

Factors to take into consideration:

1.   The sentences for public protection must be considered in all cases. They are designed to ensure that sexual offenders are not released into the community if they present a significant risk of serious harm.

2.   In a case where no substantive sexual offence has in fact been committed, the main dimension of seriousness will be the offender's intention – the more serious the offence intended, the higher the offender's culpability.

3.   The harm to the victim in such cases will invariably be less than that resulting from a completed offence, although the risk to which the victim has been put is always a relevant factor.

4.   In some cases, where the offender has come quite close to fulfilling his or her intention, the victim may have been put in considerable fear, and physical injury to the victim is a possible feature.

5.   In addition to the generic aggravating factors identified in the Council guideline on seriousness, the main factors determining the seriousness of a preparatory offence are:

- the seriousness of the intended offence (which will affect both the offender's culpability and the degree of risk to which the victim has been exposed);
- the degree to which the offence was planned;
- the sophistication of the grooming;
- the determination of the offender;
- how close the offender came to success;
- the reason why the offender did not succeed, i.e. whether it was a change of mind or whether someone or something prevented the offender from continuing; and
- any physical or psychological injury suffered by the victim.

6.   The starting point should be commensurate with that for the preparatory offence actually committed, with an enhancement to reflect the nature and severity of the intended sexual offence.

Sexual grooming

THIS IS A SERIOUS OFFENCE FOR THE PURPOSES OF SECTION 224 CJA 2003

Meeting a child following sexual grooming etc (section 15): An offender aged 18 or over meeting, or travelling to meet, a child under 16 (having met or communicated with the child on at least two previous occasions) with the intention of committing a sexual offence against the child

Maximum penalty: 10 years

Type/nature of activity	Starting points	Sentencing ranges
Where the intent is to commit an assault by penetration or rape	4 years custody if the victim is under 13	3–7 years custody
	2 years custody if the victim is 13 or over but under 16	1–4 years custody
Where the intent is to coerce the child into sexual activity	2 years custody if the victim is under 13	1–4 years custody
	18 months custody if the victim is 13 or over but under 16	12 months–2 years 6 months custody

Additional aggravating factors	Additional mitigating factors
1. Background of intimidation or coercion	
2. Use of drugs, alcohol or other substance to facilitate the offence	
3. Offender aware that he or she is suffering from a sexually transmitted infection	
4. Abduction or detention	

An offender convicted of this offence is automatically subject to notification requirements.[1]

---

1   In accordance with the SOA 2003, s.80 and schedule 3

Committing another offence with intent

Factors to take into consideration:

This guideline assumes that the intended sexual offence was not committed.

1.   The sentences for public protection must be considered in all cases. They are designed to ensure that sexual offenders are not released into the community if they present a significant risk of serious harm. Within any indeterminate sentence, the minimum term will generally be half the appropriate determinate sentence. The starting points will be relevant, therefore, to the process of fixing any minimum term that may be necessary.

2.   In a case where no substantive sexual offence has in fact been committed, the main dimension of seriousness will be the offender's intention – the more serious the offence intended, the higher the offender's culpability.

3.   The harm to the victim in such cases will invariably be less than that resulting from a completed offence, although the risk to which the victim has been put is always a relevant factor.

4.   In some cases, where the offender has come quite close to fulfilling his or her intention, the victim may have been put in considerable fear, and physical injury to the victim is a possible feature.

5.   In addition to the generic aggravating factors identified in the Council guideline on seriousness, the main factors determining the seriousness of a preparatory offence are:

- the seriousness of the intended offence (which will affect both the offender's culpability and the degree of risk to which the victim has been exposed);
- the degree to which the offence was planned;
- the determination of the offender;
- how close the offender came to success;
- the reason why the offender did not succeed, i.e. whether it was a change of mind or whether someone or something prevented the offender from continuing; and
- any physical or psychological injury suffered by the victim.

6.   The starting point should be commensurate with that for the preparatory offence actually committed, with an enhancement to reflect the nature and severity of the intended sexual offence.

Committing another offence with intent

THIS IS A SERIOUS OFFENCE FOR THE PURPOSES OF SECTION 224 CJA 2003

Committing an offence with intent to commit a sexual offence (section 62)

Maximum penalty: Life imprisonment if offence is kidnapping or false imprisonment; 10 years for any other criminal offence

Type/nature of activity	Starting points and sentencing ranges
Any offence committed with intent to commit a sexual offence, e.g. assault (see item 4 of 'Factors to take into consideration' above)	The starting point and sentencing range should be commensurate with that for the preliminary offence actually committed, but with an enhancement to reflect the intention to commit a sexual offence. The enhancement will need to be varied depending on the nature and seriousness of the intended sexual offence, but 2 years is suggested as a suitable enhancement where the intent was to commit rape or an assault by penetration.

Additional aggravating factors	Additional mitigating factors
1. Use of drugs, alcohol or other substance to facilitate the offence 2. Offender aware that he or she is suffering from a sexually transmitted infection (where the intended offence would have involved penile penetration)	1. Offender decides, of his or her own volition, not to proceed with the intended sexual offence 2. Incident of brief duration

An offender convicted of this offence is automatically subject to notification requirements.[2]

---

2   In accordance with the SOA 2003, s.80 and schedule 3

Trespass with intent

Factors to take into consideration:

1.   The sentences for public protection must be considered in all cases. They are designed to ensure that sexual offenders are not released into the community if they present a significant risk of serious harm.

2.   In a case where no substantive sexual offence has in fact been committed, the main dimension of seriousness will be the offender's intention – the more serious the offence intended, the higher the offender's culpability.

3.   The harm to the victim in such cases will invariably be less than that resulting from a completed offence, although the risk to which the victim has been put is always a relevant factor.

4.   In some cases, where the offender has come quite close to fulfilling his or her intention, the victim may have been put in considerable fear, and physical injury to the victim is a possible feature.

5.   In addition to the generic aggravating factors identified in the Council guideline on seriousness, the main factors determining the seriousness of a preparatory offence are:

- the seriousness of the intended offence (which will affect both the offender's culpability and the degree of risk to which the victim has been exposed);
- the degree to which the offence was planned;
- the determination of the offender;
- how close the offender came to success;
- the reason why the offender did not succeed, i.e. whether it was a change of mind or whether someone or something prevented the offender from continuing; and
- any physical or psychological injury suffered by the victim.

6.   The starting point should be commensurate with that for the preparatory offence actually committed, with an enhancement to reflect the nature and severity of the intended sexual offence.

Trespass with intent

THIS IS A SERIOUS OFFENCE FOR THE PURPOSES OF SECTION 224 CJA 2003

Trespass with intent to commit a sexual offence (section 63): Knowingly or recklessly trespassing on any premises with intent to commit a sexual offence on those premises

Maximum penalty: 10 years

Type/nature of activity	Starting points	Sentencing ranges
The intention is to commit rape or an assault by penetration	4 years custody	3–7 years custody
The intended sexual offence is other than rape or assault by penetration	2 years custody	1–4 years custody

Additional aggravating factors	Additional mitigating factors
1. Offender aware that he or she is suffering from a sexually transmitted infection (where intended offence would have involved penile penetration) 2. Targeting of a vulnerable victim 3. Significant impact on persons present in the premises	1. Offender decides, of his or her own volition, not to commit the intended sexual offence

An offender convicted of this offence is automatically subject to notification requirements.[3]

---

3 In accordance with the SOA 2003, s.80 and schedule 3

Administering a substance with intent

Factors to take into consideration:

1.   The sentences for public protection must be considered in all cases. They are designed to ensure that sexual offenders are not released into the community if they present a significant risk of serious harm.

2.   In a case where no substantive sexual offence has in fact been committed, the main dimension of seriousness will be the offender's intention – the more serious the offence intended, the higher the offender's culpability. This is equally so where the offence is committed by an offender for the benefit of another.

3.   The harm to the victim in such cases will invariably be less than that resulting from a completed offence, although the risk to which the victim has been put is always a relevant factor.

4.   In some cases, where the offender has come quite close to fulfilling his or her intention, the victim may have been put in considerable fear, and physical injury to the victim is a possible feature, in particular for this offence.

5.   In addition to the generic aggravating factors identified in the Council guideline on seriousness, the main factors determining the seriousness of a preparatory offence are:

- the seriousness of the intended offence (which will affect both the offender's culpability and the degree of risk to which the victim has been exposed);
- the degree to which the offence was planned;
- the determination of the offender;
- how close the offender came to success;
- the reason why the offender did not succeed, i.e. whether it was a change of mind or whether someone or something prevented the offender from continuing; and
- any physical or psychological injury suffered by the victim.

6.   The starting point should be commensurate with that for the preparatory offence actually committed, with an enhancement to reflect the nature and severity of the intended sexual offence.

Administering a substance with intent

THIS IS A SERIOUS OFFENCE FOR THE PURPOSES OF SECTION 224 CJA 2003

Administering a substance with intent (section 61): Administering a substance, without the consent of the victim, with the intention of overpowering or stupefying the victim in order to enable any person to engage in sexual activity involving the victim

Maximum penalty: 10 years

Type/nature of activity	Starting points	Sentencing ranges
If intended offence is rape or assault by penetration	8 years custody if the victim is under 13	6–9 years custody
	6 years custody otherwise	4–9 years custody
If intended offence is any sexual offence other than rape or assault by penetration	6 years custody if the victim is under 13	4–9 years custody
	4 years custody otherwise	3–7 years custody

Additional aggravating factors	Additional mitigating factors
1. Threats to prevent the victim reporting an offence 2. Abduction or detention 3. Offender aware that he or she, or the person planning to commit the sexual offence, is suffering from a sexually transmitted infection 4. Targeting of the victim	1. Offender intervenes to prevent the intended sexual offence from taking place

An offender convicted of this offence is automatically subject to notification requirements.[4]

---

4 In accordance with the SOA 2003, s.80 and schedule 3

PART 5: OTHER OFFENCES

5.1   This category covers a small number of relatively minor offences, none of which involves direct sexual contact with a person who was not consenting:

- Prohibited adult sexual relationships: sex with an adult relative
- Sexual activity in a public lavatory
- Exposure
- Voyeurism
- Intercourse with an animal
- Sexual penetration of a corpse

Prohibited adult sexual relationships: sex with an adult relative

Factors to take into consideration:

1.   The sentences for public protection must be considered in all cases. They are designed to ensure that sexual offenders are not released into the community if they present a significant risk of serious harm.

2.   The two offences within this category are triable either way and carry a maximum penalty of 2 years' imprisonment on conviction on indictment. The relatively low maximum penalty for these offences reflects the fact that they involve sexual relationships between consenting adults.

3.   For these offences, unlike those against child family members, the relationship between offender and victim is narrowly defined in terms of close blood relationships only: 'a parent, grandparent, child, grandchild, brother, sister, half-brother, half-sister, uncle, aunt, nephew or niece'.

4.   It is a defence to both offences that the offender was unaware of the blood relationship, unless it is proved that he or she could reasonably have been expected to be aware of it.

5.   These offences could be charged in a wide range of circumstances and the most important issue for the sentencer to consider is the particular circumstances in which an offence has taken place and the harm that has been caused or risked:

- Where an offence involves no harm to a victim (other than the offensiveness of the conduct to society at large), the starting point for sentencing should normally be a community order.
- Where there is evidence of the exploitation of a victim or significant aggravation, the normal starting point should be a custodial sentence.
- The presence of certain aggravating factors should merit a higher custodial starting point.

6.   Examples of aggravating factors especially relevant to these offences include:

- high level of coercion or humiliation of the victim;
- imbalance of power;
- evidence of grooming;
- age gap between the parties;
- history of sexual offending;
- sexual intercourse with the express intention of conceiving a child or resulting in the conception of a child; and
- no attempt taken to prevent the transmission of a sexual infection.

626 *Sexual Offences*

Prohibited adult sexual relationships: sex with an adult relative

THESE ARE SPECIFIED OFFENCES FOR THE PURPOSES OF SECTION 224 CJA 2003

1.   Sex with an adult relative: penetration (section 64): Intentional penetration of the vagina or anus of an adult blood relative with a body part or object; or penetration of the vagina, anus or mouth with the penis

2.   Sex with an adult relative: consenting to penetration (section 65): Consenting to intentional penetration of the vagina or anus by an adult blood relative with a body part or object; or penetration of the vagina, anus or mouth with the penis

Maximum penalty for both offences: 2 years

Type/nature of activity	Starting points	Sentencing ranges
Where there is evidence of long-term grooming that took place at a time when the person being groomed was under 18	12 months custody if offender is 18 or over	26 weeks–2 years custody
Where there is evidence of grooming of one party by the other at a time when both parties were over the age of 18	Community order	An appropriate non-custodial sentence*
Sexual penetration with no aggravating factors	Community order	An appropriate non-custodial sentence*

* 'Non-custodial sentence' in this context suggests a community order or a fine. In most instances, an offence will have crossed the threshold for a community order. However, in accordance with normal sentencing practice, a court is not precluded from imposing a financial penalty where that is determined to be the appropriate sentence.

Additional aggravating factors	Additional mitigating factors
1. Background of intimidation or coercion	1. Small disparity in age between victim and offender
2. Use of drugs, alcohol or other substance to facilitate the offence	2. Relationship of genuine affection
3. Threats to prevent the victim reporting an offence	
4. Evidence of long-term grooming	
5. Offender aware that he or she is suffering from a sexually transmitted infection	
6. Where there is evidence that no effort was made to avoid pregnancy or the sexual transmission of infection	

An offender convicted of these offences is automatically subject to notification requirements.[1]

---

1   In accordance with the SOA 2003, s.80 and schedule 3

Sexual Offences – Part 5

Sexual activity in a public lavatory

Factors to take into consideration:

1.   This offence has been introduced to give adults and children the freedom to use public lavatories for the purpose for which they are designed, without the fear of being an unwilling witness to overtly sexual behaviour of a kind that most people would not expect to be conducted in public.

2.   This offence, being a public order offence rather than a sexual offence, carries the lowest maximum penalty in the SOA 2003 – 6 months' imprisonment – and the starting point for sentencing reflects this.

3.   More detailed guidance is provided in the Magistrates' Court Sentencing Guidelines (MCSG).

Sexual activity in a public lavatory

Sexual activity in a public lavatory (section 71): Intentionally engaging in sexual activity in a public lavatory

Maximum penalty: 6 months

Type/nature of activity	Starting points	Sentencing ranges
Repeat offending and/or aggravating factors	Community order	An appropriate non-custodial sentence*
Basic offence as defined in the SOA 2003, assuming no aggravating or mitigating factors	Fine	An appropriate non-custodial sentence*

* 'Non-custodial sentence' in this context suggests a community order or a fine. In most instances, an offence will have crossed the threshold for a community order. However, in accordance with normal sentencing practice, a court is not precluded from imposing a financial penalty where that is determined to be the appropriate sentence.

Additional aggravating factors	Additional mitigating factors
1.　Intimidating behaviour/threats of violence to member(s) of the public	

Sexual Offences – Part 5

Exposure

Factors to take into consideration:

1.   The sentences for public protection must be considered in all cases. They are designed to ensure that sexual offenders are not released into the community if they present a significant risk of serious harm.

2.   The offence replaces section 4 of the Vagrancy Act 1824 and section 28 of the Town Police Clauses Act 1847. It is gender neutral (covering exposure of male or female genitalia to a male or female witness) and carries a maximum penalty of 2 years' imprisonment.

3.   These offences are sometimes more serious than they may, at first, appear. Although there is no physical contact with the victim, the offence may cause serious alarm or distress, especially when the offender behaves aggressively or uses obscenities.

4.   A pre-sentence report,[2] which can identify sexually deviant tendencies, will be extremely helpful in determining the most appropriate disposal. It will also help determine whether an offender would benefit from participation in a programme designed to help them address those tendencies.

5.   A person convicted of this offence is subject to notification requirements.[3]

6.   Where this offence is being dealt with in a magistrates' court, more detailed guidance is provided in the Magistrates' Court Sentencing Guidelines (MCSG).

---

2   As defined in the Criminal Justice Act 2003, s.158
3   In accordance with the Sexual Offences Act 2003, s.80 and schedule 3

Exposure

THIS IS A SPECIFIED OFFENCE FOR THE PURPOSES OF SECTION 224 CJA 2003

Exposure (section 66): Intentional exposure of the offender's genitals, intending that someone will see them and be caused alarm or distress

Maximum penalty: 2 years

Type/nature of activity	Starting points	Sentencing ranges
Repeat offender	12 weeks custody	4 weeks–26 weeks custody
Basic offence as defined in the SOA 2003, assuming no aggravating or mitigating factors, or some offences with aggravating factors	Community order	An appropriate non-custodial sentence*

* 'Non-custodial sentence' in this context suggests a community order or a fine. In most instances, an offence will have crossed the threshold for a community order. However, in accordance with normal sentencing practice, a court is not precluded from imposing a financial penalty where that is determined to be the appropriate sentence.

Additional aggravating factors	Additional mitigating factors
1. Threats to prevent the victim reporting an offence	
2. Intimidating behaviour/threats of violence	
3. Victim is a child	

An offender convicted of this offence is automatically subject to notification requirements.[4]

---

4   In accordance with the SOA 2003, s.80 and schedule 3

Voyeurism

Factors to take into consideration:

1.   The sentences for public protection must be considered in all cases. They are designed to ensure that sexual offenders are not released into the community if they present a significant risk of serious harm.

2.   The offence of voyeurism covers cases where someone who has a reasonable expectation of privacy is secretly observed. The offence may be committed in a number of ways:

- by direct observation on the part of the offender;
- by operating equipment with the intention of enabling someone else to observe the victim;
- by recording someone doing a private act, with the intention that the recorded image will be viewed by the offender or another person; or
- by installing equipment or constructing or adapting a structure with the intention of enabling the offender or another person to observe a private act.

3.   In all cases the observation, or intended observation, must be for the purpose of obtaining sexual gratification and must take place, or be intended to take place, without the consent of the person observed.

4.   The SOA 2003 defines a 'private act', in the context of this offence, as an act carried out in a place which, in the circumstances, would reasonably be expected to provide privacy, and where the victim's genitals, buttocks or breasts are exposed or covered only in underwear; or the victim is using a lavatory; or the person is 'doing a sexual act that is not of a kind ordinarily done in public'.

5.   The harm inherent in this offence is intrusion of the victim's privacy. Whilst less serious than non-consensual touching, it may nevertheless cause severe distress, embarrassment or humiliation to the victim, especially in cases where a private act is not simply observed by one person, but where an image of it is disseminated for wider viewing. A higher sentencing starting point is recommended for cases where the offender records and shares images with others.

6.   For offences involving the lowest level of offending behaviour, i.e. spying on someone for private pleasure, a non-custodial sentence is recommended as the starting point.

7.   A pre-sentence report,[5] which can identify sexually deviant tendencies, will be extremely helpful in determining the most appropriate disposal. It will also help determine whether an offender would benefit from participation in a programme designed to help them address those tendencies.

8.   Where this offence is being dealt with in a magistrates' court, more detailed guidance is provided in the Magistrates' Court Sentencing Guidelines (MCSG).

---

5   As defined in the Criminal Justice Act 2003, s.158

Voyeurism

THIS IS A SPECIFIED OFFENCE FOR THE PURPOSES OF SECTION 224 CJA 2003

Voyeurism (section 67): For the purpose of obtaining sexual gratification, and knowing that the other person does not consent to being observed, observing another person engaged in a private act

Maximum penalty: 2 years

Type/nature of activity	Starting points	Sentencing ranges
Offence with serious aggravating factors such as recording sexual activity and placing it on a website or circulating it for commercial gain	12 months custody	26 weeks–2 years custody
Offence with aggravating factors such as recording sexual activity and showing it to others	26 weeks custody	4 weeks–18 months custody
Basic offence as defined in the SOA 2003, assuming no aggravating or mitigating factors, e.g. the offender spies through a hole he or she has made in a changing room wall	Community order	An appropriate non-custodial sentence*

* 'Non-custodial sentence' in this context suggests a community order or a fine. In most instances, an offence will have crossed the threshold for a community order. However, in accordance with normal sentencing practice, a court is not precluded from imposing a financial penalty where that is determined to be the appropriate sentence.

Additional aggravating factors	Additional mitigating factors
1. Threats to prevent the victim reporting an offence 2. Recording activity and circulating pictures/videos 3. Circulating pictures or videos for commercial gain – particularly if victim is vulnerable, e.g. a child or person with a mental or physical disorder 4. Distress to victim, e.g. where the pictures/videos are circulated to people known to the victim	

An offender convicted of this offence is automatically subject to notification requirements.[6]

6   In accordance with the SOA 2003, s.80 and schedule 3

Intercourse with an animal

Factors to take into consideration:

1.   The sentences for public protection must be considered in all cases. They are designed to ensure that sexual offenders are not released into the community if they present a significant risk of serious harm.

2.   This replaces the previous offence of 'buggery' with an animal, for which the maximum penalty was life imprisonment. The maximum penalty of 2 years' imprisonment attached to this offence is sufficient to recognise an offender's predisposition towards unnatural sexual activity.

3.   A custodial sentence for an adult for this offence will result in an obligation to comply with notification requirements and this seems to be the most appropriate course of action for a repeat offender. The offence can be charged in addition to existing offences relating to cruelty to animals.

4.   A pre-sentence report,[7] which can identify sexually deviant tendencies, will be extremely helpful in determining the most appropriate disposal. It will also help determine whether an offender would benefit from participation in a programme designed to help them address those tendencies.

---

7   As defined in the Criminal Justice Act 2003, s.158

Intercourse with an animal

THIS IS A SPECIFIED OFFENCE FOR THE PURPOSES OF SECTION 224 CJA 2003

Intercourse with an animal (section 69): Intentionally penetrating a live animal's anus or vagina with the offender's penis; or intentionally causing or allowing a person's anus or vagina to be penetrated by the penis of a live animal

Maximum penalty: 2 years

Type/nature of activity	Starting points	Sentencing range
Basic offence as defined in the SOA 2003, assuming no aggravating or mitigating factors	Community order	An appropriate non-custodial sentence*

* 'Non-custodial sentence' in this context suggests a community order or a fine. In most instances, an offence will have crossed the threshold for a community order. However, in accordance with normal sentencing practice, a court is not precluded from imposing a financial penalty where that is determined to be the appropriate sentence.

Additional aggravating factors	Additional mitigating factors
1. Recording activity and/or circulating pictures or videos	1. Symptom of isolation rather than depravity

An offender convicted of this offence is automatically subject to notification requirements.[8]

---

8 In accordance with the SOA 2003, s.80 and schedule 3

Sexual penetration of a corpse

Factors to take into consideration:

1. The sentences for public protection must be considered in all cases. They are designed to ensure that sexual offenders are not released into the community if they present a significant risk of serious harm.

2. Necrophilia is associated with 'other very deviant behaviour', and killers who use the bodies of their victims for sexual gratification cannot, under the existing law, be formally recognised as, or treated as, sexual offenders.

3. A pre-sentence report[9] (and in some cases a psychiatric report), which can identify sexually deviant tendencies, will be extremely helpful in determining the most appropriate disposal. It will also help determine whether an offender would benefit from participation in a programme designed to help them address those tendencies.

---

9   As defined in the Criminal Justice Act 2003, s.158

Sexual penetration of a corpse

THIS IS A SPECIFIED OFFENCE FOR THE PURPOSES OF SECTION 224 CJA 2003

Sexual penetration of a corpse (section 70): Intentional sexual penetration of part of the body of a dead person with a part of the offender's body or an object

Maximum penalty: 2 years

Type/nature of activity	Starting points	Sentencing ranges
Repeat offending and/or aggravating factors	26 weeks custody	4 weeks–18 months custody
Basic offence as defined in the SOA 2003, assuming no aggravating or mitigating factors	Community order	An appropriate non-custodial sentence*

* 'Non-custodial sentence' in this context suggests a community order or a fine. In most instances, an offence will have crossed the threshold for a community order. However, in accordance with normal sentencing practice, a court is not precluded from imposing a financial penalty where that is determined to be the appropriate sentence.

Additional aggravating factors	Additional mitigating factors
1. Distress caused to relatives or friends of the deceased	
2. Physical damage caused to body of the deceased	
3. The corpse was that of a child	
4. The offence was committed in a funeral home or mortuary	

An offender convicted of this offence is automatically subject to notification requirements.[10]

---

10 In accordance with the SOA 2003, s.80 and schedule 3

PART 6: EXPLOITATION OFFENCES

6.1   Whilst all sexual offences involve, to a greater or lesser degree, the exploitation or abuse of a victim or victims, the specific sexual exploitation offences involve a high degree of offender culpability, with offenders intentionally exploiting vulnerable individuals. In some cases, for example the prostitution offences, the sexual acts themselves may not be unlawful, but the purpose of the legislation is to address the behaviour of those who are prepared to exploit others by causing, inciting or controlling their sexual activities, whether or not for gain.

The harm caused by the offences

6.2   Section 54 of the SOA 2003 defines 'gain' as:

(a) any financial advantage, including the discharge of an obligation to pay or the provision of goods or services (including sexual services) gratuitously or at a discount; or
(b) the goodwill of any person which is, or appears likely, in time, to bring financial advantage.

6.3   The sexual exploitation offences cover a range of offending behaviour that is broken down into four groups in the SOA 2003:

(i) indecent photographs of children;
(ii) abuse of children through prostitution and pornography;
(iii) exploitation of prostitution; and
(iv) trafficking.

6.4   Groups (i) and (ii) specifically relate to the exploitation and abuse of children; for the purposes of these offences, 'child' means anyone under the age of 18.

6.5   The 'exploitation of prostitution' offences relate to adult victims. The offences in group (iii) include the specific element that the activity was carried out 'for gain'. However, whether or not it is implicit in the offence that the prosecution is seeking to prove, in most cases someone will secure an advantage from the exploitation.

6.6   The 'trafficking' offences are designed to protect victims of all ages.

6.7   The term 'prostitution', which is used in most of the offences in these groups, is defined as 'providing sexual services for payment or promise of payment' and 'payment' is defined as being 'any financial advantage'.

6.8   The offences that do not require the prosecution to prove that the offender acted 'for gain' have the effect that offenders cannot avoid prosecution by claiming that they did not stand to benefit by their involvement. For these offences, the starting points for sentencing are based solely on the criminality of taking part in sexual exploitation without taking into account any benefits, financial or otherwise, that the defendant may receive.

> Where a sexual exploitation offence does not require the prosecution to prove
> that the offender acted for gain, the degree of personal involvement of the
> offender and the levels of personal or financial gain should be treated as
> aggravating factors for sentencing.

6.9   Confiscation and compensation orders have particular relevance in the context of
exploitation offences, where it is extremely likely both that there will be property that can be
seized from the offender and also that exploited victims will have been caused a degree of
harm that might merit compensation.

6.10   The 'for gain' element is inherent in the 'exploitation of prostitution' offences;
therefore, it cannot be treated as an aggravating factor and is reflected in the starting points
for sentencing. This group of offences relates to offenders who control the activities of those
over the age of consent, and the maximum penalties are lower than for offences where the
prosecution is not required to prove that the defendant acted 'for gain'. However, the
commercial sexual exploitation of another person's vulnerability is serious and socially
unacceptable offending behaviour, and the starting point for these offences should still be
significant.

> Where a sexual exploitation offence requires the prosecution to prove that the
> offender acted for personal gain and this is already reflected in the starting point
> for sentencing, evidence of substantial financial or other advantage to a value in
> the region of £5000 and upwards (in line with the provisions of section 75(4) of
> the Proceeds of Crime Act 2002) should be treated as an aggravating factor.

6.11   Although the courts must bear in mind the actual 'recoverable amount'[1] when making
a confiscation order, they can legitimately take into account, as an aggravating factor for
sentencing purposes, not only the benefits secured by the offender in fact, but also the
benefits that he or she would have accrued from the offence had the activity not been
intercepted or disrupted. Courts should also take into account non-monetary profits such as
payment in kind, gifts or favours, which will need to be carefully assessed in each individual
case.[2]

The offender's culpability

6.12   In the Council's guideline on seriousness, it is stated that, in broad terms, an
intention to cause harm is at the highest level of criminal culpability – the worse the harm
intended, the higher the offender's culpability – and planning an offence makes the offender
more highly culpable than impulsive offending.

6.13   The common thread of the exploitation offences is the planned abuse of vulnerable
victims, with the main purpose of the offender being to secure some form of personal
advantage, whether this is financial gain or reward, sexual services or personal sexual
gratification (as in the offence of 'paying for sexual services of a child').

---

1   Proceeds of Crime Act 2002, s.9
2   ibid. ss.79–81

6.14 As the combination of culpability with harm determines the seriousness of an offence, it follows that the offences covered in this section are at the higher end of the scale of seriousness, and robust sentencing provisions are needed.

Evidence of an offender's involvement in, or management of, a well-planned or large-scale commercial operation resulting in sexual exploitation should be treated as an aggravating factor for sentencing: the greater the offender's degree of involvement, the more serious the offence.

The age of the victim

- In general, the younger the age of the child, the higher the sentence should be for an offence involving the sexual exploitation of a child.
- In particular, the starting points for sentencing should be higher where the victim is under 13. The starting points for offences involving victims aged 16 or 17 should be lower than those for victims aged 13 or over but under 16, to recognise that they are over the legal age of consent, but any evidence of grooming, coercion, threats or intimidation should increase a sentence in line with that which would apply if the victim were aged 13 or over but under 16.

The risk of re-offending

6.15 The sexual exploitation offences are of a level of seriousness that suggests a custodial sentence will normally be appropriate, but the way in which the risk of re-offending should be addressed will depend on the nature of, and the motivation for, the offences committed.

6.16 A person found guilty of, for example, 'paying for sexual services of a child' or, in some cases, 'causing or inciting child prostitution or pornography' may very well benefit from taking part in a sex offender treatment programme, which will help the offender to recognise and control sexually deviant tendencies. There is a need to ensure that offenders are assessed for their suitability to take part in such programmes and that periods spent on licence in the community are of a sufficient length to enable such programmes to take place.

6.17 However, different issues arise where the courts are sentencing someone whose behaviour has nothing to do with personal sexual deviance but instead involves the exploitation of the sexual appetites or deviancies of others, whether or not for gain. In such cases, sex offender treatment programmes are unlikely to be appropriate. The use of fines or community orders containing requirements such as a curfew, residence, unpaid work and prohibited activity may be effective in discouraging future offending.

PART 6A: INDECENT PHOTOGRAPHS OF CHILDREN

6A.1 The SOA 2003 makes amendments to the Protection of Children Act 1978 and the Criminal Justice Act 1988. It is now a crime to take, make, permit to take, distribute, show, possess, possess with intent to distribute, or to advertise indecent photographs or pseudo-photographs of any person below the age of 18.

6A.2 The levels for sentencing of offences involving pornographic images were established in the case of R v Oliver, Hartrey and Baldwin.[3] These levels have been reviewed in terms of the nature of the images falling into each level:

- Images depicting non-penetrative activity are less serious than images depicting penetrative activity.
- Images of non-penetrative activity between children are generally less serious than images depicting non-penetrative activity between adults and children.
- All acts falling within the definitions of rape and assault by penetration, which carry the maximum life penalty, should be classified as level 4.

The levels of seriousness (in ascending order) for sentencing for offences involving pornographic images are:

Level 1	Images depicting erotic posing with no sexual activity
Level 2	Non-penetrative sexual activity between children, or solo masturbation by a child
Level 3	Non-penetrative sexual activity between adults and children
Level 4	Penetrative sexual activity involving a child or children, or both children and adults
Level 5	Sadism or penetration of, or by, an animal

Offences involving any form of sexual penetration of the vagina or anus, or penile penetration of the mouth (except where they involve sadism or intercourse with an animal, which fall within level 5), should be classified as activity at level 4.

6A.3 Pseudo-photographs should generally be treated as less serious than real images. However, they can be just as serious as photographs of a real child, for example where the imagery is particularly grotesque and beyond the scope of normal photography.

6A.4 The aggravating and mitigating factors set out in the case of Oliver remain relevant and are included in the guideline for this offence.

6A.5 An adult (aged 18 or over) who is given any sentence (including a conditional discharge) in relation to offences involving a victim or victims aged under 16 will be subject to registration requirements.

---

3 [2003] 2 Cr App R(S) 15

6A.6   Courts have the discretion to make an order disqualifying an offender
(adult or juvenile) from working with children regardless of the sentence imposed.[4]

Possession of indecent photographs where the child depicted is aged 16 or 17

6A.7   The starting points for sentencing should reflect the fundamental facts of a case,
including that the victim is over the legal age of consent.

> Sentences should be lower than those involving photographs of children under 16
> where:
>
> - an offender possesses only a few indecent photographs, none of which
>   includes sadism or penetration of, or by, an animal; and
> - the images are of children aged 16 or 17; and
> - the photographs are retained solely for the use of the offender.

6A.8   The presence of any aggravating factors will substantially increase a sentence, and
the principle of lower sentences should not be applied where an offender possesses images
at level 5 as these will involve either non-consensual or unlawful activity.

6A.9   Where it cannot be established that a victim was under 13, penalties will need to
be based on the sentencing starting points for children aged 13 or over but under 16. In
many cases, however, the extreme youth of the child in a photograph or pseudo-photograph
will either be a matter of proven fact or will be a question that is beyond reasonable doubt.
Where the nature of the image indicates that the victim is likely to have suffered particularly
serious harm, this should always aggravate the sentence.

> Starting points for sentencing for possession of indecent photographs should be
> higher where the victim is a child under 13.

6A.10 The court cannot make inferences about the status of unknown material, because of
the fundamental principle that a person may only be convicted and sentenced according to
the facts that have been proved. However, if an offender has used devices to destroy or hide
material then it falls within the general aggravating factor 'An attempt to conceal or dispose
of evidence'.

Showing or distributing and the element of financial gain

6A.11 The starting points in the guideline reflect the differences in terms of relative
seriousness and maximum penalty available for possessing indecent photographs or pseudo-
photographs (5 years) and taking or making, distributing or showing, etc such photographs
(10 years).

6A.12 Showing or distributing indecent photographs or pseudo-photographs, even on a very
small scale, is regarded as serious offending behaviour. Wide-scale distribution is in the
most serious category of offending behaviour.

---

4   Criminal Justice and Court Services Act 2000, s.29A as inserted by the Criminal Justice Act 2003, schedule 30

642   *Sexual Offences*

Sexual Offences – Part 6A

6A.13 Where the material is shown or distributed without the victim's consent, the fact that the victim is over the age of consent should not have any bearing on sentencing levels, even if the material was originally taken and possessed with his or her consent.

6A.14 Where the offence involves a victim aged 16 or 17, the starting points for sentencing should reflect the fact that the victim is above the age of consent. The fact that the victim was not coerced or forced into the activity must be relevant for sentencing purposes, and starting points should be lower to encourage consistency. Any evidence of threats or intimidation to induce consent should have the effect of increasing sentence in an individual case.

6A.15 Any profit for the victim, financial or otherwise, actual or anticipated, should be neutral for sentencing purposes.

The showing or distribution of pornographic images of children under 16, or of children aged 16 or 17 without their consent, is an aggravating factor for sentencing purposes.

111

Sexual Offences – Part 6A

Indecent photographs of children

Factors to take into consideration:

1.   The levels of seriousness (in ascending order) for sentencing for offences involving pornographic images are:

Level 1   Images depicting erotic posing with no sexual activity

Level 2   Non-penetrative sexual activity between children, or solo masturbation
                 by a child

Level 3   Non-penetrative sexual activity between adults and children

Level 4   Penetrative sexual activity involving a child or children, or both children
                 and adults

Level 5   Sadism or penetration of, or by, an animal

2.   Offences involving any form of sexual penetration of the vagina or anus, or penile penetration of the mouth (except where they involve sadism or intercourse with an animal, which fall within level 5), should be classified as activity at level 4.

3.   Pseudo-photographs generally should be treated less seriously than real photographs.

4.   Sentences should be lower than those involving photographs of children under 16 where:

- an offender possesses only a few indecent photographs, none of which includes sadism or penetration of, or by, an animal; and
- the images are of children aged 16 or 17; and
- the photographs are retained solely for the use of the offender.

5.   The fact that the subject of the indecent photograph(s) is aged 16 or 17 has no impact on sentencing starting points where the activity depicted is at level 5.

6.   Starting points for sentencing for possession of indecent photographs should be higher where the subject of the indecent photograph(s) is a child under 13.

7.   Registration requirements attach to a conviction for this offence dependent upon the age of the subject portrayed in the indecent photograph(s) and the sentence imposed.

8.   Courts should consider making an order disqualifying an offender (adult or juvenile) from working with children regardless of the sentence imposed.

9.   Courts should consider making an order for the forfeiture of any possessions (for example, computers or cameras) used in connection with the commission of the offence.

Indecent photographs of children

THESE OFFENCES ARE SERIOUS OFFENCES FOR THE PURPOSES OF SECTION 224 CJA 2003, EXCEPT WHERE THEY INVOLVE ONLY POSSESSION, WHEN THEY ARE SPECIFIED OFFENCES FOR THE PURPOSES OF SECTION 227

Indecent photographs of children (section 1 of the Protection of Children Act 1978 and section 160 of the Criminal Justice Act 1988, as amended by section 45 of the SOA 2003): Taking, making, permitting to take, possessing, possessing with intent to distribute, distributing or advertising indecent photographs or pseudo-photographs of children under 18.

Maximum penalty: 5 years for possession; otherwise 10 years

Type/nature of activity	Starting points	Sentencing ranges
Offender commissioned or encouraged the production of level 4 or 5 images Offender involved in the production of level 4 or 5 images	6 years custody	4–9 years custody
Level 4 or 5 images shown or distributed	3 years custody	2–5 years custody
Offender involved in the production of, or has traded in, material at levels 1–3	2 years custody	1–4 years custody
Possession of a large quantity of level 4 or 5 material for personal use only Large number of level 3 images shown or distributed	12 months custody	26 weeks–2 years custody
Possession of a large quantity of level 3 material for personal use Possession of a small number of images at level 4 or 5 Large number of level 2 images shown or distributed Small number of level 3 images shown or distributed	26 weeks custody	4 weeks–18 months custody

Sexual Offences – Part 6A

Type/nature of activity	Starting points	Sentencing ranges
Offender in possession of a large amount of material at level 2 or a small amount at level 3 Offender has shown or distributed material at level 1 or 2 on a limited scale Offender has exchanged images at level 1 or 2 with other collectors, but with no element of financial gain	12 weeks custody	4 weeks–26 weeks custody
Possession of a large amount of level 1 material and/or no more than a small amount of level 2, and the material is for personal use and has not been distributed or shown to others	Community order	An appropriate non-custodial sentence*

* 'Non-custodial sentence' in this context suggests a community order or a fine. In most instances, an offence will have crossed the threshold for a community order. However, in accordance with normal sentencing practice, a court is not precluded from imposing a financial penalty where that is determined to be the appropriate sentence.

Additional aggravating factors	Additional mitigating factors
1. Images shown or distributed to others, especially children	1. A few images held solely for personal use
2. Collection is systematically stored or organised, indicating a sophisticated approach to trading or a high level of personal interest	2. Images viewed but not stored
3. Images stored, made available or distributed in such a way that they can be inadvertently accessed by others	3. A few images held solely for personal use and it is established both that the subject is aged 16 or 17 and that he or she was consenting
4. Use of drugs, alcohol or other substance to facilitate the offence of making or taking	
5. Background of intimidation or coercion	
6. Threats to prevent victim reporting the activity	
7. Threats to disclose victim's activity to friends or relatives	
8. Financial or other gain	

An offender convicted of these offences is automatically subject to notification requirements.[5]

5 In accordance with the SOA 2003, s.80 and schedule 3

114

PART 6B: ABUSE OF CHILDREN THROUGH PROSTITUTION AND PORNOGRAPHY

6B.1 The four offences in this category are:

- Paying for sexual services of a child
- Causing or inciting child prostitution or pornography
- Controlling a child prostitute or a child involved in pornography
- Arranging or facilitating child prostitution or pornography

Paying for sexual services of a child

Factors to take into consideration:

1.   The sentences for public protection must be considered in all cases. They are designed to ensure that sexual offenders are not released into the community if they present a significant risk of serious harm. Within any indeterminate sentence, the minimum term will generally be half the appropriate determinate sentence. The starting points will be relevant, therefore, to the process of fixing any minimum term that may be necessary.

2.   The offence of 'paying for sexual services of a child' is the only offence in this group that involves actual physical sexual activity between an offender and a victim.

3.   It carries staged maximum penalties according to the age of the victim (in this case under 16, or over 16 but under 18) and also, specifically in relation to victims under 13, whether the sexual services provided or offered involved penetrative activity.

4.   The starting points for sentencing for the offence of 'paying for sexual services of a child', where the victim is aged 13 or over but under 16, are higher than those for the offence of 'sexual activity with a child', to reflect the fact that the victim has been commercially exploited.

5.   Starting points for victims aged 16 or 17 are lower than the equivalent starting points for victims aged 13 to 15, in line with the difference in the maximum penalty, to reflect the fact that the victim is above the legal age of consent.

6.   The starting points where the victim is aged 13 or over but under 16 are higher than those for the offence of 'sexual activity with a child', to reflect the fact that the victim has been commercially exploited.

7.   The starting points for sentencing for the offence of 'paying for sexual services of a child' where the victim is under 13 are higher than those for the specific 'under 13' offences covering the same type of sexual activity, to reflect the fact that the victim has been commercially exploited.

8.   The offence of 'paying for sexual services of a child' includes higher maximum penalties to cater for those (albeit rare) cases where the age of the victim is only established during the course of a trial. The same principle has been applied to the starting points for sentencing.

Sexual Offences

Paying for sexual services of a child

THIS IS A SERIOUS OFFENCE FOR THE PURPOSES OF SECTION 224 CJA 2003

Paying for sexual services of a child (section 47): Intentionally obtaining the sexual services of a child having made or promised payment or knowing that another person has made or promised payment

Maximum penalty: Life imprisonment for offences involving penetration where the child is under 13, otherwise 14 years; 14 years where the child is aged 13 or over but under 16; 7 years where the child is aged 16 or 17

Type/nature of activity	Starting points	Sentencing ranges
History of paying for penetrative sex with children under 18	If the victim is under 13, the offence of 'rape of a child under 13' or 'assault of a child under 13 by penetration' would normally be charged. Any commercial element to the offence and any history of repeat offending would be aggravating factors. However, if this offence is charged – 15 years custody	13–19 years custody
	7 years custody if the victim is 13 or over but under 16	5–10 years custody
	3 years custody if the victim is aged 16 or 17	2–5 years custody
Penile penetration of the vagina, anus or mouth or penetration of the vagina or anus with another body part or an object	If the victim is under 13, the offence of 'rape of a child under 13' or 'assault of a child under 13 by penetration' would normally be charged. Any commercial element to the offence would be an aggravating factor. However, if this offence is charged – 12 years custody	10–16 years custody
	5 years custody if the victim is 13 or over but under 16	4–8 years custody
	2 years custody if the victim is aged 16 or 17	1–4 years custody

Sexual Offences – Part 6B

Type/nature of activity	Starting points	Sentencing ranges
Sexual touching falling short of penetration	If the victim is under 13, the offence of 'sexual assault of a child under 13' would normally be charged. Any commercial element to the offence would be an aggravating factor. However, if this offence is charged – 5 years custody	4–8 years custody
	4 years custody if the victim is 13 or over but under 16	3–7 years custody
	12 months custody if the victim is aged 16 or 17	26 weeks–2 years custody

Additional aggravating factors	Additional mitigating factors
1. Use of drugs, alcohol or other substance to secure the victim's compliance	
2. Abduction or detention	
3. Threats to prevent victim reporting the activity	
4. Threats to disclose victim's activity to friends or relatives	
5. Offender aware that he or she is suffering from a sexually transmitted infection	

An offender convicted of this offence is automatically subject to notification requirements.[6]

---

6   In accordance with the SOA 2003, s.80 and schedule 3

Child prostitution or pornography

Factors to take into consideration:

1.   The sentences for public protection must be considered in all cases. They are designed to ensure that sexual offenders are not released into the community if they present a significant risk of serious harm.

2.   Three offences fall within this group:

- Causing or inciting child prostitution or child pornography
- Controlling a child prostitute or a child involved in pornography
- Arranging or facilitating child prostitution or pornography

3.   The level of involvement of the offender is a fundamental element of the 'abuse of children through prostitution and pornography' offences.

4.   Financial reward may not always be a factor in someone's involvement in these offences. Thus the offences cover anyone who takes part in any way, for whatever reason, in a child's involvement in prostitution or pornography. However, most offenders will stand to gain in some way from their involvement, and sentencing starting points need to be relatively high, in line with established principles about the serious nature of commercial exploitation.

5.   The courts should consider making an order confiscating any profits stemming from the offender's criminal lifestyle or forfeiting any possessions (for example cameras, computers, property) used in connection with the commission of the offence.

6.   Evidence of an offender's involvement in, or management of, a well-planned or large-scale commercial operation resulting in sexual exploitation should be treated as an aggravating factor for sentencing: the greater the offender's degree of involvement, the more serious the offence.

7.   The starting point for the child prostitution and pornography offences will always be a custodial sentence.

8.   The same starting points apply whether the activity was caused or incited. Where an offence was incited but did not take place as a result of the voluntary intervention of the offender, that is likely to reduce the severity of the sentence imposed.

9.   The presence of any of the general aggravating factors identified in the Council guideline on seriousness or any of the additional factors identified in the guidelines will indicate a sentence above the normal starting point.

10.   In cases where a number of children are involved, consecutive sentences may be appropriate, leading to cumulative sentences significantly higher than the suggested starting points for individual offences.

11.   In cases where the offender is, to a degree, another victim, a court may wish to take a more lenient stance. A court might consider whether the circumstances of the offender should mitigate sentence. This will depend on the merits of each case.

Child prostitution and pornography

THESE ARE SERIOUS OFFENCES FOR THE PURPOSES OF SECTION 224 CJA 2003

1.   Causing or inciting child prostitution or pornography (section 48): Intentionally causing or inciting a child to become a prostitute, or to be involved in pornography, anywhere in the world

2.   Controlling a child prostitute or a child involved in pornography (section 49): Intentionally controlling any of the activities of a child under 18 where those activities relate to child's prostitution, or involvement in pornography, anywhere in the world

3.   Arranging or facilitating child prostitution or pornography (section 50): Intentionally arranging or facilitating the prostitution of a child, or the child's involvement in pornography, anywhere in the world

Maximum penalty for all offences: 14 years

Type/nature of activity	Starting points	Sentencing ranges
Penetrative activity Organised commercial exploitation	If the victim is under 13, the offence of 'causing or inciting a child under 13 to engage in sexual activity' would normally be charged. The commercial element of the offence would be an aggravating factor. However, if this offence is charged – 10 years custody	8–13 years custody
	8 years custody if the victim is 13 or over but under 16	6–11 years custody
	4 years custody if the victim is aged 16 or 17	3–7 years custody
Penetrative activity Offender's involvement is minimal and not perpetrated for gain	If the victim is under 13, the offence of 'causing or inciting a child under 13 to engage in sexual activity' would normally be charged. The commercial element of the offence would be an aggravating factor. However, if this offence is charged – 8 years custody	6–11 years custody
	5 years custody if the victim is 13 or over but under 16	4–8 years custody
	2 years custody if the victim is aged 16 or 17	1–4 years custody

Sexual Offences – Part 6B

Type/nature of activity	Starting points	Sentencing ranges
Non-penetrative activity Organised commercial exploitation	If the victim is under 13, the offence of 'causing or inciting a child under 13 to engage in sexual activity' would normally be charged. The commercial element of the offence would be an aggravating factor. However, if this offence is charged – 8 years custody	6–11 years custody
	6 years custody if the victim is 13 or over but under 16	4–9 years custody
	3 years custody if the victim is aged 16 or 17	2–5 years custody
Non-penetrative activity Offender's involvement is minimal and not perpetrated for gain	If the victim is under 13, the offence of 'causing or inciting a child under 13 to engage in sexual activity' would normally be charged. The commercial element of the offence would be an aggravating factor. However, if this offence is charged – 6 years custody	4–9 years custody
	3 years custody if the victim is aged 13 or over but under 16	2–5 years custody
	12 months custody if the victim is aged 16 or 17	26 weeks–2 years custody

Additional aggravating factors	Additional mitigating factors
1. Background of threats or intimidation	1. Offender also being controlled in prostitution or pornography and subject to threats or intimidation
2. Large-scale commercial operation	
3. Use of drugs, alcohol or other substance to secure the victim's compliance	
4. Induced dependency on drugs	
5. Forcing a victim to violate another person	
6. Victim has been manipulated into physical and emotional dependence on the offender	
7. Abduction or detention	
8. Threats to prevent victim reporting the activity	
9. Threats to disclose victim's activity to friends or relatives	
10. Storing, making available or distributing images in such a way that they can be inadvertently accessed by others	
11. Images distributed to other children or persons known to the victim	
12. Financial or other gain	

An offender convicted of these offences is automatically subject to notification requirements.[7]

---

7   In accordance with the SOA 2003, s.80 and schedule 3

PART 6C: EXPLOITATION OF PROSTITUTION

6C.1   The offences in this section relate to the exploitation of adults who work as prostitutes, replacing gender-specific offences in the Sexual Offences Act 1956. Offenders who cause, incite or control the activities of a prostitute for their own gain, or for the gain of a third person, can be prosecuted under two new offences.

6C.2   The offences 'causing or inciting prostitution for gain' and 'controlling prostitution for gain' cover two levels of criminal activity:

(i) the coercion of another person into prostitution; and
(ii) controlling his or her activities for gain.

Exploitation of prostitution

Factors to take into consideration:

1.   The sentences for public protection must be considered in all cases. They are designed to ensure that sexual offenders are not released into the community if they present a significant risk of serious harm.

2.   The degree of coercion, both in terms of recruitment and subsequent control of a prostitute's activities, is highly relevant to sentencing.

3.   The degree to which a victim is exploited or controlled, the harm suffered as a result, the level of involvement of the offender, the scale of the operation and the timescale over which it has been run will all be relevant in terms of assessing the seriousness of the offence.

4.   Where an offender has profited from his or her involvement in the prostitution of others, the courts should always consider making a confiscation order approximately equivalent to the profits enjoyed.

5.   The presence of any of the general aggravating factors identified in the Council guideline on seriousness or any of the additional factors identified in the guidelines will indicate a sentence above the normal starting point.

6.   Where there is evidence that an offender convicted of an exploitation of prostitution offence is not actively involved in the coercion or control of the victim(s), that he or she acted through fear or intimidation and that he or she is trying to exit prostitution, the courts may wish to consider whether, in the particular circumstances of the case, this should mitigate sentence.

7.   The starting points are the same whether prostitution was caused or incited and whether or not the incited activity took place. Where the offence was incited, the sentencer should begin from the starting point that the offence was incited, taking account of the nature of the harm that would have been caused had the offence taken place and calculating the final sentence to reflect that no actual harm was occasioned to the victim, but being mindful that the intended victim may have suffered as a result of knowing or believing the offence would take place.

8.   The starting point for the exploitation of prostitution offences where an offender's involvement was minimal, and he or she has not actively engaged in the coercion or control of those engaged in prostitution, is a non-custodial sentence.

9.   A fine may be more appropriate for very minimal involvement.

10.   Where an offender has profited from his or her involvement in the prostitution of others, the court should consider making a confiscation order[8] approximately equivalent to the profits enjoyed.

11.   Where this offence is being dealt with in a magistrates' court, more detailed guidance is provided in the Magistrates' Court Sentencing Guidelines (MCSG).

---

8   Criminal Justice Act 1988 as amended by the Proceeds of Crime Act 2002

Exploitation of prostitution

THESE ARE SPECIFIED OFFENCES FOR THE PURPOSES OF SECTION 227 CJA 2003

1.   Causing or inciting prostitution for gain (section 52): Intentionally causing or inciting another person to become a prostitute anywhere in the world

2.   Controlling prostitution for gain (section 53): Intentionally controlling any of the activities of another person relating to that person's prostitution in any part of the world

Maximum penalty for both offences: 7 years

Type/nature of activity	Starting points	Sentencing ranges
Evidence of physical and/or mental coercion	3 years custody	2–5 years custody
No coercion or corruption, but the offender is closely involved in the victim's prostitution	12 months custody	26 weeks–2 years custody
No evidence that the victim was physically coerced or corrupted, and the involvement of the offender was minimal	Community order	An appropriate non-custodial sentence*

* 'Non-custodial sentence' in this context suggests a community order or a fine. In most instances, an offence will have crossed the threshold for a community order. However, in accordance with normal sentencing practice, a court is not precluded from imposing a financial penalty where that is determined to be the appropriate sentence.

Additional aggravating factors	Additional mitigating factors
1. Background of threats, intimidation or coercion 2. Large-scale commercial operation 3. Substantial gain (in the region of £5000 and upwards) 4. Use of drugs, alcohol or other substance to secure the victim's compliance 5. Induced dependency on drugs 6. Abduction or detention 7. Threats to prevent victim reporting the activity 8. Threats to disclose victim's activity to friends or relatives	1. Offender also being controlled in prostitution and subject to threats or intimidation

Keeping a brothel used for prostitution

Factors to take into consideration:

1.   The sentences for public protection must be considered in all cases. They are designed to ensure that sexual offenders are not released into the community if they present a significant risk of serious harm.

2.   The offence covers anyone who keeps, manages or acts or assists in the management of a brothel. The degree of coercion, both in terms of recruitment and subsequent control of a prostitute's activities, is highly relevant to sentencing.

3.   The degree to which a victim is exploited or controlled, the harm suffered as a result, the level of involvement of the offender, the scale of the operation and the timescale over which it has been run will all be relevant in terms of assessing the seriousness of the offence.

4.   The presence of any of the general aggravating factors identified in the Council guideline on seriousness or any of the additional factors identified in the guidelines will indicate a sentence above the normal starting point.

5.   Where there is evidence that an offender convicted of an exploitation of prostitution offence is not actively involved in the coercion or control of the victim(s), that he or she acted through fear or intimidation and that he or she is trying to exit prostitution, the courts may wish to consider whether, in the particular circumstances of the case, this should mitigate sentence.

6.   The starting points are the same whether prostitution was caused or incited and whether or not the incited activity took place. Where the offence was incited, the sentencer should begin from the starting point that the offence was incited, taking account of the nature of the harm that would have been caused had the offence taken place and calculating the final sentence to reflect that no actual harm was occasioned to the victim, but being mindful that the intended victim may have suffered as a result of knowing or believing the offence would take place.

7.   A non-custodial sentence may be appropriate for very minimal involvement.

8.   Where an offender has profited from his or her involvement in the prostitution of others, the courts should always consider making a confiscation order approximately equivalent to the profits enjoyed.

9.   Where this offence is being dealt with in a magistrates' court, more detailed guidance is provided in the Magistrates' Court Sentencing Guidelines (MCSG).

Keeping a brothel used for prostitution

Keeping a brothel used for prostitution (section 33A of the Sexual Offences Act 1956
as inserted by section 55 of the SOA 2003): Keeping, managing, or acting or assisting in the
management of a brothel

Maximum penalty: 7 years

Type/nature of activity	Starting points	Sentencing ranges
Offender is the keeper of a brothel and has made substantial profits in the region of £5000 and upwards	2 years custody	1–4 years custody
Offender is the keeper of the brothel and is personally involved in its management	12 months custody	26 weeks–2 years custody
Involvement of the offender was minimal	Community order	An appropriate non-custodial sentence*

* 'Non-custodial sentence' in this context suggests a community order or a fine. In most instances,
an offence will have crossed the threshold for a community order. However, in accordance with normal
sentencing practice, a court is not precluded from imposing a financial penalty where that is determined
to be the appropriate sentence.

Additional aggravating factors	Additional mitigating factors
1. Background of threats, intimidation or coercion 2. Large-scale commercial operation 3. Personal involvement in the prostitution of others 4. Abduction or detention 5. Financial or other gain	1. Using employment as a route out of prostitution and not actively involved in exploitation 2. Coercion by third party

SENTENCERS ARE REMINDED THAT A NUMBER OF FINANCIAL ORDERS CAN BE MADE
IN ADDITION TO THE SENTENCE IMPOSED FOR THIS OFFENCE (see Part 1, paragraph
1.32 above).

PART 6D: TRAFFICKING

Factors to take into consideration:

1. The sentences for public protection must be considered in all cases. They are designed to ensure that sexual offenders are not released into the community if they present a significant risk of serious harm.

2. The type of activity covered by the various trafficking offences in the SOA 2003 is broadly the same, the only difference being the geographical area within which the trafficked persons are moved. The harm being addressed is sexual exploitation, but here either children or adults may be involved as victims.

3. The offences are designed to cover anyone involved in any stage of the trafficking operation, whether or not there is evidence of gain. This is serious offending behaviour, which society as a whole finds repugnant, and a financial or community penalty would rarely be an appropriate disposal.

4. The degree of coercion used and the level of control over the trafficked person's liberty will be relevant to assessing the seriousness of the offender's behaviour. The nature of the sexual exploitation to which the victim is exposed will also be relevant, as will the victim's age and vulnerability.

5. In general terms the greater the level of involvement, the more serious the crime. Those at the top of an organised trafficking chain may have very little personal involvement with day-to-day operations and may have no knowledge at all of individual victims. However, being in control of a money-making operation that is based on the degradation, exploitation and abuse of vulnerable people may be equally, if not more, serious than the actions of an individual who is personally involved at an operational level.

6. The presence of any of the general aggravating factors identified in the Council guideline on seriousness or any of the additional factors identified in the guidelines will indicate a sentence above the normal starting point.

7. Circumstances such as the fact that the offender is also a victim of trafficking and that their actions were governed by fear could be a mitigating factor if not accepted as a defence.

8. The starting point for sentencing for offences of trafficking for sexual exploitation should be a custodial sentence. Aggravating factors such as participation in a large-scale commercial enterprise involving a high degree of planning, organisation or sophistication, financial or other gain, and the coercion and vulnerability of victims should move sentences towards the maximum 14 years.

9. In cases where a number of children are involved, consecutive sentences may be appropriate, leading to cumulative sentences significantly higher than the suggested starting points for individual offences.

10. Where an offender has profited from his or her involvement in the prostitution of others, the court should consider making a confiscation order[9] approximately equivalent to the profits enjoyed.

11. The court may order the forfeiture of a vehicle used, or intended to be used, in connection with the offence.[10]

9 Proceeds of Crime Act 2002, part 2
10 Sexual Offences Act 2003, s.60A as inserted by the Violent Crime Reduction Act 2006, s.54 and schedule 4

Trafficking

THESE ARE SERIOUS OFFENCES FOR THE PURPOSES OF SECTION 224 CJA 2003

Trafficking into/within/out of the UK for sexual exploitation (sections 57, 58 and 59): Intentionally arranging or facilitating a person's arrival/travel within/departure from the UK, intending or believing that a sexual offence will be committed

Maximum penalty for all offences: 14 years

Type/nature of activity	Starting point	Sentencing range
Involvement at any level in any stage of the trafficking operation where the victim was coerced	6 years custody	4–9 years custody
Involvement at any level in any stage of the trafficking operation where there was no coercion of the victim	2 years custody	1–4 years custody

Note: If the victim is under 13, one of the specific under-13 offences would normally be charged. Any commercial exploitation element would be an aggravating factor.

Additional aggravating factors	Additional mitigating factors
1. Large-scale commercial operation	1. Coercion of the offender by a third party
2. High degree of planning or sophistication	
3. Large number of people trafficked	2. No evidence of personal gain
4. Substantial financial (in the region of £5000 and upwards) or other gain	3. Limited involvement
5. Fraud	
6. Financial extortion of the victim	
7. Deception	
8. Use of force, threats of force or other forms of coercion	
9. Threats against victim or members of victim's family	
10. Abduction or detention	
11. Restriction of victim's liberty	
12. Inhumane treatment	
13. Confiscation of victim's passport	

PART 7: SENTENCING YOUNG OFFENDERS – OFFENCES WITH A LOWER STATUTORY MAXIMUM

7.1   The SOA 2003 makes special provision in respect of the maximum sentence that can be imposed for certain offences where committed by a person under the age of 18 (a young offender). The sentencing framework that applies to the sentencing of young offenders is also different.

7.2   This section deals with those offences within the context of the framework that currently applies. Many cases will be sentenced in the youth court, but a significant proportion may also be dealt with in the Crown Court. The essential elements of each offence, relevant charging standards and any other general issues pertaining to the offence are set out in the offence guidelines at pages 135–139.

7.3   The offences with which Part 7 is concerned are:

   (i) Sexual activity with a child
   (ii) Causing or inciting a child to engage in sexual activity
   (iii) Engaging in sexual activity in the presence of a child
   (iv) Causing a child to watch a sexual act
   (v) Sexual activity with a child family member
   (vi) Inciting a child family member to engage in sexual activity

7.4   In relation to each offence, the maximum sentence for an offence committed by a young offender is 5 years' custody compared with a maximum of 14 years or 10 years for an offender aged 18 or over. Offences under (i), (ii), (v) and (vi) above can be committed to the Crown Court where it is considered that sentencing powers greater than those available in a magistrates' court may be needed.[1]

7.5   The provisions relating to the sentencing of dangerous offenders apply to young offenders with some variation and, where appropriate, cases should be sent for trial or committed for sentence in the Crown Court. The offences in this section are 'serious' offences for the purposes of the provisions. Where the significant harm criterion is met, the court is required[2] to impose one of the sentences for public protection, which in the case of those under 18 are discretionary detention for life, indeterminate detention for public protection or an extended sentence.

7.6   The following guidelines are for those offences where the court considers that the facts found by the court justify the involvement of the criminal law – these findings may be different from those on which the decision to prosecute was made.

7.7   The sentencing framework that applies to young offenders is different from that for adult offenders. The significant factors are set out below.

7.8   For each offence, the circumstances that would suggest that a custodial sentence should be passed where it is available to the court and those that would suggest that a case should be dealt with in the Crown Court (as 'grave crimes') are set out. As for adult

---

1   Powers of Criminal Courts (Sentencing) Act 2000, s.91
2   Criminal Justice Act 2003, ss.226 and 228

offenders, these guidelines relate to sentencing on conviction for a first-time offender after a plea of not guilty.

7.9   The principal aim for all involved in the youth justice system is to prevent offending by children and young persons.[3]

7.10   A court imposing sentence on a youth must have regard to the welfare,[4] maturity, sexual development and intelligence of the youth. These are always important factors.

7.11   Where a young offender pleads guilty to one of these offences and it is the first offence of which they are convicted, a youth court may impose an absolute discharge, a mental health disposal, a custodial sentence, or make a referral order.

7.12   Except where the dangerous offender provisions apply:

   (i) Where the young offender is aged 12, 13 or 14, a custodial sentence may only be imposed if the youth is a 'persistent offender' or has committed a 'grave crime' warranting detention for a period in excess of 2 years.[5]
   (ii) Where a young offender is aged 10 or 11, no custodial sentence is available in the youth court.
   (iii) Where a custodial sentence is imposed in the youth court, it must be a Detention and Training Order (DTO), which can only be for 4/6/8/10/12/18 or 24 months.
   (iv) Where a custodial sentence is imposed in the Crown Court, it may be a DTO or it may be detention for a period up to the maximum for the offence.

---

3   Crime and Disorder Act 1998, s.37
4   Children and Young Persons Act 1933, s.44
5   Powers of Criminal Courts (Sentencing) Act 2000, s.100

Sexual activity with a child
(when committed by a person under the age of 18)

THIS IS A SPECIFIED OFFENCE FOR THE PURPOSES OF SECTION 224 CJA 2003

Intentional sexual touching of a person under 16 (section 9 and section 13)

Maximum penalty: 5 years (14 years if offender is 18 or over)

The starting points below are based upon a first-time offender aged 17 years old who pleaded not guilty. For younger offenders, sentencers should consider whether a lower starting point is justified in recognition of the offender's age or immaturity.

Type/nature of activity	Starting points	Sentencing ranges
Offence involving penetration where one or more aggravating factors exist or where there is a substantial age gap between the parties	Detention and Training Order 12 months	Detention and Training Order 6–24 months
CUSTODY THRESHOLD		
Any form of sexual activity (non-penetrative or penetrative) not involving any aggravating factors	Community order	An appropriate non-custodial sentence*

* 'Non-custodial sentence' in this context suggests a youth community order (as defined in the Criminal Justice Act 2003, section 147(2)) or a fine. In most instances, an offence will have crossed the threshold for a community order. However, in accordance with normal sentencing practice, a court is not precluded from imposing a financial penalty where that is determined to be the appropriate sentence.

Aggravating factors	Mitigating factors
1. Background of intimidation or coercion	1. Relationship of genuine affection
2. Use of drugs, alcohol or other substance to facilitate the offence	2. Youth and immaturity of offender
3. Threats to prevent victim reporting the incident	
4. Abduction or detention	
5. Offender aware that he or she is suffering from a sexually transmitted infection	

An offender convicted of this offence is automatically subject to notification requirements when sentenced to imprisonment for a term of at least 12 months.[6]

---

6   In accordance with the SOA 2003, s.80 and schedule 3

Causing or inciting a child to engage in sexual activity
(when committed by a person under the age of 18)

THIS IS A SPECIFIED OFFENCE FOR THE PURPOSES OF SECTION 224 CJA 2003

Intentional causing/inciting of person under 16 to engage in sexual activity (section 10 and section 13)

Maximum penalty: 5 years (14 years if offender is 18 or over)

The same starting points apply whether the activity was caused or incited and whether or not the incited activity took place.

The starting points below are based upon a first-time offender aged 17 years old who pleaded not guilty. For younger offenders, sentencers should consider whether a lower starting point is justified in recognition of the offender's age or immaturity.

Type/nature of activity	Starting points	Sentencing ranges
Offence involving penetration where one or more aggravating factors exist or where there is a substantial age gap between the parties	Detention and Training Order 12 months	Detention and Training Order 6–24 months
CUSTODY THRESHOLD		
Any form of sexual activity (non-penetrative or penetrative) not involving any aggravating factors	Community order	An appropriate non-custodial sentence*

* 'Non-custodial sentence' in this context suggests a youth community order (as defined in the Criminal Justice Act 2003, section 147(2)) or a fine. In most instances, an offence will have crossed the threshold for a community order. However, in accordance with normal sentencing practice, a court is not precluded from imposing a financial penalty where that is determined to be the appropriate sentence.

Aggravating factors	Mitigating factors
1. Background of intimidation or coercion	1. Relationship of genuine affection
2. Use of drugs, alcohol or other substance to facilitate the offence	2. Offender intervenes to prevent incited offence from taking place
3. Threats to prevent victim reporting the incident	3. Youth and immaturity of offender
4. Abduction or detention	
5. Offender aware that he or she is suffering from a sexually transmitted infection	

An offender convicted of this offence is automatically subject to notification requirements when sentenced to imprisonment for a term of at least 12 months.[7]

7 In accordance with the SOA 2003, s.80 and schedule 3

Engaging in sexual activity in the presence of a child
(when committed by a person under the age of 18)

THIS IS A SPECIFIED OFFENCE FOR THE PURPOSES OF SECTION 224 CJA 2003

Intentionally, and for the purpose of obtaining sexual gratification, engaging in sexual activity in the presence of a person under 16, knowing or believing that the child is aware of the activity (section 11 and section 13)

Maximum penalty: 5 years (10 years if offender is 18 or over)

The starting points below are based upon a first-time offender aged 17 years old who pleaded not guilty. For younger offenders, sentencers should consider whether a lower starting point is justified in recognition of the offender's age or immaturity.

Type/nature of activity	Starting points	Sentencing ranges
Sexual activity involving penetration where one or more aggravating factors exist	Detention and Training Order 12 months	Detention and Training Order 6–24 months
CUSTODY THRESHOLD		
Any form of sexual activity (non-penetrative or penetrative) not involving any aggravating factors	Community order	An appropriate non-custodial sentence*

* 'Non-custodial sentence' in this context suggests a youth community order (as defined in the Criminal Justice Act 2003, section 147(2)) or a fine. In most instances, an offence will have crossed the threshold for a community order. However, in accordance with normal sentencing practice, a court is not precluded from imposing a financial penalty where that is determined to be the appropriate sentence.

Aggravating factors	Mitigating factors
1. Background of intimidation or coercion	1. Youth and immaturity of offender
2. Use of drugs, alcohol or other substance to facilitate the offence	
3. Threats to prevent victim reporting the incident	
4. Abduction or detention	

An offender convicted of this offence is automatically subject to notification requirements when sentenced to imprisonment for a term of at least 12 months.[8]

---

8   In accordance with the SOA 2003, s.80 and schedule 3

Causing a child to watch a sexual act
(when committed by a person under the age of 18)

THIS IS A SPECIFIED OFFENCE FOR THE PURPOSES OF SECTION 224 CJA 2003

Intentionally causing a person under 16 to watch sexual activity or look at a photograph or pseudo-photograph of sexual activity, for the purpose of obtaining sexual gratification (section 12 and section 13)

Maximum penalty: 5 years (10 years if offender is 18 or over)

The starting points below are based upon a first-time offender aged 17 years old who pleaded not guilty. For younger offenders, sentencers should consider whether a lower starting point is justified in recognition of the offender's age or immaturity.

Type/nature of activity	Starting points	Sentencing ranges
Live sexual activity	Detention and Training Order 8 months	Detention and Training Order 6–12 months
CUSTODY THRESHOLD		
Moving or still images of people engaged in sexual acts involving penetration	Community order	An appropriate non-custodial sentence*
Moving or still images of people engaged in sexual acts other than penetration	Community order	An appropriate non-custodial sentence*

* 'Non-custodial sentence' in this context suggests a youth community order (as defined in the Criminal Justice Act 2003, section 147(2)) or a fine. In most instances, an offence will have crossed the threshold for a community order. However, in accordance with normal sentencing practice, a court is not precluded from imposing a financial penalty where that is determined to be the appropriate sentence.

Aggravating factors	Mitigating factors
1. Background of intimidation or coercion	1. Youth and immaturity of offender
2. Use of drugs, alcohol or other substance to facilitate the offence	
3. Threats to prevent victim reporting the incident	
4. Abduction or detention	
5. Images of violent activity	

An offender convicted of this offence is automatically subject to notification requirements when sentenced to imprisonment for a term of at least 12 months.[9]

---

9 In accordance with the SOA 2003, s.80 and schedule 3

Sexual activity with a child family member and
Inciting a child family member to engage in sexual activity
(when committed by a person under the age of 18)

THESE ARE SERIOUS OFFENCES FOR THE PURPOSES OF SECTION 224 CJA 2003

Intentional sexual touching with a child family member (section 25)

Intentionally inciting sexual touching by a child family member (section 26)

Maximum penalty for both offences: 5 years (14 years if offender is 18 or over)

The starting points below are based upon a first-time offender aged 17 years old who pleaded not guilty. For younger offenders, sentencers should consider whether a lower starting point is justified in recognition of the offender's age or immaturity.

Type/nature of activity	Starting points	Sentencing ranges
Offence involving penetration where one or more aggravating factors exist or where there is a substantial age gap between the parties	Detention and Training Order 18 months	Detention and Training Order 6–24 months
CUSTODY THRESHOLD		
Any form of sexual activity that does not involve any aggravating factors	Community order	An appropriate non-custodial sentence*

* 'Non-custodial sentence' in this context suggests a youth community order (as defined in the Criminal Justice Act 2003, section 147(2)) or a fine. In most instances, an offence will have crossed the threshold for a community order. However, in accordance with normal sentencing practice, a court is not precluded from imposing a financial penalty where that is determined to be the appropriate sentence.

Additional aggravating factors	Additional mitigating factors
1. Background of intimidation or coercion	1. Small disparity in age between victim and offender
2. Use of drugs, alcohol or other substance	2. Relationship of genuine affection
3. Threats deterring the victim from reporting the incident	3. Youth and immaturity of offender
4. Offender aware that he or she is suffering from a sexually transmitted infection	

An offender convicted of this offence is automatically subject to notification requirements when sentenced to imprisonment for a term of at least 12 months.[10]

---

10 In accordance with the SOA 2003, s.80 and schedule 3

INDEX

References are to paragraph numbers.